Questions of Life
and Death

Questions of Life and Death

Readings in Practical Ethics

Christopher W. Morris
University of Maryland, College Park

New York   Oxford
OXFORD UNIVERSITY PRESS

Oxford University Press, Inc., publishes works that further Oxford University's objective of excellence in research, scholarship, and education.

Oxford   New York
Auckland   Cape Town   Dar es Salaam   Hong Kong   Karachi
Kuala Lumpur   Madrid   Melbourne   Mexico City   Nairobi
New Delhi   Shanghai   Taipei   Toronto

With offices in
Argentina   Austria   Brazil   Chile   Czech Republic   France   Greece
Guatemala   Hungary   Italy   Japan   Poland   Portugal   Singapore
South Korea   Switzerland   Thailand   Turkey   Ukraine   Vietnam

For titles covered by Section 112 of the U.S. Higher Education Opportunity Act, please visit www.oup.com/us/he for the latest information about pricing and alternate formats.

Published by Oxford University Press, Inc.
198 Madison Avenue, New York, New York 10016
http://www.oup.com

Library of Congress Cataloging-in-Publication Data
Questions of life and death : readings in practical
ethics / [compiled by] Christopher W. Morris.
    p.   cm.
Includes bibliographical references.
ISBN 978-0-19-515698-0
1. Death—Moral and ethical aspects—Textbooks.
I. Morris, Christopher W.
BJ1409.5.Q47   2012
179.7—dc23   2011021042

9 8 7 6 5 4 3 2 1

Printed in the United States of America
on acid-free paper

Dedicated to
the FDNY, the NYPD,
and all of the other rescue workers of 9/11

BRIEF CONTENTS

CONTENTS

PREFACE

Questions of Life and Death is a reader intended for university courses in practical or applied ethics. It is different from most textbooks of its kind. The topics covered all have to do with life and death and the ethics of killing and saving lives, and there is an emphasis on what might be called middle-level moral theorizing.

TOPICS

Virtually all introductory readers in practical ethics cover a wide array of topics—for example, abortion, euthanasia, civil disobedience, the death penalty, sexual morality, affirmative action, privacy, animals, the environment. This is not unreasonable given the interest in these topics. There are, however, few if any theoretical connections between all of these topics, and this makes it much harder for students to see the implications of one discussion for another. The questions covered in this reader virtually all concern life and death. It is easy to teach these topics in a way that allows students to determine the implications of their positions on any particular question for others. They may discover, for example, that certain arguments for restricting abortion commit one to opposing the death penalty and nuclear deterrence; that opposition to terrorism may imply that the "terror bombings" of World War II were wrong; that certain positions on the wrongness of killing humans may lead one to think that killing animals is often evil or that famine relief is obligatory. A reader with a focus on questions about life and death makes possible a well-integrated course. Concepts and distinctions introduced for one topic may be equally useful with regard to another.

MIDDLE-LEVEL MORAL THEORY

Most anthologies for practical ethics courses contain selections from works of classical and/or contemporary moral philosophy. The idea is often that moral ideas and principles—or "moral theories"—are to be *applied* to particular questions or controversies. There are, however, several problems with this standard approach. One is that the theories or principles in question are so abstract that they may not yield determinate practical conclusions and may in fact be used to defend a number of different and opposing conclusions, which often leads students to think that the theories or principles in question are not particularly useful. This conception of "applied ethics" can also encourage a somewhat mechanical approach to thinking about difficult questions. In addition, the students usually know too little about the theories or principles in question to understand them very well; it may be better, for instance, to invoke everyday queries asking "what if everyone did that?" than an ill-understood Categorical Imperative. What is more useful for contemporary controversies about life and death is what we might think of as "middle-level moral theory," the kind of reflection found in many of the essays included in this reader. At the least, theorizing should start at this middle level. As the reader will see, few of our authors bring in developed moral theories to reach their conclusions.

Because different kinds of moral relativism and skepticism are commonplace among university students, many readers include discussions of "relativism" and "subjectivism." I refrain from following suit in part because these matters are in fact too complex and difficult to take up in the short amount of time one normally has. More important, though, I do not find it necessary to say much about these matters if the course is focused on questions about killing and letting die and is well designed. In my experience, students tend not to be attracted to relativist or skeptical positions *in practice* if they remain focused on the questions at hand, especially if one pushes them to figure out what they think about the topic.[1] I have yet to meet someone who did not think that killing is generally wrong or that certain particular acts of killing are clearly wrong. There appears to be no disagreement here; no one makes any of the standard relativist noises about shooting children in a cafeteria, and no one hesitates to think such acts to be evil. Best to plunge right into the questions and debates, starting from the uncontroversial assumption that there is something wrong about killing or that there are some cases of killing that are indisputably wrong.

SELECTIONS

I have attempted to include excellent writings, of different levels of difficulty, with contrasting positions. In particular I have tried to include several selections from a number of philosophers so as to enable students to get a sense of the positions that particular thinkers take on different topics. Many of the philosophers included in the reader are represented by two or more selections.

In most courses of philosophy, instructors focus on thinking and reasoning. Readings typically raise questions, explain controversies, introduce ideas, put forward claims or theses, defend these, consider objections, and the like. Contemporary philosophers emphasize ideas and arguments, and much that students learn to do involves analyzing ideas and evaluating arguments. As we all know, some bad ideas can be defended by some impressive or at least clever arguments, and some good ideas are hard to defend. Ideally, good philosophers put forward good ideas supported by good arguments. Most of the readings in this book do this, but some do better with one than with the other. I have not hesitated to include selections that seem weak on argument because they present ideas that are important or interesting. Not everything in here is meant to be a model for emulation. For similar pedagogical reasons I have included readings of differing degrees of difficulty.[2] Lastly, I have also included a number of religious or theistic selections. Given the influence of Judeo-Christian ideas on our thinking, it seemed odd to omit such readings. And given that a good number of our students are religious, it seemed equally peculiar to do so. It does not seem to me a bad idea for religious students to learn how to think and reason in a secular manner, and for nonbelievers to do the same with regard to religious texts.

---

1. It is sometimes important to encourage students to figure out what they wish to say. When students tell me that "some people say this or that," I tell them that's very interesting but that I want to hear what *they* think and why they think it ("Don't tell me that there's much disagreement about the bombing of Dresden or Hiroshima. Tell me what *you* think and why").

2. Most of the readings should be accessible to a variety of students. I have taught versions of this kind of course at more than half a dozen universities. But instructors will have to take note of the more difficult selections and judge whether the students in question can handle them.

A COMMENT ABOUT THE ORDER OF THE TOPICS

Instructors may teach the sections and topics in any order they wish. But it might be worth it to explain the order given, which is as follows:

Why is killing usually wrong?
Why is death an evil?
What makes our lives go well?
Saving lives: famine
Killing in war
Terrorism
Capital punishment
Animals
Suicide
Euthanasia
When do we die?
Abortion
Making people: cloning
Future generations
Moral theories

The placement of the first three sections should be evident; they raise abstract questions about death and killing, about the significance of well-being, autonomy, and the like. They are representative of the middle-level theory distinctive of this reader. The fourth section is on famine; it is meant to serve in part as an introduction to contemporary practical ethics. Singer's article is well known, and it is a testimony to its excellence that it reads well many decades later. It has many virtues, but one is that of showing the importance and practical import of a certain kind of serious thinking about contemporary problems and controversies. Students are rarely left indifferent by it.

Note also that I place abortion quite late, and this might strike some instructors as unusual. I place this topic after animals and euthanasia, as well as some of the more "political" topics such as the ethics of war. First-year students usually have been exposed to discussions of abortion, and they often have some unfortunate preconceptions about the debate (e.g., that there are only "two sides" and that people's views are determined mainly by their religious beliefs). So I do not find it helpful to talk about it early in the term. But my main reason for teaching it late in a typical one-semester course is that it seems to me the most complex and difficult topic in the reader. I have found it much easier to teach when students have already given some thought to a number of questions that arise with other topics—for example, moral standing and the status of animals, killing in self-defense, different kinds of "innocence" (from the ethics of war), and a number of end-of-life questions.

I have ended the volume not with a selection of classical texts in moral theory but with an excellent essay on moral theories written for another Oxford reader. As I noted, I find that students often do not acquire a good understanding of moral theories from their short exposure to them in courses on practical ethics. It is often better to give them a clear presentation of many of the different theories, one that does not pose interpretative difficulties. I was going to use some notes of mine before I came across Mark Timmons's excellent "primer." Instructors may wish to assign parts of this essay at different stages of the course.

I welcome comments and suggestions, however critical, from instructors and students. My e-mail address is cwmorris@umd.edu.

SOME ACKNOWLEDGMENTS

I am grateful to many people for helpful evaluations of the proposal for this reader: George Agich, R. G. Frey, Thomas May, Jeff McMahan, L. W. Sumner, Ted Warfield, and more than half a dozen anonymous reviewers. My editor Robert Miller has been helpful as well as remarkably patient. My favorite editor, my wife Elissa, has helped in many ways, one of them signing me up for the project in the first place.

Most of the writings on the topics in this reader are relatively new, having been written in the last forty years. For much of the twentieth century, Anglo-American philosophers did not write very much about particular moral and political controversies. In the late sixties and early seventies a number of important thinkers, well represented in this volume, began to write about practical ethics. We are all grateful for the work of philosophers such as Thomas Nagel, James Rachels, Peter Singer, Judith Thomson, and Michael Walzer. I am indebted to them all, and especially to Ray Frey and Wayne Sumner for helping me think about many of these topics.

Christopher W. Morris
July 2010

Why Is Killing Usually Wrong?

Controversies about killing or letting die are of interest to us because we think that killing is usually or almost always wrong. There is in fact very little disagreement about *this*, not only in the United States but also in the world. Every known society has strict rules prohibiting killing except in rare or special cases. This reader focuses on controversies having to do with life and death. So it is natural that we start by thinking about the wrongness of killing.

We believe that killing is usually wrong? Why?

The question needs some clarification. Someone might answer by noting that we have been raised and taught that killing is usually wrong. That is true. But this is not the question we need to answer. What we want to know is whether what we have been taught, that killing is (usually) wrong, is true or trustworthy. Supposing we have been taught that killing is wrong, what reason do we have to maintain this belief?

If we wish to think critically about a range of controversies having to do with life and death, we need to think about the grounds for thinking killing usually to be wrong. Different answers can be given to this question, and it will make a difference which are the most plausible. It may be that some of what divides us on some of the controversies discussed in this text—for example, euthanasia, killing in war—turns on the different answers we give to the question of why killing is usually wrong.

So why is killing usually wrong? One way of answering this question is by examining some cases of killings that are obviously or uncontroversially wrong. People instead often start thinking about the sorts of controversies that are discussed in texts such as this one. But these cases are very *controversial*. They are cases about which we disagree or about which we are puzzled. Examining these cases won't help us at the outset of our inquiries. Instead, we should look at cases of killings that are clearly wrong; we should start with the simpler questions.

Consider the following cases. Two young men are curious about what it is like to kill someone; they order some pizzas to be delivered to an abandoned building in a run-down part of town, where they kill the pizza-delivery man. A second case: A man, angry with his wife who is divorcing him, goes to her house and kills her and their three children. The first case is based on a true story; the second is familiar from stories we may read not infrequently in the papers. Both are examples of obviously wrongful killings. No one reading the descriptions of these acts thinks that they were *permissible* or *justified*, much less *admirable* or *praiseworthy*. Indeed, we rarely spend time thinking about their wrongfulness; that we simply take for granted.[1]

So, when a killing is clearly wrong, what is it exactly that makes it wrong? Let us briefly look at some answers, most of which will occur to the reader. But it might be best for students reading this introduction to stop at this point and think about the question before reading further. (*Exercise*: What are the different reasons why you think killings like these are wrong? Write down your answers.[2])

Here are some common answers. The first might be simply that killing (in cases like these) is against the law. In every society with a legal system there are laws prohibiting killings like these. These laws are not always fairly enforced, which raises a question about enforcement. When one says that the existence of a law makes a killing wrong, is it the legal norm itself or the sanction attached to its violation that makes it wrong? If one imagines having a conversation with an acquaintance who turns out to be unbalanced and homicidal, one might be tempted to cite the fact that the acquaintance is likely to be caught and severely punished if he carries out his plan to kill his philosophy instructor—someone already plotting a murder is unlikely to be deterred by the mere fact that it would be wrong to kill. But the previous suggestion, that killing is wrong because it is against the law, seems different. It suggests that killing might be wrong because of the existence of a law prohibiting it.

This suggestion raises the question whether the law *makes* killing wrong. That is, is killing wrong *because* it is against the law, or might it be wrong *independently* of the law? We might have laws prohibiting killing because we think that killing is wrong, not the other way around. So the question we are asking is related to another: Why have laws that prohibit killing?

A second reason why killing is (usually[3]) wrong might be that it is against God's will. This reason presupposes that there is a deity, as many people believe. In the Jewish and Christian Bibles, one of God's Ten Commandments is "Thou shalt not kill." Might this commandment be what makes killing wrong? There is controversy among experts about how to translate the Hebrew term "*rasah*" used in the Sixth Commandment. Older translations use "kill," while newer ones use "murder." The latter usually means something like wrongful killing with malice. Many biblical scholars now think that the best translation of the

---

1. Someone might try to suggest that the killers were not wrong in acting as they did. Perhaps the pizza-delivery person was an enemy spy about to plant a powerful bomb; suppose the discontented wife was a creature from another planet and the children like those from the British film *Village of the Damned* (1960). But these suppositions challenge the examples only by changing the story.

2. Note: You should not answer, "Many people think that . . ." or "Someone might say that . . ." Rather, note why *you* think that these kinds of killings are wrong.

3. Killing might *always* be wrong, but I add "usually" as we should focus initially on what is clear and obvious (as it is not obvious that killing is always wrong).

commandment would not rule out suicide or the death penalty, much less killing in war. We cannot resolve these interpretive questions, much less the theological debates associated with them. Our interest is in the idea that wrongful killing is wrong *because* the Deity has forbidden it. This idea is hard to evaluate in a short space. Some dismiss it quickly, but it is in fact quite complicated. We merely raise the question and move to another.

Suppose the Deity forbids killing. Why might He do this? What are the reasons for His prohibition? What is it about *us* that we are to be protected by a divine prohibition of this kind?[4]

Let us pause and consider briefly another possible answer to our question. Killing someone can be difficult and unpleasant; the act as well as its anticipation can be stressful. These considerations are reasons not to kill. But surely they are not the sort of reasons we are looking for when we ask why it is wrong to kill. The fact that it is likely to be very diffi-cult to kill someone whose wealth you wish to possess has little to do with the wrongness of the act! Similar killings remain wrong even when they are not difficult or messy.

A similar but more serious proposal is that killing someone changes the killer and makes him or her a worse individual, defective in some ways. Killing damages a person's character. Again, there is more that needs to be said to explore this idea. But just as we don't think that killing is made wrong by being difficult or unpleasant (for the killer), so it is hard to believe that killing is made wrong solely by its effects on the killer's character. It seems odd to think that the effects on the killer are the main reasons that killing is wrong (though there is much more that needs to be said here). Surely character is harmed or corrupted because killing is independently wrong. One might think that the wrongness of killing has more to do with the effects on the victim.

Let us ask then what happens when someone is killed. What are the typical effects or consequences of a killing? Let me list a number of obvious ones:

- the suffering and grief of friends and family
- greater fear and anxiety in the larger population
- losses, especially economic, to the community

These are effects of many if not most killings. But note a feature of them: They all are effects on people other than the victim. Again, it is hard to believe that the principal reasons that killing is wrong solely or even primarily have to do with the effects on others. Let us ask about the effects on the victim.

Typically, when someone is killed (wrongfully), the victim did not want to die. And typically the victim would have preferred many other alternatives to being killed. This sug-gests one or both of two possibilities. The first is that (wrongful) killings seriously *harm* the victim. The second is that they do something to the victim that he or she does not want done to him or her; it seriously infringes the victim's freedom or autonomy. There are two ideas here that we may want to distinguish and explore. Killings, at least wrongful ones, either harm or infringe upon the freedom of their victims. The wrongfulness of killing may have something to do with one or other of these effects on the victim.

On both accounts the wrong is a serious one. It is sometimes said that killing someone is the greatest harm that can be done to them. That has to be an exaggeration; however, it is

---

4. Atheists and agnostics may not find these questions pressing. However, it is instructive to reason about difficult questions from different assumptions, if only to understand how others might see things.

typically a very great harm and a great infringement of the person's autonomy. We need to explore these thoughts. For now, notice that we are focusing on the effects of a killing on the victim (see also the readings in section II). And these effects seem to have something to do with why we think killing is usually wrong.

Something may still be left out. To kill is to take away or destroy life. Life is valuable, and that fact seems to have something to do with the wrongness of killing. In what ways is life valuable? Generally, life has instrumental value; it is a means to other goods. Many goods for us depend on our being alive. Life is thus valuable as an instrument, as a means to other things. Does life also have intrinsic value? Is it also valuable in itself? The distinction here between something being valuable as a means to something else (*instrumental value*) and being valuable in itself (*intrinsically valuable*) is an old one. Some things have only instrumental value (money?), while others (friendship) clearly have both. Is life both instrumentally and intrinsically valuable? Is its great value due to its intrinsic value? The question is important for the controversies this reader explores, as many associate the wrongfulness of killing with the intrinsic value of life, at least human life.

To summarize, the question we are asking is why killing is usually wrong. That is, what is it that makes wrongful killings wrong? We have uncovered several possibilities, and I list them in a different order than that in which they were presented. Killing might be wrong because:

1. it harms the victim
2. it infringes the victim's freedom or autonomy
3. it destroys something of great intrinsic value
4. it harms others (friends and family, community, others)
5. of the effects it has on the killer (e.g., his or her character)
6. it is legally forbidden
7. it is against God's will.

There are other possibilities or, most certainly, other ways of framing the ones I have mentioned. We need to consider these possibilities, as the answers to many of the debates discussed in the rest of the reader will be affected by what we think.

1. What Is Life?

R. M. HARE

Richard Mervyn Hare (1919–2002) was an English philosopher whose accounts of morality were especially influential in the second half of the twentieth century. Much of his work develops his well-known "prescriptivist" account of moral language. But he also wrote widely on a number of questions of practical ethics. Hare was White's Professor of Moral Philosophy at the University of Oxford from 1966 until 1983 and later taught at the University of Florida. Although a pacifist at the start of World War II, Hare enlisted in the Royal Artillery and served in the Malayan Campaign. He was prisoner of war of the Japanese for three years, first in Singapore, and then working on the Burma-Thailand railway. This experience marked him considerably, forming his belief in the importance of ethics. Hare trained some very important moral philosophers, including Peter Singer.

In this short article, Hare raises some simple questions about the taking of life and killing, suggesting that they are not as simple as we might think at first. He argues that "we are on a wild-goose-chase if we are looking for a set of a few simple rules, without exceptions, which will give us the right answer to all moral problems." Determining what is right to do in unusual cases requires us "to think hard about why it is right to do what most of us do in the ordinary cases. . . . and this is how moral philosophy begins."

Life presents us with many problems; but is "What is Life?" one of them? Don't we all know what life is? Or do we? Surgeons have recently learnt how, in certain cases, to start a man's heart working after it has stopped; this has long been possible with the breathing, which was once thought to be a criterion of life—"If that her breath will mist or stain the stone, why then she lives," says King Lear. What then is the state of the man who has stopped breathing, and whose heart has stopped beating, but who is subsequently resuscitated? Is he alive or dead? If we say he is alive, why do we not apply the same term to another man, in a precisely similar condition, who does not happen to be lucky enough to have his seizure when there is a surgeon at hand, and who is therefore not resuscitated? How would we *date* the death of the second man? If we say that his life ended when he had the seizure, we ought in consistency to say that the first man, too, died when he had the seizure, and was subsequently brought back to life. But then is death not "the undiscover'd country from whose bourn no traveller returns"? We feel an aversion to saying that man has been dead, if he subsequently "comes to life again."

What, again, are we to say about the lady in Montreal who recently stopped breathing after having been in a coma since a traffic accident twelve years previously? Suppose that during these twelve years we knew for certain that she could never recover consciousness. In that case, some would claim that her life ended at the time of the accident,

From R. M. Hare, "What Is Life?" *Crucible* (1965). Reprinted with permission of the Estate of R. M. Hare.

and that her subsequent state was one of, at the most, "arrested death." Patients whose brain has been injured by accident or disease are nowadays kept breathing for long periods in respirators without the hope of ever regaining consciousness.

Suppose that some person had administered poison to the Montreal patient between the time of the accident and the time when she stopped breathing twelve years later. Would he have been guilty of murder? Or suppose that a man's heart has stopped beating, but could be restarted; and that, before this is done, somebody shoots him through the head. If the man is no longer alive, then the man who shoots him can hardly be said to be guilty of murder; for you cannot murder a man without killing him, and you cannot kill a man who is not alive. Yet we feel that some sort of crime has been committed more serious than that of mutilating a corpse.

Here is another very similar problem, which is important for the same sort of reasons. A child is born deformed. Is it a man? On what does the answer to this question depend? Suppose that the child has only rudimentary limbs; does that entitle me to say that it is not human? Or suppose that it appears physically normal, but turns out to have the mind of an animal. Suppose, even, to take a fantastic extreme case, that what is born is a perfectly formed puppy. Perhaps nobody would say, in the last-mentioned case, that a man who took the life of the puppy would be guilty of murder. In the recent tragic series of deformed births due to thalidomide, there were those who held that extreme deformity entitled us to say that a child was not human, and therefore that to take its life would not be murder. Most of us shrank from this conclusion. What seemed to be needed was a definition of "human"; the question "What is Man?" like the question "What is Life?" began to look like a crucial, and at the same time an insoluble, question.

So let us ask, more fundamentally, what it is about our thinking that has got us into trouble. The fault lies in our unreasonable wish to have simple rules for our conduct in a complex world. We are on a wild-goose-chase if we are looking for a set of a few simple rules, without exceptions, which will give us the right answer to all moral problems. Life is too

complicated for that. There is no substitute for careful thought about particular cases. The Israelites, who started with the Ten Commandments, ended up with the books of Leviticus, Numbers and Deuteronomy.

If we are seeking a simple rule, the command "Thou shalt do no murder" looks like a strong candidate. It has not got quite the simplicity of "Thou shalt not kill"; but the latter has seemed obviously *too* simple to most people except the followers of Tolstoy and some Oriental sects. "Thou shalt do no murder" looks at first sight more promising. It allows us to kill the people that most of us think it is all right to kill, and forbids us to kill anybody else. The concept "murder" is, indeed, tailored to do just this. At the moment most people think it is not murder to kill one's country's enemies in battle. But if we all became pacifists, and thought that it was wrong to kill people even in battle, we might start calling it murder to do so. The word "murder" scarcely serves to identify the cases in which it is wrong to kill; all it does is to docket or catalogue the most important class of them in a conveniently simple way—provided that we are dealing only with ordinary cases and not with the queer cases mentioned earlier. When we come to them, we have to think again. Even in the case of killing in battle, which is familiar enough, try settling the question of whether it is wrong by asking the question whether it is murder. We at once realise that we cannot know whether it is murder until we have already decided whether it is wrong.

So, when we consider whether it is all right to kill a child without arms and legs, or one even more seriously deformed, or whether it is wrong to stop feeding artificially a patient who will remain unconscious until he ceases to breathe years later, the word "murder" is not going to help us. We have to consider the case before us. If it were analogous in all respects to more normal cases, then we should not be in the quandary we are in. If, instead of considering the peculiarities of the particular case, we confuse ourselves by trying to force it into ready-made categories like "murder," "alive," "human," etc., which were not designed to deal with it, we shall go on being puzzled—go on asking the apparently insoluble questions "What is Murder?" "What is Life?" "What is Man?" But the moral question we are asking cannot really depend on definitions of words. If what we want are definitions of words, we can have plenty. There are any number of ways in which "life" might be defined. Each defines a slightly different concept. Different people, for different purposes (of medical or legal practice, or biological research, or theological or moral discussion) will choose different definitions. None of these gives *the* meaning of the word "life." The people we have described are alive in some senses, in others not. Provided we keep these senses distinct, and thus are clear about the facts of a situation, there may be some hope of arriving at an answer to the moral question that will satisfy us.

This advice will cause some people to despair. They will say, "We have learnt from our parents and priests the simple rule 'Thou shalt do no murder'; if you take this away from us, how shall we ever know that it is wrong to kill anybody? You tell us to consider particular cases; but how are we supposed to do this?" The answer to this is a Socratic one: "You do not know that it is wrong to kill anybody; you have only taken it on trust from your parents and priests. If you wish to understand how to decide what it is right to do in the queer cases, you will have to think hard about why it is right to do what most of us do in the ordinary cases." And that is how moral philosophy begins. But it is not likely to produce any simple labour-saving rules; for life is not like that.

QUESTIONS

1. Why is it hard sometimes to answer the question, "What is life?" Why is it important in these instances to answer this question?
2. How much guidance are we given by the rule, "Thou shalt not kill," or, "Thou shalt not murder"?

2. Of Murder

THOMAS AQUINAS

*S*t. *Thomas Aquinas* (ca. 1225–1274) was a member of the Dominican Order, a Christian priest, and a very influential philosopher. He is sometimes thought of as the philosopher of the Roman Catholic Church. He studied at the University of Paris, founded in the 1100s. His two major works are the *Summa Theologica* and the *Summa contra Gentiles*. His work attempts to combine the philosophy of Aristotle with Christian theology.

In our excerpts from his discussion of murder, Aquinas asks about the killing of living things (especially plants and animals), of innocent people, and in self-defense. He argues

Thomas Aquinas, *Summa Theologica* (Benziger Bros. edition, 1947), translated by Fathers of the English Dominion Province.

that the killing of plants and animals for our use is not wrong, but that killing innocent people is wrong. He also argues that killing in self-defense can be permissible.

Aquinas's discussion of killing in self-defense introduces an important distinction. He distinguishes between the intended and unintended (or "accidental") effects of an action. In killing in self-defense one need intend only to save oneself, not the death of the attacker. As long as one intends only to save one's life and one's act is not "out of proportion to the end," then killing in self-defense is not unlawful. The account Aquinas gives here develops into what is called the doctrine of double effect (see chapter 67). A common statement of the doctrine distinguishes four parts: for any act with two effects, one good (e.g., saving one's life) and one bad (e.g., killing an aggressor), the act is not prohibited if the following conditions are satisfied: (1) the act, in itself, is not morally impermissible, (2) the bad effect of the act is not the means to the good effect, (3) the bad effect is not intended, and (4) the bad effect does not outweigh the good effect (proportionality).

A note on the text. All but one of the excerpts included in this reader are from the *Summa Theologica.* A large work, never completed, it was a "summary of theology," of everything known (God's existence, His creation, Man's end), intended as a manual of study for students. Each "Article" has a standard format, representing the teaching technique of the University of Paris. Articles start with a title (e.g., "Whether it is unlawful to kill any living thing?"). Immediately following are several *objections* (to Aquinas's yet-to-be-stated thesis or conclusion). This is followed by a counter-statement ("on the contrary . . ."), citing Scripture or an important philosopher, and then Aquinas's thesis ("I answer that . . ."). Individual replies to the initial objections are then given. In the following as well as most of the excerpts only the title question and Aquinas's thesis and main argument are given. Chapters 21 (on war) and 46 (suicide) do not omit the objections and responses. The format of Aquinas's *Summa* indicates the importance he gave to the consideration of arguments for and against a position. The objections also indicate to us the positions that he was resisting, some very influential in philosophical and theological thought.

Q64. Of Murder

Art. I Whether It Is Unlawful to Kill Any Living Thing?

Augustine says (De Civ. Dei i, 20): "When we hear it said, 'Thou shalt not kill,' we do not take it as referring to trees, for they have no sense, nor to irrational animals, because they have no fellowship with us. Hence it follows that the words, 'Thou shalt not kill' refer to the killing of a man."

[. . .] There is no sin in using a thing for the purpose for which it is. Now the order of things is such that the imperfect are for the perfect, even as in the process of generation nature proceeds from imperfection to perfection. Hence it is that just as in the generation of a man there is first a living thing, then an animal, and lastly a man, so too things, like the plants, which merely have life, are all alike for animals, and all animals are for man. Wherefore it is not unlawful if man use plants for the good of animals, and animals for the good of man, as the Philosopher states (Polit. i, 3).

Now the most necessary use would seem to consist in the fact that animals use plants, and men use animals, for food, and this cannot be done unless these be deprived of life: wherefore it is lawful both to take life from plants for the use of animals, and from animals for the use of men. In fact this is in keeping with the commandment of God Himself: for it is written (Gn. 1:29,30): "Behold I have given you every herb . . . and all trees . . . to be your meat, and to all beasts of the earth": and again (Gn. 9:3): "Everything that moveth and liveth shall be meat to you."

Art. 6 Whether It Is Lawful to Kill the Innocent?

It is written (Ex. 23:7): "The innocent and just person thou shalt not put to death."

[. . .] An individual man may be considered in two ways: first, in himself; secondly, in relation to something else. If we consider a man in himself, it is unlawful to kill any man, since in every man though he be sinful, we ought to love the nature which God has made, and which is destroyed by slaying him. Nevertheless, as stated above (A[2]) the slaying of a sinner becomes lawful in relation to the common good, which is corrupted by sin. On the other hand the life of righteous men preserves and forwards the common good, since they are the chief part of the community. Therefore it is in no way lawful to slay the innocent.

Art. 7 Whether It Is Lawful to Kill a Man in Self-Defense?

It is written (Ex. 22:2): "If a thief be found breaking into a house or undermining it, and be wounded so as to die; he that slew him shall not be guilty of blood." Now it is much more lawful to defend one's life than one's house. Therefore neither is a man guilty of murder if he kill another in defense of his own life.

[. . .] Nothing hinders one act from having two effects, only one of which is intended, while the other is beside the intention. Now moral acts take their species according to what is intended, and not according to what is beside the intention, since this is accidental as explained above (Q[43], A[3]; FS, Q[12], A[1]). Accordingly the act of self-defense may have two effects, one is the saving of one's life, the other is the slaying of the aggressor. Therefore this act, since one's intention is to save one's own life, is not unlawful, seeing that it is natural to everything to keep itself in "being," as far as possible. And yet, though proceeding from a good intention, an act may be rendered unlawful, if it be out of proportion to the end. Wherefore if a man, in self-defense, uses more than necessary violence, it will be unlawful: whereas if he repel force with moderation his defense will be lawful, because according to the jurists [*Cap. Significasti, De Homicid. volunt. vel casual.], "it is lawful to repel force by force, provided one does not exceed the limits of a blameless defense." Nor is it necessary for salvation that a man omit the act of moderate self-defense in order to avoid killing the other man, since one is bound to take more care of one's own life than of another's. But as it is unlawful to take a man's life, except for the public authority acting for the common good, as stated above (A[3]), it is not lawful for a man to intend killing a man in self-defense, except for such as have public authority, who while intending to kill a man in self-defense, refer this to the public good, as in the case of a soldier fighting against the foe, and in the minister of the judge struggling with robbers, although even these sin if they be moved by private animosity.

QUESTIONS

1. Why is the killing of plants or animals permissible? Does Aquinas's argument permit all killings of plants or animals?
2. For what reasons is the killing of the innocent wrong? How many does Aquinas offer?
3. Why (and when) is killing in self-defense permissible?

3. The Natural State of Men

JOHN LOCKE

*J*ohn Locke (1632–1704) was an important early modern English philosopher, one of the British Empiricists. His political writings were very influential in his time and were well known in the American colonies at the time of the American Revolution; the rights asserted in the second paragraph of the American Declaration of Independence seem quite Lockean. His political thought remains very influential to this day. These extracts, from his famous *Second Treatise of Government*, state his basic assumptions about the laws of nature and the rights and duties that flow from them.

In the *Second Treatise of Government*, Locke gives a description of the "State all men are naturally in" in the absence of government. This condition is "a *State of perfect Freedom* to order their Actions, and dispose of their Possessions, and Persons as they think fit, within the bounds of the Law of Nature, without asking leave or depending upon the Will of any other Man." In these short extracts, he says that the laws of nature obligate us not "to harm another in his life, health, liberty, or possessions . . ." In addition, we have a right to punish transgressors of these laws of nature.

The natural law account of our basic rights and duties that Locke sketches is different from the other moral theories that are discussed in this reader, and it may have quite different implications for the controversies covered here. (See the presentations of natural law and rights-based theories in chapter 67.)

Sect. 6. But though this be a state of liberty, yet it is not a state of licence: though man in that state have an uncontroulable liberty to dispose of his person or possessions, yet he has not liberty to destroy himself, or so much as any creature in his possession, but where some nobler use than its bare preservation calls for it. The state of nature has a law of nature to govern it, which obliges every one: and reason, which is that law, teaches all mankind, who will but consult it, that being all equal and independent, no one ought to harm another in his life, health, liberty, or possessions: for men being all the workmanship of one omnipotent, and infinitely wise maker; all the servants of one sovereign master, sent into the world by his order, and about his business; they are his property, whose workmanship they are, made to last during his, not one another's pleasure: and being furnished with like faculties, sharing all in one community of nature, there cannot be supposed any such subordination among us, that may authorize us to destroy one another, as if we were made for one another's uses, as the inferior ranks of creatures are for our's. Every one, as he is bound to preserve himself, and not to quit his station wilfully, so by the like reason, when his own preservation comes not in competition, ought he, as much as he can, to preserve the rest of mankind, and may not, unless it be to do justice on an offender, take away, or impair the

From *Second Treatise of Government* (1690).

life, or what tends to the preservation of the life, the liberty, health, limb, or goods of another.

Sect. 7. And that all men may be restrained from invading others rights, and from doing hurt to one another, and the law of nature be observed, which willeth the peace and preservation of all mankind, the execution of the law of nature is, in that state, put into every man's hands, whereby every one has a right to punish the transgressors of that law to such a degree, as may hinder its violation: for the law of nature would, as all other laws that concern men in this world be in vain, if there were no body that in the state of nature had a power to execute that law, and thereby preserve the innocent and restrain offenders. And if any one in the state of nature may punish another for any evil he has done, every one may do so: for in that state of perfect equality, where naturally there is no superiority or jurisdiction of one over another, what any may do in prosecution of that law, every one must needs have a right to do.

QUESTIONS

1. What does the law of nature require us to do? Make a list of our natural obligations or duties.
2. Locke's arguments for these are compressed. Try to state them.

---

4. Thou Shall Not Kill

JOHN PAUL II

John Paul II, born Karol Józef Wojtyla (1920–2005), was pope of the Roman Catholic Church from 1978 until his death. His influence, both in religious affairs and in late-twentieth-century politics, was enormous. He is widely viewed as having been instrumental in the collapse of communism in Eastern and Central Europe. He held doctoral degrees in theology as well as in philosophy, and he was fluent in many languages, including his native Polish and more than half a dozen others. As pope he strengthened the Church's stance against abortion and euthanasia and wrote a number of papers, one of the more important being the *Evangelium vitae,* "On the Value and Inviolability of Human Life" (1995).

In these excerpts from the *Evangelium vitae,* John Paul affirms the position of "the absolute inviolability of innocent human life" and argues that the "deliberate decision to deprive an innocent human being of his life is always morally evil and can never be licit either as an end in itself or as a means to a good end." The position he develops here and in other parts of this document (see also chapters 35, 48, and 56) is influential today. John Paul defends his position by reference to Christian doctrine. Non-Christians and nonbelievers

From John Paul II, *Evangelium vitae,* 1995.

will not find the religious premises plausible, but it is still important both to learn about influential doctrines and to examine the relations between the religious premises and conclusions. It is also the case that some non-Christians or nonbelievers have been attracted to similar positions.

53. "Human life is sacred because from its beginning it involves 'the creative action of God,' and it remains forever in a special relationship with the Creator, who is its sole end. God alone is the Lord of life from its beginning until its end: no one can, in any circumstance, claim for himself the right to destroy directly an innocent human being."[1] With these words the Instruction Donum Vitae sets forth the central content of God's revelation on the sacredness and inviolability of human life.

Sacred Scripture in fact presents the precept "You shall not kill" as a divine commandment (Ex 20:13; Dt 5:17). As I have already emphasized, this commandment is found in the Decalogue, at the heart of the Covenant which the Lord makes with his chosen people; but it was already contained in the original covenant between God and humanity after the purifying punishment of the Flood, caused by the spread of sin and violence (cf. Gen 9:5–6).

God proclaims that he is absolute Lord of the life of man, who is formed in his image and likeness (cf. Gen 1:26–28). Human life is thus given a sacred and inviolable character, which reflects the inviolability of the Creator himself. Precisely for this reason God will severely judge every violation of the commandment "You shall not kill," the commandment which is at the basis of all life together in society. He is the "goel," the defender of the innocent (cf. Gen 4:9–15; Is 41:14; Jer 50:34; Ps 19:14). God thus shows that he does not delight in the death of the living (cf. Wis 1:13). Only Satan can delight therein: for through his envy death entered the world (cf. Wis 2:24). He who is "a murderer from the beginning," is also "a liar and the father of lies" (Jn 8:44). By deceiving man he leads him to projects of sin and death, making them appear as goals and fruits of life.

54. As explicitly formulated, the precept "You shall not kill" is strongly negative: it indicates the extreme limit which can never be exceeded. Implicitly, however, it encourages a positive attitude of absolute respect for life; it leads to the promotion of life and to progress along the way of a love which gives, receives and serves. The people of the Covenant, although slowly and with some contradictions, progressively matured in this way of thinking, and thus prepared for the great proclamation of Jesus that the commandment to love one's neighbour is like the commandment to love God; "on these two commandments depend all the law and the prophets" (cf. Mt 22:36–40). Saint Paul emphasizes that "the commandment . . . you shall not kill . . . and any other commandment, are summed up in this phrase: 'You shall love your neighbour as yourself'" (Rom 13:9; cf. Gal 5:14). Taken up and brought to fulfilment in the New Law, the commandment "You shall not kill" stands as an indispensable condition for being able "to enter life" (cf. Mt 19:16–19). In this same perspective, the words of the Apostle John have a categorical ring: "Anyone who hates his brother is a murderer, and you know that no murderer has eternal life abiding in him" (1 Jn 3:15).

From the beginning, the living Tradition of the Church—as shown by the Didache, the most ancient non-biblical Christian writing—categorically repeated the commandment "You shall not kill": "There are two ways, a way of life and a way of death; there is a great difference between them . . . In accordance with the precept of the teaching: you shall not kill . . . you shall not put a child to death by abortion nor kill it once it is born . . . The way of death is this: . . . they show no compassion for the poor, they do not suffer with the suffering, they do not acknowledge their Creator, they kill their children and by abortion cause God's creatures to perish; they drive away the needy, oppress the suffering, they are advocates of the rich and unjust judges of the poor; they are filled with every sin. May you be able to stay ever apart, o children, from all these sins!"[2]

As time passed, the Church's Tradition has always consistently taught the absolute and unchanging value of the commandment "You shall not kill." It is a known fact that in the first centuries, murder was put among the three most serious sins—along with apostasy and adultery—and required a particularly heavy and lengthy public penance before the repentant murderer could be granted forgiveness and readmission to the ecclesial community.

55. This should not cause surprise: to kill a human being, in whom the image of God is present, is a particularly serious sin. Only God is the master of life! Yet from the beginning, faced with the many and often tragic cases which occur in the life of individuals and society, Christian reflection has sought a fuller and deeper understanding of what God's commandment prohibits and prescribes.[3] There are in fact situations in which values proposed by God's Law seem to involve a genuine paradox. This happens for example in the case of legitimate defence, in which the right to protect one's own life and the duty not to harm someone else's life are difficult to reconcile in practice. Certainly, the intrinsic value of life and the duty to love oneself no less than others are the basis of a true right to self-defence. The demanding commandment of love of neighbour, set forth in the Old Testament and confirmed by Jesus, itself presupposes love of oneself as the basis of comparison: "You shall love your neighbour as yourself" (Mk 12:31). Consequently, no one can renounce the right to self-defence out of lack of love for life or for self. This can only be done in virtue of a heroic love which deepens and transfigures the love of self into a radical self-offering, according to the spirit of the Gospel Beatitudes (cf. Mt 5:38–40). The sublime example of this self-offering is the Lord Jesus himself.

Moreover, "legitimate defence can be not only a right but a grave duty for someone responsible for another's life, the common good of the family or of the State."[4] Unfortunately it happens that the need to render the aggressor incapable of causing harm sometimes involves taking his life. In this case, the fatal outcome is attributable to the aggressor whose action brought it about, even though he may not

be morally responsible because of a lack of the use of reason.[5]

57. If such great care must be taken to respect every life, even that of criminals and unjust aggressors, the commandment "You shall not kill" has absolute value when it refers to the innocent person. And all the more so in the case of weak and defenceless human beings, who find their ultimate defence against the arrogance and caprice of others only in the absolute binding force of God's commandment.

In effect, the absolute inviolability of innocent human life is a moral truth clearly taught by Sacred Scripture, constantly upheld in the Church's Tradition and consistently proposed by her Magisterium. This consistent teaching is the evident result of that "supernatural sense of the faith" which, inspired and sustained by the Holy Spirit, safeguards the People of God from error when "it shows universal agreement in matters of faith and morals."[6]

Faced with the progressive weakening in individual consciences and in society of the sense of the absolute and grave moral illicitness of the direct taking of all innocent human life, especially at its beginning and at its end, the Church's Magisterium has spoken out with increasing frequency in defence of the sacredness and inviolability of human life. The Papal Magisterium, particularly insistent in this regard, has always been seconded by that of the Bishops, with numerous and comprehensive doctrinal and pastoral documents issued either by Episcopal Conferences or by individual Bishops. The Second Vatican Council also addressed the matter forcefully, in a brief but incisive passage.[7]

Therefore, by the authority which Christ conferred upon Peter and his Successors, and in communion with the Bishops of the Catholic Church, I confirm that the direct and voluntary killing of an innocent human being is always gravely immoral. This doctrine, based upon that unwritten law which man, in the light of reason, finds in his own heart (cf. Rom 2:14-15), is reaffirmed by Sacred Scripture, transmitted by the Tradition of the Church and taught by the ordinary and universal Magisterium.[8]

The deliberate decision to deprive an innocent human being of his life is always morally evil and can never be licit either as an end in itself or as a means to a good end. It is in fact a grave act of disobedience to the moral law, and indeed to God himself, the author and guarantor of that law; it contradicts the fundamental virtues of justice and charity. "Nothing and no one can in any way permit the killing of an innocent human being, whether a fetus or an embryo, an infant or an adult, an old person, or one suffering from an incurable disease, or a person who is dying. Furthermore, no one is permitted to ask for this act of killing, either for himself or herself or for another person entrusted to his or her care, nor can he or she consent to it, either explicitly or implicitly. Nor can any authority legitimately recommend or permit such an action."[9]

As far as the right to life is concerned, every innocent human being is absolutely equal to all others. This equality is the basis of all authentic social relationships which, to be truly such, can only be founded on truth and justice, recognizing and protecting every man and woman as a person and not as an object to be used. Before the moral norm which prohibits the direct taking of the life of an innocent human being "there are no privileges or exceptions for anyone. It makes no difference whether one is the master of the world or the 'poorest of the poor' on the face of the earth. Before the demands of morality we are all absolutely equal."[10]

Notes

1. Congregation for the Doctrine of the Faith, Instruction on Respect for Human Life in Its Origin and on the Dignity of Procreation *Donum Vitae* (22 February 1987), Introduction, No. 5: *AAS* 80 (1988), 76–77; cf. *Catechism of the Catholic Church*, No. 2258.
2. *Didache*, I, 1; II, 1–2; V, 1 and 3: *Patres Apostolici*, ed. F. X. Funk, I, 2–3, 6–9, 14–17; cf. *Letter of Pseudo-Barnabas*, XIX, 5: loc. cit., 90–93.
3. Cf. *Catechism of the Catholic Church*, Nos. 2263–2269; cf. also *Catechism of the Council of Trent* III, §§ 327–332.
4. *Catechism of the Catholic Church*, No. 2265.
5. Cf. Saint Thomas Aquinas, *Summa Theologiae*, II–II, q. 64, a. 7; Saint Alphonsus De' Liguori, *Theologia Moralis*, 1. III, tr. 4, c. 1, dub.3.
6. Second Vatican Ecumenical Council, Dogmatic Constitution on the Church *Lumen Gentium*, 12.
7. Second Vatican Ecumenical Council, Pastoral Constitution on the Church in the Modern World *Gaudium et Spes*, 27.
8. Second Vatican Ecumenical Council, Dogmatic Constitution on the Church *Lumen Gentium*, 25.
9. Congregation for the Doctrine of the Faith, Declaration on Euthanasia *Iura et Bona* (5 May 1980), II: *AAS* 72 (1980), 546.
10. Encyclical Letter *Veritatis Splendor* (6 August 1993), 96: *AAS* 85 (1993), 1209.

QUESTIONS

1. What exactly is John Paul's position regarding the killing of innocent humans? What do the terms "absolute" and "inviolable" mean?
2. What are the different considerations John Paul uses to defend his conclusions? Which ones depend on religious premises and which do not?

5. The Value of a Man Is His Price

THOMAS HOBBES

Thomas Hobbes (1588–1679) was an important seventeenth-century English philosopher and one of the most important political thinkers of all time. His major work is the *Leviathan* (1649), a long work stating his views on the nature of the world and of human beings, and developing an important account of the nature of the modern state. He defended the absolute rule of sovereigns and denied any right to rebellion, but the premises of his argument are widely thought to be unfavorable to unlimited government. His political thought is now studied in most courses in modern political philosophy.

We often say that life or human life has great value or is valuable in itself (intrinsically). Pope John Paul in the previous chapter asserts that human life is sacred. We also often disapprove of those who treat others as mere means to their ends (instrumentally). Hobbes seems to challenge these common thoughts and boldly claims that the "Value, or WORTH of a man, is . . . his Price." It follows from this thought that different people will have different worth. This conclusion seems to follow from Hobbes's views about value and rationality, which are not laid out in this brief chapter. However, merely thinking about his challenge to commonly accepted ideas will require us to think about what we mean when we talk about the value of human life.

The Value, or WORTH of a man, is as of all other things, his Price; that is to say, so much as would be given for the use of his Power: and therefore is not absolute; but a thing dependant on the need and judgement of another. An able conductor of Souldiers, is of great Price in time of War present, or imminent; but in Peace not so. A learned and uncorrupt Judge, is much Worth in time of Peace; but not so much in War. And as in other things, so in men, not the seller, but the buyer determines the Price. For let a man (as most men do,) rate themselves as the highest Value they can; yet their true Value is no more than it is esteemed by others.

The manifestation of the Value we set on one another, is that which is commonly called Honouring, and Dishonouring. To Value a man at a high rate, is to Honour him; at a low rate, is to Dishonour him. But high, and low, in this case, is to be understood by comparison to the rate that each man setteth on himselfe.

The publique worth of a man, which is the Value set on him by the Common-wealth, is that which men commonly call DIGNITY. And this Value of him by the Common-wealth, is understood, by offices of Command, Judicature, publike Employment; or by Names and Titles, introduced for distinction of such Value.

From Thomas Hobbes, *Leviathan* (1649).

QUESTIONS

1. What does Hobbes mean when he says that the value of a person is his or her price? What implications might this have for ethics and some of the controversies in this book?

2. Hobbes says that something's price is "dependant on the need and judgement of another." This is a hint as to the conception of value that leads to his conception of the value of a person. Is the value of *everything* dependent on the needs and judgments of others? This is a very difficult question.

6. Killing

JEFF McMAHAN

*J*eff McMahan (1954–) is professor of philosophy at Rutgers University. He writes about the ethics of life and death. The extracts in this reader all come from his *Ethics of Killing: Problems at the Margins of Life* (Oxford, 2002). He is the author also of *Killing in War* (Oxford, 2009), *The Values of Lives* (Oxford, 2009), and *The Ethics of Killing: Self-Defense, War, and Punishment* (Oxford, forthcoming).

In this chapter, taken from his book on the ethics of killing, McMahan takes up the question of the wrongness of killing and distinguishes between two accounts. The first is the *Harm-Based Account*, which is defended by many people, including James Rachels. This view "holds that acts of killing are normally wrong principally because of the harm they inflict on the victims." It also holds that the degree of wrongness varies with the degree of harm caused, other things being equal. This account McMahan associates with an influential thesis in the ethics of killing, namely, the thesis that the common distinction between killing someone and letting someone die is not morally significant. The debate about this thesis will be taken up in later sections. The second view of the wrongness of killing is what McMahan calls the *Time-Relative Interest Account*, which identifies the principal feature of killing that makes it wrong, namely the fact that it frustrates the victim's interest in continuing to live. The interest in continuing to live is "time-relative," that is, the interests a person has at a particular time. The distinction between these two accounts is part of a case McMahan makes against the influential Harm-Based Account, in that it presupposes an implausible account of the badness of death. The discussion in this chapter is more abstract and difficult than that in the other chapters in section I of the reader.

The Wrongness of Killing and the Badness of Death

1.1. Two Accounts

There is no moral belief that is more universal, stable, and unquestioned, both across different societies and throughout history, than the belief that killing people is normally wrong. Yet no one, to my knowledge, has ever offered an account of why killing is wrong that even begins to do justice to the full range of commonsense beliefs about the morality of killing. Perhaps the overwhelming obviousness of the general belief—its luminous self-evidence—discourages inquiry into its foundations. Yet it does not appear to be a basic or ultimate moral belief—that is, one that cannot be derived from or justified by reference to some more fundamental moral principle or principles. Rather, the belief that killing is normally wrong seems susceptible of defense or justification: reasons can be given that purport to explain why killing is wrong.

It might be thought that an understanding of why killing is wrong is merely of academic interest. From a practical point of view, the important piece of knowledge—that in general killing *is* wrong—is already known with sufficient certainly that it would be idle to offer clever proofs that trace the belief to its source in more fundamental beliefs or principles. What could be gained from an exercise in demonstrating the obvious?

There is in fact an answer to this, which is that an understanding of why killing is normally wrong should help us to identify the conditions in which killing may *not* be wrong. For, in cases of killing in which the reasons that make killing normally wrong do not apply, there may be no objection to killing: it may be permissible or, if there are moral reasons that favor it, even morally required. And there may be other cases involving killing in which the reasons that normally militate against killing are present but only to a weaker degree, or in which some reasons apply while others do not. In either case, the presumption against killing may he correspondingly weaker, or more readily overridden by countervailing considerations.

Understanding the basis of the wrongness of killing is therefore of considerable practical

significance. How might we seek to deepen our understanding of the morality of killing? One approach is to compare the killing of persons with the killing of animals. (Recall that by "persons" I mean individuals who are self-conscious, irrespective of species. By "animals" I mean nonhuman animals. In general, I will use the word "people" as the plural of "person" rather than as the plural of "human being." Thus "people" could conceivably include some nonhuman individuals. But in general I will treat "people" and "animals" as categories that do not overlap. Thus, in most of what follows, one should assume that "animals" refers to animals that are not only nonhuman but also not persons. For simplicity, I will put aside, for the time being, the questions that are raised by the possibility that there are nonhuman animals that—or who—are persons.)

It is uncontroversial that the killing of an animal is normally less seriously wrong than the killing of a person. If we could determine *why* this is so, this could illuminate the reasons why killing is in general wrong. Either some of the reasons why killing a person is wrong do not apply in the case of animals, or the reasons that apply in the case of persons apply less strongly in the case of animals. Or both could be true. If we could identify what is missing in the case of animals, this would reveal why killing people is normally *more* wrong. And that would provide a substantial part of the explanation of why killing people is wrong at all.

The idea that wrongness is a matter of degree may seem puzzling. This is the result of an ambiguity in the notion of wrongness. In the most familiar sense of the term, to say that an act is wrong is to say that it ought not to be done, all things considered. In this sense, wrongness is not a matter of degree, for it either is or is not the case that an act ought not to be done. There is, however, another sense of the term, according to which the wrongness of an act is just its moral objectionableness. An act may have various morally objectionable or, as some have said, "wrong-making" features. These features may, in certain contexts, be outweighed by other considerations, so that the act, though morally objectionable in some respects, may be permissible, or not wrong (in the sense that it ought not to be done), all things considered. But if the reasons why it is morally objectionable are not outweighed (or nullified or otherwise overcome), it will be wrong, in the sense that it ought not to be done. Still, the degree to which it is morally objectionable is variable. If the moral objections to it, or the reasons why it ought not to be done, are very strong and are not substantially opposed by countervailing considerations, we say that the act would be seriously wrong. If, by contrast, the objections to it are weak, or are almost counterbalanced by countervailing moral considerations, it may be only slightly wrong.

Return now to the claim that killing people is generally more wrong than killing animals. One strikingly obvious difference between killing a person and killing an animal is that a person who is killed normally thereby suffers a significantly greater harm than an animal does if it is killed. And it seems obvious that there is a close connection between the wrongness of killing and the fact that killing normally involves the infliction of a grievous harm on the victim. Indeed, many people think that it is precisely because killing harms its victim that it is morally wrong. James Rachels, for example, contends that, "[i]f we should not kill, it is because in killing we are harming someone. That is the reason killing is wrong. The rule against killing has as its point the protection of the victims."[1] And in a well-known article on abortion, Don Marquis echoes Rachels's claim: "What primarily makes killing wrong is . . . its effect on the victim. The loss of one's life is one of the greatest losses one can suffer. The loss of one's life deprives one of all the experiences, activities, projects, and enjoyments that would otherwise have constituted one's future. Therefore, killing someone is wrong, primarily because the killing inflicts (one of) the greatest possible losses on the victim."[2] With one further assumption, this view of the morality of killing offers a tidy and plausible explanation of why killing people is normally more wrong than killing animals. What Rachels, Marquis, and others claim is that killing is wrong because it harms the individual who is killed. But of the great many acts that are harmful, few if any are as seriously wrong as killing. Why is killing more gravely wrong than most other acts that also cause harm? For someone sympathetic to the account offered by

Rachels and Marquis, the answer is obvious. As Marquis notes in the passage just quoted, the harm inflicted by killing is normally very great. If we assume that the degree to which a harmful act is wrong varies with the degree of harm it causes, this would explain why killing is normally more seriously wrong than other harmful acts. It would also explain why some acts of killing are more wrong than others—in particular, it would explain why killing a person is normally more wrong than killing an animal.

The assumption that is needed to generate these explanations may take a weaker or a stronger form. According to the weaker version, if an act of killing is wrong, or morally objectionable, at least in part because it harms its victim, then another act that is the same in all relevant respects except that it harms its victim to an even greater extent will be wrong, or morally objectionable, to a greater degree. Call this *the assumption of correlative variation*. The stronger version is that, if an act of killing is wrong, or morally objectionable, at least in part because it harms its victim, then another act that is the same in all relevant respects except that it harms its victim to an even greater extent will be more wrong, or more morally objectionable, *in proportion to* the extent to which the amount of harm it causes is greater. Call this *the assumption of proportional variation*. Because the assumption of correlative variation is weaker and is entailed by the assumption of proportional variation, it has a better chance of being true. Hence in the subsequent discussion I will focus primarily on it.

In order to explain why killing people is in general more seriously wrong than killing animals, we can combine the view articulated by Rachels and Marquis with the assumption of correlative variation. The resulting view, which we may call the *Harm-Based Account* of the wrongness of killing, holds that acts of killing are normally wrong principally because of the harm they inflict on the victims, and that the degree to which an act of killing is wrong varies with the degree of harm it causes to the victim, other things being equal. (This account has to be refined in order to account for the wrongness of attempted, unsuccessful killing, presumably by focusing on expected or intended rather than actual harm. Though important, this refinement need not detain us here.) According to this account, killing people is usually gravely wrong, for death is typically among the worst harms a person can suffer. By contrast, the harm an animal suffers in dying is considerably less; hence killing the animal is less seriously wrong.

The Harm-Based Account of the morality of killing is naturally associated with the denial of moral significance to the distinction between killing and letting die. If it is the harm that the victim suffers that explains why killing is wrong, then letting someone die should also be wrong, if other things are equal, for the same reason. For the harm that results when one lets someone die—namely, death—is the same as the harm caused by killing.[3] The idea that letting a person die is, other things being equal, as objectionable as killing is not, however, *entailed* by the Harm-Based Account. That view does not claim that the only factor relevant to assessing the morality of killing is the amount of harm suffered by the victim. It claims only that the *fundamental* explanation of the wrongness of killing appeals to the wrongness of inflicting harm. It is compatible with that claim to suppose that the way in which an agent is instrumental in the occurrence of harm could make a moral difference.

The Harm-Based Account has certain virtues. For example, it offers a credible explanation not only of why the killing of persons is in general more seriously wrong than the killing of animals but also of why the killing of animals of certain types is generally more objectionable than the killing of animals of other types. Because animals vary considerably in their capacities for well-being, some may be harmed to a greater extent by death than others. For example, because a dog's life is normally richer (in pleasure, social relations, and so on) than a frog's, dogs generally suffer a greater harm in dying. Therefore the Harm-Based Account implies that it is normally more wrong to kill a dog than it is to kill a frog. These claims—that the killing of persons is normally more seriously wrong than the killing of animals and that the killing of higher animals is generally more seriously wrong than the killing of lower animals—are ones that our account of the wrongness of killing should be able to explain and defend.

Despite these virtues, however, the Harm-Based Account faces certain objections. There is only one we need to consider, since it alone is sufficient to undermine the account. This is that the Harm-Based Account presupposes that identity is what matters. For the harm involved in death is equivalent to the extent to which the death is worse for the individual who dies—that is, the extent to which the death makes the life as a whole worse than it would otherwise have been. In short, the Harm-Based Account presupposes a Life Comparative Account of the badness of death. Its implications for certain cases are consequently profoundly counterintuitive. For example, it implies that, if other things are equal, the killing of a fetus or infant is more seriously wrong than the killing of an older child or adult, because the death of the fetus or infant involves a greater harm—that is, the effect of the death on the value of the life as a whole is worse.

Some advocates of the Harm-Based Account have embraced the conclusion that abortion is wrong for the same reason that the killing of adults is normally wrong.[4] Others have sought to evade this conclusion by various stratagems—for example, by asserting a conceptual link between harm and desire and arguing that a fetus cannot be harmed by death because it cannot desire to continue to live.[5] But another option is to abandon the assumption that identity is the rational basis of egoistic concern. If we recognize that identity is not what really matters, our moral concern ought not to follow identity but ought instead to follow what really matters. If morality requires us to be concerned for an individual for his own sake, it should direct our concern to what he has most egoistic reason to care about—that is, to his time-relative interests. These, as I have noted, may diverge from his interests, which are what would be best for his life as a whole. The divergence is, of course, most striking in hypothetical cases involving division. These cases can raise moral questions that may assist us to see the appropriateness of focusing our concern on an individual's time-relative interests rather than on his interests.

Spontaneous Division. Suppose that people sometimes spontaneously divide. (Readers may imagine their own details, which will have to be rather bizarre. The sole constraint is that the process of division must preserve the prudential unity relations: between the original person and each of his successors, there must be sufficient physical, functional, and organizational continuity of the brain to support a degree of psychological unity over time comparable to that within the life of an ordinary person over the same period of time.) The process of spontaneous division is preceded by the person's lapsing into a coma. In the early phases, while the person is comatose, the process can be reversed and division prevented. Suppose a person suddenly enters this process without having indicated whether she would prefer to be prevented from dividing. Suppose, too, that we know that, if she does not divide, she will die in about a year but that, if she divides, her successors will both be able to live for many years.

Ought we to prevent this person from dividing or ought we to allow it to happen? We cannot consult her preferences, for she is comatose. It would be against her interests to divide, for she would cease to exist now rather than in a year. What does she have most egoistic reason to want? She might, of course, have contingent egoistic reasons to want not to divide—for example, she might greatly value the relation she has with her husband, a relation that could not be sustained by both of her successors. But suppose there are no such reasons. Suppose, on the contrary, that she has been vacillating between becoming a concert pianist and becoming a historian and has been frustrated by her inability to do both, given the amount of time that each would require. If she were to divide, one of her successors could become a pianist while the other could engage in historical research. In these circumstances, she has strong egoistic reason to want to divide. For if she divides, she will be related in the ways that matter to *two* future lives, in each of which her successor would be able to achieve one of her ambitions. And each of her successors would live much longer than she would if she were not to divide. If the prudential unity relations, and not identity, are what matter, it would be perverse to prevent her from dividing.

The only actual cases in which an individual's time-relative interests may diverge from his interests are cases in which the prudential unity relations would be conspicuously weak. In these cases, the divergence is considerably less pronounced than in cases involving division. And in most of these cases this weaker divergence is of little or no practical significance. This is because morality requires us to show the same respect for an individual's future time-relative interests as we must show for his present ones. So, for example, even if an individual's present time-relative interest in some future event is weak, it may be that our treatment of him should be the same as it would be if we were guided by a concern for his interests; for we can now anticipate that his *later* time-relative interest in that event will be strong. [. . .]

Among the actual cases in which there may be significant divergence between an individual's interests and his time-relative interests, the only ones that are common are those involving a choice that will affect whether an individual will continue to exist and in which the prudential unity relations linking that individual to himself in the future would be weak. In these cases, the individual's present time-relative interest in continuing to live may be weak even if his interest in continuing to live is strong. And the present time-relative interest is the only one that would be frustrated by the individual's ceasing to exist, for his ceasing to exist would prevent his having any future time-relative interests. In these cases, it can make an enormous difference whether we are guided by a concern for the individual's interests or his time-relative interests. I claim that, if identity is not what matters, it would be a mistake to be guided by a concern for his interests, just as it would be in the case of Spontaneous Division. It would therefore be a mistake to be guided by the Harm-Based Account.

It is, however, obviously possible to formulate an alternative account of the wrongness of killing that captures the spirit of the Harm-Based Account but rejects the assumption that identity is what matters. Like the Harm-Based Account, this alternative account would explain what is fundamentally wrong about killing in terms of the effect on the victim. But it would insist that it is the prudential unity relations, which may hold to varying degrees, that matter. Therefore it will explain the wrongness of killing in terms of the effect on the victim's time-relative interests. According to this account, what is fundamentally wrong about killing, when it is wrong, is that it frustrates the victim's time-relative interest in continuing to live. It should incorporate its own assumption of correlative variation, which holds that the degree to which an act of killing is wrong varies, other things being equal, with the strength of the victim's time-relative interest in continuing to live. (Substituting for this an assumption of proportional variation would yield a more determinate, slightly more controversial account.) Call this the *Time-Relative Interest Account* of the wrongness of killing. (The label is, of course, the same as that of the parallel account of the badness of death. I [. . .] normally rely on the context to indicate to which account I will be referring.)

As was true of the Harm-Based Account, the Time-Relative Interest Account does not claim that the factor that it identities as fundamental is the only factor relevant to the morality of an act of killing. It is compatible with this account to accept that a variety of other factors can affect the moral status of an act of killing and that these factors can interact in complex ways. Relevant factors divide into several distinct types, among which are the agent's motives, intentions, and mode of agency, side effects, whether the victim is responsible in a way that makes him liable to be killed as a matter of justice, whether the victim consents to be killed, whether the agent is specially related to the victim, and so on. [. . .]

Notes

1. James Rachels, *The End of Life: Euthanasia and Morality* (Oxford University Press, 1986), p. 6.
2. Don Marquis, "Why Abortion Is Immoral," *Journal of Philosophy* 86 (1989): 183–203, p. 189.
3. This is denied in Matthew Hanser, "Why Are Killing and Letting Die Wrong?" *Philosophy and Public Affairs* 24: 175–201.
4. For example, Marquis, "Why Abortion Is Immoral."
5. For an argument along these lines, see Peter Singer, *Practical Ethics*, 2nd ed. (Cambridge University Press, 1993), chs. 4 and 5.

QUESTIONS
1. Describe the two accounts of the wrongness of killing.
2. McMahan's objection to the influential harm account is explained in the paragraph that begins, "Despite these virtues . . ." Formulate the objection.

7. Not Playing God

JONATHAN GLOVER

*J*onathan Glover (1941–) is an important British philosopher who writes about ethics and politics and a number of other subjects. His recent books include *Humanity: A Moral History of the Twentieth Century* (1999) and *Choosing Children: The Ethical Dilemmas of Genetic Intervention* (2006). He is also the author of *Ethics of New Reproductive Technologies: The Glover Report to the European Commission* (1989).

From *Causing Death and Saving Lives* (Penguin, 1977).

In this chapter, a brief selection from his influential book, *Causing Death and Saving Lives* (1977), Glover describes a case of a decision in wartime to cause a large number of people to be saved by causing a different, smaller number of people to perish. Many react by thinking that we cannot make such choices, that doing so would be "playing God." Glover's case is important to think about in the context of a discussion of the wrongness of killing, for we need to be clearer about the matter of whether it is ever permissible to kill someone in order to save many. Glover's case is formulated in terms of causing death, and one question that will arise in the course of this reader is whether killing consists in more than causing death.

A case in which there was a choice between saving the lives of two different lots of people occurred during the Second World War.[1] A German "spy ring" in Britain consisted of a double agent on the British side and a string of fictitious people. It was on this supposed network of agents that the German government relied for information about where the V1 and V2 rockets were falling. The aiming was broadly accurate, hitting the target of London. It was proposed that the double agent should send back reports indicating that most of them had fallen well north of London, so that the rocket ranges would correct their aim a number of miles to the south. The result of this would have been to make most of the rockets fall in Kent, Surrey or Sussex, killing far fewer people than they did in London. This proposal is said to have been resisted successfully by Herbert Morrison, on the grounds that the British government was not justified in choosing to sacrifice one lot of citizens in order to save another lot.

Note

1. Sefton Delmer: *The Counterfeit Spy*, London, 1971, Ch. 12.

QUESTIONS
1. What is the exact choice facing the double agent in the story?
2. What arguments can you construct for the different options facing the double agent?

II

Why Is Death an Evil?

Typically we do not want to die, and those who care about us do not want us to die. Death seems to be something bad or an evil. We might think, as was said in the last section, that death is usually a harm to the victim (as well as to others). Why is death usually bad for the victim? The question turns out to be difficult to answer.

Life is valuable, as we noted in section I. Death deprives us of life. So death may be bad because of the value of life (of which it deprives us). But the loss of life is not like many other losses, for instance, the loss of a leg or of one's sight. Much more is lost when one dies. On some accounts, it seems as if everything is lost with death. That is a lot, but it also suggests something puzzling: the fact that the deceased won't mind.

We usually fear death. We need to be a bit clearer about what we mean here. A distinction must be made at the outset between death and dying. The latter is an experience, one that may well be fearful. Our interest for now is in death, the *state*, not the *process* of dying (coming to be dead). We may fear death, as well as dying.

In section XI we will take up the question of "when do we die." This question is confused with that of "the definition of death." The two are connected. But determining what death *is*, how the term is to be defined, may not tell us *when* we die, much less how we can tell when someone is in fact dead. It is becoming increasingly important for us, especially in medical contexts, to refine our *criteria* of death—for example, heart-lung or cardiopulmonary criteria and brain-death criteria (see the readings in section XI). But for now our interest is in understanding what death is.

We just said that death deprives us of life. But many people believe in "life after death"; they believe that we are immortal and will live on. Many religious traditions assert something like this, and presumably this thought will affect other beliefs about the harmfulness of killing or the misfortune of death. Suppose we think we have immortal souls. Then we will survive death. Many if not most people would consider this good news. We usually do not want to die. We could treat the belief that we are immortal as a denial that we die.

23

Explaining why the discovery that we are immortal is good news will then require an explanation of why death *would* be a bad thing were it to happen to us.

If we think of death as the end of life but are convinced that there is life after death, it will sometimes be confusing to talk about "death." Usually we mean death "in this world." So it might be best to talk about this-worldly death, in which case death is the end of life in this world. For some that is the end of things, for others it is not. We need to proceed slowly here because religious people who believe in an afterlife may think differently of the evil of death (in this world), and we do not want to beg any important questions.

What is death, then, in this world? The question that will preoccupy us in section XI is when does death happen. The two are related, but we'll try here to address mainly the first. The simplest thought would be this: death (in this world) is the permanent end of life (in this world). When we die, our lives end. Some will object, saying that we might be able to bring people back to life some time in the future. It's not clear, however, what this might mean. If something like this were possible we could talk of "suspended animation." Usually, if we revive someone who fell into a freezing lake, we do not say, except metaphorically, that we brought them back to life. So it seems reasonable to talk about death being the permanent end of life in this world. The difficult question of *when* this happens, to be taken up in section XI, may change what we say here.

Why then is death typically something bad or an evil? To kill someone is to end his or her life in this world; if there is no afterlife, it is to end his or her life. Presumably death is worse in the absence of an afterlife. Note that I say *worse*; if there is an afterlife, then killing someone might be an additional offense against the Deity and possibly a greater *wrong*. We are focusing now only on the question of the harm of death. A conjecture might be that death is one of the greatest harms we can suffer. With death we might say that we lose everything (in this life). Since most of us are attached to other things—people, projects, places— there are worse things that can befall us. But death seems pretty bad.

If we say that death is bad because we lose everything with death, there is a puzzle. Let us suppose that we are not immortal and don't live on after this life. What kind of loss does death bring? Death deprives us of our life. But this loss is different from other losses. You lose your car or your hearing—that is bad—but *you* are still here. *You* are the subject of these losses. Death (without an afterlife) is different. With this loss *you* cease to be. Thus, there is no subject of death. Death is not analogous to normal losses; it is not a state like unconsciousness. You are no longer around, in existence. We think that death is a bad thing for us. But this thought is puzzling. The Greek philosopher Epicurus (341–270 BCE) pointed to this puzzling fact long ago: "So death, the most terrifying of ills, is nothing to us, since so long as we exist, death is not with us; but when death comes, then we do not exist." The process of dying may be bad, but why is death bad? Epicurus points out that we do not mind our nonexistence prior to our birth. Why should we mind the state of nonexistence after our death? We need to think about this puzzle.

Our interest in understanding the evil or harm of death is in large part tied to our inquiries into the ethics of killing and letting die. We think of killing as usually wrong and a much more serious wrong than many others. A conjecture we might make is that one of the greatest harms is to destroy another's life.[1]

---

1. Is this a lesser harm (to the victim) if it turns out that we are immortal? As we noted, if there is a Creator, then killing someone presumably would (also) be a wrong against Him.

8. Death and Evil

JAMES RACHELS

*J*ames Rachels (1941–2003) was an American moral philosopher. His work helped stimulate interest in practical or applied ethics. He edited the very first course reader in the subject, *Moral Problems* (1971), and some of his articles have been very influential. His book *The End of Life* (1986), from which this chapter and chapter 49 are taken, develops his views about euthanasia. The best-selling *Elements of Moral Philosophy*, now in its sixth edition, is one of the best texts of its kind. More information about him and his work is available at http://www.jamesrachels.org/.

In this chapter from *The End of Life*, Rachels asks why killing someone is usually wrong. He thinks the answer has something to do with the fact that death is bad for the victim. This leads him to confront the puzzling idea defended by the Greek philosopher Epicurus (341–270 BCE) that death is not bad or evil. Considering Epicurus's doctrine leads Rachels to a discussion of *hedonism*, the doctrine that "the only things intrinsically good or bad for a person are pleasant or unpleasant experiences" (e.g., feeling pleasure, suffering pain, being embarrassed). Rachels concludes that death is an evil for the person who dies because of the possibilities it forecloses. This topic is taken up again in the other readings in section II.

Death and Suffering

Why is it wrong to kill people? No doubt the question is too simple, because killing people is not *always* wrong; the rule has exceptions. However, there is always a strong presumption that it is wrong, and this presumption may be set aside only in special cases and for powerful reasons. Thus, when we ask why killing is wrong, we mean: why is there such a strong presumption against it?

It is a strange question, for two reasons. First, it brings into question something that we usually take for granted; the wrongness of killing may seem too obvious to need explanation. Second, it is an *unclear* question, in the way that philosophical questions are often unclear, at least when they are first posed. It is hard to tell, in advance, just what a satisfactory answer will be like. It is unlike questions such as

"What is the specific gravity of aluminium?" Here we know that the answer will be a number, and, moreover, we know how to go about discovering which number is the right one. There is a well-established procedure which, if followed faithfully, will yield the correct answer. But how will we recognize the correct answer to the question "Why is it wrong to kill people?" if we find it? Here, as often happens in philosophy, we are to some extent groping in the dark, or better, in a kind of half-light, in which we can see that there is a problem, but not the exact shape of the problem.

Nevertheless, it is obvious enough where to start. The wrongness of killing is undoubtedly connected with the fact that the victim ends up dead. But why is *that* such a bad thing? Why is it bad to die? It is easy to see why it may be bad for people other than

From James Rachels, *The End of Life* (1986), reprinted by permission of Oxford University Press.

the victim himself. Those who love him may grieve over his death, and those who were depending on him for one thing or another may suffer because, being dead, he will be unable to perform as expected. But considerations of this kind will not provide a full account of why killing is wrong. Killing is wrong because of what is done to the victim himself, and not merely because of what happens to the survivors. A satisfactory account of the wrongness of killing must be based on an explanation of why death is a bad thing *for the person who dies*.

Epicurus' Argument

Not everyone has agreed that death is bad. Some philosophers have argued that there is nothing evil about death, and that fearing it is therefore irrational. The most famous argument to this effect was devised by Epicurus, and repeated with approval by such figures as Lucretius and Montaigne. Epicurus' equanimity did not come from any optimistic view of death as merely a passage to a different and better life. If "death" *were* followed by some sort of afterlife, then what we think of it should depend on what sort of life follows—if we go to heaven, death might be a splendid thing; and if we go to hell, it is clearly terrible for that very obvious reason. But Epicurus held no such view. He thought of death as annihilation, the absolute end of one's existence. Yet he still believed there was nothing bad about it. In a letter to one of his followers, he wrote:

> Become accustomed to the belief that death is nothing to us. For all good and evil consists in sensation, but death is deprivation of sensation . . . So long as we exist death is not with us; but when death comes, then we do not exist. It does not then concern either the living or the dead, since for the former it is not, and the latter are no more.

The argument presented in this passage has three main steps.

1. First there is the hedonistic principle which says that the only things intrinsically good or bad for a person are pleasant or unpleasant experiences—"all good and evil consists in sensation." It is unpleasant, for example, to suffer pain, or to feel depressed, worried, embarrassed, frustrated, frightened, or bored. So these are all intrinsically bad. But, according to this principle, things *other than* experiences are bad only in so far as they cause one to have unpleasant experiences. Disease, for example, is bad because it causes pain, and, when it is incapacitating, because it causes one to feel frustrated at being unable to do what one wants. Goods are explained in a similar manner: pleasant experiences are intrinsically good, and other things are good only in so far as they cause pleasant experiences.

2. Does death cause one to have unpleasant experiences? (Or for that matter, pleasant ones?) Epicurus points out that "So long as we exist death is not with us; but when death comes, then we do not exist." A person's death cannot cause him to have unpleasant experiences while he is alive because his death has not yet occurred; and after he dies it cannot cause him unpleasant experiences because he no longer exists, and has no experiences at all.

3. Therefore, although a person's death may be a bad thing for others—it may cause them to feel grief or frustration—it cannot be a bad thing for the person himself.

This argument is an example of one of the most fascinating philosophical phenomena: like Zeno's arguments for the unreality of motion, it attempts to prove false something that we all know—or think we know—to be true. Therefore, it is tempting to dismiss it as mere sophistry, for surely, one might think, there must be *something* wrong with it. That is an understandable reaction. However, like Zeno's arguments, there may be something to be learned by asking *what* is wrong with it.

Death, Dying, and Being Dead (with a Digression on the Time of Death)

An obvious but misguided reaction to the argument is to object that, contrary to what Epicurus says, death can be quite painful—think for example of the agony experienced by someone dying of a horrible disease. This objection is misguided because it confuses *death* with *dying*, which are different notions. The difference is that dying is a process, which goes on through a period of time, while death is an event which occurs *at* a certain time. While he is dying, a person is still alive: the process of dying, and not the event of death, is the source of the pain.

In the literature on medical ethics, the idea that death is an event is sometimes resisted on the grounds that there is no one point in the process of dying which is *the* point at which death takes place. The transition from living person to corpse is often a very gradual one, involving various changes. When is the exact moment death occurs? When spontaneous respiration ceases? When the heart stops? When the patient has an isoelectric electroencephalogram? As an empirical matter, the choice seems arbitrary. Therefore, it is concluded, there is no one event which is death.

There is obviously something to this, but it is important to keep the conceptual as well as the medical facts straight. The logical relation between dying and death is analogous to the relation between travelling towards a destination and arriving. By asking the same questions, we might come to doubt whether *arriving* is an event. Exactly when does an air traveller arrive in Philadelphia? When the aeroplane first broaches the space over the city? When the plane touches the airport runway? When the passenger sets foot off the plane? It seems arbitrary which moment we designate the moment of arrival; nevertheless, the *concept* of arrival is the concept of a momentary event. It is a fact about language that we cannot say, with good sense, "She arrived in Philadelphia from 12.18 to 12.33," but must rather say, "She arrived *at* 12.33." The example of arrival shows that the exact time at which an event takes place may be underdetermined by the facts.

Death is like this. The concept of death is the concept of a momentary event; but precisely when it takes place is underdetermined by the physiological facts, so that we are free, within limits, to set the time of death where we choose. In making this choice, practical considerations may come into play. One such practical consideration has to do with organ-transplant surgery. When a transplant is in the offing, we want to remove the donor's organs as soon as possible, before they begin to deteriorate; but of course we do not want to remove them before he is dead.

When is the organ-donor *really* dead? That, as we have seen, is the wrong question to ask, because it assumes there is some one moment which is *the* moment of death. Instead, we may ask, "At what point is it morally all right to declare him dead?" or even, "At what point is it morally all right to remove his organs?" That may help us to decide among the several possible "moments of death." At what point does the donor no longer have any use for the organs? The most reasonable answer is when he has lost all consciousness and there is no possibility of his ever regaining it. At that point, his life is over, and we cannot possibly be harming him by removing his heart or kidney or whatever. Therefore, there is no moral reason (at least, none having to do with *his* welfare) why we should not fix the time of death as soon as possible after the permanent cessation of consciousness.

Medical expertise comes in to tell us which of the possible "times of death" is associated with the irrevocable loss of consciousness. Studies show that consciousness is possible when and only when certain sorts of brain activity are possible. This means that "brain death" precludes any restoration of consciousness: at that point, we can be sure the donor's organs are no longer of any use to him. So, it is morally all right to fix the time of death at that point.

"Brain death" is currently the most popular option among physicians and legislators who must choose when to declare people dead. I believe this is the best approach; but it is not commonly understood *why* it is best. It is not because "the facts" dictate that a person is dead when and only when he suffers brain death. It is not that a person *really* dies then. Empirical considerations only establish limits within which a decision must be made. The final decision is determined by moral considerations, which argue for fixing the time of death at the point at which consciousness is no longer possible.

At any rate, the importance of the distinction between death and dying or Epicurus' argument is clear enough. A person who is dying is still alive, and so is able to suffer; his death, whenever it occurs, is simply the termination of this process, after which suffering is no longer possible. Epicurus' argument maintains that death cannot be the source of unhappiness, but it does not imply that dying cannot be unpleasant.

There is one other related notion to be distinguished, that of *being dead*. Epicurus interprets the fear of death as based on the misconception of death as some sort of mysterious, possibly unpleasant condition. We may ask, "What is it like to be dead?" and, being unable to answer, find it a strange and unsettling prospect. Against this, Epicurus assumes that the question itself is radically misconceived: being dead isn't like anything at all; it is simply the *absence* of experience. The "state" you will be in after you die is exactly comparable to the "state" you were in before you were born, and it is "unimaginable" to you for exactly the same reason, namely, that there is nothing to imagine.

The Fear of Death

So dying—which is a process that takes place while one is still alive—but not death or being dead, can be the source of unhappiness. So far, Epicurus' argument seems unassailable. But we have not yet taken notice of the fact that the *anticipation* of death can cause one unhappiness. People, after all, can know in advance that they are going to die, and they dread it; so mustn't we admit that, contrary to what Epicurus says, death can be the source of unhappiness?

This objection is not hard to answer. People do fear their own deaths, but they fear a great many other things as well, and we do not always conclude that a thing is bad merely because it is feared. Some people fear enclosed places, but we do not assume on that account that there is anything bad about being in an enclosed space. Rather, because there *isn't* anything bad about it, we conclude that there is something wrong with those people. They may not be able to help themselves, of course; one does not choose to be claustrophobic. Nevertheless their fears are unfounded, since there is no good reason to fear enclosures.

The point of Epicurus' argument is to show that, in the same way, there is no good reason to fear death. If death is not an evil when it comes, we ought not to fear it in advance. The fact that some people do fear it is irrelevant; for the explanation of their fear might be their own ignorance or irrationality, and not the "evil" of death itself. To show that death is bad we will have to show not only that some fear it, but that there is reason to fear it. As Epicurus put it,

The man speaks but idly who says that he fears death not because it will be painful when it comes,

but because it is painful in anticipation. For that which gives no trouble when it comes, is but an empty pain in anticipation.

I believe Epicurus was right in what he said about death and suffering. Except possibly for the pain of anticipation, death cannot cause suffering for the person who dies, and the pain of anticipation cannot be invoked as evidence that death is bad. If we assume, then, that "all good and evil consists in sensation," Epicurus was right: death is not an evil.

The Unanswered Question about Killing

Epicurus intended his argument as a contribution to human happiness: by removing death from the list of things we worry about, he meant to make us more contented with our lot. That is a laudable enough intention. But the argument, if successful, would do more than that: it has another, less benign consequence. It would not only remove a certain rationale for fearing death; it would deprive us of any adequate rationale for the prohibition of murder. If death is not an evil, why should we object to killing? If, in killing someone, we are doing something that "is nothing to him," then why is it wrong? We would be left with three possible reasons why murder might be prohibited, but each of them is inadequate:

First, we could still object to killings in which the victim is made to suffer a lot of pain before he dies. But then we would be objecting to the infliction of pain and not to the killing. This would not provide an adequate justification for the prohibition on murder because quick, painless killing would still be unobjectionable. Second, we could object to killing people whose survivors would suffer on account of their deaths—but again, on this way of looking at things, the killing of people without dependants would be all right.

There remains only one way, within the hedonistic framework, of trying to explain what is wrong with killing. We might appeal to the idea that, in causing someone's death, we prevent him from enjoying pleasures in the future: we might say that killing someone is wrong because it deprives him of pleasures he *would have* experienced had he continued to live. This is also unsatisfactory, though, since it would permit the killing of people simply on the grounds that their future lives could be expected to contain less happiness than unhappiness. But the wrongness of killing does not depend on the victim's future expectations in this way. If someone *wants* to go on living, even though his life is unhappy, killing him is simple murder.

Our conclusion about Epicurus' argument is, therefore, this: once the hedonistic conception of good and evil, expressed in the first step, is granted, his conclusion follows; and with that conclusion we are unable to account for either the evil of death or the wrongness of killing. It is the hedonistic conception of good and evil that leads to these problems.

Hedonism

Hedonism is, without doubt, the most elegant theory of good and evil ever conceived. It is, first of all, beautifully *simple*. Only one thing is taken as fundamentally good, and only one as fundamentally evil. The assumption of other basic goods and evils is unnecessary, since all other goods and evils are to be explained in terms of suffering and enjoyment. Moreover, because only one thing is viewed as fundamentally good, and one as fundamentally evil, there is a theoretically pleasing *unity* among all goods and evils: no matter how disparate the group of things we regard as good or bad, in the end they must all be seen as good or bad *for the same reason*, namely, because of their connection with enjoyment or suffering. And there is even a connection between enjoyment and suffering, since they are both states of consciousness, or, as Epicurus put it, "sensations." So there is an even deeper kind of unity in the fundamental conception.

In addition, there is no mystery about *why* the basic good is good, or why the basic evil is evil. Suffering is so obviously an evil, just on account of what it is like, that argument would be superfluous; and the same goes for enjoyment as a good. Moreover, no matter how much people disagree about "values," we can expect every rational person to agree about this. It is no wonder, then, that hedonism has been such an appealing view, even to the present day.

But is hedonism *true*? One might doubt that it is true simply because of the problems it creates in connection with killing. But we need to see, in a more systematic way, what its deficiencies are. There are, in my opinion, two principal mistakes involved in this view. They might be called the *logical* mistake and the *metaphysical* mistake.

The Logical Mistake

Wonmug was a somewhat stupid but very vain college student interested in physics. The other students would amuse themselves by making fun of him; but to his face they pretended to have great respect for his intellect. As a result, Wonmug came to believe himself to be their intellectual leader. The others thought this very funny.

Soon Wonmug's teachers joined in the joke, giving him much higher grades than he deserved and writing effusive comments on his papers. When he applied for admission to graduate school, the physicists enlisted their friends at other universities. Gradually, the entire scientific establishment came to participate in the charade. Wonmug was given a Ph.D. "with distinction," and offered a faculty position at a distinguished university. His research was in fact inconsequential, but it was acclaimed by all his colleagues, and he didn't know the difference.

Eventually the whole world was playing along, and the joke continued for forty-five years. Wonmug was cheered at scientific meetings; his picture was twice on the cover of *Time*; and he was fêted at the White House. Finally, he was awarded the Nobel Prize. As Wonmug delivered his pompous acceptance speech, the woman he loved, but who ridiculed him behind his back, sat beside him beaming with false pride, and the members of the Swedish Academy could barely keep from laughing. When Wonmug died he sincerely believed himself to have been the greatest and most beloved figure in science since Einstein.

This ludicrous story is, of course, fictitious, but it is worth thinking about in connection with hedonism. Was Wonmug a fortunate individual, or an unfortunate one? Did he have a good life, or not? In an obvious way he was very fortunate. He received honours that most of us can only dream about. But of course there was something radically wrong. Although he *thought* he achieved great things in science, he really achieved nothing. Although he *thought* he had many friends, he really had no friends. But what is wrong with that? Hedonism says that all the things we value—knowledge, achievement, the love and respect of other people—are good *only in that they cause pleasant states of consciousness.* It is only the states of consciousness that are good "in themselves." Wonmug, in fact, had all the states of consciousness associated with achievement, respect, and the rest. So according to hedonism he had everything good associated with those things. His life was just as good as Einstein's, and maybe even better.

Hedonism seems mistaken on this point, but how can the mistake be explained? From the outside, knowing about the deception, we see him as a pathetic figure, the butt of an elaborate joke. He is happy only because he is ignorant of what is going on. And if he were to discover what is really happening, he would also come to see himself in this way, and his happiness would be shuttered. But why would his happiness be diminished? The answer is that what *he* values (and what we value too) is such things as achievement and friendship. It is because he values these things, and because he thinks he has them, that he is happy. His happiness would be diminished because he would learn that he really does not have the things he values.

This is what I termed the "logical mistake." In saying that achievement and friendship are good because they make us happy, hedonism gets things the wrong way round. They are not good because they make us happy. Rather, having them (and other things like them) makes us happy because we recognize them *as goods.* To explain their value, then, we have to look elsewhere than to the conscious states that accompany them.

Death is like this. It is a bad thing for the person who dies, but not because of the conscious states that accompany it. (As Epicurus observed, there are no conscious states that accompany it.) Its evil is to be explained in other ways. *What* other ways is suggested by considering the second kind of hedonistic mistake.

The Metaphysical Mistake

To assess a theory such as hedonism, we may consider some of the particular kinds of misfortune that a person may sustain, and ask whether in fact those misfortunes can adequately be explained in the recommended terms.

One kind of misfortune, which should be "home ground" for hedonism, is physical injury—a broken arm, for example. Suppose we ask why it is a misfortune to be physically injured. Part of the answer will indeed be found in the pain and misery which go with it: a broken arm hurts, and that is bad. But this is only part of the answer. There are also the activities from which one is barred by the injury; these must be considered as well. A broken arm is a greater misfortune for an athlete than for a scholar because it will disrupt his normal activities to a greater degree. The scholar's life may go on as usual, with only a minimum of inconvenience; the athlete, however, will not be able to go about his normal business. This is bad for him not merely because he will fret and worry over it—on the contrary, even if he were quite cheerful about the mishap, the fact that a portion of his life has been upset in a way that he would not have wished would still constitute a misfortune for him.

The more severe the injury, the more important this sort of consideration becomes: think of a promising young pianist whose hands are permanently damaged in an automobile accident, so that she can no longer play. It is tempting to think this is a misfortune for her simply because it will make her so unhappy. But this is surely an anaemic view of the matter, and not merely because stronger language would be required to do justice to her despair. If we dwell exclusively on her distress over what happened, we miss the essential nature of the tragedy. To see why this is a tragedy, we must pay attention to what she is unhappy *about,* and to the life she could have led were it not for the accident. She could have had a life as a concert pianist, but now she cannot. *That* is the tragedy. Once again, even if she is unhappy over this, we must not think her unfortunate *merely* on that account. This confuses the order of things: it is not that she is unfortunate because she is so unhappy, but that she is unhappy because she recognizes a misfortune—the loss of the ability to play—for the bad thing it is. We could not eliminate her misfortune by getting her to cheer up.

Thus hedonism makes a kind of *metaphysical* error. It implies that, in order to understand the goods and evils to which people are subject, the only elements of human nature we need to consider are the capacities to suffer and enjoy: it is only the capacity for suffering that makes people vulnerable to misfortune, and it is only the capacity for enjoyment that enables anything to be good for them. The example of the pianist suggests that this is too impoverished a picture. To understand some evils, we need to consider people as more than receptacles of happiness and unhappiness. We need to consider them as beings who have hopes, aspirations, and desires that may or may not be fulfilled; we need to consider them as the subjects of lives with possibilities that may or may not be realized. Something may be bad for a person, not only because it causes unhappiness, but because it disappoints a hope, or precludes a possibility for his life.

The evil of death is like this. When a person dies, not merely some but *all* his hopes, aspirations, and desires are frustrated, and all the possibilities for his life are cancelled. Actually, the "all" here is a little too sweeping; some qualification is needed, and I will come to that shortly. Nevertheless, this points us in the right direction. To see why death is an evil, we need to examine the concept of a life, and see how death may affect a life badly, by putting an end to it.

The Concept of a Life

Generally speaking, death is a misfortune for the person who dies because it puts an end to his life. Like many philosophical theses, this is more complicated than it first appears. Death is a misfortune, not because it puts an end to one's *being alive* (in the biological sense), but because it ends one's *life* (in the biographical sense). To explain the thesis—to show how the termination of one's life can be a bad thing—we need to examine some aspects of what it means to have a life.

Complete and Incomplete Lives

The contingencies of human existence determine the general shape of our lives. Because we are born physically weak and without knowledge or skills, the first part of our lives is a process of growth, learning, and general maturation. Because we will

not live much longer than seventy-five years, and because in the last years we will decline mentally and physically, the projects and activities that will fill our lives cannot be planned for much longer than that. The forms of life within human society are adjusted to these dimensions: families care for children while they are small and are acquiring a basic understanding of the world; schools continue the educational process; careers last about forty years; and people normally retire some time between sixty and seventy.

A life can, therefore, be complete or incomplete; it can run its course, or be cut short. Bertrand Russell lived an extraordinarily full life. Born in 1872, he lived ninety-seven years, during which time he was twice married and raised a family; he travelled the world and enjoyed the friendship of such as George Bernard Shaw, H. G. Wells, and Ludwig Wittgenstein; he published seventy-one books and pamphlets, including many that made fundamental contributions to human thought, and was awarded the Nobel Prize; and he was internationally famous as a political and moral propagandist. Compare this with the life of another philosopher, Frank P. Ramsey, who died in 1930 at the age of twenty-six. Ramsey's life had hardly begun; he had achieved only a little of what he could have achieved. The two deaths were, therefore, very different. Ramsey's death was a tragedy, while Russell's death was only the occasion for solemn reflection on a life well lived.

The tragedy of Ramsey's death was threefold. First, there was the sense of *incompleteness*. It was as though a story was only half-told; we had the beginning, and intimations of the middle, but no idea of what the ending might be. Second, there was the sense of futility connected with the fact that Ramsey's life to that point had been *training* him for something that now could not take place. He had been educated and studied philosophy and the foundations of mathematics; prepared now for fundamental work in these fields, he died before he could do it. And third, there was the sense of unfulfilled promise: Ramsey *could have* done great things; but death prevented it. None of this could be said of Russell, whose life was complete, and so Russell's death was not comparably tragic.

This does not mean that Russell's death was not a bad thing in its own way, but we must be careful in describing how it was bad. Even Russell's personal friends, saddened by his passing, must have realized that his life was rich, successful, and in some important sense complete. If there was anything bad about the death, it is because we are able to view a life as in principle open-ended, as always having further possibilities that still might be realized, if only it could go on. There were still desires that Russell could have satisfied; there were still ambitions he might have accomplished. These thoughts make sense of seeing evil even in this death.

Our equanimity about his death, however, is due to our conception of life as bounded by the natural human contingencies. If those contingencies were different, our conception of a life's possibilities would be different. In reality, the possibilities for Russell's life had been exhausted by age and the feebleness it brings; thus thoughts about what he still might have done are largely fanciful. But suppose people lived to be a hundred and fifty, and at ninety-seven Russell was still vigorous and only half-done with the tasks he could naturally expect to accomplish. Then his death would be as tragic as Ramsey's; but then, too, our conception of what a life can contain would be changed, and so the reasons for judging the death tragic would be changed.

The Stages of a Life

The stages of a life are not isolated or self-contained parts. They bear relations to one another that must be understood if any part of the life is to be understood.

We cannot understand what a medical student is doing, for example, if we do not appreciate the way in which her present activity is preparation for the stages of her life which will come later. She wants to be a doctor, and live the kind of life that doctors have: apart from that, her present activity makes no sense. (Thus death at an early age renders this part of the life *pointless.*)

Moreover, the *evaluation* of one stage of a life may require reference to what came before. To be a door-keeper, with a small but steady income sufficient to pay the rent on a modest apartment, might

be a laudable achievement for one who previously was a homeless drunk; but for one who was a vice-president of the United States, caught taking bribes, the same existence might be a sign of failure and disgrace. (This is of course a fictitious example, since we know this is not what happens to American vice-presidents caught taking bribes.)

Thus the fact that people have memories, and are able to contemplate their futures, is important in explaining why they are able to have lives. Without these capacities, one could not see one's present condition as part of a larger, temporally extended existence; and one could have neither regrets nor aspirations.

Consider the plight of someone in whom the connections of memory have been severed. A striking example of this is described by Oliver Sacks, a professor of neurology at the Albert Einstein School of Medicine. Sacks has a patient, whom he calls Jimmie R., suffering from Korsakov's syndrome, which is associated with braindamage produced by alcohol. Jimmie remembers his life vividly up to 1945, when he was nineteen years old. After that, he remembers nothing. He is a bright, alert man who will talk to you intelligently when you are introduced; but two minutes later he will not remember having met you before and the conversation will start again. (Dr. Sacks has been "re-meeting" him regularly for nine years.) He believes he is still nineteen and that it is still 1945; but this is not because he is deluded in the way of someone who thinks he is Napoleon. He is rational enough; he simply has no memory of anything that has happened between then and now. When shown himself in the mirror he panics and thinks something terrible has happened to his face. Soon, though, he forgets having seen the mirror and the worry disappears.

Of course, Jimmie cannot have a normal life because he cannot do any of the things that constitute a life—he cannot relate normally to other people, hold a job, or even take care of his basic needs by shopping for food. (He is cared for in an institution.) But his lack of memory deprives him of a life in a deeper sense: without memory, he cannot conceive of his present state as connected with any other part of himself; plans, even intentional actions become impossible in any but a truncated sense.

Without these connections, even the simplest feelings and attitudes lose their objects and meaning. Sacks recorded this conversation with Jimmie:

"How do you feel?"

"How do I feel," he repeated, and scratched his head.

"I cannot say I feel ill. But I cannot say I feel well. I cannot say I feel anything at all."

"Are you miserable?" I continued.

"Can't say I am."

"Do you enjoy life?"

"I can't say I do . . ."

"You don't enjoy life," I repeated, hesitating somewhat. "How then *do* you feel about life?"

"I can't say I feel anything at all."

"You feel alive though?"

"'Feel alive' . . . Not really. I haven't felt alive for a very long time."

After nine years of trying to deal with this case, Dr. Sacks's own conclusion is continuing bafflement about ". . . whether, indeed, one [can] speak of an 'existence,' given so absolute a privation of memory or continuity." We can, of course, speak of an "existence"—Jimmie R. exists. But Dr. Sacks's point is clear enough. Without the continuity that memory makes possible, a life, in any but the most rudimentary sense, is unattainable.

Multiple Lives

We sometimes speak of a person's having more than one life: a bigamist may be said to "lead two lives." This is not merely an idle way of speaking; it has a point. Lives are characterized by sets of interconnected projects, concerns, and relationships. A person may be said to "lead two lives" when there are two such sets, held rigidly separate, with little or no interaction between elements of the sets. The bigamist has two sets of relationships which must be kept absolutely apart—it is important that the members of one household not even know of the other's existence. Thus it is natural to speak of him as going back and forth between two lives.

Similarly, someone who moves to a distant city to start a new profession may be said to take up "a new life." Suppose a woman who was a prostitute in Miami moves to Los Angeles to become the proprietor of a clothing shop. She will spend her time on an entirely new set of activities, she will have a new set of friends—everything will be different. Like the bigamist, she may not even want her friends in Los Angeles to know about her life in Miami. Hence, a new life.

On some occasions, the effect of physical injury is to leave a patient alive and able to lead a life, but not the same life he had before. The famous "Texas burn case," often discussed in the literature of medical ethics, is a case of this type. In 1973 a young man known as "Donald C." was horribly burned over 68 per cent of his body by an exploding gas line, and left blind, crippled, without fingers, and deformed in other ways as well. He was kept alive in the hospital for two years by a series of extraordinary and painful treatments; but all these treatments were against his will. Wanting to die, he continually demanded to be removed from the protective environment of the hospital. The doctors refused. He attempted to commit suicide, but was physically unable to bring it off. Finally, to justify keeping him in the hospital against his wishes, a psychiatrist was brought in to examine him, in the expectation that he would testify that Donald was incompetent. But, after interviewing him, the psychiatrist refused to do that, pronouncing—to the surprise of the physicians—that the patient was perfectly rational. So the young man was given the right to leave the hospital. But then, in a dramatic reversal, he changed his mind, and he is still alive today.

Now what could be said in defence of the judgement that this man's desire to die was rational? I believe focusing on the notion of his *life* (in the biographical sense) points us in the right direction. He was, among other things, a rodeo performer, a pilot, and what used to be called a "ladies' man." His life was not the life of a scholar or a solitary dreamer. What his injury had done, from his point of view, was to destroy his ability to lead the life that made him the distinctive individual he was. There could be no more rodeos, no more aeroplanes, no more dancing with the ladies, and a lot more. Donald's position was that if he could not lead *that* life, he didn't want to live.

Donald's physicians, in resisting his demand to die, argued in effect that he could take up a different sort of life, and that this different life might come to have some value for him. That is what he eventually did. The physicians may naturally think that these later developments vindicate their refusal to let Donald die, but Donald himself disagrees. Nine years after his ordeal, he appeared before a group of medical students to insist, with some bitterness, that the doctors had been wrong to refuse his demand. Although one may feel some sympathy with the doctors' view, it isn't hard to see Donald's point. We may applaud the courage he eventually showed in making a new life for himself, but we shouldn't miss noticing that his old life was gone. That is why his despair was not merely a temporary hysterical reaction to his situation.

The Temporal Boundaries of a Life

L. C. Morris was a 63-year-old Miami man who was shot in the head one night in 1970 when police mistook him for a roof-top sniper. The damage to his brain was extensive, but he did not die. He lived on, after a fashion, in a nursing home, where for more than three years he was fed through a tube running to his stomach and periodically turned to prevent bedsores. His body had private attendants round the clock; the cost of maintaining it alive was $2,600 per month. The emotional cost to Mrs. Morris cannot be calculated. Under the strain of daily visits to see him, her health deteriorated and she too had to be hospitalized. When told in 1972 that her husband might live for two more years, she replied, "He died back in 1970. We know that."

At the same time that Mr. Morris was in his coma, Miguel Martinez was also lying unconscious in a hospital. Martinez, a well-known Spanish athlete, had been injured in a soccer game in 1964 and remained in a coma until he died eight years later. When he died, his family announced, "Miguel died at the age of 34 after having lived 26 years."

Mrs. Morris's statement that her husband died in 1970 was simply false. The Martinezes' melodramatic statement was paradoxical. Yet it is easy to see the point in both cases. The *lives* of these two men were over when they entered the comas, even though both remained alive for some time longer. Both families realized that being alive, in the absence of having a life, was not very important.

These cases illustrate that the temporal boundaries of one's life need not be the same as the temporal boundaries of one's being alive—one may remain alive long after one's life is over. Now some people, as we have noted, do not want to be kept alive in such circumstances; they may even leave specific instructions to this effect in "living wills." It is an interesting question why these instructions should be respected. If hedonism were true, there would be no reason for respecting these wishes *having to do with the person's own interests*. Because the person will never know whether he lived on in the coma, he cannot be angry or otherwise unhappy about it; so no harm is done to him even if he is kept alive indefinitely. But I have argued that hedonism is mistaken on this point. People are vulnerable to misfortune, not only because they are capable of suffering unhappiness, but because they may have desires that may be frustrated; and, moreover, the misfortune of frustrated desire does not *consist in* the unhappiness this might cause, even if unhappiness is caused. Thus the way is open for us to regard ignoring the patient's wishes in this matter as an offence to *him*. He will not know that we have ignored his wishes, but that does not matter; for even if he did know, the wrongness of it would not depend on his being unhappy about it.

This has the following strange consequence: a person may suffer misfortune even after he is dead. Suppose, for example, a person's life has been spent in trying to accomplish projects to which he attaches great value. Whether the life is a success or a failure may depend, partly, on the success of these projects; and he may or may not live to see the outcome. There is no good reason (unless one is under the spell of a view such as hedonism) to think it is any *less* a misfortune for him if the crucial events occur after he dies. Of course, he will not *know* what has happened to his projects; but what of that?

One man who suffered such misfortune is Nietzsche. In writing about him Philippa Foot was not concerned with any of the matters we have been considering, but she found it natural to say that

Few philosophers can ever have suffered more than Nietzsche those special misfortunes that may come to a man after his death. That his unpublished manuscripts should have been in the hands of an unscrupulous sister ready to twist his doctrines to serve the cause of an anti-semitism that he loathed; that he should have been taken as a prophet by an intellectually and morally despicable regime; that he should have been execrated not only for those parts of his writings that are, precisely, execrable, but also on account of numberless misunderstandings; that even his non-Nazi disciples should have often defended him in a childish, hysterical way.

These perversions of Nietzsche's work are now widely recognized for what they are, and so his reputation has risen. If my account is correct, this is a good thing, not just for posterity, but for him.

More and Less Complex Lives

In discussing non-human animals, I observed that some of them do apparently have lives, and that those lives range from very simple to quite complex, although none approach the social, emotional, or intellectual complexity of (normal) human lives. And I suggested that the natural moral conclusion should be that their lives are to be protected by the rule against killing in proportion to the complexity of the life—the more complex the life, the more objectionable the killing.

But why does complexity matter? Why is it morally important? This question has not often been discussed by moral philosophers. One philosopher who has discussed it is Edward Johnson; he thinks that, in fact, mental complexity does *not* count for anything. Why, he asks, should we think that the life of a creature is less valuable simply because its mental capacities are not as complex as our own? He can think of three possible answers—that more complex beings experience greater pleasures and pains; that they are capable of different sorts of personal relationships; and that mental complexity is intrinsically valuable—and rejects each of them in turn.

But there is another, more natural explanation that Johnson does not consider. Complexity matters because, when a mentally complex being dies, much more can be said about why its death was a bad thing. A young woman dies: it is bad because she will not get to raise her children, finish her novel, learn French, improve her backhand, or do what she wanted for Oxfam; her talents will remain undeveloped, her aspirations unfulfilled. Not nearly so much of this kind could be said about a less sophisticated being. Her death is worse because there are *more reasons* for regretting it. Thus, if we had to choose between the death of a human and the death of a dog, there is reason to choose in favour of the human.

When comparisons are made between humans and other animals, this idea may be easy enough to accept. As I remarked before, it conforms fairly well to what we already instinctively feel about the animals. It explains not only why we feel that killing a human is worse than killing a dog, but why killing a dog is a more morally serious matter than squashing a bug. However, there are other implications of this idea that are more unsettling. Let me mention two such implications, one less radical and one more radical.

The less radical, but still somewhat unsettling, implication is that in most cases the life of a "normal" human is to be preferred to the life of a mentally retarded human. This is contrary to the thought that every human life is equally sacred. Thus, it may be a hard idea to accept, for on the face of it it *sounds like* an unacceptable denigration of the mentally handicapped.

But it does not imply that the lives of the mentally handicapped are to be held cheap, or that they may be killed at will. It implies only a comparison that might come into play in a theoretical situation of "forced choice." The life of a mentally defective human will typically be simpler than the life of a normal human, in the same way that the life of a non-human animal is simpler; and so this idea would dictate that, in a situation of forced choice—if you *must choose* between the death of the retarded person and the death of the normal person—there is reason to choose in favour of the normal person. The reasoning is exactly the same as in the earlier comparison: where the life of the mentally more complex creature is at issue, there are more reasons why the death would be a bad thing.

I call this the "less radical" implication because it is not quite so contrary to our normal views as it may at first appear to be. Although we may be inclined to endorse "the equal worth of all human lives" almost by reflex—it sounds so noble, who could deny it?—not many of us really believe this high-sounding principle. Suppose you were to hear of the death of a severely retarded person at the same time as you heard of the death of the young woman in the previous example. Would you think the two deaths equally tragic? You would not have to be an especially radical thinker to see that there are important differences.

The more radical implication becomes apparent when we remember that severely retarded humans might have *less* complex mental abilities than those of some non-human animals. Then, according to the principle we are considering, there would be reason to prefer the life of the animal to that of the human.

This may seem at first wildly implausible, for on the traditional view the lives of humans have special value simply because they are human, independent of any other considerations.

Conclusion

Death is an evil for the person who dies because it forecloses possibilities for his or her life; because it eliminates the chance for developing abilities and talents, because it frustrates desires, hopes, and aspirations; and because it leaves parts of lives pointless and whole lives incomplete.

QUESTIONS

1. Why does Rachels think that killing is usually wrong?
2. What is the distinction between *death* and *dying*, and why is it important?
3. Why does he object to Epicurus's doctrine? What exactly is wrong with it?
4. On the view that Rachels develops, might the killing of some people be worse than the killing of others?

9. Death

THOMAS NAGEL

*T*homas Nagel (1937–), professor at New York University, is an important American philosopher who writes about most areas of philosophy. His many books include *The Possibility of Altruism* (1970), *Mortal Questions* (1979), *The View from Nowhere* (1986), and an introductory book, *What Does It All Mean? A Very Short Introduction to Philosophy* (1987).

In this influential essay Nagel asks, if we think of death as the unequivocal and permanent end of our existence, why is it bad to die? It has to be bad because of that which death deprives us of, what we lose by dying. Nagel considers the difficulties this kind of answer faces. In exploring and addressing these difficulties, Nagel illuminates our complex attitudes toward death.

From "Death," *Nous* 4, 1 (1970), pp. 73–80. Reprinted by permission of Blackwell Publishing.

The syllogism he had learnt from Kiesewetter's Logic: "Caius is a man, men are mortal, therefore Caius is mortal," had always seemed to him correct as applied to Caius, but certainly not as applied to himself . . . What did Caius know of the smell of that striped leather ball Vanya had been so fond of?

—Tolstoy, *The Death of Ivan Ilych*

If, as many people believe, death is the unequivocal and permanent end of our existence, the question arises whether it is a bad thing to die. There is conspicuous disagreement about the matter: some people think death is dreadful; others have no objection to death per se, though they may hope their own will be neither premature nor painful.

Those in the former category tend to think those in the latter are blind to the obvious, while the latter suppose the former to be prey to some sort of confusion. On the one hand it can be said that life is all one has, and the loss of it is the greatest loss one can sustain. On the other hand it may be objected that death deprives this supposed loss of its subject, and that if one realizes that death is not an unimaginable condition of the persisting person, but a mere blank, one will see that it can have no value whatever, positive or negative.

Since I want to leave aside the question whether we are, or might be, immortal in some form, I shall simply use the word "death" and its cognates in this discussion to mean *permanent* death, unsupplemented by any form of conscious survival. I wish to consider whether death is in itself an evil; and how great an evil, and of what kind, it might be. This question should be of interest even to those who believe that we do not die permanently, for one's attitude towards immortality must depend in part on one's attitude towards death.

Clearly if death is an evil at all, it cannot be because of its positive features, but only because of what it deprives us of. I shall try to deal with the difficulties surrounding the natural view that death is an evil because it brings to an end all the goods that life contains. An account of these goods need not occupy us here, except to observe that some of them, like perception, desire, activity, and thought, are so general as to be constitutive of human life. They are widely regarded as formidable benefits in themselves, despite the fact that they are conditions of misery as well as happiness, and that a sufficient quantity of more particular evils can perhaps outweigh them.

I wish to add only two observations. First, the value of life and its contents does not attach to mere organic survival: almost everyone would be indifferent (other things equal) between immediate death and immediate coma followed by death twenty years later without reawakening. And secondly, like most goods, this one can be multiplied by time: more is better than less. (It should be remarked that the added quantities need not be temporally continuous. People are attracted to the possibility of long-term suspended animation or freezing, followed by the resumption of conscious life, because they can regard it from within simply as a *continuation* of their present life. If these techniques are ever perfected, what from outside appeared as a dormant interval of three hundred years could be experienced by the subject as nothing more than a sharp discontinuity in the character of his experiences.)

If we turn from what is good about life to what is bad about death, the case is completely different. Essentially, though there may be problems about their specification, what we find desirable in life are certain states, conditions, or types of activity. It is *being* alive, *doing* certain things, having certain experiences, that we consider good. But if death is an evil, it is the *loss of life,* rather than the state of being dead, or non-existent, or unconscious, that is objectionable. This asymmetry is important. If it is good to be alive, that advantage can be attributed to a person at each point of his life. It is a good of which Bach had more than Schubert, simply because he lived longer. Death, however, is not an evil of which Shakespeare has so far received a larger portion than Proust. If death is a disadvantage, it is not easy to say when a man suffers it.

Two other facts indicate that we do not object to death merely because it involves long periods of nonexistence. First, as has been mentioned, most of us would not regard the *temporary* suspension of life, even for substantial intervals, as in itself a misfortune. If it develops that people can be frozen without reduction of the conscious lifespan, it will be inappropriate to pity those who are temporarily out of circulation. Secondly, none of us existed before we were born (or conceived), but few regard that as a misfortune. I shall have more to say about this later.

The point that death is not regarded as an unfortunate *state* enables us to refute a curious but very common suggestion about the origin of the fear of death. It is often said that those who object to death have made the mistake of trying to imagine what it is like to *be* dead. It is alleged that the failure to realize that this task is logically impossible (for the banal reason that there is nothing to imagine) leads to the conviction that death is a mysterious and therefore terrifying prospective *state*. But this diagnosis is evidently false, for it is just as impossible to imagine being totally unconscious as to imagine being dead (though it is easy enough to imagine oneself, from the outside, in either of those conditions). Yet people who are averse to death are not usually averse to unconsciousness (so long as it does not entail a substantial cut in the total duration of waking life).

If we are to make sense of the view that to die is bad, it must be on the ground that life is a good and death is the corresponding deprivation or loss, bad not because of any positive features but because of the desirability of what it removes. We must now turn to the serious difficulties which this hypothesis raises, difficulties about loss and privation in general, and about death in particular.

Essentially there are three types of problem. First, doubt may be raised whether *anything* can be bad for a man without being positively unpleasant to him: specifically, it may be doubted that there are any evils which consist merely in the deprivation or absence of possible goods, and which do not depend on someone's *minding* that deprivation. Secondly, there are special difficulties, in the case of death, about how the supposed misfortune is to be assigned to a subject at all. There is doubt both as to *who* its subject is, and as to *when* he undergoes it. So long as a person exists, he has not yet died, and once he has died, he no longer exists; so there seems to be no time when death, if it is a misfortune, can be ascribed to its unfortunate subject. The third type of

difficulty concerns the asymmetry, mentioned above, between our attitudes to posthumous and prenatal nonexistence. How can the former be bad if the latter is not?

It should be recognized that if these are valid objections to counting death as an evil, they will apply to many other supposed evils as well. The first type of objection is expressed in general form by the common remark that what you don't know can't hurt you. It means that even if a man is betrayed by his friends, ridiculed behind his back, and despised by people who treat him politely to his face, none of it can be counted as a misfortune for him so long as he does not suffer as a result. It means that a man is not injured if his wishes are ignored by the executor of his will, or if, after his death, the belief becomes current that all the literary works on which his fame rests were really written by his brother, who died in Mexico at the age of twenty-eight. It seems to me worth asking what assumptions about good and evil lead to these drastic restrictions.

All the questions have something to do with time. There certainly are goods and evils of a simple kind (including some pleasures and pains) which a person possesses at a given time simply in virtue of his condition at that time. But this is not true of all the things we regard as good or bad for a man. Often we need to know his history to tell whether something is a misfortune or not; this applies to ills like deterioration, deprivation, and damage. Sometimes his experiential *state* is relatively unimportant—as in the case of a man who wastes his life in the cheerful pursuit of a method of communicating with asparagus plants. Someone who holds that all goods and evils must be temporally assignable states of the person may of course try to bring difficult cases into line by pointing to the pleasure or pain that more complicated goods and evils cause. Loss, betrayal, deception, and ridicule are on this view bad because people suffer when they learn of them. But it should be asked how our ideas of human value would have to be constituted to accommodate these cases directly instead. (This would enable us to explain *why* their discovery causes suffering.) One possible account is that most good and ill fortune has as its subject a person identified by his history and his possibilities, rather than merely by his categorical state of the moment—and that while this subject can be exactly located in a sequence of places and times, the same is not necessarily true of the goods and ills that befall him.

These ideas can be illustrated by an example of deprivation whose severity approaches that of death. Suppose an intelligent person receives a brain injury that reduces him to the mental condition of a contented infant, and that such desires as remain to him are satisfied by a custodian, so that he is free from care. Such a development would be widely regarded as a severe misfortune, not only for his friends and relations, or for society, but also, and primarily, for the person himself. This does not mean that a contented infant is unfortunate. The intelligent adult who has been *reduced* to this condition is the subject of the misfortune. He is the one we pity, though of course he does not mind his condition—there is some doubt, in fact, whether he can be said to exist any longer.

The view that such a man has suffered a misfortune is open to the same objections which have been raised in regard to death. He does not mind his condition. It is in fact the same condition he was in at the age of three months, except that he is bigger. If we did not pity him then, why pity him now; in any case, who is there to pity? The intelligent adult has disappeared, and for a creature like the one before us, happiness consists in a full stomach and a dry diaper.

If these objections are invalid, it must be because they rest on a mistaken assumption about the temporal relation between the subject of a misfortune and the circumstances which constitute it. If, instead of concentrating exclusively on the oversized baby before us, we consider the person he was, and the person he *could* be now, then his reduction to this state and the cancellation of his natural adult development constitute a perfectly intelligible catastrophe.

This case should convince us that it is arbitrary to restrict the goods and evils that can befall a man to nonrelational properties ascribable to him at particular times. As it stands, that restriction excludes not only such cases of gross degeneration, but also a good deal of what is important about success and failure, and other features of a life that have the character of processes. I believe we can go further, however. There are goods and evils which are irreducibly relational; they are features of the relations between a person, with spatial and temporal boundaries of the usual sort, and circumstances which may not coincide with him either in space or in time. A man's life includes much that does not transpire within the boundaries of his body and his mind, and what happens to him can include much that does not take place within the boundaries of his life. These boundaries are commonly crossed by the misfortunes of being deceived, or despised, or betrayed. (If this is correct, there is a simple account of what is wrong with breaking a deathbed promise. It is an injury to the dead man. For certain purposes it is possible to regard time as just another type of distance.) The case of mental degeneration shows us an evil that depends on a contrast between the reality and the possible alternatives. A man is the subject of good and evil as much because he has hopes which may or may not be fulfilled, or possibilities which may or may not be realized, as because of his capacity to suffer and enjoy. If death is an evil, it must be accounted for in these terms, and the impossibility of locating it within life should not trouble us.

When a man dies we are left with his corpse, and while a corpse can suffer the kind of mishap that may occur to an article of furniture, it is not a suitable object for pity. The man, however, is. He has lost his life, and if he had not died, he would have continued to live it, and to possess whatever good there is in living. If we apply to death the account suggested for the case of dementia, we shall say that although the spatial and temporal locations of the individual who suffered the loss are clear enough, the misfortune itself cannot be so easily located. One must be content just to state that his life is over and there will never be any more of it. That *fact*, rather than his past or present condition, constitutes his misfortune, if it is one. Nevertheless if there is a loss, someone must suffer it, and *he* must have existence and specific spatial and temporal location even if the loss itself does not. The fact that Beethoven had no children may have been a cause of regret to him, or a sad thing for the world, but it cannot be described as a misfortune for the children that he never had. All of us, I believe, are fortunate to have been born. But unless good and ill can be assigned to an embryo, or even to an unconnected pair of gametes, it cannot be said that not to be born is a misfortune. (That is a factor to be considered in deciding whether abortion and contraception are akin to murder.)

This approach also provides a solution to the problem of temporal asymmetry, pointed out by Lucretius. He observed that no one finds it disturbing to contemplate the eternity preceding his own birth, and he took this to show that it must be irrational to fear death, since death is simply the mirror image of the prior abyss. That is not true, however, and the difference between the two explains why it is reasonable to regard them differently. It is true that both the time before a man's birth and the time after his death are times when he does not exist. But the time after his death is time of which his death deprives him. It is time in which, had he not died then, he would be alive. Therefore any death entails the loss of *some* life that its victim would have led had he not died at that or any earlier point. We know perfectly well what it would be for him to have had it instead of losing it, and there is no difficulty in identifying the loser.

But we cannot say that the time prior to a man's birth is time in which he would have lived had he been born not then but earlier. For aside from the brief margin permitted by premature labor, he *could* not have been born earlier: anyone born substantially earlier than he was would have been someone else. Therefore the time prior to his birth is not time in which his subsequent birth prevents him from living. His birth, when it occurs, does not entail the loss to him of any life whatever.

The direction of time is crucial in assigning possibilities to people or other individuals. Distinct possible lives of a single person can diverge from a common beginning, but they cannot converge to a common conclusion from diverse beginnings. (The latter would represent not a set of different possible lives of one individual, but a set of distinct possible individuals, whose lives have identical conclusions.) Given an identifiable individual, countless possibilities for his continued existence are imaginable, and we can clearly conceive of what it would be for him

to go on existing indefinitely. However inevitable it is that this will not come about, its possibility is still that of the continuation of a good for him, if life is the good we take it to be.

We are left, therefore, with the question whether the non-realization of this possibility is in every case a misfortune, or whether it depends on what can naturally be hoped for. This seems to me the most serious difficulty with the view that death is always an evil. Even if we can dispose of the objections against admitting misfortune that is not experienced, or cannot be assigned to a definite time in the person's life, we still have to set some limits on *how* possible a possibility must be for its nonrealization to be a misfortune (or good fortune, should the possibility be a bad one). The death of Keats at 24 is generally regarded as tragic; that of Tolstoy at 82 is not. Although they will both be dead forever, Keats's death deprived him of many years of life which were allowed to Tolstoy; so in a clear sense Keats's loss was greater (though not in the sense standardly employed in mathematical comparison between infinite quantities). However, this does not prove that Tolstoy's loss was insignificant. Perhaps we record an objection only to evils which are gratuitously added to the inevitable; the fact that it is worse to die at 24 than at 82 does not imply that it is not a terrible thing to die at 82, or even at 806. The question is whether we can regard as a misfortune any limitation, like mortality, that is normal to the species. Blindness is not a misfortune for a mole, nor would it be for a man, if that were the natural condition of the human race.

The trouble is that life familiarizes us with the goods of which death deprives us. If we put aside doubts about their status as goods and grant that their quantity is in part a function of their duration, the question remains whether death, no matter when it occurs, can be said to deprive its victim of what is in the relevant sense a possible continuation of life. The situation is an ambiguous one. Observed from without, human beings obviously have a natural lifespan and cannot live much longer than a hundred years. A man's sense of his own experience, on the other hand, does not embody this idea of a natural limit. His existence defines for him an essentially open-ended possible future, containing the usual mixture of goods and evils that he has found so tolerable in the past. Having been gratuitously introduced to the world by a collection of natural, historical, and social accidents, he finds himself the subject of a *life*, with an indeterminate and not essentially limited future. Viewed in this way, death, no matter how inevitable, is an abrupt cancellation of indefinitely extensive possible goods. Normality seems to have nothing to do with it, for the fact that we will all inevitably die in a few score years cannot by itself imply that it would not be good to live longer. If there is no limit to the amount of life that it would be good to have, then it may be that a bad end is in store for us all.

QUESTIONS
1. Why think of death as "the unequivocal and permanent end of our existence"?
2. State Nagel's answer to the question why it is bad to die.
3. What are the problems his answer faces? How does he address each problem?

10. Death

ROBERT NOZICK

Robert Nozick (1938–2002) was professor of philosophy at Harvard University until his untimely death. He thought and wrote about most areas of philosophy and was reputed never to have taught the same course twice. His most famous work, *Anarchy, State, and Utopia* (1974), explores questions about the justification of states and defends a classical liberal conception of justice and of the minimal state.

In the next few pages, excerpted from a long book about a number of philosophical questions, Nozick reflects on our mortality and the meaning of life. He considers the possibility that the fact we die might deprive our lives of meaning—or that immortality might instead rob them of meaning. He points to the importance we find in "traces," the marks our lives leave on the world. We want to have made a difference; we do not want it to be that we changed nothing. We leave traces with our children, our artistic creations, the students we have taught, the bridges we have built. Nozick asks why traces are important.

It is often assumed that there is a problem about the meaning of life because of our mortality. Why does the fact that all people die create a special problem? (If life were to go on forever, would there then be no problem about its meaning?) One opposite view has been proposed that welcomes the fact of death and makes a virtue of its apparently grim necessity. Victor Frankl writes that "death itself is what makes life

Reprinted by permission of the publisher from "Philosophy and the Meaning of Life," in *Philosophical Explanations*, by Robert Nozick, pp. 579–585, Cambridge, Mass.: The Belknap Press of Harvard University Press, Copyright © 1981 by Robert Nozick.

meaningful," arguing for this startling view as follows. "What would our lives be like if they were not finite in time, but infinite? If we were immortal, we could legitimately postpone every action forever. It would be of no consequence whether or not we did a thing now; every act might just as well be done tomorrow or the day after or a year from now or ten years hence. But in the face of death as absolute *finis* to our future and boundary to our possibilities, we are under the imperative of utilizing our lifetimes to the utmost, not letting the singular opportunities—whose 'finite' sum constitutes the whole of life—pass by unused."[1] It would appear, then, that persons who were or could become immortal should choose to set a temporal limit to their lives in order to escape meaninglessness; scientists who discovered some way to avoid natural death should suppress their discoveries.*

Frankl assumes our only desire is to have done certain things, to put certain things somewhere on our record. Because we shall die, if we are to have done these things by the end of our lives, we had better get on with them. However, we may desire to *do* things; our desire need not be merely to have done them.[2] Moreover, if we had an infinite life, we might view it as a whole, as something to organize, shape and do something with. (Will this require us to be tolerant of very long gaps?) Persons who are immortal need not be limited to the desires and designs of mortals; they might well think up new plans that, in Parkinsonian fashion, expand to fill the available time. Despite his clear sympathy for religious thought, Frankl seems never to wonder or worry whether unlimited existence presents a problem of meaningfulness for God.

---

*For the firm statement of the opposite view, see Alan Harrington, *The Immortalist* (Random House, New York, 1969). Frankl might avoid the consequences drawn in the text, by saying that though immortality would involve a sacrifice of meaningfulness, the other things gained might be even more important and so justify that sacrifice. Nevertheless, Frankl makes some parochial assumptions, and limits his vision of human possibilities. Even on his own terms, perhaps, you do best thinking you are mortal and very long-lived (having no good idea of approximately when the end would come, whether after 200 or 2,000 or 20,000 years), while in fact being immortal.

Whatever appeal Frankl's view has depends upon the more general assumption that certain limits, certain preexisting structures into which things can be poured, are necessary for meaningful organization. Similar things often are said in discussions of particular art forms, such as the sonnet and the sonata.[3] Even were this general assumption true, though, death constitutes only one kind of structural limitation: finiteness in time. Other kinds are possible too, and we well might welcome these others somewhat more. The dual assumption that some limitation is necessary for meaning, and limitation in time is the only one that can serve, is surely too ill established to convince anyone that mortality is good for him— unless he is willing to grasp at any straw. If we are going to grasp at things, let them not be straws.*

---

*There seems to be no limit to the flimsiness of what philosophers will grasp at to disarm the fact of death. It has been argued that if death is bad, bad because it ends life, that can only be because what it ends is good. It cannot be that life, because it ends in death, is bad, for if it were bad then death, ending a bad thing, itself would be good and not bad. The argument concludes that the badness of death presupposes the goodness of the life that it ends. (See Paul Edwards, "Life, Meaning and Value of," *Encyclopedia of Philosophy*, Macmillan, New York, 1967, Vol. 4. pp. 469–470.)

Why think that the badness of death resides in and depends upon the goodness of what it ends rather than in the goodness of what it prevents? When an infant dies three minutes after delivery, is its death bad because of the goodness of those three minutes that it ends, or because of the goodness of the longer life which it prevents? Similarly, suppose that only an infinite life could be good; death then would be bad because it prevented this. It would not follow or be presupposed that the finite portion itself was good. I do not say here that only an infinite life can be good, merely that this argument, purporting to show that the badness of death presupposes the goodness of a finite life, fails.

Even stranger arguments about death have been produced. We find Epicurus saying, "Death is nothing to us . . . it does not concern either the living or the dead, since for the former it is not, and the latter are no more." Epicurus asks who death is bad for, and answers that it is not bad for anyone—not for anyone alive, for that person is not dead, and not for anyone dead, for

Granting that our life ending in death is in tension, at least, with our existence having meaning, we have not yet isolated why this is so. We can pursue this issue by considering a puzzle raised by Lucretius, which runs as follows. No one is disturbed by there being a time before which they did not exist, before their birth or conception, although if the past is infinite, there was an infinite amount of time before you were born when you didn't exist. So why should you be disturbed by the fact that after you are dead, there also will be an infinite amount of time when you will not exist? What creates the asymmetry between the time before we were born and the time after we die, leading us to different attitudes toward these two periods?[4]

Is it that death is bad because it makes our lives finite in duration? We can sharpen this issue with an extreme supposition. Imagine that the past is infinite and that you have existed throughout all of it, having forgotten most. If death, even in this case, would disturb you, this is not because it makes you merely finite, since you are not, we are supposing, merely finite in the past direction. What then is so especially distressing about a finite future? Is it that an extended future gives you a chance for further improvement and growth, the opportunity to build from what you are now, whereas an infinite past that culminates only in what you now are might seem puny indeed? We can test whether this accounts for any difference in our attitudes toward infinite future and infinite past by imagining two cases that are mirror images. The infinite future of one is the mirror image of the other's infinite past; each has heights to match the heights of the other. If we had existed infinitely long until now, done all and seen all (though now the memory is dim), would we be disturbed at dying? Perhaps not, perhaps then the asymmetry between past and future would disappear. Nevertheless, this view does not explain why

there is an asymmetry between the past and future for finite beings. Why don't we bemoan our late (relative to the infinite past) birth, just as we bemoan our early death? Is the answer that we take the past as given and fixed already, and since, at the present juncture, it is what will happen that settles our fate, we therefore focus upon this?

In the mirror image situation, however, if we were satisfied with the life whose future was finite, that need not be simply because it contained an infinite past existence. That past existence must be specified as one in which we had done all, seen all, known all, been all. An infinite but monotonous past would not make death welcome, except perhaps as a deserved closing. Is the crucial fact about death not that it makes us finite or limits our future, but that it limits the possibilities (of those we would choose) that we can realize? On this view, death's sting lies not in its destroying or obliterating our personality, but in thwarting it. Nonetheless, underneath many phenomena there seems to lurk not simply the desire to realize other possibilities, but the desire and the hope to endure beyond death, perhaps forever.

Traces

Death wipes you out. Dead, you are no longer around—around *here* at any rate—and if there is nowhere else where you'll be (heaven, hell, with the white light) then all that will be left of you is your effects, leavings, traces. People do seem to think it important to continue to be around somehow. The root notion seems to be this one: it shouldn't *ever* be as if you had never existed at all. A significant life leaves its mark on the world. A significant life is, in some sense, permanent; it makes a permanent difference to the world—it leaves traces. To be wiped out completely, traces and all, goes a long way toward destroying the meaning of one's life. Endurance, however, even if a necessary condition for a meaningful life, is certainly not sufficient. We shall have to ask what kind of trace is important, and why that kind is not important even when very evanescent. First, though, let us explore some of the ramifications of the notion that it shouldn't ever be as if one had never lived or existed at all.

---

dead people do not exist any more, and something can be bad only for someone who exists. Since there is no one for whom death is bad, Epicurus concludes, why should we fear it or even view it unfavorably? We shall not pause to unravel this argument, but note that it does have a limited point: if we believe death obliterates us, we should not fear it as if it were a bad *experience*.

People sometimes speak of achieving immortality through their children. (Will this include achieving immortality through a child, himself childless, who achieves it in some other way? Did Kant's parents do so by siring Kant?) It is puzzling that people speak of achieving immortality by leaving descendants, since they do not believe that their chain of descendants, although perhaps very extended, is going to be infinite. So how do descendants bring immortality rather than a somewhat extended mortality? Perhaps the situation is this: while infinite continuation is best, any continuation is better than none. When a ninety-year-old's only child dies childless at the age of sixty-eight, we feel sad for this parent who now will not be leaving behind that (expected) trace.

There are many manifestations of the desire not to sink completely into oblivion. Artists often strive to leave behind permanent masterpieces, thereby achieving what is called immortality—a goal rejected by the dadaists in their temporary "art-for-a-day." People erect tombstones for others, and some make that provision for themselves. Tombstones are continuing marks upon the world; through them people know where your remains are, and remember you—hence, they are called *memorials*.

When funeral orators say, "he will live in our hearts," the assumption is not that the listeners will live forever, thereby immortalizing the dead person. Nor is it assumed that "living on in the hearts of" is a transitive relation, so that the dead person will continue to live on in the further hearts where the listeners themselves will live on. Permanent survival is not involved here, but neither is it sufficient merely to continue on somewhat, however little. Imagine that the funeral orator had said, "he will continue on in our minds until we leave this building whereupon we all promptly will forget him."

Another phrase sometimes heard is: "as long as people survive, this man will not be forgotten, his achievements and memory will live on." Presumably, one would want to add the proviso that people *will* live on for a long time. This, perhaps, is as close to immortality as a person can get. Some people are disturbed by the thought that life will go on for others, yet without themselves in any way. They are forgotten, and left out; those who follow later will live

as if you never had. Here, permanent survival is not the goal, only survival as long as life goes on. More modest reference groups than all of humanity might be picked; you can hope to be remembered as long as your relations, friends, and acquaintances survive. In these cases it is not temporal enduringness that is crucial, but rather a certain sort of enduringness as shown in relationships to others.

When people desire to leave a trace behind, they want to leave a certain kind of trace. We all do leave traces, causal effects reverberate down: our voices move molecules which have their effects, we feed the worms, and so on. The kind of trace one wishes to leave is one that people know of in particular and that they know is due to you,[5] one due (people know) to some action, choice, plan of yours, that expresses something you take to be important about the kind of person you are, such that people respect or positively evaluate both the trace and that aspect of yourself. We want somehow to live on, but not as an object lesson for others. Notice also that wanting to live on by leaving appropriate traces need not involve wanting continuous existence; you want there to be some time after which you continue to leave a mark, but this time needn't be precisely at your death. Artists as well as those who anticipate resurrection are quite willing to contemplate and tolerate a gap.

Why are traces important? There are several possibilities. First, the importance of traces might lie not in themselves but (only) in what they indicate. Traces indicate that a person's life had a certain meaning or importance, but they are not infallible signs of this—there may be traces without meaning, or meaning without traces. For instance, to "live on" in the memory of others indicates one's effect on these others. It is the effect that matters; even if each of them happened to die first, there still would have been that effect. On this first view, it is a mistake to scrutinize traces in an attempt to understand how life has or can have meaning, for at best traces are a symptom of a life's meaning. Second, traces might be an expression of something important about a life, but it might be important and valuable in addition that this be expressed.

Third, it might be thought that the leaving of traces is intrinsically important. A philosophical tradition going back to Plato holds that the perma-nent and unchanging is more valuable by virtue of being permanent and unchanging. For Plato, the changing objects of our ordinary everyday world were less valuable and less real than the unchanging permanent Forms or Ideas. These latter not only served an explanatory purpose, they were to be val-ued, respected, and even venerated. Therefore, when Socrates is asked whether distinct Forms corre-spond to "such things as hair, mud, dirt, or anything else which is vile and paltry," he is unwilling to say they do.[6] Forms of such things do not seem very exalted, valuable or important, in contrast to the Forms of the Good, the Just, and the Beautiful. Some mathematicians have this attitude toward the per-manent and unchanging mathematical objects and structures they study, investigate, and explore. (Other mathematicians, in contrast, think they have created this realm, or are engaged merely in the combinatorial manipulation of meaningless marks on paper or blackboard.)

Despite the pedigree of the tradition, it is difficult to discover why the more permanent is the more valuable or meaningful, why permanence or long-lastingness, why duration in itself, should be impor-tant. Consider those things people speak of as permanent or eternal. These include (apart from God) numbers, sets, abstract ideas, space-time itself. Would it be better to be one of these things? The question is bizarre; how could a concrete person become an abstract object? Still, would anyone wish they *could* become the number 14 or the Form of Justice, or the null set? Is anyone pining to lead a setly existence?

Yet, it cannot be denied that some are gripped by the notion of traces continuing forever. Hence, we find some people disturbed over thermodynamics, worrying that millions of years from now the uni-verse will run down into a state of maximum entropy, with no trace remaining of us or of what we have done. In their view, this eventuality makes human existence absurd; the eventual obliteration of all our traces also obliterates or undermines the meaningfulness of our existence. An account or theory of the meaning of life should find a place for this feeling, showing what facet of meaning it gets a grip upon; an adequate theory should explain the force of this feeling, even if it does not endorse or justify it.[7]

Notes

1. Victor Frankl, *The Doctor and the Soul* (Alfred Knopf, New York, 1957), p. 73.
2. Compare Frankl's discussion to Ludwig Von Mises' attempt to derive time preference from the essence of human action (*Human Action,* Regnery, Chicago, 1966, ch. 5), critically discussed in part IV of my essay "On Austrian Methodology," *Synthese,* Vol. 36, 1977, pp. 353–392.
3. A recent instance is E. H. Gombrich's critical argu-ment about modern painting, "The Vogue of Abstract Art" in his *Meditations on a Hobby Horse* (Phaidon, London, 1963), pp. 143–150.
4. Let us distinguish this question from others close by. We do have different attitudes toward our own past and future. Suppose you have gone into the hospital for a very painful operation. No anesthetic can be given for this operation, though something can be given immediately afterwards causing you to forget the trauma. This puts you to sleep, and when you awake you will not remember what happened. Each night of the preliminary stay in the hospital, you are given a sedative to induce sleep; each morning you wake up and wonder whether the tremendously pain-ful operation has happened already or is still to come. Are you indifferent as to which it is, counting pain in your life as the same, whenever it happens? No, you hope it has happened already and is behind you. If the nurse comes in and tells you the operation is over, you are relieved; if she says that today is the day, you are fearful. Although in any case it is three hours of ago-nizing pain that you undergo, you want it to be over and done. However, if another person is in this situa-tion, with no danger involved, only pain, it does not matter to you whether he had it yesterday or will have it tomorrow. (I owe this example to Derek Parfit.)

Why is there an asymmetry between the future and past in the first-person case but none in the third-person case? It seems plausible to think that the key is fear, which is not to be understood merely as a negative evaluation of something—usually we are not afraid of something that is past even when we negatively evalu-ate it. Yet if fear is the explanation of the phenomenon in the hospital case, it cannot be the whole explanation of the asymmetry about existence. For not only do we not fear our past nonexistence, antiquarians aside, we do not even negatively evaluate it.

Also, we should avoid the answer that before you exist, in contrast to afterwards, you cannot even be referred to; in consequence, no one could have said earlier that *you* did not exist then, while after your death that can be said. First, why isn't it sadder that not only did you not exist earlier but you could not even be referred to then? (There could have been a list of everyone who existed earlier, and that list would not have included you.) Second, you can be referred to now, and so now we can say that you didn't exist then.

5. Here lurk complicated problems about what someone must know to identify you. To know merely that an effect is due to "the person who caused the effect" is not to know to whom it is due. Fortunately, these problems need not divert us here.

6. Plato, *Parmenides*, 130.

7. For another treatment of the subject of traces, see my "R.S.V.P.—a Story," *Commentary*, Vol. 53, No. 3, March 1972, pp. 66–68.

QUESTIONS

1. What is Nozick's reaction to Victor Frankl's thesis that death is what makes life meaningful?

2. In a long footnote Nozick challenges the thought "that if death is bad because it ends life, that can only be because what it ends is good." Are Rachels's or Nagel's views subject to Nozick's criticisms of this thought?

3. What traces might you want to leave? Why?

III

What Makes Our Lives Go Well?

In the introduction to section I we distinguished between accounts of the wrongness of killing that focus on the harm to the victim and on the infringement of the victim's freedom or autonomy. Distinguishing these different kinds of accounts will be important for some of the controversies discussed in this reader, especially suicide and euthanasia. For harms and threats to freedom can come apart. Someone might choose and consent to a genuine harm, perhaps in order to benefit family members. So we might face the choice of respecting his or her autonomy or preventing a harm.

There is also the difficult question of determining what are genuine harms. Consider people who ride motorcycles without helmets. Suppose some do so fully understanding the risks. They may say that they strongly prefer a life of risk-taking unprotected on the back of a motorcycle, with their hair blowing in the wind, to other alternatives. Think also of people who neglect their safety or health and who tell us that these things are not in fact valuable. Now consider someone who says that something is good or bad for us only insofar as we care about it. These cases all raise questions about what constitutes genuine harms or, more generally, goods or evils for us. Some think that people's (informed) desires or preferences determine whether something is good or bad for them. Others deny this. Some think that all that matters are one's experiences, and others deny that.

There are difficult questions about what makes someone's life go well, about human well-being, about our ends, questions that are interesting and important in their own right but that are also central to many of the topics discussed in this reader.

11. Happiness

THOMAS AQUINAS

For a description of the author and a note on the text, see chapter 2.

In these lengthy excerpts, Aquinas raises and answers four sets of questions: What things make up human happiness? What is happiness? What things are required for happiness? Can we attain happiness? He defends a theistic view: "Final and perfect happiness can consist in nothing else than the vision of the Divine Essence." The view that human happiness is to be achieved mostly in the afterlife may have important implications for some of the controversies taken up in this reader. But many of Aquinas's reflections in these pages may stand independently of his theism.

Q1 Of Those Things in Which Man's Happiness Consists

Art. 1 Whether Man's Happiness Consists in Wealth?

It is impossible for man's happiness to consist in wealth. For wealth is twofold, as the Philosopher says (Polit. i, 3), viz. natural and artificial. Natural wealth is that which serves man as a remedy for his natural wants: such as food, drink, clothing, cars, dwellings, and such like, while artificial wealth is that which is not a direct help to nature, as money, but is invented by the art of man, for the convenience of exchange, and as a measure of things salable.

Now it is evident that man's happiness cannot consist in natural wealth. For wealth of this kind is sought for the sake of something else, viz. as a support of human nature: consequently it cannot be man's last end, rather is it ordained to man as to its end. Wherefore in the order of nature, all such things are below man, and made for him, according to Ps. 8:8: "Thou hast subjected all things under his feet."

And as to artificial wealth, it is not sought save for the sake of natural wealth; since man would not seek it except because, by its means, he procures for himself the necessaries of life. Consequently much less can it be considered in the light of the last end. Therefore it is impossible for happiness, which is the last end of man, to consist in wealth.

Art. 2 Whether Man's Happiness Consists in Honors?

It is impossible for happiness to consist in honor. For honor is given to a man on account of some excellence in him; and consequently it is a sign and attestation of the excellence that is in the person honored. Now a man's excellence is in proportion, especially to his happiness, which is man's perfect good; and to its parts, i.e. those goods by which he has a certain share of happiness. And therefore honor can result from happiness, but happiness cannot principally consist therein.

Thomas Aquinas, *Summa Theologica* (Benziger Bros. edition, 1947), translated by Fathers of the English Dominion Province.

Art. 4 Whether Man's Happiness Consists in Power?

It is impossible for happiness to consist in power; and this for two reasons. First because power has the nature of principle, as is stated in Metaph. v, 12, whereas happiness has the nature of last end. Secondly, because power has relation to good and evil: whereas happiness is man's proper and perfect good. Wherefore some happiness might consist in the good use of power, which is by virtue, rather than in power itself.

Now four general reasons may be given to prove that happiness consists in none of the foregoing external goods. First, because, since happiness is man's supreme good, it is incompatible with any evil. Now all the foregoing can be found both in good and in evil men. Secondly, because, since it is the nature of happiness to "satisfy of itself," as stated in Ethic. i, 7, having gained happiness, man cannot lack any needful good. But after acquiring any one of the foregoing, man may still lack many goods that are necessary to him; for instance, wisdom, bodily health, and such like. Thirdly, because, since happiness is the perfect good, no evil can accrue to anyone therefrom. This cannot be said of the foregoing: for it is written (Eccles. 5:12) that "riches" are sometimes "kept to the hurt of the owner"; and the same may be said of the other three. Fourthly, because man is ordained to happiness through principles that are in him; since he is ordained thereto naturally. Now the four goods mentioned above are due rather to external causes, and in most cases to fortune; for which reason they are called goods of fortune. Therefore it is evident that happiness nowise consists in the foregoing.

Art. 5 Whether Man's Happiness Consists in Any Bodily Good?

It is impossible for man's happiness to consist in the goods of the body; and this for two reasons. First, because, if a thing be ordained to another as to its end, its last end cannot consist in the preservation of its being. Hence a captain does not intend as a last end, the preservation of the ship entrusted to him, since a ship is ordained to something else as its end, viz. to navigation. Now just as the ship is entrusted to the captain that he may steer its course, so man is given over to his will and reason; according to Ecclus. 15:14: "God made man from the beginning and left him in the hand of his own counsel." Now it is evident that man is ordained to something as his end: since man is not the supreme good. Therefore the last end of man's reason and will cannot be the preservation of man's being.

Secondly, because, granted that the end of man's will and reason be the preservation of man's being, it could not be said that the end of man is some good of the body. For man's being consists in soul and body; and though the being of the body depends on the soul, yet the being of the human soul depends not on the body, as shown above (FP, Q[75], A[2]); and the very body is for the soul, as matter for its form, and the instruments for the man that puts them into motion, that by their means he may do his work. Wherefore all goods of the body are ordained to the goods of the soul, as to their end. Consequently happiness, which is man's last end, cannot consist in goods of the body.

Art. 6 Whether Man's Happiness Consists in Pleasure?

Because bodily delights are more generally known, "the name of pleasure has been appropriated to them" (Ethic. vii, 13), although other delights excel them: and yet happiness does not consist in them. Because in every thing, that which pertains to its essence is distinct from its proper accident: thus in man it is one thing that he is a mortal rational animal, and another that he is a risible animal. We must therefore consider that every delight is a proper accident resulting from happiness, or from some part of happiness; since the reason that a man is delighted is that he has some fitting good, either in reality, or in hope, or at least in memory. Now a fitting good, if indeed it be the perfect good, is precisely man's happiness: and if it is imperfect, it is a share of happiness, either proximate, or remote, or at least apparent. Therefore it is evident that neither is delight, which results from the perfect good, the very essence of happiness, but something resulting therefrom as its proper accident.

But bodily pleasure cannot result from the perfect good even in that way. For it results from a good apprehended by sense, which is a power of the soul, which power makes use of the body. Now good pertaining to the body, and apprehended by sense, cannot be man's perfect good. For since the rational soul excels the capacity of corporeal matter, that part of the soul which is independent of a corporeal organ, has a certain infinity in regard to the body and those parts of the soul which are tied down to the body: just as immaterial things are in a way infinite as compared to material things, since a form is, after a fashion, contracted and bounded by matter, so that a form which is independent of matter is, in a way, infinite. Therefore sense, which is a power of the body, knows the singular, which is determinate through matter: whereas the intellect, which is a power independent of matter, knows the universal, which is abstracted from matter, and contains an infinite number of singulars. Consequently it is evident that good which is fitting to the body, and which causes bodily delight through being apprehended by sense, is not man's perfect good, but is quite a trifle as compared with the good of the soul. Hence it is written (Wis. 7:9) that "all gold in comparison of her, is as a little sand." And therefore bodily pleasure is neither happiness itself, nor a proper accident of happiness.

Art. 7 Whether Some Good of the Soul Constitutes Man's Happiness?

As stated above (Q[1], A[8]), the end is twofold: namely, the thing itself, which we desire to attain, and the use, namely, the attainment or possession of that thing. If, then, we speak of man's last end, it is impossible for man's last end to be the soul itself or something belonging to it. Because the soul, considered in itself, is as something existing in potentiality: for it becomes knowing actually, from being potentially knowing; and actually virtuous, from being potentially virtuous. Now since potentiality is for the sake of act as for its fulfilment, that which in itself is in potentiality cannot be the last end. Therefore the soul itself cannot be its own last end.

In like manner neither can anything belonging to it, whether power, habit, or act. For that good which

is the last end, is the perfect good fulfilling the desire. Now man's appetite, otherwise the will, is for the universal good. And any good inherent to the soul is a participated good, and consequently a portioned good. Therefore none of them can be man's last end.

But if we speak of man's last end, as to the attainment or possession thereof, or as to any use whatever of the thing itself desired as an end, thus does something of man, in respect of his soul, belong to his last end: since man attains happiness through his soul. Therefore the thing itself which is desired as end, is that which constitutes happiness, and makes man happy; but the attainment of this thing is called happiness. Consequently we must say that happiness is something belonging to the soul; but that which constitutes happiness is something outside the soul.

Art. 8 Whether Any Created Good Constitutes Man's Happiness?

It is impossible for any created good to constitute man's happiness. For happiness is the perfect good, which lulls the appetite altogether; else it would not be the last end, if something yet remained to be desired. Now the object of the will, i.e. of man's appetite, is the universal good; just as the object of the intellect is the universal true. Hence it is evident that naught can lull man's will, save the universal good. This is to be found, not in any creature, but in God alone; because every creature has goodness by participation. Wherefore God alone can satisfy the will of man, according to the words of Ps. 102:5: "Who satisfieth thy desire with good things." Therefore God alone constitutes man's happiness.

Q3 What Is Happiness?

Art. 5 Whether Happiness Is an Operation of the Speculative, or of the Practical Intellect?

Happiness consists in an operation of the speculative rather than of the practical intellect. This is evident for three reasons. First because if man's happiness is an operation, it must needs be man's highest operation. Now man's highest operation is that of his highest power in respect of its highest object: and his highest power is the intellect, whose highest object is the Divine Good, which is the object, not of the practical but of the speculative intellect. Consequently happiness consists principally in such an operation, viz. in the contemplation of Divine things. And since that "seems to be each man's self, which is best in him," according to Ethic. ix, 8, and x, 7, therefore such an operation is most proper to man and most delightful to him.

Secondly, it is evident from the fact that contemplation is sought principally for its own sake. But the act of the practical intellect is not sought for its own sake but for the sake of action: and these very actions are ordained to some end. Consequently it is evident that the last end cannot consist in the active life, which pertains to the practical intellect.

Thirdly, it is again evident, from the fact that in the contemplative life man has something in common with things above him, viz. with God and the angels, to whom he is made like by happiness. But in things pertaining to the active life, other animals also have something in common with man, although imperfectly.

Therefore the last and perfect happiness, which we await in the life to come, consists entirely in contemplation. But imperfect happiness, such as can be had here, consists first and principally, in an operation of the practical intellect directing human actions and passions, as stated in Ethic. x, 7, 8.

Art. 8 Whether Man's Happiness Consists in the Vision of the Divine Essence?

Final and perfect happiness can consist in nothing else than the vision of the Divine Essence. To make this clear, two points must be observed. First, that man is not perfectly happy, so long as something remains for him to desire and seek: secondly, that the perfection of any power is determined by the nature of its object. Now the object of the intellect is "what a thing is," i.e. the essence of a thing, according to De Anima iii, 6. Wherefore the intellect attains perfection, in so far as it knows the essence of a thing. If therefore an intellect knows the essence of some effect, whereby it is not possible to know the essence of the cause, i.e. to know of the cause "what it is"; that intellect cannot be said to reach that cause

simply, although it may be able to gather from the effect the knowledge of that the cause is. Consequently, when man knows an effect, and knows that it has a cause, there naturally remains in the man the desire to know about the cause, "what it is." And this desire is one of wonder, and causes inquiry, as is stated in the beginning of the Metaphysics (i, 2). For instance, if a man, knowing the eclipse of the sun, consider that it must be due to some cause, and know not what that cause is, he wonders about it, and from wondering proceeds to inquire. Nor does this inquiry cease until he arrive at a knowledge of the essence of the cause.

If therefore the human intellect, knowing the essence of some created effect, knows no more of God than "that He is"; the perfection of that intellect does not yet reach simply the First Cause, but there remains in it the natural desire to seek the cause. Wherefore it is not yet perfectly happy. Consequently, for perfect happiness the intellect needs to reach the very Essence of the First Cause. And thus it will have its perfection through union with God as with that object, in which alone man's happiness consists, as stated above (AA[1],7; Q[2], A[8]).

Q4 Of Those Things That Are Required for Happiness

Art. 4 Whether Rectitude of the Will Is Necessary for Happiness?

Rectitude of will is necessary for Happiness both antecedently and concomitantly. Antecedently, because rectitude of the will consists in being duly ordered to the last end. Now the end in comparison to what is ordained to the end is as form compared to matter. Wherefore, just as matter cannot receive a form, unless it be duly disposed thereto, so nothing gains an end, except it be duly ordained thereto. And therefore none can obtain Happiness, without rectitude of the will. Concomitantly, because as stated above (Q[3], A[8]), final Happiness consists in the vision of the Divine Essence, Which is the very essence of goodness. So that the will of him who sees the Essence of God, of necessity, loves, whatever he loves, in subordination to God; just as the will of him who sees not God's Essence, of necessity, loves whatever he loves, under the common notion of good which he knows. And this is precisely what makes the will right. Wherefore it is evident that Happiness cannot be without a right will.

Art. 5 Whether the Body Is Necessary for Man's Happiness?

Happiness is twofold; the one is imperfect and is had in this life; the other is perfect, consisting in the vision of God. Now it is evident that the body is necessary for the happiness of this life. For the happiness of this life consists in an operation of the intellect, either speculative or practical. And the operation of the intellect in this life cannot be without a phantasm, which is only in a bodily organ, as was shown in the FP, Q[84], AA[6],7. Consequently that happiness which can be had in this life, depends, in a way, on the body. But as to perfect Happiness, which consists in the vision of God, some have maintained that it is not possible to the soul separated from the body; and have said that the souls of saints, when separated from their bodies, do not attain to that Happiness until the Day of Judgment, when they will receive their bodies back again. And this is shown to be false, both by authority and by reason. By authority, since the Apostle says (2 Cor. 5:6): "While we are in the body, we are absent from the Lord"; and he points out the reason of this absence, saying: "For we walk by faith and not by sight." Now from this it is clear that so long as we walk by faith and not by sight, bereft of the vision of the Divine Essence, we are not present to the Lord. But the souls of the saints, separated from their bodies, are in God's presence; wherefore the text continues: "But we are confident and have a good will to be absent . . . from the body, and to be present with the Lord." Whence it is evident that the souls of the saints, separated from their bodies, "walk by sight," seeing the Essence of God, wherein is true Happiness.

Again this is made clear by reason. For the intellect needs not the body, for its operation, save on account of the phantasms, wherein it looks on the intelligible truth, as stated in the FP, Q[84], A[7]. Now it is evident that the Divine Essence cannot be seen by means of phantasms, as stated in the FP, Q[12], A[3]. Wherefore, since man's perfect Happiness consists in the vision of the Divine Essence, it does not depend on the body. Consequently, without the body the soul can be happy.

We must, however, notice that something may belong to a thing's perfection in two ways. First, as constituting the essence thereof; thus the soul is necessary for man's perfection. Secondly, as necessary for its well-being: thus, beauty of body and keenness of perfection belong to man's perfection. Wherefore though the body does not belong in the first way to the perfection of human Happiness, yet it does in the second way. For since operation depends on a thing's nature, the more perfect is the soul in its nature, the more perfectly it has its proper operation, wherein its happiness consists. Hence, Augustine, after inquiring (Gen. ad lit. xii, 35) "whether that perfect Happiness can be ascribed to the souls of the dead separated from their bodies," answers "that they cannot see the Unchangeable Substance, as the blessed angels see It; either for some other more hidden reason, or because they have a natural desire to rule the body."

Art. 7 Whether Any External Goods Are Necessary for Happiness?

For imperfect happiness, such as can be had in this life, external goods are necessary, not as belonging to the essence of happiness, but by serving as instruments to happiness, which consists in an operation of virtue, as stated in Ethic. i, 13. For man needs in this life, the necessaries of the body, both for the operation of contemplative virtue, and for the operation of active virtue, for which latter he needs also many other things by means of which to perform its operations.

On the other hand, such goods as these are nowise necessary for perfect Happiness, which consists in seeing God. The reason of this is that all such-like external goods are requisite either for the support of the animal body; or for certain operations which belong to human life, which we perform by means of the animal body: whereas that perfect Happiness which consists in seeing God, will be either in the soul separated from the body, or in the soul united to the body then no longer animal but spiritual. Consequently these external goods are nowise necessary for that Happiness, since they are ordained to the animal life. And since, in this life, the felicity of contemplation, as being more Godlike, approaches nearer than that of action to the likeness of that perfect Happiness, therefore it stands in less need of these goods of the body as stated in Ethic. x, 8.

Art. 8 Whether the Fellowship of Friend Is Necessary for Happiness?

If we speak of the happiness of this life, the happy man needs friends, as the Philosopher says (Ethic. ix, 9), not, indeed, to make use of them, since he suffices himself; nor to delight in them, since he possesses perfect delight in the operation of virtue; but for the purpose of a good operation, viz. that he may do good to them; that he may delight in seeing them do good; and again that he may be helped by them in his good work. For in order that man may do well, whether in the works of the active life, or in those of the contemplative life, he needs the fellowship of friends.

But if we speak of perfect Happiness which will be in our heavenly Fatherland, the fellowship of friends is not essential to Happiness; since man has the entire fulness of his perfection in God. But the fellowship of friends conduces to the well-being of Happiness. Hence Augustine says (Gen. ad lit. viii, 25) that "the spiritual creatures receive no other interior aid to happiness than the eternity, truth, and charity of the Creator. But if they can be said to be helped from without, perhaps it is only by this that they see one another and rejoice in God, at their fellowship."

Q5 Of the Attainment of Happiness

Art. 1 Whether Man Can Attain Happiness

Happiness is the attainment of the Perfect Good. Whoever, therefore, is capable of the Perfect Good can attain Happiness. Now, that man is capable of the Perfect Good, is proved both because his intellect can apprehend the universal and perfect good, and because his will can desire it. And therefore man can attain Happiness. This can be proved again from the fact that man is capable of seeing God, as stated in FP, Q[12], A[1]: in which

vision, as we stated above (Q[3], A[8]) man's perfect Happiness consists.

Art. 3 Whether One Can Be Happy in This Life?

A certain participation of Happiness can be had in this life: but perfect and true Happiness cannot be had in this life. This may be seen from a twofold consideration.

First, from the general notion of happiness. For since happiness is a "perfect and sufficient good," it excludes every evil, and fulfils every desire. But in this life every evil cannot be excluded. For this present life is subject to many unavoidable evils; to ignorance on the part of the intellect; to inordinate affection on the part of the appetite, and to many penalties on the part of the body; as Augustine sets forth in De Civ. Dei xix, 4. Likewise neither can the desire for good be satiated in this life. For man naturally desires the good, which he has, to be abiding. Now the goods of the present life pass away; since life itself passes away, which we naturally desire to have, and would wish to hold abidingly, for man naturally shrinks from death. Wherefore it is impossible to have true Happiness in this life.

Secondly, from a consideration of the specific nature of Happiness, viz. the vision of the Divine Essence, which man cannot obtain in this life, as was shown in the FP, Q[12], A[11]. Hence it is evident that none can attain true and perfect Happiness in this life.

Art. 5 Whether Man Can Attain Happiness by His Natural Powers?

Imperfect happiness that can be had in this life, can be acquired by man by his natural powers, in the same way as virtue, in whose operation it consists: on this point we shall speak further on (Q[63]). But man's perfect Happiness, as stated above (Q[3], A[8]), consists in the vision of the Divine Essence. Now the vision of God's Essence surpasses the nature not only of man, but also of every creature, as was shown in the FP, Q[12], A[4]. For the natural knowledge of every creature is in keeping with the mode of his substance: thus it is said of the intelligence (De Causis; Prop. viii) that "it knows things that are above it, and things that are below it, according to the mode of its substance." But every knowledge that is according to the mode of created substance, falls short of the vision of the Divine Essence, which infinitely surpasses all created substance. Consequently neither man, nor any creature, can attain final Happiness by his natural powers.

QUESTIONS
1. What is Aquinas's conception of happiness? Is it the same as ours?
2. In Q1, Art. 6, he challenges the view that happiness consists of pleasure. Compare his challenges to those mounted by Rachels against hedonism in chapter 8.

12. Felicity

THOMAS HOBBES

For a description of the author, see chapter 5.

In these brief passages, Hobbes lays out his conception of "felicity" or happiness. It contrasts with that of Thomas Aquinas or other influential thinkers of his time. The basis for some of our attitudes toward things is our "appetites and aversions." "[W]hatsoever is the object of any man's appetite or desire . . . [is what he] calleth *good*: and the object of his hate and aversion, *evil*." It follows that good and bad are relative to the person's desires. (This kind of conception of good and bad makes value "agent-relative.") This is the conception of good that leads Hobbes to conclude that "the Value of a man is his price" (chapter 5).

From this conception of good and bad, Hobbes concludes that a person's "felicity" (or happiness) can only be "continual success" in satisfying his or her desires. The last sentence of the selected passage is a criticism of Thomas Aquinas's conception as taught in Hobbes's time by university teachers; it is said to be unintelligible given that we cannot know anything about the hereafter. Hobbes's conception of "continual prospering" is similar to conceptions of happiness found in economics and policy studies today.

Of appetites and aversions, some are born with men; as appetite of food, appetite of excretion, and exoneration, which may also and more properly be called aversions, from somewhat they feel in their bodies; and some other appetites, not many. The rest, which are appetites of particular things, proceed from experience, and trial of their effects upon themselves or other men. For of things we know not at all, or believe not to be, we can have no further desire, than to taste and try. But aversion we have for things, not

From Thomas Hobbes, *Leviathan* (1649).

only which we know have hurt us, but also that we do not know whether they will hurt us, or not. [. . .]

Those things which we neither desire, nor hate, we are said to *contemn*; contempt being nothing else but an immobility, or contumacy of the heart, in resisting the action of certain things; and proceeding from that the heart is already moved otherwise, by other more potent objects; or from want of experience of them. And because the constitution of a man's body is in continual mutation, it is impossible that all the same things should always cause in him the same appetites, and aversions: much less can all men consent, in the desire of almost any one and the same object.

But whatsoever is the object of any man's appetite or desire, that is it which he for his part calleth *good*: and the object of his hate and aversion, *evil*; and of his contempt, *vile* and *inconsiderable*. For these words of good, evil, and contemptible, are ever used with relation to the person that useth them: there being nothing simply and absolutely so; nor any common rule of good and evil, to be taken from the nature of the objects themselves; but from the person of the man, where there is no commonwealth; or, in a commonwealth, from the person that representeth it; or from an arbitrator or judge, whom men disagreeing shall by consent set up, and make his sentence the rule thereof. [. . .]

Continual success in obtaining those things which a man from time to time desireth, that is to say, continual prospering, is that men call felicity; I mean the felicity of this life. For there is no such thing as perpetual tranquillity of mind, while we live here; because life itself is but motion, and can never be without desire, nor without fear, no more than without sense. What kind of felicity God hath ordained to them that devoutly honour Him, a man shall no sooner know, than enjoy; being joys, that now are as incomprehensible, as the word of school-men *beatifical vision* is unintelligible.

QUESTIONS

1. Why are "these words of good, evil, and contemptible . . . [always] used with relation to the person that useth them"? Why are they "agent-relative"?
2. Why can there be no "perpetual tranquillity of mind, while we live here"?

---

13. The Experience Machine

ROBERT NOZICK

For a description of the author, see chapter 10.

We characterized hedonism earlier as the view that "the only things intrinsically good or bad for a person are pleasant or unpleasant experiences" (chapter 8, Rachels). A broader view might just have it that the only things that are intrinsically good or bad are experiences.

From Robert Nozick, *Anarchy, State, and Utopia* (New York: Basic Books, 1974). Reprinted by permission of the Perseus Book Group.

Or, we might say that only experiences tell us whether something is good or bad. Hobbes's view is a version of the latter.

Nozick develops a criticism of views that suppose that experiences are all that matter. It may matter how things feel "from the inside." However, this is not all that matters. Nozick's thought experiment is worth considering.

There are also substantial puzzles when we ask what matters other than how *people's* experiences feel "from the inside." Suppose there were an experience machine that would give you any experience you desired. Superduper neuropsychologists could stimulate your brain so that you would think and feel you were writing a great novel, or making a friend, or reading an interesting book. All the time you would be floating in a tank, with electrodes attached to your brain. Should you plug into this machine for life, preprogramming your life's experiences? If you are worried about missing out on desirable experiences, we can suppose that business enterprises have researched thoroughly the lives of many others. You can pick and choose from their large library or smorgasbord of such experiences, selecting your life's experiences for, say, the next two years. After two years have passed, you will have ten minutes or ten hours out of the tank, to select the experiences of your *next* two years. Of course, while in the tank you won't know that you're there; you'll think it's all actually happening. Others can also plug in to have the experiences they want, so there's no need to stay unplugged to serve them. (Ignore problems such as who will service the machines if everyone plugs in.) Would you plug in? *What else can matter to us, other than how our lives feel from the inside?* Nor should you refrain because of the few moments of distress between the moment you've decided and the moment you're plugged. What's a few moments of distress compared to a lifetime of bliss (if that's what you choose), and why feel any distress at all if your decision *is* the best one?

What does matter to us in addition to our experiences? First, we want to *do* certain things, and not just have the experience of doing them. In the case of certain experiences, it is only because first we want to do the actions that we want the experiences of doing them or thinking we've done them. (But

why do we want to do the activities rather than merely to experience them?) A second reason for not plugging in is that we want to *be* a certain way, to be a certain sort of person. Someone floating in a tank is an indeterminate blob. There is no answer to the question of what a person is like who has long been in the tank. Is he courageous, kind, intelligent, witty, loving? It's not merely that it's difficult to tell; there's no way he is. Plugging into the machine is a kind of suicide. It will seem to some, trapped by a picture, that nothing about what we are like can matter except as it gets reflected in our experiences. But should it be surprising that what *we are* is important to us? Why should we be concerned only with how our time is filled, but not with what we are?

Thirdly, plugging into an experience machine limits us to a man-made reality, to a world no deeper or more important than that which people can construct. There is no *actual* contact with any deeper reality, though the experience of it can be simulated. Many persons desire to leave themselves open to such contact and to a plumbing of deeper significance.* This clarifies the intensity of the conflict over psychoactive drugs, which some view as mere local experience machines, and

----

*Traditional religious views differ on the *point* of contact with a transcendent reality. Some say that contact yields eternal bliss or Nirvana, but they have not distinguished this sufficiently from merely a *very* long run on the experience machine. Others think it is intrinsically desirable to do the will of a higher being which created us all, though presumably no one would think this if we discovered we had been created as an object of amusement by some superpowerful child from another galaxy or dimension. Still others imagine an eventual merging with a higher reality, leaving unclear its desirability, or where that merging leaves *us*.

others view as avenues to a deeper reality; what some view as equivalent to surrender to the experience machine, others view as following one of the reasons *not* to surrender!

We learn that something matters to us in addition to experience by imagining an experience machine and then realizing that we would not use it. We can continue to imagine a sequence of machines each designed to fill lacks suggested for the earlier machines. For example, since the experience machine doesn't meet our desire to *be* a certain way, imagine a transformation machine which transforms us into whatever sort of person we'd like to be (compatible with our staying us). Surely one would not use the transformation machine to become as one would wish, and thereupon plug into the experience machine!* So something matters in addition to one's experiences *and* what one is like. Nor is the reason merely that one's experiences are unconnected with what one is like. For the experience machine might be limited to provide only experiences possible to the sort of person plugged in. Is it that we want to make a difference in the world? Consider then the result machine, which produces in the world any result you would produce and injects your vector input into any joint activity. We shall not pursue here the fascinating details of these or other machines. What is most disturbing about them is their living of our lives for us. Is it misguided to search for *particular* additional functions beyond the competence of machines to do for us? Perhaps what we desire is to live (an active verb) ourselves, in contact with reality. (And this, machines cannot do *for* us.) Without elaborating on the implications of this, which I believe connect surprisingly with issues about free will and causal accounts of knowledge, we need merely note the intricacy of the question of what matters *for people* other than their experiences. Until one finds a satisfactory answer, and determines that this answer does not *also* apply to animals, one cannot reasonably claim that only the felt experiences of animals limit what we may do to them.

QUESTIONS

1. If you were given the option to be plugged into an "experience machine"—what we now think of virtual reality machines that simulate reality—for life, would you choose to? Why?

2. What implications might Nozick's thought experiment have for the nature of happiness or well-being?

---

*Some wouldn't use the transformation machine at all; it seems like *cheating*. But the one-time use of the transformation machine would not remove all challenges; there would still be obstacles for the new us to overcome, a new plateau from which to strive even higher. And is this plateau any the less earned or deserved than that provided by genetic endowment and early childhood environment? But if the transformation machine could be used indefinitely often, so that we could accomplish anything by pushing a button to transform ourselves into someone who could do it easily, there would remain no limits we *need* to strain against or try to transcend. Would there be anything left *to do?* Do some theological views place God outside of time because an omniscient omnipotent being couldn't fill up his days?

14. A Conception of the Human Being: The Central Human Capabilities

MARTHA NUSSBAUM

*M*artha Nussbaum (1947–) is professor of law and ethics at the University of Chicago, with appointments in philosophy, law, and divinity as well as classics and political science. She writes on a wide variety of topics, theoretical and practical, in moral and political philosophy. She recently published *Liberty of Conscience: In Defense of America's Tradition of Religious Equality* (2008).

A good life for a geranium, a turtle, or a dog is different from that of a human. We are different from these other living things; we are more complex and can do more complex things. What sorts of things—what sorts of "capabilities"—are characteristically human? Martha Nussbaum has developed an understanding of human capabilities in terms of the "activities [or "functionings"] characteristically performed by human beings [that] are so central that they seem definitive of a life that is truly human." Nussbaum's influential work on this topic differs from that of the economist Amartya Sen in part because of her list of central human functional capabilities. These she thinks are such "that a life that lacks any one of these capabilities, no matter what else it has, will fall short of being a good human life."

It is important to distinguish between two distinct claims that Nussbaum makes. The first is that there is a list of central human capabilities that tell us what "good" for humans is. The second is that the list is one she has developed. The second claim Nussbaum readily admits is fallible; she may have omitted something important or included something that should not be on the list. So her second claim—the items on the list—could be mistaken without falsifying the first.

IV. A Conception of the Human Being: The Central Human Capabilities

The list of basic capabilities is generated by asking a question that from the start is evaluative: What activities[1] characteristically performed by human beings are so central that they seem definitive of a life that is truly human? In other words, what are the functions without which (meaning, without the availability of which) we would regard a life as not, or not fully, human?[2] We can get at this question better if we approach it via two somewhat more concrete questions that we often really ask ourselves. First is a question about personal continuity. We ask ourselves which changes or transitions are compatible with the continued existence of that being as a member of the human kind and which are not. Some functions can fail to be present without threatening our sense that we still have a human being on our hands; the absence of others seems to signal the end of a human life. This question is asked regularly, when we attempt to make medical definitions of death in a situation in which some of the functions of life persist, or to decide,

From *Sex and Social Justice* (2000). By permission of Oxford University Press.

for others or (thinking ahead) for ourselves, whether a certain level of illness or impairment means the end of the life of the being in question.[3]

The other question is a question about kind inclusion. We recognize other humans as human across many differences of time and place, of custom and appearance. We often tell ourselves stories, on the other hand, about anthropomorphic creatures who do not get classified as human, on account of some feature of their form of life and functioning. On what do we base these inclusions and exclusions? In short, what do we believe must be there, if we are going to acknowledge that a given life is human?[4] The answer to these questions points us to a subset of common or characteristic human functions, informing us that these are likely to have a special importance for everything else we choose and do.

Note that the procedure through which this account of the human is derived is neither ahistorical nor a priori. It is the attempt to summarize empirical findings of a broad and ongoing cross-cultural inquiry. As such, it is both open-ended and humble; it can always be contested and remade. Nor does it claim to read facts of "human nature" from biological observation; it takes biology into account as a relatively constant element in human experience.[5] It is because the account is evaluative from the start that it is called a conception of the good.

It should also be stressed that, like John Rawls's account of primary goods in *A Theory of Justice*,[6] this list of good functions, which is in some ways more comprehensive than his own list, is proposed as the object of a specifically political consensus.[7] The political is not understood exactly as Rawls understands it because the nation state is not assumed to be the basic unit, and the account is meant to have broad applicablity to cross-cultural deliberations. This means, given the current state of world politics, that many of the obligations to promote the adequate distribution of these goods must rest with individuals rather than with any political institution, and in that way its role becomes difficult to distinguish from the role of other norms and goals of the individual. Nonetheless, the point of the list is the same as that of Rawlsian primary goods: to put forward something that people from many different traditions, with many different fuller conceptions of the good, can agree on, as the necessary basis for pursuing their good life. That is why the list is deliberately rather general.[8] Each of its components can be more concretely specified in accordance with one's origins, religious beliefs, or tastes. In that sense, the consensus that it hopes to evoke has many of the features of the "overlapping consensus" described by Rawls.[9]

Having isolated some functions that seem central in defining the very presence of a human life, we do not rest content with mere bare humanness. We want to specify a life in which fully human functioning, or a kind of basic human flourishing, will be available. For we do not want politics to take mere survival as its goal; we want to describe a life in which the dignity of the human being is not violated by hunger or fear or the absence of opportunity. (The idea is very much Marx's idea, when he used an Aristotelian notion of functioning to describe the difference between a merely animal use of one's faculties and a "truly human use."[10]) The following list of central human functional capabilities is an attempt to specify this basic notion of the good. All citizens should have these capabilities, whatever else they have and pursue.[11] I introduce this as a list of capabilities rather than of actual functionings, because I shall argue that capability, not actual functioning, should be the goal of public policy.

Central Human Functional Capabilities

1. *Life.* Being able to live to the end of a human life of normal length;[12] not dying prematurely or before one's life is so reduced as to be not worth living

2. *Bodily health and integrity.* Being able to have good health, including reproductive health; being adequately nourished;[13] being able to have adequate shelter[14]

3. *Bodily integrity.* Being able to move freely from place to place; being able to be secure against violent assault, including sexual assault, marital rape, and domestic violence; having opportunities for sexual satisfaction and for choice in matters of reproduction

4. *Senses, imagination, thought.* Being able to use the senses; being able to imagine, to think, and to reason—and to do these things in a "truly human" way, a way informed and cultivated by an adequate education, including, but by no means limited to, literacy and basic mathematical and scientific training; being able to use imagination and thought in connection with experiencing and producing expressive works and events of one's own choice (religious, literary, musical, etc.); being able to use one's mind in ways protected by guarantees of freedom of expression with respect to both political and artistic speech and freedom of religious exercise; being able to have pleasurable experiences and to avoid nonbeneficial pain

5. *Emotions.* Being able to have attachments to things and persons outside ourselves; being able to love those who love and care for us; being able to grieve at their absence; in general, being able to love, to grieve, to experience longing, gratitude, and justified anger; not having one's emotional developing blighted by fear or anxiety. (Supporting this capability means supporting forms of human association that can be shown to be crucial in their development.[15])

6. *Practical reason.* Being able to form a conception of the good and to engage in critical reflection about the planning of one's own life. (This entails protection for the liberty of conscience.)

7. *Affiliation.* (a) Being able to live for and in relation to others, to recognize and show concern for other human beings, to engage in various forms of social interaction; being able to imagine the situation of another and to have compassion for that situation; having the capability for both justice and friendship. (Protecting this capability means, once again, protecting institutions that constitute such forms of affiliation, and also protecting the freedoms of assembly and political speech.) (b) Having the social bases of self-respect and nonhumiliation; being able to be treated as a dignified being whose worth is equal to that of others. (This entails provisions of nondiscrimination.)

8. *Other species.* Being able to live with concern for and in relation to animals, plants, and the world of nature[16]

9. *Play.* Being able to laugh, to play, to enjoy recreational activities

10. *Control over one's environment.* (a) *Political:* being able to participate effectively in political choices that govern one's life; having the rights of political participation, free speech, and freedom of association (b) *Material:* being able to hold property (both land and movable goods); having the right to seek employment on an equal basis with others; having the freedom from unwarranted search and seizure.[17] In work, being able to work as a human being, exercising practical reason and entering into meaningful relationships of mutual recognition with other workers.

The "capabilities approach," as I conceive it,[18] claims that a life that lacks any one of these capabilities, no matter what else it has, will fall short of being a good human life. Thus it would be reasonable to take these things as a focus for concern, in assessing the quality of life in a country and asking about the role of public policy in meeting human needs. The list is certainly general—and this is deliberate, to leave room for plural specification and also for further negotiation. But like (and as a reasonable basis for) a set of constitutional guarantees, it offers real guidance to policymakers, and far more accurate guidance than that offered by the focus on utility, or even on resources.[19]

The list is, emphatically, a list of separate components. We cannot satisfy the need for one of them by giving a larger amount of another one. All are of central importance and all are distinct in quality. This limits the trade-offs that it will be reasonable to make and thus limits the applicability of quantitative cost-benefit analysis. At the same time, the items on the list are related to one another in many complex ways. Employment rights, for example, support health, and also freedom from domestic violence, by giving women a better bargaining position in the family. The liberties of speech and association turn up at several distinct points on the list, showing their fundamental role with respect to several distinct areas of human functioning.

Notes

1. The use of this term does not imply that the functions all involve doing something especially "active." See here A. Sen, "Capability and Well-Being," in *The Quality of Life*, ed. M. Nussbaun and A. Sen (Oxford: Clarendon Press, 1993), 30–53. In Aristotelian terms, and in mine, being healthy, reflecting, and being pleased are all "activities."

2. For further discussion of this point, and for examples, see Martha Nussbaum, "Aristotle on Human Nature and the Foundation of Ethics," in *World, Mind and Ethics: Essays on the Ethical Philosophy of Bernard Williams*, ed. J. E. J. Altham and Ross Harrison (Cambridge: Cambridge University Press, 1995), 86–131, hereafter HN.

3. Could one cease to be one's individual self without ceasing to be human? Perhaps, in cases of profound personality or memory change, but I shall leave such cases to one side here. This is ruled out, I think, in Aristotle's conception but is possible in some other metaphysical conceptions.

4. See HN for a more extended account of this procedure and how it justifies.

5. Nor does it deny that experience of the body is shaped by culture. See Martha Nussbaum, "Non-Relative Virtues: An Aristotelian Approach," in *The Quality of Life*, ed. M. Nussbaum and A. Sen (Oxford: Clarendon Press, 1993).

6. John Rawls, *A Theory of Justice* (Cambridge, MA: Harvard University Press, 1971), 90, 95, 396–7.

7. This was implicit in Martha Nussbaum, "Aristotelian Social Democracy," in *Liberalism and the Good*, ed. R. B. Douglas et al. (New York: Routledge, 1990), 203–53 (hereafter ASD), but has become more prominent in recent essays. See A. Sen, "Freedoms and Needs," *New Republic*, January 10/17, 1994, 31–38; Martha Nussbaum, "The Good as Discipline, the Good as Freedom," in *The Ethics of Consumption and Global Stewardship*, ed. D. Crocker and T. Linden (Lanham, MD: Rowman and Littlefield, 1998), 312–41.

8. In ASD I call it "the thick vague theory of the good."

9. John Rawls, *Political Liberalism* (New York: Columbia University Press, 1993; paperback ed. 1996). Note that the consensus is defined in terms of a normative notion of reasonableness. Thus, the failure of some real individuals to agree will not be fatal to the view.

10. On this relationship, see HN.

11. The current version of this list reflects changes-suggested to me by discussions during my visits to women's development projects in India. These include a new emphasis on bodily integrity, on employment, on property rights, and on dignity and nonhumiliation.

12. Although "normal length" is clearly relative to current human possibilities and may need, for practical purposes, to be to some extent relativized to local conditions, it seems important to think of it—at least at a given time in history—in universal and comparative terms, as the *Human Development Report* does, to give rise to complaint in a country that has done well with some indicators of life quality but badly on life expectancy. And although some degree of relativity may be put down to the differential genetic possibilities of different groups (the "missing women" statistics, for example, allow that on the average women live somewhat longer than men), it is also important not to conclude prematurely that inequalities between groups—for example, the growing inequalities in life expectancy between blacks and whites in the United States—are simply genetic variation, not connected with social injustice.

13. The precise specification of these health rights is not easy, but the work currently being done on them in drafting new constitutions in South Africa and Eastern Europe gives reasons for hope that the combination of a general specification of such a right with a tradition of judicial interpretation will yield something practicable. It should be noticed that I speak of health, not just health care; and health itself interacts in complex ways with housing, with education, with dignity. Both health and nutrition are controversial as to whether the relevant level should be specified universally, or relatively to the local community and its traditions. For example, is low height associated with nutritional practices to be thought of as "stunting" or as felicitous adaptation to circumstances of scarcity? For an excellent summary of this debate, see S. R. Osmani, ed., *Nutrition and Poverty* (Oxford: Clarendon Press, WIDER series, 1990), especially the following papers: on the relativist side, T. N. Srinivasan, "Undernutrition: Concepts, Measurements, and Policy Implications," 97–120; on the universalist side, C. Gopalan, "Undernutrition: Measurement and Implications," 17–48; for a compelling adjudication of the debate, coming out on the universalist side, see

Osmani, "On Some Controversies in the Measurement of Undernutrition," 121–61.

14. There is a growing literature on the importance of shelter for health; for example, that the provision of adequate housing is the single largest determinant of health status for HIV-infected persons. Housing rights are increasingly coming to be constitutionalized, at least in a negative form—giving squatters grounds for appeal, for example, against a landlord who would bulldoze their shanties. On this as a constitutional right, see proposed Articles 11, 12, and 17 of the South African Constitution, in a draft put forward by the African National Congress (ANC) committee adviser Albie Sachs, where this is given as an example of a justiciable housing right.

15. Some form of intimate family love is central to child development, but this need not be the traditional Western nuclear family. In the development of citizens it is crucial that the family be an institution characterized by justice as well as love. See Susan Moller Okin, *Justice, Gender, and the Family* (New York: Basic Books, 1989).

16. In terms of cross-cultural discussion, this item has proven the most controversial and elusive on the list. It also properly raises the question whether the list ought to be anthropocentric at all, or whether we should seek to promote appropriate capabilities for all living things. I leave further argument on these questions for another occasion.

17. ASD argues that property rights are distinct from, for example, speech rights, in the sense that property is a tool of human functioning and not an end in itself. See also Martha Nussbaum, "Capabilities and Hyman Rights," *Fordham Law Review* 66 (1997), 273–300.

18. Sen has not endorsed any such specific list of the capabilities.

19. See A. Sen, "Gender Inequality and Theories of Justice," in *Women, Culture, and Development*, ed. M. Nussbaum and J. Glover (Oxford: Clarendon Press, 1995), 259–73; Gary Becker, "The Economic Way of Looking at Behavior," in *The Essence of Becker*, ed. R. Febrero and P. Schwartz (Stanford, CA: Hoover Institution Press, 1995), 633–658.

QUESTIONS

1. What are human functionings? Human capabilities?
2. What is Nussbaum's list of capabilities supposed to tell us?
3. Are there errors in the list?

15. What Makes Someone's Life Go Best?

DEREK PARFIT

*D*erek Parfit (1942–) is an important British philosopher, well known for his work on ethics, personal identity, rationality, and especially on the relation among them. His first book, *Reasons and Persons* (1984), from which our extracts are taken, is widely influential. His forthcoming book, *On What Matters,* has circulated for several years in manuscript and may now be one of the best-read *un*published books.

From *Reason and Persons* (1984). By permission of Oxford University Press.

The excerpt below is an appendix to *Reasons and Persons*. It is a useful classification and description of the wide variety of accounts of "what makes someone's life go best." Many of the questions this reader takes up will require us to reflect on what makes our lives go well or badly, and there are several different kinds of accounts that purport to answer this question. Parfit's discussion is especially helpful, though it may be hard-reading for some, and instructors may wish to assign only some parts of it.

What would be best for someone, or would be most in this person's interests, or would make this person's life go, for him, as well as possible? Answers to this question I call *theories about self-interest.* There are three kinds of theory. On *Hedonistic Theories,* what would be best for someone is what would make his life happiest. On *Desire-Fulfilment Theories,* what would be best for someone is what, throughout his life, would best fulfil his desires. On *Objective List Theories,* certain things are good or bad for us, whether or not we want to have the good things, or to avoid the bad things.

Narrow Hedonists assume, falsely, that pleasure and pain are two distinctive kinds of experience. Compare the pleasures of satisfying an intense thirst or lust, listening to music, solving an intellectual problem, reading a tragedy, and knowing that one's child is happy. These various experiences do not contain any distinctive common quality.

What pains and pleasures have in common are their relations to our desires. On the use of "pain" which has rational and moral significance, all pains are when experienced unwanted, and a pain is worse or greater the more it is unwanted. Similarly, all pleasures are when experienced wanted, and they are better or greater the more they are wanted. These are the claims of *Preference-Hedonism.* On this view, one of two experiences is more pleasant if it is preferred.

This theory need not follow the ordinary uses of the words "pain" and "pleasure." Suppose that I could go to a party to enjoy the various pleasures of eating, drinking, laughing, dancing, and talking to my friends. I could instead stay at home and read *King Lear.* Knowing what both alternatives would be like, I prefer to read *King Lear.* It extends the ordinary use to say that this would give me more pleasure. But on Preference-Hedonism, if we add some further assumptions given below, reading *King Lear*

would give me a better evening. Griffin cites a more extreme case. Near the end of his life Freud refused pain-killing drugs, preferring to think in torment than to be confusedly euphoric. Of these two mental states, euphoria is more pleasant. But on Preference-Hedonism thinking in torment was, for Freud, a better mental state. It is clearer here not to stretch the meaning of the word "pleasant." A Preference-Hedonist should merely claim that, since Freud preferred to think clearly though in torment, his life went better if it went as he preferred.[1]

Consider next Desire-Fulfilment Theories. The simplest is the *Unrestricted* Theory. This claims that what is best for someone is what would best fulfil *all* of his desires, throughout his life. Suppose that I meet a stranger who has what is believed to be a fatal disease. My sympathy is aroused, and I strongly want this stranger to be cured. Much later, when I have forgotten our meeting, the stranger is cured. On the Unrestricted Desire-Fulfilment Theory, this event is good for me, and makes my life go better. This is not plausible. We should reject this theory.

Another theory appeals only to someone's desires about his own life. I call this the *Success Theory.* This theory differs from Preference-Hedonism in only one way. The Success Theory appeals to all of our preferences about our own lives. A Preference-Hedonist appeals only to preferences about those present features of our lives that are introspectively discernible. Suppose that I strongly want not to be deceived by other people. On Preference-Hedonism it would be better for me if I believe that I am not being deceived. It would be irrelevant if my belief is false, since this makes no difference to my state of mind. On the Success Theory, it would be worse for me if my belief is false. I have a strong desire about my own life—that I should not be deceived in this way. It is bad for me if this desire is not fulfilled, even if I falsely believe that it is.

When this theory appeals only to desires that are about our own lives, it may be unclear what this excludes. Suppose that I want my life to be such that all of my desires, whatever their objects, are fulfilled. This may seem to make the Success Theory, when applied to me, coincide with the Unrestricted Desire-Fulfilment Theory. But a Success Theorist should claim that this desire is not really about my own life. This is like the distinction between a real change in some object, and a so-called *Cambridge-change*. An object undergoes a Cambridge-change if there is any change in the true statements that can be made about this object. Suppose that I cut my cheek while shaving. This causes a real change in me. It also causes a change in Confucius. It becomes true, of Confucius, that he lived on a planet on which later one more cheek was cut. This is merely a Cambridge-change.

Suppose that I am an exile, and cannot communicate with my children. I want their lives to go well. I might claim that I want to live the life of someone whose children's lives go well. A Success Theorist should again claim that this is not really a desire about my own life. If unknown to me one of my children is killed by an avalanche, this is not bad for me, and does not make my life go worse.

A Success Theorist *would* count some similar desires. Suppose that I try to give my children a good start in life. I try to give them the right education, good habits, and psychological strength. Once again, I am now an exile, and will never be able to learn what happens to my children. Suppose that, unknown to me, my children's lives go badly. One finds that the education that I gave him makes him unemployable, another has a mental breakdown, another becomes a petty thief. If my children's lives fail in these ways, and these failures are in part the result of mistakes I made as their parent, these failures in my children's lives would be judged to be bad for me on the Success Theory. One of my strongest desires was to be a successful parent. What is now happening to my children, though it is unknown to me, shows that this desire is not fulfilled. My life failed in one of the ways in which I most wanted it to succeed. Though I do not know this fact, it is bad for me, and makes it true that I have had a worse life. This is like the case where I strongly want not to be deceived. Even if I never know, it is bad for me both if I am deceived and if I turn out to be an unsuccessful parent. These are not introspectively discernible differences in my conscious life. On Preference-Hedonism, these events are not bad for me. On the Success Theory, they are.

Because they are thought by some to need special treatment, I mention next the desires that people have about what happens after they are dead. For a Preference-Hedonist, once I am dead, nothing bad can happen to me. A Success Theorist should deny this. Return to the case where all my children have wretched lives, because of the mistakes I made as their parent. Suppose that my children's lives all go badly only after I am dead. My life turns out to have been a failure, in the one of the ways I cared about most. A Success Theorist should claim that, here too, this makes it true that I had a worse life.

Some Success Theorists would reject this claim. Their theory ignores the desires of the dead. I believe this theory to be indefensible. Suppose that I was asked, "Do you want it to be true, even after you are dead, that you were a successful parent?" I would answer "Yes." It is irrelevant to my desire whether it is fulfilled before or after I am dead. These Success Theorists count it as bad for me if my desire is not fulfilled, even if, because I am an exile, I never know this. How then can it matter whether, when my desire is not fulfilled, I am dead? All that my death does is to *ensure* that I will never know this. If we think it irrelevant that I never know about the non-fulfilment of my desire, we cannot defensibly claim that my death makes a difference.

I turn now to questions and objections which arise for both Preference-Hedonism and the Success Theory.

Should we appeal only to the desires and preferences that someone actually has? Return to my choice between going to a party or staying at home to read *King Lear*. Suppose that, knowing what both alternatives would be like, I choose to stay at home. And suppose that I never later regret this choice. On one theory, this shows that staying at home to read *King Lear* gave me a better evening. This is a mistake. It might be true that, if I had chosen to go to the party, I would never have regretted that choice. According to this theory, this would have shown that going to the party gave me a better evening. This theory thus implies that each alternative would have been better than the other. Since this theory implies such contradictions, it must be revised. The obvious revision is to appeal not only to my actual preferences, in the alternative I choose, but also to the preferences that I would have had if I had chosen otherwise.[2]

In this example, whichever alternative I choose, I would never regret this choice. If this is true, can we still claim that one of the alternatives would give me a better evening? On some theories, when in two alternatives I would have such contrary preferences, neither alternative is better or worse for me. This is not plausible when one of my contrary preferences would have been much stronger. Suppose that, if I choose to go to the party, I shall be only mildly glad that I made this choice, but that, if I choose to stay and read *King Lear*, I shall be extremely glad. If this is true, reading *King Lear* gives me a better evening.

Whether we appeal to Preference-Hedonism or the Success Theory, we should not appeal only to the desires or preferences that I actually have. We should also appeal to the desires and preferences that I would have had, in the various alternatives that were, at different times, open to me. One of these alternatives would be best for me if it is the one in which I would have the strongest desires and preferences fulfilled. This allows us to claim that some alternative life would have been better for me, even if throughout my actual life I am glad that I chose this life rather than this alternative.

There is another distinction which applies both to Preference-Hedonism and to the Success Theory. These theories are *Summative* if they appeal to all of someone's desires, actual and hypothetical, about his own life. In deciding which alternative would produce the greatest total net sum of desire-fulfilment, we assign some positive number to each desire that is fulfilled, and some negative number to each desire that is not fulfilled. How great these numbers are depends on the intensity of the desires in question. (In the case of the Success Theory, which appeals to past desires, it may also depend on how long these desires were had. [. . .] This may be a weakness in this theory. The issue does not arise for Preference-Hedonism, which appeals only to desires about one's

present state of mind.) The total net sum of desire-fulfilment is the sum of the positive numbers minus the negative numbers. Provided that we can compare the relative strength of different desires, this calculation could in theory be performed. The choice of a unit for the numbers makes no difference to the result.

Another version of both theories does not appeal, in this way, to all of a person's desires and preferences about his own life. It appeals only to *global* rather than *local* desires and preferences. A preference is global if it is about some part of one's life considered as a whole, or is about one's whole life. The *Global* versions of these theories I believe to be more plausible.

Consider this example. Knowing that you accept a Summative theory, I tell you that I am about to make your life go better. I shall inject you with an addictive drug. From now on, you will wake each morning with an extremely strong desire to have another injection of this drug. Having this desire will be in itself neither pleasant nor painful, but if the desire is not fulfilled within an hour it would then become extremely painful. This is no cause for concern, since I shall give you ample supplies of this drug. Every morning, you will be able at once to fulfil this desire. The injection, and its after-effects, would also be neither pleasant nor painful. You will spend the rest of your days as you do now.

What would the Summative theories imply about this case? We can plausibly suppose that you would not welcome my proposal. You would prefer not to become addicted to this drug, even though I assure you that you will never lack supplies. We can also plausibly suppose that, if I go ahead, you will always regret that you became addicted to this drug. But it is likely that your initial desire not to become addicted, and your later regrets that you did, would not be as strong as the desires you have each morning for another injection. Given the facts as I described them, your reason to prefer not to become addicted would not be very strong. You might dislike the thought of being addicted to anything. And you would regret the minor inconvenience that would be involved in remembering always to carry with you, like a diabetic, sufficient supplies. But these desires might be far weaker than the desires you would have each morning for a fresh injection.

On the Summative Theories, if I make you an addict, I would be increasing the sum-total of your desire-fulfilment. I would be causing one of your desires not to be fulfilled: your desire not to become an addict, which, after my act, becomes a desire to be cured. But I would also be giving you an indefinite series of extremely strong desires, one each morning, all of which you can fulfil. The fulfilment of all these desires would outweigh the non-fulfilment of your desires not to become an addict, and to be cured. On the Summative Theories, by making you an addict, I would be benefiting you—making your life go better.

This conclusion is not plausible. Having these desires, and having them fulfilled, are neither pleasant nor painful. We need not be Hedonists to believe, more plausibly, that it is in no way better for you to have and to fulfil this series of strong desires.

Could the Summative Theories be revised, so as to meet this objection? Is there some feature of the addictive desires which would justify the claim that we should ignore them when we calculate the sum total of your desire-fulfilment? We might claim that they can be ignored because they are desires that you would prefer not to have. But this is not an acceptable revision. Suppose that you are in great pain. You now have a very strong desire not to be in the state that you are in. On our revised theory, a desire does not count if you would prefer not to have this desire. This must apply to your intense desire not to be in the state you are in. You would prefer not to have this desire. If you did not dislike the state you are in, it would not be painful. Since our revised theory does not count desires that you would prefer not to have, it implies, absurdly, that it cannot be bad for you to be in great pain.

There may be other revisions which could meet these objections. But it is simpler to appeal to the Global versions of both Preference-Hedonism and the Success Theory. These appeal only to someone's desires about some part of his life, considered as a whole, or about his whole life. The Global Theories give us the right answer in the case where I make you an addict. You would prefer not to become addicted, and you would later prefer to

cease to be addicted. These are the only preferences to which the Global Theories appeal. They ignore your particular desires each morning for a fresh injection. This is because you have yourself taken these desires into account in forming your global preference.

This imagined case of addiction is in its essentials similar to countless other cases. There are countless cases in which it is true both (1) that, if someone's life goes in one of two ways, this would increase the sum total of his local desire-fulfilment, but (2) that the other alternative is what he would globally prefer, *whichever* way his actual life goes.

Rather than describing another of the countless actual cases, I shall mention an imaginary case. This is the analogue, within one life, of the *Repugnant Conclusion*. [. . .] Suppose that I could either have fifty years of life of an extremely high quality, or an indefinite number of years that are barely worth living. In the first alternative, my fifty years would, on any theory, go extremely well. I would be very happy, would achieve great things, do much good, and love and be loved by many people. In the second alternative my life would always be, though not by much, worth living. There would be nothing bad about this life, and it would each day contain a few small pleasures.

On the Summative Theories, if the second life was long enough, it would be better for me. In each day within this life I have some desires about my life that are fulfilled. In the fifty years of the first alternative, there would be a very great sum of local desire-fulfilment. But this would be a finite sum, and in the end it would be outweighed by the sum of desire-fulfilment in my indefinitely long second alternative. A simpler way to put this point is this. The first alternative would be good. In the second alternative, since my life is worth living, living each extra day is good for me. If we merely add together whatever is good for me, some number of these extra days would produce the greatest total sum.

I do not believe that the second alternative would give me a better life. I therefore reject the Summative Theories. It is likely that, in both alternatives, I would globally prefer the first. Since the Global Theories would then imply that the first alternative gives me a better life, these theories seem to me more plausible.[3]

Turn now to the third kind of theory that I mentioned: the Objective List Theory. According to this theory, certain things are good or bad for people, whether or not these people would want to have the good things, or to avoid the bad things. The good things might include moral goodness, rational activity, the development of one's abilities, having children and being a good parent, knowledge, and the awareness of true beauty. The bad things might include being betrayed, manipulated, slandered, deceived, being deprived of liberty or dignity, and enjoying either sadistic pleasure, or aesthetic pleasure in what is in fact ugly.[4]

An Objective List Theorist might claim that his theory coincides with the Global version of the Success Theory. On this theory, what would make my life go best depends on what I would prefer, now and in the various alternatives, if I knew all of the relevant facts about these alternatives. An Objective List Theorist might say that the most relevant facts are what his theory claims—what would in fact be good or bad for me. And he might claim that anyone who knew these facts would want what is truly good for him, and want to avoid what would be bad for him.

If this was true, though the Objective List Theory would coincide with the Success Theory, the two theories would remain distinct. A Success Theorist would reject this description of the coincidence. On his theory, nothing is good or bad for people, whatever their preferences are. Something is bad for someone only if, knowing the facts, he wants to avoid it. And the relevant facts do not include the alleged facts cited by the Objective List Theorist. On the Success Theory it is, for instance, bad for someone to be deceived if and because this is not what he wants. The Objective List Theorist makes the reverse claim. People want not to be deceived because this is bad for them.

As these remarks imply, there is one important difference between on the one hand Preference-Hedonism and the Success Theory, and on the other hand the Objective List Theory. The first two kinds of theory give an account of self-interest which is entirely factual, or which does not appeal to facts about value. The account appeals to what a person does and would prefer, given full knowledge of the purely non-evaluative facts about the alternatives. In contrast, the Objective List Theory appeals directly to facts about value.

In choosing between these theories, we must decide how much weight to give to imagined cases in which someone's fully informed preferences would be bizarre. If we can appeal to these cases, they cast doubt on both Preference-Hedonism and the Success Theory. Consider the man that Rawls imagined who wants to spend his life counting the numbers of blades of grass in different lawns. Suppose that this man knows that he could achieve great progress if instead he worked in some especially useful part of Applied Mathematics. Though he could achieve such significant results, he prefers to go on counting blades of grass. On the Success Theory, if we allow this theory to cover all imaginable cases, it could be better for this person if he counts his blades of grass rather than achieves great and beneficial results in Mathematics.

The counter-example might be more offensive. Suppose that what someone would most prefer, knowing the alternatives, is a life in which, without being detected, he causes as much pain as he can to other people. On the Success Theory, such a life would be what is best for this person.

We may be unable to accept these conclusions. Ought we therefore to abandon this theory? This is what Sidgwick did, though those who quote him seldom notice this. He suggests that "a man's future good on the whole is what he would now desire and seek on the whole if all the consequences of all the different lines of conduct open to him were accurately foreseen and adequately realised in imagination at the present point of time."[5] As he comments: "The notion of 'Good' thus attained has an ideal element: it is something that *is* not always actually desired and aimed at by human beings: but the ideal element is entirely interpretable in terms of *fact,* actual or hypothetical, and does not introduce any judgement of value." Sidgwick then rejects this account, claiming that what is ultimately good for someone is what this person would desire if his desires were in harmony with reason. This last phrase is needed, Sidgwick thought, to exclude the cases where someone's desires are irrational. He assumes that there are some things that we have good reason to desire, and others that we have good reason not to desire. These might be the things which are held to be good or bad for us by Objective List Theories.

Suppose we agree that, in some imagined cases, what someone would most want both now and later, fully knowing about the alternatives, would *not* be what would be best for him. If we accept this conclusion, it may seem that we must reject both Preference-Hedonism and the Success Theory. Perhaps, like Sidgwick, we must put constraints on what can be rationally desired.

It might be claimed instead that we can dismiss the appeal to such imagined cases. It might be claimed that what people would in fact prefer, if they knew the relevant facts, would always be something that we could accept as what is really good for them. Is this a good reply? If we agree that in the imagined cases what someone would prefer might be something that is bad for him, in these cases we have abandoned our theory. If this is so, can we defend our theory by saying that, in the actual cases, it would not go astray? I believe that this is not an adequate defence. But I shall not pursue this question here.

This objection may apply with less force to Preference-Hedonism. On this theory, what can be good or bad for someone can only be discernible features of his conscious life. These are the features that, at the time, he either wants or does not want. I asked above whether it is bad for people to be deceived because they prefer not to be, or whether they prefer not to be deceived because this is bad for them. Consider the comparable question with respect to pain. Some have claimed that pain is intrinsically bad, and that this is why we dislike it. As I have suggested, I doubt this claim. After taking certain kinds of drugs, people claim that the quality of their sensations has not altered, but they no longer dislike these sensations. We would regard such drugs as effective analgesics. This suggests that the badness of a pain consists in its being disliked, and that it is not disliked because it is bad. The disagreement between these views would need much more

discussion. But, if the second view is better, it is more plausible to claim that whatever someone wants or does not want to experience—however bizarre we find his desires—should be counted as being for this person truly pleasant or painful, and as being for that reason good or bad for him. There may still be cases where it is plausible to claim that it would be bad for someone if he enjoys certain kinds of pleasure. This might be claimed, for instance, about sadistic pleasure. But there may be few such cases.

If instead we appeal to the Success Theory, we are not concerned only with the experienced quality of our conscious life. We are concerned with such things as whether we are achieving what we are trying to achieve, whether we are being deceived, and the like. When considering this theory, we can more often plausibly claim that, even if someone knew the facts, his preferences might go astray, and fail to correspond to what would be good or bad for him.

Which of these different theories should we accept? I shall not attempt an answer here. But I shall end by mentioning another theory, which might be claimed to combine what is most plausible in these conflicting theories. It is a striking fact that those who have addressed this question have disagreed so fundamentally. Many philosophers have been convinced Hedonists; many others have been as much convinced that Hedonism is a gross mistake.

Some Hedonists have reached their view as follows. They consider an opposing view, such as that which claims that what is good for someone is to have knowledge, to engage in rational activity, and to be aware of true beauty. These Hedonists ask, "Would these states of mind be good, if they brought no enjoyment, and if the person in these states of mind had not the slightest desire that they continue?" Since they answer No, they conclude that the value of these states of mind must lie in their being liked, and in their arousing a desire that they continue.

This reasoning assumes that the value of a whole is just the sum of the value of its parts. If we remove the part to which the Hedonist appeals, what is left seems to have no value, hence Hedonism is the truth.

Suppose instead that we claim that the value of a whole may not be a mere sum of the value of its parts. We might then claim that what is best for people is a composite. It is not just their being in the conscious states that they want to be in. Nor is it just their having knowledge, engaging in rational activity, being aware of true beauty, and the like. What is good for someone is neither just what Hedonists claim, nor just what is claimed by Objective List Theorists. We might believe that if we had *either* of these, *without the other*, what we had would have little or no value. We might claim, for example, that what is good or bad for someone is to have knowledge, to be engaged in rational activity, to experience mutual love, and to be aware of beauty, while strongly wanting just these things. On this view, each side in this disagreement saw only half of the truth. Each put forward as sufficient something that was only necessary. Pleasure with many other kinds of object has no value. And, if they are entirely devoid of pleasure, there is no value in knowledge, rational activity, love, or the

awareness of beauty. What is of value, or is good for someone, is to have both; to be engaged in these activities, and to be strongly wanting to be so engaged.

Notes

1 J. P. Griffin, "Are There Incommensurable Values?" *Philosophy and Public Affairs* 7, No. 1, Fall 1977.
2. See "Prudence" by P. Bricker, *Journal of Philosophy*, July 1980.
3. See, for example, G. E. Moore, *Principia Ethica* (Cambridge: Cambridge University Press, 1903), and W. D. Ross, *The Foundations of Ethics* (Oxford: The Clarendon Press, 1939).
4. H. Sidgwick, *The Methods of Ethics* (London: Macmillan, 1907).
5. See R. B. Edwards, *Pleasures and Pains* (Ithaca, NY: Cornell University Press, 1979). A similar suggestion is made by Plato in *The Philebus*. For a deeper discussion of the different theories about self-interest, see J. Griffin, *Welfare*, forthcoming.

QUESTIONS
1. Parfit distinguishes three kinds of accounts of what would be best for someone. What are they, and how are they different?
2. How should some of the authors in section III of this reader (as well as Rachels and Nozick) be classified according to Parfit's taxonomy?

16. The Meaning of Life

THOMAS NAGEL

For a description of the author, see chapter 9.

In this brief chapter taken from his short book—an excellent introduction, accessible to readers without a background in philosophy—Nagel raises a number of difficult questions about the meaning of life. He contrasts looking at one's life from "within" or "inside" with looking at it from "the outside." From this latter perspective it may seem that it has no meaning. He considers a number of possibilities, including religious ones, and seems to find them wanting. At the very end of the chapter he entertains the possibility that we may be somewhat ridiculous and that life may be absurd.

Perhaps you have had the thought that nothing really matters, because in two hundred years we'll all be dead. This is a peculiar thought, because it's not clear why the fact that we'll be dead in two hundred years should imply that nothing we do now really matters.

The idea seems to be that we are in some kind of rat race, struggling to achieve our goals and make something of our lives, but that this makes sense only if those achievements will be permanent. But they won't be. Even if you produce a great work of literature which continues to be read thousands of years from now, eventually the solar system will cool or the universe will wind down or collapse, and all trace of your efforts will vanish. In any case, we can't hope for even a fraction of this sort of immortality. If there's any point at all to what we do, we have to find it within our own lives.

Why is there any difficulty in that? You can explain the point of most of the things you do. You work to earn money to support yourself and perhaps your family. You eat because you're hungry, sleep because you're tired, go for a walk or call up a friend because you feel like it, read the newspaper to find out what's going on in the world. If you didn't do any of those things you'd be miserable; so what's the big problem?

The problem is that although there are justifications and explanations for most of the things, big and small, that we do *within* life, none of these explanations explain the point of your life as a whole—the whole of which all these activities, successes and failures, strivings and disappointments are parts. If you think about the whole thing, there seems to be no point to it at all. Looking at it from the outside, it wouldn't matter if you had never existed. And after you have gone out of existence, it won't matter that you did exist.

Of course your existence matters to other people—your parents and others who care about you—but taken as a whole, their lives have no point either, so it ultimately doesn't matter that you matter to them. You matter to them and they matter to you, and that may give your life a feeling of significance, but you're just taking in each other's washing, so to speak. Given that any person exists, he has needs and concerns which make particular things and people within his life matter to him. But the *whole thing* doesn't matter.

But does it matter that it doesn't matter? "So what?" you might say. "It's enough that it matters whether I get to the station before my train leaves, or whether I've remembered to feed the cat. I don't

From *What Does It All Mean? A Very Short Introduction to Philosophy.* By permission of Oxford University Press.

need more than that to keep going." This is a perfectly good reply. But it only works if you really can avoid setting your sights higher, and asking what the point of the whole thing is. For once you do that, you open yourself to the possibility that your life is meaningless.

The thought that you'll be dead in two hundred years is just a way of seeing your life embedded in a larger context, so that the point of smaller things inside it seems not to be enough—seems to leave a larger question unanswered. But what if your life as a whole did have a point in relation to something larger? Would that mean that it wasn't meaningless after all?

There are various ways your life could have a larger meaning. You might be part of a political or social movement which changed the world for the better, to the benefit of future generations. Or you might just help provide a good life for your own children and their descendants. Or your life might be thought to have meaning in a religious context, so that your time on Earth was just a preparation for an eternity in direct contact with God.

About the types of meaning that depend on relations to other people, even people in the distant future, I've already indicated what the problem is. If one's life has a point as a part of something larger, it is still possible to ask about that larger thing, what is the point of *it*? Either there's an answer in terms of something still larger or there isn't. If there is, we simply repeat the question. If there isn't, then our search for a point has come to an end with something which has no point. But if that pointlessness is acceptable for the larger thing of which our life is a part, why shouldn't it be acceptable already for our life taken as a whole? Why isn't it all right for your life to be pointless? And if it isn't acceptable there, why should it be acceptable when we get to the larger context? Why don't we have to go on to ask, "But what is the point of all *that*?" (human history, the succession of the generations, or whatever).

The appeal to a religious meaning to life is a bit different. If you believe that the meaning of your life comes from fulfilling the purpose of God, who loves you, and seeing Him in eternity, then it doesn't seem appropriate to ask, "And what is the point of *that*?" It's supposed to be something which is its own point, and can't have a purpose outside itself. But for this very reason it has its own problems.

The idea of God seems to be the idea of something that can explain everything else, without having to be explained itself. But it's very hard to understand how there could be such a thing. If we ask the question, "Why is the world like this?" and are offered a religious answer, how can we be prevented from asking again, "And why is *that* true?" What kind of answer would bring all of our "Why?" questions to a stop, once and for all? And if they can stop there, why couldn't they have stopped earlier?

The same problem seems to arise if God and His purposes are offered as the ultimate explanation of the value and meaning of our lives. The idea that our lives fulfil God's purpose is supposed to give them their point, in a way that doesn't require or admit of any further point. One isn't supposed to ask "What is the point of God?" any more than one is supposed to ask, "What is the explanation of God?"

But my problem here, as with the role of God as ultimate explanation, is that I'm not sure I understand the idea. Can there really be something which gives point to everything else by encompassing it, but which couldn't have, or need, any point itself? Something whose point can't be questioned from outside because there is no outside?

If God is supposed to give our lives a meaning that we can't understand, it's not much of a consolation. God as ultimate justification, like God as ultimate explanation, may be an incomprehensible answer to a question that we can't get rid of. On the other hand, maybe that's the whole point, and I am just failing to understand religious ideas. Perhaps the belief in God is the belief that the universe is intelligible, but not to us.

Leaving that issue aside, let me return to the smaller-scale dimensions of human life. Even if life as a whole is meaningless, perhaps that's nothing to worry about. Perhaps we can recognize it and just go on as before. The trick is to keep your eyes on what's in front of you, and allow justifications to come to an end inside your life, and inside the lives of others to whom you are connected. If you ever ask yourself the question, "But what's the point of being alive at all?"—leading the particular life of a student or bartender or whatever you happen to be—you'll answer

"There's no point. It wouldn't matter if I didn't exist at all, or if I didn't care about anything. But I do. That's all there is to it."

Some people find this attitude perfectly satisfying. Others find it depressing, though unavoidable. Part of the problem is that some of us have an incurable tendency to take ourselves seriously. We want to matter to ourselves "from the outside." If our lives as a whole seem pointless, then a part of us is dissatisfied— the part that is always looking over our shoulders at what we are doing. Many human efforts, particularly those in the service of serious ambitions rather than just comfort and survival, get some of their energy from a sense of importance—a sense that what you are doing is not just important to you, but important in some larger sense: important, period. If we have to give this up, it may threaten to take the wind out of our sails. If life is not real, life is not earnest, and the grave is its goal, perhaps it's ridiculous to take ourselves so seriously. On the other hand, if we can't help taking ourselves so seriously, perhaps we just have to put up with being ridiculous. Life may be not only meaningless but absurd.

QUESTIONS
1. Why might it make a difference whether one views one's life from the "inside" or the "outside"? What are these two perspectives?
2. Why might life be absurd?

Saving Lives: Famine

If it is usually bad for people to die, then it will usually be bad for them to die from starvation. We think it is usually wrong to kill someone. Sometimes we can save someone, and often we can do so quite easily. Is it wrong to refrain from saving someone when one can do so easily? Surely it is usually good to save someone from dying of starvation. We admire people who do so, especially when they make considerable sacrifices to help others. Is it wrong for the rest of us not to do so?

It seems wrong for the lifeguard to let someone die from drowning while on duty, and it may be wrong for health-care providers to allow some to die. People in these professions and situations have duties to help or rescue others. To fail to do so is usually wrong. Do the rest of us have duties to help others, at least when doing so is fairly easy?

Some think that all or most of our duties to others are essentially "negative," to refrain from doing certain things (e.g., that are harmful, that violate their rights). Duties to rescue are "positive"; they require us not merely to refrain from harming but also to benefit. We need to consider if we have any such duties and if so what might be their nature.

Famine is also one of the greatest evils of the lives of humans—the other being war. In the last centuries millions of people died from starvation. The causes of mass starvation turn out to be more complicated than the simple "lack of food." All the great famines of the twentieth century took place while there was enough food in the country in question. The causes of mass starvation are more political than meteorological. We normally think we have a responsibility to rescue people in distress. Do we have duties to help the starving? And if so, how extensive are they?

17. Famine, Affluence, and Morality

PETER SINGER

Peter Singer (1946–) is a well-known and controversial Australian philosopher, now professor of bioethics at Princeton University. Along with that of James Rachels (see chapter 8), his writings helped revive interest in practical or applied ethics. His widely read book *Animal Liberation* (1975) helped publicize the case for according moral standing to animals. His popular *Practical Ethics* (1979) is an accessible treatment of many of the topics covered in this reader. He has written extensively on famine and poverty, starting with the famous article reprinted in this section. More recently he has published *One World: The Ethics of Globalization* (2002) and *The Life You Can Save: Acting Now to End World Poverty* (2009) (see www.thelifeyoucansave.com). Singer's views are controversial, perhaps in part because he is a moral utilitarian (see chapter 67). But he is sometimes misrepresented or misunderstood by the public and has been publicly attacked for views he does not accept.

If someone saves the life of another, we normally think that good. We often praise such people. But sometimes not saving someone seems wrong. In a classic article published in 1972—hence the dated references to famines now long ago—Singer argues that for most of us, not to contribute to famine relief when this would save lives is wrong. He thinks our normal ways of thinking about famine relief are mistaken, that the "traditional distinction between duty and charity cannot be drawn, or at least not in the place we normally draw it." We need to help the starving, and we need to change the way we think and act about these matters.

As I write this, in November 1971, people are dying in East Bengal from lack of food, shelter, and medical care. The suffering and death that are occurring there now are not inevitable, not unavoidable in any fatalistic sense of the term. Constant poverty, a cyclone, and a civil war have turned at least nine million people into destitute refugees; nevertheless, it is not beyond the capacity of the richer nations to give enough assistance to reduce any further suffering to very small proportions. The decisions and actions of human beings can prevent this kind of suffering. Unfortunately, human beings have not made the necessary decisions. At the individual level, people have, with very few exceptions, not responded to the situation in any significant way. Generally speaking, people have not given large sums to relief funds; they have not written to their parliamentary representatives demanding increased government assistance; they have not demonstrated in the streets, held symbolic fasts, or done anything else directed toward providing the refugees with the means to satisfy their essential needs. At the government level, no government has given the sort of massive aid that would enable the refugees to survive for more than a few days. Britain, for instance, has given rather more than most countries. It has, to

From "Famine, Affluence, and Morality," *Philosophy and Public Affairs* 1, 1 (1972): 229–243. Reprinted by permission of Blackwell Publishing.

date, given £14,750,000. For comparative purposes, Britain's share of the nonrecoverable development costs of the Anglo-French Concorde project is already in excess of £275,000,000, and on present estimates will reach £440,000,000. The implication is that the British government values a supersonic transport more than thirty times as highly as it values the lives of the nine million refugees. Australia is another country which, on a per capita basis, is well up in the "aid to Bengal" table. Australia's aid, however, amounts to less than one-twelfth of the cost of Sydney's new opera house. The total amount given, from all sources, now stands at about £65,000,000. The estimated cost of keeping the refugees alive for one year is £464,000,000. Most of the refugees have now been in the camps for more than six months. The World Bank has said that India needs a minimum of £300,000,000 in assistance from other countries before the end of the year. It seems obvious that assistance on this scale will not be forthcoming. India will be forced to choose between letting the refugees starve or diverting funds from her own development program, which will mean that more of her own people will starve in the future.[1]

These are the essential facts about the present situation in Bengal. So far as it concerns us here, there is nothing unique about this situation except its magnitude. The Bengal emergency is just the latest and most acute of a series of major emergencies in various parts of the world, arising both from natural and from manmade causes. There are also many parts of the world in which people die from malnutrition and lack of food independent of any special emergency. I take Bengal as my example only because it is the present concern, and because the size of the problem has ensured that it has been given adequate publicity. Neither individuals nor governments can claim to be unaware of what is happening there.

What are the moral implications of a situation like this? In what follows, I shall argue that the way people in relatively affluent countries react to a situation like that in Bengal cannot be justified; indeed, the whole way we look at moral issues—our moral conceptual scheme—needs to be altered, and with it, the way of life that has come to be taken for granted in our society.

In arguing for this conclusion I will not, of course, claim to be morally neutral. I shall, however, try to argue for the moral position that I take, so that anyone who accepts certain assumptions, to be made explicit, will, I hope, accept my conclusion.

I begin with the assumption that suffering and death from lack of food, shelter, and medical care are bad. I think most people will agree about this, although one may reach the same view by different routes. I shall not argue for this view. People can hold all sorts of eccentric positions, and perhaps from some of them it would not follow that death by starvation is in itself bad. It is difficult, perhaps impossible, to refute such positions, and so for brevity I will henceforth take this assumption as accepted. Those who disagree need read no further.

My next point is this: if it is in our power to prevent something bad from happening, without thereby sacrificing anything of comparable moral importance, we ought, morally, to do it. By "without sacrificing anything of comparable moral importance" I mean without causing anything else comparably bad to happen, or doing something that is wrong in itself, or failing to promote some moral good, comparable in significance to the bad thing that we can prevent. This principle seems almost as uncontroversial as the last one. It requires us only to prevent what is bad, and to promote what is good, and it requires this of us only when we can do it without sacrificing anything that is, from the moral point of view, comparably important. I could even, as far as the application of my argument to the Bengal emergency is concerned, qualify the point so as to make it: if it is in our power to prevent something very bad from happening, without thereby sacrificing anything morally significant, we ought, morally, to do it. An application of this principle would be as follows: if I am walking past a shallow pond and see a child drowning in it, I ought to wade in and pull the child out. This will mean getting my clothes muddy, but this is insignificant, while the death of the child would presumably be a very bad thing.

The uncontroversial appearance of the principle just stated is deceptive. If it were acted upon, even in its qualified form, our lives, our society, and our world would be fundamentally changed. For the principle takes, firstly, no account of proximity or distance. It makes no moral difference whether the person I can help is a neighbor's child ten yards from me or a Bengali whose name I shall never know, ten thousand miles away. Secondly, the principle makes no distinction between cases in which I am the only person who could possibly do anything and cases in which I am just one among millions in the same position.

I do not think I need to say much in defense of the refusal to take proximity and distance into account. The fact that a person is physically near to us, so that we have personal contact with him, may make it more likely that we *shall* assist him, but this does not show that we *ought* to help him rather than another who happens to be further away. If we accept any principle of impartiality, universalizability, equality, or whatever, we cannot discriminate against someone merely because he is far away from us (or we are far away from him). Admittedly, it is possible that we are in a better position to judge what needs to be done to help a person near to us than one far away, and perhaps also to provide the assistance we judge to be necessary. If this were the case, it would be a reason for helping those near to us first. This may once have been a justification for being more concerned with the poor in one's town than with famine victims in India. Unfortunately for those who like to keep their moral responsibilities limited, instant communication and swift transportation have changed the situation. From the moral point of view, the development of the world into a "global village" has made an important, though still unrecognized, difference to our moral situation. Expert observers and supervisors, sent out by famine relief organizations or permanently stationed in famine-prone areas, can direct our aid to a refugee in Bengal almost as effectively as we could get it to someone in our own block. There would seem, therefore, to be no possible justification for discriminating on geographical grounds.

There may be a greater need to defend the second implication of my principle—that the fact that there are millions of other people in the same position, in respect to the Bengali refugees, as I am, does not make the situation significantly different from a situation in which I am the only person who can prevent something very bad from occurring. Again, of course, I admit that there is a psychological difference between the cases; one feels less guilty about doing nothing if one can point to others, similarly placed, who have also done nothing. Yet this can make no real difference to our moral obligations.[2] Should I consider that I am less obliged to pull the drowning child out of the pond if on looking around I see other people, no further away than I am, who have also noticed the child but are doing nothing? One has only to ask this question to see the absurdity of the view that numbers lessen obligation. It is a view that is an ideal excuse for inactivity; unfortunately most of the major evils—poverty, overpopulation, pollution—are problems in which everyone is almost equally involved.

The view that numbers do make a difference can be made plausible if stated in this way: if everyone in circumstances like mine gave £5 to the Bengal Relief Fund, there would be enough to provide food, shelter, and medical care for the refugees; there is no reason why I should give more than anyone else in the same circumstances as I am; therefore I have no obligation to give more than £5. Each premise in this argument is true, and the argument looks sound. It may convince us, unless we notice that it is based on a hypothetical premise, although the conclusion is not stated hypothetically. The argument would be sound if the conclusion were: if everyone in circumstances like mine were to give £5, I would have no obligation to give more than £5. If the conclusion were so stated, however, it would be obvious that the argument has no bearing on a situation in which it is not the case that everyone else gives £5. This, of course, is the actual situation. It is more or less certain that not everyone in circumstances like mine will give £5. So there will not be enough to provide the needed food, shelter, and medical care. Therefore by giving more than £5 I will prevent more suffering than I would if I gave just £5.

It might be thought that this argument has an absurd consequence. Since the situation appears to be that very few people are likely to give substantial amounts, it follows that I and everyone else in similar circumstances ought to give as much as possible, that is, at least up to the point at which by giving more one would begin to cause serious suffering for oneself and one's dependents—perhaps even beyond this point to the point of marginal utility, at which by giving more one would cause oneself and one's dependents as much suffering as one would prevent in Bengal. If everyone does this, however, there will be more than can be used for the benefit of the refugees, and some of the sacrifice will have been unnecessary. Thus, if everyone does what he ought to do, the result will not be as good as it would be if everyone did a little less than he ought to do, or if only some do all that they ought to do.

The paradox here arises only if we assume that the actions in question—sending money to the relief funds—are performed more or less simultaneously, and are also unexpected. For if it is to be expected that everyone is going to contribute something, then clearly each is not obliged to give as much as he would have been obliged to had others not been giving too. And if everyone is not acting more or less simultaneously, then those giving later will know how much more is needed, and will have no obligation to give more than is necessary to reach this amount. To say this is not to deny the principle that people in the same circumstances have the same obligations, but to point out that the fact that others have given, or may be expected to give, is a relevant circumstance: those giving after it has become known that many others are giving and those giving before are not in the same circumstances. So the seemingly absurd consequence of the principle I have put forward can occur only if people are in error about the actual circumstances—that is, if they think they are giving when others are not, but in fact they are giving when others are. The result of everyone doing what he really ought to do cannot be worse than the result of everyone doing less than he ought to do, although the result of everyone doing what he reasonably believes he ought to do could be.

If my argument so far has been sound, neither our distance from a preventable evil nor the number of other people who, in respect to that evil, are in the same situation as we are, lessens our obligation to mitigate or prevent that evil. I shall therefore take as established the principle I asserted earlier. As I have already said, I need to assert it only in its qualified form: if it is in our power to prevent something very bad from happening, without thereby sacrificing anything else morally significant, we ought, morally, to do it.

The outcome of this argument is that our traditional moral categories are upset. The traditional distinction between duty and charity cannot be drawn, or at least, not in the place we normally draw it. Giving money to the Bengal Relief Fund is regarded as an act of charity in our society. The bodies which collect money are known as "charities." These organizations see themselves in this way—if you send them a check, you will be thanked for your "generosity." Because giving money is regarded as an act of charity, it is not thought that there is anything wrong with not giving. The charitable man may be praised, but the man who is not charitable is not condemned. People do not feel in any way ashamed or guilty about spending money on new clothes or a new car instead of giving it to famine relief. (Indeed, the alternative does not occur to them.) This way of looking at the matter cannot be justified. When we buy new clothes not to keep ourselves warm but to look "well-dressed" we are not providing for any important need. We would not be sacrificing anything significant if we were to continue to wear our old clothes, and give the money to famine relief. By doing so, we would be preventing another person from starving. It follows from what I have said earlier that we ought to give money away, rather than spend it on clothes which we do not need to keep us warm. To do so is not charitable, or generous. Nor is it the kind of act which philosophers and theologians have called "supererogatory"—an act which it would be good to do, but not wrong not to do. On the contrary, we ought to give the money away, and it is wrong not to do so.

I am not maintaining that there are no acts which are charitable, or that there are no acts which it would be good to do but not wrong not to do. It may be possible to redraw the distinction between duty and charity in some other place. All I am arguing here is that the present way of drawing the distinction, which makes it an act of charity for a man living at the level of affluence which most people in the "developed nations" enjoy to give money to save someone else from starvation, cannot be supported. It is beyond the scope of my argument to consider whether the distinction should be redrawn or abolished altogether. There would be many other possible ways of drawing the distinction—for instance, one might decide that it is good to make other people as happy as possible, but not wrong not to do so.

Despite the limited nature of the revision in our moral conceptual scheme which I am proposing, the revision would, given the extent of both affluence and famine in the world today, have radical implications. These implications may lead to further objections, distinct from those I have already considered. I shall discuss two of these.

One objection to the position I have taken might be simply that it is too drastic a revision of our moral scheme. People do not ordinarily judge in the way I have suggested they should. Most people reserve their moral condemnation for those who violate some moral norm, such as the norm against taking another person's property. They do not condemn those who indulge in luxury instead of giving to famine relief. But given that I did not set out to present a morally neutral description of the way people make moral judgments, the way people do in fact judge has nothing to do with the validity of my conclusion. My conclusion follows from the principle which I advanced earlier, and unless that principle is rejected, or the arguments are shown to be unsound, I think the conclusion must stand, however strange it appears. It might, nevertheless, be interesting to consider why our society, and most other societies, do judge differently from the way I have suggested they should. In a well-known article, J. O. Urmson suggests that the imperatives of duty, which tell us what we must do, as distinct from what it would be good to do but not wrong not to do, function so as to prohibit behavior that is intolerable if men are to live together in society.[3] This may explain the origin and continued existence of the present division between acts of duty and acts of charity. Moral attitudes are shaped by the needs of society, and no doubt society needs people who will observe the rules that make social existence tolerable. From the point of view of a particular society, it is essential to prevent violations of norms against killing, stealing, and so on. It is quite inessential, however, to help people outside one's own society.

If this is an explanation of our common distinction between duty and supererogation, however, it is not a justification of it. The moral point of view requires us to look beyond the interests of our own society. Previously, as I have already mentioned, this may hardly have been feasible, but it is quite feasible now. From the moral point of view, the prevention of the starvation of millions of people outside our society must be considered at least as pressing as the upholding of property norms within our society.

It has been argued by some writers, among them Sidgwick and Urmson, that we need to have a basic moral code which is not too far beyond the capacities of the ordinary man, for otherwise there will be a general breakdown of compliance with the moral code. Crudely stated, this argument suggests that if we tell people that they ought to refrain from murder and give everything they do not really need to famine relief, they will do neither, whereas if we tell them that they ought to refrain from murder and that it is good to give to famine relief but not wrong not to do so, they will at least refrain from murder. The issue here is: Where should we draw the line between conduct that is required and conduct that is good although not required, so as to get the best possible result? This would seem to be an empirical question, although a very difficult one. One objection to the Sidgwick-Urmson line of argument is that it takes insufficient account of the effect that moral standards can have on the decisions we make. Given a society in which a wealthy man who gives 5 percent of his income to famine relief is regarded as most generous, it is not surprising that a proposal that we all ought to give away half our incomes will be thought to be absurdly unrealistic. In a society which held that no man should have more than enough while others have less than they need, such a proposal might seem narrow-minded. What it is possible for a man to do and what he is likely to do are both, I think, very greatly influenced by what people around him are doing and expecting him to do. In any case, the possibility that by spreading the idea that we ought to be doing very much more than we are to relieve famine we shall bring about a general breakdown of moral behavior seems remote. If the stakes are an end to widespread starvation, it is worth the risk. Finally, it should be emphasized that these considerations are relevant only to the issue of what we should require from others, and not to what we ourselves ought to do.

The second objection to my attack on the present distinction between duty and charity is one which has from time to time been made against utilitarianism. It follows from some forms of utilitarian theory that we all ought, morally, to be working full time to increase the balance of happiness over misery. The position I have taken here would not lead to this conclusion in all circumstances, for if there were no bad occurrences that we could prevent without sacrificing something of comparable moral importance, my argument would have no application. Given the present conditions in many parts of the world, however, it does follow from my argument that we ought, morally, to be working full time to relieve great suffering of the sort that occurs as a result of famine or other disasters. Of course, mitigating circumstances can be adduced—for instance, that if we wear ourselves out through overwork, we shall be less effective than we would otherwise have been. Nevertheless, when all considerations of this sort have been taken into account, the conclusion remains: we ought to be preventing as much suffering as we can without sacrificing something else of comparable moral importance. This conclusion is one which we may be reluctant to face. I cannot see, though, why it should be regarded as a criticism of the position for which I have argued, rather than a criticism of our ordinary standards of behavior. Since most people are self-interested to some degree, very few of us are likely to do everything that we ought to do. It would, however, hardly be honest to take this as evidence that it is not the case that we ought to do it.

It may still be thought that my conclusions are so wildly out of line with what everyone else thinks and has always thought that there must be something wrong with the argument somewhere. In order to show that my conclusions, while certainly contrary to contemporary Western moral standards, would not have seemed so extraordinary at other times and in other places, I would like to quote a passage from a writer not normally thought of as a way-out radical, Thomas Aquinas.

> Now, according to the natural order instituted by divine providence, material goods are provided for the satisfaction of human needs. Therefore the division and appropriation of property, which proceeds from human law, must not hinder the satisfaction of man's necessity from such goods. Equally, whatever a man has in superabundance is owed, of natural right, to the poor for their sustenance. So Ambrosius says, and it is also to be found in the *Decretum Gratiani*: "The bread which you withhold belongs to the hungry; the clothing you shut away, to the naked; and the money you bury in the earth is the redemption and freedom of the penniless."[4]

I now want to consider a number of points, more practical than philosophical, which are relevant to the application of the moral conclusion we have reached. These points challenge not the idea that we ought to be doing all we can to prevent starvation, but the idea that giving away a great deal of money is the best means to this end.

It is sometimes said that overseas aid should be a government responsibility, and that therefore one ought not to give to privately run charities. Giving privately, it is said, allows the government and the noncontributing members of society to escape their responsibilities.

This argument seems to assume that the more people there are who give to privately organized famine relief funds, the less likely it is that the government will take over full responsibility for such aid. This assumption is unsupported, and does not strike me as at all plausible. The opposite view—that if no one gives voluntarily, a government will assume that its citizens are uninterested in famine relief and would not wish to be forced into giving aid—seems more plausible. In any case, unless there were a definite probability that by refusing to give one would be helping to bring about massive government assistance, people who do refuse to make voluntary contributions are refusing to prevent a certain amount of suffering without being able to point to any tangible beneficial consequence of their refusal. So the onus of showing how their refusal will bring about government action is on those who refuse to give.

I do not, of course, want to dispute the contention that governments of affluent nations should be giving many times the amount of genuine, no-strings-attached aid that they are giving now. I agree, too, that giving privately is not enough, and that we ought to be campaigning actively for entirely new standards for both public and private contributions to famine relief. Indeed, I would sympathize with someone who thought that campaigning was more important than giving oneself, although I doubt whether preaching what one does not practice would be very effective. Unfortunately, for many people the idea that "it's the government's responsibility" is a reason for not giving which does not appear to entail any political action either.

Another, more serious reason for not giving to famine relief funds is that until there is effective population control, relieving famine merely postpones starvation. If we save the Bengal refugees now, others, perhaps the children of these refugees, will face starvation in a few years' time. In support of this, one may cite the now well-known facts about the population explosion and the relatively limited scope for expanded production.

This point, like the previous one, is an argument against relieving suffering that is happening now, because of a belief about what might happen in the future; it is unlike the previous point in that very good evidence can be adduced in support of this belief about the future. I will not go into the evidence here. I accept that the earth cannot support indefinitely a population rising at the present rate. This certainly poses a problem for anyone who thinks it important to prevent famine. Again, however, one could accept the argument without drawing the conclusion that it absolves one from any obligation to do anything to prevent famine. The conclusion that should be drawn is that the best means of preventing famine, in the long run, is population control. It would then follow from the position reached earlier that one ought to be doing all one can to promote population control (unless one held that all forms of population control were wrong in themselves, or would have significantly bad consequences). Since there are organizations working specifically for population control, one would then support them rather than more orthodox methods of preventing famine.

A third point raised by the conclusion reached earlier relates to the question of just how much we all ought to be giving away. One possibility, which has already been mentioned, is that we ought to give until we reach the level of marginal utility—that is, the level at which, by giving more, I would cause as much suffering to myself or my dependents as I would relieve by my gift. This would mean, of course, that one would reduce oneself to very near the material circumstances of a Bengali refugee. It will be recalled that earlier I put forward both a strong and a moderate version of the principle of preventing bad occurrences. The strong version, which required us to prevent bad things from happening unless in doing so we would be sacrificing something of comparable moral significance, does seem to require reducing ourselves to the level of marginal utility. I should also say that the strong version seems to me to be the correct one. I proposed the more moderate version—that we should prevent bad occurrences unless, to do so, we had to sacrifice something morally significant—only in order to show that, even on this surely undeniable principle, a great change in our way of life is required. On the more moderate principle, it may not follow that we ought to reduce ourselves to the level of marginal utility, for one might hold that to reduce oneself and one's family to this level is to cause something significantly bad to happen. Whether this is so I shall not discuss, since, as I have said, I can see no good reason for holding the moderate version of the principle rather than the strong version. Even if we accepted the principle only in its moderate form, however, it should be clear that we would have to give away enough to ensure that the consumer society, dependent as it is on people spending on trivia rather than giving to famine relief, would slow down and perhaps disappear entirely. There are several reasons why this would be desirable in itself. The value and necessity of economic growth are now being questioned not only by conservationists, but by economists as well.[5] There is no doubt, too, that the consumer society has had a distorting effect on the goals and purposes of its members. Yet looking at the matter purely from the point of view of overseas aid, there must be a limit to the extent to which we should deliberately slow down our economy; for it might be the case that if we gave away, say, 40 percent of our Gross National Product, we would slow down the economy so much that in absolute terms we would be giving less than if we gave 25 percent of the much larger GNP that we would have if we limited our contribution to this smaller percentage.

I mention this only as an indication of the sort of factor that one would have to take into account in working out an ideal. Since Western societies generally consider 1 percent of the GNP an acceptable level for overseas aid, the matter is entirely academic. Nor does it affect the question of how much an individual should give in a society in which very few are giving substantial amounts.

It is sometimes said, though less often now than it used to be, that philosophers have no special role to play in public affairs, since most public issues depend primarily on an assessment of facts. On questions of fact, it is said, philosophers as such have no special expertise, and so it has been possible to engage in philosophy without committing oneself to any position on major public issues. No doubt there are some issues of social policy and foreign policy about which it can truly be said that a really expert assessment of the facts is required before taking sides or acting, but the issue of famine is surely not one of these. The facts about the existence of suffering are beyond dispute. Nor, I think, is it disputed that we can do something about it, either through orthodox methods of famine relief or through population control or both. This is therefore an issue on which philosophers are competent to take a position. The issue is one which faces everyone who has more money than he needs to support himself and his dependents, or who is in a position to take some sort of political action. These categories must include practically every teacher and student of philosophy in the universities of the Western world. If philosophy is to deal with matters that are relevant to both teachers and students, this is an issue that philosophers should discuss.

Discussion, though, is not enough. What is the point of relating philosophy to public (and personal) affairs if we do not take our conclusions seriously? In this instance, taking our conclusion seriously means acting upon it. The philosopher will not find it any easier than anyone else to alter his attitudes and way of life to the extent that, if I am right, is involved in doing everything that we ought to be doing. At the very least, though, one can make a start. The philosopher who does so will have to sacrifice some of the benefits of the consumer society, but he can find compensation in the satisfaction of a way of life in which theory and practice, if not yet in harmony, are at least coming together.

Postscript

The crisis in Bangladesh that spurred me to write the above article is now of historical interest only, but the world food crisis is, if anything, still more serious. The huge grain reserves that were then held by the United States have vanished. Increased oil prices have made both fertilizer and energy more expensive in developing countries, and have made it difficult for them to produce more food. At the same time, their population has continued to grow. Fortunately, as I write now, there is no major famine anywhere in the world; but poor people are still starving in several countries, and malnutrition remains very widespread. The need for assistance is, therefore, just as great as when I first wrote, and we can be sure that without it there will, again, be major famines.

The contrast between poverty and affluence that I wrote about is also as great as it was then. True, the affluent nations have experienced a recession, and are perhaps not as prosperous as they were in 1971. But the poorer nations have suffered as least as much from the recession, in reduced government aid (because if governments decide to reduce expenditure, they regard foreign aid as one of the expendable items, ahead of, for instance, defense or public construction projects) and in increased prices for goods and materials they need to buy. In any case, compared with the difference between the affluent nations and the poor nations, the whole recession was trifling; the poorest in the affluent nations remained incomparably better off than the poorest in the poor nations.

So the case for aid, on both a personal and a governmental level, remains as great now as it was in 1971, and I would not wish to change the basic argument that I put forward then.

There are, however, some matters of emphasis that I might put differently if I were to rewrite the article, and the most important of these concerns the population problem. I still think that, as I wrote then, the view that famine relief merely postpones starvation unless something is done to check population growth is not an argument against aid, it is only an argument against the *type* of aid that should be given. Those who hold this view have the same obligation to give to prevent starvation as those who do not; the difference is that they regard assisting population control schemes as a more effective way of preventing starvation in the long run. I would now, however, have given greater space to the discussion of the population problem; for I now think that there is a serious case for saying that if a country refuses to take any steps to slow the rate of its population growth, we should not give it aid. This is, of course, a very drastic step to take, and the choice it represents is a horrible choice to have to make; but if, after a dispassionate analysis of all the available information, we come to the conclusion that without population control we will not, in the long run, be able to prevent famine or other catastrophes, then it may be more humane in the long run to aid those countries that are prepared to take strong measures to reduce population growth, and to use our aid policy as a means of pressuring other countries to take similar steps.

It may be objected that such a policy involves an attempt to coerce a sovereign nation. But since we are not under an obligation to give aid unless that aid is likely to be effective in reducing starvation or malnutrition, we are not under an obligation to give aid to countries that make no effort to reduce a rate of population growth that will lead to catastrophe. Since we do not force any nation to accept our aid, simply making it clear that we will not give aid where it is not going to be effective cannot properly be regarded as a form of coercion.

I should also make it clear that the kind of aid that will slow population growth is not just assistance with the setting up of facilities for dispensing contraceptives and performing sterilizations. It is also necessary to create the conditions under which people do not wish to have so many children. This will involve, among other things, providing greater economic security for people, particularly in their old age, so that they do not need the security of a large family to provide for them. Thus, the requirements of aid designed to reduce population growth

and aid designed to eliminate starvation are by no means separate; they overlap, and the latter will often be a means to the former. The obligation of the affluent is, I believe, to do both. Fortunately, there are now many people in the foreign aid field, including those in the private agencies, who are aware of this.

One other matter that I should now put forward slightly differently is that my argument does, of course, apply to assistance with development, particularly agricultural development, as well as to direct famine relief. Indeed, I think the former is usually the better long-term investment. Although this was my view when I wrote the article, the fact that I started from a famine situation, where the need was for immediate food, has led some readers to suppose that the argument is only about giving food and not about other types of aid. This is quite mistaken, and my view is that the aid should be of whatever type is most effective.

On a more philosophical level, there has been some discussion of the original article which has been helpful in clarifying the issues and pointing to the areas in which more work on the argument is needed. In particular, as John Arthur has shown in "Rights and the Duty to Bring Aid" [in William Aiken and Hugh Le Follette, eds., *World Hunger and Moral Obligation* (Englewood Cliffs, NJ: Prentice Hall, 1977)], something more needs to be said about the notion of "moral significance." The problem is that to give an account of this notion involves nothing less than a full-fledged ethical theory; and while I am myself inclined toward a utilitarian view, it was my aim in writing "Famine, Affluence, and Morality" to produce an argument which would appeal not only to utilitarians, but also to anyone who accepted the initial premises of the argument, which seemed to me likely to have a very wide acceptance. So I tried to get around the need to produce a complete ethical theory by allowing my readers to fill in their own version—within limits—of what is morally significant, and then see what the moral consequences are. This tactic works reasonably well with those who are prepared to agree that such matters as being fashionably dressed are not really of moral significance; but Arthur is right to say that people could take the opposite view without being obviously irrational. Hence, I do not accept Arthur's claim that the weak principle implies little or no duty of benevolence, for it will imply a significant duty of benevolence for those who admit, as I think most nonphilosophers and even off-guard philosophers will admit, that they spend considerable sums on items that by their own standards are of no moral significance. But I do agree that the weak principle is nonetheless too weak, because it makes it too easy for the duty of benevolence to be avoided.

On the other hand, I think the strong principle will stand, whether the notion of moral significance is developed along utilitarian lines, or once again left to the individual reader's own sincere judgment. In either case, I would argue against Arthur's view that we are morally entitled to give greater weight to our own interests and purposes simply because they are our own. This view seems to me contrary to the idea, now widely shared by moral philosophers, that some element of impartiality or universalizability is inherent in the very notion of a moral judgment. (For a discussion of the different formulations of this idea, and an indication of the extent to which they are in agreement, see R. M. Hare, "Rules of War and Moral Reasoning," *Philosophy and Public Affairs* 1, no. 2 [1972].) Granted, in normal circumstances, it may be better for everyone if we recognize that each of us will be primarily responsible for running our own lives and only secondarily responsible for others. This, however, is not a moral ultimate, but a secondary principle that derives from consideration of how a society may best order its affairs, given the limits of altruism in human beings. Such secondary principles are,

I think, swept aside by the extreme evil of people starving to death.

Notes

1. There was also a third possibility: that India would go to war to enable the refugees to return to their lands. Since I wrote this paper, India has taken this way out. The situation is no longer that described above, but this does not affect my argument, as the next paragraph indicates.
2. In view of the special sense philosophers often give to the term, I should say that I use "obligation" simply as the abstract noun derived from "ought," so that "I have an obligation to" means no more, and no less, than "I ought to." This usage is in accordance with the definition of "ought" given by the *Shorter Oxford English Dictionary*: "the general verb to express duty or obligation." I do not think any issue of substance hangs on the way the term is used; sentences in which I use "obligation" could all be rewritten, although somewhat clumsily, as sentences in which a clause containing "ought" replaces the term "obligation."
3. J. O. Urmson, "Saints and Heroes," in *Essays in Moral Philosophy*, ed. Abraham I. Melden (Seattle: University of Washington Press, 1958), p. 214. For a related but significantly different view see also Henry Sidgwick, *The Methods of Ethics*, 7th ed. (London: Dover Press, 1907), pp. 220–211, 492–493.
4. *Summa Theologica*, II-II, Question 66, Article 7, in Aquinas, *Selected Political Writings*, ed. A. P. d'Entrèves, trans. J. G. Dawson (Oxford: Basil Blackwell, 1948), p. 171.
5. See, for instance, John Kenneth Galbraith, *The New Industrial State* (Boston: Houghton Mifflin, 1967); and E. J. Mishan, *The Costs of Economic Growth* (New York: Praeger, 1967).

QUESTIONS

1. Outline as carefully as you can Singer's argument for the conclusion that "we ought to give the money away [to help the starving], and that it is wrong not to do so."
2. If you disagree with Singer's conclusion, where exactly does his argument go wrong?
3. If you agree with Singer's conclusion, how has that affected your life?

18. Islands in a Sea of Obligation: Limits of the Duty to Rescue

DAVID SCHMIDTZ

David Schmidtz (1955–) is a professor of philosophy and economics at the University of Arizona and director of its Freedom Center. He writes extensively in moral and political philosophy. His books include *Rational Choice and Moral Agency* (1995), *Elements of Justice* (2006), and *A Brief History of Liberty*, coauthored with J. Brennan (2010). His reader, *Environmental Ethics: What Really Matters, What Really Works*, coedited with E. Willott, was published by Oxford University Press (2002).

Schmidtz raises the question, if we have a duty to rescue people nearby, in an emergency, "must we also have a duty to rescue people from chronic famine in foreign countries?" He challenges arguments like Singer's in a number of ways, arguing that the duty to rescue is limited. He also raises important questions about the role of thought experiments in ethical discussions.

I. Marooned

John Harris muses, "If we sometimes take comfort from the reflection that no man is an island, we may sometimes ponder just how, or how far, we are involved in mankind."[1] I cite Harris's musing not as a preface to criticizing it but simply because I find it fascinating. I have tried to imagine what it would be like to take comfort from the reflection that no man is an island. I am involved in certain patterns of interdependence, and not others. The bare fact of being so involved seems neither lamentable nor comforting. To be sure, I am glad I can depend on others in the ways I do, but I equally am glad I need not depend on others in the ways I do not.

It is a near-miraculous fact that I live in a society that can support full-time intellectuals. Making a living as an intellectual means that in some ways

I am not an island. So be it. I take no comfort from that. Is it only in some ways that I am not an island? I do not know why some people will find that thought disturbing, but I realize they will. I take no comfort from that either.

My main question is: if we have a duty to rescue in a local emergency, must we also have a duty to rescue people from chronic famine in foreign countries? Most of the literature in this area seems to consist of reflections on thought experiments. It's not my style, but it seems apt for this topic, so I follow custom here. The basic puzzle is illustrated by the following pair of cases.

> ACCIDENT: You come across a traffic accident. You know that one of the victims will survive if and only if you stop to help. You also know that if you stop to help, it will cost you a hundred dollars.

From "Islands in a Sea of Obligation: Limits of the Duty to Rescue," *Law and Philosophy* 19 (2000), pp. 683–705. Reprinted with permission of Springer Science & Business Media.

Compare this to:

> FAMINE: You receive a letter in the mail asking you to send a hundred dollars in support of a famine relief effort. You know that a life will be saved if and only if you contribute.

Are these cases morally different? Even if they are—even if it is obvious that they are—it is not obvious why. This essay leaves open whether we actually have a duty to rescue in local emergencies. Assuming for argument's sake that we have such duties, the question is whether that premise entails that we also have a duty to participate in famine relief efforts. Or are there obstacles blocking any easy move from such a premise to such a conclusion? I consider obstacles pertaining to beneficiaries: what we must do and what we must not do in the face of uncertainty about whether intervention will do more harm than good. Second, I consider obstacles pertaining to the self: the difference between duties we accept so as to make life meaningful and duties we must, for the same reason, reject. Finally, I consider obstacles pertaining to institutional frameworks that help to determine what we ought to expect from one another.

II. Regarding the Beneficiaries

A. Uncertainty

Peter Unger notes that in a case like ACCIDENT you see the situation for yourself whereas in a case like FAMINE, you get information indirectly, via someone's report. According to Unger, this difference in "informative directness" is morally irrelevant. We know this because it is "common sense."[2] Maybe so, but the real issue is reliability, not directness. The information you get in FAMINE is produced not by a trusted researcher but rather by an advertising agency whose purpose is to raise money. If the money raised by the appeal were used to buy guns to shore up a pro-western military dictator, it would be neither the first time nor the last. Not relevant? You decide.

Unger insists we flesh out our cases in the most boring way possible, such that nothing is at stake other than what Unger specifically says is at stake (p. 26). Unfortunately, what Unger calls boring is

not realistic. For better or worse, the real world is interesting. When I recently crossed the border from Zimbabwe into Zambia, a large sign warned that bringing second-hand clothing into Zimbabwe from Zambia is prohibited. Puzzled, I wondered whether second-hand clothing might carry some disease. When I passed through the town of Livingstone, just north of the border, I asked what the sign was about, and I was told by three different sources (two white men, one black woman, all local residents) that Livingstone had until recently been the hub of Zambia's textile industry. Cotton was grown, processed, and woven into cloth there. However, a few years ago, in the wake of a severe and highly publicized drought, international relief agencies decided that what Zambia needed was planeloads of second-hand clothing. Livingstone manufacturers could not compete with free clothing, though. Today, the unemployment rate in Livingstone is ninety percent.

This particular relief effort was more thoughtful than most, undertaken by people who understood how much damage has been done by would-be saviors from the North. We remembered that money sent to Somalia had been used to buy guns. We remembered that grain sent to India had become infested with plague-carrying rats, and that when the hordes of people arriving in search of free food realized they were being exposed to the plague, they fled back to their villages, carrying the plague with them. With such experiences in mind, we sent clothing to Zambia because we meant to ensure above all that this time we did no harm.

Everywhere I went, in South Africa, Botswana, and Zimbabwe as well as Zambia, the people I met (blacks as much as whites, women as much as men) spoke of international aid as having done considerable short-term good in isolated cases but as having the larger and longer-range result of corrupting and ultimately crippling their country's cultures and economies. So, Unger can stipulate that, in his thought experiment, the influx of international aid is not driving third-world farmers out of business and into the cities. But stipulating it does not make it so.

Unger acknowledges that research is needed. Having your heart in the right place is not enough.

Doing the research, though, is not a small cost. Famines are so much less clear-cut than roadside emergencies, which themselves are not especially clear-cut in the real world. At a real accident scene, I do not know what ACCIDENT says I know. Indeed, police urge motorists *not* to feel certain and *not* to stop at highway accident scenes, but rather to notify the police, lest they be set up for a robbery. In our thought experiments, we are omniscient. At a real accident scene, we have no idea what will happen if we stop.[3]

The real world is opaque in interesting ways, morally relevant ways. The opacity not only obscures our responsibilities. It changes them. Real-world morality makes us more responsible for situations we know best and less responsible for situations others know best. Why would morality do that? My thought is, morality would do that so as to be conducive to our living good lives.

B. Token-Benefit and Type-Benefit

> TRAGIC COMMONS: A baby is drowning in the pool beside you. You can save the baby by a process that involves giving the baby's family a hundred dollars. If you do not save the baby, the baby will die. You save the baby. A crowd begins to gather. Seeing what you have done, two onlookers throw their babies into the pool. The babies will drown unless you give each of their families a hundred dollars. More onlookers begin to gather, waiting to see what you do.

I am not saying our world is like TRAGIC COMMONS. I would say, though, that TRAGIC COMMONS is not a world we have any good reason to want to live in. And we could make our world more like TRAGIC COMMONS if we acted as Unger and Peter Singer say we should.[4]

TRAGIC COMMONS illustrates one kind of type-token issue. In TRAGIC COMMONS, the token-benefit is a saved life, but this token-benefit is wildly misleading as a characterization of your action's real consequences. The token-result of your action is a saved life, but the type-result is an escalating catastrophe. Knowing that foreign aid has a history of driving such wedges between token-benefits and type-disasters, I now get a letter asking me to participate in what may be another commons tragedy in the making. I have to make a decision. Should I accept a theorist's or professional fundraiser's verbal assurance that if we turn on the spigots in response to problems and turn them off in response to solutions, we'll eventually have fewer problems and more solutions? Is that what morality requires of me? Or is that what morality forbids?

To whatever extent we take responsibility for other people as well as ourselves, our actions are encouraging people to depend on us rather than on themselves. Act-utilitarianism usually would not permit people to arrange circumstances so that our act-utilitarian commitments require us to support them, but unless they too are committed act-utilitarians, that will not stop them from doing it. Theories often have implications other than ones they formally acknowledge. A theory can stipulate an action guide and an intended result. But a theory cannot stipulate that following its action guide will have its intended result, for that is an empirical matter. So it is with maximizing utility. One can say that trying to maximize utility actually tends to maximize utility, but saying it does not make it so. A simple maximizing strategy like Singer's or Unger's may tend to lead to the best possible outcome for beings like us in situations like ours. Then again, it may not. It has no history of doing so.

It is worth noting that Unger's argument is not as overtly utilitarian as Singer's. Instead, Unger presents a series of cases, telling us over and over again that his way of reacting to a case is common sense or otherwise intuitively compelling.[5] Unger makes it clear, though, that the intuitions he expects us to share are relentlessly act-utilitarian. For example, Unger dismisses our (intuitive!) tendency to divide the world into insiders to whom we are more obligated and outsiders to whom we are less obligated. Unger finds this intuitive separation indefensible on the grounds that it is *intuitively* indefensible (p. 97).

The problem is, in relying on intuitions, we miss everything that isn't a mere intuition. The case for dividing the world into insiders to whom we owe more, and outsiders to whom we owe less, is based not on intuition but on what happens when we fail to distinguish between insiders and outsiders.

It may be intuitive that we can do more good by allocating our resources to those who need them more, and thus correspondingly intuitive that we should throw our doors open to anyone anywhere who needs our stuff more than we do. No matter what our intuitions say, though, the fact remains that no good comes from pouring resources down the sink of an open access commons. Trying unconstrainedly to satisfy all demands results in greater demand, not greater satisfaction.

III. Regarding the Self

A. Selective Focus

Is there any simple connection between premises about how bad someone's problem is and conclusions about what we ought to do about it?

> FAST PAIN RELIEF: There is a button you could push. If you push it, all sentient life will painlessly vanish from existence. You will, of course, minimize suffering in the process.

FAST PAIN RELIEF shows us that minimizing suffering is not the only thing that matters. Nor is it always what matters most. Further, there are things (e.g., all sentient life) that ought not to be sacrificed merely to minimize suffering.

What FAST PAIN RELIEF leaves open is whether minimizing suffering matters a lot, or relatively little, in the cosmic scheme of things. However, we need not settle that, because suffering could matter quite a lot without it being true that we ought to spend quite a lot of our lives working to put an end to it. Let me approach the point obliquely, beginning with a story. Environmental activist Paul Watson, founder of the Sea Shepherd Society, confronted a Japanese fishing fleet in 1982 and negotiated a halt to a netting process that was killing dolphins. During the discussion, a fisherman asked Watson which is of more value, the life of a dolphin or a life of a human?

> I answered that, in my opinion, the life of a dolphin was equal in value to the life of a human. The fisherman then asked. "If a Japanese fisherman and a dolphin were both caught in a net and you could save the life of one, which would you save?"

All the fishermen in the room smirked. They had me pegged for a liberal and felt confident that I would say I would save the fisherman, thus making a mockery of my declaration that humans and dolphins are equal. I looked about the room and smiled. "I did not come to Japan to save fishermen; I am here to save dolphins."[6]

There is power in Watson's response. It is no mere philosophical inconsistency. We can learn from it. It is a pivotal feature of our moral psychology that when we focus on something, it takes on added moral significance to us. We can call it the phenomenon of *selective focus*. A lot of people are consumed by one burning issue or another, and most of them think everyone ought to be consumed by the same issue. In fact, we freely choose to be consumed by one issue rather than another. Peter Singer may think what he has chosen to focus on is the thing on which we are all obliged to focus, but it only looks that way when you already are focusing on the same thing. What Paul Watson was telling the Japanese fishermen was that although he may be philosophically committed to viewing humans and dolphins as equals, he has no obligation to be preoccupied by that particular commitment. He is committed to *respecting* humans and dolphins alike, but he is not committed to giving them equal time when deciding how to plan his life.

Even if, counterfactually, everyone who thought hard about Singer's puzzles came to the same conclusions as Singer, that would not imply everyone will come to Singer's conclusions, for not everyone will think hard about famine (and some will think very hard, and that too will lead to different conclusions). Not everyone will focus as Singer does. Some people focus on environmental degradation and wonder how Singer can fail to see that if a billion humans were to starve, the world would be a better place. Or perhaps the one true moral problem is sexism. Or atheism. Whatever. Selective focus. It makes complicated lives seem so simple. It makes overly simple solutions seem so righteous.

I believe in fighting injustice. Does that commit me to fighting injustice wherever I find it? Not at all. There is injustice everywhere I turn. Am I committed to fighting whichever injustice happens to be firing the imagination of Peter Singer? Not at all. That's not what I'm here for. Like Singer, I decide for myself where to make my stand.

Generally speaking, the 1960's slogan "if you aren't part of the solution, you're part of the problem" is a false dichotomy. If the problem is real, morality imposes constraints that require us to avoid being part of it. In addition, morality asks us to form and pursue goals that make life meaningful within those constraints. Which is to say, morality requires us not only to avoid being part of that problem but also to be part of the solution either to that or to other real problems—to take some aspect of the problem of making the world a better place to live and make that problem our own.

I believe in small efforts that save lives—performing them, not just talking about them. So, I give blood several times per year. I do not believe I am required to give blood, and I would not compel people to give blood. I would not give blood if I had no idea whether I was saving lives or spreading a fatal disease. For the record, I also give a few thousand a year to charitable organizations, and I am sure my donations do some good. However, my main obligation to the world concerns not how I spend my paycheck, but rather what I do to earn it.

B. Token-Cost and Type-Cost

We noted that even when the token-benefit is desirable, the type-benefit may be no benefit at all, but may instead be a nightmare. This section offers a complementary warning about the difference between token-cost and type-cost.

> VAN GOGH IN THE LAKE: You find yourself in a lifeboat. Are you obliged to throw a Van Gogh painting overboard to make room for a drowning person?[7]

Compare this to:

> VAN GOGH AT THE AUCTION: You find yourself at an auction. Are you obliged to auction off the same Van Gogh to raise money to save starving people?

What is the difference? Token-cost is the cost of a particular rescue. Type-cost is the cost of undertaking a kind of rescue whenever the occasion comes up in the course of our lives. One difference between

VAN GOGH IN THE LAKE and VAN GOGH AT THE AUCTION (likewise between ACCIDENT and FAMINE) is a difference in cost. In a sense, of course, that cannot be true, since by hypothesis the cost is identical. But the cost that is stipulated to be identical is token-cost. Type-cost is another matter.

Is distance per se important? Frances Kamm says it is. She may be right. I don't know. What surely matters, though, is this: distant problems are types of which there are innumerable tokens. Local emergencies are simply tokens. If one falls in your lap today, you can be fairly sure there won't be another in your mailbox tomorrow. You help and that's the end of it. Life goes on.[8]

When professional fund-raisers exhort us to help relieve famine, they talk about token-cost (although not by that name), going into some detail explaining how a hundred dollar donation can change a recipient's life. Yet, it is no particular token of the type "starving person" they have in mind. It is the type itself, and famine relief's type-cost is not small. If we embrace the duty to relieve famine in the way Singer and Unger say we should, life does not just go on.

In fact, Singer says, "if it is in our power to prevent something bad from happening, without thereby sacrificing anything of comparable moral importance, we ought, morally, to do it" (p. 231). The strong version of this principle requires "reducing ourselves to the level of marginal disutility," by which he means "the level at which, by giving more, I would cause as much suffering to myself or my dependents as I would relieve by my gift. This would mean, of course, that one would reduce oneself to very near the material circumstances of a Bengali refugee." Singer adds, "I should also say that the strong version seems to me to be the correct one" (p. 241).

Unger likewise ultimately asks us not to contribute a hundred dollars to famine relief but rather to contribute 51% of our wealth (p. 138). Now, perhaps 51% would satisfy Unger, but according to Unger's theory, satisfying Unger is not good enough, for there is nothing in Unger's theory to make this a one-shot game. After giving 51%, what justifies failing to give half again of what we have left? Is there a point when we can consider ourselves to have done our share and can think of the plight of the still-starving millions to be someone else's problem? Is Unger mistaken in asking us to contribute (only) 51% of our wealth, or is he mistaken in presenting us with a theory that asks us to contribute virtually everything we have? Or are we to think of 51% as the real request and of the theory as a gambit meant only to soften us up in preparation for the real request?

Unger does not distinguish between type-cost and token-cost, but he does say we must liberate ourselves from the paralysis of "futility thinking." Futility thinking involves thinking of people who need help as constituting an overwhelmingly large group. From that group's perspective, helping a single person is roughly the same as not helping at all. Overwhelmed, we give up (pp. 75–76). As therapy for futility thinking, Unger gives us another case (p. 77):

> AIRPORT: There are ten bombs about to explode in ten busy airports. We can stop one (but only one) of the bombs from going off and killing several people.

Of course, we should defuse the one bomb. So what? The point is, Unger wants us to see FAMINE as a single hundred dollar problem, and not see it as a problem we failed to solve with yesterday's donation and again will fail to solve with each new day. We are meant to draw that lesson by seeing it as analogous to AIRPORT, in which the right course was to forget nine problems we couldn't solve and just tackle one we could. But the ten problems in AIRPORT do not constitute an endless series. By hypothesis, nine of the problems will never be ours, no matter how much we might wish to make them ours. By hypothesis, there is one action for us to perform, after which there will be nothing left to do. The crisis will be over.

I think Unger must be missing what it is about FAMINE that stops us. I know when I can regard AIRPORT as a solved problem. I do not know when I can regard FAMINE as a solved problem. In AIRPORT, I know exactly when it will be time to get on with my own life. In FAMINE, I have no idea. The face that FAMINE presents to me tomorrow will be indistinguishable from the face it presents to me today, no matter what I do.

I discussed differences in how much good we might be doing in ACCIDENT as compared to FAMINE. There is also a difference in cost: a difference in what kind of life we have left after meeting the purported obligation. In ACCIDENT, the problem goes away and leaves you alone once you fix it. In FAMINE, the problem is a permanent feature of your moral landscape no matter what you do.

Back to VAN GOGH IN THE LAKE. If you had two seats, each occupied by a Van Gogh, and there were two people in the water, would it be okay to throw one painting overboard, save one person, let the other drown, and still have one painting left? I suppose not. The issue of type-cost, though, is not about one-shot emergencies involving one person rather than two. The type-cost worry is not about the obligation's multiple nature so much as its serial nature. The issue is about a situation where, no matter what you do, there always will be someone in the water. Having thrown a Van Gogh overboard, there is no point in ever acquiring another one: no point in ever trying to have a life of your own, because there won't ever be room for it. It will always be the thing that went overboard.

Unger wants to help people get past futility thinking. What would help? I suppose we could use a better theory—a theory that identifies nonarbitrary limits of obligation compatible with living a recognizably good life. Singer stresses that pious talk is not enough. "What is the point of relating philosophy to public (and personal) affairs if we do not take our conclusions seriously? In this instance, taking our conclusion seriously means acting upon it" (p. 242). Indeed. Singer's conclusion cannot be taken seriously in this sense. Late in *Living High and Letting Die*, after admitting he has not given up the high life, Unger assures us that as long as we have a "multidimensional context-sensitive semantics," it is fine to embrace both "my severe Liberationist judgment of the Envelope's behavior and my lenient ordinary judgment of the same behavior" (p. 170).[9] But it is not okay. If Unger's theory could be taken seriously in Singer's sense, then Unger would not need an Orwellian semantics to excuse the discrepancy between word and deed. Shelly Kagan once said at a public lecture that he did not live up to standards proposed by Unger and Singer and himself. Kagan insisted, though, that he ought to be and in fact was ashamed of himself for so failing.[10] I can see how the discrepancy between theory and behavior would lead Kagan to conclude he should be ashamed of something, but why assume the behavior is shameful? Why not the theory?

How much should we give? Unger's theory gives the easy answer: more. To get past futility thinking, and to get to something we can take seriously in Singer's sense, we have to do better than that. Theorists need to realize that moral theorizing isn't a game you win by having the most demanding theory.

IV. Regarding Institutions

A. Institutional Expectations

The remaining sections consider roles that institutions play in determining how likely people are to be rescued, and to be in need of rescue in the first place.

> TROLLEY: You know the story. A trolley is rolling down the track on its way to killing five people. If you switch the trolley to another track on which there is only one person, you will be saving five and killing one.

Compare this to:

> HOSPITAL: Five patients lie on operating tables about to die for lack of suitable organ donors. A UPS delivery person just walked into the office. She is a suitable organ donor for all five patients. If you kidnap her and harvest her organs, you will be saving five and killing one.

HOSPITAL may appear to be nothing more than a TROLLEY in a surgical mask, but it is quite different. TROLLEY is about one versus five. HOSPITAL is not. HOSPITAL is about trust. What gives society its utility for those who live in it? The answer is, trust. We can't trust people who assume a right to harvest our liver whenever we stray too close to a hospital. HOSPITAL and TROLLEY differ because hospitals cannot serve their purpose unless people can trust hospitals to treat people as rights-bearers. Institutions have utility by creating conditions under which people can trust each other *not* to operate in an act-utilitarian way.[11]

Act-utilitarian philosophers sometimes seem blind to the fact that there literally is no such thing

as maximization per se. Maximization necessarily is relative to a set of constraints. How much good our actions actually can do depends on the constraints. If we want to live in a good society, a society whose members can flourish, the primary imperative is to get the constraints right, so that constraints within which individuals pursue goals have the effect of leading them to formulate and pursue their goals in peaceful and mutually supporting ways. For example, we need constraints that enable patients and doctors to trust each other. If those constraints also stop doctors from killing one patient to save five, that is good, because doctors who can be trusted to respect that constraint will save more lives than doctors who cannot. From a consequentialist standpoint, the utility of particular act-tokens is a secondary issue at best.

Some utilitarians say they consider it a mystery why morality would incorporate any constraints beyond a requirement to do whatever maximizes the good.[12] But there is no mystery why it is moral for institutions (including cultural norms) to constrain individual action. Moral institutions constrain the good's pursuit because the good is pursued by individuals. If the good is to be realized, then institutions—legal, political, economic, and cultural institutions—must get the constraints right, so as to put individuals in a position to pursue the good in a manner conducive to the good's production in general. Institutions do that by (a) curbing people's tendency to pursue their good in a partial manner, and by (b) helping to make people more predictable to each other, thereby helping them avoid wasting resources on projects that needlessly put them in each other's way.

There are interesting parallels between rational agents and moral institutions in terms of how they operate in the face of real-world complexity. Moral institutions respond to people as they are. Similarly, rational agents respond to themselves as they are. Both are sensitive to their own limitations. For example, individuals adopt satisficing strategies in pursuit of particular goals. They impose constraints on local goals so as to bring their various goals into better harmony with each other, thereby making life as a whole go as well as possible.[13] Likewise, moral institutions get the best result not so much by aiming at the best result as by imposing constraints on individual pursuits so as to bring individual pursuits into better harmony with each other. Institutions (hospitals, for example) serve the common good by leaving well enough alone—creating opportunities for mutual benefit, then trusting individuals to take advantage of them. That is how (even from a utilitarian perspective) institutions have a moral mandate to serve the common good that does not translate (or collapse) into a mandate for ordinary moral agents to maximize utility.[14] In effect, there are two sides to the sense in which institutional utility is based on trust. First, people have to be able to trust their society to treat them as rights-bearers. Second, society has to trust people to make use of the opportunities that people have as rights-bearers within society.

Let me stress, this appeal to consequences is not a plea for social engineering. I am not asking what to maximize but rather what to respect. The kind of consequentialism I have in mind does not ask us to maximize utility. Instead, it asks us to show respect for existing customs and institutional arrangements that truly have utility. A reflective consequentialist morality is not about one versus five. It is not even about costs versus benefits. It is about how we need to live in order to be glad we are neighbors. It's about getting on with our lives in a way that complements rather than hinders our neighbors' efforts to get on with their own.

B. Institutional Limits of Positive Rights

If we can impose legal constraints that keep people from tearing out each other's throats, why not go all the way? Why not impose a legal obligation not merely to abstain from violence but to *minimize* violence? Thomas Nagel doubts that morality requires agents to be thoroughly impartial. Yet, Nagel asks, "How can there be a reason not to twist someone's arm which is not equally a reason to prevent his arm from being twisted by someone else?"[15] The question is not rhetorical. For Nagel, there is a real puzzle here.

Nagel's question is answerable, though, when considered in an institutional context. For the sake of argument, let us suppose that the impartial reason to refrain from arm twisting is, as Nagel suspects, equally a reason to prevent arms from being twisted. Thus, the same reasons why an institution should

not twist arms are also reasons why it should *prevent* arms from being twisted.

How, then, do institutions prevent arms from being twisted? One way in which institutions prevent arm twisting is by *forbidding* it. Institutions carry out their mandate to prevent harm precisely by imposing constraints against causing harm. In addition, and in conjunction with the general imposition of constraints against causing harm, legal and political institutions give selected citizens the mandate to prevent harm by enforcing laws that forbid causing it.

The psychological fact is that most of us are averse to doing evil—to twisting arms. And it serves the common good for institutions to work with rather than against that psychological fact.[16] We do not have the same aversion to failing to prevent harm as we do to causing it. Thus, from a structural viewpoint, positive duties to prevent harm and negative duties not to cause harm are not symmetrical. Social structure has psychologically potent material to work with in inducing compliance with negative duties; it has less to work with in inducing compliance with positive duties. Institutions serve the common good by working mainly (if not only) with the psychological aversion to causing harm, reinforcing that aversion as best they can.

Some would say a distinction between acts and omissions is psychologically salient only because of cultural contingency; that is, people are beguiled by false moral theory or false religion into thinking the distinction is important. But the origin and contingency of the distinction's salience is beside the point. I am not saying our tendency to distinguish between acts and omissions is hard-wired; I assume only that the tendency is real, and that a society that ignored this tendency would be dysfunctional.[17]

I explained how a theoretical endorsement of the prevention of arm twisting might manifest itself, at the action-guiding level, as a stringent prohibition of arm twisting. The upshot is that if we as a society have duties to prevent arm twisting, we are meeting those obligations when we create institutions that effectively prohibit arm twisting. That is *how* we prevent arm twisting. Indeed, it likely is our best way, regardless of whether it is our only way. Again, the point is not that there are no grounds for requiring harm prevention but rather that structurally embedded constraints against causing harm can be grounded in an institutional obligation to prevent harm.

Whether institutions also should try to compel us to be good Samaritans—whether they should compel us to donate blood, for example—depends in part on whether that is the best way of inducing people to be good Samaritans. It may not be. There are empirical issues here that need sorting out. By way of general observation, though, it is relatively easy to argue that people have positive obligations to children, especially their own children. The dependency warned of earlier is, in young children, innocuous, indeed appropriate. Enforcing special responsibilities of adults to their children need not undermine the recipients' sense of personal responsibility. Positive rights grounded in such relationships are not prescriptions for commons tragedies. Their only cost is a token-cost.

Beyond that, there are going to be some serious moral constraints on the potential scope of positive rights. Real positive rights are not "open-access." The only defensible positive rights are those compatible with human flourishing, and the only ones compatible with human flourishing are those that do not reconstitute morality as an open access commons.

This suggests that the only credible positive rights are rights grounded in relationships to which access is not open—where the class of potential claimants is small. Or, if the class of people who can invoke the obligation is not sharply limited, then it is the nature of the obligation itself that will be sharply limited. The issue is more complicated than that, however, because even in the context of special relationships, there has to be a limit to the nature and extent of the obligation. A relationship is not healthy unless both givers and receivers respect the separate personhood of the givers. Free riding and seemingly limitless need often are painfully evident in even the most intimate relationships.[18] Self-respect sometimes requires a person to ask herself when she ought to quit.[19]

In the end, it seems inescapable that emergencies and chronic problems are two different things. When we assume a burden of long-term care, we give up the life we had. When we help out in a one-shot emergency, we are inconvenienced, maybe even at risk, but we are not abandoning life as a member of a kingdom of ends and replacing it with a new life as a mere means.

C. Liberationism

Unger imagines a future world in which "whenever well-off folks learn of people in great need, they promptly move to meet the need, almost no matter what the financial cost. So, at this later date, the basic needs of almost all the world's people will be met almost all the time. . . . What's more, should any of these descendants find herself facing such preventable suffering as now actually obtains, she'd devote almost all her energy and resources toward lessening the suffering" (p. 20).

I am left wondering whether this vision is coherent. It has the following logic. The productive output of the western world is put up for grabs. A worldwide competition ensues. And the way for a country's leaders to win the competition for that output is to have a population that needs (or seems to need) it more than anyone else. But if we are devoting almost all our energy and resources to meeting such need, then how is it that we are well off?

Imagine what our community would be like if a lot of us voluntarily did as Unger asks. There were about five thousand people in the nearest town when I was growing up on a farm in Saskatchewan. Suppose farmers gave up that part of our crop we would have cashed in to buy movie tickets. The Towne Theater goes out of business. No big deal, perhaps. The half dozen employees seek work elsewhere, although suffice it to say that in a town of five thousand, opportunities are limited. Maybe they find work at the Princess or Lucky Cafes. Fine, but we are not done. We also stop cashing in grain for hamburgers at the cafe, instead sending that part of our crop abroad. The cafes close, over a dozen people are out of work, and we exceed our town's ability to find work for them.

Unger says we would not have nice cars and nice homes (p. 145). We send away that part of our crop that would have bought new cars. Fine. The car dealers and their employees are out of work. They no longer send money to foreign countries; nor do they support local merchants, critical services aside. The furniture shop and the clothing store shut down.

They stop repaying business loans. Their employees stop making mortgage payments. Banks begin to foreclose on houses. There is no one to buy the houses, though, so the banks close too, and I don't know what happens to their employees. Perhaps they become refugees.

One last thing. The shippers we relied on to ship our grain to foreign countries? We no longer have the money to pay them to ship the grain, and in any case the overall volume of business in our town has spiraled down to a point where servicing our community is no longer feasible. Nor is there any local market for our grain. We eat what we can until it spoils. Police begin to crack down on "hoarders." They work on commission; there is no money for salaries. We do not bother to plant next year's crop. The police would just take it, anyway.

Singer would allow that we have to keep doing our part to maintain our incomes so that we remain able to send money overseas. But in the above thought experiment, the problem isn't that we aren't working as hard but that we aren't doing as much business. It is the lack of business that shuts down the theater and the coffee shops. Moreover, the experiment is not merely a thought experiment. Historically, with few exceptions, this is how communal societies end, unless they switch to some other way of doing business first.[20]

There is more. Unger advocates not only that we contribute our own resources to famine relief, but that we contribute our neighbors' resources, too, with or without permission (p. 62). Unger says he believes this is morally required but will argue only that it is permissible forcibly to divert other people's money to famine relief (p. 63). As Unger puts it, "to lessen serious suffering, it's good to take what's rightfully another's" (p. 63). What Unger thinks is good sounds like a recipe for chaos. Indeed, it is chaos wherever it has been a general practice, which is why we still have "developing" countries that will not develop until people in those countries can count on being able to control the wealth they create.

It seems relevant that what Unger calls Liberationism—the view that we need liberating from goals or scruples that stop us from throwing our whole lives into the minimization of suffering—has never done any good in the world while the morality he rejects has produced the civilization he wants to tap. Unger and Singer give the distinct impression that they are not keen on western civilization and indeed would be glad to help accelerate its decline and fall.[21] For some, perhaps, that is the point of being a Liberationist. If they respected western civilization, they would respect the morality that makes it work.

D. Structural Violence

John Harris defines the Marxist conception of violence as holding, first, that people are causally responsible for harm they could have prevented, and second, that such harm is a form of *violence* (pp. 192–193). Harris says, "If we have a duty not to kill others, it would be strange indeed if the duty not to kill by positive actions was somehow stronger than the duty not to kill by negative actions" (p. 211). Yet, no morality that ever has formed the backbone of a viable civilization has ever put simply failing to aid on a moral par with killing.[22] So, is it "strange indeed" to think my duty to send money to African famine relief is less stringent than my duty not to shoot people for fun when I go on safari in Africa? Harris seems not to notice that the lumping together of responsibility for actions and nonactions could be seen as leaving us with an absurdly nondemanding theory. Perhaps he thinks a prohibition of murder is the common-sense bedrock to which he can anchor what otherwise is a concerted attack on common sense morality. But Harris is not entitled to assume without argument that while everything else shifts around in response to his attack, his anchor remains unmoved. If murder becomes no worse than declining to send your movie money to a third-world dictator, then murder has moved to a new place in the realm of moral wrongs. There is no warrant for assuming that, at the end of its odyssey, murder is as wrong as ever.

I mentioned I was raised on a Canadian farm. I don't know much about violence. (I know a little. Writing this reminds me I once was shot at by a poacher.) In that sense I have lived a privileged and sheltered life. However, I do know about being poor. My parents grew up in houses with dirt floors. I was the fifth of six children and the first born into a house with electricity. Running water and an indoor toilet came a little later. I remember when water was delivered and sewage was removed by truck. Given the expense, our parents did not allow our toilet to be flushed more than once a day (and it served a family of eight). We didn't feel sorry for ourselves. We didn't ask America to rescue us. We didn't see ourselves as victims of violence. Lucky for us. Had we been taught to see ourselves as victims, it would have ruined us, for such teaching is poisonous, doing more violence to a poor person's mind than mere lack of money ever could.

V. Conclusion

None of the preceding discussion is meant to suggest we have no duty to rescue. However, taking that duty seriously requires us to understand its limits. We must draw lines, with or without the aid of moral theory. First, we have to learn how to lend aid so as to enhance rather than undermine our sense that being moral is an integral part of living a life that is worth living. Second, we have to recognize that even if being in situation X were unjust, that does not mean any particular agent is obligated to dedicate his or her life to helping people escape from situation X. Morality presents us with options when choosing goals around which we organize our lives within relatively less flexible moral constraints.

Third, we have to take responsibility for distinguishing between aid that helps beneficiaries resume meaningful lives and aid that turns people into seekers of aid. Relief efforts in Africa have a history of failure in this regard. Fourth, the world is opaque in morally relevant ways. When we may well be utterly wrong about the nature of the problem and about what truly would help solve it, that uncertainty affects what we ought to do.[23] The thought experiments that dominate discussion in this field often suppose we know all relevant facts, which makes them unreliable as ways of shedding light on real-world obligations.

Fifth, we have to understand that a reflective consequentialist morality is not (even in emergencies) about numbers but about how we need to live so that our relationships constitute a good community. Finally, we have to understand that when we respect institutions that forbid causing harm, we thereby play a role in our community being a preventer of harm. Institutional arrangements that give priority to our duty not to cause harm, seemingly slighting our duty to prevent harm, may not be slighting the latter duty at all. Such institutions may instead be fulfilling their duty to prevent harm by stopping us from causing it. We do not excuse doing less by claiming we were trying to do more.

Notes

For their many thoughtful comments, I thank participants at the Duty to Rescue conference at Georgia State University, especially my commentator Gerald Postema. Thanks also to conference organizer Kit Wellman and assistant Irene Pierce for their consummate professionalism and hospitality. Finally, I want to thank Joel Feinberg for years of friendship, mentorship, and philosophical leadership on this and so many other topics.

1. John Harris, "The Marxist Conception of Violence," *Philosophy and Public Affairs* 3 (1974), pp. 192–220, here p. 211.

2. Peter Unger, *Living High and Letting Die: Our Illusion of Innocence* (New York: Oxford University Press, 1996), p. 36.

3. We are similarly uncertain of what to do about local homelessness. We can find literature on the plight of street people every bit as convincing as anything Unger says about more distant crises. Yet when we actually meet street people, in a town like Tucson where the current unemployment rate is under three percent and where every second or third storefront displays a "Now Hiring" sign, the majority appear to be young and able-bodied people of normal intelligence who simply prefer not to be tied down by a job. Some openly admit they want the money for alcohol or drugs, thinking their honesty will touch a chord among those who long to be stoned themselves. Despite knowing relatively more about this situation, it remains hard to know what to do, other than the obvious: don't give them money. (On occasion, I see someone who seems horrified to be on the street, rather than comfortable with it, and I buy them groceries.)

4. Peter Singer, "Famine, Affluence, and Morality," *Philosophy and Public Affairs* 1 (1972), pp. 229–243.

5. For further discussion of Unger's "Method of Moral Intuitions," see Robert Hanna, "Must We Be Good Samaritans?" *Canadian Journal of Philosophy* 28 (1998), pp. 453–470.

6. Paul Watson, "Tora! Tora! Tora!" *Earth Ethics,* edited by James Sterba (Englewood Cliffs: Prentice Hall, 1995), pp. 341–346, here p. 341.

7. This case is inspired by Susan Wolf, "Morality and the View from Here," *Journal of Ethics* 3, 3 (1999): 203–223.

8. I thank Arthur Ripstein for the intriguing suggestion that we think in terms of psychological rather than physical distance. Nearness, Ripstein suggests, is not a matter of where you happen to be but rather of where you live your life. If I think of my town as my town, then I may have the attitude that no one drowns in my town if I can help it. It is because I think of it as my space that what occurs within it is psychologically near.

9. What Unger calls Envelope is comparable to what I call FAMINE.

10. Spring of 1993, Yale University.

11. I think it generally is understood that the trolley conductor is not using the lone victim as a mere means of saving five. TROLLEY's victim simply is in the wrong place at the wrong time, unlike the victim in HOSPITAL who in effect is being hunted down for use as a mere resource. The seminal article on this point probably is Philippa Foot, "The Problem of Abortion and the Doctrine of Double Effect," *Oxford Review* 5 (1967), pp. 5–15. Foot argues persuasively against attaching too much weight to the idea of double effect, but see the discussion of acts and omissions in Horacio Spector, *Autonomy and Rights* (Oxford: Oxford University Press, 1992). See also Jean Beer Blumenfeld, "Causing Harm and Bringing Aid," *American Philosophical Quarterly* 18 (1981), pp. 323–329. For a classic discussion of HOSPITAL-type cases, see Judith Jarvis Thomson, "Killing, Letting Die, and the Trolley Problem," *Monist* 59 (1976), 204–217.

12. See Shelly Kagan, *The Limits of Morality* (New York: Oxford University Press, 1989), pp. 121–127. Samuel Scheffler, *The Rejection of Consequentialism* (New York: Oxford University Press, 1982), p. 129, expresses similar skepticism, despite departing from utilitarianism in other respects.

13. For extended discussion, see David Schmidtz, "Rationality within Reason," *Journal of Philosophy* 89 (1992), pp. 445–466.

14. For discussion of the broader theoretical framework of the ideas here and in the following paragraphs, see Chapter 7 of David Schmidtz, *Rational Choice and Moral Agency* (Princeton: Princeton University Press, 1995).

15. Thomas Nagel, *Equality and Partiality* (New York: Oxford University Press, 1986), p. 178.

16. For purposes of this discussion, I assume some part of morality is bound up with the idea of serving the common good. (See Chapter 7 of my *Rational Choice and Moral Agency* for some argument and explication.) One thing that would serve the common good (plausibly construed) would be the general prevention of arm twisting. Prohibiting arm twisting might not be an end in itself, but if it serves to prevent arm twisting, that goes a long way toward justifying the prohibition.

Note also that taking on a duty to help people in trouble would be only one way of minimizing harm. Another way would consist of taking on a duty to minimize the likelihood of people being in trouble in the first place. That is why, for example, insurance companies have compelling reason to structure policies so as to give clients an incentive to avoid accidents.

17. In general, when can we properly speak of a failure to act as causing harm? Christopher Wellman, "Liberalism, Samaritanism, and Political Legitimacy," *Philosophy and Public Affairs* 25 (1996), pp. 211–237, explains why we should not accept Joel Feinberg's claim that failing to aid a person in need amounts to a causing of harm. Withholding aid is withholding aid, period. It may constitute a failure to stop a process that is causing harm, but it is not itself the process that is causing the harm (pp. 228–229). Alison McIntyre, "Guilty Bystanders? On the Legitimacy of Duty to Rescue Statutes," *Philosophy and Public Affairs* 23 (1994), pp. 157–191, adds that many crimes do not depend on causing harm (p. 172). McIntyre agrees with Wellman that we should stop trying to fit the wrongness of omissions into a causal paradigm (p. 191). We need not get into the metaphysics of harm and causation to determine when a refraining is morally tantamount to murder.

18. I owe this observation to Gerald Postema and Frances Kamm. See also Jean Hampton, "Selflessness and the Loss of Self," *Social Philosophy and Policy* 10(1) (1993), pp. 135–165.

19. Liam Murphy proposes a Cooperative Principle that, were it correct, would limit our liabilities without embedding them in special relationships. First, Murphy intuits that morality is a cooperative project, and that our obligation as part of that project does not

depend on how much other people contribute. (See "The Demands of Beneficence," *Philosophy and Public Affairs* 22 [1993], pp. 267–292, here p. 267.) Whatever others actually contribute, our own obligation is to contribute our fair share (p. 278). As Murphy acknowledges, though, this principle is incorrect. If you and another person are walking past a pond in which two babies are drowning, Murphy's Cooperative Principle says your fair share involves saving one baby. However, Murphy admits that if the other person does not save one, *then* your obligation is to save both. Thus, the other person's action does affect what morality requires of you. This undermines not only Murphy's Cooperative Principle, but also the driving initial intuition that morality does not demand more as others contribute less. Murphy says we may need to appeal to special obligations in cases occurring at our feet, reserving the Cooperative Principle for distant cases (p. 292). But given that the Cooperative Principle does not distinguish between local and distant cases and given that the Principle is incorrect in local cases squarely within its domain as formulated, we need something different both for local and distant cases.

20. See David Schmidtz, "The Institution of Property," *Social Philosophy and Policy* 11 (1994), pp. 42–62, for some exceptions to this historical rule and also for some explanation of why it is the rule.

21. If this seems too implausible, then let Singer speak for himself. Having endorsed the redistributive principle in its strong form, as per section III B above, Singer adds, "Even if we accepted the principle only in its moderate form, however, it should be clear that we would have to give away enough to ensure that the consumer society, dependent as it is on people spending on trivia rather than giving to famine relief, would slow down and perhaps disappear entirely. There are several reasons why this would be desirable in itself" (p. 241). Now, if this is the *moderate* principle's predictable result, what happens if we follow the *strong* principle Singer favors? What else disappears along with consumer society? Books? Art? Presumably spending *time* on "trivia" would be no more allowable than spending money on it.

22. We can distinguish between something we simply did not do and something we refrained from doing with the intent that a harm occur. See Heidi Malm, "Killing, Letting Die, and Simple Conflicts," *Philosophy and Public Affairs* 18 (1989), pp. 238–258, here p. 239. Malm convincingly argues that the moral difference between killing and letting die neither entails nor corresponds to any moral difference between acting and refraining. For a detailed response to Harris's view that people cause harm by failing to prevent it, see Eric Mack, "Bad Samaritanism and the Causation of Harm," *Philosophy and Public Affairs* 9 (1980), 230–259.

23. Charlie Wilmot is a pilot for AirServ International, working out of Maputo, Mozambique. AirServ provides transportation (funded by USAid) for organizations such as Save the Children. I met him in Johannesburg in July of 1999. Wilmot told me that Canada donated a de Haviland aircraft to Guinea a few years ago. Guinea used the craft until it needed servicing. They asked Canada to service it. Canada refused. Now the plane sits idle, because Guinea believes they are better off waiting for someone to give them another airplane. Wilmot says relief efforts always are meant to help African countries become self-sustaining, but that is not what African governments want. The authorities have too much to lose. Their first priority is to keep the money coming in.

QUESTIONS

1. What are the limits on our duty to rescue?
2. Does Schmidtz show that Singer's argument is mistaken?
3. What according to Schmidtz are some of the problems with the kind of thought experiments that are common in contemporary ethics?

Killing in War

As we noted in the introduction to the last section, the second great killer of men and women has been war. In the last century the destruction caused by war broke new records. The estimates of deaths caused by the Second World War range from fifty to more than seventy million people. We are all interested in war; war always seems to be with us. As the famous quotation, misattributed to Trotsky, notes: "You may not be interested in war, but war is interested in you."

There are multiple ethical questions to be raised about killing in war. The big questions are when, if ever, is it permissible. The literature on the ethics of war is substantial and, not surprisingly, goes back some time in history. Wars have long been with us, and people have reflected on them for a long time. It has become customary to distinguish between questions about the evaluation of wars (is this war permissible?) and about the conduct of a war (is this action permissible?). In the influential just war tradition, the first set of questions is dubbed "the justice *of* war" (*jud ad bellum*) and the second "justice *in* war" (*jus in bello*). It is controversial how separate the two sets of questions in fact are, but the distinction helps to organize the large number of questions that may be asked about the morality of war.

Given the importance of war, a number of questions about peace will also attract our attention, though it will be hard to devote much attention to them in this reader. The first chapter, "Notes on War and Peace," provides an introduction to traditional concerns with and questions about war. In particular, it contrasts different traditions or schools of thought—pacifist, just war, and "realist."

One particular question that is raised by some of the authors is of general interest, namely whether there are some acts of killing—for instance, intentionally killing the innocent—that are such that they are *never* permissible, no matter what the consequences. Some think that the prohibition on intentionally killing the innocent is *absolute* or *indefeasible*, that is, not to be done whatever the consequences. Others think, especially in wartime, that we may sometimes kill the innocent.

19. Notes on War and Peace

CHRISTOPHER W. MORRIS

Christopher W. Morris (1949–) is professor of philosophy at the University of Maryland, College Park. He writes about a number of topics in moral and political philosophy, practical ethics, and practical rationality. He is the author of *An Essay on the Modern State* (1998) and the editor, with R. G. Frey, of *Violence, Terrorism, and Justice* (1991).

In these notes, Morris considers war and peace and the ethical controversies that they engender. He offers an overview of "just war" theory, the account of the moral norms that are widely thought to govern war, both its conduct and its justification. This tradition has been remarkably influential. It has been countered by the "realist" tradition, which Morris also characterizes. This tradition is skeptical about moral conduct in international affairs. At the other end of the continuum of positions is pacifism. There are many kinds of pacifists, some believing that all wars and all violence are wrong, others believing that most wars are wrong. These notes attempt to frame some of the major theoretical controversies about war.

War—large-scale violent conflict between groups, countries, or states—is a constant of human life. It is not surprising, therefore, that war and peace have been the object of human reflection for millennia. Given the suffering and miseries caused by war, it raises innumerable moral questions, and reflection on these is also ancient. At different times, often following extraordinary conflicts, there have been major efforts at establishing "perpetual peace," and some of these merit philosophical attention.

1. War and Peace

Jean-Jacques Rousseau's well-known characterization of war is often a starting point for analysis: "War is not a relation between men, but a relation between states . . ." (*Social Contract*, I, iv). But there have been wars long before there were states. Clausewitz's famous "definition"—"an act of force/violence [*die Gewalt*] to compel our enemy to do our will" (*On War*, 1, 2)—is better but still incomplete. Some acts of

force or violence do not constitute war. But "definitions" are not always helpful or useful. Our general characterization of war as large-scale violent conflict between groups, countries, or states suffices to focus our attention on the relevant questions. The characterization of peace is more problematic, reflecting perhaps the elusive nature of the phenomenon. Negatively, peace is the absence of war. Negative characterizations are commonplace (see Hobbes, *Leviathan*, xiii). The question is whether more can be said.

There are many different sorts of wars: limited and total wars, insurgencies, guerrilla wars, cold wars, nuclear wars, and so on. And these distinctions raise a number of questions (Can wars be limited? Is the notion of a nuclear war coherent?). Some of these questions are about the causes of war. Two distinct modern traditions regard war as a consequence of conflict between states. One is exemplified by Clausewitz's celebrated claim that war is "a continuation of political intercourse, carried on with

By permission of the author.

other means" (*On War*, 1, 24). Hegel emphasized the importance of war to "the ethical health of peoples" (*Elements of the Philosophy of Right*, paragraph 324). The other tradition is that of modern pacifism, which often claims that the control, if not the abolition, of states will bring about peace. But some proponents of these modern views tie in war with features or flaws of human nature and thus connect with older views about the sources of war. Heraclitus is believed to have thought that "war [ὁ πόλεμος] is the father and king of all" and that "all things happen by strife and necessity." Nietzsche, in his mature works, may be read as glorifying war or at least understanding it as something natural to humans (*Thus Spake Zarathustra*). Hobbes also understood conflict to be endemic to the human situation, but he had no wish to praise or glorify war. Even though for him there need be no injustice in war, there was little to be desired in large-scale conflict. Hobbes, of course, was especially concerned with the religious origins of many wars, and his justification of states is linked to their role in alleviating this, as well as other, sources of conflict and disorder. In the Christian tradition, there is a tendency to link war not so much with religious disagreement, as with the imperfect and fallen nature of humans. Many pacifists, Christian and other, have linked the abolition of war with the transformation of human nature. By contrast, the Marxist tradition tends to understand modern war as connected to forms of economic and political organization. With the abolition of class exploitation, war should cease (*Manifesto of the Communist Party*). But this change in human society may bring about a transformation of human nature, at least on some readings.

The word "peace" derives from the Latin *pax* and *pais*. Our notions of peace are related but different from certain classical notions of *pax*. The *pax romana* was an order imposed by conquest, imposing the *jus gentium* on subjects (but non-citizens) of Rome. This and modern counterparts (e.g., the *pax britannica*) may suggest that peace is order imposed by the powerful. By contrast, peace has often been understood in modern times as a set of relations between more or less equal sovereign states. And many modern proposals for "perpetual peace" have reflected this view. Some of these were motivated by

distinctly European or Christian concerns (e.g., unity against the Turks). Others were designed to bring about world peace. One of the first was proposed by Pierre Dubois (*De Recuperatione Terre Sancte*, 1305–1307), involving the unification of Europe. The Duke of Sully, minister to Henri IV, proposed a European federation ("*Grand dessein*," 1620–1635). Emeric Crucé envisaged some form of international representative government (*The New Cyneas*, 1623). Better known is the *Project to Make Peace in Europe Perpetual* (1713) of the abbot of Saint-Pierre, elaborating the Duke of Sully's plan. The abbot proposed a confederation of European states with a perpetual congress. Rousseau's application of the abbot plan in his *Project for a Perpetual Peace* (1761) expressed scepticism about its success in the absence of radical changes.

The lack of attention to institutional and political means to bringing about peace was a concern of Kant in his famous *Perpetual Peace: A Philosophical Sketch* (1795). He claimed that peace was in fact guaranteed by "nature" or fate, or rather various features of the development of the world. Part of his essay is written as a statement of various articles for a treaty. The most interesting and fruitful idea is that expressed in the first Article: "The civil constitution of every state shall be republican." This idea has gained power in the two centuries since Kant's essay, in large part due to the notable fact that there have been no wars between democracies in this time. While twentieth century alliances for peace (the League of Nations, the United Nations) are not always "federation of free states" as Kant required, the idea that serious prospects for universal peace require democratic governance is now very widely accepted.

The nineteenth- and twentieth-century peace movement is too diverse and complex to be adequately covered here. Nineteenth-century liberalism introduced the idea that peace between states may result from increasing commercial relations and interdependence, another idea with great currency today. This liberalism was consistent with the internationalism of many proponents of peace in both centuries. Also of some philosophical interest are some of the forms of pacifism that developed in these times (see later discussion). Some of these challenge the common view that war is endemic to the human condition or reflects a failing in human nature. While not a pacifist, Erasmus already had challenged these claims (*Anti-polemus, or the Plea of Reason, Religion and Humanity against War*, 1510). One of the philosophical interests of pacifism is the possibility of a non-negative characterization of peace. In Augustine we find such a view of peace: "The peace among human beings is ordered concord . . . The peace of all things is the tranquility of order" (*City of God*, XIX, 13). In Thoreau, Tolstoy, and Gandhi we also find non-negative conceptions of peace. A wider, richer conception is reflected, for instance, as well in the Hebrew word *shalom*.

2. Just War Theory

One of the oldest bodies of moral reflection on war is *just war theory*, and contemporary discussions usually start with the principles and distinctions of this tradition. Just war theory is, in certain respects, a moderate position; it holds some wars to be justified, others not. The just war tradition consequently has two main adversaries. The first is *pacifism*, a position that no war is justified or that all wars are wrong. There are many different versions of pacifism; none have developed the sophisticated body of theory characteristic of the just war tradition. The other main adversary one might logically expect to just war theory would be the view that *all* wars are justified. But such a position would be implausible at the very outset. Rather, the second adversary is a tradition called "realism" that denies the possibility of moral evaluation or justification in certain situations—for instance, situations of extreme conflict. "Realists" thus do not affirm that all wars are just; rather, they say that none are *un*just. Moral evaluations have there no place. Realism, like pacifism, comes in several different versions, none particularly well-worked out theoretically. These three positions represent the main theoretical alternatives on the central moral questions of war and peace.

The just war tradition is old, with roots in ancient Hebraic, Greek, and Roman conventions and reflections on war. Early Christian thinkers, such as Ambrose and Augustine, developed some of these ideas, introducing Christian elements.

Thomas Aquinas, Vitoria, Suarez, and Grotius are principally responsible for refining and formalizing the body of ideas and principles that make up what is now commonly referred to as "just war theory." (See Ambrose, *Duties of the Clergy*; Augustine, *City of God*; Thomas Aquinas, *Summa Theologica*, II-II, Q. 40; Vitoria, *De Indis*, and *De Jure Belli*; Suarez, *The Three Theological Virtues*, XIII; Grotius, *De Jure Belli ac Pacis*.) There is some disagreement about the content of the theory and the precise formulation of its principles. But we can ignore many of the controversies and focus on the core ideas and distinctions.

Classical just war theory has two parts, each corresponding to a different set of questions we might pose about war. We might inquire as to what wars, if any, are just. This and related questions are answered by the theory of "justice of war," *jus ad bellum*. We might also inquire about how wars may be fought. For answers to such questions we turn to the theory of "justice in war," *jus in bello*. The first part of just war theory consists of a number of conditions which must be satisfied if a war is to be just, that is, if a country or state is to be justified in waging it. Roughly, a war must be fought for the right reasons, with the right means, if it is to be just. Most contemporary versions of *jus ad bellum* agree on something like the following conditions. A war is just if (1) it is declared by a *competent authority*, fought (2) for a *just cause*, (3) with a *just intention*, (4) using means that are *proportionate* to the ends, (5) with a *reasonable expectation of success*, and (6) as a last *resort*.

The main principles of *jus in bello* are *proportionality* (condition 4 in the previous paragraph) and *discrimination*, a prohibition of direct attacks on non-combatants. (Some versions add a condition requiring the use of *minimal force*: only that force which is needed to achieve one's just military objectives is permissible.) As with *jus ad bellum*, the disagreements amongst partisans are in the details.

There is some controversy as to how to understand these conditions and how to apply them, especially in circumstances of imperfect information. For instance, while self-defense is regarded as a paradigmatic just cause, there is less agreement about other candidates—e.g., assistance to others, responses to threats, rescue of victims of massacres, assistance to (just) secessionist movements. Similarly, the conditions of *jus in bello* have been the subject of considerable debate. The discrimination principle prohibits direct attacks on noncombatants and is related to the well-known "doctrine of double effect" (see later in this selection). It prohibits direct (or intentional) attacks on noncombatants. Stated in this manner, the principle presupposes a distinction between combatants and noncombatants. While we may be able to distinguish easily enough between most soldiers and most civilians, there will be problem cases (e.g., supply troops, political leaders). Modern guerrilla wars employ tactics designed to push this distinction to the limit.

The classical discrimination principle has its origins in a natural law concern with the innocent. We may think of the discrimination requirement as an instantiation of the natural law prohibition on intentionally harming the innocent. Noncombatants are not to be targeted, as they are innocent. Reflection on the fact that most soldiers, especially those conscripted to fight, may be equally innocent may be thought to undermine this strategy of basing discrimination on a prior, more fundamental moral concern. However, the term "innocence" is ambiguous here, and one needs to distinguish two meanings it may have in these contexts. The usual one is the moral/juridical sense of non-culpability, used to designate some individual who is not guilty of moral or legal wrongdoing. By contrast, in discussing what are called "innocent threats"—for instance, an approaching infant who unwittingly is booby trapped with explosives—it is common to distinguish a "technical" or "causal" sense of "innocence." Someone lacks innocence in this second sense insofar as they threaten or are causally harmful, whatever their culpability (e.g., a fetus whose continued growth threatens the life of the woman). If the classical prohibition on harming the innocent is understood, in these contexts, to rule out harming the causally innocent, then it can underpin the different status accorded by just war theory to combatants and noncombatants. The latter, at least when not causally harmful, are protected; combatants, at least while in uniform and carrying their weapons, are threatening and may be harmed.

It is no part, however, of *jus in bello* to rule out all harm to noncombatants. It may be expected that, in most wars, civilians and other innocents (in the causal sense, as well as the moral/juridical sense) will be hurt and even killed. In keeping with the natural law theory from which it emerges, the concern of just war theory is primarily with *intended* harm. Unintended harms are not necessarily prohibited by the discrimination principle, originally stated in terms of a prohibition on *direct* attacks on noncombatants or the (causally) innocent. Intended deaths of the innocent are ruled out; merely foreseen deaths are not. Reference is made, at least implicitly, to the well-known *doctrine of double effect*. For any act with two effects, one good (e.g., destroying an enemy munitions factory), one bad (e.g., killing innocent civilians), the act is not one of *direct* killing and thus prohibited if the following conditions are satisfied: (1) the act, in itself, is not morally impermissible, (2) the bad effect of the act is not the *means* to the good effect, (3) the bad effect is not intended, and (4) the bad effect does not outweigh the good effect (proportionality). Bombing a munitions factory, thus, would not be prohibited, even if one foresaw the deaths of some noncombatants, provided the numbers harmed were not disproportionate to the good effect and the harm was neither intended nor a means to the end. (See the discussion later in section 4.)

3. Realism

One of the main adversaries of just war theory is the "realist" tradition. This tradition is largely modern, but its ancestry is ancient, some finding the roots of this sort of realism in Thucydides and Machiavelli. (See especially the "Melian dialogue" of *The Peloponnesian War*. For Machiavelli, see especially *The Prince*.) We characterized it earlier as a denial of the possibility of moral evaluation or justification in certain situations, e.g., of war. (Realism in this sense, it is important to understand, bears *no* relation to other philosophical realism; in fact, it is the antithesis of "moral realism.") On this understanding, realists do not claim that all wars are just; rather, they say that none are *un*just. Moral evaluations have there no place. As Hobbes argued, "To this war of every man against every man, this also is consequent: that nothing can be unjust. The notions of right and wrong, justice and injustice have there no place. Where there is no common power, there is no law; where no law, no injustice. Force and fraud are in war the two cardinal virtues" (*Leviathan*, xiii).

This is, however, one amongst many interpretations. The realist tradition, while priding itself on being "realistic" about the scope and force of moral evaluation, is neither uniform nor clear in its statements of positions. (See Morgenthau, *Politics amongst Nations*.) Some realists seem to be moral sceptics, denying the possibility of moral judgment. Others seem merely to espouse some sort of moral relativism, denying the possibility of moral judgments across cultures or societies (or, more exactly, states). Some members of this tradition are statists; they may accord to states permission to pursue their interests by whatever means they please, or they may even claim that a state's pursuit of its interests is its supreme or unique moral end. One might find a basis for this realism in Hegel's account of the state: "The state is the actuality of the ethical Idea . . . [I]f no agreement can be reached between particular wills, conflicts between states can be settled only by war" (*Elements of the Philosophy of Right*, paragraphs 257, 334). The view that states are the ultimate sources of right is also associated with the continental traditions of realpolitik and of *raison d'État*. And some realists seem to hold a number of different positions, not all compatible. The problem is, in part, that realism has not been carefully developed by philosophers and jurists over a long period; rather, it is a position associated very much with political leaders and theorists of diplomacy. It would not be an exaggeration, however, to say that the tradition is dominant amongst policy leaders and most heads of state.

Our initial interpretation has realists denying the meaningfulness or applicability of moral judgments in certain contexts such as war. As such realism is a philosophically interesting challenge to just war theory as well as to any alternative moral assessment of war. Why might we think of war as something beyond good and evil, as it were? There is an old tradition, exemplified by Hobbes and Hume, which holds that justice does not bind in situations of complete conflict. The idea here is that expressed (badly) in the old saying, "all's fair in love and war" (a better statement would be: "nothing is unfair in love and war"). In situations of complete conflict, where one party's gain is

always another's loss—what are called "zero-sum games" in game theory—it may be thought that people could not be motivated or have reason to respect moral constraints on the pursuit of their ends. Hobbes, Hume, and others have thought that the virtue of justice presupposes the possibility of mutually beneficial behavior; in the absence of this, justice does not bind. As Hume argues in the *Enquiry Concerning the Principles of Morals* (1751), when in "the society of ruffians, remote from the protection of laws and government," or during the "rage and violence of public war," the conventions of justice are suspended: "The laws of war, which then succeed to those of equity and justice, are rules calculated for the *advantage* and *utility* of that particular state, in which men are now placed. And were a civilized nation engaged with barbarians, who observed no rules even of war, the former must also suspend their observance of them, where they no longer serve to any purpose; and must render every action or rencounter as bloody and pernicious as possible to the first aggressors."

It is hard, however, to see how such a view could support the realist contention that war cannot be judged morally. For even twentieth-century "total wars" do not constitute situations of *complete* conflict of interests. In the Second World War, for instance, all parties had an interest in not allowing the use of gas warfare, in refraining from mistreating prisoners, and the like.

Sometimes realists invoke the famous saying "war is hell" (attributed to the U.S. civil war general Sherman), suggesting that the horrors of war justify or excuse almost any act necessary to vanquish the enemy. But this is to invoke a *moral* position, perhaps some sort of *consequentialism*, according to which certain ends may justify (or excuse) certain means. So this sort of justification is not available to our sort of realist.

The doctrine of *military necessity*, the view that actions "indispensable" to subduing the adversary quickly are permissible, should also not be confused with realism. For the former presupposes that acts not required for military objectives are morally prohibited; realism, as we have been understanding the tradition, *morally* prohibits nothing.

It is also important to note that realism cannot be based on a general scepticism about the *normative*, as opposed to moral scepticism. Realists certainly do not challenge the veracity of judgments, e.g., concerning *rational* action or those regarding *appropriate* or *efficient* military action. It is not clear what the ground of this general sort of scepticism could be.

The realist tradition in this century is partly a reaction to what was thought to be excessive optimism or "idealism" on the part of certain world leaders (e.g., President Wilson), and this may help in understanding the tradition. A more "realistic" assessment of the prospects for change and of the "real" interests of the relevant actors, it was thought, would reduce tensions and lessen the chances of war. But partisans of just war theory or defenders of international morality need not be naive or uninformed. Being "realistic" in this sense is something available to all, just war theorists and sceptics alike. It is not clear what relevance the accusation of excessive "idealism" has to the question of the justice of war.

Realism, as we have characterized it, denies the two parts of just war theory: there can be no moral assessment of the ends of war and there are no moral constraints on the means with which wars are fought. Many of the arguments realists have used to defend these points are weak, and different questions are often confused in the literature. Nevertheless, the general position is widely influential in policy circles, and it represents an interesting challenge to just war theory and to other attempts to assess war morally.

4. Pacifism

Pacifism is, like realism, a diverse tradition or movement. There are many different sorts of pacifists. Few, however, have been disposed to the development of a systematic theory of pacifism. In the context of a discussion of the morality of war, we may think of pacifism as the view that all wars are unjust. For some this may be because political authorities (especially modern states) are always illegitimate, and their acts consequently are unjust. For others it may be simply because the conditions that could justify war are never met in practice, and possibly never could be. The former is a type of anarchism, while the latter could be an interpretation of the implications of just war theory. Indeed, some

pacifists are anarchists (e.g., Tolstoy), and the early roots of just war theory are responses to Christian opposition to warfare (cf. the injunction to turn the other cheek in *Matthew*).

It may be more useful in the context of our discussion of just wars to consider pacifism as an opposition to deliberate, organized violence. Pacifists thus considered oppose wars and usually recommend non-violent means of resisting evil and fighting for justice. One needs at the outset to distinguish between pacifism or a commitment to non-violence as a (mere) tactic and as a matter of principle. In many occasions it may be most efficacious to adopt non-violent tactics, even if one is not in any way committed to pacifism. Our concern will be with principled pacifism. (See Thoreau, "Resistance to Civil Government," 1849; Tolstoy, "Patriotism," 1896.)

Pacifists have been the subject of ridicule (e.g., lack of courage). They have been frequently criticized for having inconsistent views (e.g., opposing war but not all uses of force). So it is important to characterize the position with some care. Pacifist opposition to war should be understood, as we said, as opposition to deliberate organized violence. Violence can be a species of *force*, getting another to do one's will by restricting their options in certain ways. In particular, violence is a form of *coercion*, a use of force (or threatened) force which operates through the victim's own agency. But not all coercion is violent; a boycott or the threatened withdrawal of one's affections may be coercive, without involving any violence. *Violence* involves the "violation" of another, the infliction of some sort of harm or injury on another. To strike a person (or animal) is to use violence against it; whereas to restrain someone physically, without injury, is non-violent coercion. It is hard to characterize these notions very precisely, and there is considerable controversy about these matters. For our purposes it is important to understand that a commitment to non-violence need not require restraint from the use of (non-violent) force or coercion. Some pacifists may reject all forms of force, but many reject *only* violence, and sometimes only deliberate, organized violence.

Opposition to violence, if principled, has to be based on the harm caused (or threatened). While noting the harm done to victims, pacifists have often stressed the harm to the actor. On this view to injure another is (also) to harm oneself. This sort of position is familiar to philosophers familiar with Socrates' famous view that one should not bestow evil on another. There are a number of ways of attempting to defend a position such as this. (Gandhi argued that "The way to peace is the way to truth . . . A truthful man cannot long remain violent" ["War or Peace," 1926].) But it is important to note its vulnerability to the sort of critical concern that is the focus of contemporary debate: in some situations one can often reduce the total amount of harm by acting so as to harm others. What if one can reduce the amount of violence by acting violently oneself? The harmfulness of violence is not enough to shore up this view. In addition proponents need to establish that it is important that violence should not be done by one's hands. The questions here join some of those raised by contemporary quarrels about the comparative merits of "consequentialism" and "deontology."

Philosophers for the most part have not been moved by the considerations and arguments made on behalf of principled pacifism, and there are few moral philosophers who are pacifists. But it is hard not to be impressed with the harms and evils of war so well catalogued by pacifists. Wars cause extraordinary harm and suffering, very often to innocent parties; they typically further the growth of state power (cf. Hegel's admiration of war), and they threaten civil liberty; wars and the violence which they characteristically involve often have a corrupting effect on societies; and, as Augustine argued, wars may reflect and reinforce love of violence and cruelty and lust for power. Recent feminist criticisms of the "manly" aspects of war echo some of these worries.

5. Contemporary Controversies

There are a number of kinds of war and conflict, characteristic of our century, that raise interesting and difficult questions. We shall mention a few that raise challenges to traditional immunities accorded noncombatants: guerrilla warfare, terrorism, sieges and other forms of blockade, bombings of urban centers, nuclear and deterrence. We shall also briefly discuss genocide and "ethnic cleansing."

First, consider what is now called "guerrilla warfare," the irregular or "non-conventional" sort of military conflict that is characteristic of many wars of our times. Guerrilla wars are fought by decentralized military units the members of which are supposed to blend in with "the people" in whose name they fight. It is hard, therefore, for their adversaries to distinguish clearly the fighters from the civilian populations. The effect of this is often to provoke the former into attacking noncombatants, either by mistake or out of frustration. Ideologically, it has been argued that these "people's wars" have other virtues as well, and there has been considerable debate in this century, especially amongst Marxists and proponents of "national liberation," about the nature of such warfare (cf., Mao, Ché Guevara, Régis Debray). Our interests lie with the intentional blurring of the traditional distinctions between combatant and noncombatant. The "people's armies" of the late eighteenth century (e.g., in the American Revolution) employed unorthodox military tactics, but they did not challenge the classical distinctions in the way characteristic of guerrilla warfare today.

Terrorism is another practice, familiar in our times, that challenges the traditional distinctions in similar ways. The characterization of the notion of terrorism is a matter of considerable controversy, given the moral and political questions that the practice raises. For our purposes let us think of terrorism as the use of violence against a variety of targets, chosen with some degree of randomness, for the purpose of creating terror amongst a population and bringing about certain political ends (e.g., overthrowing a regime, expelling "foreign" rulers, changing the political order). Terrorism, thus understood, need not be a practice restricted to individuals and to the weak; it can be an instrument of state rule. While some terrorists insist that "there are no innocents," the effectiveness of terrorism depends to some extent on targeting noncombatants. Were military units the only target, the civilian population would not be "terrorized," and the resulting pressures and destabling effects would be lessened. It is especially this feature of terrorism, its intentional targeting of noncombatants, that has it challenge the traditional moral distinctions.

Sieges and blockades are old tactics. In olden times cities would be besieged until they fell. Traditionally, the attackers were often thought to be obligated to allow certain classes of individuals to leave the city at different stages of the siege (e.g., women and children, the elderly). Modern sieges are in many ways similar, albeit sometimes more ruthless (e.g., Leningrad). But it should be noted that, in the absence of some special treatment of noncombatants, sieges, like blockades, target noncombatants along with every one else. Indeed, the effectiveness of sieges and blockades often depends on the suffering of noncombatants to pressure the leaders to capitulate. The deprivations imposed on the bulk of the population are one of the central means through which the objectives of the siege or blockade are achieved (e.g., the blockade of Germany in the First World War). Trade embargoes today work similarly (e.g., Cuba, Iraq).

Guerrilla warfare and, more obviously, terrorism and sieges and blockades are instruments of war that challenge the traditional distinctions between combatant and noncombatant. It is also useful to consider them in terms of the distinctions of the traditional doctrine of double effect. To target an anonymous crowd of civilians in a public space or to cause severe deprivations in a large civilian population, for the purpose of bringing about certain political ends, *is* to intend the bad effects of one's act (i.e., harming the noncombatants) and to intend them as means to one's ends. The matter of proportionality, whether the bad effects are outweighed by the good effects, is not one about which one can pronounce a priori. But it seems clear that targeting civilians with the end of putting pressure on political leaders or of destabilizing a regime is both to intend the harm thus caused and to have it as a means to one's end. Proponents of these instruments of war seem committed to a rejection of the values or principles that make up the classical doctrine of double effect. Most likely, they are committed to some species of moral consequentialism: just ends justify the means. (It is, of course, possible that few of these tactics can be justified by reasonable forms of consequentialism.)

Consider now the practice, developed during the Second World War, of bombing civilian centers of population. Initially, the practice of "strategic bombing" (as it was called) was to break the will of the civilian populations supporting an enemy regime. The doctrine was developed in the closing year of the First World War and put into practice two decades later (e.g., Guernica). In ways similar to the practices mentioned previously (e.g., terrorism), the bombing of civilian centers appears to raise the same moral questions about the status of noncombatants. Indeed, during the Second World War many partisans of the traditional views or of the doctrine of double effect were troubled by these new bombing practices; many of these sceptics included military leaders. Often it is Hiroshima and Nagasaki that are singled out for attention. But the bombings of the German and Japanese cities generally raise these questions, and the casualties, e.g., of the bombings of Tokyo exceeded those of the atomic bombings. The main question is when, if ever, may one use weapons of mass destruction on civilian populations? The traditional principles of just war theory, especially the doctrine of double effect, would appear to rule out virtually all of the bombings in question. The death and mutilation of civilians could not plausibly be construed as an unintended side-effect of targeting military centers, as these civilians were explicitly targeted and the military rationale had to do with undermining support for the war. (The destruction of Dresden appears to be a clear exception, given the late date of the bombing. It should also be mentioned that great improvements were made in precision bombing during the course of the war, and that these affect the morality of the acts in question.)

President Truman's defense of the atomic bombings is instructive. He claimed in defense of his decision that the Japanese were the aggressors in the war against the U.S., that they disregarded the accepted conventional rules of war, that the bombings saved hundreds of thousands of American lives that would have been lost in an invasion of Japan, and that several million Japanese lives, both military and civilian, were also saved (at the cost of fewer than two hundred thousand immediate deaths from the atomic bombings). The claims, whether or not true, are interesting. In terms of the classical distinction of just war theory, the argument Truman gave was that the adversary was fighting an unjust war (*jus ad bellum*), using unjust means (*jus in bello*), and that the expected consequences in terms of lives saved favored the bombings over invasion. The individual claims, especially that regarding expected casualties, are the subject of much controversy today. It is the nature of the claims that concern us here. Truman's defense, thus stated, uses classical distinctions but challenges the classical doctrines. In the just war tradition, it is usually thought that the rules governing the conduct of war (*jus in bello*) obligate independently of the considerations establishing the justice of the war (*jus ad bellum*). Further, the former are usually thought to bind even against adversaries that do not respect them; they are not conditional in this way. Additionally, and most importantly, noncombatants are simply not legitimate targets of war, irrespective of the behavior of political leaders.

The sort of justification attempted by Truman suggests an alternative position which would bring in considerations of total suffering. Consequentialist moral theories, of course, propose to do just this. Another possibility is that defended by Michael Walzer, which is to suggest that certain situations of "supreme emergency," when the survival of one's society (or civilization) is at stake, then the normal rules of warfare may be suspended (see selection 25 in this volume). It is possible that Britain faced such a situation in the early years of the Second World War when its survival was at stake, and that its leaders might have had a justification for attacking German cities that would not otherwise been available.

In addition to raising all of these questions about targeting civilians and using instruments of mass destruction, the use of nuclear weapons, especially the doctrine of nuclear deterrence, is obviously controversial. Nuclear weapons may be used (i.e., launched and detonated) or their use may be threatened. Nuclear deterrence is the policy of attempting to dissuade a potential adversary from attacking by threatening with nuclear retaliation in the event of an attack. "Basic deterrence" is the policy of threatening nuclear retaliation to nuclear attack; "extended deterrence" threatens nuclear retaliation to any attack, nuclear or "conventional." NATO policy was extended in this sense: nuclear retaliation

was threatened in response to any attack by Soviet or Warsaw Pact forces on NATO allies. As a species of deterrence, this policy raises some of the same questions as deterrence accounts of punishment. (It is, of course, possible to think of nuclear retaliation as a form of *retribution*, as with punishment.) But the important difference is that the targets are not likely to be culpable of any wrong.

A retaliatory nuclear strike seems morally questionable if civilian centers of population are targeted. If military targets alone are struck, and these are distant from cities (as it is unlikely), then they may be justifiable. Suppose that the form of retaliation contemplated is unjust. May one *threaten* to do what is unjust? Suppose also that the benefits of nuclear deterrence are considerable: namely, averting war between superpowers. (Many argue that nuclear deterrence also prevented smaller conflicts from developing into war during the Cold War.) If the benefits of threatening to do what would be wrong are considerable, may one do so? Affirmative answers to this question have been thought to be paradoxical by some philosophers (e.g., Kavka). Nuclear deterrence is the domain of many apparent paradoxes of rationality: it may be rational to threaten to do what it would not be rational to do (e.g., retaliate after a nuclear strike). There may be moral paradoxes as well. To threaten to do something requires the conditional *intention* to do it; "threatening," without intention—insincere threatening—is bluffing. (Many, included some important political leaders, have argued that the deterrent policies of many states, especially during the time of the policy of threatened massive retaliation known as "mutual assured destruction," or MAD, were essentially bluffs.) May one then intend to do something that it would be wrong to do? (There is also the question of whether a moral person is *capable* of so intending, without corrupting himself or herself.)

Partisans of classical just war theory have been very uncomfortable with nuclear deterrence given their commitment to the wrongness of targeting civilians and to the importance of intention in the moral assessment of action and character. They usually accept what is now called the "wrongful intentions principle": it would be wrong to intend to do that which it would be wrong to do. Some moralists have tried to justify intending to do wrong and thereby the policy of nuclear deterrence. But virtually none claim to find a justification for carrying out the threatened retaliation (except for limited strikes against military targets). Neo-Hobbesians may argue that in the event of a massive attack by an adversary, one would be plunged into "a state of nature," circumstances in which justice no longer binds; in this situation nuclear retaliation would not be unjust. They could thus argue that it is morally permissible to threaten to do what would not be wrong to do under the circumstances contemplated. This is a possible position, one which has some affinities with the realist tradition, but it is not a position that many moral philosophers find plausible. Some have defended "existential deterrence," the policy of possessing nuclear weapons but refraining from intending to use them. But it is unclear that such a policy bears any relation to the practices of nuclear states. On the matter of nuclear deterrence, the worlds of heads of state and policy leaders and of moral theorists are rather far apart.

The twentieth century has witnessed several of the most extraordinary genocides. In one sense, the Armenian genocide or the Holocaust pose no ethical *problem* or raise no special moral question. On virtually all accounts, they are instances of extraordinary injustice and their perpetrators evil. There is relatively little controversy about this. The only theoretical problem they may pose is to the Hobbesian or to the realist who may want to claim that, in such situations, "The notions of right and wrong, justice and injustice have there no place." Such a theorist cannot condemn such atrocities as wrong or unjust (or just). To some philosophers this implication is the *reductio ad absurdum* of these positions.

These atrocities of the last century, even if they raise no special moral problem, do clearly require us to ask disturbing questions about the propensity of humans to do evil. And they must shatter our confidence in the moral progress of humanity. The "ethnic cleansing" following the demise of the Yugoslavian federal state makes inquiries into these matters of the utmost urgency.

Note

The text of these notes borrows from the entry on "War and Peace" written for the *Dictionnaire d'éthique et de philosophie morale*, edited by Monique Canto-Sperber (Paris: Presses universitaires de France, 1996; 4th ed. 2004). References to classical works, which exist in many editions, are given parenthetically.

QUESTIONS

1. How do realists and defenders of just war theory disagree?
2. How do pacifists and defenders of just war theory disagree?
3. Is intentionally killing the innocent always impermissible in times of war? What answers do just war theorists have to this question?

20. War of Every One against Every One

THOMAS HOBBES

For a description of the author, see chapter 5.

In this short excerpt from the first part of the *Leviathan*, Hobbes describes the "state of nature," the condition that people find themselves in when there is no state or government. He argues that this condition is a "state of war," a notion that he characterizes in the first paragraph. He tells us that this natural condition is about as bad as it can be; the famous second paragraph, widely cited, is Hobbes's description of the human condition in the absence of a state.

Some say that there never was such a state of nature, but Hobbes denies this claim, noting that "Kings and persons of Soveraigne authority" are in such a condition with each other. Hobbes is thus a "realist" about international relations. His last paragraph draws a controversial conclusion: "To this Warre of every man against every man . . . nothing can be Unjust. The notions of Right and Wrong, Justice and Injustice have there no place." No developed argument is offered in this short excerpt, but it is important to have a clear statement of this radical realist position.

Hereby it is manifest, that during the time men live without a common Power to keep them all in awe, they are in that condition which is called Warre; and such a warre, as is of every man, against every man. For Warre, consisteth not in Battell onely, or the act of fighting; but in a tract of time, wherein the Will to contend by Battell is sufficiently known: and therefore the notion of *Time*, is to be considered in the nature of Warre; as it is in the nature of Weather. For as the nature of Foule weather, lyeth not in a showre or two of rain; but in an inclination thereto of many dayes together; So the nature of War, consisteth not in actuall fighting; but in the known disposition thereto, during all the time there is no assurance to the contrary. All other time is Peace.

Whatsoever therefore is consequent to a time of Warre, where every man is Enemy to every man; the same is consequent to the time, wherein men live without other security, than what their own strength, and their own invention shall furnish them withall. In such condition, there is no place for Industry; because the fruit thereof is uncertain: and consequently no Culture of the Earth; no Navigation, nor use of the commodities that may be imported by Sea; no commodious Building; no Instruments of moving, and removing such things as require much force; no Knowledge of the face of the Earth; no account of Time; no Arts; no Letters; no Society; and which is worst of all, continuall feare, and danger of violent death; And the life of man, solitary, poore, nasty, brutish, and short.

It may seem strange to some man, that has not well weighed these things; that Nature should thus dissociate, and render men apt to invade, and destroy one another: and he may therefore, not trusting to this Inference, made from the Passions, desire perhaps

From Thomas Hobbes, *Leviathan* (1649)

to have the same confirmed by Experience. Let him therefore consider with himselfe, when taking a journey, he armes himselfe, and seeks to go well accompanied; when going to sleep, he locks his dores; when even in his house he locks his chests; and this when he knowes there bee Lawes, and publike Officers, armed, to revenge all injuries shall bee done him; what opinion he has of his fellow subjects, when he rides armed; of his fellow Citizens, when he locks his dores; and of his children, and servants, when he locks his chests. Does he not there as much accuse mankind by his actions, as I do by my words? But neither of us accuse mans nature in it. The Desires, and other Passions of man, are in themselves no Sin. No more are the Actions, that proceed from those Passions, till they know a Law that forbids them: which till Lawes be made they cannot know: nor can any Law be made, till they have agreed upon the Person that shall make it.

It may peradventure be thought, there was never such a time, nor condition of warre as this; and I believe it was never generally so, over all the world: but there are many places, where they live so now. For the savage people in many places of *America*, except the government of small Families, the concord whereof dependeth on naturall lust, have no government at all; and live at this day in that brutish manner, as I said before. Howsoever, it may be perceived what manner of life there would be, where there were no common Power to feare; by the manner of life, which men that have formerly lived under a peacefull government, use to degenerate into, in a civill Warre.

But though there had never been any time, wherein particular men were in a condition of warre one against another; yet in all times, Kings, and Persons of Soveraigne authority, because of their Independency, are in continuall jealousies, and in the state and posture of Gladiators; having their weapons pointing, and their eyes fixed on one another; that is, their Forts, Garrisons, and Guns upon the Frontiers of their Kingdomes; and continuall Spyes upon their neighbours; which is a posture of War. But because they uphold thereby, the Industry of their Subjects; there does not follow from it, that misery, which accompanies the Liberty of particular men.

To this warre of every man against every man, this also is consequent; that nothing can be Unjust. The notions of Right and Wrong, Justice and Injustice have there no place. Where there is no common Power, there is no Law: where no Law, no Injustice. Force, and Fraud, are in warre the two Cardinall vertues. Justice, and Injustice are none of the Faculties neither of the Body, nor Mind. If they were, they might be in a man that were alone in the world, as well as his Senses, and Passions. They are Qualities, that relate to men in Society, not in Solitude. It is consequent also to the same condition, that there be no Propriety, no Dominion, no *Mine* and *Thine* distinct; but onely that to be every mans, that he can get; and for so long, as he can keep it. And thus much for the ill condition, which man by meer Nature is actually placed in; though with a possibility to come out of it, consisting partly in the Passions, partly in his Reason.

QUESTIONS

1. Hobbes thought it very important to determine the correct definition of terms. What is his definition of war?
2. Why does he think that some people (e.g., kings and sovereigns) are in a state or condition of war with one another?
3. What does he mean by "the notions of Right and Wrong, Justice and Injustice have there no place"? Do you think that might be true?

21. Of War

THOMAS AQUINAS

For a description of the author and a note on the text, see chapter 2.

The following excerpt is one of the first major statements of just war theory, the influential account of the rules governing war. The objections and Aquinas's answers are included as it is important to understand that Aquinas, as well as his predecessor St. Augustine (354–430), were arguing against influential Christian pacifists who widely believed that "it is always sinful to wage war." Today just war theorists defend themselves mainly against realists.

Aquinas lays out three conditions that must be met for a war to be just (in the paragraph starting, "I answer that . . . "). These conditions remain at the center of just war theory today.

Q40. Of War

Art. 1 Whether It Is Always Sinful to Wage War?

Objection 1: It would seem that it is always sinful to wage war. Because punishment is not inflicted except for sin. Now those who wage war are threatened by Our Lord with punishment, according to Mat. 26:52: "All that take the sword shall perish with the sword." Therefore all wars are unlawful.

Objection 2: Further, whatever is contrary to a Divine precept is a sin. But war is contrary to a Divine precept, for it is written (Mat. 5:39): "But I say to you not to resist evil"; and (Rom. 12:19): "Not revenging yourselves, my dearly beloved, but give place unto wrath." Therefore war is always sinful.

Objection 3: Further, nothing, except sin, is contrary to an act of virtue. But war is contrary to peace. Therefore war is always a sin.

Objection 4: Further, the exercise of a lawful thing is itself lawful, as is evident in scientific exercises. But warlike exercises which take place in tournaments are forbidden by the Church, since those who are slain in these trials are deprived of ecclesiastical burial. Therefore it seems that war is a sin in itself.

On the contrary, Augustine says in a sermon on the son of the centurion [*Ep. ad Marcel. cxxxviii]: "If the Christian Religion forbade war altogether, those who sought salutary advice in the Gospel would rather have been counselled to cast aside their arms, and to give up soldiering altogether. On the contrary, they were told: 'Do violence to no man . . . and be content with your pay' [*Lk. 3:14]. If he commanded them to be content with their pay, he did not forbid soldiering."

I answer that, In order for a war to be just, three things are necessary. First, the authority of the sovereign by whose command the war is to be waged. For it is not the business of a private individual to declare war, because he can seek for redress of his rights from the tribunal of his superior. Moreover it is not the business of a private individual to summon together the people, which has to be done in wartime. And as the care of the common weal is committed to those who are in authority, it is their business to watch over the common weal of the city, kingdom or province subject to them. And just as it is lawful for them to

Thomas Aquinas, *Summa Theologica* (Benziger Bros. edition, 1947), translated by Fathers of the English Dominion Province.

have recourse to the sword in defending that common weal against internal disturbances, when they punish evil-doers, according to the words of the Apostle (Rom. 13:4): "He beareth not the sword in vain: for he is God's minister, an avenger to execute wrath upon him that doth evil"; so too, it is their business to have recourse to the sword of war in defending the common weal against external enemies. Hence it is said to those who are in authority (Ps. 81:4): "Rescue the poor: and deliver the needy out of the hand of the sinner"; and for this reason Augustine says (Contra Faust. xxii, 75): "The natural order conducive to peace among mortals demands that the power to declare and counsel war should be in the hands of those who hold the supreme authority."

Secondly, a just cause is required, namely that those who are attacked, should be attacked because they deserve it on account of some fault. Wherefore Augustine says (QQ. in Hept., qu. x, super Jos.): "A just war is wont to be described as one that avenges wrongs, when a nation or state has to be punished, for refusing to make amends for the wrongs inflicted by its subjects, or to restore what it has seized unjustly."

Thirdly, it is necessary that the belligerents should have a rightful intention, so that they intend the advancement of good, or the avoidance of evil. Hence Augustine says (De Verb. Dom. [*The words quoted are to be found not in St. Augustine's works, but Can. Apud. Caus. xxiii, qu. 1]): "True religion looks upon as peaceful those wars that are waged not for motives of aggrandizement, or cruelty, but with the object of securing peace, of punishing evil-doers, and of uplifting the good." For it may happen that the war is declared by the legitimate authority, and for a just cause, and yet be rendered unlawful through a wicked intention. Hence Augustine says (Contra Faust. xxii, 74): "The passion for inflicting harm, the cruel thirst for vengeance, an unpacific and relentless spirit, the fever of revolt, the lust of power, and such like things, all these are rightly condemned in war."

Reply to Objection 1: As Augustine says (Contra Faust. xxii, 70): "To take the sword is to arm oneself in order to take the life of anyone, without the command or permission of superior or lawful authority." On the other hand, to have recourse to the sword (as a private person) by the authority of the sovereign or judge, or (as a public person) through zeal for justice, and by the authority, so to speak, of God, is not to "take the sword," but to use it as commissioned by another, wherefore it does not deserve punishment. And yet even those who make sinful use of the sword are not always slain with the sword, yet they always perish with their own sword, because, unless they repent, they are punished eternally for their sinful use of the sword.

Reply to Objection 2: Such like precepts, as Augustine observes (De Serm. Dom. in Monte i 19), should always be borne in readiness of mind, so that we be ready to obey them, and, if necessary, to refrain from resistance or self-defense. Nevertheless it is necessary sometimes for a man to act otherwise for the common good, or for the good of those with whom he is fighting. Hence Augustine says (Ep. ad Marcellin. cxxxviii): "Those whom we have to punish with a kindly severity, it is necessary to handle in many ways against their will. For when we are stripping a man of the lawlessness of sin, it is good for him to be vanquished, since nothing is more hopeless than the happiness of sinners, whence arises a guilty impunity, and an evil will, like an internal enemy."

Reply to Objection 3: Those who wage war justly aim at peace, and so they are not opposed to peace, except to the evil peace, which Our Lord "came not to send upon earth" (Mat. 10:34). Hence Augustine says (Ep. ad Bonif. clxxxix): "We do not seek peace in order to be at war, but we go to war that we may have peace. Be peaceful, therefore, in warring, so that you may vanquish those whom you war against, and bring them to the prosperity of peace."

Reply to Objection 4: Manly exercises in warlike feats of arms are not all forbidden, but those which are inordinate and perilous, and end in slaying or plundering. In olden times warlike exercises presented no such danger, and hence they were called "exercises of arms" or "bloodless wars," as Jerome states in an epistle [*Reference incorrect: cf. Veget., De Re Milit. i].

QUESTIONS

1. State the conditions of just war.
2. How does Aquinas's conditions of a just war answer his pacifist opponents?

22. Address to the American People, 9 August 1945

HARRY TRUMAN

*H*arry Truman (1884–1972) was the thirty-third president of the United States (1945–1953). He had been vice president for only eighty-two days when President Franklin Roosevelt died in April 1945. Roosevelt had not talked much to Truman or kept him informed about the conduct of World War II or the development of atomic weapons. Truman made the decision to drop the newly developed bomb on the Japanese. On 6 August 1945, the B-29 bomber *Enola Gay* dropped one on Hiroshima, and, having not heard from the Japanese, another B-29 dropped a second bomb three days later on Nagasaki. The Japanese agreed to surrender on 14 August.

President Truman made few public statements about the atomic bombings of Japan. They occurred at the end of the war, after months of conventional bombardments of Japanese cities, especially Tokyo, which lay in rubble after seven months of bombing. As the Japanese would not surrender—"unconditionally," as was demanded—the Americans planned an invasion of Japan. Given the ferocious fighting on the Pacific Islands, the estimates of casualties for an invasion were very high. The war had ended in Europe, and there was great weariness, as well as anger, on the part of the forces fighting the Axis powers.

These excerpts from a radio address that Truman gave a few days after the first atomic bombing, on the day of the second bombing, contain a number of points that may be relevant to a possible defense of the bombings. The first paragraph makes the point that the Japanese have been warned. The second paragraph makes a number of important points. One is that Hiroshima was "a military base," which was true, although the relative number of civilians was large. (Nagasaki was a large southern seaport, of military importance.) Truman says that the wish was "to avoid, insofar as possible, the killing of civilians."

In the penultimate paragraph, Truman says that the United States used the bomb (1) "against those who attacked us without warning at Pearl Harbor," and (2) "against those who have starved and beaten and executed American prisoners of war, against those who have abandoned all pretense of obeying international laws of warfare." The first point is relevant to the question of the justice of the war (the first part of just war theory), the second to the question of the justice of the conduct of (or in) war (the second part of just war theory). Lastly, Truman claims that (3) the bomb was used to shorten the war and to save thousands of American lives. He might have added, as he did elsewhere, that (4) the bombings also saved Japanese lives that would have been lost in an invasion. All of these points could figure in a defense of the bombings, though how they would is a matter of considerable controversy.

The British, Chinese, and United States Governments have given the Japanese people adequate warning of what is in store for them. We have laid down the general terms on which they can surrender. Our warning went unheeded; our terms were rejected. Since then the Japanese have seen what our atomic bomb can do. They can foresee what it will do in the future.

The world will note that the first atomic bomb was dropped on Hiroshima, a military base. That was because we wished in this first attack to avoid, insofar as possible, the killing of civilians. But that attack is only a warning of things to come. If Japan does not surrender, bombs will have to be dropped on her war industries and, unfortunately, thousands of civilian lives will be lost. I urge Japanese civilians to leave industrial cities immediately, and save themselves from destruction.

I realize the tragic significance of the atomic bomb.

Its production and its use were not lightly undertaken by this Government. But we knew that our enemies were on the search for it. We know now how close they were to finding it. And we knew the disaster, which would come to this Nation, and to all peace-loving nations, to all civilization, if they had found it first.

That is why we felt compelled to undertake the long and uncertain and costly labor of discovery and production.

We won the race of discovery against the Germans. Having found the bomb we have used it. We have used it against those who attacked us without warning at Pearl Harbor, against those who have starved and beaten and executed American prisoners of war, against those who have abandoned all pretense of obeying international laws of warfare. We have used it in order to shorten the agony of war, in order to save the lives of thousands and thousands of young Americans.

We shall continue to use it until we completely destroy Japan's power to make war. Only a Japanese surrender will stop us.

QUESTIONS

1. How might the different elements of the relevant parts of Truman's address be a defense of the atomic bombings?
2. What would be the weak points of this defense?

23. Fifty Years after Hiroshima

JOHN RAWLS

*J*ohn Rawls (1921–2002) was an influential American philosopher and widely thought of as the most important political philosopher of the last century. His influence on contemporary moral and political thought is hard to underestimate. His major works are *A Theory of Justice* (1971) and *Political Liberalism* (1993). After graduating from college in 1943, Rawls joined the Army and served as an infantryman in New Guinea, the Philippines, and Japan.

"Fifty years after Hiroshima" reprinted by permission of the publishers from *John Rawls: Collected Papers*, edited by Samuel Freeman, pp. 565–572, Cambridge, Mass.: Harvard University Press, Copyright © 1999 by the President and Fellows of Harvard College. Originally published in *Dissent* (Summer 1995): 323–327.

The experience of combat, witnessing the aftermath of the bombing of Hiroshima, and learning of the Holocaust marked him deeply.

Fifty years after the atomic bombings and the end of World War II, John Rawls published his reflections—those of an important moral and political thinker but also of a foot soldier in the Pacific campaign—on the morality of the bombings. He argues that the bombings, including the fire-bombings of other Japanese cities, were very great wrongs.

Rawls's case against the bombings makes use of an influential contemporary restatement of the principles of just war, that due to the political thinker Michael Walzer (see chapter 25). He also includes elements of his own account of the morality of international relations. Of note is Rawls's repudiation of two "nihilistic doctrines" at the end of his essay.

The fiftieth year since the bombing of Hiroshima is a time to reflect about what one should think of it. Is it really a great wrong, as many now think, and many also thought then, or is it perhaps justified after all? I believe that both the fire-bombing of Japanese cities beginning in the spring of 1945 and the later atomic bombing of Hiroshima on August 6 were very great wrongs, and rightly seen as such. In order to support this opinion, I set out what I think to be the principles governing the conduct of war—*jus in bello*—of democratic peoples. These peoples[1] have different ends of war than nondemocratic, especially totalitarian, states, such as Germany and Japan, which sought the domination and exploitation of subjected peoples, and in Germany's case, their enslavement if not extermination.

Although I cannot properly justify them here, I begin by setting out six principles and assumptions in support of these judgments. I hope they seem not unreasonable; and certainly they are familiar, as they are closely related to much traditional thought on this subject.

1. The aim of a just war waged by a decent democratic society is a just and lasting peace between peoples, especially with its present enemy.
2. A decent democratic society is fighting against a state that is not democratic. This follows from the fact that democratic peoples do not wage war against each other;[2] and since we are concerned with the rules of war as they apply to such peoples, we assume the society fought against is nondemocratic and that its expansionist aims threatened the security and free institutions of democratic regimes and caused the war.[3]

3. In the conduct of war, a democratic society must carefully distinguish three groups: the state's leaders and officials, its soldiers, and its civilian population. The reason for these distinctions rests on the principle of responsibility: since the state fought against is not democratic, the civilian members of the society cannot be those who organized and brought on the war. This was done by its leaders and officials assisted by other elites who control and staff the state apparatus. They are responsible, they willed the war, and for doing that, they are criminals. But civilians, often kept in ignorance and swayed by state propaganda, are not.[4] And this is so even if some civilians knew better and were enthusiastic for the war. In a nation's conduct of war many such marginal cases may exist, but they are irrelevant. As for soldiers, they, just as civilians, and leaving aside the upper ranks of an officer class, are not responsible for the war, but are conscripted or in other ways forced into it, their patriotism often cruelly and cynically exploited. The grounds on which they may be attacked directly are not that they are responsible for the war but that a democratic people cannot defend itself in any other way, and defend itself it must do. About this there is no choice.

4. A decent democratic society must respect the human rights of the members of the other side, both civilians and soldiers, for two reasons. One is because they simply have these rights by the law of peoples. The other reason is to teach enemy soldiers and civilians the content of those rights by the example of how

they hold in their own case. In this way their significance is best brought home to them. They are assigned a certain status, the status of the members of some human society who possess rights as human persons.[5] In the case of human rights in war the aspect of status as applied to civilians is given a strict interpretation. This means, as I understand it here, that they can never be attacked directly except in times of extreme crisis, the nature of which I discuss below.

5. Continuing with the thought of teaching the content of human rights, the next principle is that just peoples by their actions and proclamations are to foreshadow during war the kind of peace they aim for and the kind of relations they seek between nations. By doing so, they show in an open and public way the nature of their aims and the kind of people they are. These last duties fall largely on the leaders and officials of the governments of democratic peoples, since they are in the best position to speak for the whole people and to act as the principle applies. Although all the preceding principles also specify duties of statesmanship, this is especially true of 4 and 5. The way a war is fought and the actions ending it endure in the historical memory of peoples and may set the stage for future war. This duty of statesmanship must always be held in view.

6. Finally, we note the place of practical means-end reasoning in judging the appropriateness of an action or policy for achieving the aim of war or for not causing more harm than good. This mode of thought—whether carried on by (classical) utilitarian reasoning, or by cost-benefit analysis, or by weighing national interests, or in other ways—must always be framed within and strictly limited by the preceding principles. The norms of the conduct of war set up certain lines that bound just action. War plans and strategies, and the conduct of battles, must lie within their limits. (The only exception, I repeat, is in times of extreme crisis.)

In connection with the fourth and fifth principles of the conduct of war, I have said that they are binding especially on the leaders of nations. They are in the most effective position to represent their people's aims and obligations, and sometimes they become statesmen. But who is a statesman? There is no office of statesman, as there is of president, or chancellor, or prime minister. The statesman is an ideal, like the ideal of the truthful or virtuous individual. Statesmen are presidents or prime ministers who become statesmen through their exemplary performance and leadership in their office in difficult and trying times and manifest strength, wisdom, and courage. They guide their people through turbulent and dangerous periods for which they are esteemed always, as one of their great statesmen.

The ideal of the statesman is suggested by the saying: the politician looks to the next election, the statesman to the next generation. It is the task of the student of philosophy to look to the permanent conditions and the real interests of a just and good democratic society. It is the task of the statesman, however, to discern these conditions and interests in practice; the statesman sees deeper and further than most others and grasps what needs to be done. The statesman must get it right, or nearly so, and hold fast to it. Washington and Lincoln were statesmen. Bismarck was not. He did not see Germany's real interests far enough into the future, and his judgment and motives were often distorted by his class interests and his wanting himself alone to be chancellor of Germany. Statesmen need not be selfless and may have their own interests when they hold office, yet they must be selfless in their judgments and assessments of society's interests and not be swayed, especially in war and crisis, by passions of revenge and retaliation against the enemy.

Above all, they are to hold fast to the aim of gaining a just peace, and avoid the things that make achieving such a peace more difficult. Here the proclamations of a nation should make clear (the statesman must see to this) that the enemy people are to be granted an autonomous regime of their own and a decent and full life once peace is securely reestablished. Whatever they may be told by their leaders, whatever reprisals they may reasonably fear, they are not to be held as slaves or serfs after surrender,[6] or denied in due course their full liberties; and they may well achieve freedoms they did not enjoy before, as the Germans and the Japanese eventually did. The statesman knows, if others do not, that all descriptions of the enemy people (not their rulers) inconsistent with this are impulsive and false.

Turning now to Hiroshima and the fire-bombing of Tokyo, we find that neither falls under the exemption of extreme crisis. One aspect of this is that since (let's suppose) there are no absolute rights—rights that must be respected in all circumstances—there are occasions when civilians can be attacked directly by aerial bombing. Were there times during the war when Britain could properly have bombed Hamburg and Berlin? Yes, when Britain was alone and desperately facing Germany's superior might; moreover, this period would extend until Russia had clearly beat off the first German assault in the summer and fall of 1941, and would be able to fight Germany until the end. Here the cutoff point might be placed differently, say the summer of 1942, and certainly by Stalingrad.[7] I shall not dwell on this, as the crucial matter is that under no conditions could Germany be allowed to win the war, and this for two basic reasons: first, the nature and history of constitutional democracy and its place in European culture; and second, the peculiar evil of Nazism and the enormous and uncalculable moral and political evil it represented for civilized society.

The peculiar evil of Nazism needs to be understood, since in some circumstances a democratic people might better accept defeat if the terms of peace offered by the adversary were reasonable and moderate, did not subject them to humiliation, and looked forward to a workable and decent political relationship. Yet characteristic of Hitler was that he accepted no possibility at all of a political relationship with his enemies. They were always to be cowed by terror and brutality, and ruled by force. From the beginning the campaign against Russia, for example, was a war of destruction against Slavic peoples, with the original inhabitants remaining, if at all, only as serfs. When Goebbels and others protested that the war could not be won that way, Hitler refused to listen.[8]

Yet it is clear that while the extreme crisis exemption held for Britain in the early stages of the war, it never held at any time for the United States in its war with Japan. The principles of the conduct of war

were always applicable to it. Indeed, in the case of Hiroshima many involved in higher reaches of the government recognized the questionable character of the bombing and that limits were being crossed. Yet during the discussions among allied leaders in June and July 1945, the weight of the practical means-end reasoning carried the day. Under the continuing pressure of war, such moral doubts as there were failed to gain an express and articulated view. As the war progressed, the heavy fire-bombing of civilians in the capitals of Berlin and Tokyo and elsewhere was increasingly accepted on the allied side. Although after the outbreak of war Roosevelt had urged both sides not to commit the inhuman barbarism of bombing civilians, by 1945 allied leaders came to assume that Roosevelt would have used the bomb on Hiroshima.[9] The bombing grew out of what had happened before.

The practical means-end reasons to justify using the atomic bomb on Hiroshima were the following:

The bomb was dropped to hasten the end of the war. It is clear that Truman and most other allied leaders thought it would do that. Another reason was that it would save lives where the lives counted are the lives of American soldiers. The lives of Japanese, military or civilian, presumably counted for less. Here the calculations of least time and most lives saved were mutually supporting. Moreover, dropping the bomb would give the Emperor and the Japanese leaders a way to save face, an important matter given Japanese samurai culture. Indeed, at the end a few top Japanese leaders wanted to make a last sacrificial stand but were overruled by others supported by the Emperor, who ordered surrender on August 12, having received word from Washington that the Emperor could stay provided it was understood that he had to comply with the orders of the American military commander. The last reason I mention is that the bomb was dropped to impress the Russians with American power and make them more agreeable with our demands. This reason is highly disputed but is urged by some critics and scholars as important.

The failure of these reasons to reflect the limits on the conduct of war is evident, so I focus on a different matter: the failure of statesmanship on the part of allied leaders and why it might have occurred. Truman once described the Japanese as beasts and to be treated as such; yet how foolish it sounds now to call the Germans or the Japanese barbarians and beasts![10] Of the Nazis and Tojo militarists, yes, but they are not the German and the Japanese people. Churchill later granted that he carried the bombing too far, led by passion and the intensity of the conflict.[11] A duty of statesmanship is not to allow such feelings, natural and inevitable as they may be, to alter the course a democratic people should best follow in striving for peace. The statesman understands that relations with the present enemy have special importance: for as I have said, war must be openly and publicly conducted in ways that make a lasting and amicable peace possible with a defeated enemy, and prepares its people for how they may be expected to be treated. Their present fears of being subjected to acts of revenge and retaliation must be put to rest; present enemies must be seen as associates in a shared and just future peace.

These remarks make it clear that, in my judgment, both Hiroshima and the fire-bombing of Japanese cities were great evils that the duties of statesmanship require political leaders to avoid in the absence of the crisis exemption. I also believe this could have been done at little cost in further casualties. An invasion was unnecessary at that date, as the war was effectively over. However, whether that is true or not makes no difference. Without the crisis exemption, those bombings are great evils. Yet it is clear that an articulate expression of the principles of just war introduced at that time would not have altered the outcome. It was simply too late. A president or prime minister must have carefully considered these questions, preferably long before, or at least when they had the time and leisure to think things out. Reflections on just war cannot be heard in the daily round of the pressure of events near the end of the hostilities; too many are anxious and impatient, and simply worn out.

Similarly, the justification of constitutional democracy and the basis of the rights and duties it must respect should be part of the public political culture and discussed in the many associations of civic society as part of one's education. It is not clearly heard in day-to-day ordinary politics, but must be presupposed as the background, not the daily subject of politics, except in special circumstances. In the same way, there was not sufficient prior grasp of the fundamental importance of the principles of just war for the expression of them to have blocked the appeal of practical means-end reasoning in terms of a calculus of lives, or of the least time to end the war, or of some other balancing of costs and benefits. This practical reasoning justifies too much, too easily, and provides a way for a dominant power to quiet any moral worries that may arise. If the principles of war are put forward at that time, they easily become so many more considerations to be balanced in the scales.

Another failure of statesmanship was not to try to enter into negotiations with the Japanese before any drastic steps such as the fire-bombing of cities or the bombing of Hiroshima were taken. A conscientious attempt to do so was morally necessary. As a democratic people, we owed that to the Japanese people—whether to their government is another matter. There had been discussions in Japan for some time about finding a way to end the war, and on June 26 the government had been instructed by the Emperor to do so.[12] It must surely have realized that with the navy destroyed and the outer islands taken, the war was lost. True, the Japanese were deluded by the hope that the Russians might prove to be their allies,[13] but negotiations are precisely to disabuse the other side of delusions of that kind. A statesman is not free to consider that such negotiations may lessen the desired shock value of subsequent attacks.

Truman was in many ways a good, at times a very good president. But the way he ended the war showed he failed as a statesman. For him it was an opportunity missed, and a loss to the country and its armed forces as well. It is sometimes said that questioning the bombing of Hiroshima is an insult to the American troops who fought the war. This is hard to understand. We should be able to look back and consider our faults after fifty years. We expect the Germans and the Japanese to do that— "*Vergangenheitsverarbeitung,*" as the Germans say. Why shouldn't we? It can't be that we think we waged the war without moral error!

None of this alters Germany's and Japan's responsibility for the war nor their behavior in conducting it. Emphatically to be repudiated are two nihilist doctrines. One is expressed by Sherman's remark, "War is hell," so anything goes to get it over with as soon as one can. The other says that we are all guilty so we stand on a level and no one can blame anyone else. These are both superficial and deny all reasonable distinctions; they are invoked falsely to try to excuse our misconduct or to plead that we cannot be condemned.

The moral emptiness of these nihilisms is manifest in the fact that just and decent civilized societies—their institutions and laws, their civil life and background culture and mores—all depend absolutely on making significant moral and political distinctions in all situations. Certainly war is a kind of hell, but why should that mean that all moral distinctions cease to hold? And granted also that sometimes all or nearly all may be to some degree guilty, that does not mean that all are equally so. There is never a time when we are free from all moral and political principles and restraints. These nihilisms are pretenses to be free of those principles and restraints that always apply to us fully.

Notes

1. I sometimes use the term "peoples" to mean the same as nations, especially when I want to contrast peoples with states and a state's apparatus.

2. I assume that democratic peoples do not go to war against each other. There is considerable evidence of this important idea. See Michael Doyle's two-part article, "Kant, Liberal Legacies, and Foreign Affairs," *Philosophy and Public Affairs*, 12 (Summer/Fall 1983): 205–235, 323–353, See especially his summary of the evidence in the first part, pp. 206–232.

3. Responsibility for war rarely falls on only one side, and this must be granted. Yet some dirty hands are dirtier than others, and sometimes even with dirty hands a democratic people would still have the right even the duty to defend itself from the other side. This is clear in World War II.

4. Here I follow Michael Walzer's *Just and Unjust Wars* (New York: Basic Books, 1977).

5. For the idea of status, I am indebted to discussions of Frances Kamm and Thomas Nagel.

6. See Churchill's remarks explaining the meaning of "unconditional surrender" in *The Hinge of Fate* (Boston: Houghton Mifflin, 1950), pp. 685–688.

7. I might add here that a balancing of interests is not involved. Rather, we have a matter of judgment as to whether certain objective circumstances are present which constitute the extreme crisis exemption. As with any other complex concept, that of such an exemption is to some degree vague. Whether or not the concept applies rests on judgment.

8. On Goebbels's and others' protests, see Alan Bullock, *Hitler: A Study in Tyranny* (London: Oldham's Press, 1952), ch. 12, sec. 5, pp. 633–644.

9. For an account of events, see David M. McCullough, *Truman* (New York: Simon and Schuster, 1992), ch. 9, sec. IV and ch. 10, pp. 390–464; and Barton Bernstein, "The Atomic Bombings Reconsidered," *Foreign Affairs*, 74 (Jan./Feb. 1995): 1.

10. See McCullough's *Truman*, p. 458, the exchange between Truman and Senator Russell of Georgia in August 1945.

11. See Martin Gilbert, *Winston Churchill: Never Despair*, vol. VIII (Boston: Houghton Mifflin, 1988), p. 259, reflecting later on Dresden.

12. See Gerhard Weinberg, *A World at Arms* (Cambridge: Cambridge University Press, 1994), pp. 886–889.

13. See ibid., p. 886.

QUESTIONS

1. What are the important moral principles that are central to Rawls's case against the bombings? Are these principles restatement of just war principles or something new?

2. Why is the distinction between statesmen and peoples important for Rawls?

24. War and Massacre

THOMAS NAGEL

For a description of the author, see chapter 9.

This essay on the ethics of war was written at a time when philosophers were returning to applied or practical ethics, after decades of neglect. The war in Vietnam pushed many American philosophers to reflect on the moral evaluation of war, and Nagel's long and difficult essay begins with some remarks about this war. Later examples from World War II are discussed. He is interested in the grounds for conventions governing war and wishes to argue that there is "a moral basis for the rules of war."

Nagel contrasts two moral views or "categories of moral reason": utilitarianism and absolutism. In moral philosophy the utilitarian tradition holds that all actions are to be evaluated in terms of their consequences, specifically on the happiness or well-being of sentient creatures (see chapter 67). It is a kind of moral consequentialism, a theory that evaluates everything by reference to the consequences of action. Often—and certainly in wartime—we think that an act that produces good or even the best consequences may still be wrong. Nagel's absolutists think this and would have us look less to the consequences of our actions than to the type of act they represent. Most absolutists think there are some things that we may never do, that are absolutely wrong. Nagel thinks the choice between these two perspectives is a dilemma, as we are pulled in two directions.

From the apathetic reaction to atrocities committed in Vietnam by the United States and its allies, one may conclude that moral restrictions on the conduct of war command almost as little sympathy among the general public as they do among those charged with the formation of U.S. military policy. Even when restrictions on the conduct of warfare are defended, it is usually on legal grounds alone: their moral basis is often poorly understood. I wish to argue that certain restrictions are neither arbitrary nor merely conventional, and that their validity does not depend simply on their usefulness. There is, in other words, a moral basis for the rules of war, even though the conventions now officially in force are far from giving it perfect expression.

I

No elaborate moral theory is required to account for what is wrong in cases like the Mylai massacre, since it did not serve, and was not intended to serve, any strategic purpose. Moreover, if the participation of the United States in the Indo-Chinese war is entirely wrong to begin with, then that engagement is incapable of providing a justification for *any* measures taken in its pursuit—not only for the measures which are atrocities in every war, however just its aims.

But this war has revealed attitudes of a more general kind, that influenced the conduct of earlier wars as well. After it has ended, we shall still be faced with the problem of how warfare may be conducted, and

From Thomas Nagel, "War and Massacre," *Philosophy and Public Affairs*, Vol. 1, No. 2 (Winter, 1972), pp. 123–144. Reprinted by permission of Blackwell Publishing.

the attitudes that have resulted in the specific conduct of this war will not have disappeared. Moreover, similar problems can arise in wars or rebellions fought for very different reasons, and against very different opponents. It is not easy to keep a firm grip on the idea of what is not permissible in warfare, because while some military actions are obvious atrocities, other cases are more difficult to assess, and the general principles underlying these judgments remain obscure. Such obscurity can lead to the abandonment of sound intuitions in favor of criteria whose rationale may be more obvious. If such a tendency is to be resisted, it will require a better understanding of the restrictions than we now have.

I propose to discuss the most general moral problem raised by the conduct of warfare: the problem of means and ends. In one view, there are limits on what may be done even in the service of an end worth pursuing—and even when adherence to the restriction may be very costly. A person who acknowledges the force of such restrictions can find himself in acute moral dilemmas. He may believe, for example, that by torturing a prisoner he can obtain information necessary to prevent a disaster, or that by obliterating one village with bombs he can halt a campaign of terrorism. If he believes that the gains from a certain measure will clearly outweigh its costs, yet still suspects that he ought not to adopt it, then he is in a dilemma produced by the conflict between two disparate categories of moral reason: categories that may be called *utilitarian* and *absolutist*.

Utilitarianism gives primacy to a concern with what will *happen*. Absolutism gives primacy to a concern with what one is *doing*. The conflict between them arises because the alternatives we face are rarely just choices between *total outcomes*: they are also choices between alternative pathways or measures to be taken. When one of the choices is to do terrible things to another person, the problem is altered fundamentally; it is no longer merely a question of which outcome would be worse.

Few of us are completely immune to either of these types of moral intuition, though in some people, either naturally or for doctrinal reasons, one type will be dominant and the other suppressed or weak. But it is perfectly possible to feel the force of both types of reason very strongly; in that case the

moral dilemma in certain situations of crisis will be acute, and it may appear that every possible course of action or inaction is unacceptable for one reason or another.

II

Although it is this dilemma that I propose to explore, most of the discussion will be devoted to its absolutist component. The utilitarian component is straightforward by comparison, and has a natural appeal to anyone who is not a complete skeptic about ethics. Utilitarianism says that one should try, either individually or through institutions, to maximize good and minimize evil (the definition of these categories need not enter into the schematic formulation of the view), and that if faced with the possibility of preventing a great evil by producing a lesser, one should choose the lesser evil. There are certainly problems about the formulation of utilitarianism, and much has been written about it, but its intent is morally transparent. Nevertheless, despite the addition of various refinements, it continues to leave large portions of ethics unaccounted for. I do not suggest that some form of absolutism can account for them all, only that an examination of absolutism will lead us to see the complexity, and perhaps the incoherence, of our moral ideas.

Utilitarianism certainly justifies *some* restrictions on the conduct of warfare. There are strong utilitarian reasons for adhering to any limitation which seems natural to most people—particularly if the limitation is widely accepted already. An exceptional measure which seems to be justified by its results in a particular conflict may create a precedent with disastrous long-term effects.[1] It may even be argued that war involves violence on such a scale that it is never justified on utilitarian grounds—the consequences of refusing to go to war will never be as bad as the war itself would be, even if atrocities were not committed. Or in a more sophisticated vein it might be claimed that a uniform policy of never resorting to military force would do less harm in the long run, if followed consistently, than a policy of deciding each case on utilitarian grounds (even though on occasion particular applications of the pacifist policy might have worse results than a specific utilitarian decision). But I shall not consider these arguments, for my concern is with reasons of a different kind, which may remain when reasons of utility and interest fail.[2]

In the final analysis, I believe that the dilemma cannot always be resolved. While not every conflict between absolutism and utilitarianism creates an insoluble dilemma, and while it is certainly right to adhere to absolutist restrictions unless the utilitarian considerations favoring violation are overpoweringly weighty and extremely certain—nevertheless, when that special condition is met, it may become impossible to adhere to an absolutist position. What I shall offer, therefore, is a somewhat qualified defense of absolutism. I believe it underlies a valid and fundamental type of moral judgment—which cannot be reduced to or overridden by other principles. And while there may be other principles just as fundamental, it is particularly important not to lose confidence in our absolutist intuitions, for they are often the only barrier before the abyss of utilitarian apologetics for large-scale murder.

III

One absolutist position that creates no problems of interpretation is pacifism: the view that one may not kill another person under any circumstances, no matter what good would be achieved or evil averted thereby. The type of absolutist position that I am going to discuss is different. Pacifism draws the conflict with utilitarian considerations very starkly. But there are other views according to which violence may be undertaken, even on a large scale, in a clearly just cause, so long as certain absolute restrictions on the character and direction of that violence are observed. The line is drawn somewhat closer to the bone, but it exists.

The philosopher who has done most to advance contemporary philosophical discussion of such a view, and to explain it to those unfamiliar with its extensive treatment in Roman Catholic moral theology, is G. E. M. Anscombe. In 1958 Miss Anscombe published a pamphlet entitled *Mr. Truman's Degree*,[3] on the occasion of the award by Oxford University of an honorary doctorate to Harry Truman. The pamphlet explained why she had opposed the decision to

award that degree, recounted the story of her unsuccessful opposition, and offered some reflections on the history of Truman's decision to drop atom bombs on Hiroshima and Nagasaki, and on the difference between murder and allowable killing in warfare. She pointed out that the policy of deliberately killing large numbers of civilians either as a means or as an end in itself did not originate with Truman, and was common practice among all parties during World War II for some time before Hiroshima. The Allied area bombings of German cities by conventional explosives included raids which killed more civilians than did the atomic attacks; the same is true of certain fire-bomb raids on Japan.

The policy of attacking the civilian population in order to induce an enemy to surrender, or to damage his morale, seems to have been widely accepted in the civilized world, and seems to be accepted still, at least if the stakes are high enough. It gives evidence of a moral conviction that the deliberate killing of noncombatants—women, children, old people—is permissible if enough can be gained by it. This follows from the more general position that any means can in principle be justified if it leads to a sufficiently worthy end. Such an attitude is evident not only in the more spectacular current weapons systems but also in the day-to-day conduct of the nonglobal war in Indochina; the indiscriminate destructiveness of antipersonnel weapons, napalm, and aerial bombardment; cruelty to prisoners; massive relocation of civilians; destruction of crops; and so forth. An absolutist position opposes to this the view that certain acts cannot be justified no matter what the consequences. Among those acts is murder—the deliberate killing of the harmless: civilians, prisoners of war, and medical personnel.

In the present war such measures are sometimes said to be regrettable, but they are generally defended by reference to military necessity and the importance of the long-term consequences of success or failure in the war. I shall pass over the inadequacy of this consequentialist defense in its own terms. (That is the dominant form of moral criticism of the war, for it is part of what people mean when they ask, "Is it worth it?") I am concerned rather to account for the inappropriateness of offering any defense of that kind for such actions.

Many people feel, without being able to say much more about it, that something has gone seriously wrong when certain measures are admitted into consideration in the first place. The fundamental mistake is made there, rather than at the point where the overall benefit of some monstrous measure is judged to outweigh its disadvantages, and it is adopted. An account of absolutism might help us to understand this. If it is not allowable to *do* certain things, such as killing unarmed prisoners or civilians, then no argument about what will happen if one doesn't do them can show that doing them would be all right.

Absolutism does not, of course, require one to ignore the consequences of one's acts. It operates as a limitation on utilitarian reasoning, not as a substitute for it. An absolutist can be expected to try to maximize good and minimize evil, so long as this does not require him to transgress an absolute prohibition like that against murder. But when such a conflict occurs, the prohibition takes complete precedence over any consideration of consequences. Some of the results of this view are clear enough. It requires us to forgo certain potentially useful military measures, such as the slaughter of hostages and prisoners or indiscriminate attempts to reduce the enemy civilian population by starvation, epidemic infectious diseases like anthrax and bubonic plague, or mass incineration. It means that we cannot deliberate on whether such measures are justified by the fact that they will avert still greater evils, for as intentional measures they cannot be justified in terms of any consequences whatever.

Someone unfamiliar with the events of this century might imagine that utilitarian arguments, or arguments of national interest, would suffice to deter measures of this sort. But it has become evident that such considerations are insufficient to prevent the adoption and employment of enormous antipopulation weapons once their use is considered a serious moral possibility. The same is true of the piecemeal wiping out of rural civilian populations in airborne antiguerrilla warfare. Once the door is opened to calculations of utility and national interest, the usual speculations about the future of freedom, peace, and economic prosperity can be brought to bear to ease the consciences of those responsible for a certain number of charred babies.

For this reason alone it is important to decide what is wrong with the frame of mind which allows such arguments to begin. But it is also important to understand absolutism in the cases where it genuinely conflicts with utility. Despite its appeal, it is a paradoxical position, for it can require that one refrain from choosing the lesser of two evils when that is the only choice one has. And it is additionally paradoxical because, unlike pacifism, it permits one to do horrible things to people in some circumstances but not in others.

IV

Before going on to say what, if anything, lies behind the position, there remain a few relatively technical matters which are best discussed at this point.

First, it is important to specify as clearly as possible the kind of thing to which absolutist prohibitions can apply. We must take seriously the proviso that they concern what we deliberately do to people. There could not, for example, without incoherence, be an absolute prohibition against *bringing about* the death of an innocent person. For one may find oneself in a situation in which, no matter what one does, some innocent people will die as a result. I do not mean just that there are cases in which someone will die no matter what one does, because one is not in a position to affect the outcome one way or the other. That, it is to be hoped, is one's relation to the deaths of most innocent people. I have in mind, rather, a case in which someone is bound to die, but who it is will depend on what one does. Sometimes these situations have natural causes, as when too few resources (medicine, lifeboats) are available to rescue everyone threatened with a certain catastrophe. Sometimes the situations are man-made, as when the only way to control a campaign of terrorism is to employ terrorist tactics against the community from which it has arisen. Whatever one does in cases such as these, some innocent people will die as a result. If the absolutist prohibition forbade doing what would result in the deaths of innocent people, it would have the consequence that in such cases nothing one could do would be morally permissible.

This problem is avoided, however, because what absolutism forbids is *doing* certain things to people, rather than bringing about certain *results*. Not every-thing that happens to others as a result of what one does is something that one has *done* to them. Catholic moral theology seeks to make this distinction precise in a doctrine known as the law of double effect, which asserts that there is a morally relevant distinction between bringing about the death of an innocent per-son deliberately, either as an end in itself or as a means, and bringing it about as a side effect of something else one does deliberately. In the latter case, even if the out-come is foreseen, it is not murder, and does not fall under the absolute prohibition, though of course it may still be wrong for other reasons (reasons of utility, for example). Briefly, the principle states that one is sometimes permitted knowingly to bring about as a side effect of one's actions something which it would be absolutely impermissible to bring about deliber-ately as an end or as a means. In application to war or revolution, the law of double effect permits a certain amount of civilian carnage as a side effect of bombing munitions plants or attacking enemy soldiers. And even this is permissible only if the cost is not too great to be justified by one's objectives.

However, despite its importance and its useful-ness in accounting for certain plausible moral judg-ments, I do not believe that the law of double effect is a generally applicable test for the consequences of an absolutist position. Its own application is not always clear, so that it introduces uncertainty where there need not be uncertainty.

In Indochina, for example, there is a great deal of aerial bombardment, strafing, spraying of napalm, and employment of pellet- or needle-spraying anti-personnel weapons against rural villages in which guerrillas are suspected to be hiding, or from which small-arms fire has been received. The majority of those killed and wounded in these aerial attacks are reported to be women and children, even when some combatants are caught as well. However, the government regards these civilian casualties as a regrettable side effect of what is a legitimate attack against an armed enemy.

It might be thought easy to dismiss this as soph-istry: if one bombs, burns, or strafes a village con-taining a hundred people, twenty of whom one believes to be guerrillas, so that by killing most of them one will be statistically likely to kill most of the

guerrillas, then isn't one's attack on the group of one hundred a *means* of destroying the guerrillas, pure and simple? If one makes no attempt to discriminate between guerrillas and civilians, as is impossible in a aerial attack on a small village, then one cannot regard as a mere side effect the deaths of those in the group that one would not have bothered to kill if more selective means had been available.

The difficulty is that this argument depends on one particular description of the act, and the reply might be that the means used against the guerrillas is not: killing everybody in the village—but rather: obliteration bombing of the *area* in which the twenty guerrillas are known to be located. If there are civil-ians in the area as well, they will be killed as a side effect of such action.[4]

Because of casuistical problems like this, I prefer to stay with the original, unanalyzed distinction between what one does to people and what merely happens to them as a result of what one does. The law of double effect provides an approximation to that distinction in many cases, and perhaps it can be sharpened to the point where it does better than that. Certainly the original distinction itself needs clarification, particularly since some of the things we do to people involve things happening to them as a result of other things we do. In a case like the one discussed, however, it is clear that by bombing the village one slaughters and maims the civilians in it. Whereas by giving the only available medicine to one of two sufferers from a disease, one does not kill the other, even if he dies as a result.

The second technical point to take up concerns a possible misinterpretation of this feature of the posi-tion. The absolutist focus on actions rather than out-comes does not merely introduce a new, outstanding item into the catalogue of evils. That is, it does not say that the worst thing in the world is the deliberate murder of an innocent person. For if that were all, then one could presumably justify one such murder on the ground that it would prevent several others, or ten thousand on the ground that they would pre-vent a hundred thousand more. That is a familiar argument. But if this is allowable, then there is no absolute prohibition against murder after all. Abso-lutism requires that we *avoid* murder at all costs, not that we *prevent* it at all costs.[5]

Finally, let me remark on a frequent criticism of absolutism that depends on a misunderstanding. It is sometimes suggested that such prohibitions depend on a kind of moral self-interest, a primary obligation to preserve one's own moral purity, to keep one's hands clean no matter what happens to the rest of the world. If this were the position, it might be exposed to the charge of self-indulgence. After all, what gives one man a right to put the purity of his soul or the cleanness of his hands above the lives or welfare of large numbers of other people? It might be argued that a public servant like Truman has no right to put himself first in that way; therefore if he is convinced that the alternatives would be worse, he must give the order to drop the bombs, and take the burden of those deaths on himself, as he must do other distasteful things for the general good.

But there are two confusions behind the view that moral self-interest underlies moral absolutism. First, it is a confusion to suggest that the need to preserve one's moral purity might be the *source* of an obligation. For if by committing murder one sacrifices one's moral purity or integrity, that can only be because there is *already* something wrong with murder. The general reason against committing murder cannot therefore be merely that it makes one an immoral person. Secondly, the notion that one might sacrifice one's moral integrity justifiably, in the service of a sufficiently worthy end, is an incoherent notion. For if one were justified in making such a sacrifice (or even morally required to make it), then one would not be sacrificing one's moral integrity by adopting that course: one would be preserving it.

Moral absolutism is not unique among moral theories in requiring each person to do what will preserve his own moral purity in all circumstances. This is equally true of utilitarianism, or of any other theory which distinguishes between right and wrong. Any theory which defines the right course of action in various circumstances and asserts that one should adopt that course, ipso facto asserts that one should do what will preserve one's moral purity, simply because the right course of action *is* what will preserve one's moral purity in those circumstances. Of course utilitarianism does not assert that this is *why*

one should adopt that course, but we have seen that the same is true of absolutism.

V

It is easier to dispose of false explanations of absolutism than to produce a true one. A positive account of the matter must begin with the observation that war, conflict, and aggression are relations between persons. The view that it can be wrong to consider merely the overall effect of one's actions on the general welfare comes into prominence when those actions involve relations with others. A man's acts usually affect more people than he deals with directly, and those effects must naturally be considered in his decisions. But if there are special principles governing the manner in which he should *treat* people, that will require special attention to the particular persons toward whom the act is directed, rather than just to its total effect.

Absolutist restrictions in warfare appear to be of two types: restrictions on the class of persons at whom aggression or violence may be directed and restrictions on the manner of attack, given that the object falls within that class. These can be combined, however, under the principle that hostile treatment of any person must be justified in terms of something *about that person* which makes the treatment appropriate. Hostility is a personal relation, and it must be suited to its target. One consequence of this condition will be that certain persons may not be subjected to hostile treatment in war at all, since nothing about them justifies such treatment. Others will be proper objects of hostility only in certain circumstances, or when they are engaged in certain pursuits. And the appropriate manner and extent of hostile treatment will depend on what is justified by the particular case.

A coherent view of this type will hold that extremely hostile behavior toward another is compatible with treating him as a person—even perhaps as an end in himself. This is possible only if one has not automatically stopped treating him as a person as soon as one starts to fight with him. If hostile, aggressive, or combative treatment of others always violated the condition that they be treated as human beings, it would be difficult to make further distinctions on that score *within* the class of hostile actions.

That point of view, on the level of international relations, leads to the position that if complete pacifism is not accepted, no holds need be barred at all, and we may slaughter and massacre to our hearts' content, if it seems advisable. Such a position is often expressed in discussions of war crimes.

But the fact is that ordinary people do not believe this about conflicts, physical or otherwise, between individuals, and there is no more reason why it should be true of conflicts between nations. There seems to be a perfectly natural conception of the distinction between fighting clean and fighting dirty. To fight dirty is to direct one's hostility or aggression not at its proper object, but at a peripheral target which may be more vulnerable, and through which the proper object can be attacked indirectly. This applies in a fist fight, an election campaign, a duel, or a philosophical argument. If the concept is general enough to apply to all these matters, it should apply to war—both to the conduct of individual soldiers and to the conduct of nations.

Suppose that you are a candidate for public office, convinced that the election of your opponent would be a disaster, that he is an unscrupulous demagogue who will serve a narrow range of interests and seriously infringe the rights of those who disagree with him; and suppose you are convinced that you cannot defeat him by conventional means. Now imagine that various unconventional means present themselves as possibilities: you possess information about his sex life which would scandalize the electorate if made public; or you learn that his wife is an alcoholic or that in his youth he was associated for a brief period with a proscribed political party, and you believe that this information could be used to blackmail him into withdrawing his candidacy; or you can have a team of your supporters flatten the tires of a crucial subset of his supporters on election day; or you are in a position to stuff the ballot boxes; or, more simply, you can have him assassinated. What is wrong with these methods, given that they will achieve an overwhelmingly desirable result?

There are, of course, many things wrong with them: some are against the law; some infringe the procedures of an electoral process to which you are presumably committed by taking part in it; very importantly, some may backfire, and it is in the interest of all political candidates to adhere to an unspoken agreement not to allow certain personal matters to intrude into a campaign. But that is not all. We have in addition the feeling that these measures, these methods of attack are *irrelevant* to the issue, between you and your opponent, that in taking them up you would not be directing yourself to that which makes him an object of your opposition. You would be directing your attack not at the true target of your hostility, but at peripheral targets that happen to be vulnerable.

The same is true of a fight or argument outside the framework of any system of regulations or law. In an altercation with a taxi driver over an excessive fare, it is inappropriate to taunt him about his accent, flatten one of his tires, or smear chewing gum on his windshield; and it remains inappropriate even if he casts aspersions on your race, politics, or religion, or dumps the contents of your suitcase into the street.[6]

The importance of such restrictions may vary with the seriousness of the case; and what is unjustifiable in one case may be justified in a more extreme one. But they all derive from a single principle: that hostility or aggression should be directed at its true object. This means both that it should be directed at the person or persons who provoke it and that it should aim more specifically at what is provocative about them. The second condition will determine what form the hostility may appropriately take.

It is evident that some idea of the relation in which one should stand to other people underlies this principle, but the idea is difficult to state. I believe it is roughly this: whatever one does to another person intentionally must be aimed at him as a subject, with the intention that he receive it as a subject. It should manifest an attitude to *him* rather than just to the situation, and he should be able to recognize it and identify himself as its object. The procedures by which such an attitude is manifested need not be addressed to the person directly. Surgery, for example, is not a form of personal confrontation but part of a medical treatment that can be offered to a patient face to face and received by him as a response to his needs and the natural outcome of an attitude toward *him*.

Hostile treatment, unlike surgery, is already addressed *to* a person, and does not take its interpersonal meaning from a wider context. But hostile acts can serve as the expression or implementation of only a limited range of attitudes to the person who is attacked. Those attitudes in turn have as objects certain real or presumed characteristics or activities of the person which are thought to justify them. When this background is absent, hostile or aggressive behavior can no longer be intended for the reception of the victim as a subject. Instead it takes on the character of a purely bureaucratic operation. This occurs when one attacks someone who is not the true object of one's hostility—the true object may be someone else, who can be attacked through the victim; or one may not be manifesting a hostile attitude toward anyone, but merely using the easiest available path to some desired goal. One finds oneself not facing or addressing the victim at all, but operating on him—without the larger context of personal interaction that surrounds a surgical operation.

If absolutism is to defend its claim to priority over considerations of utility, it must hold that the maintenance of a direct interpersonal response to the people one deals with is a requirement which no advantages can justify one in abandoning. The requirement is absolute only if it rules out any calculation of what would justify its violation. I have said earlier that there may be circumstances so extreme that they render an absolutist position untenable. One may find then that one has no choice but to do something terrible. Nevertheless, even in such cases absolutism retains its force in that one cannot claim *justification* for the violation. It does not become *all right*.

As a tentative effort to explain this, let me try to connect absolutist limitations with the possibility of justifying *to the victim* what is being done to him. If one abandons a person in the course of rescuing several others from a fire or a sinking ship, one *could* say to him, "You understand, I have to leave you to save the others." Similarly, if one subjects an unwilling child to a painful surgical procedure, one can say to him, "If you could understand, you would realize that I am doing this to help you." One could *even* say, as one bayonets an enemy soldier, "It's either you or me." But one cannot really say while torturing a prisoner, "You understand, I have to pull out your fingernails because it is absolutely essential that we have the names of your confederates"; nor can one say to the victims of Hiroshima, "You understand,

we have to incinerate you to provide the Japanese government with an incentive to surrender."

This does not take us very far, of course, since a utilitarian would presumably be willing to offer justifications of the latter sort to his victims, in cases where he thought they were sufficient. They are really justifications to the world at large, which the victim, as a reasonable man, would be expected to appreciate. However, there seems to me something wrong with this view, for it ignores the possibility that to treat someone else horribly puts you in a special relation to him, which may have to be defended in terms of other features of your relation to him. The suggestion needs much more development; but it may help us to understand how there may be requirements which are absolute in the sense that there can be no justification for violating them. If the justification for what one did to another person had to be such that it could be offered to him specifically, rather than just to the world at large, that would be a significant source of restraint.

If the account is to be deepened, I would hope for some results along the following lines. Absolutism is associated with a view of oneself as a small being interacting with others in a large world. The justifications it requires are primarily interpersonal. Utilitarianism is associated with a view of oneself as a benevolent bureaucrat distributing such benefits as one can control to countless other beings, with whom one may have various relations or none. The justifications it requires are primarily administrative. The argument between the two moral attitudes may depend on the relative priority of these two conceptions.[7]

VI

Some of the restrictions on methods of warfare which have been adhered to from time to time are to be explained by the mutual interests of the involved parties: restrictions on weaponry, treatment of prisoners, etc. But that is not all there is to it. The conditions of directness and relevance which I have argued apply to relations of conflict and aggression apply to war as well. I have said that there are two types of absolutist restrictions on the conduct of war: those that limit the legitimate targets of hostility and those that limit its character, even when the target is acceptable. I shall say something about each of these. As will become clear, the principle I have sketched does not yield an unambiguous answer in every case.

First let us see how it implies that attacks on some people are allowed, but not attacks on others. It may seem paradoxical to assert that to fire a machine gun at someone who is throwing hand grenades at your emplacement is to treat him as a human being. Yet the relation with him is direct and straightforward.[8] The attack is aimed specifically against the threat presented by a dangerous adversary, and not against a peripheral target through which he happens to be vulnerable but which has nothing to do with that threat. For example, you might stop him by machine-gunning his wife and children, who are standing nearby, thus distracting him from his aim of blowing you up and enabling you to capture him. But if his wife and children are not threatening your life, that would be to treat them as means with a vengeance.

This, however, is just Hiroshima on a smaller scale. One objection to weapons of mass annihilation—nuclear, thermonuclear, biological, or chemical—is that their indiscriminateness disqualifies them as direct instruments for the expression of hostile relations. In attacking the civilian population, one treats neither the military enemy nor the civilians with that minimal respect which is owed to them as human beings. This is clearly true of the direct attack on people who present no threat at all. But it is also true of the character of the attack on those who *are* threatening you, viz., the government and military forces of the enemy. Your aggression is directed against an area of vulnerability quite distinct from any threat presented by them which you may be justified in meeting. You are taking aim at them through the mundane life and survival of their countrymen, instead of aiming at the destruction of their military capacity. And of course it does not require hydrogen bombs to commit such crimes.

This way of looking at the matter also helps us to understand the importance of the distinction between combatants and noncombatants, and the irrelevance of much of the criticism offered against its intelligibility and moral significance. According to an absolutist position, deliberate killing of the innocent is murder, and in warfare the role of the innocent is filled by noncombatants. This has been thought to raise two sorts of problems: first, the widely imagined difficulty of making a division, in modern warfare, between combatants and noncombatants; second, problems deriving from the connotation of the word "innocence."

Let me take up the latter question first.[9] In the absolutist position, the operative notion of innocence is not moral innocence, and it is not opposed to moral guilt. If it were, then we would be justified in killing a wicked but noncombatant hairdresser in an enemy city who supported the evil policies of his government, and unjustified in killing a morally pure conscript who was driving a tank toward us with the profoundest regrets and nothing but love in his heart. But moral innocence has very little to do with it, for in the definition of murder "innocent" means "currently harmless," and it is opposed not to "guilty" but to "doing harm." It should be noted that such an analysis has the consequence that in war we may often be justified in killing people who do not deserve to die, and unjustified in killing people who do deserve to die, if anyone does.

So we must distinguish combatants from noncombatants on the basis of their immediate threat or harmfulness. I do not claim that the line is a sharp one, but it is not so difficult as is often supposed to place individuals on one side of it or the other. Children are not combatants even though they may join the armed forces if they are allowed to grow up. Women are not combatants just because they bear children or offer comfort to the soldiers. More problematic are the supporting personnel, whether in or out of uniform, from drivers of munitions trucks and army cooks to civilian munitions workers and farmers. I believe they can be plausibly classified by applying the condition that the prosecution of conflict must direct itself to the cause of danger, and not to what is peripheral. The threat presented by an army and its members does not consist merely in the fact that they are men, but in the fact that they are armed and are using their arms in the pursuit of certain objectives. Contributions to their arms and logistics are contributions to this threat; contributions to their mere existence as men are not. It is therefore wrong to direct an attack against those who merely serve the combatants' needs as human beings, such as farmers and food suppliers, even though survival as a human being is a necessary condition of efficient functioning as a soldier.

This brings us to the second group of restrictions: those that limit what may be done even to combatants. These limits are harder to explain clearly. Some of them may be arbitrary or conventional, and some may have to be derived from other sources; but I believe that the condition of directness and relevance in hostile relations accounts for them to a considerable extent.

Consider first a case which involves both a protected class of noncombatants and a restriction on the measures that may be used against combatants. One provision of the rules of war which is universally recognized, though it seems to be turning into a dead letter in Vietnam, is the special status of medical personnel and the wounded in warfare. It might be more efficient to shoot medical officers on sight and to let the enemy wounded die rather than be patched up to fight another day. But someone with medical insignia is supposed to be left alone and permitted to tend and retrieve the wounded. I believe this is because medical attention is a species of attention to completely general human needs, not specifically the needs of a combat soldier, and our conflict with the soldier is not with his existence as a human being.

By extending the application of this idea, one can justify prohibitions against certain particularly cruel weapons: starvation, poisoning, infectious diseases (supposing they could be inflicted on combatants only), weapons designed to maim or disfigure or torture the opponent rather than merely to stop him. It is not, I think, mere casuistry to claim that such weapons attack the men, not the soldiers. The effect of dum-dum bullets, for example, is much more extended than necessary to cope with the combat situation in which they are used. They abandon any attempt to discriminate in their effects between the combatant and the human being. For this reason the use of flamethrowers and napalm is an atrocity in all circumstances that I can imagine, whoever the target may be. Burns are both extremely painful and extremely disfiguring—far more than any other category of wound. That this well-known fact plays no (inhibiting) part in the determination

of U.S. weapons policy suggests that moral sensitivity among public officials has not increased markedly since the Spanish Inquisition.[10]

Finally, the same condition of appropriateness to the true object of hostility should limit the scope of attacks on an enemy country: its economy, agriculture, transportation system, and so forth. Even if the parties to a military conflict are considered to be not armies or governments but entire nations (which is usually a grave error), that does not justify one nation in warring against every aspect or element of another nation. That is not justified in a conflict between individuals, and nations are even more complex than individuals, so the same reasons apply. Like a human being, a nation is engaged in countless other pursuits while waging war, and it is not in those respects that it is an enemy.

The burden of the argument has been that absolutism about murder has a foundation in principles governing all one's relations to other persons, whether aggressive or amiable, and that these principles, and that absolutism, apply to warfare as well, with the result that certain measures are impermissible no matter what the consequences.[11] I do not mean to romanticize war. It is sufficiently utopian to suggest that when nations conflict they might rise to the level of limited barbarity that typically characterizes violent conflict between individuals, rather than wallowing in the moral pit where they appear to have settled, surrounded by enormous arsenals.

VII

Having described the elements of the absolutist position, we must now return to the conflict between it and utilitarianism. Even if certain types of dirty tactics become acceptable when the stakes are high enough, the most serious of the prohibited acts, like murder and torture, are not just supposed to require unusually strong justification. They are supposed *never* to be done, because no quantity of resulting benefit is thought capable of *justifying* such treatment of a person.

The fact remains that when an absolutist knows or believes that the utilitarian cost of refusing to adopt a prohibited course will be very high, he may hold to his refusal to adopt it, but he will find it difficult to feel that a moral dilemma has been satisfactorily resolved. The same may be true of someone who rejects an absolutist requirement and adopts instead the course yielding the most acceptable consequences. In either case, it is possible to feel that one has acted for reasons insufficient to justify violation of the opposing principle. In situations of deadly conflict, particularly where a weaker party is threatened with annihilation or enslavement by a stronger one, the argument for resorting to atrocities can be powerful, and the dilemma acute.

There may exist principles, not yet codified, which would enable us to resolve such dilemmas. But then again there may not. We must face the pessimistic alternative that these two forms of moral intuition are not capable of being brought together into a single, coherent moral system, and that the world can present us with situations in which there is no honorable or moral course for a man to take, no course free of guilt and responsibility for evil.

The idea of a moral blind alley is a perfectly intelligible one. It is possible to get into such a situation by one's own fault, and people do it all the time. If, for example, one makes two incompatible promises or commitments—becomes engaged to two people, for example—then there is no course one can take which is not wrong, for one must break one's promise to at least one of them. Making a clean breast of the whole thing will not be enough to remove one's reprehensibility. The existence of such cases is not morally disturbing, however, because we feel that the situation was not unavoidable: one had to do something wrong in the first place to get into it. But what if the world itself, or someone else's actions, could face a previously innocent person with a choice between morally abominable courses of action, and leave him no way to escape with his honor? Our intuitions rebel at the idea, for we feel that the constructibility of such a case must show a contradiction in our moral views. But it is not in itself a contradiction to say that someone can do X or not do X, and that for him to take either course would be wrong. It merely contradicts the supposition that *ought* implies *can*—since presumably one ought to refrain from what is wrong, and in such a case it is impossible to do so.[12] Given the limitations on human action, it is naïve to suppose that there is

a solution to every moral problem with which the world can face us. We have always known that the world is a bad place. It appears that it may be an evil place as well.

Notes

This paper grew out of discussions at the Society for Ethical and Legal Philosophy, and I am indebted to my fellow members for their help.

1. Straightforward considerations of national interest often tend in the same direction: the inadvisability of using nuclear weapons seems to be overdetermined in this way.

2. These reasons, moreover, have special importance in that they are available even to one who denies the appropriateness of utilitarian considerations in international matters. He may acknowledge limitations on what may be done to the soldiers and civilians of other countries in pursuit of his nation's military objectives, while denying that one country should in general consider the interests of nationals of other countries in determining its policies.

3. (Privately printed.) See also her essay "War and Murder," in *Nuclear Weapons and Christian Conscience,* ed. Walter Stein (London, 1963). The present paper is much indebted to these two essays throughout. These and related subjects are extensively treated by Paul Ramsey in *The Just War* (New York, 1968). Among recent writings that bear on the moral problem are Jonathan Bennett, "Whatever the Consequences," *Analysis* 26, no. 3 (1966): 83–102; and Philippa Foot, "The Problem of Abortion and the Doctrine of the Double Effect," *Oxford Review* 5 (1967): 5–15. Miss Anscombe's replies are "A Note on Mr. Bennett," *Analysis* 26, no. 3 (1966): 208, and "Who Is Wronged?" *Oxford Review* 5 (1967): 16–17.

4. This counterargument was suggested by Rogers Albritton.

5. Someone might of course acknowledge the *moral relevance* of the distinction between deliberate and nondeliberate killing, without being an absolutist. That is, he might believe simply that it was *worse* to bring about a death deliberately than as a secondary effect. But that would be merely a special assignment of value, and not an absolute prohibition.

6. Why, on the other hand, does it seem appropriate, rather than irrelevant, to punch someone in the mouth if he insults you? The answer is that in our

culture it is an insult to punch someone in the mouth, and not just an injury. This reveals, by the way, a perfectly unobjectionable sense in which convention may play a part in determining exactly what falls under an absolutist restriction and what does not. I am indebted to Robert Fogelin for this point.

7. Finally, I should mention a different possibility, suggested by Robert Nozick: that there is a strong general presumption against benefiting from the calamity of another, whether or not it has been deliberately inflicted for that or any other reason. This broader principle may well lend its force to the absolutist position.

8. It has been remarked that according to my view, shooting at someone establishes an I-thou relationship.

9. What I say on this subject derives from Anscombe.

10. Beyond this I feel uncertain. Ordinary bullets, after all, can cause death, and nothing is more permanent than that. I am not at all sure why we are justified in trying to kill those who are trying to kill us (rather than merely in trying to stop them with force which may also result in their deaths). It is often argued that incapacitating gases are a relatively humane weapon (when not used, as in Vietnam, merely to make people easier to shoot). Perhaps the legitimacy of restrictions against them must depend on the dangers of escalation, and the great utility of maintaining *any* conventional category of restriction so long as nations are willing to adhere to it.

Let me make clear that I do not regard my argument as a defense of the moral immutability of the Hague and Geneva Conventions. Rather, I believe that they rest partly on a moral foundation, and that modifications of them should also be assessed on moral grounds.

But even this connection with the actual laws of war is not essential to my claims about what is permissible and what is not. Since completing this paper I have read an essay by Richard Wasserstrom entitled "The Laws of War" (*The Monist*, 56, 1 (1972): 1–19), which argues that the existing laws and conventions do not even attempt to embody a decent moral position: that their provisions have been determined by other interests, that they are in fact immoral in substance, and that it is a grave mistake to refer to them as standards in forming moral judgments about warfare. This possibility deserves serious consideration, and I am not sure what to say about it, but it does not affect my view of the moral issues.

11. It is possible to draw a more radical conclusion, which I shall not pursue here. Perhaps the technology and organization of modern war are such as to make it impossible to wage as an acceptable form of interpersonal or even international hostility. Perhaps it is too impersonal and large-scale for that. If so, then absolutism would in practice imply pacifism, given the present state of things. On the other hand, I am skeptical about the unstated assumption that a technology dictates its own use.

12. This was first pointed out to me by Christopher Boorse.

QUESTIONS

1. Nagel does not clearly characterize his two views, utilitarianism and absolutism. Try to formulate clear characterizations given what he says about these views in the text.

2. Is the choice between these two perspectives a genuine dilemma? Does Nagel think it can be resolved?

25. Supreme Emergency

MICHAEL WALZER

Michael Walzer (1935–) is a well-known political thinker and public intellectual. He is professor emeritus of the Institute for Advanced Study in Princeton, New Jersey, and editor of the quarterly review *Dissent*. He has written important works on war, nationalism, justice, tolerance, Jewish political thought, and other subjects. His books include *Just and Unjust Wars* (1977), *Spheres of Justice* (1983), *What It Means to Be an American* (1992), and *Arguing about War* (2004).

Just and Unjust Wars, now in its third edition, is the most influential contemporary statement and defense of just war theory. In the following excerpt Walzer raises questions about situations he calls "supreme emergency" where some of the rules of war may be overridden, or so he argues. He is thinking of the situation, mentioned by Rawls in chapter 23, confronting the British in the early years of World War II, when the survival and freedom of British society was threatened. Walzer argues that threats against "the survival and freedom of political communities . . . are the highest values of international society" and may justify overriding the rules of war. His case has been enormously controversial and the subject of much discussion.

The Nature of Necessity

Everyone's troubles make a crisis. "Emergency" and "crisis" are cant words, used to prepare our minds for acts of brutality. And yet there are such things as critical moments in the lives of men and women and in the history of states. Certainly, war is such a time: every war is an emergency, every battle a possible turning point. Fear and hysteria are always latent in combat, often real, and they press us toward fearful measures and criminal behavior. The war convention is a bar to such measures, not always effective, but there nevertheless. In principle at least, as we have seen, it resists the ordinary crises of military life. Churchill's description of Britain's predicament in 1939 as a "supreme emergency" was a piece of rhetorical heightening designed to overcome that resistance. But the phrase also contains an argument:

that there is a fear beyond the ordinary fearfulness (and the frantic opportunism) of war, and a danger to which that fear corresponds, and that this fear and danger may well require exactly those measures that the war convention bars. Now, a great deal is at stake here, both for the men and women driven to adopt such measures and for their victims, so we must attend carefully to the implicit argument of "supreme emergency."

Though its use is often ideological, the meaning of the phrase is a matter of common sense. It is defined by two criteria, which correspond to the two levels on which the concept of necessity works: the first has to do with the imminence of the danger and the second with its nature. The two criteria must both be applied. Neither one by itself is sufficient as an account of extremity or as a defense of

From Michael Walzer, *Just and Unjust Wars* (New York: Basic Books, 1977). Reprinted by permission of the Perseus Book Group.

the extraordinary measures extremity is thought to require. Close but not serious, serious but not close—neither one makes for a supreme emergency. But since people at war can rarely agree on the seriousness of the dangers they face (or pose for one another), the idea of closeness is sometimes made to do the job alone. Then we are offered what might best be called the back-to-the wall argument: that when conventional means of resistance are hopeless or worn out, anything goes (anything that is "necessary" to win). Thus British Prime Minister Stanley Baldwin, writing in 1932 about the dangers of terror bombing:[1]

> Will any form of prohibition of bombing, whether by convention, treaty, agreement, or anything you like, be effective in war? Frankly, I doubt it, and in doubting it, I make no reflection on the good faith of either ourselves or any other country. If a man has a potential weapon and has his back to the wall and is going to be killed, he will use that weapon, whatever it is and whatever undertaking he has given about it.

The first thing that has to be said about this statement is that Baldwin does not mean his domestic analogy to be applied literally. Soldiers and statesmen commonly say that their backs are to the wall whenever military defeat seems imminent, and Baldwin is endorsing this view of extremity. The analogy is from survival at home to victory in the international sphere. Baldwin claims that people will necessarily (inevitably) adopt extreme measures if such measures are necessary (essential) either to escape death or to avoid military defeat. But the argument is wrong at both ends. It is simply not the case that individuals will always strike out at innocent men and women rather than accept risks for themselves. We even say, very often, that it is their duty to accept risks (and perhaps to die); and here as in moral life generally, "ought" implies "can." We make the demand knowing that it is possible for people to live up to it. Can we make the same demand on political leaders, acting not for themselves but for their countrymen? That will depend upon the dangers their countrymen face. What is it that defeat entails? Is it some minor territorial adjustment, a loss of face (for the leaders), the payment of heavy

indemnities, political reconstruction of this or that sort, the surrender of national independence, the exile or murder of millions of people? In such cases, one's back is always to the wall, but the dangers one confronts take very different forms, and the different forms make a difference.

If we are to adopt or defend the adoption of extreme measures, the danger must be of an unusual and horrifying kind. Such descriptions, I suppose, are common enough in time of war. One's enemies are often thought to be—at least they are often said to be—unusual and horrifying.[2] Soldiers are encouraged to fight fiercely if they believe that they are fighting for the survival of their country and their families, that freedom, justice, civilization itself are at risk. But this sort of thing is only sometimes plausible to the detached observer, and one suspects that its propagandistic character is also understood by many of the participants. War is not always a struggle over ultimate values, where the victory of one side would be a human disaster for the other. It is necessary to be skeptical about such matters, to cultivate a wary disbelief of wartime rhetoric, and then to search for some touchstone against which arguments about extremity might be judged. We need to make a map of human crises and to mark off the regions of desperation and disaster. These and only these constitute the realm of necessity, truly understood. Once again, I am going to use the experience of World War II in Europe to suggest at least the rough contours of the map. For Nazism lies at the outer limits of exigency, at a point where we are likely to find ourselves united in fear and abhorrence.

That is what I am going to assume, at any rate, on behalf of all those people who believed at the time and still believe a third of a century later that Nazism was an ultimate threat to everything decent in our lives, an ideology and a practice of domination so murderous, so degrading even to those who might survive, that the consequences of its final victory were literally beyond calculation, immeasurably awful. We see it—and I don't use the phrase lightly—as evil objectified in the world, and in a form so potent and apparent that there could never have been anything to do but fight against it. I obviously cannot offer an account of Nazism in these pages.

But such an account is hardly necessary. It is enough to point to the historical experience of Nazi rule. Here was a threat to human values so radical that its imminence would surely constitute a supreme emergency; and this example can help us understand why lesser threats might not do so.

In order to get the map right, however, we must imagine a Nazi-like danger somewhat different from the one the Nazis actually posed. When Churchill said that a German victory in World War II "would be fatal, not only to ourselves, but to the independent life of every small country in Europe," he was speaking the exact truth. The danger was a general one. But suppose it had existed for Britain alone. Can a supreme emergency be constituted by a particular threat—by a threat of enslavement or extermination directed against a single nation? Can soldiers and statesmen override the rights of innocent people for the sake of their own political community? I am inclined to answer this question affirmatively, though not without hesitation and worry. What choice do they have? They might sacrifice themselves in order to uphold the moral law, but they cannot sacrifice their countrymen. Faced with some ultimate horror, their options exhausted, they will do what they must to save their own people. That is not to say that their decision is inevitable (I have no way of knowing that), but the sense of obligation and of moral urgency they are likely to feel at such a time is so overwhelming that a different outcome is hard to imagine.

Still, the question is difficult, as its domestic analogue suggests. Despite Baldwin, it is not usually said of individuals in domestic society that they necessarily will or that they morally can strike out at innocent people, even in the supreme emergency of self-defense.[3] They can only attack their attackers. But communities, in emergencies, seem to have different and larger prerogatives. I am not sure that I can account for the difference, without ascribing to communal life a kind of transcendence that I don't believe it to have. Perhaps it is only a matter of arithmetic: individuals cannot kill other individuals to save themselves, but to save a nation we can violate the rights of a determinate but smaller number of people. But then large nations and small ones would have different entitlements in such cases, and I

doubt very much that that is true. We might better say that it is possible to live in a world where individuals are sometimes murdered, but a world where entire peoples are enslaved or massacred is literally unbearable. For the survival and freedom of political communities—whose members share a way of life, developed by their ancestors, to be passed on to their children—are the highest values of international society. Nazism challenged these values on a grand scale, but challenges more narrowly conceived, *if they are of the same kind,* have similar moral consequences. They bring us under the rule of necessity (and necessity knows no rules).

I want to stress again, however, that the mere recognition of such a threat is not itself coercive; it neither compels nor permits attacks on the innocent, so long as other means of fighting and winning are available. Danger makes only half the argument; imminence makes the other half. Now let us consider a time when the two halves came together: the terrible two years that followed the defeat of France, from the summer of 1940 to the summer of 1942, when Hitler's armies were everywhere triumphant.

Overriding the Rules of War

The Decision to Bomb German Cities

There have been few decisions more important than this one in the history of warfare. As a direct result of the adoption of a policy of terror bombing by the leaders of Britain, some 300,000 Germans, most of them civilians, were killed and another 780,000 seriously injured. No doubt, these figures are low when compared to the results of Nazi genocide; but they were, after all, the work of men and women at war with Nazism, who hated everything it stood for and who were not supposed to imitate its effects, even at lagging rates. And the British policy had further consequences: it was the crucial precedent for the fire-bombing of Tokyo and other Japanese cities and then for Harry Truman's decision to drop atomic bombs on Hiroshima and Nagasaki. The civilian death toll from Allied terrorism in World War II must have exceeded half a million men, women, and children. How could the initial choice of this ultimate weapon ever have been defended?

The history is a complex one, and it has already been the subject of several monographic analyses.[4] I can review it only briefly, attending especially to the arguments put forward at the time by Churchill and other British leaders, and always remembering what sort of a time it was. The decision to bomb cities was made late in 1940. A directive issued in June of that year had "specifically laid down that targets had to be identified and aimed at. Indiscriminate bombing was forbidden." In November, after the German raid on Coventry, "Bomber Command was instructed simply to aim at the center of a city." What had once been called indiscriminate bombing (and commonly condemned) was now required, and by early 1942, aiming at military or industrial targets was barred: "the aiming points are to be the built-up areas, *not,* for instance, the dockyards or aircraft factories."[5] The purpose of the raids was explicitly declared to be the destruction of civilian morale. Following the famous minute of Lord Cherwell in 1942, the means to this demoralization were specified: working-class residential areas were the prime targets. Cherwell thought it possible to render a third of the German population homeless by 1943.[6]

Before Cherwell provided his "scientific" rationale for the bombing, a number of reasons had already been offered for the British decision. From the beginning, the attacks were defended as reprisals for the German blitz. This is a very problematic defense, even if we leave aside the difficulties of the doctrine of reprisals (which I have already canvassed). First of all, it appears possible, as one scholar has recently argued, that Churchill deliberately provoked the German attacks on London—by bombing Berlin—in order to relieve pressure on R.A.F. installations, until then the major *Luftwaffe* target.[7] Nor was it Churchill's purpose, once the blitz began, to deter the German attacks or to establish a policy of mutual restraint.[8]

> We ask no favor of the enemy. We seek from them no compunction. On the contrary, if tonight the people of London were asked to cast their votes whether a convention should be entered into to stop the bombing of all cities, the overwhelming majority would cry, "No, we will mete out to the Germans the measure, and more than the measure, that they have meted out to us."

Needless to say, the people of London were not in fact asked to vote on such a convention. Churchill assumed that the bombing of German cities was necessary to their morale and that they wanted to hear (what he told them in a radio broadcast of 1941) that the British air force was making "the German people taste and gulp each month a sharper dose of the miseries they have showered upon mankind."[9] This argument has been accepted by many historians: there was "a popular clamor" for revenge, one of them writes, which Churchill had to satisfy if he was to maintain a fighting spirit among his own people. It is especially interesting to note, then, that a 1941 opinion poll showed that "the most determined demand for [reprisal raids] came from Cumberland, Westmoreland, and the North Riding of Yorkshire, rural areas barely touched by bombing, where some three-quarters of the population wanted them. In central London, conversely, the proportion was only 45 percent."[10] Men and women who had experienced terror bombing were less likely to support Churchill's policy than those who had not—a heartening statistic, and one which suggests that the morale of the British people (or perhaps better, their conventional morality) allowed for political leadership of a different sort than Churchill provided. The news that Germany was being bombed was certainly glad tidings in Britain; but as late as 1944, according to other opinion surveys, the overwhelming majority of Britishers still believed that the raids were directed solely against military targets. Presumably, that is what they wanted to believe; there was by then quite a bit of evidence to the contrary. But that says something, again, about the character of British morale. (It should also be said that the campaign against terror bombing, run largely by pacifists, attracted very little popular support.)

Reprisal was a bad argument; revenge was a worse one. We must concentrate now on the military justifications for terror bombing, which were presumably paramount in Churchill's mind, whatever he said on the radio. I can discuss these only in a general way. There was a great deal of dispute at the time, some of it technical, some of it moral in character. The calculations of the Cherwell minute, for example, were sharply attacked by a group of scientists whose opposition to terrorism may well have had moral grounds, but whose position, to the best of my knowledge, was never stated in moral terms.[11] Explicit moral disagreement developed most importantly among the professional soldiers involved in the decision-making process. These disagreements are described, in characteristic fashion, by a strategic analyst and historian who has studied the British escalation: "The . . . debate had been beclouded by emotion on one side of the argument, on the part of those who as a matter of moral principle objected to making war on civilians."[12] The focus of these objections seems to have been some version of the doctrine of double effect. (The arguments had, to the mind of the strategic analyst, "a curiously scholastic flavor.") At the height of the blitz, many British officers still felt strongly that their own air attacks should be aimed only at military targets and that positive efforts should be made to minimize civilian casualties. They did not want to imitate Hitler, but to differentiate themselves from him. Even officers who accepted the desirability of killing civilians still sought to maintain their professional honor: such deaths, they insisted, were desirable "only insofar as [they] remained a by-product of the primary intention to hit a military target . . ."[13] A tendentious argument, no doubt, yet one that would drastically have limited the British offensive against cities. But all such proposals ran up against the operational limits of the bomber technology then available.

Early in the war, it became clear that British bombers could fly effectively only at night and, given the navigational devices with which they were equipped, that they could reasonably aim at no target smaller than a fairly large city. A study made in 1941 indicated that of those planes that actually succeeded in attacking their target (about two-thirds of the attacking force), only one-third dropped their bombs within five miles of the point aimed at.[14] Once this was known, it would seem dishonest to claim that the intended target was, say, this aircraft factory and that the indiscriminate destruction around it was only an unintended, if foreseeable, consequence of the justified attempt to stop the production of planes. What was really unintended but foreseeable was that the factory itself would probably escape harm. If any sort of strategic bombing offensive was to be maintained, one would have to

plan for the destruction that one could and did cause. Lord Cherwell's minute was an effort at such planning. In fact, of course, navigational devices were rapidly improved as the war went on, and the bombing of specific military targets was an important part of Britain's total air offensive, receiving top priority at times (before the June 1944 invasion of France, for example) and cutting into the resources allowed for attacks on cities. Today many experts believe that the war might have ended sooner had there been a greater concentration of air power against targets such as the German oil refineries.[15] But the decision to bomb cities was made at a time when victory was not in sight and the specter of defeat ever present. And it was made when no other decision seemed possible if there was to be any sort of military offensive against Nazi Germany.

Bomber Command was the only offensive weapon available to the British in those frightening years, and I expect there is some truth to the notion that it was used simply because it was there. "It was the only force in the West," writes Arthur Harris, chief of Bomber Command from early 1942 until the end of the war, "which could take offensive action against . . . Germany, our only means of getting at the enemy in a way that would hurt at all."[16] Offensive action could have been postponed until (or in hope of) some more favorable time. That is what the war convention would require, and there was also considerable military pressure for postponement. Harris was hard-pressed to keep his Command together in the face of repeated calls for tactical air support—which would have been coordinated with ground action largely defensive in character, since the German armies were still advancing everywhere. Sometimes, in his memoirs, he sounds like a bureaucrat defending his function and his office, but obviously he was also defending a certain conception of how the war might best be fought. He did not believe that the weapons he commanded should be used because he commanded them. He believed that the tactical use of bombers could not stop Hitler and that the destruction of cities could. Later in the war, he argued that only the destruction of cities could bring the fighting to a quick conclusion. The first of these arguments, at least, deserves a careful examination. It was apparently accepted by the Prime Minister. "The bombers alone," Churchill had said as early as September 1940, "provide the means of victory."[17]

The bombers alone—that poses the issue very starkly, and perhaps wrongly, given the disputes over strategy to which I have already referred. Churchill's statement suggested a certainty to which neither he nor anyone else had any right. But the issue can be put so as to accommodate a degree of skepticism and to permit even the most sophisticated among us to indulge in a common and a morally important fantasy: suppose that I sat in the seat of power and had to decide whether to use Bomber Command (in the only way that it could be used systematically and effectively) against cities. Suppose further that unless the bombers were used in this way, the probability that Germany would eventually be defeated would be radically reduced. It makes no sense at this point to quantify the probabilities; I have no clear notion what they actually were or even how they might be calculated given our present knowledge; nor am I sure how different figures, unless they were very different, would affect the moral argument. But it does seem to me that the more certain a German victory appeared to be in the absence of a bomber offensive, the more justifiable was the decision to launch the offensive. It is not just that such a victory was frightening, but also that it seemed in those years very close; it is not just that it was close, but also that it was so frightening. Here was a supreme emergency, where one might well be required to override the rights of innocent people and shatter the war convention.

Given the view of Nazism that I am assuming, the issue takes this form: should I wager this determinate crime (the killing of innocent people) against that immeasurable evil (a Nazi triumph)? Obviously, if there is some other way of avoiding the evil or even a reasonable chance of another way, I must wager differently or elsewhere. But I can never hope to be sure; a wager is not an experiment. Even if I wager and win, it is still possible that I was wrong, that my crime was unnecessary to victory. But I can argue that I studied the case as closely as I was able, took the best advice I could find, sought out available alternatives. And if all this is true, and my perception of evil and imminent danger not hysterical or self-serving, then surely I must wager. There is no

option; the risk otherwise is too great. My own action is determinate, of course, only as to its direct consequences, while the rule that bars such acts is founded on a conception of rights that transcends all immediate considerations. It arises out of our common history; it holds the key to our common future. But I dare to say that our history will be nullified and our future condemned unless I accept the burdens of criminality here and now.

This is not an easy argument to make, and yet we must resist every effort to make it easier. Many people undoubtedly found some comfort in the fact that the cities being bombed were German and some of the victims Nazis. In effect, they applied the sliding scale and denied or diminished the rights of German civilians so as to deny or diminish the horror of their deaths. This is a tempting procedure, as we can see most clearly if we consider again the bombing of occupied France. Allied fliers killed many Frenchmen, but they did so while bombing what were (or were thought to be) military targets. They did not deliberately aim at the "built-up areas" of French cities. Suppose such a policy had been proposed. I am sure that we would all find the wager more difficult to undertake and defend if, through some strange combination of circumstances, it required the deliberate slaughter of Frenchmen. For we had special commitments to the French; we were fighting on their behalf (and sometimes the bombers were flown by French pilots). But the status of the civilians in the two cases is no different. The theory that distinguishes combatants from noncombatants does not distinguish Allied from enemy noncombatants, at least not with regard to the question of their murder. I suppose it makes sense to say that there were more people in German than in French cities who were responsible (in some fashion) for the evil of Nazism, and we may well be reluctant to extend to them the full range of civilian rights. But even if that reluctance is justified, there is no way for the bombers to search out the right people. And for all the others, terrorism only reiterates the tyranny that the Nazis had already established. It assimilates ordinary men and women to their government as if the two really made a totality, and it judges them in a totalitarian way. If one is forced to bomb cities, it seems to me, it is best to acknowledge that one has also been forced to kill the innocent.

Once again, however, I want to set radical limits to the notion of necessity even as I have myself been using it. For the truth is that the supreme emergency passed long before the British bombing reached its crescendo. The greater number by far of the German civilians killed by terror bombing were killed without moral (and probably also without military) reason. The decisive point was made by Churchill in July of 1942:[18]

> In the days when we were fighting alone, we answered the question: "How are you going to win the war?" by saying: "We will shatter Germany by bombing." Since then the enormous injuries inflicted on the German Army and manpower by the Russians, and the accession of the manpower and munitions of the United States, have rendered other possibilities open.

Surely, then, it was time to stop the bombing of cities and to aim, tactically and strategically, only at legitimate military targets. But that was not Churchill's view: "All the same, it would be a mistake to cast aside our original thought . . . that the severe, ruthless bombing of Germany on an ever-increasing scale will not only cripple her war effort . . . but will create conditions intolerable to the mass of the German population." So the raids continued, culminating in the spring of 1945—when the war was virtually won—in a savage attack on the city of Dresden in which something like 100,000 people were killed.[19] Only then did Churchill have second thoughts. "It seems to me that the moment has come when the question of bombing German cities simply for the sake of increasing the terror, though under other pretexts, should be reviewed . . . The destruction of Dresden remains a serious query against the conduct of Allied bombing."[20] Indeed it does, but so does the destruction of Hamburg and Berlin and all the other cities attacked simply for the sake of terror.

The argument used between 1942 and 1945 in defense of terror bombing was utilitarian in character, its emphasis not on victory itself but on the time and price of victory. The city raids, it was claimed by men such as Harris, would end the war sooner than it would otherwise end, and, despite the large number of civilian casualties they inflicted, at a lower cost in human life. Assuming this claim to be true (I have already indicated that precisely opposite claims are made by some historians and strategists), it is nevertheless not sufficient to justify the bombing. It is not sufficient, I think, even if we do nothing more than calculate utilities. For such calculations need not be concerned only with the preservation of life. There is much else that we might plausibly want to preserve: the quality of our lives, for example, our civilization and morality, our collective abhorrence of murder, even when it seems, as it always does, to serve some purpose. Then the deliberate slaughter of innocent men and women cannot be justified simply because it saves the lives of other men and women. I suppose it is possible to imagine situations where that last assertion might prove problematic from a utilitarian perspective, where the number of people involved is small, the proportions are right, the events hidden from the public eye, and so on. Philosophers delight in inventing such cases in order to test out our moral doctrines. But their inventions are somehow put out of our minds by the sheer scale of the calculations necessary in World War II. To kill 278,966 civilians (the number is made up) in order to avoid the deaths of an unknown but probably larger number of civilians and soldiers is surely a fantastic, godlike, frightening, and horrendous act.*

I have said that such acts can probably be ruled out on utilitarian grounds, but it is also true that

---

* George Orwell has suggested an alternative utilitarian rationale for the bombing of German cities. In a column written for the leftist journal *Tribune* in 1944, he argued that the bombing brought the true character of contemporary combat home to all those people who supported the war, even enjoyed it, only because they never felt its effects. It shattered "the immunity of civilians, one of the things that have made war possible," and so it made war less likely in the future. See *The Collected Essays, Journalism and Letters of George Orwell,* ed. Sonia Orwell and Ian Angus, New York, 1968, Vol. 3, pp. 151–152. Orwell assumes that civilians had really been immune in the past, which is false. In any case, I doubt that his argument would lead anyone to begin bombing cities. It is an apology after the fact, and not a convincing one.

utilitarianism as it is commonly understood, indeed, as Sidgwick himself understands it, encourages the bizarre accounting that makes them (morally) possible. We can recognize their horror only when we have acknowledged the personality and value of the men and women we destroy in committing them. It is the acknowledgment of rights that puts a stop to such calculations and forces us to realize that the destruction of the innocent, whatever its purposes, is a kind of blasphemy against our deepest moral commitments. (This is true even in a supreme emergency, when we cannot do anything else.) But I want to look at one more case before concluding my argument—a case where the utilitarian accounting, however bizarre, seemed so radically clear-cut to the decision-makers as to leave them, they thought, no choice but to attack the innocent.

The Limits of Calculation

Hiroshima

"They all accepted the 'assignment' and produced The Bomb," Dwight Macdonald wrote in August 1945 of the atomic scientists. "Why?" It is an important question, but Macdonald poses it badly and then gives the wrong answer. "Because they thought of themselves as specialists, technicians, and not as complete men."[21] In fact, they did not accept the assignment; they sought it out, taking the initiative, urging upon President Roosevelt the critical importance of an American effort to match the work being done in Nazi Germany. And they did this precisely because they were "complete men," many of them European refugees, with an acute sense of what a Nazi victory would mean for their native lands and for all mankind. They were driven by a deep moral anxiety, not (or not most crucially) by any kind of scientific fascination; they were certainly not servile technicians. On the other hand, they were men and women without political power or following, and once their own work was done, they could not control its use. The discovery in November 1944 that German scientists had made little progress ended their own supreme emergency, but it did not end the program they had helped to launch. "If I had known that the Germans would not succeed in constructing the atom bomb," Albert Einstein said, "I would

never have lifted a finger."[22] By the time he found that out, however, the scientists had largely finished their work; now indeed technicians were in charge, and the politicians in charge of them. And in the event, the bomb was not used against Germany (or to deter its use by Hitler, which is what men like Einstein had in mind), but against the Japanese, who had never posed such a threat to peace and freedom as the Nazis had.[†]

Still, it was an important feature of the American decision that the President and his advisors believed the Japanese to be fighting an aggressive war and, moreover, to be fighting it unjustly. Thus Truman's address to the American people on August 12, 1945:

> We have used [the bomb] against those who attacked us without warning at Pearl Harbor, against those who have starved and beaten and executed American prisoners of war, against those who have abandoned all pretense of obeying international laws of warfare. We have used it in order to shorten the agony of war . . .

Here again, the sliding scale is being used to open the way for utilitarian calculations. The Japanese have forfeited (some of) their rights, and so they cannot complain about Hiroshima so long as the destruction of the city actually does, or could reasonably be expected to, shorten the agony of war. But had the Japanese exploded an atomic bomb over an American city, killing tens of thousands of civilians and thereby shortening the agony of war, the action would clearly have been a crime, one more for Truman's list. This distinction is only

---

[†] In his novel *The New Men*, C. P. Snow describes the discussions among atomic scientists as to whether or not the bomb should be used. Some of them, his narrator says, answered that question with "an absolute no," feeling that if the weapon were used to kill hundreds of thousands of innocent people, "neither science nor the civilization of which science is bone and fibre, would be free from guilt again." But the more common view was the one I have been defending: "Many, probably the majority, gave a conditional no with much the same feeling behind it, but if there were *no other way* of saving the war against Hitler, they would be prepared to drop the bomb." *The New Men*, New York, 1954, p. 177 (Snow's emphasis).

plausible, however, if one renders a judgment not only against the leaders of Japan but also against the ordinary people of Hiroshima and insists at the same time that no similar judgment is possible against the people of San Francisco, say, or Denver. I can find, as I have said before, no way of defending such a procedure. How did the people of Hiroshima forfeit their rights? Perhaps their taxes paid for some of the ships and planes used in the attack on Pearl Harbor; perhaps they sent their sons into the navy and air force with prayers for their success; perhaps they celebrated the actual event, after being told that their country had won a great victory in the face of an imminent American threat. Surely there is nothing here that makes these people liable to direct attack. (It is worth noting, though the fact is not relevant in judging the Hiroshima decision, that the raid on Pearl Harbor was directed entirely against naval and army installations: only a few stray bombs fell on the city of Honolulu.)[23]

But if Truman's argument on August 12 was weak, there was a worse one underlying it. He did not intend to apply the sliding scale with any precision, for he seems to have believed that, given Japanese aggression, the Americans could do anything at all to win (and shorten the agony of war). Along with most of his advisors, he accepted the "war is hell" doctrine; it is a constant allusion in defenses of the Hiroshima decision. Thus Henry Stimson:[24]

As I look back over the five years of my service as Secretary of War, I see too many stern and heart-rending decisions to be willing to pretend that war is anything else but what it is. The face of war is the face of death; death is an inevitable part of every order that a wartime leader gives.

And James Byrnes, Truman's friend and his Secretary of State:[25]

. . . war remains what General Sherman said it was.

And Arthur Compton, chief scientific advisor to the government:[26]

When one thinks of the mounted archers of Ghengiz Khan . . . the Thirty Years War . . . the millions of Chinese who died during the Japanese invasion . . .

the mass destruction of western Russia . . . one realizes that in whatever manner it is fought, war is precisely what General Sherman called it.

And Truman himself:[27]

Let us not become so preoccupied with weapons that we lose sight of the fact that war itself is the real villain.

War itself is to blame, but also the men who begin it . . . while those who fight justly merely participate in the hell of war, choicelessly, and there are no moral decisions for which they can be called to account. This is not, or not necessarily, an immoral doctrine, but it is radically one-sided; it evades the tension between *jus ad bellum* and *jus in bello;* it undercuts the need for hard judgments; it relaxes our sense of moral restraint. When he was choosing a target for the first bomb, Truman reports, he asked Stimson which Japanese cities were "devoted exclusively to war production."[28] The question was reflexive; Truman did not want to violate the "laws of war." But it wasn't serious. Which American cities were devoted exclusively to war production? It is possible to ask such questions only when the answer doesn't matter. If war is hell however it is fought, then what difference can it make how we fight it? And if war itself is the villain, then what risks do we run (aside from the strategic risks) when we make decisions? The Japanese, who began the war, can also end it; only they can end it, and all we can do is fight it, enduring what Truman called "the daily tragedy of bitter war." I don't doubt that that was really Truman's view; it was not a matter of convenience but of conviction. But it is a distorted view. It mistakes the actual hellishness of war, which is particular in character and open to precise definition, for the limitless pains of religious mythology. The pains of war are limitless only if we make them so—only if we move, as Truman did, beyond the limits that we and others have established. Sometimes, I think, we have to do that, but not all the time. Now we must ask whether it was necessary to do it in 1945.

The only possible defense of the Hiroshima attack is a utilitarian calculation made without the sliding scale, a calculation made, then, where there was no room for it, a claim to override the rules of war and the rights of Japanese civilians. I want to state this argument as strongly as I can. In 1945, American policy was fixed on the demand for the unconditional surrender of Japan. The Japanese had by that time lost the war, but they were by no means ready to accept this demand. The leaders of their armed forces expected an invasion of the Japanese main islands and were preparing for a last-ditch resistance. They had over two million soldiers available for the fighting, and they believed that they could make the invasion so costly that the Americans would agree to a negotiated peace. Truman's military advisors also believed that the costs would be high, though the public record does not show that they ever recommended negotiations. They thought that the war might continue late into 1946 and that there would be as many as a million additional American casualties. Japanese losses would be much higher. The capture of Okinawa in a battle lasting from April to June of 1945 had cost almost 80,000 American casualties, while virtually the entire Japanese garrison of 120,000 men had been killed (only 10,600 prisoners were taken).[29] If the main islands were defended with a similar ferocity, hundreds of thousands, perhaps millions, of Japanese soldiers would die. Meanwhile, the fighting would continue in China and in Manchuria, where a Russian attack was soon due. And the bombing of Japan would also continue, and perhaps intensify, with casualty rates no different from those anticipated from the atomic attack. For the Americans had adopted in Japan the British policy of terrorism: a massive incendiary raid on Tokyo early in March 1945 had set off a firestorm and killed an estimated 100,000 people. Against all this was set, in the minds of American decision-makers, the impact of the atomic bomb—not materially more damaging but psychologically more frightening, and holding out the promise, perhaps, of a quick end to the war. "To avert a vast, indefinite butchery . . . at the cost of a few explosions," wrote Churchill in support of Truman's decision, "seemed, after all our toils and perils, a miracle of deliverance."[30]

"A vast indefinite butchery" involving quite probably the deaths of several million people: surely this is a great evil, and if it was imminent, one could reasonably argue that extreme measures might be warranted to avert it. Secretary of War Stimson thought

it was the sort of case I have already described, where one had to wager; there was no option. "No man, in our position and subject to our responsibilities, holding in his hand a weapon of such possibilities for . . . saving those lives, could have failed to use it."[31] This is by no means an incomprehensible or, on the surface at least, an outrageous argument. But it is not the same as the argument I suggested in the case of Britain in 1940. It does not have the form: if we don't do *x* (bomb cities), they will do *y* (win the war, establish tyrannical rule, slaughter their opponents). What Stimson argued is very different. Given the actual policy of the U.S. government, it amounts to this: if we don't do *x*, *we* will do *y*. The two atomic bombs caused "many casualties," James Byrnes admitted, "but not nearly so many as there would have been had our air force continued to drop incendiary bombs on Japan's cities."[32] Our purpose, then, was not to avert a "butchery" that someone else was threatening, but one that we were threatening, and had already begun to carry out. Now, what great evil, what supreme emergency, justified the incendiary attacks on Japanese cities?

Even if we had been fighting in strict accordance with the war convention, the continuation of the struggle was not something forced upon us. It had to do with our war aims. The military estimate of casualties was based not only on the belief that the Japanese would fight almost to the last man, but also on the assumption that the Americans would accept nothing less than unconditional surrender. The war aims of the American government required either an invasion of the main islands, with enormous losses of American and Japanese soldiers and of Japanese civilians trapped in the war zones, or the use of the atomic bomb. Given that choice, one might well reconsider those aims. Even if we assume that unconditional surrender was morally desirable because of the character of Japanese militarism, it might still be morally undesirable because of the human costs it entailed. But I would suggest a stronger argument than this. The Japanese case is sufficiently different from the German so that unconditional surrender should never have been asked. Japan's rulers were engaged in a more ordinary sort of military expansion, and all that was morally required was that they be defeated, not that they be conquered and totally overthrown. Some restraint upon their war-making power might be justified, but their domestic authority was a matter of concern only to the Japanese people. In any case, if killing millions (or many thousands) of men and women was militarily necessary for their conquest and overthrow, then it was morally necessary—in order not to kill those people—to settle for something less. I have made this argument before; here is a further example of its practical application. If people have a right not to be forced to fight, they also have a right not to be forced to continue fighting beyond the point when the war might justly be concluded. Beyond that point, there can be no supreme emergencies, no arguments about military necessity, no cost-accounting in human lives. To press the war further than that is to re-commit the crime of aggression. In the summer of 1945, the victorious Americans owed the Japanese people an experiment in negotiation. To use the atomic bomb, to kill and terrorize civilians, without even attempting such an experiment, was a double crime.[33]

These, then are the limits of the realm of necessity. Utilitarian calculation can force us to violate the rules of war only when we are face-to-face not merely with defeat but with a defeat likely to bring disaster to a political community. But these calculations have no similar effects when what is at stake is only the speed or the scope of victory. They are relevant only to the conflict between winning and fighting well, not to the internal problems of combat itself. Whenever that conflict is absent, calculation is stopped short by the rules of war and the rights they are designed to protect. Confronted by those rights, we are not to calculate consequences, or figure relative risks, or compute probable casualties, but simply to stop short and turn aside.

Notes

1. Quoted in George Quester, *Deterrence before Hiroshima* (New York, 1966), p. 67.
2. See J. Glenn Gray, *The Warriors: Reflections on Men in Battle* (New York, 1967), ch. 5: "Images of the Enemy."
3. But the claim that one can never kill an innocent person abstracts from questions of coercion and consent.
4. See Quester, *Deterrence*, and F. M. Sallagar, *The Road to Total War: Escalation in World War II* (Rand Corporation Report, 1969); also the official history by Sir Charles Webster and Noble Frankland, *The Strategic Air Offensive against Germany* (London, 1961).
5. Noble Frankland, *Bomber Offensive: The Devastation of Europe* (New York, 1970), p. 41.
6. The Story of the Cherwell minute is told, most unsympathetically, in C. P. Snow, *Science and Government* (New York, 1962).
7. Quester, pp. 117–18.
8. Quoted in Quester, p. 141.
9. Quoted in Angus Calder, *The People's War: 1939–1945* (New York, 1969), p. 491
10. Calder, p. 229; the same poll is cited by Vera Brittain, a courageous opponent of British bombing policy: *Humiliation with Honor* (New York, 1943). p. 91.
11. ". . . it was not [Cherwell's] ruthlessness that worried us most, it was his calculations." Snow, *Science and Government*, p. 48. Cf. P. M. S. Blackett's postwar critique of the bombing, worked out in narrowly strategic terms: *Fear, War, and the Bomb* (New York, 1949), ch. 2.
12. Sallagar, p. 127.
13. Sallagar, p. 128.
14. Frankland, *Bomber Offensive*, pp. 38–39.
15. Frankland, *Bomber Offensive*, p. 134.
16. Sir Arthur Hartis, *Bomber Offensive* (London, 1947), p. 74
17. Calder, p. 229.
18. Winston Churchill, *The Second World War*, Vol. 4: *The Hinge of Fate* (New York, 1950), p. 770.
19. For a detailed account of this attack, see David Irving, *The Destruction of Dresden* (New York, 1963).
20. Quoted in Quester, p. 156.
21. Dwight Macdonald, *Memoirs of a Revolutionist* (New York, 1957), p. 178.
22. Robert C. Batchelder, *The Irreversible Decision: 1939–1950* (New York, 1965), p. 38. Batchelder's is the best historical account of the decision to drop the bomb, and the only one that treats the moral issues in a systematic way.
23. A. Russell Buchanan, *The United States and World War II* (New York, 1964). I, 75.
24. Henry Stimson, "The Decision to Use the Atomic Bomb," *Harpers Magazine* (February, 1947), repr. in *The Atomic Bomb: The Great Decision*, ed. Paul R. Baker (New York, 1968), p. 21.
25. James Byrnes, *Speaking Frankly* (New York, 1947), p. 261.

26. Arthur Compton, *Atomic Quest* (New York, 1956), p. 247.
27. Harry Truman, *Mr. Citizen* (New York, 1960), p. 267. I owe this group of quotations to Gerald McElroy.
28. Batchelder, p. 159.
29. Batchelder, p. 149.
30. Winston Churchill, *Triumph and Tragedy* (New York, 1962), p. 639.
31. Stimson, p. 21.
32. Byrnes, p. 264.
33. The case would be even worse if the bomb were used for political rather than military reasons (with the Russians rather than the Japanese in mind): on this point, see the careful analysis of Martin J. Sherwin, *A World Destroyed: The Atomic Bomb and the Grand Alliance* (New York, 1975).

QUESTIONS

1. What exactly is a supreme emergency and what rules of war may be overridden in such situations? Why?
2. Would Walzer's doctrine permit the atomic bombings of Japan?

26. On the Futility of Limiting War

GEORGE ORWELL

George Orwell (1903–1950), born Eric Arthur Blair, was an English writer, well known for his novels *Animal Farm* (1945) and *Nineteen Eighty-Four* (1949). He wrote well and forcefully about injustice and the horrors of totalitarianism. He was a great essayist, and his views about writing, expressed in his famous essay, "Politics and the English Language" (1946), are always worth considering.

Now, no one in his senses regards bombing, or any other operation of war, with anything but disgust. On the other hand, no decent person cares tuppence for the opinion of posterity. And there is something very distasteful in accepting war as an instrument and at the same time wanting to dodge responsibility for its more obviously barbarous features. Pacifism is a tenable position, provided that you are willing to take the consequences. But all talk of "limiting" or "humanizing" war is sheer humbug, based on the fact that the average human being never bothers to examine catchwords.

The catchwords used in this connexion are "killing civilians," "massacre of women and children" and "destruction of our cultural heritage." It is tacitly assumed that air bombing does more of this kind of thing than ground warfare.

When you look a bit closer, the first question that strikes you is: Why is it worse to kill civilians than soldiers? Obviously one must not kill children if it is in any way avoidable. [. . .]

War is not avoidable at this stage of history, and since it has to happen it does not seem to me a bad thing that others should be killed besides young men. [. . .] The immunity of the civilian, one of the things that have made war possible, has been shattered. Unlike Miss Brittain, I don't regret that. I can't feel that war is "humanized" by being confined to the slaughter of the young and becomes "barbarous" when the old get killed as well.

As to international agreements to "limit" war, they are never kept when it pays to break them. Long before the last war the nations had agreed not to use gas, but they used it all the same. This time they have refrained, merely because gas is comparatively ineffective in a war of movement, while its use against civilian populations would be sure to provoke reprisals in kind. Against an enemy who can't hit back, e.g. the Abyssinians, it is used readily enough. War is of its nature barbarous, it is better to admit that. If we see ourselves as the savages we are, some improvement is possible, or at least thinkable.

QUESTIONS

1. How do you react to Orwell's attack on traditional constraints of the conduct of war?
2. "War is of its nature barbarous, it is better to admit that. If we see ourselves as the savages we are, some improvement is possible, or at least thinkable." Is that true?

---

27. Conventions and the Morality of War

GEORGE I. MAVRODES

George I. Mavrodes is professor emeritus of philosophy at the University of Michigan, Ann Arbor. He is the author of *Belief in God: A Study in the Epistemology of Religion* (1970) and *Revelation in Religious Belief* (1988).

In an important early essay, Mavrodes examines the basis for the traditional rules protecting civilians. He is critical of some defenses of civilian immunity and proposes an alternative view. The immunity of noncombatants, he argues, is "convention-dependent." We are obligated by a convention that seeks to tame or limit war, by in effect substituting a form of limited combat for warfare.

The point of this paper is to introduce a distinction into our thinking about warfare, and to explore the moral implications of this distinction. I shall make two major assumptions. First, I shall assume without discussion that under some circumstances and for some ends warfare is morally justified. These conditions I shall lump together under such terms as "justice" and "just cause," and say no more about them. I shall also assume that in warfare some means, including some killing, are morally justified. I sometimes call such means "proportionate," and in general I say rather little about them. These assumptions, incidentally, are common to all of the philosophers whom I criticize here.

George I. Mavrodes, "Conventions and the Morality of War," *Philosophy and Public Affairs*, Vol. 4, No. 2 (Winter, 1975), pp. 117–131. Reprinted by permission of Blackwell Publishing.

The distinction which I introduce can be thought of either as dividing wars into two classes, or else as distinguishing wars from certain other international combats. I have no great preference for one of these ways of speaking over the other, but I shall generally adopt the latter alternative. I am particularly interested in the moral significance of this distinction, and I shall explore in some detail its bearing on one moral question associated with warfare, that of the intentional killing of noncombatants.

My paper has two main parts. In the first I examine three closely related treatments of this moral question: the arguments of Elizabeth Anscombe, John C. Ford, and Paul Ramsey. These treatments seem to ignore the distinction which I will propose. I argue that on their own terms, and without reference to that distinction, they must be counted as unsatisfactory.

In the second part of the paper I propose and explain my distinction. I then explore what I take to be some of its moral implications, especially with reference to the alleged immunity of noncombatants, and I argue that it supplies what was missing or defective in the treatments previously criticized.

I. The Immunity Theorists

A number of philosophers have held that a large portion of the population of warring nations have a special moral status. This is the *noncombatant* segment of the population, and they have a moral immunity from being intentionally killed. This view seems to have been especially congenial to philosophers who have tried to apply Christian ethics to the problems of warfare. Among the philosophers who have held this view are Elizabeth Anscombe, John C. Ford, and Paul Ramsey. I shall refer to this trio of thinkers as the *immunity theorists*.

Perhaps we should indicate a little more in detail just what the immunity theorists appear to hold, specifying just what segment of the population is being discussed and just what their immunity consists in. The immunity theorists commonly admit that there is some difficulty in specifying exactly who are the noncombatants.[1] Roughly, they are those people who are not engaged in military operations and whose activity is not immediately and directly related to the war effort. Perhaps we could say that if a person is engaged only in the sort of activities which would be carried on even if the nation were not at war (or preparing for war) then that person is a noncombatant. So generally farmers, teachers, nurses, firemen, sales people, housewives, poets, children, etc. are noncombatants.[2] There are, of course, difficult cases, ranging from the high civilian official of the government to the truck driver (either military or civilian) who hauls vegetables toward the front lines. But despite the hard cases it is held that warring nations contain large numbers of readily identifiable people who are clearly noncombatants.

What of their immunity? The writers whom I consider here make use of the "principle of double-effect."[3] This involves dividing the consequences of an act (at least the foreseeable consequences) into two classes. Into the first class go those consequences which constitute the goal or purpose of the act, what the act is done for, and also those consequences which are means to those ends. Into the other class go those consequences which are neither the sought-after ends nor the means to those ends. So, for example, the bombing of a rail yard may have among its many consequences the following: the flow of supplies toward the front is disrupted, several locomotives are damaged, and a lot of smoke, dust, etc. is discharged into the air. The disruption of transport may well be the end sought by this action, and perhaps the damage to locomotives is sought as a means of disrupting transport. If so, these consequences belong in the first class, a class which I shall generally mark by using the words "intentional" or "intended." The smoke, on the other hand, though as surely foreseeable as the other effects, may be neither means nor end in this situation. It is a side-effect, and belongs in the second class (which I shall sometimes call "unintentional" or "unintended").

Now, the moral immunity of noncombatants consists, according to these writers, in the fact that their death can never, morally, be made the intended consequence of a military operation. Or to put it another way, any military operation which seeks the death of noncombatants either as an end or a means is immoral, regardless of the total good which it might accomplish.

The *unintended* death of noncombatants, on the other hand, is not absolutely forbidden. A military operation which will foreseeably result in such deaths, neither as means nor ends but as side effects, may be morally acceptable according to these writers. It will be morally acceptable if the good end which it may be expected to attain is of sufficient weight to overbalance the evil of these noncombatant deaths (as well as any other evils involved in it). This principle, sometimes called the principle of proportionality, apparently applies to foreseen but unintended noncombatant deaths in just the same way as it applies to the intended death of combatants, the destruction of resources, and so on. In all of these cases it is held to be immoral to cause many deaths, much pain, etc., in order to achieve minor goals. Here combatant and noncombatant stand on the same moral ground, and their deaths are weighed in the same balances. But when the slaying of noncombatants is envisioned as an end or, more commonly, as a means—perhaps in order to reduce the production of foodstuffs or to damage the morale of troops—then there is an unqualified judgment that the projected operation is flatly immoral. The intentional slaying of combatants, on the other hand, faces no such prohibition. This, then, is the place where the moral status of combatant and noncombatant differ sharply.

Now, if a scheme such as this is not to appear simply arbitrary it looks as though we must find some morally relevant basis for the distinction. It is perhaps worthwhile to notice that in this context the immunity of noncombatants cannot be supported by reference to the sanctity or value of human life, nor by reference to a duty not to kill our brothers, etc. For these authors recognize the moral permissibility, even perhaps the duty, of killing under certain circumstances. What must be sought is the ground of a distinction, and not merely a consideration against killing.

Such a ground, however, seems very hard to find, perhaps unexpectedly so. The crucial argument proposed by the immunity theorists turns on the notions of guilt and innocence. Anscombe, for example, says:

> Now, it is one of the most vehement and repeated teachings of the Judaeo-Christian tradition that the

shedding of innocent blood is forbidden by the divine law. No man may be punished except for his own crime, and those "whose feet are swift to shed innocent blood" are always represented as God's enemies.[4]

Earlier on she says, "The principal wickedness which is a temptation to those engaged in warfare is the killing of the innocent,"[5] and she has titled one of the sections of her paper, "Innocence and the Right to Kill Intentionally." Clearly enough the notion of innocence plays a large role in her thinking on this topic. Just what that role is, or should be, will be considered shortly. Ford, in the article cited earlier, repeatedly couples the word "innocent" with "civilian" and "noncombatant." His clearest statement, however, is in another essay. There he says:

> Catholic teaching has been unanimous for long centuries in declaring that it is never permitted to kill directly noncombatants in wartime. Why? Because they are innocent. That is, they are innocent of the violent and destructive action of war, or of any close participation in the violent and destructive action of war. It is such participation *alone* that would make them legitimate targets of violent repression themselves.[6]

Here we have explicitly a promising candidate for the basis of the moral distinction between combatants and noncombatants. It is promising because innocence itself seems to be a moral property. Hence, if we could see that noncombatants were innocent while combatants were not it would be plausible to suppose that this fact made it morally proper to treat them in different ways.

If we are to succeed along this line of thought, then we must meet at least two conditions. First, we must find some one sense of "innocence" such that all noncombatants are innocent and all combatants are guilty. Second, this sense must be morally relevant, a point of the greatest importance. We are seeking to ground a moral distinction, and the facts to which we refer must therefore be morally relevant. The use of a morally tinged word, such as "innocent," does not of itself guarantee such relevance.

Well, is there a suitable sense for "innocent"? Ford said that noncombatants "are innocent of the violent and destructive action of war." Anscombe, writing of the people who can properly be attacked with deadly force, says, "What is required, for the people attacked to be noninnocent in the relevant sense, is that they themselves be engaged in an objectively unjust proceeding which the attacker has the right to make his concern; or—the commonest case—should be unjustly attacking him." On the other hand, she speaks of "people whose mere existence and activity supporting existence by growing crops, making clothes, etc.," might contribute to the war effort, and she says, "such people are innocent and it is murderous to attack them, or make them a target for an attack which he judges will help him towards victory."[7] These passages contain, I think, the best clues we have as to the sense of "innocent" in these authors.

It is probably evident enough that this sense of "innocent" is vague in a way parallel to the vagueness of "noncombatant." It will leave us with troublesome borderline cases. In itself, that does not seem to me a crucial defect. But perhaps it is a clue to an important failing. For I suspect that there is this parallel vagueness because "innocent" here is just a synonym for "noncombatant."

What can Ford mean by saying that some people are "innocent of the violent and destructive action of war" except that those people are not engaged in the violence of war? Must not Anscombe mean essentially the same thing when she says that the noninnocent are those who are themselves "engaged in an objectively unjust proceeding"? But we need not rely wholly on these rhetorical questions. Ramsey makes this point explicitly. He first distinguishes between close and remote cooperation in military operations, and then he alludes to the distinction between the "guilty" and the "innocent." Of this distinction he says, "These are very misleading terms, since their meaning is exhaustively stated under the first contrast, and is reducible to degrees of actual participation in hostile force."[8] In this judgment Ramsey certainly seems to me to be right.

Now, we should notice carefully that a person may be an enthusiastic supporter of the unjust war and its unjust aims, he may give to it his voice and his vote, he may have done everything in his power to procure it when it was yet but a prospect, now that it is in progress he may contribute to it both his savings and the work which he knows best how to do, and he may avidly hope to share in the unjust gains which will follow if the war is successful. But such a person may clearly be a noncombatant, and (in the sense of the immunity theorists) unquestionably "innocent" of the war. On the other hand, a young man of limited mental ability and almost no education may be drafted, put into uniform, trained for a few weeks, and sent to the front as a replacement in a low-grade unit. He may have no understanding of what the war is about, and no heart for it. He might want nothing more than to go back to his town and the life he led before. But he is "engaged," carrying ammunition, perhaps, or stringing telephone wire or even banging away ineffectually with his rifle. He is without doubt a combatant, and "guilty," a fit subject for intentional slaughter. Is it not clear that "innocence," as used here, leaves out entirely all of the relevant moral considerations—that it has no moral content at all? Anscombe suggests that intentional killing during warfare should be construed on the model of punishing people for their crimes, and we must see to it, if we are to be moral, that we punish someone only for his own crime and not for someone else's. But if we construe the criminality involved in an unjust war in any reasonable moral sense then it must either be the case that many noncombatants are guilty of that criminality or else many combatants are innocent. In fact, it will probably be the case that *both* of these things are true. Only if we were to divest "crime" of its moral bearings could we make it fit the combatant/noncombatant distinction in modern wars.

The fact that both Anscombe and Ramsey[9] use the analogy of the criminal in discussing this topic suggests that there is an important fact about warfare which is easily overlooked. And that is that warfare, unlike ordinary criminal activity, is not an activity in which individuals engage qua individuals or as members of voluntary associations. They enter into war as members of nations. It is more proper to say that the nation is at war than that its soldiers are at war. This does not, of course, entail that individuals have no moral responsibility for their acts in war. But it does suggest that moral responsibility may not be distributed between combatant and noncombatant in the same way as between a criminal and his children. Many of the men who are soldiers, perhaps most of them, would not be engaged in military operations at all if they did not happen to be citizens of a warring nation. But noncombatants are citizens of warring nations in exactly the same sense as are soldiers. However these facts are to be analyzed they should warn us not to rely too heavily on the analogy with ordinary criminality.

We seem, then, to be caught in a dilemma. We can perhaps find some sense for notions such as *innocence* and *criminality* which will make them fit the distinction in which we are interested. But the price of doing so seems to be that of divesting these notions of the moral significance which they require if they are to justify the moral import of the distinction itself. In the ordinary senses, on the other hand, these notions do have the required moral bearings. But in their ordinary senses they do not fit the desired distinction. In neither way, therefore, can the argument from innocence be made to work, and the alleged moral immunity of noncombatants seems to be left as an arbitrary claim.

II. Convention-Dependent Morality

Despite the failure of these arguments I have recently come to think that there may be something of importance in this distinction after all, and even that it may have an important moral bearing. How might this be?

Imagine a statesman reflecting on the costliness of war, its cost in human life and human suffering. He observes that these costs are normally very high, sometimes staggering. Furthermore, he accepts the principle of proportionality. A consequence of this is that he sometimes envisions a just war for a just cause, but nevertheless decides not to prosecute that war even though he believes it could be won. For the cost of winning would be so high as to outweigh the good which would be attained. So he must sometimes let oppression flourish and injustice hold sway. And even in those wars which can be prosecuted the costs eat very seriously into the benefits.

Then he has an idea. Suppose—just suppose—that one could replace warfare with a less costly substitute. Suppose, for example, that one could introduce a convention—and actually get it accepted and followed by the nations—a convention which replaced warfare with single combat. Under this convention, when two nations arrived at an impasse which would otherwise have resulted in war they would instead choose, each of them, a single champion (doubtless a volunteer). These two men would then meet in mortal combat, and whoever won, killing his opponent or driving him from the field, would win for his nation. To that nation would then be ceded whatever territory, influence, or other prize would have been sought in the war, and the nation whose champion was defeated would lose correspondingly.

Suppose, too, that the statesman believes that if such a convention were to come into force his own nation could expect to win and lose such combats in about the same proportion as it could now expect to win and lose ordinary wars. The same types of questions would be settled by such combats as would otherwise be settled by war (though perhaps more questions would be submitted to combat than would be submitted to war), and approximately the same resolutions would be arrived at. The costs, however—human death and suffering—would be reduced by several orders of magnitude. Would that not be an attractive prospect? I think it would.

While the prospect may seem attractive it may also strike us as hopelessly utopian, hardly to be given a serious thought. There seems to be some evidence, however, that exactly this substitution was actually attempted in ancient times. Ancient literature contains at least two references to such attempts. One is in the Bible, I Samuel 17, the combat between David and Goliath. The other is in the *Iliad*, book 3, where it is proposed to settle the siege of Troy in the very beginning by single combat between Menelaus and Paris. It may be significant that neither of these attempts appears to have been successful. The single combats were followed by bloodier and more general fighting. Perhaps this substitute for warfare is too cheap; it cannot be made practical, and nations just will not consent in the end to abide by this convention. But consider, on the one hand, warfare which is limited only by the moral requirements that the ends sought should be just and that the means used should be proportionate, and, on the other hand, the convention of single combat as a substitute for warfare. Between these extremes there lie a vast number of other possible conventions which might be canvassed in the search for a less costly substitute for war. I suggest that the long struggle, in the western world at least, to limit military operations to "counter-forces" strategies, thus sparing civilian populations, is just such an attempt.

If I am right about this, then the moral aspects of the matter must be approached in a way rather different from that of the immunity theorists. Some, but not all, of their conclusions can be accepted, and somewhat different grounds must be given for them. These thinkers have construed the immunity of non-combatants as though it were a moral fact which was independent of any actual or envisioned convention or practice. And they have consequently sought to support this immunity by argument which makes no reference to convention. I have already argued that their attempts were failures. What I suggest now is that all such attempts *must* be failures, for they mistake the sort of moral requirement which is under consideration. Let me try to make this clearer.

I find it plausible to suppose that I have a moral obligation to refrain from wantonly murdering my neighbors. And it also seems plausible to discuss this, perhaps in utilitarian terms, or in terms of the will of God, or of natural law, or in terms of a rock-bottom deontological requirement, but in any case without essential reference to the laws and customs of our nation. We might, indeed, easily imagine our laws and customs to be other than they are with respect to murder. But we would then judge the moral adequacy and value of such alternative laws and customs by reference to the moral obligation I have mentioned and not vice versa. On the other hand, I may also have a moral obligation to pay a property tax or to drive on the right side of the street. It does not seem plausible to suppose, however, that one can discuss these duties without immediately referring to our laws and customs. And it seems likely that different laws would have generated different moral duties, e.g. driving on the left. These latter are examples of "convention-dependent" moral obligations. More formally, I will say that a given moral obligation is convention-dependent if and only if (1) given that a certain convention, law, custom, etc., is actually in force one really does have an obligation to act in conformity with that convention, and (2) there is an alternative law, custom, etc. (or lack thereof) such that if that had been in force one would not have had the former obligation.

At this point, before developing the way in which it may apply to warfare, let me forestall some possible misunderstandings by a series of brief comments on this notion. I am not claiming, nor do I believe, that all laws, customs, etc., generate corresponding moral obligations. But some do. I am not denying that one may seek, and perhaps find, some more general moral law, perhaps independent of convention, which explains why this convention generates the more specific obligation. I claim only that one cannot account for the specific obligation apart from the convention. Finally, I am not denying that one might have an obligation, perhaps independent of convention, to try to change a convention of this sort. For I think it possible that one might simultaneously have a moral obligation to conform to a certain convention and also a moral obligation to replace that convention, and thus to eliminate the first obligation.

Now, the core of my suggestion with respect to the immunity of noncombatants is this. The immunity of noncombatants is best thought of as a convention-dependent obligation related to a convention which substitutes for warfare a certain form of limited combat. How does this bear on some of the questions which we have been discussing?

To begin with, we might observe that the convention itself is presumably to be justified by its expectable results. (Perhaps we can refer to some moral rule to the effect that we should minimize social costs such as death and injury.) It seems plausible to suppose that the counter-forces convention, if followed, will reduce the pain and death involved in combat—will reduce it, that is, compared to unlimited warfare. There are surely other possible conventions which, if followed, would reduce those costs still more, e.g. the substitution of single combat. Single combat, however, is probably not a live contender because there is almost no chance that such a convention would actually be followed. It is possible, however, that there is some practical convention which is preferable to the present counter-forces convention. If so, the fact that it is preferable is a strong reason in favor of supposing that there is a moral obligation to promote its adoption.

It does not follow, however, that we now have a duty to act in conformity with this other possible convention. For the results of acting in conformity with a preferable convention which is not widely observed may be much worse than the results of acting in conformity with a less desirable convention which is widely observed. We might, for example, discover that a "left-hand" pattern of traffic flow would be preferable to the present system of "right-hand" rules, in that it would result in fewer accidents, etc. The difference might be so significant that we really would be morally derelict if we did not try to institute a change in our laws. We would be acquiescing in a very costly procedure when a more economical one was at hand. But it would be a disaster, and, I suspect, positively immoral, for a few of us to begin driving on the left before the convention was changed. In cases of convention-dependent obligations the question of what convention is actually in force is one of considerable moral import. That one is reminded to take this question seriously is one of the important differences between this approach and that of the immunity theorists.

Perhaps the counter-forces convention is not really operative now in a substantial way. I do not know. Doubtless it suffered a severe blow in World War II, not least from British and American bombing strategies. Traffic rules are embedded in a broad, massive, comparatively stable social structure which makes their status comparatively resistant to erosion by infraction. Not so, however, for a convention of warfare. It has little status except in its actual observance, and depends greatly on the mutual trust of the belligerents; hence it is especially vulnerable to abrogation by a few contrary acts. Here arises a related difference with the immunity theorists. Taking the obligation to be convention-independent they reject argument based on the fact that "the enemy did it first," etc.[10] If the obligation were independent they would be correct in this. But for convention-dependent obligations, what one's opponent does, what "everyone is doing," etc., are facts of great moral importance. Such facts help to determine within what convention, if any, one is operating, and thus they help one to discover what his moral duties are.

If we were to decide that the counter-forces convention was dead at present, or, indeed, that no convention at all with respect to warfare was operative now, it would not follow that warfare was immoral. Nor, on the other hand, would it follow that warfare was beyond all moral rules, an area in which "anything goes." Instead, we would simply go back to warfare per se, limited only by independent moral requirements, such as those of justice and proportionality. That would, on the whole, probably be a more costly way of handling such problems. But if we live in a time when the preferable substitutes are not available, then we must either forgo the goods or bear the higher costs. If we had no traffic laws or customs, traffic would be even more dangerous and costly than it is now. Traveling, however, might still be justified, if the reason for traveling were sufficiently important.

In such a case, of course, there would be no obligation to drive on the right, or in any regular manner, nor would there be any benefit in it. Probably the best thing would be to drive in a completely ad hoc way, seeking the best maneuver in each situation as it arose. More generally, and ignoring for the moment a final consideration which will be discussed below, there is no obligation and no benefit associated with the unilateral observance of a convention. If one's cause is unjust then one ought not to kill noncombatants. But that is because of the independent moral prohibition against prosecuting such a war at all, and has nothing to do with any special immunity of noncombatants. If one's cause is just, but the slaying of noncombatants will not advance it to any marked degree, then one ought not to slay them. But this is just the requirement of proportionality, and applies equally and in the same way to combatants. If one's cause is just and the slaying of noncombatants would advance it—if, in other words, one is not prevented by considerations of justice and proportionality—this is the crucial case. If one refrains unilaterally in this situation then he seems to choose the greater of two evils (or the lesser of two goods). By hypothesis, the good achieved, i.e. the lives spared, is not as weighty as the evil which he allows in damage to the prospects for justice or in the even more costly alternative measures, e.g. the slaying of a larger number of combatants, which he must undertake. Now, if the relevant convention were operative, then his refraining from counter-population strategies here would be related to his enemy's similar restraint, and indeed it would be related to the strategies which would be used in future wars. These larger considerations might well tip the balance in the other direction. But by hypothesis we are considering the case in which there is no such convention, and so these larger considerations do not arise. One acts unilaterally. In such a situation it certainly appears that one would have chosen the worse of the two alternatives. It is hard to suppose that one is morally obligated to do so.

I said above that we were ignoring for the moment one relevant consideration. It should not be ignored forever. I have already called attention to the fact that conventions of warfare are not, like traffic rules, embedded in a more massive social structure. This makes them especially precarious, as we have noted. But it also bears on the way in which they may be adopted. One such way, perhaps a rather important way, is for one party to the hostilities to signal his willingness to abide by such a convention by undertaking some unilateral restraint on his own part. If the opponent does not reciprocate, then the offer has failed and it goes no further. If the opponent does reciprocate, however, then the area of restraint may be broadened, and a kind of mutual respect and confidence may grow up between the belligerents. Each comes to rely on the other to keep the (perhaps unspoken) agreement, and therefore each is willing to forgo the immediate advantage which might accrue to him from breaking it. If this happens, then a new convention has begun its precarious life. This may be an event well worth seeking.

Not only may it be worth seeking, it may be worth paying something for it. For a significant increase in the likelihood that a worthwhile convention will be adopted it may be worth accepting an increased risk or a higher immediate cost in lives and suffering. So there may be some justification in unilateral restraint after all, even in the absence of a convention. But this justification is prospective and finite. It envisions the possibility that such a convention may arise in the future as a result of this restraint. Consequently, the justification should be proportioned to some judgment as to the likelihood of that event, and it should be reevaluated as future events unfold.

III. Convention vs. Morality

I began by examining some attempts to defend a certain alleged moral rule of war, the immunity of noncombatants. These defenses have in common the fact that they construe this moral rule as independent of any human law, custom, etc. I then argued that these defenses fail because they leave a certain distinction without moral support, and yet the distinction is essential to the rule. Turning then to the task of construction rather than criticism, I suggested that the immunity of noncombatants is not an independent moral rule but rather a part of a convention which sets up a morally desirable alternative to war. I argued then that some conventions, including this one, generate special moral obligations which cannot be satisfactorily explained and defended without reference to the convention. And in the final pages I explored some of the special features of the obligation at hand and of the arguments which are relevant to it.

The distinction I have drawn is that between warfare per se on the one hand, and, on the other hand, international combats which are limited by convention and custom. But the point of the distinction is to clarify our thinking about the *morality* of such wars and combats. That is where its value must be tested.

Notes

1. Elizabeth Anscombe, "War and Murder," *War and Morality* ed. Richard A. Wasserstrom (Belmont, Calif., 1970), p. 52; John C. Ford, "The Morality of Obliteration Bombing," ibid., pp. 19–23; Paul Ramsey, *The Just War* (New York, 1968), pp. 157, 158.
2. Ford gives a list of over 100 occupations whose practitioners he considers to be "almost without exception" noncombatants.
3. Anscombe, pp. 46, 50, 51; Ford, pp. 26–28; Ramsey, pp. 347–358.
4. Anscombe, p. 49.
5. Ibid., p. 44.

6. John C. Ford, "The Hydrogen Bombing of Cities," *Morality and Modern Warfare* ed. William J. Nagle (Baltimore: Helicon Press, 1960), p. 98.

7. Anscombe, p. 45.

8. Ramsey, p. 153.

9. Ibid., p. 144.

10. For example, Ford, "The Morality of Obliteration Bombing," pp. 20, 33.

QUESTIONS

1. What are Mavrodes's criticisms of "the immunity theorists"?

2. Is he right in thinking "that the immunity of noncombatants is not an independent moral rule but rather part of a convention that sets up a morally desirable alternative to war"?

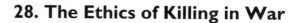

28. The Ethics of Killing in War

JEFF McMAHAN

For a description of the author, see chapter 6.

This essay is a statement of an attack on just war theory that McMahan has been developing for several years. Traditional just war has two parts, one governing the justice of war (*jus ad bellum*), the second the ethics of the conduct of war (*jus in bello*), and views each as independent of the other. Thus soldiers fighting an unjust war are not prohibited from firing on their adversaries. McMahan argues, against just war theory, that if a war is unjust, then combatants act wrongly in attacking enemy soldiers. He also argues that combatants fighting a just war may sometimes target noncombatants who are responsible for wrongs. This carefully argued but difficult essay is for advanced readers.

The Traditional Theory of the Just War

The traditional theory of the just war comprises two sets of principles, one governing the resort to war (*jus ad bellum*) and the other governing the conduct of war (*jus in bello*). The two set of principles are regarded, in Michael Walzer's words, as "logically independent. It is perfectly possible for a just war to be fought unjustly and for an unjust war to be fought in strict accordance with the rules." (Walzer, 1977, p 21).[1] Let us say that those who fight in a just war are *just combatants,* while those who fight in a war that is unjust because it lacks a just cause are *unjust combatants.* (A just cause is an aim that can contribute to the justification for war and that may permissibly be pursued by means of war.) The most important implication of the idea that *jus in bello* is independent of *jus ad bellum* is that it makes no difference to the permissibility of an unjust combatant's conduct

Jeff McMahan, "The Ethics of Killing in War," *Philosophia*, vol. 34, No. 1 (January 2006), pp. 23–41. Reprinted by permission of Springer Science & Business Media.

in war that he fights without a just cause. Unjust combatants do not do wrong merely by participating in an unjust war. They do wrong only if they violate the principles of *jus in bello*. So the moral position of unjust combatants is indistinguishable from that of just combatants—a condition that Walzer refers to as "the moral equality of soldiers" (Walzer, 1977, p. 34). Both just and unjust combatants have "an equal right to kill" (Walzer, 1977, p. 41).

They do not, of course, have a right to kill just anyone. According to the traditional theory, combatants are permitted to kill only opposing combatants. This is, indeed, the traditional understanding of the central requirement of *jus in bello*: the requirement of discrimination. All combatants, just and unjust alike, must discriminate between combatants and noncombatants, intentionally attacking only the former and not the latter.

In this paper I will challenge all three foundational tenets of the traditional theory I have identified: (1) that the principles of *jus in bello* are independent of those of *jus ad bellum*, (2) that unjust combatants can abide by the principles of *jus in bello* and do not act wrongly unless they fail to do so, and (3) that combatants are permissible targets of attack while noncombatants are not. I will begin by examining certain arguments that have been offered in support of these tenets. I will then argue that the tenets cannot be correct. Finally, I will sketch the outlines of a revisionist understanding of the just war that I believe is more consistent and plausible, as well as better grounded, than the traditional theory.

The Presumed Permissibility of Defensive Force

According to the traditional theory, we are all initially "morally immune" to attack. Those who do nothing to lose their right against attack are commonly said to be *innocent*. Yet, as Thomas Nagel observes, in the tradition "'innocent' means 'currently harmless,' and it is opposed not to 'guilty' but to 'doing harm'" (Nagel, 1985, p. 69). Those who retain their immunity to attack are therefore those who are not threatening. In the context of war, the innocent are those who do not contribute to the prosecution of the war—that is, noncombatants.

The noninnocent are those who pose a threat to others—that is, combatants. They lose their immunity and are liable to attack.

These observations help to reveal how the three tenets of the traditional theory follow from a general principle of the permissibility of defensive force. Because just combatants threaten unjust combatants, they are noninnocent and lose their right not to be attacked. For "that right," according to Walzer, "is lost by those who bear arms 'effectively' because they pose a danger to other people" (Walzer, 1977, p. 145). It does not matter that they have done no wrong: "Simply by fighting," just combatants lose "their title to life and liberty, . . . even though, unlike aggressor states, they have committed no crime" (Walzer, 1977, p. 136). This is why unjust combatants do no wrong in attacking them. But just combatants are also permitted, for the same reason, to attack the unjust combatants who threaten them. The fact that just combatants fight in a just war while unjust combatants do not is irrelevant to their respective justifications for fighting; hence the independence of *jus in bello* from *jus ad bellum*. Finally, the distinction between combatants and noncombatants is significant because combatants pose a threat and so may be the target of defensive force, while noncombatants do not pose a threat and thus cannot be the target of defensive force (though of course they can be used instrumentally in defensive efforts directed against threats posed by others).

The attempt to ground the tenets of just war theory in the permissibility of defensive force cannot succeed, however, because it is simply false that all defensive force is permissible. Consider a case at the individual level of a surprise attack. Suppose a villain attacks you, entirely without justification or excuse, but that the initial attack fails to overcome you. Rightly believing that he will otherwise kill you, you justifiably attack him in self-defense. If all necessary and proportionate defensive force is permissible, the fact that you now pose a threat to your attacker makes it permissible for him to attack you—even to kill you if your defensive counterattack threatens his life. Hobbes accepted this conclusion, but he was one of the last people to accept it. Most find it impossible to believe that, by unjustifiably attacking you and thereby making it justifiable for you to engage in self-defense, your attacker can create the conditions in which it becomes permissible for him to attack you. Most of us believe that, in these circumstances, your attacker has no right not to be attacked by you, that your attack would not wrong him in any way, and that he therefore has no right of self-defense against your justified, defensive attack (McMahan, 1994a, p. 257). But if your attacker has no right of self-defense, then not all defensive force is permissible.

Walzer recognizes this. He implicitly rejects the suggestion that the three foundational tenets of the traditional theory derive from a principle of the permissibility of defensive force. Indeed, he supplies his own counterexample to such a principle: "In the course of a bank robbery, a thief shoots a guard reaching for his gun. The thief is guilty of murder, even if he claims that he acted in self-defense. Since he had no right to rob the bank, he also had no right to defend himself against the bank's defenders" (Walzer, 1977, p. 128).[2] In general, Walzer believes, there is no right to self-defense in the course of criminal activity. And he concedes that "aggression is . . . a criminal activity" (Walzer, 1977, p. 128). Yet he contends that participation in unjust, aggressive war differs in a morally significant way from participation in domestic criminal activities. In the domestic context, "the idea of necessity doesn't apply to criminal activity: it was not necessary to rob the bank in the first place" (Walzer, 1977, p. 128). But the idea of necessity does, he argues, apply to war, and this makes a difference to the morality of participation in an unjust war. "Personal choice," he contends, "effectively disappears as soon as fighting becomes a legal obligation and a patriotic duty. . . . For the state decrees that an army of a certain size be raised, and it sets out to find the necessary men, using all the techniques of coercion and persuasion at its disposal" (Walzer, 1977, p. 28). Because those who become combatants are subject to a variety of forces that compel their will—manipulation, deception, coercion, their own sense of the moral authority of the government that commands them to fight, uncertainty about the conditions of justice in the resort to war, and so on—they cannot be held responsible for

merely participating in an unjust war As Walzer puts it, "their war is not their crime"; for "the war itself, . . . soldiers are not responsible" (Walzer, 1977, pp. 37–38).

These claims about the necessity of participation in an unjust war support the contention that such participation differs *in permissibility* from ordinary criminal activity *only* if they provide a basis for claiming that participation is *justified*. But it seems that they are best understood as *excuses*. They may show that a particular unjust combatant is not a criminal and is not to be blamed or punished for what he does, but they do not show that he acts permissibly. If, however, unjust combatants are at best merely excused for fighting, while just combatants are justified, two of the central tenets of traditional just war theory must be rejected. It is false that unjust combatants do no wrong to fight provided they respect the rules of engagement. And it is false, a fortiori, that *jus in bello* is independent of *jus ad bellum*.

Are Unjust Combatants Justified in Fighting?

The best argument of which I am aware for the claim that participation in an unjust war can be morally justified appeals to institutional considerations. There are institutions that are necessary to achieve certain important social goods—for example, coordinated decision-making, security, and so on. We therefore have moral reason to support these institutions. But they cannot operate to produce social goods unless people are willing to participate in them even when they require that people do what they believe to be wrong, and may actually *be* wrong. For example, democratic decision-making may require voting, but voting is pointless unless people will abide by the outcome of the vote, even if it commits them to support policies or participate in activities they believe to be wrong. Similarly, domestic security requires laws that, to be effective, must be enforced. Police, judges, prison officials, and others must therefore enforce the laws, including those they believe, perhaps rightly, to be unjust. For the legal system could not function if individuals were permitted selectively to enforce only those laws they believed to be just.

Similar considerations apply to participation in military institutions. It may be rational both epistemically and practically to establish an institutional division of moral labor that assigns responsibility for important decisions such as whether to go to war to those who have access to the relevant information, are positioned to coordinate an effective response to external threats, and can be held accountable for their decisions. Military institutions themselves may thus demand that only those with the assigned authority should make decisions pertaining to *jus ad bellum*. If the institutions are to survive and carry out their functions, others within them must fulfill their assigned roles even if they disagree with the decisions reached by those responsible for matters of *jus ad bellum*.

By participating in such institutions as the legal system and the military, individuals risk becoming instruments of injustice. But if the institutions are sufficiently important, this is a risk that individuals morally ought to take.

This argument, while forceful, cannot vindicate the traditional view that unjust combatants do wrong only if they violate the rules of *jus in bello*. For it grounds an unjust combatant's justification for fighting in his duty to support certain institutions and in his duties to his fellow participants in these institutions; but these duties arise only in the case of institutions that are genuinely just and important. Thus when unjust combatants are compelled by governments or military organizations that lack legitimacy to fight in wars that lack democratic authorization, they have no institutional obligations that can justify their fighting. According to this argument, therefore, some unjust combatants are justified in fighting while others are not. And this is not what the traditional view claims.

Can the appeal to institutional obligations show that at least *some* unjust combatants are justified in fighting? It seems clear that there are cases in which such considerations as the importance of an institution in securing social goods, the importance of the individual's contribution to the survival and integrity of the institution, and the individual's obligations to other participants in the institution together make it permissible, all things considered, for the individual to do what would otherwise be wrong, and may be unjust to those who are victims of the action. In such cases, the conflict between the individual's duties is resolved in favor of the institutional duties, though the individual may also be morally required to call attention to and protest against the malfunctioning of the institution.

There are, however, some types of act that are so seriously objectionable that they cannot become permissible even if they are demanded by institutions that are both just and important. For example, while it may be permissible or even obligatory for agents of a legal system that is just overall to enforce an unjust law (especially when people can choose whether to accept the risks involved in violating that law), it may not be permissible for them to punish, and would certainly be impermissible for them to execute, a person they know to be innocent of violating the law, even if that is what their institutional role requires. The same is true of the sorts of act required by participation in an unjust war—namely, killing people who have done no wrong, collaborating in the destruction of their political institutions and way of life, and so on. These acts are beyond the limits of what can be made permissible by a person's institutional obligations. This is in part because of the gravity of the harms inflicted; but it is also, and equally essentially, because of the moral status of the victims. Just combatants, in taking up arms in a just cause—most commonly, defense against unjust aggression—do nothing to lose their right not to be attacked or killed or to make themselves morally liable to attack; they are innocent in the relevant sense. Merely posing a threat to the unjust combatants who have attacked them is, as we have seen, not enough to make them liable. So in fighting against just combatants, unjust combatants would be attacking and killing the innocent. It is generally believed to be wrong, except in the direst circumstances, to kill the innocent even as a means of averting a greater evil. How, then, could it be permissible to kill the innocent as a means of achieving aims that are *unjust*?

It is often suggested that if some soldiers or draftees refuse on moral grounds to fight in an unjust war, this could compromise the efficient functioning and perhaps even threaten the survival of valuable institutions to which these people would rightly be committed. But even if this is true, those who create, serve, and are served by valuable institutions must themselves bear the burdens when those institutions malfunction, thereby causing or threatening unjust harm to others. It would be unjust to impose the costs of their own mistakes or wrongdoing on others.

Yet the consequences for just institutions of people refusing to fight in unjust wars are unlikely to be calamitous. If the refusal to cooperate were sufficiently extensive or widespread, it could seriously degrade the ability of the aggressor (as I will call a country that fights an unjust war) to prosecute the unjust war and could even contribute to its defeat. This might be bad for the aggressor overall, but there are reasons for doubting whether it would be bad for the aggressor's just institutions—and it is just institutions rather than overall national self-interest that is the focus of the argument we are considering. Victory in an unjust war may serve the national interest but is likely on balance to have a corrupting effect on just institutions. Would just institutions in Germany, for example, have benefited from victory in World War II?

Why *Jus in Bello* Cannot Be Independent of *Jus Ad Bellum*

Recall that the *jus ad bellum* requirement of just cause is a constraint on the *type* of good that may permissibly be pursued by means of war. Just cause is an extrapolation into the domain of war of the insistence that one may not seriously harm or kill another person except for certain highly specific reasons, such as to defend oneself or another against an unjust threat of extreme gravity. Just as one may not kill a person as a means of promoting certain goods, no matter how great those goods would be, so there are many goods—for example, economic growth—that may not be pursued by means of war, no matter how effective war would be in promoting them.[3]

I will argue that whether people fighting in a war have a just cause makes a great difference to whether their acts of war can satisfy the *jus in bello* requirement of proportionality. This requirement holds that for an act of war to be permissible, its bad effects must not be out of proportion to its good effects. Yet, if the requirement of just cause specifies the types of good that may legitimately be pursued by means of war, it is hard to see how, in the absence of a just cause, there can be *any* goods to weigh against the harms that the acts of unjust combatants cause. For goods that may not legitimately be pursued by means of war cannot contribute to the justification for an act of war and thus cannot figure in the proportionality calculation for that act of war.

There are, however, some goods that combatants may legitimately pursue in the course of war even when their war aims are otherwise unjust. These are the goods that would be secured by preventing just combatants from engaging in acts of war that would be wrong. There are two basic ways in which just combatants may act wrongly in fighting. One is to pursue their just cause by wrongful means—that is, by force or violence that is unnecessary, excessive, disproportionate, or indiscriminate. The other is to pursue a subordinate aim that is unjust within a war that is just overall because its guiding aims are just. As an example of the former, suppose that just combatants were to attempt to coerce the surrender of their opponents by attacking a population of innocent civilians. It would be permissible, if necessary, for unjust combatants to use military force against the just combatants to prevent this. By posing an unjust threat by their own belligerent action, the just combatants would, as I will argue later, make themselves liable to attack. In these circumstances, the good that the unjust combatants' action would achieve—saving the lives of innocents—would weigh against the harm it would cause to the just combatants, thereby making the action proportionate. This, therefore, is an act of war by unjust combatants against just combatants that is proportionate and permissible.

This, however, is of negligible significance for the defense of the traditional theory of the just war. For unjust war cannot consist entirely, or even predominantly, of acts that prevent wrongful acts by just combatants. In practice only a small proportion of the acts constitutive of an unjust war could be of this sort. If this is right, then an unjust war *cannot* be fought "in strict accordance with the rules." For except in the limited range of cases in which unjust combatants act to prevent wrongful acts by just combatants, their acts of war cannot satisfy the proportionality requirement, and satisfaction of this requirement is a necessary condition of permissible conduct in war.[4] In general, therefore, unjust combatants cannot participate in war without doing wrong. Since this is not true of just combatants, *jus in bello* cannot be independent of *jus ad bellum*. In short, the first two foundational tenets of the traditional theory are mistaken.

If the range of goods that can make the action of unjust combatants proportionate is restricted to the prevention of harms that would otherwise be unjustly inflicted by just combatants, what have just war theorists been assuming when they have claimed that acts of war by unjust combatants can be proportionate in the same way that acts of war of just combatants can? What goods have they thought might weigh against the harms caused?

Sidgwick gives a neutral statement of the requirement of proportionality, one he assumes can be satisfied by just and unjust combatants alike. He states that the "moral combatant" will seek as his end "to disable his opponent, and force him into submission," but that he must not "do him . . . any mischief of which the conduciveness to the end is slight in comparison with the amount of the mischief" (Sidgwick, 1891, p. 254). Walzer interprets this passage as claiming that the "mischief" caused by an act of war must be weighed against the act's contribution to "the end of victory" (Walzer, 1977, p. 129). And this is the orthodox view: the harm caused must be weighed against the "military value" of the act, which is measured by its contribution to the defeat of the enemy.

But one cannot weigh the bad effects that one would cause against the contribution one's act would make to the end of victory without having some sense of what the good effects of victory would be. Without that, it is hard to see how there can be any constraint at all. One cannot evaluatively weigh the "mischief" caused by an act of war against the contribution the act would make to the probability of a mere *event*; one must also have some sense of the importance or value of the event. If one's cause is unjust, the value of the event—victory—would presumably be negative, not positive. How, for example, could a Nazi soldier weigh the harms he would cause to enemy combatants against the end of victory by the Nazis without assigning any value to that victory? If he believes a Nazi victory would be a great good, he is mistaken.

Perhaps some have assumed that, given the inevitable uncertainties about just cause, it is important to encourage all combatants to exercise restraint by keeping their action proportionate to what they *believe* will be its good effects. This is indeed plausible but, so understood, the requirement of proportionality is, in its application to unjust combatants, not a genuine moral requirement but merely a device that serves the moral purpose of limiting the violence of those who ought not to be engaged in warfare at all.

Another possibility is that what proportionality requires is just a neutral comparison between the harm an act of war inflicts and that which it averts *on the battlefield*. It is not concerned with the larger aims of the war at all but weighs the harms inflicted on enemy forces against the magnitude of the threat they pose to one's own forces in combat.

This view does not, however, match most people's intuitions—even though these intuitions favor the view that proportionality is a neutral requirement that can be satisfied or violated by just and unjust combatants alike. Most people believe, for example, that it would be permissible to kill ten enemy combatants (or twenty, or a hundred) to prevent the killing of a single member of one's own forces. This is in part because the threat from enemy combatants is not confined to the threat they pose to one's own forces; they also threaten the aims one has in fighting.

This view is tantamount to the claim that the good to be weighed in the proportionality calculation is the self-preservation of the unjust combatants themselves. But unjust combatants are entitled to weigh the good of their own preservation against the harms they might cause only if this good is one that it is permissible for them to pursue in the circumstances. And the assumption that it is permissible for them to use force even in self-defense is precisely what I have challenged. Those they have attacked, and who in consequence now threaten them in return, have done nothing to lose their right not to be attacked. Recall that in the individual case a culpable attacker has no right of self-defense against the defensive force of his victim. This should be true of unjust combatants as well unless the circumstances of war fundamentally alter the morality of defensive force.[5] I believe that the morality of defense in war is continuous with the morality of individual self-defense. Indeed, justified warfare just *is* the collective exercise of individual rights of self- and other-defense in a coordinated manner against a common threat.[6]

Two further points deserve mention here. First, self-defense by unjust combatants in general fails to meet the necessity requirement for permissible self-defense. They need not kill in order to avoid harm to themselves when they have the option of surrender. They are unjustified in killing in self-defense when they could preserve their lives simply by stopping their own wrongful action.

Second, even if acts of war by unjust combatants could in some instances be proportionate because the goods secured by self-defense would outweigh the harms caused, it remains true that no unjust war could consist entirely in justified acts of individual self- and other-defense. While a series of acts of individual self-defense might in combination count as war, it would in the nature of the case be a just rather than unjust war. Even if there can be just wars of aggression, an unjust war of defense would involve resistance to the aggressor's just cause and not just the defense of individual lives.

In summary, it is still rather mysterious what traditional just war theorists have been assuming in their supposition that unjust combatants can satisfy the requirement of proportionality in the same way that just combatants can. If, as I have argued, unjust combatants can satisfy that requirement in only a narrow range of cases, and if, as just war theorists assert, the satisfaction of the proportionality requirement is a necessary condition of permissible conduct in war, it follows that in practice no unjust war can be fought in a permissible manner, that in general unjust combatants do wrong merely by fighting, and that because a just war *can* be fought entirely in a permissible manner, *jus in bello* cannot be independent of *jus ad bellum*.

The Requirement of Discrimination

The arguments I have advanced also challenge the third foundational tenet of the traditional theory: the requirement of discrimination. They do not challenge that requirement in its most generic formulation, which is simply that combatants must discriminate between legitimate and illegitimate targets. Rather, they challenge the assumption that the distinction between legitimate and illegitimate targets coincides with that between combatants and noncombatants. For I have argued that it is *not* permissible for unjust combatants to attack just combatants, except to prevent just combatants from engaging in wrongdoing that makes them morally liable to attack. For unjust combatants, therefore, there are, with few exceptions, *no* legitimate targets of belligerent action. In general, noncombatants *and* just combatants are alike impermissible targets for unjust combatants.

What, then, is the correct interpretation of the requirement? There must be one, for even if in general there are no legitimate targets for unjust combatants, there must, unless pacifism is true, be legitimate targets for just combatants, but also limits to what they may permissibly attack. That a just combatant's action may serve a just cause does not mean that he or she may treat anyone as fair game.

One possibility is that even if the traditional requirement is unacceptable in its application to unjust combatants, it is nevertheless correct in its application to just combatants. It might be, in other words, that just combatants are permitted to attack unjust combatants but not to conduct intentional attacks against noncombatants.[7] This view has, moreover, an obvious foundation in a more general and seemingly compelling principle. This principle is a significantly qualified variant of the principle rejected earlier that asserts the permissibility of defensive force. The qualified principle holds that, if other things are equal, it is permissible to use defensive force against anyone who poses an *unjust* threat. Because unjust combatants pose an unjust threat (except on those occasions when they are defending themselves or others against wrongful action by just combatants) but enemy noncombatants do not, it follows from the qualified general principle that enemy combatants are in general legitimate targets for just combatants but that enemy noncombatants are not.

This position has the clear advantage of being able to recognize the impermissibility of self-defense against what I have elsewhere called a Just Attacker—that is, a person who is justified in attacking another and whose victim lacks a right not to be attacked by him and is therefore not wronged by the attack. Thus, whereas the more orthodox view of Walzer and most others in the just war tradition has to assert that the conditions of war fundamentally alter the morality of defensive force, this alternative position holds that the same basic principle—the permissibility of defensive force against unjust threats—applies equally and without modification both in domestic society and in war. And although this alternative view is fundamentally antagonistic to the more orthodox view because it offers no justification for most acts of war by unjust combatants, it, or at least something very close to it, is not unfamiliar in the just war tradition.[8]

I will, however, argue against this alternative understanding as well, despite its greater plausibility. I will argue that even in its application to just combatants, the requirement of discrimination cannot take the relevant distinction to be that between combatants and noncombatants.

This alternative understanding of the requirement of discrimination asserts that it is *posing an unjust threat* that makes a person morally liable to defensive force or, to put it another way, makes the person lack a right not to be attacked in self- or other-defense. I claim, by contrast, that posing an unjust threat is neither necessary nor sufficient for liability. It is possible to pose an unjust threat without being liable to attack and possible to be liable to attack without posing an unjust threat, and indeed without posing a threat at all.

How could it be that one could pose an unjust threat to another without losing one's right not to be attacked—that is, without it becoming permissible for one's potential victim to attack in self-defense? I believe—though I concede that the implications are counterintuitive—that one does not lose one's right not to be attacked by posing an unjust threat to another *if one is in no way morally responsible for this fact.*

Consider an example drawn from science fiction:

The Implacable Pursuer A person is drugged and kidnapped while sleeping by a villain who then implants a device in her brain that *irresistibly* directs her will to the task of killing you. As a result, she will implacably pursue your death until she kills you, at which time the device will automatically deactivate itself.

Let us stipulate that the original person will continue to exist throughout the period in which her will is controlled by the device. Indeed it seems coherent to suppose that, while she pursues you, a part of her conscious mind could observe her own behavior with horror but be powerless to exert control over the movements of her body.

I claim that the Pursuer, who is what I call a *Non-Responsible Threat,* has done nothing to lose any rights or to make herself morally liable to attack. Although she is causally implicated in the threat to you, that is a wholly external fact about her position in the local causal architecture. It has no more moral significance than the fact that an innocent bystander might, through no fault of her own, occupy a position in the causal architecture that makes your killing her the only means by which you could save your own life. If you would not be permitted to kill the innocent bystander as a means of self-preservation, you are also not permitted to kill the Non-Responsible Threat in self-defense. For a Non-Responsible Threat is morally indistinguishable from an innocent bystander.[9] (There *are* lesser harms you could permissibly inflict on an innocent bystander as a means of self-preservation. Whatever harms you would be permitted to inflict on an innocent bystander in order to save your life, you would also be permitted to inflict on a Non-Responsible Threat in self-defense.)

The claim that one may not kill a Non-Responsible Threat in self-defense is contrary to common sense. It is not, however, directly relevant to the requirement of discrimination or to the morality of war, since unjust combatants are almost invariably morally responsible at least to some degree for the unjust threats they pose. Nevertheless, the case of the Pursuer does suggest that moral responsibility is important to liability. If the Pursuer were in some measure responsible for the unjust threat she poses, that would establish an obviously relevant moral asymmetry between you and her and would constitute a sufficient basis for the permissibility of your killing her if that were necessary to defend your life.

We ought not to conclude, however, that it is a person's being responsible for posing an unjust threat that makes it permissible to use force against that person in order to eliminate the threat. For a person may be morally liable to such force simply by virtue of being morally responsible for an unjust threat, even if he does not himself *pose* the threat. Consider again the case of the Pursuer. Suppose that the person who programmed and implanted the mind-control device—call him the *Initiator*—has suffered an accident and is now bedridden and tethered to a respirator. You go to plead with him only to discover that he is powerless to stop the Pursuer.[10] At that point, you see the approach of the Pursuer, who has followed you to the Initiator's house. You have only two options for saving yourself. One is to shoot the Pursuer as she approaches. The other is to flee in the Initiator's car. This car, however, is battery-powered and the only available battery is the one that is supplying power to the respirator. In order to flee the Pursuer, you must remove the power supply from the Initiator's respirator, thereby killing him.

What ought you to do: allow yourself to be killed, kill the Pursuer, who poses an unjust threat but is not responsible, or kill the Initiator, who now poses no threat but is morally responsible for the threat posed by the Pursuer? It would be permissible for you to allow yourself to be killed but in the circumstances that is not morally required. The view that asserts the permissibility of defense against unjust threats implies that you may kill the Pursuer but not the Initiator. Intuitively, however, it seems that if you must kill one or the other to save your life, you *must* kill the Initiator rather than the Pursuer. Because the Initiator is the one who is morally responsible for the fact that someone must die, he should, as a matter of justice, bear the costs of his own voluntary and culpable action. (We can assume that, if you evade the Pursuer on this occasion, she can be subdued by the police and the device can then be removed from her brain.)

In summary, what the case of the Implacable Pursuer suggests is that *posing* an unjust threat is

neither necessary nor sufficient for moral liability to force or violence that is necessary to eliminate the threat. Rather, what makes a person morally liable to force or violence that is necessary to eliminate an unjust threat is *moral responsibility* for initiating or sustaining the threat (or perhaps, in some cases, for failing to eliminate the threat).

The Criterion of Liability and Its Application to Unjust Combatants

This account of the basis of liability to defensive force has implications for the nature of the requirement of discrimination. If it is moral responsibility for an unjust threat that is the principal basis of liability to defensive (or preservative) force, it seems to follow that what makes a person a legitimate target in war is moral responsibility for an unjust threat. This assumes that permissible force in war always involves defense against an unjust threat; but it may be that there are some types of just cause for war that are not defensive, such as offensive action to recover territory or other goods that were lost to previous unjust aggression. To accommodate these possibilities, our claim should be broadened to assert that what makes a person a legitimate target in war is moral responsibility for an unjust threat or, more generally, for a wrong that provides a just cause for war. The requirement of discrimination should then hold that combatants must discriminate between those who are morally responsible for an unjust threat, or for a wrong that provides a just cause, and those who are not. It should state that while it is permissible to attack the former, it is not permissible intentionally to attack the latter—or if, more plausibly, we think that the requirement should not be absolute, it should state that there is a strong moral presumption against the permissibility of intentionally attacking those who are not responsible for an unjust threat or for a wrong that provides a just cause.

According to this understanding of the requirement of discrimination, all unjust combatants who are morally responsible for posing an unjust threat are legitimate targets of defensive or preservative attack by just combatants. This means that virtually all unjust combatants are legitimate targets because virtually all are moral agents, and because even those who are in rear areas or are asleep and are therefore not presently attacking nevertheless pose a threat by virtue of their participation in a continuing attack that has many phases coordinated over time.

It is important for understanding these claims to note that the understanding of "responsibility" employed here is eccentric.[11] Responsibility—for an unjust threat, for instance—is often assumed to require some degree of culpability, which involves both fault in the act and fault in the agent. As I will use the term, however, responsibility does not presuppose or entail culpability. If a morally responsible agent—that is, an agent with the capacity for autonomous deliberation and action—creates an unjust threat through voluntary action that is wrongful but fully excused, she is to some extent responsible for that threat even though she is not blamable.[12] In such a case there is fault in the act but not in the agent. I believe, moreover, that there can be responsibility even in the absence of fault in the act—that is, even when a person acts permissibly. If, for example, a person voluntarily engages in a permissible but foreseeably risk-imposing activity, such as driving a car, that person will be responsible if, contrary to reasonable expectation and through no fault on the part of the agent, that activity creates a threat or causes harm to which the victim is in no way liable. It is important to bear these points in mind; for it is sometimes thought that if we reject the view that the innocent in war are simply those who pose no threat, the alternative must be to accept that innocence means *moral* innocence, which contrasts with moral guilt or culpability. According to this latter view, it is *culpable* responsibility for an unjust threat that is the basis of moral liability to defensive force. This, however, is not the view defended here.[13]

Unjust combatants pose an unjust threat. But they may, as we noted earlier, have one or more of a variety of excuses: for example, they may have been deceived, manipulated, indoctrinated, or coerced or compelled by threats, or perhaps they just believed, reasonably but mistakenly, in the moral authority of their government. In some cases, these excusing conditions will be strong enough to absolve an unjust combatant of all culpability for participation

in an unjust war. But conditions of this sort are never sufficient to absolve him of all *responsibility* for his participation, or for the unjust threat he poses. Thus, even if he is *morally* innocent, he is not innocent in the sense that is relevant to the requirement of discrimination. Only the absence of a capacity for moral agency could absolve him of all responsibility for his action and thus make him innocent in the latter sense.[14]

Moral responsibility, however, is a matter of degree and the degree of an unjust combatant's responsibility for posing an unjust threat is reduced by such excuses as nonculpable ignorance and duress. And it is reasonable to assume that the extent to which a person is morally liable to defensive force varies with the degree of his responsibility for the existence of, or for posing, an unjust threat. But how are we to understand the idea that liability varies in degree? It seems that either a person is a legitimate target or he is not; either it is permissible to attack him or it is not.

A person becomes a legitimate target in war by being to some degree morally responsible for an unjust threat, or for a wrong that provides a just cause for war. But there are various constraints, such as minimal force and proportionality, that apply even to attacks on legitimate targets. The way that variations in the degree of a person's liability to defensive force are manifested is in variations in the strength or stringency of these constraints. For example, a level of harm that it might be proportionate to inflict on unjust combatants who are culpable might not be proportionate if inflicted on unjust combatants known to be largely innocent.

It may be objected that, while this might be true in principle, it is irrelevant in practice since it is normally impossible to know, of any particular unjust combatant, the degree to which he is morally responsible for the unjust threat he poses or for whatever grievance constitutes the just cause for war. This is largely true. But, as in the case of individual self-defense, reasonable agents in war have to act on the basis of presumptions that are as well grounded as possible in the circumstances. And there is occasionally good reason to presume that one group of unjust combatants bears a greater degree of liability than another. In the first

American war against Iraq, for example, all Iraqi combatants were unjust combatants because they fought to resist the reversal of their country's unjust invasion and occupation of Kuwait. Yet some bore a greater degree of responsibility than others. It was reasonable to assume that members of the Iraqi Republican Guard, a highly-paid, elite volunteer force loyal to the regime, were responsible for their action to a higher degree than poorly armed conscripts who had been compelled by threats to themselves and their families to take up positions in the desert. I believe that the proportionality requirement applied differently to attacks against these different groups. Forces of the coalition against Iraq were entitled to inflict as much harm on the Republican Guard as was necessary to eliminate the threat the guard posed to them; but they may have been morally required to accept greater risks to themselves to reduce the harm inflicted on conscripts, in something like the way that combatants are obliged to accept greater risks in order to minimize incidental harm to innocent civilians.

More generally, it is true of most unjust combatants that their conduct is excused to varying degrees by the sorts of consideration Walzer mentions in arguing that they are not criminals and that these excuses diminish their liability to varying degrees. This is in itself an important consideration that affects the way that the requirements of minimal force and proportionality apply to the use of force even in a just war. Even just wars should be fought with more restraint than might be required if it were reasonable to assume that unjust combatants were criminals or villains rather than the victims of duress and delusion.

Noncombatant Liability

Recall that the example of the Initiator offers intuitive support for the claim that one need not pose an unjust threat or currently be part of that threat in order to be morally responsible for it. And it should be obvious that in war there are some who occupy a position analogous to that of the Initiator: namely, noncombatants who bear significant responsibility for initiating or sustaining an unjust war, or for the wrong whose redress is the just cause for war. Some

of these may be responsible to a greater degree than any combatant. In 1954, for example, executives of the United Fruit Company persuaded the Eisenhower administration to organize and direct a coup that overthrew the democratic government of Guatemala and installed a new regime that returned to the company some uncultivated lands that had been nationalized in an effort to aid the peasants. This is a paradigm of an unjust war and it is reasonable to suppose that the executives bore at least as great a degree of responsibility for the killing and the violation of national self-determination as the soldiers who carried it out.[15] According to the understanding of the requirement of discrimination I have advanced—which I will refer to as the *responsibility criterion*—the executives were liable; they were legitimate targets. If attacking them would have been as effective as attacking soldiers in preventing the coup, the responsibility criterion implies that, other things being equal, it would have been permissible to attack them, and that that might have been preferable to attacking combatants, particularly if it would have meant that fewer people had to be killed.

The responsibility criterion denies both the permission and the prohibition asserted by the traditional requirement. Because it claims that it is in general impermissible for unjust combatants to attack just combatants, it denies the traditional claim that all combatants are permissible targets; because it claims that some noncombatants are permissible targets, it denies the traditional prohibition of intentional attacks on noncombatants.

Perhaps some may not find it appalling to suppose that in the case of United Fruit, certain civilians could be morally liable to attack. But for most people, the general suggestion that civilians can be legitimate targets in war will seem pernicious. The best way to address this understandable reaction is to respond to a couple of the more obvious objections to the responsibility criterion.[16]

One worry is that because moral responsibility is a matter of degree, it is difficult to identify a lower bound or threshold for responsibility for an unjust threat or other grievance that provides a just cause for war. Because of this, the responsibility criterion threatens to be utterly promiscuous in its assignment of liability in war. For in an unjust war many voters and perhaps all taxpayers must surely bear *some* degree of responsibility for their country's action. But if the responsibility criterion implies that a great many or even most ordinary citizens in a country fighting an unjust war are legitimate targets, it can hardly be regarded as a principle of *discrimination* at all.

The first part of the reply to this objection is that the same objection applies in a more seriously damaging way to the traditional requirement of discrimination. According to the traditional requirement of discrimination, noncombatants are those who are not threatening, who do not contribute to the threat posed by their country. The problem of drawing the line between those who contribute to the threat and those who do not is a familiar one in the just war literature. The typical response is to try to find a basis for drawing the distinction between combatants and noncombatants in a way that limits liability in war to soldiers, those who directly supply them with the instruments of war (including, perhaps, workers in munitions factories, but *only* while they are at work), and those who occupy positions in the military chain of command.[17] It is sometimes said, for instance, that if a person who makes a material contribution to the war is doing the same thing she would be doing if war were not in progress, she is not a combatant. But such criteria of combatant status never correspond to the tradition's own generic notion of a combatant, which is simply the notion of a person who poses a threat or contributes to the threat his country poses—the latter clause being necessary for the inclusion of military personnel who occupy roles that do not involve participation in combat or the firing of weapons. And the class of those who contribute, even quite directly, to their country's war effort is in fact considerably more extensive than the class of military personnel. It includes, for example, doctors who heal wounded soldiers and return them to combat.

So the line-drawing problem is not unique to the responsibility criterion. But on what basis can I claim that this problem is more seriously damaging to the traditional requirement of discrimination? The reason is that on the traditional view, the criterion of liability is all-or-nothing: either one is a combatant or one is not, a legitimate target or not a legitimate target. There are no degrees of liability. The only constraints on attacking legitimate targets (combatants) are the requirements of necessity, minimal force, and proportionality, and the proportionality calculation takes account of only two variables: the gravity of the threat that the combatant poses and the magnitude of the harm that defensive force would inflict. According to the responsibility criterion, by contrast, the proportionality calculation has to take account of *three* variables: The gravity of the threat, the amount of harm that would be inflicted, and the degree of the potential target's moral liability. Thus a use of force that would be proportionate according to the traditional requirement of discrimination might be disproportionate according to the responsibility criterion if the person at whom it would be directed was only weakly responsible for the threat (or other wrong) that was the basis of his liability. In short, even though the responsibility criterion (like the traditional requirement) implies that many civilians are permissible targets *in principle,* in the vast majority of cases a civilian's degree of liability will be so low that to attack him or her *militarily* would be wholly disproportionate. While voters or taxpayers might be morally liable, for example, to the effects of certain kinds of economic sanction, they would not be appropriate targets for military force. This conclusion is reinforced by the fact that, in contrast to unjust combatants, even morally responsible noncombatants normally make only a very slight causal contribution to their country's unjust war, so that attacking them would do little to diminish the threat their country poses or to advance the just cause.

A second objection is that, just as it is normally impossible to have accurate information about an unjust combatant's responsibility for the threat he poses, so it is normally impossible to have detailed information about whether and to what extent a particular noncombatant is responsible for her country's unjust war. Again, this is true. But it does not show that noncombatants cannot be liable, but only that just combatants can seldom know which ones are responsible or to what extent they are responsible. And this drastically restricts the practical significance of the responsibility criterion's implication that some noncombatants may be legitimate targets in war. For, while a few noncombatants may bear a high degree of responsibility for their country's unjust war and many may be responsible to a much weaker degree, there are also many others who are not responsible at all. Because one cannot normally distinguish among the highly responsible, the minimally responsible, and those who are not responsible at all, just combatants should in general err on the side of caution by acting on the presumption that noncombatants are innocent—that is, devoid of responsibility for their country's unjust war (just as just combatants may act on the presumption that unjust combatants *are* responsible for the threat they pose). And even if, on some occasions, just combatants were to have sufficient information to be able to distinguish between responsible and nonresponsible noncombatants, the responsible ones would normally be intermingled among the nonresponsible, making it impossible to direct force, or even economic sanctions, against the responsible ones only. And this is a further reason why military action can very rarely if ever be proportionate against civilian targets. In this respect, attacks on civilian populations are again importantly different from attacks against groups of unjust combatants, for *all* of the latter are (or may reasonably be presumed to be) to some degree liable to defensive force.

The Laws of War

Doubtless most readers retain a strong sense that opening the door to intentional attacks on noncombatants is profoundly dangerous. As with the other three objections I have canvassed, this is true. It is important that combatants should always experience deep inhibitions against attacking noncombatants. As I have argued, it is very seldom permissible, even according to the responsibility criterion, to attack noncombatants. Yet the temptation to attack them is very strong, both among those with political grievances who lack military power and among those who control powerful military forces. Because most soldiers, just and unjust alike, believe their cause is just, they will be strongly disposed to kill civilians if they believe that it is permissible to kill

enemy civilians who are responsible for an unjust war. It therefore seems better to discourage even those few attacks on noncombatants that could in principle be morally justified.

This suggests that there is indeed a role for the traditional requirement of discrimination. Although it is false as a criterion of moral liability to attack in war, it ought nevertheless to be upheld as a convention to which all combatants are bound. Thus far in this essay I have focused on what I will refer to as the "deep" morality of war: the criterion of moral liability to attack, the relation between just cause and the *jus in bello* requirement of proportionality, and so on. But there is another dimension to the morality of war that I have not explored: the laws of war, or conventions established to mitigate the savagery of war. It is in everyone's interests that such conventions be recognized and obeyed. But, although the conventions have their point in considerations of consequences, they can have a role even in a non-consequentialist account of the morality of war, such as the one I offer here. Given that general adherence to certain conventions is better for everyone, all have a moral reason to recognize and abide by these conventions. For it is rational for each side in a conflict to adhere to them only if the other side does. Thus if one side breaches the understanding that the conventions will be followed, it may cease to be rational or morally required for the other side to persist in its adherence to them. A valuable device for limiting the violence will thereby be lost, and that will be worse for all.

It is important to understand that the account I have developed of the deep morality of war is *not* an account of the laws of war. The formulation of the laws of war is a wholly different task, one that I have not attempted and that has to be carried out with a view to the consequences of the adoption and enforcement of the laws or conventions. It is, indeed, entirely clear that the laws of war must diverge significantly from the deep morality of war as I have presented it. Perhaps most obviously, the fact that most combatants believe that their cause is just means that the laws of war must, at least for the most part, be neutral between just and unjust combatants, as the traditional theory insists that the requirements of *jus in bello* are. Consider, for example, the question of punishment in the aftermath of a war. I have argued that according to the deep morality of war, unjust combatants in general cannot obey certain requirements of *jus in bello* and therefore act wrongly by participating in an unjust war. While many are fully excused, some may be culpable to varying degrees, and some may even deserve punishment, even if they have confined their attacks to military targets. But it would be counterproductive and indeed disastrous to permit the punishment of ordinary soldiers merely for their participation in an unjust war. This is so for several reasons.

First, it is simply impossible for one country, or even an international body, to provide fair trials for all the members of an army. Second, there is the problem of "victor's justice": the winning side will declare its war to have been just and will be tempted to seek vengeance against vanquished soldiers under the guise of punishment. Finally, if all combatants have to fear this fate, they may be deterred from surrendering; and it is irrational to establish incentives to protract wars rather than to terminate them.

It is, however, important to be able to punish just combatants who act wrongly in the way they conduct a war. The solution, it seems, must be to reserve punishment for infractions of the conventions or laws of war, which must be neutral between just and unjust combatants, rather than for violations of the deeper principles of *jus in bello,* which are not neutral.

It is possible that the traditional rules of *jus in bello* coincide rather closely with the laws that would be optimal for regulating conduct in battle. These rules have evolved over many centuries and have been refined, tested, and adapted to the experience of war as the nature of war has itself evolved. They may, in particular, be well suited to the regulation of the conduct of war in conditions in which there are few institutional constraints, so that the restraining effects have to come from the content of the rules rather than from institutions in which the rules might be embedded.[18]

It is also possible that these rules are not ideal. They are the products not only of modern battlefields but also of ancient chivalric engagements, religious wars, and Medieval Catholic philosophy.

(Just war theory is unique in contemporary practical ethics in two respects. It is widely and uncritically accepted and differs very little in content from what Western religious thinkers have believed from the Middle Ages to the present.) The account of the deep morality of war I have sketched provides a basis for the reevaluation of the rules we have inherited. Ideally we should establish laws of war best suited to get combatants on both sides to conform their action as closely as possible to the constraints imposed by the deep morality of war. Yet it is dangerous to tamper with rules that already command a high degree of allegiance. The stakes are too high to allow for much experimentation with alternatives.

There are, moreover, objections to the idea that we can distinguish between the deep morality of war and the laws of war. One such objection has been forcefully stated by Walzer: "No limit is accepted simply because it is thought that it will be useful. The war convention must first be morally plausible . . .; it must correspond to our sense of what is right."[19]

This may not be a problem for some of the conventional laws of war. The idea that it is wrong to attack noncombatants, for instance, already corresponds to most people's sense of what is right. Moreover, it *does* seem that people can accept limits, even in war, on the ground that respect for these limits serves everyone's interests. It is not obvious, for example, that poison gas is inherently more objectionable morally than artillery, provided that its use is confined to the battlefield; yet the convention that prohibits its use is widely obeyed, mainly because we all sense that it would be worse for everyone, ourselves included, were the taboo to be breached.

Suppose, however, that I am wrong about this and that, in general, if combatants are to be sufficiently motivated to obey certain rules in the conduct of war, they will have to believe that those rules really do constitute the deep morality of war. If it is imperative to get them to respect certain conventions, must we present the conventions as the deep morality of war and suppress the genuine deeper principles? Must the morality of war be self-effacing in this way?[20] I confess that I do not know what to say about this, though my inclination is to think that what is most important is not that the correct account of the morality of war should meet the publicity condition, or that combatants not be deceived, but that wars, when inevitable, should be fought as decently and with as little harm, especially to the innocent, as possible.

One further objection to distinguishing between the deep morality of war and the laws of war is that there are bound to be circumstances in which the deeper morality and the conventions will conflict—for example, when morality requires an attack on noncombatants while the conventional requirement of discrimination forbids it. How ought such conflicts to be resolved? In order for morality to require the violation of the convention in a particular case, it must take into account not only the positive reasons for attacking noncombatants but also the effect that the violation of the convention would be likely to have on general respect for the convention. For it is widely accepted that the violation of a convention by one side tends to release the other side from its commitment to respect the convention. If, however, this consideration is factored in and morality still requires the violation of the convention, it seems that the convention ought to be violated. Yet there is so much scope for self-deception in these matters that this is a conclusion that one ought never to accept with complacency.

If, despite these problems, it is right that there must be laws of war that diverge from the deep morality of war, then war is normatively governed by two sets of principles that operate at different levels. It may seem, however, that it is really the conventions that must be action-guiding in the conduct of war and, if so, that raises the question whether the deeper morality of war has any practical significance at all. Are the judgments it issues of merely academic interest?

I think not. If nothing else, the deep morality of war is a guide to individual conscience. It demands of potential volunteers, potential conscripts, and active military personnel that they consider with the utmost seriousness whether any war in which they might fight is just and to refuse to fight unless they can be confident that it is. The effects of this demand

are hard to predict. It might simply prompt governments to become ever more subtle and clever in the lies they tell their citizens. If so, it is a corollary of the account I have offered that greater efforts must be made to ensure openness in government. Yet I think that the main effect would be to make it harder for governments to fight unjust wars.

Notes

1. Compare Henry Sidgwick's claim that "the rules which civilised opinion should attempt to impose on combatants . . . must abstract from all consideration of the justice of the war." (Sidgwick, 1891, pp 253–254)
2. See also the discussion on Walzer's pp. 38–39.
3. Here I draw on the argument in McMahan and McKim (1993), pp. 502–506, 512–513.
4. I believe that in the same cases in which they cannot satisfy the requirement of proportionality, unjust combatants also cannot satisfy the requirement of discrimination. But this claim presupposes a conception of the requirement of discrimination different from the orthodox conception. I will defend the alternative conception in the following section.
5. In an earlier paper, I claimed that "a case can perhaps be made" for the view that morally innocent unjust combatants can be "justified in engaging in self-defense against the defensive counterattack by the victims of their initial attack" (McMahan, 1994b). Because I now attribute less significance than I did earlier to the distinction between moral innocence and moral culpability, I believe that this earlier claim is mistaken. Two philosophers who have argued persuasively against my earlier position on self-defense by morally innocent unjust combatants against just combatants are Richard Arneson ("Just Warfare Theory and Noncombatant Immunity," manuscript) and McPherson (2004).
6. This is, of course, a controversial claim that I lack space to defend here, though I do so in a manuscript in progress called *The Ethics of Killing: Self-Defense, War, and Punishment*. I defend the claim against important objections in McMahan (2004).
7. I believe, contrary to the traditional assumption, that there can be rare instances in which both sides in a war have a just cause and are justified in fighting. For present purposes I leave it an open

question what the requirement of discrimination should say about attacks by just combatants against just combatants in such cases.

8. See, for example, Anscombe (1981), p. 53.

9. A mistaken variant of this claim is defended in McMahan (1994a). A better argument is in McMahan (2002). Others who argue that there is no right of self-defense against a Non-Responsible Threat are Zohar (1993), Otsuka (1994) and Rodin (2002).

10. I am indebted to Monsignor Stuart Swetland and to Richard Arneson for making me see the importance of this detail. If the Initiator could eliminate the threat to you, he could be regarded as continuing to *pose* the threat by having set it in motion and then refusing to stop it. For an ancestor of this kind of case that differs from it in that the person in the position of the Initiator remains a necessary cause of the threat, see Alexander (1985), p. 100.

11. For further elucidation, see McMahan (2002), pp. 402–403.

12. Since writing the longer version of this paper, I have modified my view about the conditions for moral responsibility for an unjust threat. I now believe that in cases in which a morally responsible agent poses an unjust threat through voluntary action but was not engaging in a risk-imposing activity and could not have foreseen that he would pose a threat, he is not responsible for the threat. See McMahan (2005).

13. It is, however, the view I defended in both "Self-Defense and the Problem of the Innocent Attacker" (McMahan, 1994a) and "Innocence, Self-Defense, and Killing in War" (McMahan, 1994b).

14. Again, my view is no longer quite so strong. See footnote 12.

15. Foa a brief but more detailed description of this episode, see McMahan (1985), 13–14.

16. Some of these responses indicate ways in which the account of the morality of war I have developed in this paper is superior to the cruder account I advanced in "Innocence, Self-Defense, and Killing in War" (McMahan, 1994b), which invites similar objections but cannot answer them in the ways suggested here.

17. For representative examples, see Nagel (1985), pp. 69–70, Walzer (1977), pp. 144–146, Finnis et al. (1987), pp. 86–90, and Oderberg (2000), pp. 217–219.

18. I am indebted here to Allen Buchanan.

19. Walzer (1977), p. 133.

20. I have been helpfully pressed to confront this and related problems by Charles Beitz, Gilbert Harman, Philip Pettit, and Peter Singer. They will be disappointed by my anemic and noncommittal response.

References

Alexander, L. (1985). Self-Defense and the Killing of Noncombatants. In Beitz, Charles R. et al. (Eds.) *International Ethics*. Princeton: Princeton University Press, pp. 98–105.

Anscombe, E. (1981). *Ethics, Religion, and Politics: Collected Philosophical Papers*, vol. 3. Minneapolis: University of Minnesota Press.

Finnis, J., Boyle, J., & Grisez, G. (1987). *Nuclear Deterrence, Morality, and Realism*. Oxford: Oxford University Press.

McMahan, J. (1985). *Reagan and the World: Imperial Policy in the New Cold War*. New York: Monthly Review Press.

McMahan, J. (1994a). Self-Defense and the Problem of the Innocent Attacker. *Ethics* 104, pp. 252–290.

McMahan, J. (1994b). Innocence, Self-Defense, and Killing in War. *Journal of Political Philosophy* 2, pp. 193–221.

McMahan, J. (2002). *The Ethics of Killing: Problems at the Margins of Life*. New York: Oxford University Press.

McMahan, J. (2004). War as Self-Defense. *Ethics and International Affairs* 18, pp. 75–80.

McMahan, J. (2005). The Basis of Moral Liability to Defensive Killing. *Philosophical Issues* 15, pp. 386–405.

McMahan, J., & McKim, R. (1993). The Just War and the Gulf War. *Canadian Journal of Philosophy* 23, pp. 501–541.

McPherson, L. (2004). Innocence and Responsibility in War. *Canadian Journal of Philosophy* 34, pp. 485–506.

Nagel, T. (1985). War and Massacre. In Beitz, Charles R. et al. (Eds.) *International Ethics*. Princeton: Princeton University Press, pp. 53–74.

Oderberg, D. (2000). *Applied Ethics*. Oxford: Blackwell.

Otsuka, M. (1994). Killing the Innocent in Self-Defense. *Philosophy and Public Affairs* 23, pp. 74–94.

Rodin, D. (2002). *War and Self-Defense*. Oxford: Clarendon Press.

Sidgwick, H. (1891). *The Elements of Politics*. London: Macmillan.

Walzer, M. (1977). *Just and Unjust Wars.* Harmondsworth: Penguin.

Zohar, N. (1993). Collective War and Individual Self-Defense: Against the Conscription of "Self-Defense." *Political Theory* 21, pp. 606–622.

QUESTIONS

1. Outline McMahan's argument for each of his three challenges to traditional just theory.
2. "The attempt to ground the tenets of just war theory in the permissibility of defensive force cannot succeed. . . ." Why not? Of what importance is this claim (and its defense) to McMahan's broader argument?

Terrorism

Few university students using this reader will not have given some thought to contemporary terrorism. This section on terrorism is continuous with the last, on war. Some of the questions raised by terrorism have already been raised by some of the readings in the last section. The "strategic bombings" of European and Japanese cities in World War II, commonly called "terror bombings," raised some of the same questions that contemporary terrorism does, for instance, about the permissibility of targeting civilian populations. If terrorism is morally condemnable, this may suggest that other practices in war are sufficiently similar to it as to be equally condemnable.

In all domains of thought it is important after some time to be clear about the phenomena and the terms one uses to describe and refer to them. And one of the things characteristic of the philosophical study of a subject is attention to terms and concepts. The question of the definition of terrorism is widely thought to be particularly problematic. It is oft said that little agreement can be secured on the definition of terrorism, that "one person's terrorist is another's freedom fighter." It's not entirely clear why someone could not be both a terrorist and a freedom fighter, but the central suggestion here is that some people will approve and others will disapprove of the acts of terrorists. This is thought to make the definition of terrorism difficult; lack of agreement on a definition, for instance, has been a major impediment to United Nations legislation on terrorism.

There are broad and narrow characterizations of terrorism. Many people favor a broad characterization; terrorism is violent political action. On this view political assassination as well as some acts of political insurgency will count as terrorism. If we think of terrorism broadly it is unlikely that it will always be wrong. Thinking of it more narrowly understands it to be a special kind of political violence, with a complex structure. Terrorism in a narrow sense is a kind of violence against property and people for certain ends or goals. But we need to say more.

To understand many acts of terrorism we need to distinguish short- from long-term ends or goals. A terrorist group might strike (e.g., blow up some targets) and make some demands (e.g., the release of political prisoners), saying their campaign will go on until the demands are met. But their long-term goals may be different (e.g., political independence). Some contemporary terrorists, notably Al Qaeda, do not make their goals or ends very clear, and sometimes do not publicly take responsibility for their acts. This makes interpreting their acts more difficult.

Missing from broad characterizations of terrorism is a reference to *terror.* The term *terrorism* comes from the Latin *terrere,* "to frighten." Terrorism is meant to terrify, and noting this is essential to understanding its structure. Terrorism, narrowly understood, typically involves (1) harming some people (e.g., victims of a bomb on a train), (2) in order to terrify a larger population (e.g., civilians who take public transport), (3) in order to affect others (e.g., a government), (4) in order to achieve (short- or long-term) ends (e.g., political demands). Terrifying a large group (most civilians?) is a means to achieving terrorists' ends. Terrorists often choose sites or victims for their attacks somewhat arbitrarily. This makes sense if they intend to terrify a larger population; instilling fear in a larger population requires violence that is seemingly arbitrary or random.

Narrow terrorism thus has several sets of victims: the people killed or injured, the people terrorized, and others whose interests are adversely affected. Most of these victims are "noncombatants," to use the term from the ethics of war. Consequently, they may be innocent.[1] The harm to the victims is intentional, something aimed at. Terrorism in this narrow sense is different from political assassination or guerrilla attacks on military targets. Summarizing, we may say that terrorism in this narrow sense is a kind of violence against property and people for certain ends or goals. It has an instrumental structure; it is virtually always a means to certain ends or goals of the perpetrators. And it has a complex structure: harming some people (civilians or noncombatants), targeted somewhat arbitrarily, in order to terrorize a larger population, perhaps in order to pressure others (or a government) in order to achieve certain (short- or long-term) ends.

Terrorism in this narrow sense raises a number of moral questions not raised by other forms of political violence.

---

1. Some writers make the innocence of the victims part of the definition of terrorism. This may be a mistake, as many terrorists claim, however implausibly, that their chosen victims are not innocent. A definition should not try to settle substantive questions like this.

29. Violence, Terrorism, and Justice

R. G. FREY AND CHRISTOPHER W. MORRIS

R. G. Frey, professor of philosophy emeritus at Bowling Green State University in Ohio, has published widely on the ethics of life and death. He is the author of *Interests and Rights* (1980) and *Rights, Killing, and Suffering* (1983) and the coeditor with Christopher Wellman of *The Companion to Applied Ethics* (2003). He will coedit with T. Beauchamp the *Oxford Handbook of Ethics and Animals.*

For a description of Christopher W. Morris, see chapter 19.

In these introductory remarks, Frey and Morris raise questions about how we should understand terrorism. (See also the last section of chapter 19.) They raise a number of questions about the moral evaluation of terrorism and the way in which different moral traditions draw the relevant distinctions. These words, as well as those in the following essay (chapter 30), were written a decade before the attacks of 9/11 made all Americans vividly aware of terrorism.

Unless one is a pacifist, one is likely to find it relatively easy to think of scenarios in which the use of force and violence against others is justified. Killing other people in self-defense, for example, seems widely condoned, but so, too, does defending our citizens abroad against attack from violent regimes. Violence in these cases appears reactive, employed to defeat aggression against or violence toward vital interests. Where violence comes to be seen as much more problematic, if not simply prohibited, is in its direct use for social/political ends. It then degenerates into terrorism, many people seem to think, and terrorism, they hold, is quite wrong. But what exactly is terrorism? And why is it wrong?

Most of us today believe terrorism to be a serious problem, one that raises difficult and challenging questions. The urgency of the problem, especially to North Americans and Western Europeans, may appear to be that terrorism is an issue that we confront from outside—that, as it were, it is an issue for us, not because violence for political ends is something approved of in our societies, but because we are the objects of such violence. The difficulty of the questions raised by contemporary terrorism has to do, we may suppose, with the complexity of issues having to do with the use of violence generally for political ends.

The first question, that of the proper characterization of terrorism, is difficult, in part because it is hard to separate from the second, evaluative question, that of the wrongness of terrorism. We may think of terrorism as a type of violence, that is, a kind of force that inflicts damage or harm on people and property. Terrorism thus broadly understood raises the same issues raised generally by the use of violence by individuals in groups. If we think of violence as being a kind of force, then the more general issues concern the evaluation of the use of force,

From R. G. Frey and Christopher W. Morris, eds., *Violence, Terrorism, and Justice* (Cambridge: Cambridge University Press, 1991). Reprinted by permission of Cambridge University Press.

coercion, and the like: When may we restrict people's options so that they have little or no choice but to do what we wish them to do? Violence may be used as one would use force, in order to obtain some end. But violence inflicts harm or damage and consequently adds a new element to the nonviolent use of force. When, then, if ever, may we inflict harm or damage on someone in the pursuit of some end? This question and the sets of issues it raises are familiar topics of moral and political philosophy.

Without preempting the varying characterizations of terrorism developed by the authors in this volume, however, we can think of it more narrowly; that is, we can think of it as a particular use of violence, typically for social/political ends, with several frequently conjoined characteristics. On this view, terrorism, as one would expect from the use of the term, usually involves creating terror or fear, even, perhaps, a sense of panic in a population. This common feature of terrorism is related to another characteristic, namely, the seemingly random or arbitrary use of violence. This in turn is related to a third feature, the targeting of the innocent or of "noncombatants." This last, of course, is a more controversial feature than the others, since many terrorists attempt to justify their acts by arguing that their victims are not (wholly) innocent.

Thus characterized, terrorism raises specific questions that are at the center of contemporary philosophical debate. When, if ever, may one intentionally harm the innocent? Is the justification of terrorist violence to be based entirely on consequences, beneficial or other? Or are terrorist acts among those that are wrong independently of their consequences? What means may one use in combating people who use violence without justification? Other questions, perhaps less familiar, also arise. What does it mean for people to be innocent, that is, not responsible for the acts, say, of their governments? May there not be some justification in terrorists' targeting some victims but not others? May terrorist acts be attributed to groups or to states? What sense, if any, does it make to think of a social system as terrorist?

Additionally, there are a variety of issues that specifically pertain to terrorists and their practices. What is the moral standing generally of terrorists?

That is, what, if any, duties do we have to them? How do their acts, and intentions, affect their standing? How does that standing affect our possible responses to them? May we, for instance, execute terrorists or inflict forms of punishment that would, in the words of the American Constitution, otherwise be "cruel and unusual"? What obligations might we, or officials of state, have in our dealings with terrorists? Is bargaining, of the sort practiced by virtually all Western governments, a justified response to terrorism? How, if at all, should our responses to terrorists be altered in the event that we admit or come to admit, to some degree, the justice of their cause?

Considered broadly, as a type of violence, or, even more generally, as a type of force, terrorism is difficult to condemn out of hand. Force is a common feature of political life. We secure compliance with law by the use and threat of force. For many, this may be the sole reason for compliance. Force is used, for instance, to ensure that people pay their taxes, and force, even violence, is commonplace in the control of crime. In many such instances, there is not much controversy about the general justification of the use of force. The matter, say, of military conscription, though endorsed by many, is more controversial. In international contexts, however, the uses of force, and of violence, raise issues about which there is less agreement. Examples will come readily to mind.

More narrowly understood, involving some or all of the three elements mentioned earlier (the creation of terror, the seemingly random use of violence, and the targeting of the innocent or of noncombatants), the justification of terrorism is more problematic, as a brief glance at several competing moral theories will reveal.

Act-consequentialists, those who would have us evaluate actions solely in terms of their consequences, would presumably condone some terrorist acts. Were some such act to achieve a desirable goal, with minimal costs, the consequentialist might approve. Care, however, must be taken in characterizing the terrorists' goals and means. For contemporary consequentialists invariably are universalists; the welfare or ends of all people (and, on some accounts, all sentient beings) are to be included. Thus, terrorists cannot avail themselves of such theories to justify furthering the ends of some small group at the cost of greater damage to the interests of others. Merely to argue that the ends justify the means, without regard to the nature of the former, does not avail to one the resources of consequentialist moral theory.

Two factors will be further emphasized. First, consequentialist moral theory will focus upon effectiveness and efficiency, upon whether terrorist acts are an effective, efficient means to achieving desirable goals. The question naturally arises, then, whether there is an alternative means available, with equal or better likelihood of success in achieving the goal at a reduced cost. If resort to terrorism is a tactic, is there another tactic, just as likely to achieve the goal, at a cost more easy for us to bear? It is here, of course, that alternatives such as passive resistance and nonviolent civil disobedience will arise and need to be considered. It is here also that account must be taken of the obvious fact that terrorist acts seem often to harden the resistance of those the terrorists oppose. Indeed, the alleged justice of the terrorists' cause can easily slip into the background, as the killing and maiming come to preoccupy and outrage the target population. Second, consequentialist moral theory will focus upon the goal to be achieved: Is the goal that a specific use of terrorism is in aid of desirable enough for us to want to see it realized in society, at the terrible costs it exacts? It is no accident that terrorists usually portray their cause as concerned with the rectification and elimination of injustice; for *this* goal seems to be one the achievement of which we might just agree was desirable enough for us to tolerate significant cost. And it is here, of course, that doubts plague us, because we are often unsure where justice with respect to some issue falls. In the battle over Ireland, and the demand of the Irish Republican Army for justice, is there nothing to be said on the English side? Is the entire matter black and white? Here, too, a kind of proportionality rule may intrude itself. Is the reunification of Ireland worth all the suffering and loss the IRA inflicts? Is this a goal worth, not only members of the IRA's dying for, but also their making other people die for? For consequentialists, it typically will not be enough that members of the IRA think so; those affected by the acts of the IRA cannot be ignored.

Finally, consequentialist moral theory will stress how unsure we sometimes are about what counts as doing justice. On the one hand, we sometimes are genuinely unsure about what counts as rectifying an injustice. For instance, is allowing the Catholics of Northern Ireland greater and greater control over their lives part of the rectification process? For the fact remains that there are many more Protestants than Catholics in the North, so that *democratic* votes may well not materially change the condition of the latter, whatever their degree of participation in the process. On the other hand, we sometimes are genuinely unsure whether we can rectify or eliminate one injustice without perpetrating another. In the Arab–Israeli conflict, for example, can we remove one side's grievances without thereby causing additional grievances on the other side? Is there *any* way of rectifying an injustice in that conflict without producing another?

Thus, while consequentialist moral theory *can* produce a justification of terrorist acts, it typically will do so here, as in other areas, only under conditions that terrorists in the flesh will find it difficult to satisfy.

It is the seeming randomness of the violence emphasized by terrorism, understood in the narrower sense, that leads many moral theorists to question its legitimacy. Many moral traditions, especially nonconsequentialist ones, impose strict limits on the harm that may be done to the innocent. Indeed, some theories, such as those associated with natural law and Kantian traditions, will impose an indefeasible prohibition on the intentional killing of the innocent, which "may not be overridden, whatever the consequences." Sometimes this prohibition is formulated in terms of the rights of the innocent not to be killed (e.g., the right to life), other times in terms merely of our duties not to take their lives. Either way the prohibition is often understood to be indefeasible.

If intentionally killing the innocent is indefeasibly wrong, that is, if it may never be done whatever the consequences, then many, if not most, contemporary terrorists stand condemned. Killing individuals who happen to find themselves in a targeted store, café, or train station may not be done, according to these traditions. Contemporary terrorists, who intend to bring about the deaths of innocent people by their acts, commit one of the most serious acts of injustice, unless, of course, they can show that these people are not innocent. Much turns on their attempts, therefore, to attack the innocence claim.

Just as natural law and Kantian moral theories constrain our behavior and limit the means we may use in the pursuit of political ends, so they constrain our responses to terrorists. We may not, for instance, intentionally kill innocent people (e.g., bystanders, hostages) while combating those who attack us. Our hands may thus be tied in responding to terrorism. Many commentators have argued that a morally motivated reluctance to use the nondiscriminating means of terrorists makes us especially vulnerable to them.

Some natural law or Kantian thinkers invoke the notions of natural or of human rights to understand moral standing, where these are rights which we possess simply by virtue of our natures or of our humanity. Now if our nature or our humanity is interpreted, as it commonly is in these traditions, as something we retain throughout our lives, at least to the extent that we retain those attributes and capacities that are characteristic of humans, then even those who violate the strictest prohibitions of justice will retain their moral standing. According to this view, a killer acts wrongly without thereby ceasing to be the sort of being that possesses moral standing. Terrorists, then, retain their moral standing, and consequently, there are limits to what we may do to them, by way either of resistance or of punishment. Conversely, though there is reason to think consequentialists, including those who reject theories of rights to understand moral standing, would not deny terrorists such standing, what may be done to terrorists may not be so easily constrained. For harming those who harm the innocent seems less likely to provoke outrage and opposition and so negative consequences.

Certainly, not every member of these nonconsequentialist traditions will agree with this analysis. John Locke, for instance, believed that a murderer has "by the unjust Violence and Slaughter he hath committed upon one, declared War against all Mankind, and therefore may be destroyed as a *Lyon* or a *Tyger*, one of those wild Savage Beasts, with whom

Men can have no Society nor Security."[1] It may, however, be argued that the analysis accords with many parts of these traditions, as well as with much of ordinary, commonsense morality.

Whether we follow these theories in understanding the prohibition on the intentional killing of the innocent to be indefeasible or not, this principle figures importantly in most moral traditions. Care, however, must be taken in its interpretation and application. Even if we understand terrorism narrowly, as involving attacks on the innocent, it may not be clear here as elsewhere exactly who is innocent. As made clear in the just war and abortion literature, the term "innocent" is ambiguous. The usual sense is to designate some individual who is not guilty of moral or legal wrongdoing, a sense usually called the moral or juridical sense of the term. By contrast, in discussing what are often called "innocent threats"—for instance, an approaching infant who unwittingly is boobytrapped with explosives, a fetus whose continued growth threatens the life of the woman—it is common to distinguish a "technical" or "causal" sense of "innocence." People lack innocence in this second sense insofar as they threaten, whatever their culpability.

Determining which sense of "innocence" is relevant (and this is not to prejudge the issue of still further, different senses) is controversial. In discussions of the ethics of war, it is often thought that "noncombatants" are not legitimate targets, because of their innocence. Noncombatants, however, may share some of the responsibility for the injustice of a war or the injustice of the means used to prosecute the war, or they may threaten the adversary in certain ways. In the first case, they would not be fully innocent in the moral or juridical sense; in the second, they would lack, to some degree, causal innocence.

This distinction is relevant to the moral evaluation of terrorist acts aimed at noncombatants. Sometimes attempts are made at justification by pointing to the victims' lack of innocence, in the first sense. Perhaps this is what Emile Henry meant when he famously said, in 1894, after exploding a bomb in a Paris café, "There are no innocents." Presumably in such cases, where the relevant notion of innocence is that of nonculpability, terrorists would strike only at members of certain national or political groups. Other times it might be argued that the victims in some way (for instance, by their financial, electoral, or tacit support for a repressive regime) posed a threat. In these cases, terrorists would view themselves as justified in striking at anyone who, say, was present in a certain location. The distinction may also be of importance in discussions of the permissibility of various means that might be used in response to terrorist acts. If the relevant sense of innocence is causal, then certain means, those endangering the lives of victims, might be permissible.

Of course it is hard to understand how the victims of the Japanese Red Army attack at Israel's Lod airport in 1972 or of a bomb in a Paris department store in 1986 could be thought to lack innocence in either sense. In the first case, the victims were travelers (e.g., Puerto Rican Christians); in the second case, the store in question was frequented by indigent immigrants and, at that time of year, by mothers and children shopping for school supplies. It is this feature of some contemporary terrorism that has led many commentators to distinguish it from earlier forms and from other political uses of violence.

The analogies here with another issue that has preoccupied moral theorists recently, that of the ethics of nuclear deterrence and conflict, are significant. The United States, of course, dropped atomic weapons on two Japanese cities at the end of the last world war. For several decades now, American policy has been to threaten the Soviet Union with a variety of kinds of nuclear strikes in the event that the latter attacked the United States or its Western allies with nuclear or, in the case of an invasion of Western Europe, merely with conventional weapons. These acts or practices involve killing or threatening to kill noncombatants in order to achieve certain ends: unconditional surrender in the case of Japan, deterrence of aggression in that of the Soviet Union. The possible analogies with terrorism have not gone unnoticed. Furthermore, just as some defenders of the atomic strikes against the Japanese have argued, those we attack, or threaten to attack, with nuclear weapons are themselves sufficiently similar to terrorists to justify our response.

A still different perspective on these issues may be obtained by turning from the usual consequentialist and natural law or Kantian theories to forms of contractarianism in ethics. Although this tradition has affinities with natural law and Kantian theories, especially with regard to the demands of justice or the content of moral principles, there are differences that are especially noteworthy in connection with the issues that are raised by terrorist violence.

According to this tradition, justice may be thought of as a set of principles and dispositions that bind people insofar as those to whom they are obligated reciprocate. In the absence of constraint by others, one has little or no duty to refrain from acting toward them in ways that normally would be unjust. Justice may be thus thought, to borrow a phrase from John Rawls, to be a sort of "cooperative venture for mutual advantage." According to this view, justice is not binding in the absence of certain conditions, one of which would be others' cooperative behavior and dispositions.

Adherents to this tradition might argue that we would be in a "state of nature," that is, a situation where few if any constraints of justice would bind us, with regard to terrorists who attack those who are innocent (in the relevant sense). As Hume argues in the *Second Enquiry,* when in "the society of ruffians, remote from the protection of laws and government," or during the "rage and violence of public war," the conventions of justice are suspended:

> The laws of war, which then succeed to these of equity and justice, are rules calculated for the *advantage* and *utility* of that particular state, in which men are now placed. And were a civilized nation engaged with barbarians, who observed no rules even of war, the former must also suspend their observance of them, where they no longer serve to any purpose; and must render every action or rencounter as bloody and pernicious as possible to the first aggressors.[2]

Unlike the earlier views, then, this view holds that terrorists who, by act or by intent, forswear the rules of justice may thereby lose the protection of those rules, and so a major part of their moral standing.

Similarly, partisans of terrorism might argue that it is the acts of their victims or of their governments that make impossible cooperative relations of fair dealing between themselves and those they attack. The acts, or intentions, of the latter remove them from the protection of the rules of justice.

In either case, the acts of terrorists and our response to them take place in a world beyond, or prior to, justice. Students of international affairs and diplomacy will recognize here certain of the implications of a family of skeptical positions called "realism."

Consequentialists, it should be noted, are likely to find this exclusive focus on the virtue of justice to be misguided, and they are likely to be less enamored of certain distinctions involving kinds of innocence or types of violence that are incorporated into contractarianism. In general, they will argue, as noted earlier, that terrorism *can* be justified by its consequences, where these must include the effects not merely on the terrorists but also on their victims (and others). As terrorist acts appear often not to produce sufficient benefits to outweigh the considerable costs they inevitably exact, there will most likely be a moral presumption, albeit defeasible, against them. But wrongful terrorism will be condemned, not because of the existence of mutually advantageous conventions of justice, but because of the overall harm or suffering caused. Consequentialists, then, will doubtless stand out as much against contractarian views here as they do against natural law or Kantian ones.

The foregoing, then, is a sketch of different ways terrorism may be understood and of different types of moral theories in which its justification may be addressed. There is serious controversy on both counts, and this fact alone, whatever other differences may exist, makes the works of philosophers and political and social scientists on terrorism contentious even among themselves.

Notes

1. John Locke, *Second Treatise of Government,* in *Two Treatises of Government,* ed. Peter Laslett (Cambridge: Cambridge University Press, 1988), p. 274 (chap. 2, sec. 11).
2. David Hume, *An Enquiry concerning the Principles of Morals,* in *Enquiries concerning Human Understanding and the Principles of Morals,* ed. L. A. Selby-Bigge, 3d ed., ed. P. H. Nidditch (Oxford: Clarendon, 1975), pp. 187–8 (sec. 3, pt. 1).

QUESTIONS

1. How do the authors characterize terrorism? Is their characterization adequate to their purposes?
2. Could there be a justification of acts of terrorism, one that would show these acts to be just? What do Frey and Morris suggest?

30. The Political Significance of Terrorism

LOREN LOMASKY

*L*oren Lomasky (1946–) is a professor of political philosophy, politics, and law at the University of Virginia. He is the author of *Persons, Rights, and the Moral Community* (1987) and the coauthor, with G. Brennan, of *Democracy and Decision: The Pure Theory of Electoral Preference* (1993).

In this essay Lomasky argues that terrorism is not ordinary, "not merely a politics that gets out of hand. . . . Rather, terrorism represents the radical rejection of civil accommodation." Writing a decade before the attacks of 9/11, Lomasky reflects on the phenomenon of terrorism common then in many parts of the world. One of his claims pertains to the *expressive*: "What it expresses is virulent and unregulated opposition to the preconditions of successful civility."

I

Q: Why do Japanese commandos fire Czech submachine guns at Puerto Rican passengers departing an Air France flight in an Israeli airport?

A: To strike at American imperialism.

It could be a bad riddle. Instead, it is one of the numerous guises in which contemporary terrorism presents itself. Although the instance[1] may seem especially bizarre, it contains many of the elements common to terrorism as practiced during the last third of the twentieth century: A party nursing a grievance lashes out violently and unpredictably against targets bearing only the most tenuous connection to the object of its animus. No melioration is brought about by the strike, nor could any rationally have been anticipated by those who organized the operation. After bodies are bagged and reporters depart, political life proceeds much as before.

The subject of this essay is how to understand and evaluate the phenomenon of terrorism. An immediate obstacle that presents itself is that any purported definition of "terrorism" will itself be laden with moral and political baggage. Most individuals who employ violent means in their political activities prefer to speak of themselves as "urban guerrilla," "revolutionary," or some such. Their admirers and supporters generally comply. Thus the bromide "One person's terrorist is another's freedom fighter." One need not accede to the implied relativism to acknowledge the absence of firm and generally accepted criteria of application for "terrorism" and its cognates.

However much this absence may concern philosophers and other political taxonomists acting in their professional capacities, it has remarkably little echo in the *vox populi*. When TWA ticket counters or Israeli schoolchildren are sprayed with bullets, when newspaper heiresses are held hostage, Turkish diplomats murdered, or airliners destroyed

From R. G. Frey and Christopher W. Morris, eds., *Violence, Terrorism, and Justice* (Cambridge: Cambridge University Press, 1991). Reprinted by permission of Cambridge University Press.

in flight by plastic bomb explosions, the events are routinely and unproblematically understood by the media and their audience to be terroristic. That is not an unimportant datum. Every day innumerable people are victimized by violent assault or natural calamity. Only rarely do these events escape the back pages of local newspapers. Yet when destructive activity dons the garb we recognize as terrorism, it ascends to extraordinary prominence. Ordinary citizens and their leaders believe that terrorism is portentous, that it is *news*. That belief is self-justifying. Events that happen halfway around the world and that directly involve only a relatively small number of heretofore obscure people take over television screens everywhere. For some reason, terrorist assault seems to *matter*. Its perceived significance is, however, totally disproportionate to any measurable effect on mortality tables or the stability of political regimes. If analysts have reason to care about definition, it is because other people care about terrorism for quite different reasons.

II

Terrorism, as commonly understood, is a species of private enterprise, albeit not the sort that Better Business Bureaus usually commend. Although states may instigate or otherwise promote terrorist attacks, the actions are carried out by individuals who are not (or at least do not present themselves as being) functionaries of a governmental apparatus.[2] That may seem to prejudice the issue, to imply that there is something especially odious about murders that do not enjoy the imprimatur of a sovereign member of the United Nations. No such ascription is intended. In a century that has witnessed Nazi genocide, Stalin's Gulag, and the immolation of Cambodia under the Khmer Rouge it would hardly seem to need mention that states are unsurpassed wielders of deadly force.

To withhold the term "terrorism" from the activities of secret police or armies is not to proffer excuse or mitigation. Rather, it is to return to the question why terrorism should seem to be so worthy of note. All the casualties of terrorism in the Middle East, arguably the most fertile ground for its exercise, represent only a minute fraction of the number of persons killed in the recently concluded Iran–Iraq war.

Although statistics are, for obvious reasons, unavailable, one may surmise that there has not been so much as one day during the previous two decades, the decades during which "international terrorism" rose to great prominence, in which the number of homicides committed by free-lance operatives has equaled the number of killings carried out by governments. Why then should we concern ourselves with terrorist activity? Assessed from a detached consequentialist perspective, fixation on terrorism may appear an indulgence.

Terrorism so understood is not the official activity of governments, but it nonetheless possesses distinct political significance.[3] Unless an individual or group represents itself as acting in the service of a political ideal or program, it will not be deemed terrorist. Charles Manson was not engaged in terrorism,[4] but the Symbionese Liberation Army was. The Mafia may routinely excite terror in individuals to secure its ends, but that does not render it terrorist in the intended sense. Again, no special imputation of moral noxiousness is either asserted or denied.

Although terrorism is a political phenomenon, its targets need not enjoy any political prominence. By far the majority of terrorist raids are aimed at individuals who are distant from positions of power and authority: airline passengers, for example, or children at play. Only occasionally is the object of attack a military unit or a high official of the despised government. In part, no doubt, that is because these individuals tend to be less easy to reach and better able to respond in kind to the employment of deadly force than private citizens. However, it is by no means obvious or even likely that choice of target is entirely a matter of expediency. A systematic program of assault on civilians constitutes a *different* sort of political enterprise than does a campaign to assassinate diplomats or to ambush military patrols, and surely terrorists are not oblivious to that fact. For one thing, it is a program that will elicit a different degree of attention from those of us who are civilians and who recognize that, but for fortune, it is we who might have been fodder for the terrorists' ambitions. It is also, in ways that will subsequently be developed, uniquely expressive of a distinctive political ethos. Thus, it is reasonable to suspect that the occurrence of civilian casualties is not merely adventitious to the practice of terrorism, and that the oft-repeated characterization of terrorism as incorporating *indiscriminate* violence can be misleading. Terrorists' failure to discriminate in their choice of victim, or rather, their failure to discriminate on the basis of standard political categories, is itself a defining feature of their enterprise.

III

Can we say, then, that terrorism is to be described as the use or threat of violence by private parties, exercised primarily on other private parties, in order to bring about desired political objectives? This understanding is called into question by available data. One of the most palpable facts about terrorist activity is the vastness of the gulf between efficacy and aspiration. In almost none of the instances of terroristic activity that come to widespread attention is there any genuine likelihood that the assault on person or property will serve to advance the claimed political ends. It is inconceivable that the Lod airport attack might have overthrown or even deflected the aims of the governments of Israel, Japan, or the United States—and, crucially, the unlikelihood was eminently knowable at the time. The murder of a dozen athletes in Munich in 1972 did not even put a halt to the Olympic Games, let alone persuade the government of Israel to alter its policies in a direction favored by Black September. Indeed, if terrorism exerts any detectable effect on the platforms and activities of governments, it is to steel them in their resolve to resist and eliminate the aggressors. Those governments that show themselves lax in pursuing the counterattack on terrorism are typically replaced by more repressive regimes of firmer will. Surviving members of the Italian Red Brigades, Baader-Meinhof, Montoneros, Tupamaros, and other such groups will attest to that fact.[5]

Two attempts at explanation suggest themselves. First, one can hypothesize that terrorists typically act with the intention of bringing about those political ends to which they declare allegiance; they are, however, in the grip of mistaken beliefs about political causation and are incapable of correcting those misbeliefs. Second, one can maintain that terrorists generally aim at *expressing support* for political outcomes without, however, intending thereby to *bring*

about those outcomes. It is the second of these hypotheses that seems better to fit the data. Although some evidence suggests a tendency toward psychological abnormality among terrorists,[6] it does not justify a conclusion that terrorists generally lack a faculty for making straightforward causal judgments. Individuals persistently unable to apprehend the sheer implausibility of toppling regimes by gunning down assorted tourists are unlikely candidates for successfully carrying out complex quasimilitary operations. In the absence of specific evidence to the contrary, it is reasonable to impute to terrorists no lesser rationality than that which social analysts routinely ascribe to other actors and which, in any event, is requisite for the conduct of their operations. Rational agents are not systematically unable to distinguish efficacious from inefficacious activity.

Indeed, it is probably the conviction that terrorists are, irrespective of their moral credentials, rational agents much like the rest of us that leads many theorists markedly to misdescribe terrorist activity. C. A. J. Coady describes terrorism as "a means or technique for the pursuit of political ends"[7] but fails to present evidence that would suggest that terrorism actually does advance avowed political ends—unless one construes those ends as something quite different from the ostensible purposes routinely cited by terrorist perpetrators as rationales for their activities. Carl Wellman defines "terrorism" as "the use or attempted use of terror as a means of coercion."[8] This is both too wide and too narrow. It is too wide in that it includes a vast range of governmental, criminal, and quite licit private activity.[9] It is too narrow in that it plainly fails to apply to instances such as the Lod airport massacre in which the three gunmen made no demands, issued no timetables, but merely opened fire. Also, there have been many instances of terrorism in which no group took "credit" for the incident, let alone presented an agenda of political demands.[10]

Nonetheless, the line taken by Coady and Wellman is common in the literature on terrorism. Despite considerable evidence to the contrary, terrorists are characterized as determined seekers of political ends by violent means. This may be the result of a misleading exercise in empathy. "What would lead *me* to contemplate, let alone carry out, the murder of uninvolved men, women, and children?" is the implicit question. For most of us the answer would either be "Nothing!" or "The pursuit of an end so momentous, so far-reaching, that failure to achieve it would be no less than a moral catastrophe." Merely to render terrorism thinkable, we must conceive of it as directed toward the attainment of an end that cannot be secured via less costly means but that *is* likely to be advanced through the employment of violence. Terrorism becomes fathomable, more easily located within the realm of recognizably political activity, if the terrorist is taken to be engaged in at least the same genus of behavior as that which we might elect were our circumstances sufficiently desperate.

Understanding should be sought via a different route. Specifically, we do better to focus on the attitudes *expressed* by terrorist activity than on the outcomes thereby achieved. It is not only the terrorist who engages in primarily expressive activity; many altogether familiar and benign activities practiced by ordinary men and women are not outcome-oriented. Consider, for example, fans seated in their bleacher seats who, in virtue of being fans and not merely spectators, cheer for their favored team during a sporting event. It is possible—barely possible—that the fans' behavior is to be explained as predicated on their belief that the marginal expected return to one more cheer justifies the cost imposed on their vocal cords. That, though, is exceedingly farfetched. (It becomes even more so if they are seated not in the bleachers but in front of their television screens.) We misidentify the situation if we regard it as the calculated result of an application of means–end rationality. For the vast majority of fans, cheering is not a cost but rather a benefit, not an investment in outcomes but a consumption good. One cheers because one wishes to express support for one's team and not because one is attempting to secure some further desired outcome.

The example is innocuous, perhaps too much so to stand as a credible analogue to the terrorist's activity. One that may seem more applicable in virtue of the higher stakes involved is the believer's voluntary acceptance of martyrdom. Individuals who refuse to contravene an article of faith even at the cost of their lives are expressing fidelity to that faith without thereby attempting to bring about some *further* religiously valuable outcome. Indeed, if such forfeiture of life is designed to advance an end beyond that of simply remaining firm in allegiance, then it is disqualified as a genuine act of martyrdom. For example, one who accepts being killed so as to secure a ticket to paradise or to gain further converts to the faith has, according to the theory of martyrology, failed. We may legitimately wonder in any particular case (as does Becket in T. S. Eliot's rendition) whether the individual has actually acted as a martyr. However, we simply fail to understand what martyrdom is if we do not conceive it as an expressive rather than outcome-oriented action.[11]

In similar fashion, terrorism should be understood as activity *supportive* of political ideals, but it need not be deliberately crafted to *bring about* favored outcomes. That is not to rule out by definitional fiat instances of terrorist activity pursued with the intention of bringing down a regime or causing it to alter its policies in a preferred direction. Clearly there are some cases of outcome-oriented terrorism, such as when hostages are taken in order to secure ransom money to be pumped back into the cause or to secure the release of imprisoned comrades.[12] Note, however, that these are intrinsically subsidiary to the main thrust of the terrorists' activity; there would neither be comrades to free nor need for money to purchase weapons were there not some prior agenda to be supported. Although terrorist activity assumes innumerable guises, it is primarily, though not exclusively, expressive in nature rather than a long-term investment in political outcomes.

It follows that utilitarian appraisals of terrorism are generally beside the point. The utilitarian, here as elsewhere, commends a cost–benefit analysis in which the costs of any particular action are estimated and then compared with the expected return (where that figure is calculated as the probability-weighted sum of the various possible outcomes). The usual caveats about one's likelihood to misestimate both costs and benefits when one's passions are engaged, damage that may be done to the actor's own generally salutary dispositions, influence on others of precedents one establishes, and so on will be duly noted.[13] Perhaps the utilitarian analyst will conclude that a sober reckoning of consequences demonstrates that terrorism is hardly ever justified; perhaps not. In either case, the bookkeeperly accounting is irrelevant. It presupposes that the terrorist's acts are engineered to produce desired political outcomes, and we have found reason to reject that understanding.[14] Rather, terrorism is to be appraised by criteria appropriate to acts that are intended to express support for envisaged scenarios but that do not thereby aim at bringing them about as consequences of the act.

That may seem to stack the deck against the terrorist. Expressive activity, one may suppose, is intrinsically of less account than are projects that directly aim at results external to the performance. One may be justified in incurring a modest cost to post a get-well card to an ailing friend, discounting entirely any therapeutic benefit that may result, but that sum is entirely disproportionate to the resources that could reasonably be expended to achieve a cure for the illness. Similarly, it is at least an open question whether one may countenance the sacrifice of the (nonconsenting) innocent when that is the price that must be paid in order to eliminate some manifest political evil. However, to sacrifice the innocent merely in order to *proclaim* the presence of an evil or to *denounce* it may seem frivolous. In both a figurative and a literal sense, expressive activity may be deemed "inconsequential."

That judgment, though, is too quick. Expressive activity need not, from the perspective of the agent, present itself as trivia, as "merely" expressive. The act of "bearing witness" to what one takes to be a moral truth is itself normatively considerable. The example of the martyr is to the point here, and although few of us may possess the stuff of which martyrs are made, we can at least recognize the depth of conviction from which the martyr acts and, under appropriate conditions, admire that expression.[15] Such recognition would not be available were it not the case that we subscribe at least in some measure to the martyr's ethic. Few of us are prepared to douse ourselves with gasoline and light a match to protest a war we hold to be grossly immoral, yet we would, I think, accuse ourselves (and others) of moral insensitivity if the perception of such an injustice never elicited protest—never, that is, except when it has been calculated that the protest will be efficacious in the requisite degree

toward eliminating that unjust state of affairs.[16] There are some evils elimination of which, as a logical matter, is impossible. We mourn, retribute, commemorate, honor, memorialize, lament, commiserate over that which is irretrievably past. An entirely forward-looking consequentialism can make no sense of these familiar contours of the moral landscape except to thrust them into a Procrustean bed from which they emerge as prophylaxis directed toward future eventualities that do remain under our control. In good Procrustean fashion, the fit is achieved only by dint of sacrificing crucial bodily parts.

It would be foolish to deny that expressively motivated activity is indeed often consequential. Typically, however, these results are achieved only because the act that generates them was not contrived with them in mind. Many individuals may be inspired by the martyr's example to take up the cause for which he or she died, but the inspiration would be obliterated were they to become convinced that the martyr accepted death precisely in order to multiply the number of disciples. I may be steeled in my determination to resist future moral horrors through participation in rites of remembrance commemorating past victims of other catastrophes, but if my engagement in those rituals is exclusively directed by my personal program for self-improvement, then I shall almost certainly fail to achieve the desired outcome.[17] Manipulative rationality has its successes but also its liabilities, chief among them that manipulation perceived is, in large measure, manipulation defused.

Terrorists have their manifestos and agendas, but more centrally, they carry with them their grievances. Although the former are usually unreadable and unintelligible, the latter must be given credence if terrorist phenomena are to be understood. By "given credence" I do not mean endorsed but rather acknowledged. Rage and righteous indignation are among the most powerful emotions in the human breast, and they would not be such were they easily confined to that domain. One who is engaged by some circumstance, justifiably or otherwise, is someone who is disposed to express that sentiment on a conspicuous canvas.

To be sure, those generally inclined to deplore violence will find it easier to sympathize with individuals who practice pacific modes of protest or who elect to employ their own bodies as the appropriate canvas rather than practice their art on the anonymous passengers of an airliner. Nonetheless, terrorists do not present themselves simply as psychotics unable morally to distinguish between burning leaves and burning people. We are informed by the killers of children that they kill precisely because their own children are denied their birthright; they are at war with all because public hostility or indifference constitutes, as the terrorists see it, a declaration of war against their own people. Because the cause for which they are willing to die—and kill—is of such gravity, they deem it mandatory to underscore the nature of the enormity they denounce with acts of a particularly flagrant and attention-commanding character: kidnapping civilians, littering an airport with bodies, transforming a recreation site into an abattoir. This sort of proportioned response to perceived injustice is entirely beyond the capacity of psychotics. It does not follow, of course, that terrorists are morally superior to psychotics. They are, however, different. And if to construe terrorism as primarily a species of expressive activity is to leave the deck stacked against terrorists, these are the cards that they have wittingly dealt.

Like terrorists, many of their respondents are best understood as operating in a predominantly expressive mode. One can hardly fail to note a disproportion between, on the one hand, the nugatory capacity of terrorist activity to disrupt political structures and, on the other hand, the fevered commentary it elicits. Former president Reagan declared international terrorism to be the United States' foremost public enemy and announced a policy, notoriously repudiated by the subsequent performance of his administration, to brook no negotiation with terrorists or their supporters. Mrs. Thatcher's response to Irish terrorism incorporated, among other measures, substantial curtailment of traditional British liberties of the press. Sober-minded persons of seasoned political judgment adopt near-apocalyptic tones when discussing the impact of terrorism. In words reminiscent of Jonathan Edwards on sin, journalist and historian Paul Johnson contends:

Terrorism is the cancer of the modern world. No state is immune to it. It is a dynamic organism which attacks the healthy flesh of the surrounding society. It has the essential hallmark of malignant cancer: unless treated, and treated drastically, its growth is inexorable, until it poisons and engulfs the society on which it feeds and drags it down to destruction.[18]

In order to understand terrorist phenomena it is necessary to understand how they can summon such striking responses.

It would, of course, be myopic to deny that terrorism has imposed severe costs within Western (and other) societies. These costs, however, have fallen far more heavily on individuals than on political institutions. An airplane crash exacts a considerable human toll whether it is the result of malfunctioning equipment or a concealed bomb. Governments survive the latter as easily as they do the former. One might expect, then, that terrorist incidents would call forth the sort of expressions of regret and mourning that accompany natural disasters, or the indignation that accompanies the commission of a heinous crime. These latter events, however, lack any significant political dimension. What requires explanation is the general perception of terrorist activity as politically portentous. A purely consequentialist account will be as inadequate for understanding the response to terrorism as it is for understanding the motivations undergirding the practice of terrorism. Terrorism is politically significant because of what it *represents* and not just because of what it *brings about*. Accordingly, the normative appraisal of terrorism must take seriously that representational dimension if it is to perceive what, from a political perspective, is most truly insidious about terrorism.

IV

A political order, whatever else it may be, is an order. That is, it necessarily embodies socially recognized distinctions such as those between citizen and alien, licit and illicit actions, states of peace and war. Where such distinctions either have never arisen or have entirely broken down, politics does not exist. Instead, one is confronted with the Hobbesian state of nature in all its brutish unloveliness: "In such a condition, every man has a right to every thing; even to one another's body. And therefore . . . there can be no security to any man."[19] For Hobbes, the establishment and preservation of security was the unique *telos* of politics, from which all prescriptions for institutional design geometrically followed as theorems. Even if one does not embrace the Hobbesian conception of the quest for order as the culmination of politics, it is at least its beginning. Absent firm distinctions between *mine* and *thine*, distinctions initially grounded in the separateness of individuals' bodies and then naturally extending to their actions and the instruments through which and for which they act, no other goods that civil society may hold forth will be attainable.

This sketchy characterization of political first principles is not meant to be controversial; rather, I take it to be entirely platitudinous. It is precisely because the status of order as a political desideratum cuts across contestable ideologies and aspirations that it can serve as a basis for contrasting the *political* with the *contra-political*. Anarchism resides—barely—within the realm of political alternatives, but nihilism does not. The anarchist maintains, maintains emphatically, that the natural distinction between individual wills has normative consequences, chief among them being the inherent repugnance of sovereignty exercised by one person over another. Nihilism is different. The nihilist acknowledges no such normative consequence of the separateness of persons and thus takes everyone and everything to be fair game, at least in the negative sense that no criteria are admitted by means of which the fair can be distinguished from the foul.

Despite the historical association, often tendentiously overstated and misdescribed, between terrorism and anarchism, terrorist activity is fundamentally nihilistic. It is the deliberate employment of principles of language and conduct corrosive of political order. Analysts work to taxonomize terrorisms as of the left or of the right, as nationalistic or internationalistic, but these categorizations possess at most a superficial validity. At bottom, terrorism is essentially contrapolitical. To commit oneself to a career of terror is to shuck off in particularly violent and blatant fashion the restraints that divide civil

society from the state of nature. This, rather than bare mortality statistics or measurable disruption of regimes, renders terrorism especially noteworthy, is that which prompts in both learned commentators and the general public a fascination that combines fear, loathing, and wonder. Terrorists lift, though more through their aspirations than through any direct effect of their deeds, a corner of the curtain screening us from the Hobbesian jungle.

That terrorists present themselves as free-lance operatives (whatever the degree of sub rosa support they may receive from sovereign states) is to the point, though not because their acts are more destructive of life and welfare than those openly carried out under the aegis of governments; as noted earlier, it is the reverse that is usually the case. Nor are bloody deeds rendered less intrinsically vile by the circumstance of their issuing from states. Violence, we may agree, is deplorable whatever its provenance—but that is precisely reason to be concerned to limit the number and variety of sources from which it emanates. The institution of government is, in its most primary function, a means for the limitation of violence. No acute study of history is needed to make us aware that this aim, even in the best of times, is realized only imperfectly. Because governments persistently prove themselves to be lukewarm or worse in their fidelity to the task of checking violence, we have reason to attempt to achieve a politics that will instill in them more restraint in their dealings both with their own citizens and with foreign countries whom they take to be competitors. The liberal tradition of political inquiry from Locke through Rawls is, in no small measure, characterized by the quest for principles through which such restraint may be secured. We may also aspire to transcend the limitations that seem inherent to national sovereignty through the establishment of supranational order-conferring political structures, although the record of organizations such as the League of Nations and United Nations affords to these hopes little encouragement. What is *not* called for, what would surely forfeit the limited degree of tranquillity we might reasonably expect to enjoy, would be a democratization of the right to perpetrate acts of violence such that each person, in pure Hobbesian state-of-nature fashion, would enjoy carte blanche to purge his or her grievances on the bodies of others.

Terrorism overtly expresses rejection of a politics that would limit the domain of authorized violence. To be sure, terrorists are neither the only nor the most prolific practitioners of nonstate violence. Professional criminals as well as common thugs daily take it upon themselves to pursue their aims through coercive means. The toll in lives and property they cumulatively exact is many times greater than that achieved by terrorists. Although I have no wish to minimize the moral evil of the former, it is nonetheless the case that ordinary crime must be understood to differ in kind from the activity of terrorists. The criminal attempts to secure through illicit means ends basically identical to those that others pursue inside the law: money chief among them, but also power, status, and a sense of achievement. Criminal activity operates within the interstices of the political order and is parasitic upon it. Where crime succeeds it does so in virtue of the fact that those upon whom it preys are, by and large, law-abiding. The standard felon does not will the collapse of civil order but, to the contrary, is pleased to take a free ride on the benefits it affords. Terrorism is different. It is the expression of disdain for the institutions of civil society in general and, specifically, for the goal of limiting the practice of violence. Terrorists do not aim to free ride but rather to destroy. Although in practice they may have little effect, the ideal they express is nihilistic.

Terrorists are sometimes spoken of as "guerrillas," as individuals engaged in internecine warfare against the established order. This characterization is erroneous. Although terrorists bear some affinity to insurgent forces, the opposition in which they set themselves is more radical. Civil war seeks the demolition of political authority for the purpose of constituting in the vacuum thereby created an improved authority. Because civil war entails a temporary retreat into the state of nature, some political theorists (Hobbes and Kant, for example) judge it to be always impermissible. Others, chief among them Locke, approve civil war, but only in conditions of utmost exigency and only to restore an order against which the current regime has itself cast the first stone. Both rejection and qualified approval issue from the same political logic. Government is instituted for the limitation of violence. Civil war is its catastrophic breakdown. Thus, on one account, it is inadmissible. However, governments can themselves become ferocious initiators of violence against persons. Therefore, maintains the other account, armed rebellion waged against gross governmental excesses is licit. Both unambiguously endorse political order, either as it in fact exists or as aspiration. Civil war is, then, the enterprise of attempting through the use of military means to replace an odious order with one that is morally (more) satisfactory. It, unlike terrorism, is outcome-oriented. The guerrilla, to be sure, avoids pitched battles until a shift in the balance of forces renders that tactic feasible. However, guerrilla warfare is genuinely warfare, that is, a politics by other means. Rebellion without any hope of melioration is not civil war; it is murder or suicide or both. Terrorists may entertain in their hearts a fantasy of the established order being laid low and subsequent securement by themselves of political control, but fantasy, even when punctuated by bullets, is not warfare.[20]

Another aspect of terrorism's contra-politics is its adherence to a policy of affirmative action for potential victims. It renounces conventional distinctions of person and place. Although soldiers or high officials of the despised regime may become targets of bombs and bullets, cruise ship passengers, office workers, men and women at prayer in a synagogue, or children asleep in their beds qualify equally well as candidates. By declaring open season on persons everywhere, terrorists underscore their rejection of familiar political categories and the limitations on violence they embody.

Although in a loose sense terrorists practice political assassination, their killings have a more esoteric flavor. Individuals are not singled out for death in virtue of the particular offices they hold, any specific complicity in the design or execution of governmental policy, or perceived wickedness attaching to their own personal conduct. Terrorists propound a sort of doctrine of original sin within which liability to the damnation they wield is universal. Ordinary assassins, by way of contrast, discriminate in quite conventional ways, holding particular individuals accountable for their own alleged misdeeds or their active participation in unjust institutions. Assassination, although an avowedly political deed, resembles ordinary crime in this way: It implicitly accepts the legitimacy of political order even as it contravenes its dictates. Assassins are, so long as they remain merely assassins, attempting to remove one officeholder or a class of officeholders in order that they be replaced by better people pursuing more acceptable policies. Within the natural law literature there exists an extended discussion of the nature of tyranny and the conditions under which tyrannicide is justifiable. All this is implicitly rejected by terrorists. They carry no specific animus against the passengers of the airliners on which they plant bombs; any other assorted collection of travelers would have done as well. Those whom fortune provides as victims are merely handy targets, ciphers for their use. Political assassination is usually an evil, but it is one of a different nature than terrorism.

When armies clash, lives are lost. Some people maintain that these killings are justified when the conditions of a just war obtain. It is not my intention either to defend traditional just war theory or to offer a replacement. In an age in which national armies are conscripted from the general citizenry and entire cities are placed in bomb sights, a doctrine of justice in warfare may have become obsolete. Still, there is a point to the distinction between soldiers and civilians, the former but not the latter being fair game for assault. The point should by now be familiar: This is a distinction responsive to the concern that violence not be unbounded. There can be little doubt that this would be a better world were there no soldiers' uniforms signifying "I am a proper target—and dispenser—of deadly force." However, that is a prospect utopian at best. If violence cannot be eliminated, it remains a matter of urgency to limit both its domain and its intensity.[21] Marking off some persons, even if entirely arbitrarily, as "soldiers" and others as "civilians" may not instantiate the highest ideals of a refined morality, but it possesses the minimal virtue of expressing a conviction that *some* people are off limits. Terrorism, by contrast, represents the endorsement of unconstrained liability to violence.[22]

Shall we then endorse the common characterization of terrorism as the employment of *indiscriminate* violence in support of political ends? That characterization is sometimes accurate, as when a random assortment of airplane passengers is blown from the sky. In such a circumstance, what matters to the terrorist is that there *be* victims; it does not matter *who* those victims are. On other occasions, though, terrorist targets are quite carefully and deliberately selected. But just as the politics of terrorism is to be understood as a contra-politics, so too are the discriminations of terrorists a kind of contra-discrimination.

When a dozen athletes are kidnapped in an Olympic village and then murdered, the terrorist has achieved, achieved with exquisite precision, an inversion of the customary categories of political order. It is precisely because the Olympic Games represent an ideal of comity among nations and competition without violence or hostility that they present themselves as a uniquely enticing opportunity for disruption. To have disrupted in similar fashion a conclave of the Hell's Angels would not have paid so rich a dividend.

The bullet placed in Pope John Paul II by Agca was similarly symbolic, as is the deliberate slaughter of children. Instances of this terrorist motif abound. Among all the passengers on the *Achille Lauro*, wheelchair-bound Leon Klinghoffer was deliberately selected for a bullet in the brain and dumping into the Mediterranean.[23] It was the elderly Lord Mountbatten, and not some active politician, who was dispatched by a bomb while on a fishing holiday. Terrence Waite, emissary of the archbishop of Canterbury, entered Lebanon to negotiate the release of victims of kidnapping; that rendered him, according to the terrorist's logic of inversion, eminently suitable for disappearance into the netherworld from which he had hoped to free others. The point seems to be that just those individuals (or venues) who, according to conventional categories, are most properly removed from the play of deadly force must be subjected to it.

The terrorist's assault on political categories is accompanied by a corresponding assault on language. As if by instruction from the Queen of Hearts, words are turned topsy-turvy to signify whatever the terrorist wants them to mean. A ragtag group of covert killers refers to itself as an "army":

for example, the Japanese Red Army, the Irish Republican Army, or, with uncharacteristic modesty, the Italian Red Brigades. Easily vanquishing all other competitors in the contest for most preposterous designation is the "Symbionese Liberation Army," which, at the time of its kidnapping of Patricia Hearst, was comprised of eight members! Whatever may have prompted either the formation or the naming of this group, it cannot be doubted that it was neither Symbionese[24] nor an army, nor had it anything whatsoever to do with liberation.

With equal imaginativeness, individual members of these organizations refer to themselves as "soldiers," "urban guerrillas," "insurgents," or, most popularly, "freedom fighters." Terrorist homicidal assaults are described as "battles" or "operations," and often are characterized as having been undertaken in "self-defense." Individuals who have the misfortune to be captured by terrorists are tried as "enemies of the people" in "people's courts" and, when found "guilty"—a foregone conclusion in a world in which none are innocent—are not simply killed but rather "executed." This transvaluation of language is not merely incidental but instead is very much of a piece with the general political nihilism that underlies terrorism. It is to invoke political and juristic terms that underlie civil society's quest for order and to bend them to the purpose of maximizing disorder. Although it is not surprising that terrorists want to include semantics among their quarries, one is hard pressed not to raise an eyebrow when the world's press shows itself woodenly content to parrot their mal-locutions as if there were nothing whatsoever fanciful or perverse to them.

V

The preceding observations have aimed at generality. That which is common to various terrorist organizations rather than that which distinguishes them has been the primary focus of attention. That is not to maintain that differences among the groups are purely nominal. Terrorists differ in their political orientation: While many situate themselves on the left, right-wing terrorism is present and, in some countries, the predominant form. Many kill out of nationalism, others in the name of proletarian internationalism. Some terrorist organizations, such as

the PLO, possess in good measure the panoply of states, while others, such as the Symbionese Liberation Army, are no more than a tiny collection of misanthropic misfits. A few groups enjoy considerable state support, a sophisticated infrastructure, and a high degree of stability, while others are no more than a blip in yesterday's news. Some terrorists routinely extort for profit and become virtually indistinguishable from participants in conventional organized crime, while others live as ascetics dedicated to the pursuit of their "ideals." And so on, and so on. Although these vicissitudes are of considerable significance to those whose job it is to catalog or to blunt particular campaigns, they can be set aside in an investigation of what it is about terrorism *as such* that renders it such a high-visibility, politically meaningful phenomenon.

I have argued that terrorism, the terrorism that plays itself out in newspapers and on television screens to rapt audiences around the world, is to be understood as activity that is primarily expressive in character rather than outcome-oriented. What it expresses is virulent and unregulated opposition to the preconditions of successful civility. If this description is accurate, then the normative verdict follows directly. Nearly all of us have a fundamental stake in the preservation of political order within which alone the pursuit of nearly all human goods is rendered feasible. Therefore, we have strong, indeed conclusive, reason to concur with Johnson's description of terrorism as a cancer to be excised. This is neither hyperbole nor vapid apocalypticism. Rather, it is to grasp with acute comprehension the animus of terrorism and to respond in strict proportion.

Some seek excuse or mitigation for the terrorist by contrasting the body count for which he or she is responsible with the considerably greater toll exacted by governments or even with the nonviolent actions of private men and women: "The amount of terror inflicted by 'terrorists,' no matter how dreadful, is a thimbleful compared to official, legally-sanctioned terror. . . . [M]ore terrorists wear three-piece suits, ride in Rolls Royces, and sit in the seats of corporate power and government than lurk in dark alleys."[25] This judgment may issue from an inconsiderate consequentialism that takes its bearings entirely from the statistics entered in official records.

Alternatively, it may bespeak a relativism that is not far distant from the nihilism of the terrorist: When some people die from bombs and others from air polluted by factories, who is in a position to assess on whom the greater blame is to be placed? The disinclination to judge may, in rare cases, spring from a deep well of pity and humility, but far more often it is symptomatic of moral impotence. It can also carry a reflexive significance: One for whom the pen rather than the bomb is the preferred instrument of expression may elect to express his or her own contempt for the wearers of three-piece suits by contrasting them unfavorably with the terrorist.

Terrorists have grievances. That is so whether they are individuals dispossessed from the land of their ancestors or the bored and spoiled children of professional families. Possession of grievances in no regard distinguishes terrorists from the remainder of humanity: Bad luck and injustice are, to one degree or another, the common human lot. One of the great curiosities of a certain desiccated strain of Western liberalism[26] is its perpetual willingness to excuse the inexcusable just so long as it issues from those who possess official standing as being among the downtrodden;[27] it takes as the foremost of moral virtues a conscientious refusal to "blame the victims." To the extent that this instinct arises from the sublimation of unease consequent on finding oneself in a favored social and economic position, it is of psychological but no analytical interest. However, this liberal reflex can also present itself as the product of a concern for distributive justice. Those who either are among the dispossessed or act as proxies on their behalf are not entirely shielded from criticism; they may, for example, be reprimanded for acting excessively or imprudently when they respond violently to social iniquities. However, in light of the evident failure of nonviolent strategies to secure redress, violence committed by those who seek meritorious ends must be sympathetically appraised. The terrorist is viewed as a sort of contemporary Robin Hood, outside the law but responsive to its best impulses.

This is radically to misidentify the logic of terrorism. Unlike Robin Hood, who, as the legends have it, practiced an outlawry that was scrupulous in the distinctions it enforced between the guilty and the innocent, between usurper and victim, terrorists either ignore such distinctions entirely or else turn them on their head. The enemy is only incidentally particular individuals who cross the terrorist's path; more fundamentally it is civil order. Because it is only within the ambit of such order that the pursuit of justice becomes feasible, the terrorist undercuts in intention and deed all basis for redress of wrongs. This is yet a further implication of the terrorist's contra-politics. Political theorists since Aristotle have been virtually unanimous in their understanding of politics as directed by a concern for melioration of bad luck and misfortunes consequent on wrongful human conduct. They have recognized that those who suffer most from the collapse of order are, almost inevitably, the poor and the weak. Insofar as terrorists repudiate this tradition, they lack standing as advocates of a program of social justice. Whatever the liberal may believe, the terrorists' ends are not those of any liberalism, no matter how attenuated and apologetic.

If self-identified progressive consciences have failed by and large to convey a clear sense of the normative standing of terrorism, print and, especially, electronic journalists have not performed conspicuously better. The abduction of an airliner or occupation of an office building by an unrestrained band of zealots is, in their perception, above all else a good story, and journalists have proved themselves willing to bear considerable financial as well as moral costs to enhance their coverage:

> In some instances, terrorists seem to have been paid by the media. In the Beirut crisis of 1985—the hijacking of TWA 847—US networks allegedly paid over $1 million a week to assure their monopoly over access to the hostage spectacular. ABC reportedly paid Amal $30,000 for sole access to a hostage interview session and $50,000 for the "farewell banquet."
>
> What did the media get in return for this investment? They received tapes from hostages in which they reported feeling fine, that the captors were nice people, and massive doses of propaganda. Only later was it revealed—as after the Tehran siege—that the hostages had by no means felt good and that some had been severely mistreated. . . . The terrorists were aware of the competition between the American networks in which a few additional

points in ratings meant huge increases in advertising revenues; they put their knowledge to good use. As a British correspondent noted at the time: "It was done quite consciously. There were graduates of media studies from American colleges at meetings at Nabih Berri's house in West Beirut while tactics were being worked out." . . . Some of the hostages bitterly resented the activities of the networks in Beirut, referring to ABC as the "Amal Broadcasting Corporation" and NBC as the "Nabih Berri Corporation."[28]

It has often been noted that this sort of journalistic feeding frenzy represents an inducement for the perpetration of yet additional terrorist attacks as well as incentive to choreograph those attacks in especially novel and garish fashion so as to hold the rapt attention of an easily jaded audience that would otherwise turn back to sitcoms. I have no wish to deny that providing an inducement for terrorism, whether in the form of publicity or cash, is morally culpable. Additionally, though, this kind of coverage is condemnable on grounds internal to journalistic practice. It is the function of the press to report the news, not to create it. Moreover, the press is responsible for applying its professional skills so as to provide its readers and viewers bona fide information, as opposed to serving as indiscriminate shills for desperate men and women who wish to deliver themselves of diatribes. A journalism both cavalier with facts and bereft of moral judgment is meretricious.

Some will contend that journalists have little choice but to act as they do, that they cannot claim for themselves a Solomonic wisdom to tailor the news as they see fit but must rather pass on to their audience whatever statements they are given. It is the task of the public and not the press to attempt to ascertain where the truth may lie. The objector contends that a free press does not engage in censorship, however odious the information with which it is presented.

The response is jejune. Journalism, like politics, is a practice that necessarily incorporates selection and discrimination. No reporter mindlessly passes on all that he sees and hears. A filtering process is inevitable; all that is in question is which criteria will be employed to distinguish news from chaff. Journalism done well discriminates between confused and clear, reliable and unreliable, informative and misleading, portentous and trivial. When these criteria give way to titillation for the sake of added rating points, journalism becomes indistinguishable from entertainment. The public deserves to be afforded the information it needs to comprehend the flux of world events, to form political judgments, and to be able to take action to avoid dangers. A free and responsible press provides such information, but that is quite distinct from plying a servile pen or camera. That reporting be free and untrammeled is a venerable principle of journalism; but so too is the principle that advertisers are to pay and not to be paid.

In fairness, journalistic distortions of the nature of terrorism are not entirely a manifestation of cynicism. Newsworthiness is not a platonic form but rather a function of human interests. Because the public is fascinated by terrorists, so too—and properly—is the press. The fascination is, in large measure, the fascination of dread. It is more than a little chilling to be confronted by individuals who seem conspicuously to lack the concerns and restraints that one has thoroughly internalized and on which sociality rests. That is why psychopathic killers such as Ted Bundy and Jack the Ripper attract considerable attention and analysis. Individuals who play out their violent role on an international stage may achieve yet greater prominence. There exists a tension between the repulsion one feels toward their deeds and one's desire to understand them as men and women ultimately not all that unlike oneself. To the extent that their motivations and designs are ones that we can sympathize with, if not share, these people need not be viewed as unremittingly threatening to the kind of life we cherish. If we allow them to speak their minds at length, and if we attend to what they have to say, perhaps the strangeness will be exorcised. Thus the tendency of the press—and not only the press[29]—to display terrorists fatuously as ordinary people, albeit with an extraordinary gripe.

Terrorists may, for all I know, indeed be ordinary, but *terrorism* is not. It is not merely a politics that gets out of hand: Cook County but somewhat more so. Rather, terrorism represents the radical rejection of civil accommodation. It takes the Hobbesian state of nature not as the problem but as the solution.

Whether terrorists do or do not love their children, whether they weep when they hear the melodies of their homelands, is irrelevant to the appraisal of terrorism. To suppose otherwise is to fail to take seriously the political significance of terrorism.

Notes

I am grateful to James Child, Robert Evans, Raymond Frey, Gerald Gaus, and an anonymous Cambridge University Press referee for helpful criticism.

1. Assault by three members of the United (Japanese) Red Army at the Lod airport, May 1972.

2. As I write, the trial of Kim Hyon Hui has opened in South Korea. According to the indictment and her own statements, while acting as an agent of the government of North Korea she planted the bomb that destroyed a (South) Korean Airlines jet near Burma in 1987. What renders the case especially fantastic is that many South Koreans voice the suspicion that she was in fact acting under orders from a *South* Korean government that hoped thereby to profit at the polls from a resurgence of anti-Communist sentiment. Whichever may prove to be the case, it is worth noting that the responsible government found it in its interest to feign an ordinary (i.e., private) terrorist attack. See *Wall Street Journal*, March 8, 1989, p. A10.

3. The way in which terrorism is political does, however, diverge radically from ordinary modes of political activity, so much so as to render terrorism the antithesis of normal politics. Section IV describes the contra-political nature of terrorism.

4. I am assuming that Manson's fixation on the deep meaning of Beatles' lyrics and the like was too jumbled and solipsistic to count as a political program.

5. The 1983 suicide attack on the U.S. Marine barracks in Lebanon is often cited as an example disconfirmatory of the thesis that terrorism is futile. President Reagan responded to the death of 241 marines by removing the American military presence in Lebanon. Although I do not deny that this event was politically consequential, the particular context within which it occurred renders it with virtual textbook clarity an exception that proves the rule. Unlike isolated terrorist attacks occurring in a country at peace, the barracks bombing was a distinctly military operation carried out in a country riven by rival armies and with only a nominally functional government.

It was directed at forces maintaining only a reluctant and peripheral commitment to the hostilities, and did not threaten that country's own political institutions. In sum, the barracks attack was only tangentially terroristic. Therefore, the U.S. departure from Lebanon cannot serve as a counterexample to the thesis that terrorism—as distinct from civil war, revolution, etc.—almost never succeeds in advancing the political aims it ostensibly serves. See Richard Falk, *Revolutionaries and Functionaries: The Dual Face of Terrorism* (New York: Dutton, 1988), pp. 34–5.

6. See, for example, Martha Crenshaw, "The Psychology of Political Terrorism," in *Psychology: Contemporary Problems and Issues*, ed. Margaret G. Hermann (San Francisco: Jossey-Bass, 1986), pp. 379–413.

7. C. A. J. Coady, "The Morality of Terrorism," *Philosophy* 60 (1985): 55.

8. Carl Wellman, "On Terrorism Itself," *Journal of Value Inquiry* 13 (1979): 250.

9. Indeed, Wellman writes, "I must confess that I often engage in nonviolent terrorism myself, for I often threaten to flunk any student who hands in his paper after the due date" (ibid., p. 252). This implausible confession represents an extreme example of the theorist's inclination to render terrorist activity continuous with that performed by agents of less sanguinary mien.

10. As I write (March 1989), no one has come forth to claim responsibility for planting the bomb that destroyed Pan Am Flight 103 in the skies over Lockerbie, Scotland, some three months previously.

11. I have argued in a series of papers written with Geoffrey Brennan that ordinary voting behavior should be understood as predominantly expressive. See G. Brennan and L. Lomasky, "Institutional Aspects of 'Merit Goods' Analysis," *Finanzarchiv* 41 (1983): 183–206; "Inefficient Unanimity," *Journal of Applied Philosophy* 1 (1984): 151–63; "The Impartial Spectator Goes to Washington: Toward a Smithian Theory of Electoral Behavior," *Economics and Philosophy* 1 (1985): 189–211; "The Logic of Electoral Preference: Response to Saraydar and Hudelson," *Economics and Philosophy* 3 (1987): 131–8; "Large Numbers, Small Costs: The Uneasy Foundations of Democratic Rule," in *Politics and Process: New Essays in Democratic Theory*, ed. G. Brennan and L. Lomasky (New York: Cambridge University Press, 1989), pp. 42–59.

12. For example, the hijacking of the *Achille Lauro* (1985).

13. For a characteristic utilitarian appraisal see R. M. Hare, "On Terrorism," *Journal of Value Inquiry* 13 (1979): 241–49.

14. Strict utilitarians may be unmoved, maintaining that the propriety of any action is a function of the value of its consequences, irrespective of whether that action is performed with the intention of bringing about those consequences. From this perspective, an inquiry into the motivational structure of terrorist (or other) activity is strictly irrelevant to its normative appraisal. Terrorists, martyrs, baseball fans, Wall Street arbitragers—the actions of each are to be evaluated via the same consequentialist standard. It would take us too far afield to place this monolithic conception of moral evaluation under scrutiny. I merely note in passing that the frequency of predominantly expressive performances across many ordinary—as well as extraordinary—practices in which we engage constitutes one reason among many to be suspicious of the credentials of utilitarianism as an all-purpose moral decision theory.

15. In the sense intended here, martyrdom is not understood as an exclusively religious calling. Indeed, some martyrs may also be terrorists, as was Bobby Sands, who starved himself during May of 1981 as an act of allegiance to the cause of the Provisional Irish Republican Army.

16. An admirable statement of this viewpoint is Stanley Benn, "The Problematic Rationality of Political Participation," in *Political Participation*, ed. Stanley Benn et al. (Canberra: Australian National University, 1978), pp. 1–22.

17. I concede that indirect strategies such as that commended by Pascal to would-be wagerers may occasionally succeed. Note, however, that they do so only insofar as they are able to transform straightforwardly outcome-oriented activity into something else. Much illuminating discussion of this theme is found in Derek Parfit, *Reasons and Persons* (Oxford: Oxford University Press, 1984), especially in chap. 1, "Theories That Are Directly Self-defeating," pp. 3–51.

18. Paul Johnson, "The Cancer of Terrorism," in *Terrorism: How the West Can Win*, ed. Benjamin Netanyahu (New York: Farrar, Straus, and Giroux, 1986), p. 31.

19. Thomas Hobbes, *Leviathan*, ed. Michael Oakeshott (New York. Macmillan, 1962), p. 103.

20. I do not maintain that there invariably exists a sharp line separating terrorists from guerrilla combatants and other genuinely political actors. The Palestine Liberation Organization, unlike, for example, the Japanese Red Army, is a group that can be thought of as straddling the fence. Although it has control of no territory within the land it claims and avoids engagement with Israeli military forces, it aspires with some realistic prospect of success to statehood and possesses a genuine political program that it endeavors to advance. The PLO has (recently) established a government-in-exile and, significantly, enjoys the aboveboard sanction of existing governments. Thus it is not mistaken to regard the PLO and, especially, some of its constituent elements as a terrorist force, *nor* is it mistaken to think of the PLO as engaged in the pursuit of genuinely political ends.

21. Nuclear warfare is especially horrifying because of the amount of destructive force it unleashes but also because it largely obliterates all distinctions between soldier and civilian. To a lesser extent, the same thing is true of chemical warfare.

22. Armies traditionally have been exclusively male organizations. More recently, under the twin spurs of changes in the technology of warfare and feminist criticism, women have been afforded entry into military careers. In the United States and several other Western countries, women may serve in armies but are neither liable for conscription nor allowed to assume combat roles. Feminists criticize these exclusions, especially the latter, holding them to be arbitrary and perpetuative of sexual stereotypes. One may concede that there is some force to this critique while nonetheless maintaining that even a thoroughly arbitrary exclusion from combat status has compensating advantages: better that some classes of the citizenry be held immune from bloodletting than that everyone be rendered vulnerable.

23. Abu Abbas, director of the *Achille Lauro* hijacking, during a November 1988 conclave of the PLO jocularly observed of Klinghoffer, "Maybe he was trying to swim for it." Evidently, the expressive potential of terrorism extends to the wry. See *New Republic* 199 (December 5, 1988): 10.

24. According to Walter Laqueur, "The name 'Symbionese' was defined as 'body of harmony of dissimilar bodies and organisms living in deep and loving harmony and partnership in the best interest of within [sic] the body.' Its emblem was a seven-headed cobra, a 170,000-year-old sign signifying God and life" (*The Age of Terrorism*, rev. and expanded ed. [Boston: Little, Brown, 1987], pp. 244–5).

25. Martin Oppenheimer, "Defining Terrorism," reprinted in *Terrorism: Opposing Viewpoints*, ed. Bonnie Szumski (St. Paul: Greenhaven Press, 1986), pp. 87–8.

26. I here use the term "liberalism" not in its ancient and honorable sense but rather in that which George Bush intended when he hurled it at his 1988 presidential campaign opponent, Michael Dukakis, and which the latter so nimbly sought to evade.

27. I say "official standing" because the list of approved causes is highly selective and, so far as any objective measure of disadvantage might indicate, quite capricious. Palestinians and, to a lesser extent, Northern Irish Catholics receive considerable sympathy and support while, for example, Tibetan and, until recently, Kurdish populations targeted for genocide have been largely ignored in Western media. Lebanese Maronites, though verifiably a beleaguered minority, are almost always reckoned on the side of the oppressors. As in baseball, one can't tell the players without a scorecard.

28. Laqueur, *The Age of Terrorism*, pp. 124–5.

29. Consider the testimony offered by the pilot of the unfortunate TWA flight 847: "I breathed. . . . a silent prayer of thanks that the hijackers were so family oriented. They cared deeply about their wives and children, so they understood that it was difficult for me to be separated from my family. . . . If there was one thing the hijackers like to talk about, besides Khomeini, it was their families. One day one man was positively giddy because he had earned a few days off and was going to be able to spend some time with his wife and two children. . . . Those were the times when I felt most strongly that, in spite of the situation we found ourselves in, we were all brothers in the family of man" (John Testrake, *Triumph over Terror on Flight 847* [Old Tappan N.J.: Fleming Revell, 1987], p. 149).

QUESTIONS

1. What is for Lomasky "the political significance of terrorism" and why is it relevant to our appraisal of the phenomenon?

2. Why is the expressive nature of terrorism significant?

31. The Evolution of the Modern Terrorist State: Area Bombing and Nuclear Deterrence

DOUGLAS LACKEY

*D*ouglas Lackey (1945–) is professor of philosophy at Baruch College, City University of New York. He is the author of *Moral Principles and Nuclear Weapons* (1984) and *The Ethics of War and Peace* (1989) and the editor of *Ethics and Strategic Defense* (1990).

The topic of area bombing, with conventional or nuclear weapons, was taken up in the previous section. Here these topics are looked at again as kinds of terrorism. Lackey argues that the bombings of German and Japanese cities in World War II were terrorism—they

Douglas Lackey, "The Evolution of the Modern Terrorist State: Area Bombing and Nuclear Deterrence," in *Terrorism: The Philosophical Issues*, ed. Igor Primoratz, reproduced by permission of Palgrave Macmillan.

used to be referred to as "terror bombings." And he argues that historical continuity exists between these practices and later nuclear strategy: "All these bombings and plans for bombings say that in certain circumstances it is acceptable to rain devastation down on a city." While Lackey's article is primarily historical, it is relevant to the question of how we should understand some uses of (massive) force and to the ethical questions raised thereby. The phenomena he examines are also relevant to the question of the characterization of terrorism. Some influential definitions make terrorism an act of nonstate agents, thus denying that there can be state terrorism. Lackey does not hesitate to describe area and nuclear bombings as terrorist.

Britain and the Area Bombing Campaigns

In the winter and spring of 1942, Allied fortunes in the war were at a low ebb. Germany had conquered most of Europe; Italy held large areas of Africa; Japan held sway over much of China, Southeast Asia, and the South Pacific. The battles of Midway, Stalingrad, el-Alamein were yet to come.

In the skies over England, British Spitfires had achieved some success against German fighters and bombers. But defense of the homeland is not offense, and all offensive measures against German forces had failed. British bombing attacks against German military facilities, in particular, had been costly and unsuccessful. The German submarine yards and other military targets selected by British bombers were hard to hit, difficult to damage, and easy to repair. British bombers were poorly armed and easily brought down by German fighters.[1] The Red Army was bearing the brunt of the fighting, and Stalin was calling for a second front in Europe. But Churchill had no interest in a second Gallipoli. Some less costly offense had to be found.

In February 1942, Churchill decided on the new offensive strategy: British bombers would raid at night, safe from fighters under cover of darkness.[2] Since little can be seen at night, British planes would bomb designated "areas," not specific military targets. In these designated areas, civilians resided. If the areas were objects of attack, then the civilians were objects of attack. The new British strategy was a strategy of terror, and cause terror it did. Giulio Douhet in 1921 had advocated "terror from the air" as an alternative to the war of attrition in the trenches.[3] The new strategy made Douhet's terror a

reality. By the war's end, 595,000 German civilians had been killed by Allied bombings, victims of Churchill and the new head of Bomber Command, Arthur Harris.[4]

The accusation that British area bombing was terrorist bombing, in violation of the international laws of war, was repeatedly made on the German radio by Josef Goebbels. The British responded that area bombing was a legitimate military operation, necessary to defeat the enemy in a just war.[5] The goal, the British said, was not to kill civilians, but to defeat Germany. The fact that Goebbels called British bombing "terror" bombing has been one of the reasons historians have been reluctant to apply the label. If Goebbels said it, it must be wrong. But consider:

(a) No document or memorandum can be found that indicates that the British, in their targeting choices, made any effort to minimize civilian casualties. In high-level memoranda, for example, circulating before the bombing of Dresden, various German *cities* are named as targets.[6] (One *sotto voce* quip among Bomber Command pilots after targeting briefings was "Target Point: Cathedral.")[7] Size and accessibility of cities seem to have been controlling factors in target selection, not the presence or absence of military facilities on the ground.

(b) When the American Eighth Air force arrived in England in 1943, a debate broke out between the Americans, who favored daylight precision bombing,[8] and the British, who insisted on the superiority of nighttime raids. That is, in 1943 the British explicitly rejected taking military facilities as targets. Similarly, in 1945, Harris argued ferociously *against* shifting the bombing campaign from German cities to quasi-military targets like oil refineries.[9]

(c) On those few occasions when the RAF did aim at a specific target rather than at areas, they chose non-military targets over military targets. On May 17–18, 1943, for example, the British bombed German dams on the Möhne, Eder, and Sorpe, even though such dams could not be considered military facilities.[10]

(d) On the night of July 24–25, 1943, British bombing, which included the use of incendiary bombs, set off an unprecedented firestorm in Hamburg, destroying the city center and taking tens of thousands of civilian lives. Fire does not discriminate between military and civilian targets. The British continued to use incendiary weapons against German cities, perhaps in the hope of igniting similar firestorms. They showed no interest is discontinuing the use of incendiary bombs even after a study of what had happened to Hamburg.[11]

(e) In the closing months of the war, depleted *Luftwaffe* fighter forces were pulled back to defend Berlin. Despite the fact that it was no longer necessary for British planes (in most cases) to fly under cover of darkness, they continued to do so, bombing the largely undefended city of Dresden during the night of February 13–14, 1945, killing at least 70,000 people.[12]

Points (a)–(e) are part of the evidence that the British knowingly targeted German civilians in their bombing campaigns in World War II, and that the campaign is properly described as terrorism. We can reach this judgement without complicated analyses of British intentions. The bombings were as indiscriminate as the fires they caused. The common soldier is not a terrorist, because the majority of his victims are soldiers and a minority of his victims are civilians. In the British bombing campaign, the majority of those killed were civilians, and a small minority of those killed were German soldiers.

Consider the following thought experiment. Suppose that nation A is engaged in a just war against nation B. In location B1 are 999 B soldiers and 1 B civilian. In location B2 are 999 B civilians and 1 B soldier. A has the capacity to obliterate B1 or B2 with bombs. If A bombs B1 *or* B2, A is "killing civilians." If A bombs B1 *or* B2, A is "killing enemy soldiers." But bombing B1 is a legitimate act of war, and bombing B2 is a terrorist act. The distinction is not found in A's intention or goals, or in the fact that civilians are killed or the fact that soldiers are killed, or in finely tuned talk about regretted side-effects. The difference is found in the ratio of military to non-military damage. I will apply this Ratio of Damage Test in what follows.

Though British bombing was terror bombing, history has not labeled Churchill a terrorist. It is interesting to consider why the historians are wrong.

To begin, heads of state are given special status by historians, and Churchill in approving area bombing was acting as head of state. But if Churchill is exempt from moral judgement as a head of state, then all heads of state are exempt from moral judgement, and there is no moral case against Hitler.

Second, the decision to begin area bombing took place in the middle of a war, while the more easily labeled terror events, like the September 11 attacks, take place in peacetime. People get psychologically brutalized by war, develop hatred of "the enemy," introduce the morally irrelevant observation that "the Germans did it first," and deploy the dismissive response that "bad things happen in war." But even the "bad things happen" response implies that killing civilians in this ratio is a bad thing, and historians in the comfort of their studies should not share the prejudices of the psychologically brutalized.

Third, the area bombings were viewed as acts against "Nazi Germany" and if the Nazis were utterly bad, it follows, in the minds of many, that anything done against "Nazi Germany," even terrorism, was utterly good. But those who insist that terrorism against Nazi Germany is a morally good thing are admitting the main point, that the bombing campaign was terrorism.

The United States and the Bombing Campaign against Japan

The Eighth Air Force arrived in England determined to do the morally right thing. American B-17s had more guns than British Lancasters, and American bombardiers had the Norden bombsight that made precision bombing possible—at least on sunny days. The Americans paid a high price for their principles. In one raid on the Schweinfurt ball-bearing factories in 1943, 10 per cent of the US bombers were shot down, and in attacks on the Ploesti synthetic oil refineries in 1943 and 1944, US forces suffered even greater losses.

Indeed, the loss rates were so high in 1943 and 1944 that it was imperative to look for alternatives. The model of area bombing, rejected with scorn by the Americans in 1943, was embraced in 1945. The Americans still bombed during the day, but the targets had become cities; the RAF bombed Dresden at night, the Americans bombed Dresden the next day, churning up rubble with high explosives.

The switch from precision bombing to area bombings in Europe had come about by slow steps. In the Pacific campaign, the change was abrupt.[13] The campaign again the Japanese mainland began in October 1944 when the XXI Bomber Command under Haywood Hansell launched B-29 bombing raids from Saipan. The raids of 1944 were precision raids against such targets as Japanese aircraft engine factories, and achieved modest success. But in 1945, when US ground forces were suffering heavy losses taking island after island, Hap Arnold, commander of the Twentieth Air Force in the Pacific Theater, recommended that the XXI Bomber Command consider taking the RAF as their model and commencing incendiary attacks on Japanese cities. When Hansell protested the requested targeting changes (echoing the 1943 American protests against British policy), he was replaced by Curtis LeMay, a man with no scruples about city attacks. The fact that a change of command was necessary in order to initiate city bombing against Japan shows that the change of policy was a deliberate choice, not a matter of target creep.

The devastation wrought by the RAF on Dresden was matched by the devastation rained on Tokyo on March 9–10, 1945, when American incendiary bombs ignited a firestorm killing at least 80,000 people and destroying 250,000 buildings.[14] Other incendiary raids followed, culminating in the attacks on Hiroshima and Nagasaki on August 6 and 9, 1945.

It has been remarked, in response to widespread moral condemnation of the Hiroshima attack, that "the raid on Tokyo killed even more people." Such remarks ignore the possibility that *both* attacks were immoral. But I will not, in this essay, develop arguments about the morality of these attacks, *all things considered*. My concern here is simply to assess whether such raids on cities were terrorist attacks.

In his radio address to the nation following the Hiroshima bombing, President Truman spoke of "destroying Japan's power to make war."[15] This remark depicts attacks on cities as attacks on the Japanese power to wage war. But if the "power to make war" means the power to attack another nation, Japan's power was destroyed by US fighting forces before these city attacks began. And if the "power to make war" means the power to engage in armed resistance, then that power persisted irrespective of the raids on Japanese cities. Suppose counter-factually that every major Japanese city had been obliterated by fire bombing as early as February 1945. Despite this, the entrenched Japanese forces on Iwo Jima and Okinawa could have, and would have, presented the same degree of furious resistance that they in fact mounted in February and April 1945. Even on the mainland, the Japanese capacity for armed resistance survived the attacks: a kamikaze squadron planned to attack the USS *Missouri* as it sailed into Tokyo harbor for the surrender ceremony on August 14. The squadron was disarmed, not by American bombing, but by a personal appeal from the brother of the Emperor.

By the Ratio of Damage standard the fire raids of 1945 were terrorist attacks. The vast majority of people killed were civilians; the vast majority of structures destroyed were non-military structures. The intent of the raids was to induce surrender by inflicting death and pain on the civilian population. About 500,000 Japanese civilians died in these raids. In nine months American bombing had killed almost as many civilians as British bombing had killed in three and a half years. If American criticisms of British bombing policy in 1943 were valid, then those criticisms apply to American attacks on Japan in 1945.

American Plans for Nuclear War

Terror bombing was employed by the United States during the Korean War, the Vietnam War, the Gulf War, and the action against Serbia in 1999. Rather than explore these later cases I wish to examine a prong of the issue stemming from the use of nuclear weapons. In the years following Hiroshima, there was considerable interest in the integration of small-size nuclear weapons into the equipment of American fighting forces. By the Ratio of Damage argument, such small nuclear weapons could be used in non-terrorist ways. But despite the deployment, or at least the storage, of thousands of tactical nuclear weapons fit for use in battle, the main post-Hiroshima use of nuclear weapons was the use of strategic (i.e. very large) nuclear weapons for the purposes of "deterrence." The root idea of nuclear deterrence was simple: leader L from nation A is led to believe, if he does bad act B, that American bombers or missiles will drop nuclear weapons on A. Fearing this, L does not do B. Note that this is not a potential use of nuclear weapons: this is an actual use, even if the weapons do not explode.

A nuclear attack is a serious business, and American planning restricted thinking about nuclear deterrence to serious bad acts. I believe that developed scenarios for counter-attacks using strategic nuclear weapons existed for (a) a Soviet attack on Western Europe, (b) a Chinese invasion of Taiwan, (c) a North Korean or Chinese attack on South Korea, and (d) an attack by either the Soviet Union or China against the territory of the United States. Of these, I will dismiss as implausible (a) to (c). The United States considered and failed to use nuclear weapons against China in response to Chinese intervention in the Korean War, an intervention that killed thousands of US troops. The fear was that if the United States began using nuclear weapons against a foreign power, then nuclear allies of that foreign power might respond by using nuclear weapons against the United States. As Henry Kissinger remarked, nations are not going to commit suicide in defense of somebody else.

The prime deterrence scheme was (d). Even here the logic was vague. Deterrence is always conditional: *if* B happens, a nuclear attack will follow against A. There were problems with the details of B, and the details of the response against A. Suppose that Soviet land forces invaded Alaska, for example. Would the United States respond with a nuclear attack on Russia? That might produce a nuclear counter-attack on New York, which had thus far been spared. But one thing seemed clear and credible: if there were a Soviet nuclear attack on the American mainland, the response would be an American nuclear attack on the Soviet Union.

In the 1950s the design of the US nuclear response to a Soviet attack on the United States was largely left to the Strategic Air Command, organized in 1946 and commanded by General LeMay from 1947 to 1958.[16] The attacks planned by SAC on Russia in the 1940s and 1950s were city-busting attacks along the lines of Hiroshima and Nagasaki. One must suppose that the thought patterns of the general who had designed city attacks on Japan carried over to the design of the Apocalypse.

In the early 1960s, when deterrence options expanded with the introduction of submarine launched missiles, the Defense Department decided to integrate US nuclear forces into a single coordinated multiservice response. The first such Single Integrated Operational Plan, or SIOP, was introduced for 1962. In the event of a bad act B, considered worthy of nuclear response, the 1962 SIOP called for massive nuclear retaliation against the Soviet Union *and China,* resulting in the deaths of at least 400 million people.

Evaluating the character of 1962 SIOP is like wrestling with the devil. Surely the attacks envisioned in the SIOP were terrorist attacks, by the Ratio of Damage argument. But what we want to evaluate is the act of setting up the SIOP, not the act of carrying it out. In contemporary moral theory, one evaluates an action by reference to intentions, consequences, and states of character expressed by the action. One could argue that the laudable intention behind the SIOP was the prevention of nuclear attack on the United States; that the laudable consequence of the SIOP was that there was no such attack, even under the pressure of the Cuban Missile Crisis, and that the laudable state of character expressed by the SIOP was a resolute and courageous commitment to do whatever was necessary to defend the United States.

I have considered such arguments at length elsewhere.[17] The problem for this essay is whether nuclear deterrence under this SIOP and its successors indicates an American commitment to terrorism. We are *not* considering the nuclear attack itself, but the threat to launch a nuclear attack under certain conditions. But I believe that the character of a threat to do X, if one is not bluffing, is found in the character of X. The moral character of doing X rubs off on sincere threats to do it. So if it is terrorism to launch a nuclear attack, then it is terrorism to threaten to launch a nuclear attack, provided that threat is no bluff.

Was the American posture under the first SIOP a bluff? Surely the SIOP did not create an automated response, the clearest case of not bluffing. Human beings, the President or his successors, remained in critical positions in the loop. Presumably, if the President chose not to launch a nuclear counter-attack, even after a nuclear attack on the United States, under the SIOP a nuclear counter-attack would not be launched. (In such circumstances, there might be a pro-response coup, overthrowing the Constitution, but such treason was not part of the SIOP.) For the SIOP to be a bluff, the President would have to have formed a fixed intention, for the duration of his Presidency, not to launch a nuclear counter-attack. I have discovered no evidence, no memoirs written late in life, that either Eisenhower or Kennedy had a fixed and persisting intention *not* to launch a nuclear counter-attack, in the face of a Soviet attack on the United States. Absent such a fixed intention, the threatened counter-attack was no bluff.

The first SIOP was unsubtle and in many ways inefficient. When McNamara was appointed Secretary of Defense in 1961, he set about upgrading efficiency on all fronts, including the SIOP. Daniel Ellsberg was brought in from RAND to design a new SIOP, which became operational in 1963. The new SIOP differed profoundly from its predecessor.[18] The first SIOP called for the same single massive response to any enemy attack that met a defined threshold: "worthy of nuclear response." The new SIOP, under the watchword "flexible response," called for different responses to different provocations. If the Soviet Union attacked Alaska, there would be a response that left most of the Soviet Union undamaged and most of American nuclear forces in reserve. Should the Soviets respond with an attack on New York, the SIOP called for an even larger, but still less than total, counter-response. Any larger Soviet attack

would produce an even larger American response; every gap in the escalation ladder was to be plugged. The Soviets, great chess players, would realize that the end-game belonged to the Americans, and so the game itself blessedly would never start.

Was "flexible response" still terrorism? Some of the planned responses, those involving limited nuclear war at sea, for example, or those involving attacks on isolated radars in Siberia, would not be terrorist attacks according to the Ratio of Damage Argument. But all other attacks, the vast majority of those planned, would involve great numbers of civilian casualties. By the Ratio of Damage argument, these "flexible" responses would be terrorist attacks.

Furthermore, the new flexible SIOP still called for attacks on cities, as attacks on cities are an integral part of the logic of deterrence. If every gap in the escalation ladder has to be plugged, then the top steps will have to consist of very large attacks. The very logic of deterrence calls for this. If the opponent realizes that it can raise the ante until the United States drops out, the capacity to execute limited responses to smaller attacks will fail to deter. Furthermore, except for nuclear attacks at sea, every step in the escalation ladder should be classified as terrorist according to the Ratio of Damage argument.

The SIOP has been revised a number of times since 1963. Nevertheless, the succeeding SIOPs were still governed by the concepts of the 1963 SIOP: "flexible response," "plugging the gaps in escalation ladder," and so forth. It is sometimes remarked that the new SIOPs, with scenarios for limited nuclear war, were designed to spare civilian life, since the number of civilians killed under flexible response is less than the number of civilians killed under massive retaliation. But the argument for replacing massive retaliation with flexible response sprung from the rationality of deterrence, not from any principle of favoring military targets over civilian targets. I have it on good authority that the Judge Advocate General's Office, during the late 1990s, conducted a legal review of the current SIOP, assessing whether targets listed in the SIOP were compatible with international law, especially laws and conventions inspired by the Principle of Non-Combatant Immunity. This was the first time that such a review had ever been conducted, proof positive that earlier SIOPs were not designed with this thought in mind. Whether the current SIOP reflects the verdicts of JAG review is something for later historians to discover.

Conclusion

There is a continuous line of historical development from Churchill's decision to commence area bombing, to the bombings of Dresden, Tokyo, Hiroshima, and Nagasaki, to Curtis LeMay and SAC plans for nuclear air attacks on Russia, and finally to the American SIOPs for nuclear war. All these bombings and plans for bombings say that in certain circumstances it is acceptable to rain devastation down on a city. The older ideal that soldiers should fight soldiers and military equipment should fight military equipment is cast aside.

I believe that the British policy of area bombing inaugurated a new era in warfare: a kind of state terrorism, now routinely added to the repertoire of policy options of powerful nations. I do not agree with Walzer and others that area bombing is just a new version of the older methods of besieging cities.[19] When the Romans besieged Carthage, when the Crusaders besieged Jerusalem, there were soldiers outside of the city throwing things in and soldiers inside the city throwing things out. A siege was often like a battlefield with a wall in the middle. But when the British bombed Dresden, when the *Enola Gay* bombed Hiroshima, there was no wall, just the planes above and the city below. If a terrorist is one who prefers killing civilians to damage to soldiers, then most of the older sieges were not terrorism, but most modern "bombing campaigns" are.

With the world's largest air force and a developing habit of preferring the lives of its soldiers over the lives of non-American civilians, the US Government has become accustomed to raining devastation from the air.[20] I suspect that Americans from 1945 to 2001 approved US bombing campaigns because they themselves had never been targets and had no first hand knowledge of the human results. On September 11, 2001, they experienced, as I did from one kilometer's distance, what a terrorist attack from the air is like. The Americans were correct to judge that the terrorists who flew those planes on September 11 were avatars of evil. What they have not realized is the degree to which their own policies, since January 1945, are more of the same.

Notes

1. For these details see the official history, Sir Charles Webster and Noble Frankland, *The Strategic Air Offensive against Germany* (London: HMSO, 1961).

2. For Churchill's complicity (and his ability to cover his tracks) see Max Hastings, *Bomber Offensive* (London: Macmillan, 1968).

3. For an English translation of Douhet, see *Command of the Air* (New York: Coward McCann, 1942).

4. For the figure, confirmed by British sources, see Hans Rumpf, *The Bombing of Germany* (London: White Lion, 1963).

5. For these moral accusations and counter-accusations, see Anthony Verrier, *The Bomber Offensive* (London: Collins, 1968).

6. For the steps leading to Dresden see Alexander McKee, *Dresden 1945: The Devil's Tinderbox* (New York: Dutton, 1982).

7. For this and other nasty sides to the campaign, see F. J. P. Veale, *Advance to Barbarism* (London: Thomson and Smith, 1948).

8. See Thomas Coffey, *Decision over Schweinfurt: The U.S. 8th Air Force Battle for Daylight Bombing* (New York: David McKay, 1977).

9. See Arthur Harris, *Bomber Offensive* (London: Collins, 1947), for Harris's battle against Sinclair over oil refinery bombings.

10. Americans with a love of blowing up things can participate (virtually) in these "dam-busting" raids by purchasing the latest CD-Rom version simulation of these attacks. In the 1954 movie, *Dam Busters,* Michael Redgrave led the raid, with no visible moral qualms.

11. See Martin Middlebrook, *The Battle of Hamburg* (New York: Scribner's, 1981), for the firestorm and its sequels.

12. Ibid.

13. For this and the following account of the American raids on Japan, see the official history, *The Army Air Forces in World War II* (Chicago: University of Chicago Press, 1948–58). A good one-volume account is Michael Sherry, *The Rise of American Air Power* (New Haven: Yale University Press, 1987).

14. Martin Caidin, *A Torch to the Enemy: The Fire Raid on Tokyo* (Baltimore, MD: Ballantine Books, 1960).

15. Barton J. Bernstein and Allen J. Matusow (eds.), *The Truman Administration: A Documentary History* (New York: Harper & Row, 1966), pp. 40–1.

16. For this and the ensuing account of the evolution of American nuclear war fighting plans see David Alan Rosenberg's magisterial article, "The Origins of Overkill," *International Security* 7 (1983).

17. Douglas P. Lackey, *Moral Principles and Nuclear Weapons* (Totowa, NJ: Rowman and Allanheld, 1984).

18. For Ellsberg and RAND and SIOP-63, see Fred Kaplan, *The Wizards of Armageddon* (New York: Simon and Schuster, 1983).

19. Michael Walzer, *Just and Unjust Wars* (New York: Basic Books, 1977), chapter 10.

20. Bill Clinton, not remembered as a militarist, used air power against the Sudan, Afghanistan, and Serbia, in the last case destroying 30 per cent of Serbian industrial capacity in 1999. Photographs of the devastation have shocked audiences and substantially aided Milošević in his defense against war crimes charges at The Hague.

QUESTIONS

1. Were the World War II bombings of cities terrorist? What changes do we have to make in our understanding of terrorism if we wish to deny that they were?
2. Is there any reason why we should not label states in some circumstances as terrorist?

32. Terrorism, Innocence, and War

ROBERT K. FULLINWIDER

Robert K. Fullinwider (1942–) is senior research scholar at the Institute for Philosophy and Public Policy, School of Public Policy, University of Maryland. He has written extensively about a number of topics in practical ethics and public policy, including the ethics of war, terrorism, education, and the debate about reparations. He is the author of *The Reverse Discrimination Controversy* (1980) and coauthor, with J. Lichtenberg, of *Leveling the Playing Field: Justice, Politics, and College Admissions* (2004).

Written in the weeks after the 9/11 attacks, Fullinwider's essay raises a number of questions about terrorism, innocence, and war. Noting that some wish to link terrorism with attacks on the innocent, he notes that the conception of innocence usually invoked in discussions of war is not that of absence of guilt; rather, in war to be innocent is to be a noncombatant, someone who does not threaten. Osama bin Laden did not fail to consider the innocent; he claimed to be acting in defense of them.

From *Philosophy and Public Policy Quarterly*, Volume 21, Number 4 (Fall 2001). Reprinted with permission of the author.

Fullinwider also stresses the terrorists' willingness to act "as a law unto themselves." Theirs is a challenge to the rule of law and its importance to civil life. "The delusion that he and God act in concert is what makes Osama bin Laden's self-election as avenging angel a special threat to humanity."

The events of September 11, 2001 defy the power of words to describe, console, or even explain. Nevertheless, because the United States must respond in one way or another, and because people must give or withhold their support to any national course of action, words necessarily come into play, words to formulate goals and words to justify the means to achieve them. "Terrorism" is one of the words ubiquitous in the aftermath of September 11, "war" another.

Carlin Romano, a philosopher and critic, writes in the *Chronicle of Higher Education* that a third word, "innocence," should get more attention than it has received. The "clarification and defense of innocence" by intellectuals, social commentators, and public officials, Romano believes, could add an important element to the fight against terrorism.

Innocence

"Innocence" links "war" and "terrorism." Terrorists are counted as murderers because they kill the innocent. Similarly, in war, military forces are prohibited by common custom and international law from targeting civilians. This prohibition "assumes innocence at its core," notes Romano. Perhaps so, but not "innocence" in the sense that underwrites Romano's initial condemnation of terrorists.

Romano insists that terrorism cannot be justified morally, no matter what its political aims, because terrorists select their victims haphazardly, without concern for innocence or guilt. Here, he construes "innocence" under a model of crime and punishment. On that model, punishment should fall on the guilty, not the innocent, on the wrongdoer, not the mere bystander. Just punishment, accordingly, must allow for some sort of antecedent "due process," in which individuals are found guilty according to evidence and only then subjected to penalties in proper proportion to their wrongs. Since the terrorist

kills "haphazardly," he doesn't fulfill this minimal demand of just punishment.

In war, however, the notion of "innocence" has nothing to do with lack of blameworthiness. Rather, it divides individuals into two classes: those who may be directly targeted by military force and those who may not. The former includes uniformed armed forces (combatants), the latter ordinary civilians (noncombatants). This division derives not from the imperatives of crime and punishment but from the imperatives of self-defense. In resisting aggression, a state may direct lethal force against the agency endangering it, and that agency is the military force of the aggressor.

From the point of view of moral-wrongdoing and just punishment, many of the aggressor's military personnel may be innocent; they may be reluctant conscripts with no sympathy for their nation's actions. Likewise, among ordinary civilians, many may actively support and favor their country's criminal aggression. They are not innocent. But *from the point of view of self-defense,* the moral quality of the conscript's reluctance and the civilian's enthusiasm is not relevant. What matters is that the former is a combatant, the latter not.

Consequently, war must be prosecuted by means that discriminate between the two classes. Specifying membership in the two classes is, of course, a difficult and somewhat arbitrary affair. Combatants are first of all those in a warring country's military service. They wear uniforms, bear arms, and are trained to be on guard. Because they wield the means of violence and destruction directed at a defending nation, such soldiers are fair targets of lethal response by that nation, even when they are in areas to the rear of active fighting and even when they are sleeping. However, not all enemy soldiers may be attacked. Those rendered *hors de combat* through injury, capture, or some other means possess the same immunities from being killed as civilian noncombatants.

Conversely, individuals not in uniform but actively participating in the war effort, such as civilian leaders and managers directing overall military policy, are fair targets of attack. They count as combatants. The operative language in the Geneva Convention of 1949 and in the U.N. Resolution on Human Rights of 1968—two legal protocols governing the prosecution of war—confers immunity on those "not taking part in hostilities." Obviously, there is plenty of room to construe this phrase in very different ways. Even so, some people—the very old and the very young, for example—clearly qualify for noncombatant immunity on any construal.

While the two points of view—of crime and punishment, on the one hand, and self-defense, on the other—understand "innocence" in different ways, either of them seems clearly to indict the perpetrators of the September 11 attacks. First, those who used hijacked passenger planes as bombs targeted civilians as such, at least in their attack on the World Trade Center. If the attackers considered themselves at war, they violated one of war's laws. Second, the attackers provided no advance notice of their plan to exact punishment from the occupants of the World Trade Center and no forum for the occupants to answer any accusations or charges. If the attackers thought of themselves as avenging angels, they violated due process.

Terrorism

That Osama bin Laden and his network stepped across a clear line marking right from wrong seems signaled by the universal condemnation of the events of September 11. Even the League of Arab States expressed its "revulsion, horror, and shock over the terrorist attacks" against America. Nevertheless, matters may not be as simple as the foregoing account suggests.

First of all, the laws of war and the distinctions they draw are creatures of *states* and *state interests*. Individuals and groups who have no states to represent their grievances, or who stand at odds to the arrangements of power imposed by the prevailing state system, are barred from using violence to vindicate their just demands (as they may see them). Indeed, whatever their cause, they are

condemned as criminals if they resort to violence. The U.N. International Convention for the Suppression of Terrorist Bombings (1997), for example, makes it a crime to explode a lethal device "in a public place" or even to attack a government facility such as an embassy. These acts, it goes on to say, constitute terrorism and "are under no circumstances justifiable by considerations of a political, philosophical, ideological, racial, ethnic, [or] religious . . . nature." No cause however good warrants violent response if the actor is an individual or group, not a state.

Since the United States is a country founded on violent rebellion against lawful authority, we can hardly endorse a blanket disavowal of the right by others violently to rebel against their own oppressors. Indeed, Thomas Jefferson offered a small paean to political violence in letters he sent to Abigail Adams, James Madison, and William Smith in 1787. "I hold that a little rebellion now and then is a good thing," Jefferson wrote, "& as necessary in the political world as storms in the physical. . . . What signify a few lives lost in a century or two? The tree of liberty must be refreshed from time to time with the blood of patriots & tyrants. It is its natural manure." The occasion of Jefferson's letters was the just-suppressed Shay's Rebellion, the violent resistance by desperate farmers in western Massachusetts against the due process of law that, in a time of economic distress, was grinding them into dust. Only a handful of lives were lost in the short affair, but it lent a degree of urgency to delegates from various states scurrying off to Philadelphia to replace the Articles of Confederation.

Nor is Jefferson alone in looking favorably at a "little rebellion" by people who resort to violence in the name of a great cause. John Brown remains for many Americans a martyr in the fight against slavery, though his actions would count as terrorism under contemporary definitions and international conventions. While leading a gang of anti-slavery guerilla fighters in eastern Kansas in 1855, Brown took revenge for an assault by slavers on the town of Lawrence by dragging five men out of the small pro-slavery settlement of Pottawatomie Creek one night and hacking them to death.

In 1859, in his ill-fated attempt to seize the United States armory at Harper's Ferry, and precipitate (he fancied) a vast slave rebellion, Brown seized sixty hostages from the neighboring precincts.

Killing "innocents"—Brown's victims at Pottawatomie Creek were not accorded any due process, nor were they combatants in uniform—and taking civilian hostages: these are the very deeds deplored and condemned by U.N. resolutions and conventions. They make Brown a quintessential terrorist. Yet many people refuse to view Brown this way because they don't accept the uncompromising U.N. position that "irregular" violence—violence initiated by individuals and groups—is "under no circumstances justifiable by considerations of a political, philosophical, ideological, racial, ethnic, [or] religious . . . nature." They believe that in some circumstances a cause *may be* sufficiently weighty to justify shedding blood, even "innocent" blood.

So, too, believes the League of Arab States. Though it condemned the September 11 attack as "terrorism," it refuses to accept an unqualified version of the U.N.'s view that, for example, exploding a lethal device "in a public place" counts always as terrorism. In its 1998 Convention for the Suppression of Terrorism, the League starts with a definition pretty much in line with the United Nation's. Terrorism is

> [a]ny act of violence, whatever its motives or purposes, that occurs in the advancement of an individual or collective criminal agenda and seeking to sow panic among people, causing fear by harming them, or placing their lives, liberty or security in danger. . . .

A "terrorist offense" is any act in furtherance of a terrorist objective.

So far, so good (though we may wonder about the force of the modifier "criminal" in reference to the terrorist's "agenda"). But the Convention then adds:

> All cases of struggle by whatever means, including armed struggle, against foreign occupation and aggression for liberation and self-determination, in accordance with the principles of international law, *shall not be regarded as an offense.*

What does this added qualification mean? Read one way (putting emphasis on the clause "in accordance with the principles of international law"), it can be taken as proscribing the same deeds outlawed by U.N. conventions. Read another way (taking account of the fact that the definition of "terrorism" is prefaced by an initial affirmation of "the right of peoples to combat foreign occupation and aggression by whatever means, in order to liberate their territories and secure their right to self determination"), it can be taken as licensing some irregular violence (that directed against foreign "occupation" and promoting Arab "self-determination") while precluding other violence (that on behalf of a "criminal agenda"). Moreover, the matter is muddied further by the fact that the U.N. itself recognizes a fundamental right to self-determination, a right to resist "colonial, foreign and alien domination." Through Osama bin Laden's eyes, the attack of September 11 fell upon an alien dominator of Arabia and bespoke a campaign that would not end "before all infidel armies leave the land of Muhammed." What could the right to self-determination mean if it tied one's hands against the very source of "humiliation and degradation" imposed upon the Islamic world from the outside for eighty years?

Carlin Romano writes that it probably never occurred to bin Laden "how awful it is to kill innocent people." But bin Laden's own self-justification indicates the contrary. "Millions of innocent children are being killed as I speak," he declared, children who are dying in Iraq as a putative consequence of the economic embargo imposed on that state by an American-led coalition. Osama bin Laden purported to act on behalf of innocence. Why should he not calculate, as Jefferson implied, that shedding the blood of a few now may save the lives and liberty of many others in the long run?

Moreover, why should he feel restrained by the conventional views of innocence? Isn't it arbitrary to immunize from attack people who may be causally implicated in the oppression one is resisting? By convention, the civilians of an aggressor nation who buy their country's war bonds are noncombatants and immune from attack. But without those war bonds, the aggressor nation would not be able to buy the guns and planes and bombs that enable it to prosecute its aggression. Why should those citizens be counted as "innocent" or made immune?

Terrorists, writes Romano, must believe in some "philosophy of innocence, however pinched." They assume the guilt of their victims, but on "transparently flimsy grounds." Obviously, their grounds won't line up with the considerations operative in the conventions of international law, but those conventions weren't endorsed by the terrorists in the first place and don't take their perspectives to heart.

Consider the infamous massacre of Israeli athletes at the 1972 Munich Olympics by Black September, a Palestinian terrorist organization. Weren't those athletes uncontrovertibly innocent? From the point of view of Black September, they were not. They were the knowing and willing representatives of Israel to an international affair where their presence would lend further international credibility and legitimacy to their state. From the point of view of their attackers, the athletes were active and informed accessories to a continuing "crime"—the support of the "criminal" state of Israel. These are not flimsy grounds for charges of "guilt," although they are grounds thoroughly contestable and clearly lying outside the scope of considerations allowed by international law.

The Rule of Law

It is too easy to dismiss the terrorist as evil incarnate, as a demon beyond the human pale. "The terrorist," claims one writer, "represents a new breed of man which takes humanity back to prehistoric times, to the times when morality was not yet born." But this characterization seems wrong. If anything, terrorists are throwbacks to a "prehistoric time" when morality was not yet under control. What is scary about terrorists is that they appeal to morality without appealing to law. They act as a law unto themselves. Let me explain.

Political theorists tell a story about the "State of Nature" to explain and defend government. The State of Nature proves to be intolerable for its inhabitants, whose lives are "solitary, poore, nasty, brutish, and short" (according to Thomas Hobbes). Contrary to common impressions, however, the problem in the State of Nature is not that people are so immoral, so lacking in any sense of justice or decency, that they prey wantonly upon one another. The problem is that people are *so moral,* so determined to vindicate rights or uphold honor at any cost that they become a menace to each other.

The distinctive feature of the State of Nature, as John Locke points out, is not the absence of morality but the absence of *law.* It is a circumstance in which the "law of nature"—the moral law—must be enforced by each individual. Each is responsible for vindicating her own rights and the rights of others. All prosecution of crime and injustice in the State of Nature is free-lance. Such a situation is the spawning ground of the never-ending chain of retaliation and counter-retaliation of the blood feud. "For every one in that state being both Judge and Executioner of the Law of Nature, Men being partial to themselves, Passion and Revenge is very apt to carry them too far, and with too much heat, in their own Cases; as well as negligence, and unconcernedness, to make them too remiss, in other Men's."

Even if persons were not biased in their own favor, the problems of enforcing justice in the State of Nature would remain deadly. How would crime be defined? How would evidence for its commission be gathered and validated? Who would be punished, and in what manner? What would constitute legitimate self-defense? Who would calculate the rectification due from unjust aggression? Nothing in the State of Nature ensures any common understanding about these questions. The contrary is the case. Private understanding pitted against private understanding produces an escalation of response and counter-response that lets violence erupt and feed on itself.

The solution, of course, is, as Locke proposed, "an establish'd, settled, known Law, received and allowed by common consent to be the Standard of Right and Wrong, and the common measure to decide all Controversies," and "a known and indifferent Judge, with Authority to determine all differences according to the established Law." This solution prevails, more or less, in the domestic case. In most states, a common law tolerably resolves disputes, even if that law is not always the product of common consent. The law does not always work well enough, however, and rebellious violence against its inflexibilities and oppressions as often elicits our sympathy as it invokes our fear and antipathy. "Irregular justice"—or vigilantism—can redirect the law toward a more just course. Moreover, sometimes the existing regime of law is so oppressive that outright revolution seems in order. At the end of the eighteenth century, a great many Americans, newly born of their own "revolution," sympathized with the revolution in France that destroyed a decadent monarchy and substituted republicanism; a great many others recoiled in horror at the revolution's excesses as it tumbled into tyranny. In the years since, Americans have both supported and resisted revolutions abroad. Our ambivalence is rooted in twin impulses: to warm to the oppressed in their liberation struggles and to fear the disorder of Private Judgment substituting for law.

At the international level, the rule of law likewise rescues the community of states from intolerable anarchy, though unlike domestic law, international law is a patchwork of treaties, conventions, and understandings among independent actors, each jealous of its sovereignty. Few tribunals exist where "a known and indifferent Judge" possesses full "Authority to determine all differences" among nations; nor is there a common agent of coercion to enforce the judge's rulings on recalcitrant parties. Still, laws and conventions bring some order to international affairs, including the laws of war and the conventions against terrorism referred to earlier. Admittedly, these laws and conventions stack the deck against non-state actors. And—as the posture of the League of Arab States indicates—some people and some states will want to support non-state actors in violent response to perceived wrongs and oppressions. But even behind such sympathizing and support lies the worrisome specter of Private Judgment. Osama bin Laden, in his isolated redoubts in the Afghan

mountains, elects himself as the vindicator of Islamic honor and rights. He answers to no one or no community but to his own sense of justice. Self-elected vigilantes on the international scene may be tolerated—or even supported—by states when their vigilantism remains a mere thorn in the sides of enemies; but when the vigilantes hold in their hands the power to destroy people by the scores and hundreds of thousands, the face of Private Judgment is hideous even to those who join in its chosen cause. When the League of Arab States proffered its condemnation of the September 11 attacks, it had not suddenly forgotten the experience of eighty years of "humiliation and degradation" noted by bin Laden, it had not suddenly abandoned the cause of Palestinian justice, it had not suddenly converted to non-violence. Rather, it had suddenly lost its taste for Private Judgment. Osama bin Laden is beholden to no one, not even to the Arab states themselves. Consequently, he is a peril to all.

Private Judgment is not only a menace when exercised by individuals but when exercised by states as well. Countries undermine the efficacy of international law by reserving to themselves Private Judgment about its application. For example, in 1928, Western powers agreed in the Kellogg-Briand Pact to outlaw war as a tool of national policy. They determined that armed aggression was henceforth a crime. But each of the Pact's signatories reserved to itself final judgment about when its acts were proper self-defense and when improper aggression against a neighbor. As a consequence, the Kellogg-Briand Pact inhibited war the way matches inhibit fire.

In the aftermath of World War II, when Nazi leaders were put on trial for war crimes, they interposed a potentially fatal objection: the Nuremberg tribunal before which they appeared had no standing to judge Germany's war policy since the Kellogg-Briand Pact reserved to each country final judgment about whether it was acting lawfully. In rebuttal, the United States joined Great Britain in arguing that although a state may be free in the first instance to decide whether it is acting in self-defense, its exercise of the right of self-defense is nevertheless ultimately subject to review by the international community. Whether this was an ingenious construction of the Kellogg-Briand Pact or an invention from whole cloth, the argument won the day and established an important principle of international law: that no state can take complete refuge in Private Judgment. Ultimately, states must face the bar of collective judgment and justify their violent conduct in terms acceptable to the common moral sense of mankind.

This new principle was an important step for international law, since a system of law in which each party can veto the application of the law to itself is no system of law at all. So long as each party remains the sole judge of its own case, the State of Nature remains in place.

Having struck a notable blow for the principle of law at Nuremberg, the United States has not always honored its own vital handiwork. For example, in 1985, when Nicaragua alleged in the World Court that we were guilty of aggression for supporting the Contras, we did not defend our support by arguing that it constituted collective self-defense. We argued instead an interpretation of the United Nations charter that made the question of whether we were acting in self-defense nonjusticiable. We argued that our actions could be reviewed only by the Security Council of the U.N., where, of course, we have a veto. In effect, the United States argued that only it could judge whether its actions were aggression or self-defense. Having so argued, our subsequent insistence that other, smaller states—states without a veto in the Security Council—must submit to the bar of collective judgment looks self-serving rather than principled. Private Judgment—whether manifested in the person of a terrorist like Osama bin Laden or in the agency of a rogue state like Iraq—increasingly reveals itself for the hazard it is. Our own interests as well as our principles demand that we put a stake through its heart. We must not claim it as our special prerogative.

Innocence Revisited

Suppose that the ideas of due process and non-combatant immunity referred to by Carlin Romano are nothing but conventions accepted within and among states. Still, they are precious ideas, hard-won in

their application. They require that legitimate institutions resort to violence in ways that discriminate between those adjudicated guilty and those not, between those taking part in hostilities and those not. These are the rules fallible humans have fashioned to keep us out of the State of Nature. They issue, in part, from our collective recognition that the partiality toward our own interests and the unconcern we feel for the interests of others—those two facets of human nature remarked on by Locke—invariably distort Private Judgment and make it unreliable.

But what if you were assured of reliable judgment? What if you were assured of infallibility? Then you would need no conventions of innocence to guide you. No conventional limitations withstand the conceit that God is on your side, since whatever God does must be right. If God orders you to war against, and to "save alive nothing that breatheth" among, an enemy; if He commands you utterly to destroy the Hittites and the Amorites, the Canaanites and the Perizzites, the Hivites and the Jebusites; then you destroy without compunction and without distinction.

When Christians, who from the Middle Ages on have developed a profoundly influential doctrine of just war that puts special emphasis on noncombatant immunity and on the innocence, particularly, of those too young, too old, and too ill to be "taking part in hostilities"—when Christians, I say, read Deuteronomy 20, they must feel a considerable indigestion. Still, the text says what it says, and if "God by revelation made the Israelites . . . the executioners of His supernatural sentence" then the "penalty was within God's right to assign, and within the Israelites' communicated right to enforce"—so reads a passage from the *Catholic Encyclopedia*. As "Sovereign Arbiter of life and death," God can take or give as he pleases, and it must be just. But we who are without God's eyes "cannot argue natural right" from these Biblical cases of wholesale slaughter, the *Encyclopedia* passage goes on to say. Indeed we cannot. We must hew to those distinctions and discriminations embedded in the conventions on war and terrorism and we must wholeheartedly strive to see them everywhere honored.

The delusion that he and God act in concert is what makes Osama bin Laden's self-election as avenging angel a special threat to humanity. Had he the power, he would not hesitate to kill all that breathes among his "enemy." He would not hesitate to destroy whole cities, entire populations. America was "hit by God," declares bin Laden in his taped message after the September 11 attacks. God has made America the enemy and bin Laden merely executes His will.

Two days after the September 11 horrors, an unnerved Jerry Falwell intemperately offered his own version of bin Laden's delirium. God, announced Falwell, had lifted the curtain of protection around America, angered by the ACLU, gays and lesbians, abortionists, pagans, secularists, and the Federal court system. "God will not be mocked," he declared. But Falwell quickly repudiated his remarks in the face of widespread criticism. He apologized for his words, pleading weariness for his thoughtlessness. "[My] September 13 comments were a complete misstatement of what I believe and what I've preached for nearly 50 years," Falwell said in an interview. "Namely, I do not believe that any mortal person knows when God is judging or not judging someone or a nation." He repeated the point: "I have no way of knowing when or if God would lift the curtain of protection" around America. "My misstatement included assuming that I or any mortal would know when God is judging or not judging a nation."

In his recantation, Falwell is surely on the mark. He does not know God's will or God's plan. Neither he, nor you, nor I know, nor does Osama bin Laden.

In limning the salutary effects of a little political violence, Thomas Jefferson posed a standard against which to reckon its justification. "What signify a few lives lost in a century or two?" he asked. He meant: the favorable course of events will let us look back from afar and tolerate the violence that set it in motion. If this is the right standard, then the United States has it within its power now, by prudent and measured action, to make sure that in a century or two the lives lost on September 11 continue to signify something—a profound and everlasting wrong.

Sources

Carlin Romano's comments occur in "Why Innocence Matters," *Chronicle of Higher Education*, 48 (October 12, 2001). The texts of the Nuremberg Laws, the Geneva Convention of 1949, and the 1968 United Nations Resolution on Human Rights can be found at www.dannen.com/decision/int-law.html. The U.N. Convention on the Suppression of Terrorist Bombing (A/RES/52/164) along with other pertinent documents such as Measures to Eliminate International Terrorism (1994) (A/RES/49/60), Human Rights and Terror (1997) (A/RES/52/133/), and Universal Realization of the Right of Peoples to Self-Determination (1997) (A/RES/52/113) can be found at www.un.org/documents/resga.htm. The statement of the League of Arab States and its 1998 Convention on the Suppression of Terrorism are available at www.leagueofarabstates.org/e_LASToday.asp. Judith Lichtenberg, "The Ethics of Retaliation," *Philosophy & Public Policy Quarterly*, vol. 21, no. 4. The characterization of terrorists as a throwback to prehistoric times is by Benzion Netanyahu, "Terrorists and Freedom Fighters," in *Terrorism: How the West Can Win*, edited by Benjamin Netanyahu (Farrar, Straus, Giroux, 1986). Osama bin Laden's statement can be found in the *Washington Post* (October 28, 2001). For the inconveniences in the State of Nature, see Thomas Hobbes, *Leviathan*, edited by Richard Tuck (Cambridge University Press, 1996), Chapters 13, 15, and 29, and John Locke, *Two Treatises of Government* (Mentor Books, 1965), Book II, Chapters 2 and 9. For Jefferson's letters, see Thomas Jefferson, *Writings* (The Library of America, 1984), pp. 881, 889, 911. For the life of John Brown, see Stephen B. Oates, *To Purge This Land with Blood: A Biography of John Brown* (Harper & Row, 1970). My discussion of the Kellogg-Briand Pact draws upon Paul W. Kahn, "From Nuremberg to the Hague: The United States Position in Nicaragua v. United States and the Development of International Law," 12 *Yale Journal of International Law*, vol. 1 (1987). The gloss on Deuteronomy 20 is taken from the 1913 edition of the *Catholic Encyclopedia*, accessible on the Web at www.newadvent.org/cathen/. Jerry Falwell's remarks can be found in Peter

Carlson, "Jerry Falwell's Awkward Apology," *Washington Post* (November 18, 2001). A few paragraphs in my text are taken from R. Fullinwider, "Understanding Terrorism." in *Problems of International Justice,* edited by Steven Luper-Foy (Westview Press, 1988), pp. 248–259 (used by permission).

QUESTIONS

1. What are some different senses of "innocence," and in what contexts are they usually invoked?
2. Why is "private judgment" a hazard that must be contained? Why might the principle or the rule of law be as important as Fullinwider claims?

VII

Capital Punishment

The death penalty is legally permissible in thirty-five U.S. states, as of this writing in 2010. In the United States widespread support exists for retaining the death penalty, although support has weakened in recent years. Most countries of the world have abolished it. However, given the large populations of the People's Republic of China, India, the United States, and Indonesia, all of which retain it, more than half of the world's population lives in states that have the death penalty. There remains considerable controversy about capital punishment.

In 1977 the United States resumed executions after a ten-year period during which none were conducted.[1] Since then, 1,170 people have been executed.[2] The rate of executions has declined since 1999, when there were 98 executions in the United States; in 2008 there were 37. It cannot be said that the death penalty is widely used in the United States. A Wikipedia article claims that "in recent years the average has been about one execution for about every 700 murders committed, or 1 execution for about every 325 murder convictions."[3] The number of people executed in the United States compared to the other

---

1. In a landmark decision the Supreme Court in *Furman v. Georgia* (1972) ruled that the death penalty is unconstitutional as then administered because of the lack of standards controlling the arbitrary imposition of death sentences. Georgia's revised statutes were approved in *Gregg v. Georgia* (1976), which lifted the moratorium on executions.

2. These figures are from Wikipedia: http://en.wikipedia.org/wiki/Capital_punishment_in_the_United_States (accessed 18 January 2011). See also the Death Penalty Information Center: http://www.deathpenaltyinfo.org/documents/FactSheet.pdf (accessed 18 January 2011).

3. See http://en.wikipedia.org/wiki/Capital_punishment_in_the_United_States#Distribution_of_sentences (accessed 18 January 2011).

leading countries that have the death penalty (China, Iran, Saudi Arabia, and Pakistan) is relatively small.[4]

Capital punishment unambiguously involves the killing of people, and, as a consequence, it is controversial. In the United States the debate over the death penalty also ranges over its legality. The Eighth Amendment to the U.S. Constitution famously forbids "cruel and unusual punishment." And there exist a number of other questions about its legality. Given the place of the Constitution in American political culture it is not always easy to separate moral and political questions. But our interest in this reader is principally in the ethical questions raised by judicial killings.

The death penalty is a form of *punishment*. Punishment is the intentional infliction of some pain or deprivation for an offense (apparently) committed by an agent. *Legal* punishment needs to be carried out by officials of the legal system for an offense against one or more laws.[5]

The most important question to raise is: Why punish? For the purpose and justification of punishment should have implications for the permissibility of judicial killing. Depending on how one groups them, there are four main accounts of punishment, though as we shall see one is not really a theory of punishment. The first two accounts are the most influential. The first is the *deterrence account*: We should punish in order to deter wrongdoing. The second is *retributivist*: Wrongdoers deserve punishment. By contrast, the third—less influential today than several decades ago—urges that we rehabilitate wrongdoers instead of punishing them. Technically it counsels replacement of punishment with reform. The last account is the *moral education theory*: punish in order to teach a (moral) lesson.

The implications of the last two accounts are straightforward: We should abolish judicial killing. One cannot rehabilitate or morally educate someone by taking his or her life. Neither account is very influential today. So much of the debate concerns the first two accounts. We need to say a bit more about each.

On the first account, the end of punishment is deterrence. What is deterrence? To deter someone is to do something that makes that person refrain from particular actions. For instance, imposing a penalty for violation of a norm may well reduce the number of violations. To deter people from doing something is to seek to change their behavior by altering some of their beliefs about the consequences of their actions. Sometimes people say of someone to be executed, "This will deter him!" But that is to confuse deterrence with prevention or incapacitation, with making it difficult or impossible for someone to commit an offense. Deterrence seeks to reduce wrongdoing by affecting people's beliefs about the likely consequences of their actions. One cannot deter someone from killing again by executing him or her (special deterrence). One may, however, be able to deter others from killing by executing a certain number of killers (general deterrence). A question is what implications this might have for the death penalty.

It seems commonsensical that the death penalty will deter homicides. It is after all a more severe punishment than imprisonment; so it should deter more effectively. There has

---

4. See http://en.wikipedia.org/wiki/Capital_punishment#Global_distribution (accessed 18 January 2011).

5. We sometimes say of someone acquitted but nevertheless guilty of an offense that he or she "has been punished enough" (e.g., by years spent in prison awaiting trial). But suffering connected to an offense is not technically punishment, much less legal punishment.

been a surprising debate on the deterrent value of capital punishment. Initial studies compared American states with and without the death penalty to determine if there were noticeable effects, but these sorts of comparisons are too crude. Increasingly sophisticated studies have come out since the late 1960s suggesting there is a fairly significant deterrent effect. And each of these studies has been subjected to strong criticism and counteranalysis. For some time now it has been difficult for nonexperts, untrained in statistical analysis and econometrics, to evaluate these debates. The only thing about which laypeople can be confident is their skepticism of those who speak with complete confidence in their view. It turns out to be quite difficult to establish that the death penalty has significant deterrent effects. The question for us will have to be conditional: *Were the death penalty to deter significantly, should we retain it?*

Whether or not the death penalty deters, many support it for retributivist reasons. The retributivist account of punishment would have us think of punishment as something that must be *deserved*. We should punish someone insofar as they deserve to be punished. Guilt is both necessary and sufficient for punishment.[6] In addition, we should punish some *proportionally* with the severity of the wrongness of their act. The ancient *lex talionis* expresses this idea with a metaphor: "A life for a life, an eye for an eye, a tooth for a tooth. . . ." Punishment should be proportional to the wrong committed. Thus some people think that homicide is fittingly punishable by death.

On this view, quite ancient, punishment is "paying back" the wrongdoer; the criminal is given what he or she deserves. The thought seems to be that punishment is called for to restore a balance upset by the wrongful act. This idea is not unfamiliar; it is found in many works of fiction, where an unpunished injustice evokes feelings of dissatisfaction, relieved only when the villain gets his or her just deserts.

An interesting contrast, important to moral philosophy, between the two accounts is the following: The deterrent account is entirely "forward-looking," while the retributivist account is entirely "backward-looking." With the first we look only to the *consequences* of punishing or refraining from doing so; with the second we look only to the past, the guilt of the person and the severity of the wrongful act. The contrast between the two accounts is sharp. It is similar to the contrast drawn between *moral consequentialism* and its critics (see chapter 67).

---

6. By contrast, unless amended, the deterrence account does not make guilt a necessary condition of just punishment, leaving room for punishing the innocent when this has deterrent effects.

33. Whether It Is Lawful to Kill Sinners?

THOMAS AQUINAS

For a description of the author and a note on the text, see chapter 2.

In this chapter Aquinas defends the death penalty against early Christian beliefs. The objections and replies are reproduced as the former are not dissimilar to many contemporary objections to the death penalty. And the Catholic Church today opposes the death penalty (see chapter 35). The argument that Aquinas uses in favor of the death penalty is, however, unpopular today. Making an analogy between the health of a body and that of the community, he compares the death penalty to the excision of a member.

Q64. Of Murder

Art. 2 Whether It Is Lawful to Kill Sinners?

Objection 1: It would seem unlawful to kill men who have sinned. For our Lord in the parable (Mat. 13) forbade the uprooting of the cockle which denotes wicked men according to a gloss. Now whatever is forbidden by God is a sin. Therefore it is a sin to kill a sinner.

Objection 2: Further, human justice is conformed to Divine justice. Now according to Divine justice sinners are kept back for repentance, according to Ezech. 33:11, "I desire not the death of the wicked, but that the wicked turn from his way and live." Therefore it seems altogether unjust to kill sinners.

Objection 3: Further, it is not lawful, for any good end whatever, to do that which is evil in itself, according to Augustine (Contra Mendac. vii) and the Philosopher (Ethic. ii, 6). Now to kill a man is evil in itself, since we are bound to have charity towards all men, and "we wish our friends to live and to exist," according to Ethic. ix, 4. Therefore it is nowise lawful to kill a man who has sinned.

On the contrary, It is written (Ex. 22:18): "Wizards thou shalt not suffer to live"; and (Ps. 100:8): "In the morning I put to death all the wicked of the land."

I answer that, As stated above (A[1]), it is lawful to kill dumb animals, in so far as they are naturally directed to man's use, as the imperfect is directed to the perfect. Now every part is directed to the whole, as imperfect to perfect, wherefore every part is naturally for the sake of the whole. For this reason we observe that if the health of the whole body demands the excision of a member, through its being decayed or infectious to the other members, it will be both praiseworthy and advantageous to have it cut away. Now every individual person is compared to the whole community, as part to whole. Therefore if a man be dangerous and infectious to the community, on account of some sin, it is praiseworthy and advantageous that he be killed in order to safeguard the common good, since "a little leaven corrupteth the whole lump" (1 Cor. 5:6).

Reply to Objection 1: Our Lord commanded them to forbear from uprooting the cockle in order to spare the wheat, i.e. the good. This occurs when the wicked cannot be slain without the good being killed with them, either because the wicked lie hidden among the good, or because they have many followers, so that they cannot be killed without danger to the good, as Augustine says (Contra Parmen. iii, 2).

Thomas Aquinas, *Summa Theologica* (Benziger Bros. edition, 1947), translated by Fathers of the English Dominion Province.

Wherefore our Lord teaches that we should rather allow the wicked to live, and that vengeance is to be delayed until the last judgment, rather than that the good be put to death together with the wicked. When, however, the good incur no danger, but rather are protected and saved by the slaying of the wicked, then the latter may be lawfully put to death.

Reply to Objection 2: According to the order of His wisdom, God sometimes slays sinners forthwith in order to deliver the good, whereas sometimes He allows them time to repent, according as He knows what is expedient for His elect. This also does human justice imitate according to its powers; for it puts to death those who are dangerous to others, while it allows time for repentance to those who sin without grievously harming others.

Reply to Objection 3: By sinning man departs from the order of reason, and consequently falls away from the dignity of his manhood, in so far as he is naturally free, and exists for himself, and he falls into the slavish state of the beasts, by being disposed of according as he is useful to others. This is expressed in Ps. 48:21: "Man, when he was in honor, did not understand; he hath been compared to senseless beasts, and made like to them," and Prov. 11:29: "The fool shall serve the wise." Hence, although it be evil in itself to kill a man so long as he preserve his dignity, yet it may be good to kill a man who has sinned, even as it is to kill a beast. For a bad man is worse than a beast, and is more harmful, as the Philosopher states (Polit. i, 1 and Ethic. vii, 6).

Art. 3 Whether It Is Lawful for a Private Individual to Kill a Man Who Has Sinned?

As stated above (A[2]), it is lawful to kill an evildoer in so far as it is directed to the welfare of the whole community, so that it belongs to him alone who has charge of the community's welfare. Thus it belongs to a physician to cut off a decayed limb, when he has been entrusted with the care of the health of the whole body. Now the care of the common good is entrusted to persons of rank having public authority: wherefore they alone, and not private individuals, can lawfully put evildoers to death.

QUESTIONS

1. Consider each of the three objections. Are Aquinas's replies effective?
2. Consider Aquinas's principal argument in favor of executing criminals. Is it persuasive?

34. The Right of Punishing

IMMANUEL KANT

Immanuel Kant (1724–1804) is widely viewed as one of the most important philosophers ever. His influence is felt in all domains of philosophy. His thinking in ethics is especially influential today. Kant spent his whole life in the Prussian city of Königsberg (now Kaliningrad, Russia). He studied at the University of Königsberg and spent the rest of his life there.

From Immanuel Kant, *The Philosophy of Law: An Exposition of the Fundamental Principles of Jurisprudence as the Science of Right*, trans. W. Hastie (Edinburgh: Clark, 1887).

Kant's moral philosophy is both very difficult and very influential (see chapter 67). His political and legal philosophy, of which his account of punishment is a part, is difficult too; and it is also separate from his moral philosophy. Three central ideas are of importance for the topics of this reader. The first is Kant's view of the grounds of judicial punishment: criminals are to be punished, not in order that some good may come of it, but simply because they have committed a crime. The second is the measure of punishment: "The Principle of Equality . . . the undeserved evil which any one commits on another, is to be regarded as perpetrated on himself." This is a principle of retribution. The last idea is the proposal that the death penalty is the appropriate punishment for homicide: "Whoever has committed Murder, must die. There is, in this case, no juridical substitute or surrogate, that can be given or taken for the satisfaction of Justice." Some of the discussions of capital punishment that follow appeal to these ideas.

I. The Right of Punishing

The Right of administering Punishment, is the Right of the Sovereign as the Supreme Power to inflict pain upon a Subject on account of a Crime committed by him. The Head of the State cannot therefore be punished; but his supremacy may be withdrawn from him. Any Transgression of the public law which makes him who commits it incapable of being a Citizen, constitutes a *Crime,* either simply as a private Crime (*crimen*), or also as a *public* Crime (*crimen publicum*). Private crimes are dealt with by a Civil Court; Public Crimes by a Criminal Court.—Embezzlement or peculation of money or goods entrusted in trade, Fraud in purchase or sale, if done before the eyes of the party who suffers, are Private Crimes. On the other hand, Coining false money or forging Bills of Exchange, Theft, Robbery, etc., are Public Crimes, because the Commonwealth, and not merely some particular individual, is endangered thereby. Such Crimes may be divided into those of a *base* character (*indolis abjectæ*) and those of a *violent* character (*indolis violentiæ*).

Judicial or Juridical Punishment (*pœna forensis*) is to be distinguished from Natural Punishment (*pœna naturalis*), in which Crime as Vice punishes itself, and does not as such come within the cognizance of the Legislator. Juridical Punishment can never be administered merely as a means for promoting another Good either with regard to the Criminal himself or to Civil Society, but must in all cases be imposed only because the individual on whom it is inflicted *has committed a Crime.* For one man ought never to be dealt with merely as a means subservient to the purpose of another, nor be mixed up with the subjects of Real Right. Against such treatment his Inborn Personality has a Right to protect him, even although he may be condemned to lose his Civil Personality. He must first be found guilty and *punishable,* before there can be any thought of drawing from his Punishment any benefit for himself or his fellow-citizens. The Penal Law is a Categorical Imperative; and woe to him who creeps through the serpent-windings of Utilitarianism to discover some advantage that may discharge him from the Justice of Punishment, or even from the due measure of it, according to the Pharisaic maxim: "It is better that *one* man should die than that the whole people should perish." For if Justice and Righteousness perish, human life would no longer have any value in the world.— What, then, is to be said of such a proposal as to keep a Criminal alive who has been condemned to death, on his being given to understand that if he agreed to certain dangerous experiments being performed upon him, he would be allowed to survive if he came happily through them? It is argued that Physicians might thus obtain new information that would be of value to the Commonweal. But a Court of Justice would repudiate with scorn any proposal of this kind if made to it by the Medical Faculty; for Justice would cease to be Justice, if it were bartered away for any consideration whatever.

But what is the mode and measure of Punishment which Public Justice takes as its Principle and Standard? It is just the Principle of Equality, by which the pointer of the Scale of Justice is made to incline no more to the one side than the other. It may be rendered by saying that the undeserved evil which any one commits on another, is to be regarded as perpetrated on himself. Hence it may be said: "If you slander another, you slander yourself; if you steal from another, you steal from yourself; if you strike another, you strike yourself; if you kill another, you kill yourself." This is the Right of Retaliation (*jus talionis*); and properly understood, it is the only Principle which in regulating a Public Court, as distinguished from mere private judgment, can definitely assign both the quality and the quantity of a just penalty. All other standards are wavering and uncertain; and on account of other considerations involved in them, they contain no principle conformable to the sentence of pure and strict Justice. It may appear, however, that difference of social status would not admit the application of the Principle of Retaliation, which is that of "Like with Like." But although the application may not in all cases be possible according to the letter, yet as regards the effect it may always be attained in practice, by due regard being given to the disposition and sentiment of the parties in the higher social sphere. Thus a pecuniary penalty on account of a verbal injury, may have no direct proportion to the injustice of slander; for one who is wealthy may be able to indulge himself in this offence for his own gratification. Yet the attack committed on the honour of the party aggrieved may have its equivalent in the pain inflicted upon the pride of the aggressor, especially if he is condemned by the judgment of the Court, not only to retract and apologize, but to submit to some meaner ordeal, as kissing the hand of the injured person. In like manner, if a man of the highest rank has violently assaulted an innocent citizen of the lower orders, he may be condemned not only to apologize but to undergo a solitary and painful imprisonment, whereby, in addition to the discomfort endured, the vanity of the offender would be painfully affected, and the very shame of his position would constitute an adequate Retaliation after the principle of "Like with Like." But how then would we render the

statement: "If you *steal* from another, you steal from yourself"? In this way, that whoever steals anything makes the property of all insecure; he therefore robs himself of all security in property, according to the Right of Retaliation. Such a one has nothing, and can acquire nothing, but he has the Will to live; and this is only possible by others supporting him. But as the State should not do this gratuitously, he must for this purpose yield his powers to the State to be used in penal labour; and thus he falls for a time, or it may be for life, into a condition of slavery.—But whoever has committed Murder, must *die*. There is, in this case, no juridical substitute or surrogate, that can be given or taken for the satisfaction of Justice. There is no *Likeness* or proportion between Life, however painful, and Death; and therefore there is no Equality between the crime of Murder and the retaliation of it but what is judicially accomplished by the execution of the Criminal. His death, however, must be kept free from all maltreatment that would make the humanity suffering in his Person loathsome or abominable. Even if a Civil Society resolved to dissolve itself with the consent of all its members—as might be supposed in the case of a People inhabiting an island resolving to separate and scatter themselves throughout the whole world—the last Murderer lying in the prison ought to be executed before the resolution was carried out. This ought to be done in order that every one may realize the desert of his deeds, and that blood-guiltiness may not remain upon the people; for otherwise they might all be regarded as participators in the murder as a public violation of Justice.

The Equalization of Punishment with Crime, is therefore only possible by the cognition of the Judge extending even to the penalty of Death, according to the Right of Retaliation. This is manifest from the fact that it is only thus that a Sentence can be pronounced over all criminals proportionate to their internal *wickedness*; as may be seen by considering the case when the punishment of Death has to be inflicted, not on account of a murder, but on account of a political crime that can only be punished capitally. A hypothetical case, founded on history, will illustrate this. In the last Scottish Rebellion there were various participators in it—such as Balmerino and others—who believed that in taking part in the Rebellion they were only discharging their duty to the House of Stuart; but there were also others who were animated only by private motives and interests. Now, suppose that the Judgment of the Supreme Court regarding them had been this: that every one should have liberty to choose between the punishment of Death or Penal Servitude for life. In view of such an alternative, I say that the Man of Honour would choose Death, and the Knave would choose servitude. This would be the effect of their human nature as it is; for the honourable man values his Honour more highly than even Life itself, whereas a Knave regards a Life, although covered with shame, as better in his eyes than not to be. The former is, without gainsaying, less guilty than the other; and they can only be proportionately punished by death being inflicted equally upon them both; yet to the one it is a mild punishment when his nobler temperament is taken into account, whereas it is a hard punishment to the other in view of his baser temperament. But, on the other hand, were they all equally condemned to Penal Servitude for life, the honourable man would be too severely punished, while the other, on account of his baseness of nature, would be too mildly punished. In the judgment to be pronounced over a number of criminals united in such a conspiracy, the best Equalizer of Punishment and Crime in the form of public Justice is Death. And besides all this, it has never been heard of, that a Criminal condemned to death on account of a murder has complained that the Sentence inflicted on him more than was right and just; and any one would treat him with scorn if he expressed himself to this effect against it. Otherwise it would be necessary to admit that although wrong and injustice are not done to the Criminal by the Law, yet the Legislative Power is not entitled to administer this mode of Punishment; and if it did so, it would be in contradiction with itself.

However many they may be who have committed a murder, or have even commanded it, or acted as art and part in it, they ought all to suffer death; for so Justice wills it, in accordance with the Idea of the juridical Power as founded on the universal Laws of Reason. But the number of the Accomplices (*correi*) in such a deed might happen to be so great that the State, in resolving to be without such criminals, would be in danger of soon also being deprived of subjects. But it will not thus dissolve itself, neither must it return to the much worse condition of Nature, in which there would be no external Justice. Nor, above all, should it deaden the sensibilities of the People by the spectacle of Justice being exhibited in the mere carnage of a slaughtering bench. In such circumstances the Sovereign must always be allowed to have it in his power to take the part of the Judge upon himself as a case of Necessity,—and to deliver a Judgment which, instead of the penalty of death, shall assign some other punishment to the Criminals, and thereby preserve a multitude of the People. The penalty of Deportation is relevant in this connection. Such a form of Judgment cannot be carried out according to a public law, but only by an authoritative act of the royal Prerogative, and it may only be applied as an act of grace in individual cases.

Against these doctrines, the Marquis Beccaria has given forth a different view. Moved by the compassionate sentimentality of a humane feeling, he has asserted that all Capital Punishment is wrong in itself and unjust. He has put forward this view on the ground that the penalty of death could not be contained in the original Civil Contract; for, in that case, every one of the People would have had to consent to lose his life if he murdered any of his fellow-citizens. But, it is argued, such a consent is impossible, because no one can thus dispose of his own life.—All this is mere sophistry and perversion of Right. No one undergoes Punishment because he has willed to be punished, but because he has willed *a punishable Action*; for it is in fact no Punishment when any one experiences what he wills, and it is impossible for any one to *will* to be punished. To say, "I *will* to be punished, if I murder any one," can mean nothing more than, "I submit myself along with all the other citizens to the Laws"; and if there are any Criminals among the People, these Laws will include Penal Laws. The individual who, as a Co-legislator, enacts *Penal Law*, cannot possibly be the same Person who, as a Subject, is punished according to the Law; for, *quâ* Criminal, he cannot possibly be regarded as having a voice in the Legislation, the Legislator being rationally viewed as just and holy. If any one, then, enact a Penal Law against himself as a

Criminal, it must be the pure juridically law-giving Reason (*homo noumenon*), which subjects him as one capable of crime, and consequently as another Person (*homo phenomenon*), along with all the others in the Civil Union, to this Penal law. In other words, it is not the People taken distributively, but the Tribunal of public Justice, as distinct from the Criminal, that prescribes Capital Punishment; and it is not to be viewed as if the Social Contract contained the Promise of all the individuals to allow themselves to be punished, thus disposing of themselves and their lives. For if the Right to punish must be grounded upon a promise of the wrongdoer,

whereby he is to be regarded as being willing to be punished, it ought also to be left to him to find himself deserving of the Punishment; and the Criminal would thus be his own Judge. The chief error (πρῶτον ψεῦδος) of this sophistry consists in regarding the judgment of the Criminal himself, necessarily determined by his Reason, that he is under obligation to undergo the loss of his life, as a judgment that must be grounded on a resolution of his *Will* to take it away himself; and thus the execution of the Right in question is represented as united in one and the same person with the adjudication of the Right.

QUESTIONS

1. Why may punishment not be used to promote a good, either to society or to the wrongdoer?
2. Why is death the appropriate punishment for murder?

35. The Death Penalty

JOHN PAUL II

For a description of the author, see chapter 4.

The late Pope John Paul rejects the death penalty in this brief excerpt. He argues that it is rarely needed for the defense of society. Interestingly, where earlier Christians might appeal to the virtue of charity in their condemnation of the death penalty, John Paul several times refers to the dignity of the human person.

56. This is the context in which to place the problem of the death penalty. On this matter there is a growing tendency, both in the Church and in civil society, to demand that it be applied in a very limited way or even that it be abolished completely. The problem must be viewed in the context of a system of penal justice ever more in line with human dignity

and thus, in the end, with God's plan for man and society. The primary purpose of the punishment which society inflicts is "to redress the disorder caused by the offence."[1] Public authority must redress the violation of personal and social rights by imposing on the offender an adequate punishment for the crime, as a condition for the offender to

From John Paul II, *Evangelium vitae*, 1995.

regain the exercise of his or her freedom. In this way authority also fulfils the purpose of defending public order and ensuring people's safety, while at the same time offering the offender an incentive and help to change his or her behaviour and be rehabilitated.[2]

It is clear that, for these purposes to be achieved, the nature and extent of the punishment must be carefully evaluated and decided upon, and ought not go to the extreme of executing the offender except in cases of absolute necessity: in other words, when it would not be possible otherwise to defend society. Today however, as a result of steady improvements in the organization of the penal system, such cases are very rare, if not practically non-existent.

In any event, the principle set forth in the new Catechism of the Catholic Church remains valid: "If bloodless means are sufficient to defend human lives against an aggressor and to protect public order and the safety of persons, public authority must limit itself to such means, because they better correspond to the concrete conditions of the common good and are more in conformity to the dignity of the human person."[3]

Notes

1. *Catechism of the Catholic Church*, No. 2266.
2. Cf. ibid.
3. No. 2267.

QUESTIONS

1. What is the end of punishment according to John Paul, and why does it rule out the death penalty in most situations?
2. What is the relevance of the value of "human dignity" to John Paul's consideration of this question?

36. The Death Penalty and the Right to Life

AMNESTY INTERNATIONAL

Amnesty International, founded in 1961, is a well-known political organization, "a worldwide movement of people who campaign for internationally recognized human rights for all." It was awarded the Nobel Peace Prize in 1977 for its campaign against torture.

For some time now, Amnesty International has campaigned for the abolition of the death penalty worldwide. In its publicity material it says little about the grounds for its opposition to the death penalty, only that it is a violation of the right to life. It is important to consider whether the death penalty is in fact a violation of this right. (I wrote the organization asking for elaboration, explaining that I wished to republish a more detailed defense of its position. I received a one-sentence reply from "Betsy Ross," who said that "Article 3 of the UN's Universal Declaration of Human Rights states that, 'Everyone has the right to life, liberty and security of person'" [e-mail, 2 August 2006].) Even if no argument is provided,

From http://www.amnesty.org/en/death-penalty

Amnesty International's assertion that the death penalty is a violation of the right to life is very interesting and worth considering.

The death penalty is the ultimate denial of human rights. It is the premeditated and cold-blooded killing of a human being by the state. This cruel, inhuman and degrading punishment is done in the name of justice.

It violates the right to life as proclaimed in the Universal Declaration of Human Rights.

Amnesty International opposes the death penalty in all cases without exception regardless of the nature of the crime, the characteristics of the offender, or the method used by the state to kill the prisoner.

QUESTIONS

1. If someone has committed a serious crime but retains a right to _____, it would be wrong to violate that right. Substitute (a) "appeal a sentence" for the blank. Is the claim true? Now substitute (b) "life." Is the claim true?
2. Is Amnesty International supposing that the right to life cannot in these circumstances be overridden or violated? Or that it can never be forfeited or taken away?

37. The Case against the Death Penalty

HUGO ADAM BEDAU

*H*ugo Adam Bedau (1926–) is professor emeritus at Tufts University. He has written extensively about the death penalty and campaigned tirelessly for its abolition. He is the editor of *The Death Penalty in America* (1964), the standard work on capital punishment in the United States, now in its fourth edition.

This article is a summary of most (all?) of the arguments against the death penalty.

In 1972, the Supreme Court declared that under then existing laws "the imposition and carrying out of the death penalty . . . constitutes cruel and unusual punishment in violation of the Eighth and Fourteenth Amendments" (*Furman v. Georgia*, 408 U.S. 238). The majority of the Court concentrated its objections on the way death-penalty laws had been applied, finding the result so "harsh, freakish, and arbitrary" as to be constitutionally unacceptable. Making the nationwide impact of its decision unmistakable, the Court summarily reversed death sentences in the many cases then before it, which involved a wide range of state statutes, crimes, and factual situations.

But within four years after the *Furman* decision, more than 600 persons had been sentenced to death under new capital-punishment statutes that provided guidance for the jury's sentencing discretion. These statutes typically require a bifurcated (two-stage) trial procedure, in which the jury first determines guilt or innocence and then chooses imprisonment or death in the light of aggravating or mitigating circumstances.

In July 1976, the Supreme Court moved in the opposite direction, holding that "the punishment of death does not invariably violate the Constitution." The Court ruled that these new statutes contained "objective standards to guide, regularize, and make rationally reviewable the process for imposing the sentence of death" (*Gregg v. Georgia*, 428 U.S. 153). Thus the states as well as Congress have had for some years constitutionally valid statutory models for death-penalty laws, and more than three dozen state legislatures have enacted death penalty statutes patterned after those the Court upheld in *Gregg*. In recent years, Congress has enacted death penalty statutes for peacetime espionage by military personnel and for drug-related murders.

Executions resumed in 1977, and by the early 1990s nearly three thousand persons were under sentence of death and more than 180 had been executed.

Despite the Supreme Court's 1976 ruling in *Gregg v. Georgia*, the ACLU [American Civil Liberties Union] continues to oppose capital punishment on moral and practical, as well as on constitutional, grounds:

- Capital punishment is cruel and unusual. It is a relic of the earliest days of penology, when slavery, branding, and other corporal punishments were commonplace. Like those other barbaric practices, executions have no place in a civilized society.
- Opposition to the death penalty does not arise from misplaced sympathy for convicted murderers. On the contrary, murder demonstrates a lack of respect for human life. For this very reason, murder is abhorrent, and any policy of state-authorized killings is immoral.
- Capital punishment denies due process of law. Its imposition is arbitrary and irrevocable. It forever deprives an individual of benefits of new evidence or new law that might warrant the reversal of a conviction or the setting aside of a death sentence.
- The death penalty violates the constitutional guarantee of the equal protection of the laws. It is applied randomly at best and discriminatorily at worst. It is imposed disproportionately upon those whose victims are white, on offenders who are people of color, and on those who are themselves poor and uneducated.
- The defects in death-penalty laws, conceded by the Supreme Court in the early 1970s, have not been appreciably altered by the shift from unfettered discretion to "guided discretion." These changes in death sentencing have proved to be largely cosmetic. They merely mask the impermissible arbitrariness of a process that results in an execution.
- Executions give society the unmistakable message that human life no longer deserves respect when it is useful to take it and that homicide is legitimate when deemed justified by pragmatic concerns.
- Reliance on the death penalty obscures the true causes of crime and distracts attention from the social measures that effectively contribute to its control. Politicians who preach the desirability of executions as a weapon of crime control deceive the public and mask their own failure to support anti-crime measures that will really work.
- Capital punishment wastes resources. It squanders the time and energy of courts, prosecuting attorneys, defense counsel, juries, and courtroom and correctional personnel. It unduly burdens the system of criminal justice, and it is therefore counterproductive as an instrument for society's control of violent crime. It epitomizes the tragic inefficacy and brutality of the resort to violence rather than reason for the solution of difficult social problems.

- A decent and humane society does not deliberately kill human beings. An execution is a dramatic, public spectacle of official, violent homicide that teaches the permissibility of killing people to solve social problems—the worst possible example to set for society. In this century, governments have too often attempted to justify their lethal fury by the benefits such killing would bring to the rest of society. The bloodshed is real and deeply destructive of the common decency of the community; the benefits are illusory.

Two conclusions buttress our entire case: Capital punishment does not deter crime, and the death penalty is uncivilized in theory and unfair and inequitable in practice.

Deterrence

The argument most often cited in support of capital punishment is that the threat of executions deters capital crimes more effectively than imprisonment. This claim is plausible, but the facts do not support it. The death penalty fails as a deterrent for several reasons.

1

Any punishment can be an effective deterrent only if it is consistently and promptly employed. Capital punishment cannot be administered to meet these conditions.

Only a small proportion of first-degree murderers is sentenced to death, and even fewer are executed. Although death sentences since 1980 have increased in number to about 250 per year,[1] this is still only 1 percent of all homicides known to the police.[2] Of all those convicted on a charge of criminal homicide, only 2 percent—about 1 in 50—are eventually sentenced to death.[3]

The possibility of increasing the number of convicted murderers sentenced to death and executed by enacting mandatory death penalty laws was ruled unconstitutional in 1976 (*Woodson v. North Carolina*, 428 U.S. 280).

Considerable delay in carrying out the death sentence is unavoidable, given the procedural safeguards required by the courts in capital cases. Starting with empaneling the trial jury, murder trials take far longer when the death penalty is involved. Post-conviction appeals in death-penalty cases are far more frequent as well. All these factors increase the time and cost of administering criminal justice.

The sobering lesson is that we can reduce such delay and costs only by abandoning the procedural safeguards and constitutional rights of suspects, defendants, and convicts, with the attendant high risk of convicting the wrong person and executing the innocent.

2

Persons who commit murder and other crimes of personal violence either premeditate them or they do not. If the crime is premeditated, the criminal ordinarily concentrates on escaping detection, arrest, and conviction. The threat of even the severest punishment will not deter those who expect to escape detection and arrest. If the crime is not premeditated, then it is impossible to imagine how the threat of any punishment could deter it. Most capital crimes are committed during moments of great emotional stress or under the influence of drugs or alcohol, when logical thinking has been suspended. Impulsive or expressive violence is inflicted by persons heedless of the consequences to themselves as well as to others.

Gangland killings, air piracy, drive-by shootings, and kidnapping for ransom are among the graver felonies that continue to be committed because some individuals think they are too clever to get caught. Political terrorism is usually committed in the name of an ideology that honors its martyrs; trying to cope with it by threatening death for terrorists is futile. Such threats leave untouched the underlying causes and ignore the many political and diplomatic sanctions (such as treaties against asylum for international terrorists) that could appreciably lower the incidence of terrorism.

The attempt to reduce murders in the illegal drug trade by the threat of severe punishment ignores this fact: Anyone trafficking in illegal drugs is already betting his life in violent competition with other dealers. It is irrational to think that the death penalty—a remote threat at best—will deter murders committed in drug turf wars or by street-level dealers.

3

If, however, severe punishment can deter crime, then long-term imprisonment is severe enough to cause any rational person not to commit violent crimes. The vast preponderance of the evidence shows that the death penalty is no more effective than imprisonment in deterring murder and that it may even be an incitement to criminal violence in certain cases.

- (a) Death-penalty states as a group do not have lower rates of criminal homicide than non–death penalty states. During the 1980s, death-penalty states averaged an annual rate of 7.5 criminal homicides per 100,000 of population; abolition states averaged a rate of 7.4.[4]
- (b) Use of the death penalty in a given state may increase the subsequent rate of criminal homicide in that state. In New York, for example, between 1907 and 1964, 692 executions were carried out. On the average, over this 57-year period, one or more executions in a given month aided a net increase of two homicides to the total committed in the next month.[5]
- (c) In neighboring states—one with the death penalty and the others without it—the one with the death penalty does not show a consistently lower rate of criminal homicide. For example, between 1972 and 1990, the homicide rate in Michigan (which has no death penalty) was generally as low as or lower than the neighboring state of Indiana, which restored the death penalty in 1973 and since then has sentenced 70 persons to death and carried out 2 executions.[6]
- (d) Police officers on duty do not suffer a higher rate of criminal assault and homicide in states that have abolished the death penalty than they do in death-penalty states. Between 1973 and 1984, for example, lethal assaults against police were not significantly more or less frequent in abolition states than in death-penalty states.

There is "no support for the view that the death penalty provides a more effective deterrent to police homicides than alternative sanctions. Not for a single year was evidence found that police are safer in jurisdictions that provide for capital punishment."[7]

- (e) Prisoners and prison personnel do not suffer a higher rate of criminal assault and homicide from life-term prisoners in abolition states than they do in death-penalty states.[8] Between 1984 and 1989, seventeen prison staff were murdered by prisoners in ten states; of these murders, 88 percent (15 of 17) occurred in death penalty jurisdictions—just as about 88 percent of all the prisoners in those ten states were in death penalty jurisdictions.[9] Evidently, the threat of the death penalty "does not even exert an incremental deterrent effect over the threat of a lesser punishment in the abolitionist state."[10]

Actual experience establishes these conclusions beyond a reasonable doubt. No comparable body of evidence contradicts them.

Three investigations since *Furman*, using methods pioneered by economists, reported findings in the opposite direction.[11] Subsequently, several qualified investigators have independently examined these claims, and all have rejected them.[12] The National Academy of Sciences, in its thorough report on the effects of criminal sanctions on crime rates, concluded: "It seems unthinkable to us to base decisions on the use of the death penalty" on such "fragile" and "uncertain" results. "We see too many plausible explanations for [these] findings . . . other than the theory that capital punishment deters murder."[13]

Furthermore, cases have been clinically documented where the death penalty actually incited the capital crimes it was supposed to deter. These include instances of the so-called suicide-by-execution syndrome—persons who wanted but feared to take their own life and committed murder so that society would kill them.[14]

It must, of course, be conceded that inflicting the death penalty guarantees that the condemned person will commit no further crimes. This is an incapacitative, not a deterrent, effect of executions. Furthermore, it is too high a price to pay when studies show that very few convicted murderers ever commit another crime of violence.[15] A recent study examined the prison and post-release records of 533 prisoners on death row in 1972 whose sentences were reduced to life by the Supreme Court's ruling in *Furman*. The research showed that 6 had committed another murder. But the same study showed that in 4 other cases, an innocent man had been sentenced to death.[16]

Recidivism among murderers does occasionally happen. But it happens less frequently than most people believe; the media rarely distinguish between a paroled murderer who murders again and other murderers who have a previous criminal record but not for homicide.

There is no way to predict which convicted murderers will kill again. Repeat murders could be prevented only by executing all those convicted of criminal homicide. Such a policy is too inhumane and brutal to be taken seriously. Society would never tolerate dozens of executions daily, yet nothing less would suffice. Equally effective but far less inhumane is a policy of life imprisonment without the possibility of parole.

Unfairness

Constitutional due process as well as elementary justice require that the judicial functions of trial and sentencing be conducted with fundamental fairness, especially where the irreversible sanction of the death penalty is involved. In murder cases (since 1930, 99 percent of all executions have been for this crime), there has been substantial evidence to show that courts have been arbitrary, racially biased, and unfair in the way in which they have sentenced some persons to prison but others to death.

Racial discrimination was one of the grounds on which the Supreme Court relied in *Furman* in ruling the death penalty unconstitutional. Half a century ago, Gunnar Myrdal, in his classic *American Dilemma* (1944), reported that "the South makes the widest application of the death penalty, and Negro criminals come in for much more than their share of the executions." Statistics confirm this discrimination, only it

is not confined to the South. Between 1930 and 1990, 4,016 persons were executed in the United States. Of these, 2,129 (or 53 percent) were black. For the crime of murder, 3,343 were executed; 1,693 (or 51 percent) were black.[17] During these years African-Americans were about 12 percent of the nation's population.

The nation's death rows have always had a disproportionately large population of African-Americans, relative to their fraction of the total population. Over the past century, black offenders, as compared with white, were often executed for crimes less often receiving the death penalty, such as rape and burglary. (Between 1930 and 1976, 455 men were executed for rape, of whom 405 [or 90 percent] were black.) A higher percentage of the blacks who were executed were juveniles; and blacks were more often executed than were whites without having their conviction reviewed by any higher court.[18]

In recent years, it has been widely believed that such flagrant discrimination is a thing of the past. Since the revival of the death penalty in the mid-1970s, about half of those on death row at any given time have been black[19]—a disproportionately large fraction given the black/white ratio of the total population, but not so obviously unfair if judged by the fact that roughly 50 percent of all those arrested for murder were also black.[20] Nevertheless, when those under death sentence are examined more closely, it turns out that race is a decisive factor after all.

An exhaustive statistical study of racial discrimination in capital cases in Georgia, for example, showed that "the average odds of receiving a death sentence among all indicted cases were 4.3 times higher in cases with white victims."[21] In 1987 these data were placed before the Supreme Court in *McCleskey v. Kemp* and the Court did not dispute the statistical evidence. The Court did hold, however, that the evidence failed to show that there was "a constitutionally significant risk of racial bias. . . ." (481 U.S. 279).

In 1990, the U.S. General Accounting Office reported to the Congress the results of its review of empirical studies on racism and the death penalty. The GAO concluded: "Our synthesis of the 28 studies shows a pattern of evidence indicating racial disparities in the charging, sentencing, and imposition of the death penalty after the Furman decision" and that "race of victim influence was found at all stages of the criminal justice system process. . . ."[22]

These results cannot be explained away by relevant non-racial factors (such as prior criminal record or type of crime), and they lead to a very unsavory conclusion: In the trial courts of this nation, even at the present time, the killing of a white is treated much more severely than the killing of a black. Of the 168 persons executed between January 1977 and April 1992, only 29 had been convicted of the killing of a non-white, and only one of these 29 was himself white.[23] Where the death penalty is involved, our criminal justice system essentially reserves the death penalty for murderers (regardless of their race) who kill white victims.

Both sex and socio-economic class are also factors that enter into determining who receives a death sentence and who is executed. During the 1980s and early 1990s, only about 1 percent of all those on death row were women,[24] even though women commit about 15 percent of all criminal homicides.[25] A third or more of the women under death sentence were guilty of killing men who had victimized them with years of violent abuse.[26] Since 1930, only 33 women (12 of them black) have been executed in the United States.[27]

Discrimination against the poor (and in our society racial minorities are disproportionately poor) is also well established. "Approximately ninety percent of those on death row could not afford to hire a lawyer when they were tried."[28] A defendant's poverty, lack of firm social roots in the community, inadequate legal representation at trial or on appeal—all these have been common factors among death-row populations. As Justice William O. Douglas noted in *Furman*, "One searches our chronicles in vain for the execution of any member of the affluent strata in this society" (408 U.S. 238).

The demonstrated inequities in the actual administration of capital punishment should tip the balance against it in the judgment of fair-minded and impartial observers. "Whatever else might be said for the use of death as a punishment, one lesson is clear from experience: this is a power that we cannot exercise fairly and without discrimination."[29]

Justice John Marshall Harlan, writing for the Court, noted: " . . . the history of capital punishment for homicides . . . reveals continual efforts, uniformly unsuccessful, to identify before the fact those homicides for which the slayer should die. . . . Those who have come to grips with the hard task of actually attempting to draft means of channeling capital sentencing discretion have confirmed the lesson taught by history. . . . To identify before the fact those characteristics of criminal homicides and their perpetrators which call for the death penalty, and to express these characteristics in language which can be fairly understood and applied by the sentencing authority, appears to be tasks which are beyond present human ability" (*McGautha v. California*, 402 U.S. 183 [1971]).

Yet in the *Gregg* decision, the majority of the Supreme Court abandoned the wisdom of Justice Harlan and ruled as though the new guided-discretion statutes could accomplish the impossible. The truth is that death statutes approved by the Court "do not effectively restrict the discretion of juries by any real standards. They never will. No society is going to kill everybody who meets certain preset verbal requirements, put on the statute books without awareness of coverage of the infinity of special factors the real world can produce."[30]

Even if these statutes were to succeed in guiding the jury's choice of sentence, a vast reservoir of unfettered discretion remains: the prosecutor's decision to prosecute for a capital or lesser crime, the court's willingness to accept or reject a guilty plea, the jury's decision to convict for second-degree murder or manslaughter rather than capital murder, the determination of the defendant's sanity, the final decision by the governor on clemency.

Discretion in the criminal-justice system is unavoidable. The history of capital punishment in American society clearly shows the desire to mitigate the harshness of this penalty by narrowing its scope. Discretion, whether authorized by statutes or by their silence, has been the main vehicle to this end. But when discretion is used, as it always has been, to mark for death the poor, the friendless, the uneducated, the members of racial minorities, and the despised, then discretion becomes injustice.

Thoughtful citizens, who in contemplating capital punishment in the abstract might support it, must condemn it in actual practice.

Inevitability of Error

Unlike all other criminal punishments, the death penalty is uniquely irrevocable. Speaking to the French Chamber of Deputies in 1830, years after the excesses of the French Revolution, which he had witnessed, the Marquis de Lafayette said, "I shall ask for the abolition of the punishment of death until I have the infallibility of human judgment demonstrated to me."[31] Although some proponents of capital punishment would argue that its merits are worth the occasional execution of innocent people, most would also insist that there is little likelihood of the innocent being executed. Yet a large body of evidence shows that innocent people are often convicted of crimes, including capital crimes and that some of them have been executed.

Since 1900, in this country, there have been on the average more than four cases per year in which an entirely innocent person was convicted of murder. Scores of these persons were sentenced to death. In many cases, a reprieve or commutation arrived just hours, or even minutes, before the scheduled execution. These erroneous convictions have occurred in virtually every jurisdiction from one end of the nation to the other. Nor have they declined in recent years, despite the new death penalty statutes approved by the Supreme Court.[32] Consider this handful of representative cases:

- In 1975, only a year before the Supreme Court affirmed the constitutionality of capital punishment, two African-American men in Florida, Freddie Pitts and Wilbert Lee, were released from prison after twelve years awaiting execution for the murder of two white men. Their convictions were the result of coerced confessions, erroneous testimony of an alleged eyewitness, and incompetent defense counsel. Though a white man eventually admitted his guilt, a nine-year legal battle was required before the governor would grant Pitts and Lee a pardon.[33] Had their execution not been stayed while the constitutional status of the death penalty was argued in the courts, these two innocent men probably would not be alive today.

- Just months after Pitts and Lee were released, authorities in New Mexico were forced to admit they had sentenced to death four white men—motorcyclists from Los Angeles—who were innocent. The accused offered a documented alibi at their trial, but the prosecution dismissed it as an elaborate ruse. The jury's verdict was based mainly on what was later revealed to be perjured testimony (encouraged by the police) from an alleged eyewitness. Thanks to persistent investigation by newspaper reporters and the confession of the real killer, the error was exposed and the defendants were released after eighteen months on death row.[34]

- In Georgia in 1975, Earl Charles was convicted of murder and sentenced to death. A surviving victim of the crime erroneously identified Charles as the gunman; her testimony was supported by a jail-house informant who claimed he had heard Charles confess. Incontrovertible alibi evidence, showing that Charles was in Florida at the very time of the crime, eventually established his innocence—but not until he had spent more than three years under death sentence. His release was owing largely to his mother's unflagging efforts.[35]

- In 1989, Texas authorities decided not to retry Randall Dale Adams after the appellate court reversed his conviction for murder. Adams had spent more than three years on death row for the murder of a Dallas police officer. He was convicted on the perjured testimony of a 16-year-old youth who was the real killer. Adams's plight was vividly presented in the 1988 docudrama, *The Thin Blue Line*, which convincingly told the true story of the crime and exposed the errors that resulted in his conviction.[36]

- Another case in Texas from the 1980s tells an even more sordid story. In 1980 a black high school janitor, Clarence Brandley, and his white co-worker found the body of a missing 15-year-old white schoolgirl. Interrogated by the police, they were told, "One of you two is going to hang for this." Looking at Brandley, the officer said, "Since you're the nigger, you're elected." In a classic case of rush to judgment, Brandley was tried, convicted, and sentenced to death. The circumstantial evidence against him was thin, other leads were ignored by the police, and the courtroom atmosphere reeked of racism. In 1986 Centurion Ministries—a volunteer group devoted to freeing wrongly convicted prisoners—came to Brandley's aid. Evidence had meanwhile emerged that another man had committed the murder for which Brandley was awaiting execution. Brandley was not released until 1990.[37]

Each of the five stories told above has a reassuring ending: The innocent prisoner is saved from execution and is released. But when prisoners are executed, no legal forum exists in which unanswered questions about their guilt can be resolved. In May 1992, Roger Keith Coleman was executed in Virginia despite widely publicized doubts surrounding his guilt and evidence that pointed to another person as the murderer—evidence that was never submitted at his trial. Not until late in the appeal process did anyone take seriously the possibility that the state was about to kill an innocent man, and then efforts to delay or nullify his execution failed. Was Coleman really innocent? At the time of his execution, his case was marked with many of the features found in other cases where the defendant was eventually cleared. Were Coleman still in prison, his friends and attorneys would have a strong incentive to resolve these questions. But with Coleman dead, further inquiry into the facts of the crime for which he was convicted is unlikely.

Overzealous prosecution, mistaken or perjured testimony, faulty police work, coerced confessions, the defendant's previous criminal record, inept defense counsel, seemingly conclusive circumstantial evidence, community pressure for a conviction—such factors help explain why the judicial system cannot guarantee that justice will never miscarry. And when it does miscarry, volunteers outside the criminal justice system—newspaper reporters, for example—and not the police or prosecutors are the ones who rectify the errors. To retain the death penalty in the face of the demonstrable failures of the system is unacceptable, especially as there are no strong counterbalancing factors in favor of the death penalty.

Barbarity

The traditional mode of execution, still available in a few states, is hanging. Death on the gallows is easily bungled: If the drop is too short, there will be a slow and agonizing death by strangulation. If the drop is too long, the head will be torn off.

Two states, Idaho and Utah, still authorize the firing squad. The prisoner is strapped into a chair, and hooded. A target is pinned to the chest. Five marksmen, one with blanks, take aim and fire.

Electrocution has been the most widely used form of execution in this country in this century. The condemned prisoner is led—or dragged—into the death chamber, strapped into the chair, and electrodes are fastened to head and legs. When the switch is thrown the body strains, jolting as the voltage is raised and lowered. Often smoke rises from the head. There is the awful odor of burning flesh. No one knows how long electrocuted individuals retain consciousness.

In 1983, the electrocution of John Evans in Alabama was described by an eyewitness as follows: "At 8:30 p.m. the first jolt of 1900 volts of electricity passed through Mr. Evans' body. It lasted thirty seconds. Sparks and flames erupted . . . from the electrode tied to Mr. Evans' left leg. His body slammed against the straps holding him in the electric chair and his fist clenched permanently. The electrode apparently burst from the strap holding it in place. A large puff of grayish smoke and sparks poured out from under the hood that covered Mr. Evans' face. An overpowering stench of burnt flesh and clothing began pervading the witness room. Two doctors examined Mr. Evans and declared that he was not dead.

"The electrode on the left leg was refastened. . . . Mr. Evans was administered a second thirty second jolt of electricity. The stench of burning flesh was nauseating. More smoke emanated from his leg and head. Again, the doctors examined Mr. Evans. [They] reported that his heart was still beating, and that he was still alive. At that time, I asked the prison commissioner, who was communicating on an open telephone line to Governor George Wallace, to grant clemency on the grounds that Mr. Evans was being subjected to cruel and unusual punishment. The request . . . was denied.

"At 8:40 p.m., a third charge of electricity, thirty seconds in duration, was passed through Mr. Evans' body. At 8:44, the doctors pronounced him dead. The execution of John Evans took fourteen minutes."[38] Afterwards, officials were embarrassed by what one observer called the "barbaric ritual." The prison spokesman remarked, "This was supposed to be a very clean manner of administering death."[39]

An attempt to improve on electrocution was the gas chamber. The prisoner is strapped into a chair, a container of sulfuric acid underneath. The chamber is sealed, and cyanide is dropped into the acid to form lethal gas. Here is an account of the 1992 execution in Arizona of Don Harding, as reported in the dissent by U.S. Supreme Court Justice John Paul Stevens:

When the fumes enveloped Don's head he took a quick breath. A few seconds later he again looked in my direction. His face was red and contorted as if he were attempting to fight through tremendous pain. His mouth was pursed shut and his jaw was clenched tight. Don then look several more quick gulps of the fumes.

At this point Don's body started convulsing violently. . . . His face and body fumed a deep red and the veins in his temple and neck began to bulge until I thought they might explode.

After about a minute Don's face leaned partially forward, but he was still conscious. Every few seconds he continued to gulp in. He was shuddering uncontrollably and his body was racked with spasms. His head continued to snap back. His hands were clenched.

After several more manuals, the most violent of the convulsions subsided. At this time the muscles along Don's left arm and back began twitching in a wavelike motion under his skin. Spittle drooled from his mouth.

Don did not stop moving for approximately eight minutes, and after that he continued to twitch and jerk for another minute. Approximately two minutes later, we were told by a prison official that the execution was complete.

Don Harding took ten minutes and thirty one seconds to die. (*Gomez v. U.S. District Court*, 112 S.Ct. 1652)

The latest mode of inflicting the death penalty, enacted into law by nearly two dozen states, is lethal injection, first used in Texas in 1982. It is easy to overstate the humaneness and efficacy of this method. There is no way of knowing that it is really painless. As the U.S. Court of Appeals observed, there is "substantial and uncontroverted evidence . . . that execution by lethal injection poses a serious risk of cruel, protracted death. . . . Even a slight error in dosage or administration can leave a prisoner conscious but paralyzed while dying, a sentient witness of his or her own asphyxiation" (*Chaney v. Heckler*, 718 F.2d 1174 [1983]).

Nor does the execution always proceed smoothly as planned. In 1985 "the authorities repeatedly jabbed needles into . . . Stephen Morin, when they had trouble finding a usable vein because he had been a drug abuser."[40] In 1988, during the execution of Raymond Landry, "a tube attached to a needle inside the inmate's right arm began leaking, sending the lethal mixture shooting across the death chamber toward witnesses."[41]

Indeed, by its veneer of decency and by subtle analogy with life-saving medical practice, death by lethal injection makes killing as punishment more acceptable to the public. Even when it prevents the struggles of the condemned person and avoids maiming the body, it is no different from hanging or shooting as an expression of the absolute power of the state over the helpless individual.

Most people observing an execution are horrified and disgusted. "I was ashamed," writes sociologist Richard Moran, who witnessed an execution in Texas in 1985. "I was an intruder, the only member of the public who had trespassed on [the condemned man's] private moment of anguish. In my face he could see the horror of his own death."[42] Revulsion at the duty to supervise and witness executions is one reason why so many prison wardens—however unsentimental they are about crime and criminals—are opponents of capital punishment.

In some people, however, executions seem to appeal to strange, aberrant impulses and give an outlet to sadistic urges. Warden Lewis Lawes wrote of the many requests he received to watch electrocutions, and told that when the job of executioner became vacant, "I received more than seven hundred applications for the position, many of them offering cut-rate prices."[43]

Public executions were common in this country during the 19th century; one of the last was in 1936 in Kentucky, when 20,000 people gathered to watch a young African-American male hanged.[44] Delight in brutality, pain, violence, and death may always be with us. But surely we must conclude that it is best for the law not to encourage these impulses. When the government sanctions, commands, and ceremoniously carries out the execution of a prisoner, it lends support to this destructive side of human nature.

More than two centuries ago, the Italian jurist Cesare Beccaria, in his highly influential treatise *On Crimes and Punishments* (1764), asserted: "The death penalty cannot be useful, because of the example of barbarity it gives men." True, and even if the death penalty were a "useful" deterrent, it would still be an "example of barbarity." No society can safely entrust the enforcement of its laws to torture, brutality, or killing. Such methods are inherently cruel and will always mock the attempt to cloak them in justice. As Supreme Court Justice Arthur J. Goldberg wrote, "The deliberate institutionalized taking of human life by the state is the greatest conceivable degradation to the dignity of the human personality."[45]

Retribution

Justice, it is often insisted, requires the death penalty as the only suitable retribution for heinous crimes. This claim will not bear scrutiny. All punishment by its nature is retributive, not only the death penalty. Whatever legitimacy, therefore, is to be found in punishment as just retribution can in principle be satisfied without recourse to executions.

It is also obvious that the death penalty could be defended on narrowly retributive grounds only for the crime of murder, and not for any of the many other crimes that have frequently been made subject to this mode of punishment (rape, kidnapping, espionage, treason, drug kingpins). Few defenders of the death penalty are willing to confine themselves consistently to the narrow scope afforded by retribution. In any case, execution is more than a punishment exacted in retribution for the taking of a life.

As Camus wrote, "For there to be equivalence, the death penalty would have to punish a criminal who had warned his victim of the date at which he would inflict a horrible death on him and who, from that moment onward, had confined him at his mercy for months. Such a monster is not encountered in private life."[46]

It is also often argued that death is what murderers deserve, and that those who oppose the death penalty violate the fundamental principle that criminals should be punished according to their deserts—"making the punishment fit the crime."

If this principle is understood to require that punishments are unjust unless they are like the crime itself, then the principle is unacceptable. It would require us to rape rapists, torture torturers, and inflict other horrible and degrading punishments on offenders. It would require us to betray traitors and kill multiple murderers again and again, punishments impossible to inflict. Since we cannot reasonably aim to punish all crimes according to this principle, it is arbitrary to invoke it as a requirement of justice in the punishment of murderers.

If, however, the principle of just deserts is understood to require that the severity of punishments must be proportional to the gravity of the crime, and that murder being the gravest crime deserves the severest punishment, then the principle is no doubt sound. But it does not compel support for the death penalty. What it does require is that crimes other than murder be punished with terms of imprisonment or other deprivations less severe than those used in the punishment of murder.

Criminals no doubt deserve to be punished, and punished with severity appropriate to their culpability and the harm they have caused to the innocent. But severity of punishment has its limits—imposed both by justice and our common human dignity. Governments that respect these limits do not use premeditated, violent homicide as an instrument of social policy.

Someone whose loved one was a murder victim believes that they cannot rest until the murderer is executed. But the feeling is by no means universal. Coretta Scott King has observed, "As one whose husband and mother-in-law have died the victims of murder assassination, I stand firmly and unequivocally opposed to the death penalty for those convicted of capital offenses. An evil deed is not redeemed by an evil deed of retaliation. Justice is never advanced in the taking of a human life. Morality is never upheld by a legalized murder."[47]

Kerry Kennedy, daughter of the slain Senator Robert Kennedy, has written: "I was eight years old when my father was murdered. It is almost impossible to describe the pain of losing a parent to a senseless murder. . . . But even as a child one thing was clear to me: I didn't want the killer, in turn, to be killed. I remember lying in bed and praying, 'Please, God. Please don't take his life, too.' I saw nothing that could be accomplished in the loss of one life being answered with the loss of another. And I knew, far too vividly, the anguish that would spread through another family—another set of parents, children, brothers, and sisters thrown into grief."[48]

Financial Costs

It is sometimes suggested that abolishing capital punishment is unfair to the taxpayer, as though life imprisonment were obviously more expensive than executions. If one takes into account all the relevant costs, the reverse is true. "The death penalty is not now, nor has it ever been, a more economical alternative to life imprisonment."[49]

A murder trial normally takes much longer when the death penalty is at issue than when it is not. Litigation costs—including the time of judges, prosecutors, public defenders, and court reporters, and the high costs of briefs—are all borne by the taxpayer.

A 1982 study showed that were the death penalty to be reintroduced in New York, the cost of the capital trial alone would be more than double the cost of a life term in prison.[50]

In Maryland, a comparison of capital trial costs with and without the death penalty for the years 1979–1984 concluded that a death penalty case costs "approximately 42 percent more than a case resulting in a non-death sentence."[51] In 1988 and 1989 the Kansas legislature voted against reinstating the death penalty after it was informed that reintroduction would involve a first-year cost of "more than $11 million."[52] Florida, with one of the nation's largest death rows, has estimated that the true cost of each execution is approximately $3.2 million, or approximately six times the cost of a life-imprisonment sentence.[53]

The only way to make the death penalty a "better buy" than imprisonment is to weaken due process and curtail appellate review, which are the defendant's (and society's) only protections against the grossest miscarriages of justice. The savings in dollars would be at the cost of justice: In nearly half of the death-penalty cases given review under federal habeas corpus, the conviction is overturned.[54]

Public Opinion

The media commonly report that the American public overwhelmingly supports the death penalty. More careful analysis of public attitudes, however, reveals that most Americans would oppose the death penalty if convicted murderers were sentenced to life without parole and were required to make some form of financial restitution. In California, for example, a Field Institute survey showed that in 1990, 82 percent approved in principle of the death penalty. But when asked to choose between the death penalty and life imprisonment plus restitution, only a small minority—26 percent—continued to favor executions.[55]

A comparable change in attitude toward the death penalty has been verified in many other states and contradicted in none.

Abolition Trends

The death penalty in the United States needs to be put into international perspective. In 1962, it was reported to the Council of Europe that "the facts clearly show that the death penalty is regarded in Europe as something of an anachronism. . . ."[56]

Today, 28 European countries have abolished the death penalty either in law or in practice. In Great Britain, it was abolished (except for treason) in 1971; France abolished it in 1981. Canada abolished it in 1976. The United Nations General Assembly affirmed in a formal resolution that, throughout the world, it is desirable to "progressively restrict the number of offenses for which the death penalty might be imposed, with a view to the desirability of abolishing this punishment."[57]

Conspicuous by their indifference to these recommendations are nations generally known for their disregard for the human rights of their citizens: China, Iraq, Iran, South Africa, and the former Soviet Union.[58] Americans ought to be embarrassed to find themselves linked with the governments of such nations in retaining execution as a method of crime control.

Opposition to the death penalty in the United States is widespread and diverse. Catholic, Jewish, and Protestant religious groups, national organizations representing people of color, and public-interest law groups are among the more than fifty national organizations that constitute the National Coalition to Abolish the Death Penalty.

Once in use everywhere and for a wide variety of crimes, the death penalty today is generally forbidden by law and widely abandoned in practice. The unmistakable worldwide trend is toward the complete abolition of capital punishment.

For Further Information and Reference

Additional copies of this pamphlet, as well as resource materials such as newsletters, books, legal and legislative information, death-row census, reprinted articles, bibliographies, and referrals to other national and state-wide anti-death penalty groups, may be obtained from the Capital Punishment Project, American Civil Liberties Union, 201 West Main Street, Suite 402, Durham, NC 27701. The National Coalition to Abolish the Death Penalty, which coordinates the work of a wide variety of organizations opposed to capital punishment, is located at 1705 De Sales Street, NW (5th floor) Washington, D.C., 20036.

No one volume on the death penalty currently serves as an up-to-date source book on all aspects of the subject. *The Death Penalty in America*, 3rd ed., ed. Hugo Adam Bedau, Oxford University Press, 1982, is still useful, and a new edition is in preparation. Many other recent volumes contain valuable information and argument, including: Welsh S. White, *The Death Penalty in the Nineties*, University of Michigan Press, 1991; Samuel R. Gross and Robert Mauro, *Death and Discrimination*, Northeastern University Press, 1989; Michael L. Radelet, ed., *Facing the Death Penalty*, Temple University Press, 1989; Kenneth C. Haas and James A. Inciardi, eds., *Challenging Capital Punishment*, Sage Publications, 1988; *United States of America—The Death Penalty*, Amnesty International Publications, 1987; Franklin E. Zimring and Gordon Hawkins, *Capital Punishment and the American Agenda*, Cambridge University Press, 1986; William J. Bowers, *Legal Homicide: Death as Punishment in America, 1864–1982*, Northeastern University Press, 1984; Charles L. Black, Jr., *Capital Punishment*, 2nd ed., W. W. Norton, 1981. The wealth of scholarly literature up through 1988 can be traced with the help of *Capital Punishment in America: An Annotated Bibliography*, Garland Publishing, 1988, edited by Michael L. Radelet and Margaret Vandiver.

Four more specialized volumes deserve mention as well: Michael L. Radelet, Hugo Adam Bedau, and Constance E. Putnam, *In Spite of Innocence: Erroneous Convictions in Capital Cases*, Northeastern University Press, 1992; Robert M. Bohm, ed., *The Death Penalty in America: Current Research*, Anderson Publishing Co., 1991; Victor T. Streib, *Death Penalty for Juveniles*, Indiana University Press, 1987; and Louis P. Masur, *Rites of Execution: Capital Punishment and the Transformation of American Culture, 1776–1865*, Oxford University Press, 1989.

Several scholarly and legal journals have devoted whole issues to various legal, sociological, and historical aspects of the problem of the death penalty, notably *Dickinson Law Review*, vol. 95, no. 4, Summer 1991; *New York University Review of Law & Social Change*, vol. 18, nos. 2 and 3, 1990–1991; *Albany Law Review*, vol. 54, nos. 3/4, 1990; *Loyola of Los Angeles Law Review*, vol. 23, no. 1, November 1989; *Journal of Contemporary Criminal Justice*, vol.

5, no. 4, December 1989; *Law and Human Behavior*, vol. 8, nos. 1/2, June 1984; *U.C. Davis Law Review*, vol. 18, no. 4, summer 1985; *Journal of Criminal Law and Criminology*, vol. 74, no. 3, fall 1983.

Among the recent U.S. government publications containing information of general interest are: "The Federal Death Penalty Act of 1989," Report of the Senate Committee on the Judiciary, 101st Congress, 1st Session, October 1989; "Death Penalty," Hearings before Committee on the Judiciary, U.S. Senate, 101st Congress, 1st Session, September–October 1989; "Establishing Constitutional Procedures for the Imposition of Capital Punishment," Report of the Senate Committee on the Judiciary, 99th Congress, 2d Session, April 1986; "Capital Punishment," Hearings before Subcommittee on Criminal Justice, U.S. House of Representatives, 99th Congress, 1st and 2d Sessions, November 1985–July 1986; "Death Penalty Legislation," Hearings before the Committee on the Judiciary, U.S. Senate, 99th Congress, 1st Session, September 1985. For earlier federal government publications, see the bibliography by Radelet and Vandiver, pp. 219–20.

Statistical information on death sentences and executions since 1930 may be obtained in the U.S. Bureau of Justice Statistics Bulletin, *Capital Punishment*, an annual report appearing under various titles since the 1950s. The NAACP Legal Defense and Educational Fund publishes *Death Row, U.S.A.*, issued since the 1970s several times a year; it reports current demographic information on executions and the death row population.

Notes

1. See U.S. Dept. Justice, *Capital Punishment*, annually, 1980 et seq.
2. See *Uniform Crime Reports*, annually, 1980 et seq.
3. See *Uniform Crime Reports*.
4. *Uniform Crime Reports*, annually, 1980–1989.
5. Bowers and Pierce, "Deterrence or Brutalization," in *Crime and Delinquency* (1980).
6. U.S. Dept. Justice, *Capital Punishment*, 1972–1990; *Uniform Crime Reports*, annually, 1972–1990; and NAACP Legal Defense and Educational Fund, *Death Row, USA*, Spring 1992.
7. Bailey and Peterson, in *Criminology* (1987), p. 22.
8. *Sourcebook of Criminal Justice Statistics—1990*.
9. Bureau of Justice Statistics, *Prisons and Prisoners in the United States* (1992), p. 1.
10. Wolfson, in Bedau, ed., *The Death Penalty in America*, 3rd ed. (1982), p. 167.
11. Ehrlich, in *American Economic Review* (1974); Phillips, in *American Journal of Sociology* (1980); and Layson, in *Southern Economic Journal* (1985).
12. Lempert, in *Crime and Delinquency* (1983); Peterson and Bailey in Chambliss, ed., *Criminal Law in Action*, 2nd ed. (1984); Bowers, in Hasse and Inciardi, eds., *Challenging Capital Punishment* (1988); Peterson and Cello, in *Social Forces* (1988); and Fox and Radelet, in *Loyola of Los Angeles Law Review* (1989).
13. Blumstein, Cohen, and Nagin, eds., *Deterrence and Incapacitation* (1975), p. 358.
14. West, Solomon, and Diamond, in Bedau and Pierce, eds., *Capital Punishment in the United States* (1976).
15. Bedau, "Recidivism, Parole, and Deterrence," in Bedau, ed., *Death Penalty in America*, 3rd ed.
16. Marquart and Sorensen, in *Loyola of Los Angeles Law Review* (1989).
17. U.S. Bureau of Justice Statistics, "Capital Punishment," 1977, and NAACP LDF, *Death Row, USA*, Spring 1992.
18. Bowers, *Legal Homicide* (1984); Streib, *Death Penalty for Juveniles* (1987).
19. *Death Row, USA*, 1976 et seq.
20. *Uniform Crime Reports*, 1972–1990.
21. Baldus, Woodworth, and Pulaski, *Equal Justice and the Death Penalty* (1990), p. 401.
22. U.S. General Accounting Office, *Death Penalty Sentencing* (1990), pp. 5, 6.
23. *Death Row, USA*, Spring 1992; and *Sourcebook of Criminal Justice Statistics—1990*.
24. U.S. Bureau of Justice Statistics, *Capital Punishment*, 1980–1990.
25. *Uniform Crime Reports*, 1980–1990.
26. Memorandum, National Coalition to Abolish the Death Penalty, January 1991.
27. U.S. Bureau of Justice Statistics, *Capital Punishment*, 1979; NAACP LDF, *Death Row, USA*, Spring 1992.
28. Tabak, in *Loyola of Los Angeles Law Review* (1989).
29. Gross and Mauro, *Death and Discrimination* (1989), p. 224.
30. Black, *Capital Punishment: The Inevitability of Caprice and Mistake*, 2nd ed. (1982).
31. Lucas Recueil des debats . . . (1831) pt. II, p. 32.

32. Radelet, Bedau, and Putnam, *In Spite of Innocence* (1992); Bedau and Radelet, "Miscarriages of Justice in Potentially Capital Cases," *Stanford Law Review* (1987).

33. Miller, *Invitation to a Lynching* (1975); also *New York Times*, Sept. 10, 1975, p. 1.

34. "Capital Punishment" Senate Hearings (1981) pp. 713–20

35. *Atlanta Weekly*, May 30, 1982.

36. Adams, Hoffer, and Hoffer, *Adams v. Texas* (1991).

37. Davies, *White Lies* (1991).

38. *Glass v. Louisiana*, 471 U.S. 1080 (1985).

39. *Boston Globe*, April 24, 1983, p. 24.

40. *New York Times*, December 14, 1988, p. A29.

41. Ibid.

42. *Los Angeles Times*, March 24, 1985, Pt. IV, p. 5.

43. Lawes, *Life and Death in Sing Sing* (1928).

44. Teeters, in *Journal of the Lancaster County Historical Society* (1960).

45. *Boston Globe*, August 16, 1976, p. 17

46. Camus, "Reflections on the Guillotine," in *Resistance, Rebellion and Death* (1960).

47. Speech to National Coalition to Abolish the Death Penalty, Washington, D.C., September 26, 1981.

48. Foreword to Gray and Stanley, *A Punishment in Search of a Crime* (1989).

49. Spangenberg and Walsh, in *Loyola of Los Angeles Law Review* (1989), p. 47

50. N.Y. State Defenders Assn., *Capital Losses* (1982).

51. U.S. Govt. Accounting Office, *Limited Data Available on Costs of Death Sentences* (1989), p. 50.

52. Cited in Spangenberg and Walsh, note 49.

53. *Miami Herald*, July 10, 1988.

54. *New York Times*, Sept. 22, 1989

55. *New York Times*, May 28, 1990; and Fox, Radelet, and Bonsteel, in *N.Y.U. Review of Law and Social Change* (1990–91).

56. Ancel, *The Death Penalty in European Countries* (1962), p. 55.

57. UN, Ecosoc, Official Records 58th Sess. (1971), Supl. 1, p. 36.

58. Hood, *The Death Penalty: A World-Wide Perspective* (1989); Amnesty International, *When the State Kills . . .* (1989).

QUESTIONS

1. How many distinct arguments does Bedau present?
2. Are any of the arguments *decisive*? That is, were a particular argument to be sound—the conclusion follows from the premises, and the premises are all true—would that settle the question of the permissibility of the death penalty? Or would it merely be one consideration to weigh against others?

38. Why the Death Penalty Is Morally Permissible

LOUIS J. POJMAN

*L*ouis *J. Pojman* (1935–2005) was professor of philosophy emeritus at the U.S. Military Academy at West Point. He held doctoral degrees in theology (Union Theological Seminary) and philosophy (Oxford). He wrote extensively about ethics, in particular the topics examined in this reader. He was the author of *Life and Death: Grappling with the Moral Dilemmas of Our Time* (2000), as well as editor of a reader with the same title.

In this essay Pojman defends the death penalty against its critics. He offers retributive as well as deterrent arguments in favor of the death penalty. And he attempts to rebut a number of other considerations brought against capital punishment.

The death penalty as punishment for the most serious crimes is morally justified. Honest people and philosophers may disagree on these matters, but I will present my reasons for supporting the retention of this practice. I have no illusions about my ability to change the minds of my ardent abolitionist opponents, but I can hope to clear the air of misperceptions and help those with an open mind come to an informed judgment of this crucial matter.

First, let me briefly comment on specific claims in Hugo Bedau's essay "An Abolitionist's Survey of the Death Penalty in America Today."[1] (1) Bedau contends that "today it ought to be impossible not to regard death in the electric chair as 'cruel and unusual punishment' in direct violation of such punishments in the Eighth Amendment in the Bill of Rights" (p. 5). Why? I take it that the idea of "cruel and unusual" simply means morally unjustified and unconscionable. If so, we need an argument for this conjunction. I fail to see that death in the electric chair is either "immoral or unconscionable." After all, the criminal has committed a heinous act of violence with malice aforethought. I would argue that

the electric chair, far from being unconscionable, is completely justified. Painless lethal injection, which is the process of choice in many states, seems too good for someone who in callous disregard for his victim shed innocent blood. Hanging or the firing squad or a painful electric shock seem more fitting to most acts of murder. (2) Along these same lines, Bedau notes that until the mid-twentieth century many jurisdictions imposed the death penalty for numerous crimes besides murder, including rape, kidnapping, and treason (p. 7). I take it that the implicit argument is that as we become more enlightened and recognize the inherent dignity of human beings, we gradually will narrow the scope of the death penalty until it covers the set of fewer crimes, to the point where it is abolished altogether. I have a different interpretation. We have suffered a loss of confidence in the ability of our society to carry out justice, a failure of nerve. A society that is inured to watching violence in movies and on TV but condemns parents for spanking their children as an act of discipline may not have the inner moral resources to discriminate between morally

From Louis P. Pojman, "Why the Death Penalty Is Morally Permissible," in *Debating the Death Penalty: Should America Have Capital Punishment? The Experts on Both Sides Make Their Case*, ed. Hugo Adam Bedau and Paul G. Cassell (New York: Oxford University Press, 2004), pp. 51–75. Reprinted by permission of Gertrude Pojman.

permissible and impermissible use of force. I suspect that a growing awareness of the sociological influences on criminals has resulted in a tendency to minimize the responsibility of criminals. Child molesters often were molested themselves, abusive people were victims of abuse. "To understand all is to forgive all." There is some truth in these generalizations, but it is a gross fallacy to infer that because we are influenced by our upbringing or heredity, we should not be held responsible for our behavior. A more robust notion of personal responsibility might lead us to extend the death penalty to those who grossly violate the public trust, to include CEOs who actively destroyed the pension plans of their employees, as was the case in 2002 with Enron and WorldCom. In 2002 Enron Corporation declared bankruptcy. It announced that thousands of lower-ranking employees would lose their retirement programs, while 29 top executives took in $1.1 billion, selling shares of company stock, with CEO Kenneth Lay scoring $101.4 million. Around the same time, at WorldCom, chief financial officer Scott Sullivan sold $45.4 million in company stock, quietly shifting $3.9 billion in expenses to make the company look more profitable. The bubble bursts; the firm declares bankruptcy and lays off 17,000 workers. The leaders of these large companies probably did more overall harm to their employees than a murderer. While it is evil to take the life of one innocent person, it is also grossly evil to destroy the pension plans of thousands of employees due to greed and dishonesty, while securing millions of dollars for oneself. The cumulative effect of such deliberate deception and disregard for one's employees may be worse than that of the single murder. If the death penalty is an appropriate punishment for those who commit treason, it is applicable to business executives who violate the public trust and undermine faith in our economic system. In applying the death penalty to white collar crimes, we would be applying it more fairly.[2] The rich, who seldom are tempted to murder, would be subject to the same capital punishment as now is usually reserved for the poor. Some cases of rape, kidnapping, treason, and white collar crimes like embezzlement of the savings of elderly and vulnerable people may well merit the death penalty. Perhaps our ancestors erred on the side of being too hard on offenders. We may be erring in being too soft on them. The goal is to seek the right golden mean, giving the criminal what he or she deserves.

(3) Bedau quotes with approval Laura Mansnerus's contention that "almost all murderers . . . studied show evidence of brain damage" (p. 10). That is too broad a category, hardly a sufficient condition to abolish punishment. Probably most adults have experienced some brain damage during their lives brought on by alcohol consumption and drug use, strokes, injuries to the head, and chemical imbalances. I read of one study in England showing that many soccer players had incurred brain damage (presumably brought on by hitting the ball with their heads). Unless we can establish a correlation between the specific brain damage and the specific crimes committed, we ought to presume that people are responsible for their behavior, that including their violent acts. Mansnerus's thesis, if confirmed, would prove too much—namely, that no one should be punished for murder since such brain-damaged people cannot be held accountable for their acts. Where we have evidence of brain damage or impaired ability, such as in the case of a retarded or (temporarily) insane criminal, we do mitigate or cancel the proposed punishment.

(4) Bedau appeals to Beccaria's principle of Minimal Invasion that given a state interest the government "must use the least restrictive means sufficient to achieve that goal or purpose" (p. 19). Bedau admits that punishment for a crime is a legitimate practice, but opts for the Minimal Invasion principle as a constraint on that punishment. I too agree that we ought to minimize suffering, all things being equal, but sometimes things are not equal, for the criminal may deserve more than a minimal punishment, deserving, in fact, the death penalty. So the Minimal Invasion principle may be overridden in the name of justice. Bedau wants to place a *ceiling* on punitive desert, but there may also be a *floor* on punishment. Sometimes nothing less than harsh punishment is justified. (5) Bedau argues against those like Attorney General John Ashcroft who hold that the death penalty produces closure in the families of the victims. He rightly notes that sometimes it doesn't bring that sense of cathartic

relief (p. 33). I agree with Bedau here and do not use the closure argument in my defense, though the families of victims often do express satisfaction that the murderer has been executed. So much the better. But this is not a sufficient argument for the death penalty. I turn now to my case for the death penalty.

A Defense of the Death Penalty

> Who so sheddeth man's blood, by man shall his blood be shed.
>
> —(Genesis 9:6)

There is an ancient tradition, going back to biblical times, but endorsed by the mainstream of philosophers, from Plato to Thomas Aquinas, from Thomas Hobbes to Immanuel Kant, Thomas Jefferson, John Stuart Mill, and C. S. Lewis, that a fitting punishment for murder is the execution of the murderer. One prong of this tradition, the *backward-looking* or deontological position, epitomized in Aquinas and Kant, holds that because human beings, as rational agents, have dignity, one who with malice aforethought kills a human being forfeits his right to life and deserves to die. The other, the *forward-looking* or consequentialist, tradition, exemplified by Jeremy Bentham, Mill, and Ernest van den Haag, holds that punishment ought to serve as a deterrent, and that capital punishment is an adequate deterrent to prospective murderers. Abolitionists like Bedau and Jeffrey Reiman[3] deny both prongs of the traditional case for the death penalty. They hold that long prison sentences are a sufficient retributive response to murder and that the death penalty probably does not serve as a deterrent or is no better deterrent than other forms of punishment. I will argue that both traditional defenses are sound and together they make a strong case for retaining the death penalty. That is, I hold a combined theory of punishment. A backward-looking judgment that the criminal has committed a heinous crime plus a forward-looking judgment that a harsh punishment will deter would-be murderers is sufficient to justify the death penalty. I turn first to the retributivist theory in favor of capital punishment.

Retribution

The small crowd that gathered outside the prison to protest the execution of Steven Judy softly sang, "We Shall Overcome" . . . But it didn't seem quite the same hearing it sung out of concern for someone who, on finding a woman with a flat tire, raped and murdered her and drowned her three small children, then said that he hadn't been "losing any sleep" over his crimes. . . .

I remember the grocer's wife. She was a plump, happy woman who enjoyed the long workday she shared with her husband in their ma-and-pa store. One evening, two young men came in and showed guns, and the grocer gave them everything in the cash register.

For no reason, almost as an afterthought, one of the men shot the grocer in the face. The woman stood only a few feet from her husband when he was turned into a dead, bloody mess.

She was about 50 when it happened. In a few years her mind was almost gone, and she looked 80. They might as well have killed her too.

Then there was the woman I got to know after her daughter was killed by a wolfpack gang during a motoring trip. The mother called me occasionally, but nothing that I said could ease her torment. It ended when she took her own life.

A couple of years ago I spent a long evening with the husband, sister and parents of a fine young woman who had been forced into the trunk of a car in a hospital parking lot. The degenerate who kidnapped her kept her in the trunk, like an ant in a jar, until he got tired of the game. Then he killed her.[4]

Human beings have dignity as self-conscious rational agents who are able to act morally. One could maintain that it is precisely their moral goodness or innocence that bestows dignity and a right to life on them. Intentionally taking the life of an innocent human being is so evil that absent mitigating circumstances, the perpetrator forfeits his own right to life. He or she deserves to die.

The retributivist holds three propositions: (1) that all the guilty deserve to be punished; (2) that only the guilty deserve to be punished; and (3) that the guilty deserve to be punished in proportion to the severity of their crime. Thomas Jefferson supported such a system of proportionality of punishment to crime:

Whosoever shall be guilty of rape, polygamy, sodomy with man or woman, shall be punished, if a man, by castration, if a woman by cutting through the cartilage of her nose a hole of one half inch in diameter at the least. [And] whosoever shall maim another, or shall disfigure him . . . shall be maimed, or disfigured in the like sort: or if that cannot be, for want of some part, then as nearly as may be, in some other part of at least equal value.[5]

Criminals like Steven Judy, Jeffrey Dahmer, Timothy McVeigh, Ted Bundy (who is reported to have raped and murdered over 100 women), John Mohammed and John Lee Malvo, who murdered 12 people in the killing spree of 2002, and the two men who gunned down the grocer (mentioned in the quotation by Royko, above) have committed capital offenses and deserve nothing less than capital punishment.[6] No doubt malicious acts like the ones committed by these criminals deserve worse punishment than death, and I would be open to suggestions of torture (why not?), but at a minimum, the death penalty seems warranted.

People often confuse *retribution* with *revenge*. Governor George Ryan, who recently commuted the sentences of all the prisoners on death row in the State of Illinois, quotes a letter from the Reverend Desmond Tutu that "to take a life when a life has been lost is revenge, it is not justice."[7] This is simply false. While moral people will feel outrage at acts of heinous crimes, such as those described above by Mike Royko, the moral justification of punishment is not *vengeance*, but *desert*. Vengeance signifies inflicting harm on the offender out of anger because of what he has done. Retribution is the rationally supported theory that the criminal deserves a punishment fitting the gravity of his crime.

The nineteenth-century British philosopher James Fitzjames Stephens thought vengeance was a justification for punishment, arguing that punishment should be inflicted "for the sake of ratifying the feeling of hatred—call it revenge, resentment, or what you will—which the contemplation of such [offensive] conduct excites in healthily constituted minds."[8] But retributivism is not based on hatred for the criminal (though a feeling of vengeance may accompany the punishment). Retributivism is the theory that the criminal *deserves* to be punished and

deserves to be punished in proportion to the gravity of his or her crime, whether or not the victim or anyone else desires it. We may all deeply regret having to carry out the punishment, but consider it warranted.

On the other hand, people do have a sense of outrage and passion for revenge directed at criminals for their crimes. Imagine that someone in your family was on the receiving end of Steven Judy's violent acts. Stephens was correct in asserting that "[t]he criminal law stands to the passion for revenge in much the same relation as marriage to the sexual appetite."[9] Failure to punish would no more lessen our sense of vengeance than the elimination of marriage would lessen our sexual appetite. When a society fails to punish criminals in a way thought to be proportionate to the gravity of the crime, the danger arises that the public would take the law into its own hands, resulting in vigilante justice, lynch mobs, and private acts of retribution. The outcome is likely to be an anarchistic, insecure state of injustice. As such, legal retribution stands as a safeguard for an orderly application of punitive desert.

Our natural instinct is for *vengeance,* but civilization demands that we restrain our anger and go through a legal process, letting the outcome determine whether and to what degree to punish the accused. Civilization demands that we not take the law into our own hands, but it should also satisfy our deepest instincts when they are consonant with reason. Our instincts tell us that some crimes, like McVeigh's, Judy's, and Bundy's, should be severely punished, but we refrain from personally carrying out those punishments, committing ourselves to the legal processes. The death penalty is supported by our gut animal instincts as well as our sense of justice as desert.

The death penalty reminds us that there are consequences to our actions, that we are responsible for what we do, so that dire consequences for immoral actions are eminently appropriate. The death penalty is such a fitting response to evil.

Deterrence

The second tradition justifying the death penalty is the utilitarian theory of deterrence. This holds that by executing convicted murderers we will deter would-be murderers from killing innocent people. The evidence for deterrence is controversial. Some scholars, like Thornstein Sellin and Bedau, argue that the death penalty is not a deterrent of homicides superior to long-term imprisonment. Others, such as Isaac Ehrlich, make a case for the death penalty as a significant deterrent.[10] Granted that the evidence is ambiguous, and honest scholars can differ on the results. However, one often hears abolitionists claiming the evidence shows that the death penalty fails to deter homicide.[11] This is too strong a claim. The sociological evidence doesn't show either that the death penalty deters or that it fails to deter. The evidence is simply inconclusive. But a commonsense case can be made for deterrence.

Imagine that every time someone intentionally killed an innocent person he was immediately struck down by lightning. When mugger Mike slashed his knife into the neck of the elderly pensioner, lightning struck, killing Mike. His fellow muggers witnessed the sequence of events. When burglar Bob pulled his pistol out and shot the bank teller through her breast, a bolt leveled Bob, his compatriots beholding the spectacle. Soon men with their guns lying next to them were found all across the world in proximity to the corpses of their presumed victims. Do you think that the evidence of cosmic retribution would go unheeded?

We can imagine the murder rate in the United States and everywhere else plummeting. The close correlation between murder and cosmic retribution would serve as a deterrent to would-be murderers. If this thought experiment is sound, we have a prima facie argument for the deterrent effect of capital punishment. In its ideal, prompt performance, the death penalty would likely deter most rational criminally minded from committing murder. The question then becomes how do we institute the death penalty so as to have the maximal deterrent effect without violating the rights of the accused.

We would have to bring the accused to trial more quickly and limit the appeals process of those found guilty "beyond reasonable doubt." Having DNA evidence should make this more feasible than hitherto. Furthermore, public executions of the convicted murderer would serve as a reminder that crime does not pay. Public executions of criminals seem an efficient way to communicate the message that if you shed innocent blood, you will pay a high price. Bedau cites Nat Hentoff's advocacy of a public execution of Timothy McVeigh in terms of being accountable for such actions (p. 4). I agree with Hentoff on the matter of accountability but also believe such publicity would serve to deter homicide.

Abolitionists like Stephen Nathanson argue that because the statistical evidence in favor of the deterrent effect of capital punishment is indecisive, we have no basis for concluding that it is a better deterrent than long prison sentences.[12] If I understand these opponents, their argument presents us with an exclusive disjunct: Either we must have conclusive statistical evidence (i.e., a proof) for the deterrent effect of the death penalty, or we have no grounds for supposing that the death penalty deters. Many people accept this argument. Recently, a colleague said to me, "There is no statistical evidence that the death penalty deters," as if to dismiss the argument from deterrence altogether. This is premature judgment, for the argument commits the fallacy of supposing that only two opposites are possible. There is a middle position that holds that while we cannot prove conclusively that the death penalty deters, the weight of evidence supports its deterrence. Furthermore, I think there are too many variables to hold constant for us to prove via statistics the deterrence hypothesis, and even if the requisite statistics were available, we could question whether they were cases of mere correlation versus causation. On the other hand, commonsense or anecdotal evidence may provide insight into the psychology of human motivation, providing evidence that fear of the death penalty deters some types of would-be criminals from committing murder.[13] Granted, people are sometimes deceived about their motivation. But usually they are not deceived, and, as a rule, we should presume they know their motives until we have evidence to the contrary. The general commonsense argument goes like this:

1. What people (including potential criminals) fear more will have a greater deterrent effect on them.
2. People (including potential criminals) fear death more than they do any other humane punishment.

3. The death penalty is a humane punishment.
4. Therefore, people (including criminals) will be deterred more by the death penalty than by any other humane punishment.

Since the purpose of this argument is to show that the death penalty very likely deters more than long-term prison sentences, I am assuming it is *humane*—that is, acceptable to the moral sensitivities of the majority in our society. Torture might deter even more, but it is not considered humane. I will say more about the significance of humaneness with regard to the death penalty below.

Common sense informs us that most people would prefer to remain out of jail, that the threat of public humiliation is enough to deter some people, that a sentence of 20 years will deter most people more than a sentence of two years, that a life sentence will deter most would-be criminals more than a sentence of 20 years. I think that we have commonsense evidence that the death penalty is a better deterrent than prison sentences. For one thing, as Richard Herrnstein and James Q. Wilson have argued in *Crime and Human Nature,* a great deal of crime is committed on a cost-benefit schema, wherein the criminal engages in some form of risk assessment as to his or her chances of getting caught and punished in some manner. If he or she estimates the punishment mild, the crime becomes inversely attractive, and vice versa.[14] The fact that those who are condemned to death do everything in their power to get their sentences postponed or reduced to long-term prison sentences, in the way *lifers* do not, shows that they fear death more than life in prison.

The point is this: Imprisonment constitutes one evil, the loss of freedom, but the death penalty imposes a more severe loss, that of life itself. If you lock me up, I may work for a parole or pardon, I may learn to live stoically with diminished freedom, and I can plan for the day my freedom will be restored. But if I believe that my crime may lead to death, or loss of freedom followed by death, then I have more to fear than mere imprisonment. I am faced with a great evil plus an even greater evil. I fear death more than imprisonment because it alone takes from me all future possibility.

I am not claiming that the fear of legal punishment is all that keeps us from criminal behavior. Moral character, good habit, fear of being shamed, peer pressure, fear of authority, or the fear of divine retribution may have a greater influence on some people. However, many people will be deterred from crime, including murder, by the threat of severe punishment. The abolitionist points out that many would-be murderers simply do not believe they will be caught. Perhaps this is true for some. While the fantastic egoist has delusions of getting away with his crime, many would-be criminals are not so bold or delusionary.

Former Prosecuting Attorney for the State of Florida, Richard Gernstein, has set forth the commonsense case for deterrence. First of all, he claims, the death penalty certainly deters the murderer from any further murders, including those he or she might commit within the prison where he is confined. Second, statistics cannot tell us how many potential criminals have refrained from taking another's life through fear of the death penalty. He quotes Judge Hyman Barshay of New York: "The death penalty is a warning, just like a lighthouse throwing its beams out to sea. We hear about shipwrecks, but we do not hear about the ships the lighthouse guides safely on their way. We do not have proof of the number of ships it saves, but we do not tear the lighthouse down."[15]

Some of the commonsense evidence is anecdotal, as the following quotation shows. British member of Parliament Arthur Lewis explains how he was converted from an abolitionist to a supporter of the death penalty:

One reason that has stuck in my mind, and which has proved [deterrence] to me beyond question, is that there was once a professional burglar in [my] constituency who consistently boasted of the fact that he had spent about one-third of his life in prison. . . . He said to me "I am a professional burglar. Before we go out on a job we plan it down to every detail. Before we go into the boozer to have a drink we say 'Don't forget, no shooters'—shooters being guns." He adds "We did our job and didn't have shooters because at that time there was capital punishment. Our wives, girlfriends and our mums said, 'Whatever you do, do not carry a shooter because if you are caught you might be topped [executed].' If you do away with capital punishment they will all be carrying shooters."

It is difficult to know how widespread this reasoning is. My own experience corroborates this testimony. Growing up in the infamous Cicero, Illinois, home of Al Capone and the Mafia, I had friends who went into crime, mainly burglary and larceny. It was common knowledge that one stopped short of killing in the act of robbery. A prison sentence could be dealt with—especially with a good lawyer—but being convicted of murder, which at that time included a reasonable chance of being electrocuted, was an altogether different matter. No doubt exists in my mind that the threat of the electric chair saved the lives of some of those who were robbed in my town. No doubt some crimes are committed in the heat of passion or by the temporally (or permanently) insane, but some are committed through a process of risk assessment. Burglars, kidnappers, traitors and vindictive people will sometimes be restrained by the threat of death. We simply don't know how much capital punishment deters, but this sort of commonsense, anecdotal evidence must be taken into account in assessing the institution of capital punishment.

John Stuart Mill admitted that capital punishment does not inspire terror in hardened criminals, but it may well make an impression on prospective murderers. "As for what is called the failure of the death punishment, who is able to judge of that? We partly know who those are whom it has not deterred; but who is there who knows whom it has deterred, or how many human beings it has saved who would have lived to be murderers if that awful association had not been thrown round the idea of murder from their earliest infancy?"[16] Mill's points are well taken: (1) Not everyone will be deterred by the death penalty, but some will; (2) the potential criminal need not consciously calculate a cost-benefit analysis regarding his crime to be deterred by the threat. The idea of the threat may have become a subconscious datum "from their earliest infancy." The repeated announcement and regular exercise of capital punishment may have deep causal influence.

Gernstein quotes the British Royal Commission on Capital Punishment (1949–53), which is one of the most thorough studies on the subject and which concluded that there was evidence that the death penalty has some deterrent effect on normal human beings. Some of its evidence in favor of the deterrence effect includes these points:

1. Criminals who have committed an offense punishable by life imprisonment, when faced with capture, refrained from killing their captor though by killing, escape seemed probable. When asked why they refrained from the homicide, quick response indicated a willingness to serve life sentence, but not risk the death penalty.
2. Criminals about to commit certain offenses refrained from carrying deadly weapons. Upon apprehension, answers to questions concerning absence of such weapons indicated a desire to avoid more serious punishment by carrying a deadly weapon, and also to avoid use of the weapon which could result in imposition of the death penalty.
3. Victims have been removed from a capital punishment State to a non-capital punishment State to allow the murderer opportunity for homicide without threat to his own life. This in itself demonstrates that the death penalty is considered by some would-be-killers.[17]

Gernstein then quotes former District Attorney of New York, Frank S. Hogan, representing himself and his associates:

We are satisfied from our experience that the deterrent effect is both real and substantial . . . for example, from time to time accomplices in felony murder state with apparent truthfulness that in the planning of the felony they strongly urged the killer not to resort to violence. From the context of these utterances, it is apparent that they were led to these warnings to the killer by fear of the death penalty which they realized might follow the taking of life. Moreover, victims of hold-ups have occasionally reported that one of the robbers expressed a desire to kill them and was dissuaded from so doing by a confederate. Once again, we think it not unreasonable to suggest that fear of the death penalty played a role in some of these intercessions.

On a number of occasions, defendants being questioned in connection with homicide have shown a striking terror of the death penalty. While these persons have in fact perpetrated homicide, we think that their terror of the death penalty must be symptomatic of the attitude of many others of their type, as a result of which many lives have been spared.[18]

It seems likely that the death penalty does not deter as much as it could due to its inconsistent and rare use. For example, out of an estimated 23,370 cases of murder, nonnegligent manslaughter, and rape in 1949, only 119 executions were carried out in the United States. In 1953, only 62 executions out of 27,000 cases for those crimes took place. Few executions were carried out in the 1960s and none at all from 1967 to 1977. Gernstein points out that at that rate a criminal's chances of escaping execution are better than 100 to 1. Actually, since Gernstein's report, the figures have become even more weighted against the chances of the death sentence. In 1993, there were 24,526 cases of murder and nonnegligent manslaughter and only 56 executions; and in 1994, there were 23,305 cases of murder and nonnegligent manslaughter and only 31 executions—for a ratio of better than 750 to 1. The average length of stay for a prisoner executed in 1994 was 10 years and two months. If potential murderers perceived the death penalty as a highly probable outcome of murder, would they not be more reluctant to kill? Gernstein notes:

> The commissioner of Police of London, England, in his evidence before the Royal Commission on Capital Punishment, told of a gang of armed robbers who continued operations after one of their members was sentenced to death and his sentence commuted to penal servitude, but the same gang disbanded and disappeared when, on a later occasion, two others were convicted of murder and hanged.[19]

Gernstein sums up his data: "Surely it is a common sense argument, based on what is known of human nature, that the death penalty has a deterrent effect particularly for certain kinds of murderers.

Furthermore, as the Royal Commission opined, the death penalty helps to educate the conscience of the whole community, and it arouses among many people a quasi-religious sense of awe. In the mind of the public there remains a strong association between murder and the penalty of death. Certainly one of the factors which restrains some people from murder is fear of punishment and surely, since people fear death more than anything else, the death penalty is the most effective deterrent."[20]

I should also point out that *given the retributivist argument* for the death penalty, based on desert, the retentionist does not have to prove that the death penalty deters *better* than long prison sentences, but if the death penalty is deemed at least as effective as its major alternative, it would be justified. If evidence existed that life imprisonment were a *more effective* deterrent, the retentionist might be hard pressed to defend it on retributivist lines alone. My view is that the desert argument plus the common-sense evidence—being bolstered by the following argument, the Best Bet Argument, strongly supports retention of the death penalty.

The late Ernest van den Haag has set forth what he called the Best Bet Argument.[21] He argued that even though we don't know for certain whether the death penalty deters or prevents other murders, we should bet that it does. Indeed, due to our ignorance, any social policy we take is a gamble. Not to choose capital punishment for first-degree murder is as much a bet that capital punishment doesn't deter as choosing the policy is a bet that it does. There is a significant difference in the betting, however, in that to bet against capital punishment is to bet against the innocent and for the murderer, while to bet for it is to bet against the murderer and for the innocent.

The point is this: We are accountable for what we let happen, as well as for what we actually do. If I fail to bring up my children properly so that they are a menace to society, I am to some extent responsible for their bad behavior. I could have caused it to be somewhat better. If I have good evidence that a bomb will blow up the building you are working in and fail to notify you (assuming I can), I am partly responsible for your death, if and when the bomb explodes. So we are responsible for what we omit doing, as well as for what we do. Purposefully to refrain from a lesser evil which we know will allow a greater evil to occur is to be at least partially responsible for the greater evil. This responsibility for our omissions underlies van den Haag's argument, to which we now return.

Suppose that we choose a policy of capital punishment for capital crimes. In this case we are betting that the death of some murderers will be more than compensated for by the lives of some innocents not being murdered (either by these murderers or others who would have murdered). If we're right, we have saved the lives of the innocent. If we're wrong, unfortunately, we've sacrificed the lives of some murderers. But say we choose not to have a social policy of capital punishment. If capital punishment doesn't work as a deterrent, we've come out ahead, but if it does work, then we've missed an opportunity to save innocent lives. If we value the saving of innocent lives more highly than the loss of the guilty, then to bet on a policy of capital punishment turns out to be rational. Since the innocent have a greater right to life than the guilty, it is our moral duty to adopt a policy that has a chance of protecting them from potential murderers.

It is noteworthy that prominent abolitionists, such as Charles Black, Hugo Adam Bedau, Ramsey Clark, and Henry Schwartzchild, have admitted to Ernest van den Haag that even if every execution were to deter a hundred murders, they would oppose it, from which van den Haag concludes, "To these abolitionist leaders, the life of every murderer is more valuable than the lives of a hundred prospective victims, for these abolitionists would spare the murderer, even if doing so will cost a hundred future victims their lives." Black and Bedau said they would favor abolishing the death penalty even if they knew that doing so would increase the homicide rate 1,000 percent.[22] This response of abolitionists is puzzling, since one of Bedau's arguments against the death penalty is that it doesn't bring back the dead. "We cannot do anything for the dead victims of crime. (How many of those who oppose the death penalty would continue to do so if, *mirabile dictu,* executing the murderer might bring the victim back to life?)"[23] Apparently, he would support the death penalty if it brought a dead victim back to life, but

not if it prevented a hundred innocent victims from being murdered.

If the Best Bet Argument is sound, or if the death penalty does deter would-be murderers, as common sense suggests, then we should support some uses of the death penalty. It should be used for those who commit first-degree murder, for whom no mitigating factors are present, and especially for those who murder police officers, prison guards, and political leaders. Many states rightly favor it for those who murder while committing another crime, such as burglary or rape. It should be used in cases of treason and terrorist bombings. It should also be considered for the perpetrators of egregious white collar crimes such as bank managers embezzling the savings of the public. The savings and loan scandals of the 1980s, involving wealthy bank officials absconding with the investments of elderly pensioners and others, ruined the lives of many people. This gross violation of the public trust warrants the electric chair. Such punishment would meet the two conditions set forth in this paper. The punishment would be deserved and it would likely deter future crimes by people in the public trust. It would also make the death penalty more egalitarian, applicable to the rich as well as the poor.

Let me consider two objections often made to the implementation of the death penalty: that it sometimes leads to the death of innocents and that it discriminates against blacks.

Objection 1: Miscarriages of justice occur. Capital punishment is to be rejected because of human fallibility in convicting innocent parties and sentencing them to death. In a survey done in 1985 Hugo Adam Bedau and Michael Radelet found[24] that of the 7,000 persons executed in the United States between 1900 and 1985, 25 were innocent of capital crimes. While some compensation is available to those unjustly imprisoned, the death sentence is irrevocable. We can't compensate the dead. As John Maxton, a member of the British Parliament puts it, "If we allow one innocent person to be executed, morally we are committing the same, or, in some ways, a worse crime than the person who committed the murder."

Response: Mr. Maxton is incorrect in saying that mistaken judicial execution is morally the same as or worse than murder, for a deliberate intention to kill the innocent occurs in a murder, whereas no such intention occurs in wrongful capital punishment.

Sometimes the objection is framed this way: It is better to let ten criminals go free than to execute one innocent person. If this dictum is a call for safeguards, then it is well taken; but somewhere there seems to be a limit on the tolerance of society toward capital offenses. Would these abolitionists argue that it is better that 50 or 100 or 1,000 murderers go free than that one innocent person be executed? Society has a right to protect itself from capital offenses even if this means taking a finite chance of executing an innocent person. If the basic activity or process is justified, then it is regrettable, but morally acceptable, that some mistakes are made. Fire trucks occasionally kill innocent pedestrians while racing to fires, but we accept these losses as justified by the greater good of the activity of using fire trucks. We judge the use of automobiles to be acceptable even though such use causes an average of 50,000 traffic fatalities each year. We accept the morality of a defensive war even though it will result in our troops accidentally or mistakenly killing innocent people.

The fact that we can err in applying the death penalty should give us pause and cause us to build a better appeals process into the judicial system. Such a process is already in most places in the American and British legal systems. That an occasional error may be made, regrettable though this is, is not a sufficient reason for us to refuse to use the death penalty, if on balance it serves a just and useful function.

Furthermore, abolitionists are simply misguided in thinking that prison sentences are a satisfactory alternative here. It's not clear that we can always or typically compensate innocent parties who waste away in prison. Jacques Barzun has argued that a prison sentence can be worse than death and carries all the problems that the death penalty does regarding the impossibility of compensation:

In the preface of his useful volume of cases, *Hanged in Error*, Mr. Leslie Hale refers to the tardy recognition of a minor miscarriage of justice—one year in jail: "The prisoner emerged to find that his wife had died and that his children and his aged parents had been removed to the workhouse. By the time a small payment had been assessed as 'compensation' the victim was incurably insane." So far we are as indignant with the law as Mr. Hale. But what comes next? He cites the famous Evans case, in which it is very probable that the wrong man was hanged, and he exclaims: "While such mistakes are possible, should society impose an irrevocable sentence?" Does Mr. Hale really ask us to believe that the sentence passed on the first man, whose wife died and who went insane, was in any sense *revocable*? Would not any man rather be Evans dead than that other wretch "emerging" with his small compensation and his reason for living gone?[25]

The abolitionist is incorrect in arguing that death is different from long-term prison sentences because it is irrevocable. Imprisonment also takes good things away from us that may never be returned. We cannot restore to the inmate the freedom or opportunities he or she lost. Suppose an innocent 25-year-old man is given a life sentence for murder. Thirty years later the error is discovered and he is set free. Suppose he values three years of freedom to every one year of life. That is, he would rather live 10 years as a free man than 30 as a prisoner. Given this man's values, the criminal justice system has taken the equivalent of 10 years of life from him. If he lives until he is 65, he has, as far as his estimation is concerned, lost 10 years, so that he may be said to have lived only 55 years.

The numbers in this example are arbitrary, but the basic point is sound. Most of us would prefer a shorter life of higher quality to a longer one of low quality. Death prevents all subsequent quality, but imprisonment also irrevocably harms one by diminishing the quality of life of the prisoner.

Objection 2: The second objection of ten made against the death penalty is that it is unjust because it discriminates against the poor and minorities, particularly African Americans, over rich people and whites. Former Supreme Court Justice William Douglas wrote that "a law which reaches that [discriminatory] result in practice has no more sanctity than a law, which in terms provides the same."[26] Nathanson argues that "in many cases, whether one is treated justly or not depends not only on what one deserves but on how other people are treated."[27] He offers the example of unequal justice in a plagiarism case. "I tell the students in my class that anyone who plagiarizes will fail the course. Three students plagiarize papers, but I give only one a failing grade. The other two, in describing their motivation, win my sympathy, and I give them passing grades." Arguing that this is patently unjust, he likens this case to the imposition of the death penalty and concludes that it too is unjust.

Response: First of all, it is not true that a law that is applied in a discriminatory manner is unjust. Unequal justice is no less justice, however uneven its application. The discriminatory application, not the law itself, is unjust. A just law is still just even if it is not applied consistently. For example, a friend once got two speeding tickets during a 100-mile trip (having borrowed my car). He complained to the police officer who gave him his second ticket that many drivers were driving faster than he was at the time. They had escaped detection, he argued, so it wasn't fair for him to get two tickets on one trip. The officer acknowledged the imperfections of the system but, justifiably, had no qualms about giving him the second ticket. Unequal justice is still justice, however regrettable. So Justice Douglas is wrong in asserting that discriminatory results invalidate the law itself. Discriminatory practices should be reformed, and in many cases they can be. But imperfect practices in themselves do not entail that the laws engendering these practices themselves are unjust.

With regard to Nathanson's analogy with the plagiarism case, two things should be said against it. First, if the teacher is convinced that the motivational factors are mitigating factors, then he or she may be justified in passing two of the plagiarizing students. Suppose that the one student did no work whatsoever, showed no interest (Nathanson's motivation factor) in learning, and exhibited no remorse in cheating, whereas the other two spent long hours seriously studying the material and, upon apprehension, showed genuine remorse for their misdeeds. To be sure, they yielded to temptation at certain—though limited—sections of their long papers, but the vast majority of their papers represented their own diligent work. Suppose, as well, that all three had C averages at this point. The teacher gives the

unremorseful, gross plagiarizer an F but relents and gives the other two D's. Her actions parallel the judge's use of mitigating circumstances and cannot be construed as arbitrary, let alone unjust.

The second problem with Nathanson's analogy is that it would have disastrous consequences for all law and benevolent practices alike. If we concluded that we should abolish a rule or practice, unless we treated everyone exactly by the same rules all the time, we would have to abolish, for example, traffic laws and laws against imprisonment for rape, theft, and even murder. Carried to its logical limits, we would also have to refrain from saving drowning victims if a number of people were drowning but we could only save a few of them. Imperfect justice is the best that we humans can attain. We should reform our practices as much as possible to eradicate unjust discrimination wherever we can, but if we are not allowed to have a law without perfect application, we will be forced to have no laws at all.

Nathanson acknowledges this latter response but argues that the case of death is different. "Because of its finality and extreme severity of the death penalty, we need to be more scrupulous in applying it as punishment than is necessary with any other punishment" (p. 67). The retentionist agrees that the death penalty is a severe punishment and that we need to be scrupulous in applying it. The difference between the abolitionist and the retentionist seems to lie in whether we are wise and committed enough as a nation to reform our institutions so that they approximate fairness. Apparently, Nathanson is pessimistic here, whereas I have faith in our ability to learn from our mistakes and reform our systems. If we can't reform our legal system, what hope is there for us?

More specifically, the charge that a higher percentage of blacks than whites are executed was once true but is no longer so. Many states have made significant changes in sentencing procedures, with the result that currently whites convicted of first-degree murder are sentenced to death at a higher rate than blacks.[28]

One must be careful in reading too much into these statistics. While great disparities in statistics should cause us to examine our judicial procedures, they do not in themselves prove injustice. For example, more males than females are convicted of violent crimes (almost 90% of those convicted of violent crimes are males—a virtually universal statistic), but this is not strong evidence that the law is unfair, for there are biological/psychological explanations for the disparity in convictions. Males are on average and by nature more aggressive (usually tied to testosterone) than females. Simply having a Y chromosome predisposes them to greater violence. Nevertheless, we hold male criminals responsible for their violence and expect them to control themselves. Likewise, there may be good explanations why people of one ethnic group commit more crimes than those of other groups, explanations that do not impugn the processes of the judicial system nor absolve rational people of their moral responsibility.

Recently, Governor George Ryan of Illinois, the state of my childhood and youth, commuted the sentences of over 150 death row inmates. Apparently, some of those convicted were convicted on insufficient evidence. If so, their sentences should have been commuted and the prisoners compensated. Such decisions should be done on a case-by-case basis. If capital punishment is justified, its application should be confined to clear cases in which the guilt of the criminal is "beyond reasonable doubt." But to overthrow the whole system because of a few possible miscarriages is as unwarranted as it is a loss of faith in our system of criminal justice. No one would abolish the use of fire engines and ambulances because occasionally they kill innocent pedestrians while carrying out their mission.

Abolitionists often make the complaint that only the poor get death sentences for murder. If their trials are fair, then they deserve the death penalty, but rich murderers may be equally deserving. At the moment only first-degree murder and treason are crimes deemed worthy of the death penalty. Perhaps our notion of treason should be expanded to include those who betray the trust of the public: corporation executives who have the trust of ordinary people, but who, through selfish and dishonest practices, ruin their lives. As noted above, my proposal is to consider broadening, not narrowing, the scope of capital punishment, to include business personnel who unfairly harm the public. The executives in the recent corporation scandals who bailed out of sinking corporations with golden, million-dollar lifeboats while the pension plans of thousands of employees went to the bottom of the economic ocean, may deserve severe punishment, and if convicted, they should receive what they deserve. My guess is that the threat of the death sentence would have a deterrent effect here. Whether it is feasible to apply the death penalty for horrendous white-collar crimes is debatable. But there is something to be said in its favor. It would remove the impression that only the poor get executed.

Conclusion

While the abolitionist movement is gaining strength due in part to the dedicated eloquence of opponents to the death penalty like Hugo Adam Bedau, Stephen Nathanson, and Jeffrey Reiman, a cogent case can be made for retaining the death penalty for serious crimes, such as first-degree murder and treason. The case primarily rests on a notion of justice as desert but is strengthened by utilitarian arguments involving deterrence. It is not because retentionists disvalue life that we defend the use of the death penalty. Rather, it is because we value human life as highly as we do that we support its continued use. The combined argument based on both backward-looking and forward-looking considerations justifies use of the death penalty. I have suggested that the application of the death penalty include not only first-degree murder but also treason (willful betrayal of one's country), including the treasonous behavior of business executives who violate the public trust.

[Abolitionists] point out the problems in applying the death penalty. We can concede that there are problems and reform is constantly needed, but since the death penalty is justified in principle, we should seek to improve its application rather than abolish a just institution. We ought not throw out the baby with the dirty bathwater.

Notes

Some of the material in the section on deterrence is adapted from my essay "For the Death Penalty" in *The Death Penalty: For and Against* by Louis P. Pojman and Jeffrey Reiman (Rowman & Littlefield, 1998). That book contains a defense of the theory of punishment discussed in this essay. It also includes a fuller defense of my theory of desert. I am indebted to Stephen Kershnar and Michel Levin for comments on an earlier draft of this essay.

1. The numbers in parentheses refer to the page numbers in Bedau's essay, "An Abolitionist's Survey of the Death Penalty in America Today," in *Debating the Death Penalty: Should America Have Capital Punishment? The Experts on Both Sides Make Their Case*, ed. Hugo Adam Bedau and Paul G. Cassell (Oxford University Press, 2004).

2. It seems that the former mayor of New York City, Fiorello LaGuardia, had this in mind when he said, "I would hang a banker who stole from the people." Quoted in Alyn Brodsky, *The Great Mayor: Fiorello LaGuardia and the Making of the City of New York* (Truman Talley Books, 2003).

3. See Hugo Adam Bedau, *The Death Penalty in America* (Oxford University Press, 1982) and his "Capital Punishment," in *Matters of Life and Death*, ed. Tom Regan (Random House, 1980); see also Jeffrey Reiman, "Why the Death Penalty Should Be Abolished in America," in *The Death Penalty: For and Against*, ed. by Louis P. Pojman and Jeffrey Reiman (Rowman & Littlefield, 1998).

4. Mike Royko, quoted in Michael Moore, "The Moral Worth of Retributivism," in *Punishment and Rehabilitation*, 3rd ed., ed. Jeffrie G. Murphy (Wadsworth, 1995): 98–99.

5. Thomas Jefferson, *Bill for Proportioning Crime and Punishments* (1779), quoted in Ernest van den Haag, *Punishing Criminals: Concerning a Very Old and Painful Question* (Basic Books, 1975): 193. I do not agree with all of Jefferson's claims, but the principle is correct.

6. These are the most notorious of recent murders, but if you agree that these culprits deserve the death penalty, the case has been made against the abolitionist who wants to abolish the death penalty altogether.

7. See his speech in Bedau and Cassell, eds., *Debating the Death Penalty*, announcing his commutation of all of Illinois's death sentences. I will comment on this toward the end of my essay. Joshua Marquis also makes some pertinent comments on this commutation in his essay in this same volume.

8. Sir James Fitzjames Stephens, *Liberty, Equality, Fraternity* (Cambridge University Press, 1967): 152.

9. Sir James Fitzjames Stephens, *A History of Criminal Law in England* (Macmillan, 1863): 80.

10. Thorstein Sellin, *The Death Penalty* (1959), reprinted in *The Death Penalty in America*, ed. Hugo Bedau (Anchor Books, 1967). Isaac Ehrlich, "The Deterrent Effect of Capital Punishment: A Question of Life and Death," *American Economic Review,* 65 (June 1975): 397–417.

11. Sophisticated abolitionists argue that the death penalty doesn't deter better than long-term prison sentences, but their less sophisticated disciples often make the broader claim. I hear the charge regularly from students that the death penalty fails to deter.

12. Nathanson, *An Eye for an Eye?* (Rowman & Littlefield, 1987): chap. 2.

13. Michael Davis offers a similar commonsense argument for the deterrent effect of the death penalty. His article is especially useful as it shows just how little the statistics of social science demonstrate and why we should take the common sense data as weightier. See his "Death, Deterrence, and the Method of Common Sense," *Social Theory and Practice,* vol. 7, no. 2 (Summer 1981).

14. Herrnstein and Wilson conclude, "To increase the disutility of crime for people in general, society must increase either the speed, the certainty, or the severity of punishment, or some combination of all three." *Crime and Human Nature* (Simon & Schuster, 1985): 397.

15. Richard E. Gernstein, "A Prosecutor Looks at Capital Punishment," *Journal of Criminal Law: Criminology and Police Science,* vol. 51, no. 2 (1960).

16. *Parliamentary Debates,* third series, April 21, 1868. Reprinted in Peter Singer, ed., *Applied Ethics* (Oxford University Press, 1986): 97–104.

17. Quoted in Gernstein, "A Prosecutor Looks at Capital Punishment."

18. Ibid.

19. Ibid.

20. Ibid.

21. Ernest van den Haag, "On Deterrence and the Death Penalty," *Ethics,* 78 (July 1968).

22. Cited in Ernest van den Haag, "The Death Penalty Once More," unpublished manuscript. In "A Response to Bedau," *Arizona State Law Journal,* 4 (1977), van den Haag states that both Black and Bedau said that they would be in favor of abolishing the death penalty even if "they knew that its abolition (and replacement by life imprisonment) would

increase the homicide rate by 10%, 20%, 50%, 100%, or 1000%. Both gentlemen continued to answer affirmatively." Bedau confirmed this in a letter to me (July 28, 1996).

23. Hugo Adam Bedau, "How to Argue about the Death Penalty," in *Facing the Death Penalty,* ed. Michael Radelet (Temple University Press, 1989): 190.

24. Hugo Adam Bedau and Michael Radelet, *Miscarriages of Justice in Potential Capital Cases* (1st draft Oct. 1985, on file at Harvard Law School Library), quoted in E. van den Haag, "The Ultimate Punishment: A Defense," *Harvard Law Review,* vol. 99, no. 7 (May 1986): 1664.

25. Jacques Barzun, "In Favor of Capital Punishment," *American Scholar,* vol. 31, no. 2 (Spring 1962).

26. Justice William Douglas in *Furman v Georgia,* 408 U.S. 238 (1972).

27. Nathanson, *An Eye for an Eye?* (Rowman & Littlefield, 1987): 62.

28. The Department of Justice's *Bureau of Justice Statistics Bulletin* for 1994 reports that between 1977 and 1994, of those arrested for murder 2,336 (51%) were white, 1,838 (40%) were black, 316 (7%) were Hispanic. Of the 257 who were executed, 140 were white, 98 (38%) were black, 17 (7%) were Hispanic, and 2 (1%) were other races. In 1994, 31 prisoners—20 white men and 11 black men—were executed although whites made up only 7,532 (41%) and blacks 9,906 (56%) of those arrested for murder. Of those sentenced to death in 1994, 158 were white men, 133 were black men, 25 were Hispanic men, 2 were Native American men, 2 were white women, and 3 were black women. Of those sentenced, relatively more blacks (72%) than whites (65%) or Hispanics (60%) had prior felony records. Overall the criminal justice system does not seem to favor white criminals over black, though it does seem to favor rich defendants over poor ones.

QUESTIONS

1. Is Pojman's retributive case for the death penalty persuasive? Does it answer Bedau's criticisms of the retributive argument?

2. In recent decades the case against the deterrent value of the death penalty has become widely accepted. Does Pojman succeed in strengthening the deterrent argument for capital punishment?

39. Punishment and Loss of Moral Standing

CHRISTOPHER W. MORRIS

For a description of the author, see chapter 19.

We often think that killing someone is a violation of their right to life. Many, including the organization Amnesty International, have said that executing criminals is a violation of their right to life. If this is true, it would be a strong reason, most likely a conclusive reason, against the death penalty. In this article Morris argues that serious wrongdoers *forfeit* some of their rights, in some cases the right to life, and that this forfeiture—this loss of moral

From "Punishment and Loss of Moral Standing," *Canadian Journal of Philosophy* 21, 1 (March 1991), 53–79. Reprinted by permission of the University of Calgary Press and of the author.

standing—is what makes the death penalty permissible. The case is made by reference to a contractarian conception of morality or justice (see chapter 67).

When any man, even in political society, renders himself by his crimes obnoxious to the public, he is punished by the laws in his goods and person; that is, the ordinary rules of justice are, with regard to him, suspended for a moment, and it becomes equitable to inflict on him, for the *benefit* of society, what otherwise he could not suffer without wrong or injury.[1]

By what authority do we punish? What permits us to deprive people of their liberty or possessions for some wrong that they have committed? Normally we may not do to people what we do when we punish wrongdoers. What exactly allows us to treat the latter as we do? The problem is clearly stated by Warren Quinn:

The major source of theoretical difficulty here is the fact that the restrictions, confinements, and deprivations of property and life that make up standard civic punishment would, if imposed in nonpenal contexts, be opposed by various important moral rights to life, liberty, and property.[2]

It might be admitted that punishment *violates* the moral rights of wrongdoers. Jeffrie Murphy, for instance, claims that

The core punishments of the criminal law (deprivation of liberty or life) represent gravely serious assaults on the fundamental *rights* of persons, stigmatize and humiliate those persons, and typically cause those persons great personal unhappiness.[3]

While punishment does adversely affect the *interests* of wrongdoers, it is not clear that it "assaults" or violates their *rights*. More importantly, to claim that punishment violates the rights of persons would, one would think, be to argue against punishment. Instead it might be said that punishment *justifiably infringes* the rights of wrongdoers. But that too seems implausible.[4] Deterrence, retribution, education may be some of the ends of our punitive practices. However, for reasons well discussed in the literature, they do not by themselves settle the matter of the moral rights of wrongdoers.[5] What then to say about the moral status of wrongdoers?

I shall argue that criminal acts alter the moral status of wrongdoers, that such acts affect their moral rights and lead to their forfeiture. Such a position is not novel. However, it is often defended (and criticized) merely at an intuitive level when what is required is a theoretical account of the relationship between action and intention and the moral status of agents. And it is this that I shall try to provide. Providing such an account, as I shall explain presently, will only be the first part of a complete theory of punishment.

I. The Moral Justification of Punishment

An institution or practice (or an individual act) of punishment is morally justified, I shall assume, if and only if (1) it is not unjust and (2) there are sufficient or compelling reasons for the practice. The reasons for the practice may be explicitly moral—e.g., retribution, moral education—though they need not be. But these will not be my concern. Rather, my focus will be on condition (1). I shall argue that wrongdoers do not possess moral rights that stand in the way of their being punished. Thus punishment of wrongdoers will not be unjust.[6]

What is punishment? The matter of the definition of punishment is complicated, as well as controversial. It will suffice for my purposes to have a general characterization of the notion. As such, punishment is the intentional imposition of some pain, unpleasantness, or deprivation for an offense committed by the culprit.[7] It may be imposed so as to teach the offender a lesson, to deter others from similar acts, or to teach the offender a lesson, to deter others from similar acts or to exact retribution. These may or may not be part of the practice. Criminal punishment will normally be authorized and carried out by the state, though this need not be the case; to make it part of the proper characterization of the notion would be to beg the question against anarchists.

Criminal penalties are often recommended or defended as effective deterrents, or as appropriate means of retribution for certain offenses or at least of expressing the seriousness with which we view them. It is usually, and quite naturally, assumed that such penalties must consequently be justified—that is, *morally* justified—if they are to be inflicted. In particular, it is usually thought that a particular kind of moral justification is required in the standard cases of punishment—namely, justification with reference to *justice*.

It is common to think of morality as having different parts or virtues. It is controversial how to understand these parts or even how to distinguish them. But it is widely thought that justice is different from the virtues of friendship, courage, moderation, and the like. More importantly, justice is usually distinguished from charity or benevolence, although there is less agreement here.[8] The standard distinction is to understand justice to pertain to what individuals are *owed,* to what they may *claim,* to what they have a *right.* Benevolence, by contrast, is a virtue that attaches itself directly to the well-being of others. It is exemplified by taking an interest in others' welfare independently of that to which they have a claim. Benevolence and justice often do not conflict, but they can. Attachment to someone's good can lead us to refuse to give them some harmful possession (e.g., drugs) to which they have a claim. Or it can make us wish to restrict another's liberty for his or her own good.[9] However we decide to handle the apparent conflicts between justice and other virtues, it seems that there is a distinction between acting from a concern for another's well-being and from a concern for another's moral rights.

Typically, infringements of liberty or intentional infliction of pain violate moral rights to be free or not to be harmed. Thus, it would normally be thought that punishment requires a rationale in terms of justice. The state's involvement, it is usually thought, will only strengthen this requirement.

Now the moral rights of criminals do not stand in the way of punishment if we may justifiably *infringe* or *override* them. I do not, however, wish to defend either of these two possibilities. Instead I shall argue that punishment will not be unjust when wrongdoers lose the moral rights that would otherwise protect them against harm or loss. I turn now

to the conception of justice that will be the basis of my approach to punishment.

II. Justice by Convention

Justice is the moral virtue that is concerned with that is *owed* or *due* to individuals. It is that to which individuals appeal when they claim that to which they have a moral *right* (though this is not to say that the domain of rights exhausts that of justice). Recent discussions of justice have focused largely on principles of distributive justice, but this narrow focus should not let us lose sight of the larger virtue.

There is a long western tradition, dating back to Antiphon, Glaucon, and Epicurus, developed by Hobbes, Hume, and Rousseau, and continued in various ways by Rawls, Harsanyi, Mackie, Harman, Scanlon, Gauthier, and Kavka that understands justice to be a type of mutually agreeable convention. According to this tradition, justice consists of principles, rules, and norms that ideally serve to advance the interests and aims of all in certain situations. This tradition is dubbed "contractarian" as it often understands the terms of justice to be the outcome of a hypothetical bargain or "social contract." It might be less misleading to think of contemporary representatives of this tradition as offering a "rational choice" conception of morality after John Rawls's famous remark, "The theory of justice is a part, perhaps the most significant part, of the theory of rational choice."[10]

The account of justice offered by this tradition is designed to answer two traditional questions: what does justice require? and why be just? In a manner characteristic of much of Western moral philosophy, the reply which members of this tradition give to the first question is determined by that which they give to the second: justice requires of us only that which we have reason to accept. What is unique to this tradition is the manner in which the structure or nature of its answer to the second question determines the answer it gives to the first. I shall briefly explain the nature of this account, as this will be important to my view of the justification of punishment.

Justice has been the virtue to give moral philosophers the greatest trouble. Plato had notorious difficulty in showing that we have reason to do what "justice in the city" requires of us. It is this special difficulty with justice that has even led some philosophers to question whether justice is a virtue in the traditional sense.

> For while prudence, courage and temperance are qualities which benefit the man who has them, justice seems rather to benefit others, and to work to the disadvantage of the just man himself . . . The point of this is . . . to suggest that we should at least consider the possibility that justice is not a virtue.[11]

The advantages of justice are, in a sense, indirect: I benefit from your acting justly toward me, and vice versa. While we may all benefit from a *system* or *practice* of just behaviour, each of us would benefit most by being the exception to such a system: I behave unjustly while everyone else behaves justly. The problem of the moral philosopher here is to show that one still has a reason to be just even though it is often the case that one would benefit most by being unjust and by taking advantage of the justice of others.

It should be emphasized that the problem does not necessarily have to do with self-interest, although both Plato's and Foot's formulations may suggest as much. The "benefits" or "advantages" of injustice to an individual need not be self-interested. Rather, the problem is that the goals or aims that give individuals reasons for action, whatever these may be, may sometimes be better served by injustice.

The indirect advantages of justice may normally be such that few individuals can wish to forego them. The advantages of injustice may, however, be sufficiently great that individuals are tempted to act unjustly. Why then is it rational to be just? The principles of conduct that would emerge from the hypothetical bargain that rational choice ethicists use to determine the requirements of justice are those to which it is rational to agree.[12] For such principles, if complied with, secure everyone's advantage. Without them, life would be nasty, brutish, and short, depending on the efficacy of alternative means of social control (e.g., law, superstition, kinship relations). However, granting that we have a reason to agree to such principles—even to grant that they define what justice is—what reason do we have to comply with their requirements?

We have reason to be just because if we have reason to accept certain principles of conduct, then we have reason to comply with them, provided the conditions under which we accepted the principles remain unchanged. That is, practical reason is to be understood as enabling rational agents to *commit* themselves to plans or policies. The rational choice ethicist must answer thus, if the latter is to be able to give the moralist reasons to be just. This is not to say that such a reply is cogent or without its difficulties; however, I shall not pursue these matters here.[13]

One of the conditions—one of the "circumstances of justice," to use Rawls's phrase[14]—giving rise to the need for justice is the possibility of mutual benefit. Others are the capacity and willingness of rational beings to impose constraints on their behaviour. In the absence of such conditions, one has no reason to abide by the constraints of justice in one's conduct toward others. This is important, for it effectively means that in the absence of (1) mutual benefit or of (2) the capacity or (3) willingness to be just, individuals are not constrained by justice in their behaviour toward one another. The answer that contractarian theorists give to the question "why be just?" commits them to the view just expressed, that in the absence of certain conditions there is no reason to act justly; we may call this view "the *doctrine* of the circumstances of justice." This doctrine is crucial to my understanding of the justification of punishment. I turn now to a brief account of *moral standing*.

Let us say that a *moral object* is something that is an object of moral consideration. A *direct* moral object is something *to* which (or to whom) that consideration is paid or owed; an *indirect* moral object is something *about* or *concerning* which moral consideration is paid. The latter is a *beneficiary* of the moral consideration. Typically direct moral objects will be beneficiaries of moral considerations owed to them; thus they will typically also be indirect moral objects. The different objects of moral duties can thus be determined by asking *to* whom/what and *regarding* whom/what are they owed. Consider the following case. Albert promises Beatrice to care for Carl. Albert's duties would be owed *to* Beatrice *regarding* Carl; the latter would be an indirect moral object of those duties. Were Albert not to care for Carl in the requisite manner, he would fail in his duties toward Beatrice and thus wrong her. Carl would merely fail to be benefited; he might be harmed but he would not be wronged thereby.

To have *moral standing* is to be owed (some) moral consideration, that is, to be a direct moral object.[15] To be a mere indirect moral object is *not* to possess moral standing. In terms of these notions and distinctions, people typically are direct moral objects and have moral standing. Protected natural sites, national monuments, significant works of art might be examples of indirect moral objects. When we destroy the latter, we may be understood to fail in our duties to other people. Animists and others could use this distinction to give a different account of whom we fail to respect when we defile nature.

We may contrast the notion of a moral object with that of a *moral subject*. The latter is something that has moral duties or may be expected to give moral consideration to direct moral objects. We usually understand adult humans to be moral subjects, while non-human animals and young infants are not so regarded; presumably *agency* would be necessary to being a moral subject.

Supposing that the "circumstances of justice" be satisfied, rational choice or contractarian moral theory understands rational humans, capable and willing to impose moral constraints on their conduct toward others, as moral subjects and direct moral objects. Thus, for this theory, as for most others, in normal circumstances adult humans have moral obligations and are owed certain moral considerations. However, it is important to note that "having moral standing" is a relation; something has moral standing in its relations to some other entity(ies). It should not be assumed that the relation holds universally, as we shall see.

Let us return to the distinction between justice and benevolence. Contractarian moral theory entails that a necessary condition for being owed the moral consideration that is part of justice is possession of the capacity to impose moral constraints on one's behaviour toward others; I shall call this capacity, or bundle of capacities, *agency*. The theory also entails that a willingness to do so is equally necessary. A being that lacks either agency or the willingness in question will not be, on this account, the sort of being to whom one owes considerations of justice.

Now such a creature could still be a proper object of the considerations that are part of benevolence. For this virtue attaches itself to the good or well-being of others, not to their rights. Thus we should want to distinguish between being the (direct) object of considerations of justice and of considerations of benevolence.

The distinction between benevolence and justice may not be all that is needed here. We may distinguish between those virtues or parts of morality which are *owed to* others and those which are not. Presumably temperance and wisdom, insofar as we consider these moral virtues, fall into the latter class. All, or most, of justice would fall into the former class. Courage, however, might be different; some, but certainly not all, exercise of this virtue may be owed to others. Benevolence as well may be similar. Some acts of benevolence may be owed to others; we may have duties of benevolence, duties which are owed to their beneficiaries, although these will not be said to have a claim or a right to be benefited. Other benevolent acts may not be so owed. Thus we should want to distinguish between being the direct object of considerations of benevolence and the mere beneficiary of benevolence.[16]

I shall now distinguish full from partial moral standing. A being has *full moral standing* insofar as it is a direct moral object both of considerations of justice and of benevolence (that is, of those considerations of benevolence that can be owed to someone). Something that is a direct moral object only of benevolence has *partial moral standing*. I take it that any creature that is a proper object of considerations of justice will also be a direct object of benevolence.[17] Something that is neither the proper direct object of considerations of justice nor of benevolence will be said to have *no moral standing*. Thus, mere indirect moral objects, although the (indirect) object of moral consideration, will lack moral standing. The Canadian flag, Yosemite Park, the Louvre, for instance, will be protected by morality by being indirect moral objects of our duties to each other; they will lack moral standing, however, since *they* are neither owed considerations of justice nor of benevolence.[18]

Now contractarian moral theory will imply that in the circumstances of justice all humans capable and willing to impose constraints on their behaviour toward others have full moral standing. Most others—e.g., humans not so capable and non-human animals—will at best have partial moral standing.[19] I shall argue that yet others—e.g., certain humans *unwilling* to impose constraints on their conduct toward others—will have *partial* or *no* moral standing.

III. Wrongdoing and Loss of Moral Standing

To have moral standing is to be owed (some) moral consideration. Justice consists in part of a set of moral rights, the most important of which, we may assume, are those to life, liberty, and property. To lose some such rights is to lose some of one's moral standing. I wish to argue that wrongdoers lose some of their rights and some of their moral standing, and that some wrongdoers lose all of their rights (or never possessed the full set) and retain at most what I have called partial moral standing. In other words, I shall defend a type of forfeiture theory, one according to which part (but only part) of the justification for punishment rests in the fact that wrongdoers lack certain rights, the presence of which would normally suffice to block the appropriate punishment.[20]

I shall defend this forfeiture account by reference to the general contractarian account of moral standing that I have sketched above. I shall argue that either one of two aspects of wrongdoing can lead to loss of (some) rights: the *act* of wrongdoing and the *unwillingness to respect the constraints of morality* that may be manifested by such wrongdoing. That is, either *acting* in violation of the constraints of morality or merely being *unwilling* to respect these constraints will suffice to cause a wrongdoer loss of certain rights.

The first way in which wrongdoers can lose rights is less controversial or novel than the second; so I shall spend less time developing it.[21] We may suppose that the conventions that determine justice, according to the contractarian tradition, have built into them provisions for penalties in the event of violation. Consider a club or organization established for the benefit of its members. It will have rules, respect of which will further the ends of the members. Without supposing duplicity on the part

of the latter, it would be reasonable for them to include sanctions, however mild, for the violation of these rules; sanctions may provide assurance that others will not take advantage of one's cooperative behaviour. Similarly, we may suppose that the rules of morality have built into them penalties, which may be applied whenever individuals act wrongly, that is, in violation of the rules.

The conception of justice characteristic of the contractarian tradition is that of an "artificial" system—to use the predicate favored by Hobbes and Hume—which ideally serves the interests of members of society. Given the imperfections of human rationality, it would be unwise to desire a system without sanctions for violations of its norms.[22] That is, since we may expect that ordinary humans, without manifesting unwillingness to abide by the constraints of justice, will violate these constraints on occasion, when the temptation proves to be difficult to resist, we build into these constraints penalties for violations.

Building sanctions into the constraints of justice must involve, on pains of incoherence, construing these constraints as not standing in the way of the administration of the penalties. There are several ways in which this can be done, some of which were mentioned at the beginning of this essay. One way would be to understand the constraints as *defeasible*. A right or duty is defeasible insofar as it may be overridden under certain conditions. So we might say that individuals' rights to, say, liberty or property may be overridden whenever they act against justice. But a right or duty which is overridden is one which is disregarded reluctantly. Indeed, in some cases those who justifiably disregard the rights of another owe the latter an apology, if not compensation. For instance, suppose that I fail to fulfil a promise to you or I damage some possession of yours because of an emergency; your overridden rights may still require the performance of certain acts, if only of contrition. So, without denying that our rights and duties are defeasible, I shall not understand this to be the property of rights and duties that leaves room for punishment.

Recall Hume's words, quoted at the beginning of this essay. Of an individual who commits crimes, Hume says that "*the ordinary rides of justice are, with regard to him, suspended for a moment,* and it becomes equitable to inflict on him . . . what otherwise he could not suffer without wrong or injury" (emphasis added). Some of the rights of wrongdoers and our duties towards them may, instead of being overridden, be "suspended for the moment." It is this suggested understanding of rights and duties, which I shall interpret as a forfeiture account, that I shall defend by reference to the contractarian account of justice I have sketched.

The normal rights of individuals, then, are suspended whenever they violate the constraints of justice. The *act* of wrongdoing may cause the wrongdoer to lose, if only temporarily, certain rights. The nature of the suspension, and its duration, I shall not examine here. Indeed, without developing or exploring further this way of losing rights, I shall move on to the second aspect of (some) acts of wrongdoing that result in loss of rights and of some moral standing. For it is this part of my thesis that is likely to be most controversial, and an explanation of its distinctive features may also serve as a defense of the first part.

Recall that on the account that I have given, the willingness to abide by certain constraints is necessary for what I have called full moral standing. Individuals unwilling to respect such constraints will lack, or lose, full moral standing. One expression of such unwillingness, we may suppose, is the intentional commitment of certain crimes. Thus, certain criminal acts will deprive their performers of some part of their moral standing.

Note how counter-intuitive this thesis is, although I do not intend this to be a counter-argument. Those who violate (some of) the moral rights of others, in ways that manifest their unwillingness to abide by the constraints of justice, lose (some of) their moral rights. That is, (some of) the latter are *forfeited* by the wrongdoer. Consider the more orthodox way of understanding fundamental moral rights. It is often claimed that we possess certain moral rights by virtue of the sort of creature that we are, that is, *by virtue of our nature.* This claim is explicit in virtually all accounts of *natural* rights and may be found in other accounts as well. Now rights that are acquired by virtue of the possession of certain (natural) attributes (e.g., ratio-

nality, self-consciousness) cannot be lost except by the loss of those very attributes. On such an account criminals retain their moral rights, as long as they do not lose their rationality or whatever natural attributes generate moral rights.[23] Moral standing is usually thus understood in terms of possession of certain attributes.[24]

While possession of certain natural attributes (e.g., rationality) is *necessary* for moral standing[25] on the account that I am offering, it is not *sufficient.* The reason for this is that justice is to be understood as a mutually beneficial convention which constrains rational agents in situations where individually rational action leads to disadvantageous outcomes. Compliance with the requirements of justice is the condition for protection by those requirements. Each person is given protection in exchange for refraining from damaging the interests of others. Barring a particular interest in the interests of others, rational agents have a reason to impose constraints on their behaviour toward others only if the latter are so willing themselves. The conditional nature of the constraints of justice is a central feature of the classical accounts of Hobbes, Hume, and Rousseau, as well as of contemporary theories such as Gauthier's. Unilaterally to impose constraints on oneself, in the absence of a particular interest in the interests of others, would be to open oneself up to exploitation.[26]

Such an account of justice entails that possession of full moral standing presupposes the willingness to comply with the requirements of justice. These requirements would have us refrain from harming the lives, liberty, and possessions of those who possess full moral standing. Further, justice presumably also requires that we assist those who possess such standing; that is, in addition to refraining from harming them, we will have duties of mutual aid, redistribution of wealth, and the like.[27] Justice will not, however, require that we so refrain from harming those who lack full moral standing. Benevolence (or prudence) may so restrain us, but justice will be silent for those who lack full moral standing.[28]

Criminal acts, then, insofar as they manifest the agent's unwillingness to comply with the requirements of justice, lead to (some) loss of moral standing. This is a simple consequence of the conditional nature of contractarian justice. What rights are thus lost? Alan H. Goldman makes the following suggestion:

> if we ask which rights are forfeited in violating rights of others, it is plausible to answer just those rights that one violates (or an equivalent set). One continues to enjoy rights only as long as one respects those rights in others: violation constitutes forfeiture. But one retains those rights which one has continued to respect in others.[29]

If the requirements of justice are not all part of a single package, if compliance with one part does not require compliance with another, then this suggestion may be plausible. One would then lose part of the standing that justice accords without necessarily losing the rest. For instance, a thief who violates the property rights of others might accordingly lose rights to his or her possessions, leaving others, perhaps through the agency of the state, at liberty to take his or her possessions. Or a thief who violates not only the property rights of others but also their rights to liberty would accordingly lose rights both to property and to liberty.

The details of such an account will depend on the structure and interrelations of the moral rights and duties of justice. Some may be separate from the rest; others may be threatened whenever any one right is violated. For instance, many property rights can be violated without any other rights being placed in jeopardy; however, violations of other property rights may significantly injure the liberty or life of an individual. So I cannot say very much about exactly how offenses will correlate with losses of moral rights without a more developed account of the rights of justice.

Further, the plausibility of Goldman's suggestions may depend on particular examples; with others, the idea may even be difficult to understand.[30] A variation on Goldman's suggestion would be that wrongdoers lose the benefits that are assured by certain rights and duties. That is, if Gerhardt violates Henrietta's right to x, Gerhardt would lose the benefits that would normally accrue to him from others' respect of his right to x.[31] In some cases this might involve loss of Gerhardt's right to x, in others loss of some different or larger set of rights. Whatever the particular account we settle on, the general idea is clear enough: violations of (some of) the moral rights of others will bring about a corresponding loss of (some of the) moral rights of the wrongdoer.

The want or forfeiture of certain moral rights opens up the way for punishment. In inflicting pain or some deprivation on a wrongdoer, we commit no injustice against this individual for he or she lacks the relevant moral rights that would otherwise make such treatment unjust. This is the first part of a justification of punishment, either of the individual act or of the practice or institution. The second part consists in the reasons we would have for punishing—e.g., retribution, deterrence, moral education. I shall not discuss this part of the justification.

I shall merely note that the standard theories of punishment are compatible with the forfeiture account that I have defended. Further, and more importantly, these theories, were they wedded to the forfeiture account, could answer some of the standard objections made by critics. For instance, deterrence theorists could defend the treatment of criminals as mere means to the ends of others by pointing to the former's loss of full moral standing.[32] Some retributivists could argue that acting on retributive sentiments is not illicit if the moral rights of the wrongdoer do not stand in the way.[33] What benefits moral education theorists could derive from a forfeiture thesis is more difficult to ascertain, for unlike deterrence theorists and retributivists, they understand the fundamental justification of punishment to be paternalistic.[34] Perhaps for such theories the forfeiture of rights will serve only to remove impediments to the justification of paternalism.

Wrongdoers, then, may lose (some of) their rights by their acts. The act alone may cause this loss insofar as the conventions of justice have penalties and the requisite suspension of duties built in. Further, the act, insofar as it manifests an unwillingness to abide by the constraints of justice, will bring about this loss; in some cases, the unwillingness revealed by the act may show that we mistakenly cooperated with the wrongdoer.[35] Inflicting pain or deprivation of property or liberty on wrongdoers as a response to their acts is not unjust for they have lost, through their acts, the moral rights that would otherwise stand in the way of such treatment. Their status is analogous to exile; they are banished, not from a physical space but from a moral space.[36] They have lost, at least in part, their membership in the moral community.

The forfeiture account may be independently appealing for retributive and other reasons. It may be thought that loss of the rights that wrongdoers violate is actually a most appropriate punishment for individuals unwilling to respect the requirements of justice. The intuitive appeal here may be similar to that of the *lex talionis* in retributive theories. Further, it might be argued that punishing wrongdoers in ways that emphasize the relation between the rights they have violated and those they have thereby lost best *expresses* the community's outrage or anger at the wrongful act. Insofar as punishment has an expressive function,[37] the criminal's forfeiture of moral rights would be both a consequence of his or her wrong doing and an expression of the moral community's consequent outrage. This and other features of the forfeiture account, however, are secondary to the main considerations that I have been offering on its behalf.[38]

Readers will note the important role played by the will in my account of the second way in which wrongful acts cause their perpetrators to lose (some of) their rights. Such an act, insofar as it manifests an unwillingness to abide by the constraints of justice, brings about the loss of (some) moral standing. I am supposing that this feature of acts and agents, that their acts may manifest certain intentions and dispositions, can be known. This is an assumption of my account, as well, one would think, of virtually all theories of punishment or responsibility. But, it would seem to be the case that if *wrongful* acts so manifest certain individuals' unwillingness to abide by the constraints of justice, so might other acts. That is, one would think that this unwillingness could be ascertainable without the agent acting wrongly. Since it is the unwillingness that triggers the loss of rights, so it may do so without a particular wrongful act. So some individuals may lose their rights, or rather, may not have any, simply by virtue of their unwillingness to abide by the constraints of justice.

On this view, the wrongful act is not so much the *reason* or *justification* for loss of certain rights as

evidence for a set of intentions and dispositions that themselves are the cause for the loss of rights. The act of wrongdoing thus functions differently in the two ways by which one may lose rights on the account I have offered. This result is simply an implication of the conditional nature of the obligations of justice in contractarian theory and certain assumptions concerning knowledge about intentions and dispositions. What I earlier called doctrine of the circumstances of justice entails that in the absence of certain conditions, justice does not bind. Acts which display unwillingness to abide by the constraints of justice reveal that some of the conditions of justice do not obtain. To reflect this feature of my account would involve reflecting the approach to the theory of justice on which it is based.

It is interesting to note, however, the accounts of the wrongness of threatening and the permissibility of preventive detention that become available upon acceptance of my account. Whatever else might be wrong about a threat, say, to harm another, we can also say that such is wrong insofar as it manifests an unwillingness to abide by the constraints of justice. The threat need not itself harm another or even violate the other's rights. For merely threatening to do something that would violate another's rights might, without violating that person's right, reveal an unwillingness to abide by the constraints of justice.

Were someone unwilling to abide by justice, then they would not possess any rights that would stand in the way of our incapacitating them in order to prevent them from harming others. We might thus have (part of) a rationale for preventive detention of certain individuals. Further, my account's emphasis on the willingness to abide by mutually beneficial constraints may offer the basis for the distinction between offenses such as civil disobedience and (genuine) mercy killing, which do not involve a rejection of the system of norms in question, and others, such as theft and most types of homicide. It may also be the case that carrying an offensive weapon—e.g., a filed screw driver, sawed-off shotgun, or fully automatic Uzi—will be a graver offense on my account than on others; weapons that have no defensive purpose presumably manifest some sort of unwillingness to abide by justice.

It is important to note, however, that these implications of my account—that mere unwillingness suffices for the loss of (some) rights—is primarily of theoretical interest. In a large society, with a workable system of criminal justice, it is unlikely that we could make or trust judgments made about the unwillingness of others to respect justice independently of their wrongful acts. Certainly we would be wary of entrusting the agents of the state to make such decisions. And it is likely that we will not reach sufficient agreement about the intentions and dispositions of agents to enable us to have an efficient system of criminal justice. The theoretical point, about the relation between willingness to respect justice and possession of moral rights, is nonetheless important.

IV. The Death Penalty

The forfeiture account may be illustrated by an application to the death penalty. A discussion of capital punishment in light of the forfeiture thesis may provide a different understanding of the issues than is usually found in the contemporary literature. Consider the cases of contract killers, war criminals, tyrants, and certain terrorists who are unwilling to abide by the constraints of justice in their conduct toward others. The individuals I am thinking of suspend considerations of justice and even of benevolence in their relations with certain others. Contract killers earn their living by eliminating others for a fee; the tyrants and war criminals of the twentieth century regarded their victims as beyond the scope of justice; and certain contemporary terrorists, those who plant bombs in crowded cafés and department stores, clearly do not view themselves as bound by the constraints of justice. Such individuals may act justly towards members of their group or clan, but in their behaviour toward us do not so constrain themselves.

What are we to say of such individuals? Some will claim that they deserve death, or worse. But I am neither concerned with desert nor with the moral assessment of the sentiments of retribution that we might have considering such cases. Rather, I am concerned with the moral status of such people. Specifically, do such individuals not lose their fundamental moral rights to life and liberty?

Such people clearly lack full moral standing on a contractarian account of justice. They show by their conduct that they are unwilling to abide by the constraints of justice with most others. With respect to the latter, they themselves lack the protection that justice normally affords people. Suppose that they are apprehended, tried, and convicted of their crimes. Would it be *unjust* to execute them? No, for they lack full moral standing and thus the protection of justice. By their unwillingness to impose the constraints of justice on their conduct toward others, they lose the protection of justice.

Would we be *justified* in executing them? I claimed earlier that punishment is justified if (1) it is not unjust and (2) there are compelling reasons to exact it. The reasons for punishing an individual need not be explicitly moral; that is, they need not themselves make reference to justice, much less to moral desert or the like.[39] It is true that normally a moral justification for an act intentionally inflicting some harm or loss of liberty on another must be one that makes reference to justice. However, in the cases of contract killers, war criminals, tyrants, and genuine terrorists, reference to justice is obviated. For by placing themselves outside of the protection of justice, these individuals relieve others of justifying their conduct toward them by reference to justice. We may be morally obligated *to one another* to explain and to justify our execution of these individuals—for instance, to demonstrate their criminal conduct, to show that executing them is consistent with public policy on these and other matters, and that doing so is consistent with our social ideals. We may have certain legal obligations to such individuals (e.g., due process). Further, their execution may not be collectively prudent.[40] However, we have no moral obligations of justice to contract killers, war criminals, tyrants, genuine terrorists, or other individuals who place themselves outside of the constraints of justice. Were it to be wrong to execute them, we would not be wronging *them* were we to do so; *they* would have no grounds of justice to complain.

We normally possess moral rights to life and to liberty. It is a controversial matter among ethicists exactly how these rights are to be understood, thus the contemporary debates over abortion, euthanasia, nuclear deterrence, and other issues. But at least part of the content of such moral rights is the obligation of others to refrain from intentionally taking one's life or from interfering with one's liberty when such is not necessary in order to protect the equal liberty of others or to serve some other important good. Such characterizations are imprecise, but they will serve my purpose.

Justice gives us our basic moral rights to life and liberty. Most theories of justice, contractarian or other, should have little trouble accounting for these rights, at least as I have characterized them.[41] Thus, normally when we intentionally take another's life or interfere with their liberty, we must justify our actions with reference to justice, given their rights to life and liberty. Since taking or thus restricting another's life or liberty appear to be violations of their moral rights to life or liberty, a moral justification, one which makes reference to justice, seems required. Usually we will seek to show that the rights in question were *overridden* by some moral consideration. To say that a right is overrideable is to say that it is *defeasible*; we need not fulfil our correlative obligation in all circumstances, there being some that morally permit us to disregard the right in question. A defeasible right continues to exist even when overridden; it merely does not obligate in such instances. Normally, when we justly restrict someone's liberty, their right to be free is overridden.

In the cases of the contract killers, war criminals, tyrants, and terrorists, I am suggesting that their moral rights to life or liberty are not overridden. (Indeed, I believe that this is not possible with respect to the moral right to life since I believe that this right is not *defeasible,* though I do not propose to argue this here.[42]) Instead I am arguing that we do not have to give standard *moral* justifications for executing contract killers, war criminals, tyrants, or terrorists because so killing them would neither be a violation nor an overriding of their moral rights to life or liberty. Rather, they no longer have, or never had, such moral rights. Thus we merely need sufficient reason to execute them.[43] To use Hobbes' language, such individuals have only the "right" of nature, that is, mere Hohfeldian liberties that entail no correlative obligations on the part of others.

Someone may object to the account I have offered of the death penalty by arguing that if it is sound it would also justify torture. Someone's loss of full moral standing, entailed by their unwillingness to abide by the constraints of justice, relieves others of justifying their actions by reference to justice. Would we be equally free to torture contract killers or terrorists? Again, let us leave aside questions of desert and retribution. Justice cannot forbid us to refrain from torturing such individuals insofar as they have lost what I have called full moral standing. Normally, torture and the like will violate the requirements of both justice and benevolence. In this case justice is silent. Suppose that the individuals in question lose all moral standing by their acts and their unwillingness to abide by the constraints of justice. Torture would be no more morally objectionable than execution. The main considerations would be matters of policy and of obligations to others.

Suppose instead that they retain partial moral standing; they are still (direct) objects of (some) considerations of benevolence. Would torture then be permissible? I do not know the (contractarian) answer to this question. The nature of benevolence is a difficult matter, one about which contemporary contractarian and other moralists are less clear than they are about justice. We might wish to argue that to the degree that the contract killers and others possess partial moral standing, to that degree benevolence would have us refrain from making them suffer.

V. Objections

Many will find my account counter-intuitive and will reject the idea that some humans, no matter how amoral, lose their rights and moral standing. And there are many objections that will, and have been, made. I shall discuss some of these.

Much crime is committed by the destitute in the urban underclass. It may be argued that the account I have offered "does not apply" to them, as "they are *outside* of the circumstances of justice to begin with and have nothing to forfeit."[44] It is unclear what exactly is the objection, for if individuals who commit crimes lack certain rights to begin with, then no rights stand in the way of their being punished for their acts, and the first part of a justification for punishment is complete. This criticism might be the same as that which finds the very idea of someone without full moral standing objectionable. Now there *is* a serious question about the implications of our moral theories for the plight of those in our cities who have no or little stake in the social order. My view is that there are compelling contractarian arguments for some redistribution to the poor and destitute to give them a stake in the social order and bring them into the circumstances of justice. But that would seem to be another matter entirely than the subject of this essay.[45]

It might be argued that the forfeiture account would permit various forms of cruel punishment—for instance, the death penalty—and that this constitutes an objection. If cruelty involves indifference to another's pain or suffering, then punishment as I have characterized it may well be cruel. However, if cruelty involves taking pleasure in another's suffering, then cruelty is not part of the account that I am offering. For on the view that I am defending, the reasons for punishment are independent of the grounds for the permissibility of punishment.

It is a criticism, however, of many of our institutions to point out that our motivations are mixed and include elements of cruelty or malice. Were we to dispose of certain amoral criminals by imprisoning or executing them, accepting the account I have offered, but do so largely from malice and revenge, then our practices would be vulnerable to criticism. Supposing that the criminal in question lacks the moral rights that justice accords, then cruelty will be an objection only insofar as (1) it is contrary to benevolence or some other virtue, (2) it is bad public policy, or (3) we have obligations to others that prohibit us from treating any human cruelly. It is likely that, e.g., torture will virtually always be ruled out for these reasons, though I do not propose to argue this here.[46]

Recently Warren Quinn has made some specific, and troublesome, criticisms of forfeiture of punishment. He supposes rightly that forfeiture of moral rights must be specifiable and intelligible independently of punishment if it is to serve as part of a justification of the latter. He then considers the following case:

The proper authorities are entitled to punish Jones, a generally decent young man who has foolishly stolen Smith's car, by depriving him of up to the amount of liberty forfeited by the theft. But suppose that before any such punishment takes place, Smith, for reasons having nothing whatever to do with the theft, kidnaps Jones and deprives him of exactly that amount of liberty.[47]

This would be to violate Jones' right to liberty, Quinn supposes. To block the response that Jones has forfeited his right *to the community,* Quinn modifies the case:

But suppose that the community in which Jones lives has the unjust practice of seizing and confining political dissenters. And suppose that shortly after his crime Jones, who happens to be a dissenter, is officially seized and, for a time, quarantined to prevent the spread of his political views (views having nothing to do with his theft).

Again, Quinn supposes, we would think that Jones' right to liberty had been violated. The conditionality of moral right that is part of the forfeiture thesis seems essentially tied to punishment; otherwise these other forms of ill-treatment cannot be blocked by a proponent of the forfeiture account. Quinn concludes,

Jones has not forfeited his right without qualification, he has forfeited it in that he may be subjected to a certain penalty (presumably the proper penalty for the crime) by certain people (presumably those with a right to punish). It seems, therefore, that the idea of forfeiture in this kind of case comes to no more than the idea that the criminal's rights do not in fact stand in the way of his being punished. The appeal to forfeiture does not, as it first seemed, provide an explanation of why this is so.[48]

It is true that it is wrong for Smith or the public authorities to restrict Jones' liberty in the ways specified. But it does not follow that Jones' right to liberty is thereby violated. Suppose that Jones is someone who seriously violates the moral rights to liberty of others and that he consequently loses his moral right to liberty. Suppose further that it is known that Jones has committed the criminal acts in question and consequently has lost his moral right to liberty. Then others would not wrong *him* by restricting his liberty in the ways imagined in the examples. This is precisely the implication of the account that I am defending.

There is, however, something wrong with the treatment accorded Jones, though it is difficult to determine whether the wrong is moral or legal. For one, presumably we would not want the state restricting *any* individual's freedom of speech.[49] So at the least we might have laws prohibiting such conduct on the part of states, laws which would possibly make Jones an indirect moral object of obligations the state would have to us. Further, we presumably would never want to allow the state to restrict the liberty of anyone without satisfying certain procedural safeguards; we might, therefore, accord *everyone* a *legal* right to due process. Smith certainly would violate such laws, though he would not thereby wrong Jones except insofar as the latter retains his procedural rights.[50] I do not find these implications counter-intuitive, although little should rest on this.

Quinn's objection, however, does not turn on the details of a hypothetical case. He objects to

> a theory of forfeiture according to which Jones' crime has to some extent made him an *outlaw*, someone whose basic moral rights do not stand in the way of a certain amount of ill-treatment whether or not it comes by way of punishment . . . On such a view, forfeiture would be restricted only in some systems of social morality; in other morally acceptable systems outlawry in some degree would be the regular consequence of crime. It is this last suggestion that I find disturbing.[51]

The thesis that moral "outlawry in some degree would be the regular consequence of crime" may very well be counter-intuitive. We normally do not presuppose such a view in our ordinary moral judgments.[52] However, note that partial *legal* outlawry does appear to be a presupposition of our ordinary legal judgments and practices. How else to understand the legal status of convicted criminals, deported suspects, or expelled diplomats? The view that legal systems are social conventions for the protection of members of society is not unusual. The contractarian tradition merely views justice and the

moral rights it accords as similar, albeit more fundamental, conventions.[53]

VI. Conclusion

Punishment, I have argued, is justified in part because wrongdoers lose the moral rights that would otherwise stand in the way of their being harmed in the manner that we do when we punish. Moral standing is to some degree lost, and moral rights are to some degree forfeited, by wrongdoers.

It might be argued that the position I have put forward does not take justice seriously. I disagree. The forfeiture account I have developed links in a certain way being a direct moral object with being a moral subject. Rational humans who are not willing to impose the constraints of justice on their conduct toward others are not themselves protected by these constraints. In my view, *that* is to take justice seriously.

Notes

Earlier versions of this essay were discussed at the UCLA Law & Philosophy Discussion Group in the spring of 1986, the Pacific meetings of the American Philosophical Association, San Francisco, March 1987, the Research Triangle Ethics Circle, September 1988, and the University of California, Riverside, January 1990. I am grateful to those present for comments and criticisms, as well as to Jacob Adler, Richard Arneson, Dorit Bar-On, David Copp, Michael Corrado, Jean Hampton, Thomas E. Hill, Jr., Gregory Kavka, Richard Mohr, Stephen Munzer, Reed Richter, Geoffrey Sayre-McCord, Keith Simmons, and the editors of this journal. And I am especially indebted to Jean Hampton, as well as to Warren Quinn, for interesting me in the subject of punishment.

1. David Hume, *Inquiry Concerning the Principles of Morals*, Section III, "Of Justice," Part I, paragraph 10.
2. Warren Quinn, "The Right to Threaten and the Right to Punish," *Philosophy & Public Affairs* 14 (1985) 327.
3. *The Philosophy of Law*, co-authored with Jules Coleman (Totowa, NJ: Rowman & Allanheld 1984), emphasis added, 113.
4. Quinn, 328.
5. Not everyone—e.g., utilitarian proponents of deterrence—will accept this. I shall simply assume, for

the standard reasons, that such theories do not give *complete* accounts of punishment.

6. The reason for formulating the first condition in terms of punishment being *not unjust,* rather than *just,* is that I shall understand these expressions as contraries, not as contradictories. My reasons for this will become clear when I explain the theoretical account of the moral status of wrongdoers that will be the basis for my argument.

7. This fairly standard characterization of punishment is provisional, as it will turn out to be incompatible with the account I develop. I am indebted to Alex Rosenberg for drawing my attention to this. I shall not, however, pursue these issues further in this essay.

8. See Philippa Foot, "Virtues and Vices," in *Virtues and Vices* (Berkeley & Los Angeles: University of California Press 1978), 1–18. For scepticism about standard ways of drawing the distinction, see Allen Buchanan, "Justice and Charity," *Ethics* 97 (1987) 558–75.

9. More frequently benevolence may tempt us to violate the constraints of justice protecting one individual for the good of another. We may, however, decide not to count an act for another's well-being as benevolent if it involves treating a third party unjustly. See Foot, "Utilitarianism and the Virtues," *Mind* 94 (1985) 205–6.

10. *A Theory of Justice* (Cambridge, MA: Harvard University Press 1971), 16; see also 172. It is clear from his most recent writings, if not from some of the elements of *A Theory of Justice,* that Rawls does not really endorse the view of moral theory expressed by his remark. The same is true of Harsanyi. David Gauthier's theory best fits Rawls's remark; see his *Morals by Agreement* (Oxford: Clarendon Press 1986).

11. Foot, "Moral Belief," reprinted in *Virtues and Vices,* 125. Foot no longer accepts the suggestion just quoted, as she now rejects the assumption made by contractarians and others that justice requires of us only that which we have reason to accept. See especially her "Introduction" to *Virtues and Vices,* xiii.

12. Hypothetical choice and agreement here has only a heuristic value. That is, it is a discovery procedure. It is not to be confused with commitment, promising, and the like, which is one of the reasons why the "social contract" label may mislead. This point will

be important later when I address some of the criticisms made of forfeiture accounts of punishment.

13. For Gauthier's controversial version of this reply, see Gauthier, Chapter 6. See also Michael Robins, *Promising, Intending, and Moral Autonomy* (Cambridge: Cambridge University Press 1984); Edward F. McClennen, "Prisoner's Dilemma and Resolute Choice," in Richmond Campbell and Lanning Sowden, eds., *Paradoxes of Rationality and Cooperation* (Vancouver: University of British Columbia Press 1985), 94–104, as well as *Rationality and Dynamic Choke* (Cambridge: Cambridge University Press 1990); and Michael Bratman, *Intention, Plans, and Practical Reason* (Cambridge, MA: Harvard University Press 1987).

14. See Rawls, 126ff. The classical accounts are to be found in Hobbes and Hume. See also H. L. A. Hart, *The Concept of Law* (Oxford: Clarendon Press 1961), 189–95.

15. The notion of moral standing I borrow and adapt from L. W. Sumner, *Abortion and Moral Theory* (Princeton: Princeton University Press 1981), 26ff.

16. The distinction here between benevolence that is owed others and benevolence which is not should not be confused with the distinction between self-regarding and other-regarding virtues. Benevolence, like justice, is an other-regarding virtue. It is simply that sometimes it may be owed others, other times not.

17. For typically only things that are capable of being benefited or harmed in the ways that humans are— or more controversially, non-human animals—can have moral rights or are owed considerations of justice. Since such things (e.g., humans) are sentient, they are also the sort of thing that can be the proper objects of considerations of benevolence. Thus, typically beings that are owed considerations of justice will also be owed considerations of benevolence, and will thereby have full moral standing. Perhaps this is not always true. We may owe considerations of justice to Scrooge, but not considerations of benevolence. This seems to have been Shakespeare's view of Shylock.

18. It should not be thought that mere indirect moral objects lack moral *value*. Moral standing may be understood as a species of moral value; the set of objects with moral value typically will be larger than that of objects with moral standing. Thus the Rocky Mountains or Chartres, while lacking moral

standing, have moral value. Note that the moral value that such objects have, while not "inherent," can be "intrinsic" in the sense of non-instrumental or ultimate value. The confusion between different senses of "intrinsic value" (e.g., inherent, non-instrumental), as well as between moral value and moral standing, as I have characterized these notions, is prevalent in ethics, especially in discussions of environmental issues.

19. A complete contractarian account of moral standing would have to discuss a second way in which something can acquire it, namely by being the object of the preferences of someone who has moral standing. For instance, Daphne may care sufficiently for Emil, who is not an agent, that she will not cooperate with Frederica unless the latter accords moral standing to Emil. My account of moral standing in this essay is importantly incomplete. I discuss this second way of acquiring moral standing in "Moral Standing and Rational Choice Contractarism," in *Contractarianism and Rational Choice: Essays on Gauthier*, Peter Vallentyne, ed. (Cambridge: Cambridge University Press 1991), 76–95.

20. It is Hume's view, as expressed by the passage quoted at the beginning of this essay. I think it is also implicit in, that is, entailed by Hobbes' account, but that may be controversial. See *Leviathan*, Chapter 28, especially paragraph 2: "the subjects did not give the Sovereign that right [to punish]; but onely in laying down theirs . . ." see as well Jean-Jacques Rousseau, *Du Contrat social*, Book II, Chapter V, paragraph 4.

    "[T]he offender, by violating the life or liberty or property of another, has lost his own right to have his life, liberty, or property respected, so that the state has no *prima facie* duty to spare him . . . It is morally at liberty to injure him as he has injured others . . ." (W. D. Ross, *The Right and the Good* [Oxford: Clarendon Press 1930], 60–1). Alan H. Goldman endorses "the possible claim that a condition of having specific rights is that one honours those rights of others (when one is able to do so). When a person violates the rights of others, he involuntarily loses his own rights . . ." ("The Paradox of Punishment," *Philosophy & Public Affairs* 9 [1979] 44). See also James Rachels, *The Elements of Moral Philosophy* (New York: Random House 1986), 130: "But why is it *permissible* to punish? The answer [of the social contract theory of morals] is that . . . by

violating the rule with respect to us, criminals release us from our obligation toward them and leave themselves open to retaliation."

21. I am especially indebted here to Geoffrey Sayre-McCord, as well as to Martin Golding, for comments and suggestions leading to my distinguishing more clearly the two ways in which rights may be lost by wrongdoers.

22. Hume, of course, emphasized the shortsightedness of humans. For a Humean reading of Hobbes, see Jean Hampton, *Hobbes and the Social Contract Tradition* (Cambridge: Cambridge University Press 1986), Chapter 3.

23. "If rights are grounded in our rational nature, how can they be lost or forfeited except by our ceasing to share in that nature?" (Sumner, 110).

24. This is especially clear in, say, the literature on abortion, where it is debated whether mere life, or sentence, or rationality (actual or merely potential) *suffice* for possession of a moral right to life.

25. More precisely, rationality is necessary only for one of two contractarian ways of acquiring moral standing. See the essay mentioned in note 19.

26. Gauthier defends this claim in a stronger form in *Morals by Agreement*, especially Chapter 6. If, contra Gauthier, we allow (non-moral) interests in the interests of others in the premises of our contractarian account of justice, the formulation of claims about exploitation becomes more complicated.

27. In the case that these (undefended) claims about positive duties be controversial, I should note that nothing in this essay depends on their truth.

28. Carl may lack full moral standing and still be protected by justice insofar as he is the beneficiary of Albert's obligations to Beatrice. Carl's status in such a case would be that of an indirect moral object (and third-party beneficiary) with regard to these obligations to Beatrice. What Carl could not be is the direct object of (these) obligations of justice.

29. Goldman, 45.

30. For instance, the loss of procedural rights when one violates the procedural rights of others.

31. I owe this suggestion to Jacob Adler.

32. Given that justice is a derived virtue for utilitarians, the concept of loss of full moral standing, as I have characterized it, should not he especially problematic for the theory. What utilitarians cannot accept is the idea of *complete* loss of moral standing for sentient beings.

33. The expression "retributive sentiments" comes from J. L. Mackie. See his "Morality and the Retributive Emotions," *Criminal Justice Ethics* 1 (1982) 3–10. Of course, retributive accounts of punishment, such as the classical theories of Kant and Hegel, that seek to understand punishment as an acknowledgement of the moral standing (and agency) of wrongdoers, will be unable to avail themselves of my full account.

34. See Herbert Morris, "A Paternalistic Theory of Punishment," *American Philosophical Quarterly* 18 (1981) 263–71; and Jean Hampton, "The Moral Education Theory of Punishment," *Philosophy & Public Affairs* 13 (1984) 208–38. Hampton argues that on her account punishment is not paternalistic in any objectionable sense; it remains, nonetheless, that the justification of the deprivations involved in punishment is the wrongdoer's good.

35. Hobbes says of the "Foole" that "He therefore that breaketh his Covenant, and consequently declareth that he thinks he may with reason do so, cannot be received into any Society . . . but by the errour of them that receive him . . ." (Hobbes, Chapter 15).

36. The analogy to exile is interesting. Consider the ancient practice of banishment. Someone violates certain fundamental norms of society (or displeases the rulers) and is stripped of citizenship and banished from the land. Socrates was offered this fate; more recently Solzhenitsyn was exiled from his native country. In these and other cases, banishment can be understood as punishment. As such it appears to be very severe: Socrates preferred death. In 1958 the U.S. Supreme Court found exile and banishment to be violations of the constitutional prohibition of "cruel and unusual punishment." See *Trop v. Dulles,* 356 U.S. 86.

    However, exile need not be thus understood. Instead one can think of it as loss of a certain status and consequent expulsion from one's society. Now banishment or exile have not historically been thus understood, or at least not entirely. Exile traditionally has been the fate reserved for those it would be politically inappropriate to execute, for instance because of their royal blood or former political status. Rarely have ordinary criminals or the poor and powerless been banished. If we focus on the elements of withdrawal of membership and expulsion that are implicit in involuntary exile, we may understand punishment in part as withdrawal of membership in society and, on occasion, as consequent expulsion.

Someone who is not a member (or citizen) of a society lacks a certain legal and political standing with respect to that society. Someone who is exiled or banished from his or her society may be understood to have had that legal and political status taken away. Similarly, something that is neither the direct object of considerations of justice nor of benevolence lacks moral standing. And someone who is unwilling to abide by certain moral constraints thereby loses his or her moral standing, either partially or completely. It is noteworthy that Chief Justice Warren rejected exile, or denationalization, as "the total destruction of the individual's status in organized society . . . In short, the expatriate has lost the right to have rights" (*Trop v. Dulles* at 101, 102). Making allowances for rhetoric, this *is* the consequence of wrongdoing on the account I am offering.

37. Joel Feinberg, "The Expressive Function of Punishment," in *Doing and Deserving* (Princeton: Princeton University Press 1970) 95–118

38. Defenders of alternatives to punishment (e.g., rehabilitation, restitution) might also avail themselves of a forfeiture account such as mine to explain how we might be justified in imposing alternative treatment on wrongdoers.

39. Though the reasons *could* appeal to justice. Some may hold that justice *requires* that certain criminals be punished. Such an account would provide reasons for punishment of a particular sort and of particular force.

40. It is often argued that execution of former tyrants makes it harder to topple present and future tyrants.

41. Of course, if one builds into the characterization of these rights certain *scope* requirements—e.g., that they be held by all humans—rational choice moral theory will not be able to generate them.

    Note, however, that such a theory may be able to generate something analogous to indefeasible or absolute moral right, that is, rights that may never be overridden, whatever the consequences. It may be that the only cases where contractarian justice does not prohibit the intentional killing of an adult human are those where the latter possesses no moral right to life to be overridden. However, the semantics of "absolute" and "defeasible" must be carefully worked out. See note 6.

42. Nor does anything in this essay turn on acceptance of this belief.

43. I should note that I am sceptical that we generally have such reasons. Thus it could be that we rationally or prudentially ought not do what we are not morally forbidden to do.

44. This objection was made to me in discussion.

45. This may also have been Hobbes' view, as he endorsed helping the poor who could not help themselves (Hobbes, Chapter 30). He also says that "When a man is destitute of food, or other thing necessary for his life, and cannot preserve himself any other way, but by some fact against the Law . . . he is totally Excused . . ." (Chapter 27).

    The redistribution I mention is defended in my "A Non-Egalitarian Defense of Redistribution," in *Social Justice, Bowling Green Studies in Applied Philosophy IV,* Michael Bradie and David Braybrooke, eds. (Bowling Green, OH: Bowling Green State University 1982), 68–84, and "A Hobbesian Welfare State?" *Dialogue* 27 (1988) 653–73.

    Marilyn Friedman and Gregory Kavka have independently expressed concern about the implications of my account for acts of wrongdoing that violate unjust laws or that take place in contexts of imperfect compliance. Addressing these concerns would require considerably more space that I have here.

46. David Falk has criticized my account for its silence regarding *mercy.* A fuller exposition of my forfeiture theory would have to discuss, and make room for, mercy. For a recent discussion, see Jeffrie G. Murphy and Jean Hampton, *Forgiveness and Mercy* (Cambridge: Cambridge University Press 1988).

47. Quinn, 332.

48. Ibid. 332–3.

49. Although note that we generally allow governments the right to restrict the freedom of speech of noncitizens and of prison inmates, though these are practices I do not endorse.

50. Would Jones lose his procedural rights by violating the procedural rights of others? This would seem to be an implication of my version of Goldman's suggestion. We might distinguish between legal rights, at least procedural ones, and basic moral rights, at least to the extent of allowing the forfeiture of one set without the loss of the other. But these matters are complex.

51. Quinn, 332n.

52. In the old English institution of outlawry, certain criminals lost protection of the law as a consequence of their acts. See Sir Frederick Pollock and Frederick William Maitland, *The History of English Law before the Time of Edward I,* 2nd ed, reissued by S. F. C. Milson (Cambridge: Cambridge University Press 1986 [1898]), Vol. I, 49, 476–8; Vol. II, 578–84.

53. Quinn considers the possibility that a forfeiture account might be defended by appeal to a contractarian theory (presumably) of justice (Quinn, 333n.). He rejects such an account for three reasons. First, the actual moral force of hypothetical agreements is unclear. Second, it would be difficult for such a theory to account for the upper limits that we place on punishment. And third, such a theory would have difficulty providing an account of the right of retaliation in a state of nature.

    The first criticism does not affect accounts such as mine, when the moral force of the conventions of justice has nothing to do with agreement or commitment as such. Hypothetical agreement is, as I mentioned in note 12, heuristic. The third criticism also has no force, as the contractarianism that I have appealed to does not suppose that we have any claim-right to punish in a state of nature; the theory is Hobbesian, not Lockean. The matter of the upper limit on punishment is more complicated and cannot be discussed adequately here. The same is true of the worries of Quinn about the appeal to reciprocity that is part of forfeiture accounts (Quinn, 333).

QUESTIONS

1. Why think that the death penalty is not permissible unless the condemned has forfeited his or her right to life?
2. Can a person lose some or all of his or her moral standing?

VIII

Animals

The numbers of animals killed every year for food alone is estimated to be huge, in the billions. In addition to providing sources of nourishment and pleasure, large numbers of nonhuman animals are used by humans for experimentation and clothing. During the Mad Cow Disease scare in the 1990s, the number of cows killed was in the millions. Today most everyone thinks that cruelty to animals is wrong. In our reader we need to take up the question to what extent is killing them wrong.

Even if the number of vegetarians has grown in recent decades, most people eat the flesh of animals and presumably do not think it is wrong to do so. Most people, as we just noted, most likely think it wrong to kill them cruelly, at least if there are feasible alternatives. The way we raise many of the animals we eat—"factory farming"—is barbaric, and movements to eliminate factory farming are under way. An important theoretical question here concerns the *status* of nonhuman animals. We usually think that people or humans *count* in a certain way. To harm or mistreat them is usually *wrong*. Indeed, we often say that such treatment *wrongs them* or is a wrong *to* them. In some cases of wrongs, we talk about violating someone's *rights*—for instance, their right not to be defamed, or their right to their property. By contrast, if someone smashes something that belongs to another (e.g., a vase), an apology or compensation may be owed to the owner of the object. The object itself is not owed anything; it is merely a thing with no standing; it does not count in the right way.

We need some technical language to express these ideas about status. The notion of *moral standing* as developed in philosophy helps us distinguish the different moral status something can have. Something has moral standing, we might say, if it is owed moral consideration, for instance, duties are owed *to* it. It merits moral consideration in its own right. Normally we think that humans, at least of a certain age, have moral standing in this sense. They have rights, duties are owed *to* them, and we must consider how our acts affect them in certain ways. By contrast, inanimate objects lack moral standing, even if they are of great *value*. A particular vase or painting may be of great value; it might even be such that we consider it to have moral value (e.g., it is associated with an important event or a great injustice). But it lacks moral standing; we do not owe *it* special treatment, even if we have duties to treat it well. The distinction between something having and something lacking moral standing is central to the debate about the ethics of the treatment of nonhuman animals.

To help sharpen the distinction, consider a human person, a valuable painting, and a piece of dirt of no particular value. The first has moral standing; we are obligated to him or her to refrain from inflicting harm, to assist at least in emergencies, and the like.[1] Contrast this person's status with the piece of dirt. We have an obligation to others not to throw the dirt at them or to use it to soil their clothes. But we have no obligations *to* the dirt itself. We don't even have a duty to make sure the dirt is used properly or something of the sort. Intermediate between these two is the painting. We do have duties regarding the painting. (If the example in question does not work, substitute another object, perhaps a country's flag or one's beloved grandmother's memoirs or a religious artifact of great significance.) The painting lacks moral standing, but we seem to have duties *regarding* it (e.g., not to destroy it). The distinction here is between a duty *owed to* something and a duty merely *regarding* something. The painting is protected not by duties owed to it, but by duties regarding it. We might express this distinction with other terms. Human persons have moral standing and thus are *direct objects* of (some) moral consideration. Valuable works of art lack moral standing but still may have some moral value; they are *indirect objects* of moral consideration.

So an important theoretical question about the status of nonhuman animals is whether some of them possess moral standing. If they do, is it wrong to kill them (or only to make them suffer)? If they do not, are they nevertheless protected by some duties we have regarding them and are thus indirect moral objects?

---

1. The duty to give aid in emergencies, to rescue, is more controversial than that to refrain from harming in certain ways. See especially chapters 17 and 18.

40. The Status of Animals

THOMAS AQUINAS

For a description of the author, see chapter 2.

In this chapter, taken from a different work, the *Summa Contra Gentiles*, Aquinas explains why it is not "a sin for man to kill dumb animals." Unintelligent beings are subordinate to intelligent ones.

The very condition of intellectual nature, whereby it is mistress of its own acts, requires the care of Providence, providing for it for its own sake: while the condition of other creatures, that have no dominion over their own act, indicates that care is taken of them not for themselves, but for their subordination to other beings. For what is worked by another is in the rank of an instrument: while what works by itself is in the rank of a prime agent. Now an instrument is not sought for its own sake, but for the use of the prime agent: hence all diligence of workmanship applied to instruments must have its end and final point of reference in the prime agent. On the other hand all care taken about a prime agent, as such, is for its own sake.

2. What has dominion over its own act, is free in acting. For he is free, who is a cause to himself of what he does: whereas a power driven by another under necessity to work is subject to slavery. Thus the intellectual nature alone is free, while every other creature is naturally subject to slavery. But under every government the freemen are provided for for their own sakes, while of slaves this care is taken that they have being for the use of the free.

3. In a system making for an end, any parts of the system that cannot gain the end of themselves must be subordinate to other parts that do gain the end and stand in immediate relation to it. Thus the end of an army is victory, which the soldiers gain by their proper act of fighting: the soldiers alone are in request in the army for their own sakes; all others in other employments in the army, such as grooms or armourers, are in request for the sake of the soldiers. But the final end of the universe being God, the intellectual nature alone attains Him in Himself by knowing Him and loving Him. Intelligent nature therefore alone in the universe is in request for its own sake, while all other creatures are in request for the sake of it.

6. Everything is naturally made to behave as it actually does behave in the course of nature. Now we find in the actual course of nature that an intelligent subsistent being converts all other things to his own use, either to the perfection of his intellect, by contemplating truth in them, or to the execution of works of his power and development of his science, as an artist develops the conception of his art in bodily material; or again to the sustenance of his body, united as that is to an intellectual soul.

Nor is it contrary to the conclusion of the aforesaid reasons, that all the parts of the universe are subordinate to the perfection of the whole. For that

From "That Rational Creatures Are Governed by Providence for Their Own Sakes, and Other Creatures in Reference to Them," *Summa Contra Gentiles*, Book III, chap. 112. *An Annotated Translation of the* Summa Contra Gentiles *of Saint Thomas Aquinas*, by J. Rickaby (London: Burns and Oates, 1905).

subordination means that one serves another: thus there is no inconsistency in saying that unintelligent natures serve the intelligent, and at the same time serve the perfection of the universe: for if those things were wanting which subsistent intelligence requires for its perfection, the universe would not be complete.

By saying that subsistent intelligences are guided by divine providence for their own sakes, we do not mean to deny that they are further referable to God and to the perfection of the universe. They are cared for for their own sakes, and other things for their sake, in this sense, that the good things which are given them by divine providence are not given them for the profit of any other creature: while the gifts given to other creatures by divine ordinance make for the use of intellectual creatures.

Hence it is said: *Look not on sun and moon and stars besides, to be led astray with delusion and to worship what the Lord thy God hath created for the service of all nations under heaven* (Deut. iv, 19):

Thou hast subjected all things under his feet, sheep and all oxen and the beasts of the field (Ps. viii, 8).

Hereby is excluded the error of those who lay it down that it is a sin for man to kill dumb animals: for by the natural order of divine providence they are referred to the use of man: hence without injustice man uses them either by killing them or in any other way: wherefore God said to Noe: *As green herbs have I given you all flesh* (Gen. ix, 3). Wherever in Holy Scripture there are found prohibitions of cruelty to dumb animals, as in the prohibition of killing the mother-bird with the young (Deut. xxii, 6, 7), the object of such prohibition is either to turn man's mind away from practising cruelty on his fellow-men, lest from practising cruelties on dumb animals one should go on further to do the like to men, or because harm done to animals turns to the temporal loss of man, either of the author of the harm or of some other; or for some ulterior meaning, as the Apostle (1 Cor. ix, 9) expounds the precept of not muzzling the treading ox.

QUESTIONS
1. Why is it not an injustice for humans to kill or otherwise use animals?
2. Why is it wrong to treat animals cruelly?

41. Duties with Regard to Animals

IMMANUEL KANT

For a description of the author, see chapter 34.

Kant draws a distinction between a duty *to* another being and one *with regard to* another being. He argues we have no duties *to* animals. This said, he says that we do have a number of duties to refrain from treating animals cruelly or violently.

From Immanuel Kant, *The Metaphysics of Morals*, trans. M. Gregor (Cambridge: Cambridge University Press, 1996), pp. 192–193.

As far as reason alone can judge, a human being has duties only to human beings (himself and others), since his duty to any subject is moral constraint by that subject's will. Hence the constraining (binding) subject must, *first,* be a person; and this person must, *second,* be given as an object of experience, since man is to strive for the end of this person's will and this can happen only in a relation to each other of two beings that exist (for a mere thought–entity cannot be the *cause* of any result in terms of ends). But from all our experience we know of no being other than a human being that would be capable of obligation (active or passive). A human being can therefore have no duty to any beings other than human beings; and if he thinks he has such duties, it is because of an *amphiboly* in his *concepts of reflection*, and his supposed duty to other beings is only a duty to himself. He is led to this misunderstanding by mistaking his duty *with regard to* other beings for a duty *to* those beings. [. . .]

With regard to the animate but nonrational part of creation, violent and cruel treatment of animals is far more intimately opposed to a human being's duty to himself, and he has a duty to refrain from this; for it dulls his shared feeling of their suffering and so weakens and gradually uproots a natural predisposition that is very serviceable to morality in one's relations with other men. The human being is authorized to kill animals quickly (without pain) and to put them to work that does not strain them beyond their capacities (such work as he himself must submit to). But agonizing physical experiments for the sake of mere speculation, when the end could also be achieved without these, are to be abhorred.—Even gratitude for the long service of an old horse or dog (just as if they were members of the household) belongs *indirectly* to a human being's duty *with regard to* these animals; considered as a *direct* duty, however, it is always only a duty of the human being *to* himself. [. . .]

QUESTIONS

1. What is the distinction that Kant makes between duties *to* and *with regard to*? Of what importance is it?
2. Why do we not have duties *to* animals?
3. Why do we have duties not to treat animals cruelly?

42. All Animals Are Equal

PETER SINGER

For a description of the author, see chapter 17.

Peter Singer is one of the founders of the animal liberation movement and the author of the very influential book *Animal Liberation* (1975). This essay restates his basic case for taking the welfare of animals into consideration. "If a being suffers, there can be no moral justification to refusing to take that suffering into consideration. No matter what the nature

From Peter Singer, "All Animals Are Equal," *Annual Proceedings of the Center for Philosophical Exchange* 1 (1994), pp. 103–11. Reprinted by permission of the author.

of the being, the principle of equality requires that its suffering be counted equally with the like suffering—in so far as rough comparisons can be made—of any other being." Note that Singer does not formulate his position in terms of "animal rights"; unlike some other proponents of animal liberation, he does not think that animals have rights (see chapter 67 for an explanation of moral utilitarianism).

In recent years a number of oppressed groups have campaigned vigorously for equality. The classic instance is the Black Liberation movement, which demands an end to the prejudice and discrimination that has made blacks second-class citizens. The immediate appeal of the black liberation movement and its initial, if limited, success made it a model for other oppressed groups to follow. We became familiar with liberation movements for Spanish-Americans, gay people, and a variety of other minorities. When a majority group—women—began their campaign, some thought we had come to the end of the road. Discrimination on the basis of sex, it has been said, is the last universally accepted form of discrimination, practiced without secrecy or pretense even in those liberal circles that have long prided themselves on their freedom from prejudice against racial minorities.

One should always be wary of talking of "the last remaining form of discrimination." If we have learnt anything from the liberation movements, we should have learnt how difficult it is to be aware of latent prejudice in our attitudes to particular groups until this prejudice is forcefully pointed out.

A liberation movement demands an expansion of our moral horizons and an extension or reinterpretation of the basic moral principle of equality. Practices that were previously regarded as natural and inevitable come to be seen as the result of an unjustifiable prejudice. Who can say with confidence that all his or her attitudes and practices are beyond criticism? If we wish to avoid being numbered amongst the oppressors, we must be prepared to re-think even our most fundamental attitudes. We need to consider them from the point of view of those most disadvantaged by our attitudes, and the practices that follow from these attitudes. If we can make this unaccustomed mental switch we may discover a pattern in our attitudes and practices that consistently operates so as to benefit one group—usually the one to which we ourselves belong—at the expense of another. In this way we may come to see that there is a case for a new liberation movement. My aim is to advocate that we make this mental switch in respect of our attitudes and practices towards a very large group of beings: members of species other than our own—or, as we popularly though misleadingly call them, animals. In other words, I am urging that we extend to other species the basic principle of equality that most of us recognize should be extended to all members of our own species.

All this may sound a little far-fetched, more like a parody of other liberation movements than a serious objective. In fact, in the past the idea of "The Rights of Animals" really has been used to parody the case for women's rights. When Mary Wollstonecraft, a forerunner of later feminists, published her *Vindication of the Rights of Women* in 1792, her ideas were widely regarded as absurd, and they were satirized in an anonymous publication entitled *A Vindication of the Rights of Brutes.* The author of this satire (actually Thomas Taylor, a distinguished Cambridge philosopher) tried to refute Wollstonecraft's reasonings by showing that they could be carried one stage further. If sound when applied to women, why should the arguments not be applied to dogs, cats, and horses? They seemed to hold equally well for these "brutes"; yet to hold that brutes had rights was manifestly absurd; therefore the reasoning by which this conclusion had been reached must be unsound, and if unsound when applied to brutes, it must also be unsound when applied to women, since the very same arguments had been used in each case.

One way in which we might reply to this argument is by saying that the case for equality between men and women cannot validly be extended to non-human animals. Women have a right to vote, for instance, because they are just as capable of making rational decisions as men are; dogs, on the other hand, are incapable of understanding the significance of voting, so they cannot have the right to vote. There are many other obvious ways in which men and women resemble each other closely, while humans and other animals differ greatly. So, it might be said, men and women are similar beings and should have equal rights, while humans and nonhumans are different and should not have equal rights.

The thought behind this reply to Taylor's analogy is correct up to a point, but it does not go far enough. There are important differences between humans and other animals, and these differences must give rise to some differences in the rights that each have. Recognizing this obvious fact, however, is no barrier to the case for extending the basic principle of equality to nonhuman animals. The differences that exist between men and women are equally undeniable, and the supporters of Women's Liberation are aware that these differences may give rise to different rights. Many feminists hold that women have the right to an abortion on request. It does not follow that since these same people are campaigning for equality between men and women they must support the right of men to have abortions too. Since a man cannot have an abortion, it is meaningless to talk of his right to have one. Since a pig can't vote, it is meaningless to talk of its right to vote. There is no reason why either Women's Liberation or Animal Liberation should get involved in such nonsense. The extension of the basic principle of equality from one group to another does not imply that we must treat both groups in exactly the same way, or grant exactly the same rights to both groups. Whether we should do so will depend on the nature of the members of the two groups. The basic principle of equality, I shall argue, is equality of consideration; and equal consideration for different beings may lead to different treatment and different rights.

So there is a different way of replying to Taylor's attempt to parody Wollstonecraft's arguments, a way which does not deny the differences between humans and nonhumans, but goes more deeply into the question of equality and concludes by finding nothing absurd in the idea that the basic principle of equality applies to so-called "brutes." I believe that we reach this conclusion if we examine the basis on which our opposition to discrimination on grounds of race or sex ultimately rests. We will then see that we would be on shaky ground if we were to demand equality for blacks, women, and other groups of oppressed humans while denying equal consideration to nonhumans.

When we say that all human beings, whatever their race, creed, or sex, are equal, what is it that we are asserting? Those who wish to defend a hierarchical, inegalitarian society have often pointed out that by whatever test we choose, it simply is not true that all humans are equal. Like it or not, we must face the fact that humans come in different shapes and sizes; they come with differing moral capacities, differing intellectual abilities, differing amounts of benevolent feeling and sensitivity to the needs of others, differing abilities to communicate effectively, and differing capacities to experience pleasure and pain. In short, if the demand for equality were based on the actual equality of all human beings, we would have to stop demanding equality. It would be an unjustifiable demand.

Still, one might cling to the view that the demand for equality among human beings is based on the actual equality of the different races and sexes. Although humans differ as individuals in various ways, there are no differences between the races and sexes as such. From the mere fact that a person is black, or a woman, we cannot infer anything else about that person. This, it may be said, is what is wrong with racism and sexism. The white racist claims that whites are superior to blacks, but this is false—although there are differences between individuals, some blacks are superior to some whites in all of the capacities and abilities that could conceivably be relevant. The opponent of sexism would say the same: a person's sex is no guide to his or her abilities, and this is why it is unjustifiable to discriminate on the basis of sex.

This is a possible line of objection to racial and sexual discrimination. It is not, however, the way that someone really concerned about equality would choose, because taking this line could, in some circumstances, force one to accept a most inegalitarian society. The fact that humans differ as individuals, rather than as races or sexes, is a valid reply to someone who defends a hierarchical society like, say, South Africa, in which all whites are superior in status to all blacks. The existence of individual variations that cut across the lines of race or sex, however, provides us with no defense at all against a more sophisticated opponent of equality, one who proposes that, say, the interests of those with I.Q. ratings above 100 be preferred to the interests of those with I.Q.s below 100. Would a hierarchical society of this sort really be so much better than one based on race or sex? I think not. But if we tie the moral principle of equality to the factual equality of the different races or sexes, taken as a whole, our opposition to racism and sexism does not provide us with any basis for objecting to this kind of inegalitarianism.

There is a second important reason why we ought not to base our opposition to racism and sexism on any kind of factual equality, even the limited kind which asserts that variations in capacities and abilities are spread evenly between the different races and sexes: we can have no absolute guarantee that these abilities and capacities really are distributed evenly, without regard to race or sex, among human beings. So far as actual abilities are concerned, there do seem to be certain measurable differences between both races and sexes. These differences do not, of course, appear in each case, but only when averages are taken. More important still, we do not yet know how much of these differences is really due to the different genetic endowments of the various races and sexes, and how much is due to environmental differences that are the result of past and continuing discrimination. Perhaps all of the important differences will eventually prove to be environmental rather than genetic. Anyone opposed to racism and sexism will certainly hope that this will be so, for it will make the task of ending discrimination a lot easier; nevertheless it would be dangerous to rest the case against racism and sexism on the belief that all significant differences are environmental in origin. The opponent of, say, racism who takes this line will be unable to avoid conceding that if differences in ability did after all prove to have some genetic connection with race, racism would in some way be defensible.

It would be folly for the opponent of racism to stake his whole case on a dogmatic commitment to one particular outcome of a difficult scientific issue which is still a long way from being settled. While attempts to prove that differences in certain selected abilities between races and sexes are primarily genetic in origin have certainly not been conclusive, the same must be said of attempts to prove that these differences are largely the result of environment. At this stage of the investigation we cannot be certain which view is correct, however much we may hope it is the latter.

Fortunately, there is no need to pin the case for equality to one particular outcome of this scientific investigation. The appropriate response to those who claim to have found evidence of genetically-based differences in ability between the races or sexes is not to stick to the belief that the genetic explanation must be wrong, whatever evidence to the contrary may turn up: instead we should make it quite clear that the claim to equality does not depend on intelligence, moral capacity, physical strength, or similar matters of fact. Equality is a moral ideal, not a simple assertion of fact. There is no logically compelling reason for assuming that a factual difference in ability between two people justifies any difference in the amount of consideration we give to satisfying their needs and interests. The principle of the equality of human beings is not a description of an alleged actual equality among humans: it is a prescription of how we should treat humans.

Jeremy Bentham incorporated the essential basis of moral equality into his utilitarian system of ethics in the formula: "Each to count for one and none for more than one." In other words, the interests of every being affected by an action are to be taken into account and given the same weight as the like interests of any other being. A later utilitarian, Henry Sidgwick, put the point in this way: "The good of any one individual is of no more importance, from the point of view (if I may say so) of the Universe, than the good of any other."[1] More recently, the leading figures in contemporary moral philosophy have shown a great deal of agreement in specifying as a fundamental presupposition of their moral theories some similar requirement which operates so as to give everyone's interests equal consideration—although they cannot agree on how this requirement is best formulated.[2]

It is an implication of this principle of equality that our concern for others ought not to depend on what they are like, or what abilities they possess—although precisely what this concern requires us to do may vary according to the characteristics of those affected by what we do. It is on this basis that the case against racism and the case against sexism must both ultimately rest; and it is in accordance with this principle that speciesism is also to be condemned. If possessing a higher degree of intelligence does not entitle one human to use another for his own ends, how can it entitle humans to exploit nonhumans?

Many philosophers have proposed the principle of equal consideration of interests, in some form or other, as a basic moral principle; but, as we shall see in more detail shortly, not many of them have recognized that this principle applies to members of other species as well as to our own. Bentham was one of the few who did realize this. In a forward-looking passage, written at a time when black slaves in the British dominions were still being treated much as we now treat nonhuman animals, Bentham wrote:

> The day may come when the rest of the animal creation may acquire those rights which never could have been witholden from them but by the hand of tyranny. The French have already discovered that the blackness of the skin is no reason why a human being should be abandoned without redress to the caprice of a tormentor. It may one day come to be recognized that the number of the legs, the villosity of the skin, or the termination of the os sacrum, are reasons equally insufficient for abandoning a sensitive being to the same fate. What else is it that should trace the insuperable line? Is it the faculty of reason, or perhaps the faculty of discourse? But a full-grown horse or dog is beyond comparison a more rational, as well as a more conversable animal, than an infant of a day, or a week, or even a month, old. But suppose they were otherwise, what would it avail? The question is not, Can they *reason*? nor, Can they *talk*? but, Can they *suffer*?[3]

In this passage Bentham points to the capacity for suffering as the vital characteristic that gives a being the right to equal consideration. The capacity for suffering—or more strictly, for suffering and/or enjoyment or happiness—is not just another characteristic like the capacity for language, or for higher mathematics. Bentham is not saying that those who

try to mark "the insuperable line" that determines whether the interests of a being should be considered happen to have selected the wrong characteristic. The capacity for suffering and enjoying things is a prerequisite for having interests at all, a condition that must be satisfied before we can speak of interests in any meaningful way. It would be nonsense to say that it was not in the interests of a stone to be kicked along the road by a schoolboy. A stone does not have interests because it cannot suffer. Nothing that we can do to it could possibly make any difference to its welfare. A mouse, on the other hand, does have an interest in not being tormented, because it will suffer if it is.

If a being suffers, there can be no moral justification for refusing to take that suffering into consideration. No matter what the nature of the being, the principle of equality requires that its suffering be counted equally with the like suffering—in so far as rough comparisons can be made—of any other being. If a being is not capable of suffering, or of experiencing enjoyment or happiness, there is nothing to be taken into account. This is why the limit of sentience (using the term as a convenient, if not strictly accurate, shorthand for the capacity to suffer or experience enjoyment or happiness) is the only defensible boundary of concern for the interests of others. To mark this boundary by some characteristic like intelligence or rationality would be to mark it in an arbitrary way. Why not choose some other characteristic, like skin color?

The racist violates the principle of equality by giving greater weight to the interests of members of his own race, when there is a clash between their interests and the interests of those of another race. Similarly the speciesist allows the interests of his own species to override the greater interests of members of other species.[4] The pattern is the same in each case. Most human beings are speciesists. I shall now very briefly describe some of the practices that show this.

For the great majority of human beings, especially in urban, industrialized societies, the most direct form of contact with members of other species is at mealtimes: we eat them. In doing so we treat them purely as means to our ends. We regard their life and well-being as subordinate to our taste for a particular kind of dish. I say "taste" deliberately—this is purely a matter of pleasing our palate. There can be no defense of eating flesh in terms of satisfying nutritional needs, since it has been established beyond doubt that we could satisfy our need for protein and other essential nutrients far more efficiently with a diet that replaced animal flesh by soy beans, or products derived from soy beans, and other high-protein vegetable products.[5]

It is not merely the act of killing that indicates what we are ready to do to other species in order to gratify our tastes. The suffering we inflict on the animals while they are alive is perhaps an even clearer indication of our speciesism than the fact that we are prepared to kill them.[6] In order to have meat on the table at a price that people can afford, our society tolerates methods of meat production that confine sentient animals in cramped, unsuitable conditions for the entire durations of their lives. Animals are treated like machines that convert fodder into flesh, and any innovation that results in a higher "conversion ratio" is liable to be adopted. As one authority on the subject has said, "cruelty is acknowledged only when profitability ceases."[7] . . .

Since, as I have said, none of these practices cater for anything more than our pleasures of taste, our practice of rearing and killing other animals in order to eat them is a clear instance of the sacrifice of the most important interests of other beings in order to satisfy trivial interests of our own. To avoid speciesism we must stop this practice, and each of us has a moral obligation to cease supporting the practice. Our custom is all the support that the meat-industry needs. The decision to cease giving it that support may be difficult, but it is no more difficult than it would have been for a white Southerner to go against the traditions of his society and free his slaves: if we do not change our dietary habits, how can we censure those slaveholders who would not change their own way of living?

The same form of discrimination may be observed in the widespread practice of experimenting on other species in order to see if certain substances are safe for human beings, or to test some psychological theory about the effect of severe punishment on learning, or to try out various new compounds just in case something turns up. . . .

In the past, argument about vivisection has often missed the point, because it has been put in absolutist terms: Would the abolitionist be prepared to let thousands die if they could be saved by experimenting on a single animal? The way to reply to this purely hypothetical question is to pose another: Would the experimenter be prepared to perform his experiment on an orphaned human infant, if that were the only way to save many lives? (I say "orphan" to avoid the complication of parental feelings, although in doing so I am being overfair to the experimenter, since the nonhuman subjects of experiments are not orphans.) If the experimenter is not prepared to use an orphaned human infant, then his readiness to use nonhumans is simple discrimination, since adult apes, cats, mice, and other mammals are more aware of what is happening to them, more self-directing and, so far as we can tell, at least as sensitive to pain, as any human infant. There seems to be no relevant characteristic that human infants possess that adult mammals do not have to the same or a higher degree. (Someone might try to argue that what makes it wrong to experiment on a human infant is that the infant will, in time and if left alone, develop into more than the nonhuman, but one would then, to be consistent, have to oppose abortion, since the fetus has the same potential as the infant—indeed, even contraception and abstinence might be wrong on this ground, since the egg and sperm, considered jointly, also have the same potential. In any case, this argument still gives us no reason for selecting a nonhuman, rather than a human with severe and irreversible brain damage, as the subject for our experiments.)

The experimenter, then, shows a bias in favor of his own species whenever he carries out an experiment on a nonhuman for a purpose that he would not think justified him in using a human being at an equal or lower level of sentience, awareness, ability to be self-directing, etc. No one familiar with the kind of results yielded by most experiments on animals can have the slightest doubt that if this bias were eliminated the number of experiments performed would be a minute fraction of the number performed today.

Experimenting on animals, and eating their flesh, are perhaps the two major forms of speciesism in our society. By comparison, the third and last form of speciesism is so minor as to be insignificant, but it is perhaps of some special interest to those for whom this article was written. I am referring to speciesism in contemporary philosophy.

Philosophy ought to question the basic assumptions of the age. Thinking through, critically and carefully, what most people take for granted is, I believe, the chief task of philosophy, and it is this task that makes philosophy a worthwhile activity. Regrettably, philosophy does not always live up to its historic role. Philosophers are human beings, and they are subject to all the preconceptions of the society to which they belong. Sometimes they succeed in breaking free of the prevailing ideology: more often they become its most sophisticated defenders. So, in this case, philosophy as practiced in the universities today does not challenge anyone's preconceptions about our relations with other species. By their writings, those philosophers who tackle problems that touch upon the issue reveal that they make the same unquestioned assumptions as most other humans, and what they say tends to confirm the reader in his or her comfortable speciesist habits.

I could illustrate this claim by referring to the writings of philosophers in various fields—for instance, the attempts that have been made by those interested in rights to draw the boundary of the sphere of rights so that it runs parallel to the biological boundaries of the species homo sapiens, including infants and even mental defectives, but excluding those other beings of equal or greater capacity who are so useful to us at mealtimes and in our laboratories. I think it would be a more appropriate conclusion to this article, however, if I concentrated on the problem with which we have been centrally concerned, the problem of equality.

It is significant that the problem of equality, in moral and political philosophy, is invariably formulated in terms of human equality. The effect of this is that the question of the equality of other animals does not confront the philosopher, or student, as an issue itself—and this is already an indication of the failure of philosophy to challenge accepted beliefs. Still, philosophers have found it difficult to discuss the issue of human equality without raising, in a paragraph or two, the question of the status of other

animals. The reason for this, which should be apparent from what I have said already, is that if humans are to be regarded as equal to one another, we need some sense of "equal" that does not require any actual, descriptive equality of capacities, talents or other qualities. If equality is to be related to any actual characteristics of humans, these characteristics must be some lowest common denominator, pitched so low that no human lacks them—but then the philosopher comes up against the catch that any such set of characteristics which covers all humans will not be possessed only by humans. In other words, it turns out that in the only sense in which we can truly say, as an assertion of fact, that all humans are equal, at least some members of other species are also equal—equal, that is, to each other and to humans. If, on the other hand, we regard the statement "All humans are equal" in some non-factual way, perhaps as a prescription, then, as I have already argued, it is even more difficult to exclude nonhumans from the sphere of equality.

This result is not what the egalitarian philosopher originally intended to assert. Instead of accepting the radical outcome to which their own reasonings naturally point, however, most philosophers try to reconcile their beliefs in human equality and animal inequality by arguments that can only be described as devious.

As a first example, I take William Frankena's well-known article "The Concept of Social Justice." Frankena opposes the idea of basing justice on merit, because he sees that this could lead to highly inegalitarian results. Instead he proposes the principle that

> all men are to be treated as equals, not because they are equal, in any respect, but simply because they are human. They are human because they have emotions and desires, and are able to think, and hence are capable of enjoying a good life in a sense in which other animals are not.[8]

But what is this capacity to enjoy the good life which all humans have, but no other animals? Other animals have emotions and desires and appear to be capable of enjoying a good life. We may doubt that they can think—although the behavior of some apes, dolphins, and even dogs suggests that some of them can—but what is the relevance of thinking? Frankena goes on to admit that by "the good life" he means "not so much the morally good life as the happy or satisfactory life," so thought would appear to be unnecessary for enjoying the good life; in fact to emphasize the need for thought would make difficulties for the egalitarian since only some people are capable of leading intellectually satisfying lives, or morally good lives. This makes it difficult to see what Frankena's principle of equality has to do with simply being human. Surely every sentient being is capable of leading a life that is happier or less miserable than some alternative life, and hence has a claim to be taken into account. In this respect the distinction between humans and nonhumans is not a sharp division, but rather a continuum along which we move gradually, and with overlaps between the species, from simple capacities for enjoyment and satisfaction, or pain and suffering, to more complex ones.

Faced with a situation in which they see a need for some basis for the moral gulf that is commonly thought to separate humans and animals, but can find no concrete difference that will do the job without undermining the equality of humans, philosophers tend to waffle. They resort to high-sounding phrases like "the intrinsic dignity of the human individual";[9] they talk of the "intrinsic worth of all men" as if men (humans?) had some worth that other beings did not,[10] or they say that humans, and only humans, are "ends in themselves," while "everything other than a person can only have value for a person."[11]

This idea of a distinctive human dignity and worth has a long history; it can be traced back directly to the Renaissance humanists, for instance to Pico della Mirandola's *Oration on the Dignity of Man*. Pico and other humanists based their estimate of human dignity on the idea that man possessed the central, pivotal position in the "Great Chain of Being" that led from the lowliest forms of matter to God himself; this view of the universe, in turn, goes back to both classical and Judeo-Christian doctrines. Contemporary philosophers have cast off these metaphysical and religious shackles and freely invoke the dignity of mankind without needing to justify the idea at all. Why should we not attribute

"intrinsic dignity" or "intrinsic worth" to ourselves? Fellow-humans are unlikely to reject the accolades we so generously bestow on them, and those to whom we deny the honor are unable to object. Indeed, when one thinks only of humans, it can be very liberal, very progressive, to talk of the dignity of all human beings. In so doing, we implicitly condemn slavery, racism, and other violations of human rights. We admit that we ourselves are in some fundamental sense on a par with the poorest, most ignorant members of our own species. It is only when we think of humans as no more than a small sub-group of all the beings that inhabit our planet that we may realize that in elevating our own species we are at the same time lowering the relative status of all other species.

The truth is that the appeal to the intrinsic dignity of human beings appears to solve the egalitarian's problems only as long as it goes unchallenged. Once we ask why it should be that all humans—including infants, mental defectives, psychopaths, Hitler, Stalin, and the rest—have some kind of dignity or worth that no elephant, pig, or chimpanzee can ever achieve, we see that this question is as difficult to answer as our original request for some relevant fact that justifies the inequality of humans and other animals. In fact, these two questions are really one: talk of intrinsic dignity or moral worth only takes the problem back one step, because any satisfactory defence of the claim that all and only humans have intrinsic dignity would need to refer to some relevant capacities or characteristics that all and only humans possess. Philosophers frequently introduce ideas of dignity, respect, and worth at the point at which other reasons appear to be lacking, but this is hardly good enough. Fine phrases are the last resource of those who have run out of arguments.

In case there are those who still think it may be possible to find some relevant characteristic that distinguishes all humans from all members of other species, I shall refer again, before I conclude, to the existence of some humans who quite clearly are below the level of awareness, self-consciousness, intelligence, and sentience, of many non-humans. I am thinking of humans with severe and irreparable brain damage, and also of infant humans. To avoid the complication of the relevance of a being's potential, however, I shall henceforth concentrate on permanently retarded humans.

Philosophers who set out to find a characteristic that will distinguish humans from other animals rarely take the course of abandoning these groups of humans by lumping them in with the other animals. It is easy to see why they do not. To take this line without re-thinking our attitudes to other animals would entail that we have the right to perform painful experiments on retarded humans for trivial reasons; similarly it would follow that we had the right to rear and kill these humans for food. To most philosophers these consequences are as unacceptable as the view that we should stop treating nonhumans in this way.

Of course, when discussing the problem of equality it is possible to ignore the problem of mental defectives, or brush it aside as if somehow insignificant.[12] This is the easiest way out.

What else remains? My final example of speciesism in contemporary philosophy has been selected to show what happens when a writer is prepared to face the question of human equality and animal inequality without ignoring the existence of mental defectives, and without resorting to obscurantist mumbo jumbo. Stanley Benn's clear and honest article "Egalitarianism and Equal Consideration of Interests"[13] fits this description.

Benn, after noting the usual "evident human inequalities" argues, correctly I think, for equality of consideration as the only possible basis for egalitarianism. Yet Benn, like other writers, is thinking only of "equal consideration of human interests." Benn is quite open in his defence of this restriction of equal consideration:

> . . . not to possess human shape is a disqualifying condition. However faithful or intelligent a dog may be, it would be a monstrous sentimentality to attribute to him interests that could be weighed in an equal balance with those of human beings . . . if, for instance, one had to decide between feeding a hungry baby or a hungry dog, anyone who chose the dog would generally be reckoned morally defective, unable to recognize a fundamental inequality of claims. This is what distinguishes our attitude to animals from our attitude to imbeciles. It would be odd to say that we ought to respect equally the dignity or personality of the imbecile and of the rational man . . . but there is nothing odd about saying that we should respect their interests equally, that is, that we should give to the interests of each the same serious consideration as claims to considerations necessary for some standard of well-being that we can recognize and endorse.

Benn's statement of the basis of the consideration we should have for imbeciles seems to me correct, but why should there be any fundamental inequality of claims between a dog and a human imbecile? Benn sees that if equal consideration depended on rationality, no reason could be given against using imbeciles for research purposes, as we now use dogs and guinea pigs. This will not do: "But of course we do distinguish imbeciles from animals in this regard," he says. That the common distinction is justifiable is something Benn does not question; his problem is how it is to be justified. The answer he gives is this:

> . . . we respect the interests of men and give them priority over dogs not *insofar* as they are rational, but because rationality is the human norm. We say it is *unfair* to exploit the deficiencies of the imbecile who falls short of the norm, just as it would be unfair, and not just ordinarily dishonest, to steal from a blind man. If we do not think in this way about dogs, it is because we do not see the irrationality of the dog as a deficiency or a handicap, but as normal for the species, The characteristics, therefore, that distinguish the normal man from the normal dog make it intelligible for us to talk of other men having interests and capacities, and therefore claims, of precisely the same kind as we make on our own behalf. But although these characteristics may provide the point of the distinction between men and other species, they are not in fact the qualifying conditions for membership, to the distinguishing criteria of the class of morally considerable persons; and this is precisely because a man does not become a member of a different species, with its own standards of normality, by reason of not possessing these characteristics.

The final sentence of this passage gives the argument away. An imbecile, Benn concedes, may have no characteristics superior to those of a dog; nevertheless this does not make the imbecile a member of "a different species" as the dog is. Therefore it would be "unfair" to use the imbecile for medical research as we use the dog. But why? That the imbecile is not rational is just the way things have worked out, and the same is true of the dog—neither is any more responsible for their mental level. If it is unfair to take advantage of an isolated defect, why is it fair to take advantage of a more general limitation? I find it hard to see anything in this argument except a defense of preferring the interests of members of our own species because they are members of our own species. To those who think there might be more to it, I suggest the following mental exercise. Assume that it has been proven that there is a difference in the average, or normal, intelligence quotient for two different races, say whites and blacks. Then substitute the term "white" for every occurrence of "men" and "black" for every occurrence of "dog" in the passage quoted; and substitute "high I.Q." for "rationality" and when Benn talks of "imbeciles" replace this term by "dumb whites"—that is, whites who fall well below the normal white I.Q. score. Finally, change "species" to "race." Now reread the passage. It has become a defense of a rigid, no-exceptions division between whites and blacks, based on I.Q. scores, not withstanding an admitted overlap between whites and blacks in this respect. The revised passage is, of course, outrageous, and this is not only because we have made fictitious assumptions in our substitutions. The point is that in the original passage Benn was defending a rigid division in the amount of consideration due to members of different species, despite admitted cases of overlap. If the original did not, at first reading strike us as being as outrageous as the revised version does, this is largely because although we are not racists ourselves, most of us are speciesists. Like the other articles, Benn's stands as a warning of the ease with which the best minds can fall victim to a prevailing ideology.

Notes

1. *The Methods of Ethics* (7th Ed.), p. 382.
2. For example, R. M. Hare, *Freedom and Reason* (Oxford, 1963), and J. Rawls, *A Theory of Justice* (Harvard, 1972); for a brief account of the essential agreement on this issue between these and other positions, see R. M. Hare, "Rules of War and Moral Reasoning," *Philosophy and Public Affairs*, vol. 1, no. 2 (1972).
3. *Introduction to the Principles of Morals and Legislation,* ch. XVII.
4. I owe the term speciesism to Richard Ryder.
5. In order to produce 1 lb. of protein in the form of beef or veal, we must feed 21 lbs. of protein to the animal. Other forms of livestock are slightly less inefficient, but the average ratio in the United States is still 1:8. It has been estimated that the amount of protein lost to humans in this way is equivalent to 90 percent of the annual world protein deficit. For a brief account, see Frances Moore Lappe, *Diet for a Small Planet* (Friends of The Earth/Ballantine, New York, 1971), pp. 4–11.
6. Although one might think that killing a being is obviously the ultimate wrong one can do to it, I think that the infliction of suffering is a clearer indication of speciesism because it might be argued that at least part of what is wrong with killing a human is that most humans are conscious of their existence over time and have desires and purposes that extend into the future. See, for instance, M. Tooley, "Abortion and Infanticide," *Philosophy and Public Affairs*, vol. 2, no. 1 (1972). Of course, if one took this view one would have to hold—as Tooley does—that killing a human infant or mental defective is not in itself wrong and is less serious than killing certain higher mammals that probably do have a sense of their own existence over time.
7. Ruth Harrison, *Animal Machines* (Stuart, London, 1964). For an account of farming conditions, see my *Animal Liberation* (New York Review Company, 1975).
8. In R. Brandt (ed.), *Social Justice* (Prentice Hall, Englewood Cliffs, 1962), p. 19.
9. Frankena, op. cit. p. 23.
10. H. A. Bedau, "Egalitarianism and the Idea of Equality," in *Nomos IX: Equality*, ed. J. R. Pennock and J. W. Chapman, New York, 1967.
11. C. Vlastos, "Justice and Equality," in Brandt, *Social Justice*, p. 48.
12. For example, Bernard Williams, "The Idea of Equality," in *Philosophy, Politics, and Society* (second series), ed. P. Laslett and W. Rundman (Blackwell, Oxford, 1962), p. 118; J. Rawls, *A Theory of Justice*, pp. 509–10.
13. *Nomos IX: Equality*; the passages quoted are on p. 62ff.

QUESTIONS

1. What exactly is the argument in favor of taking animal suffering into consideration?
2. Why don't the positions of Aquinas and Kant, both of whom argue that we should not treat animals cruelly, appeal to Singer?

43. Against the Moral Standing of Animals

PETER CARRUTHERS

Peter Carruthers (1952–) is professor of philosophy at the University of Maryland, College Park. His main areas of research have been the philosophy of mind and cognitive science, especially theories of consciousness and self-knowledge, the role of natural language in human cognition, and modularity of mind. He is the author of a book on the moral status of animals, *The Animals Issue: Moral Theory in Practice* (1992).

In this essay, written for this volume, Carruthers presents and develops his case against the moral standing of animals. He assumes the correctness of a contractualist conception of morality (see chapter 67) and argues that only humans have moral standing.

I shall argue in this essay that the lives and sufferings of nonhuman animals (hereafter "animals") make no direct moral claims on us. At the same time I shall argue that the lives and sufferings of human infants and senile old people *do* make such claims on us. In short: I shall argue that no animals possess *moral standing*, while arguing all human beings possess such standing. I shall allow, however, that some of the things that one might do (or fail to do) to an animal might attract justified moral criticism. But this will be criticism of an indirect (and perhaps culturally local) sort, not deriving from any violations of the rights that the animal might possess. On the contrary, because animals lack standing, they have no rights.

I. Assumptions

In this section I shall lay out two sets of assumptions that form the background to my argument. One is about the mental lives and cognitive capacities of animals; the other is about the correct framework for moral theory. While I shall make no attempt to defend these assumptions here, they are quite widely shared, and each is, I believe, fully defensible.

1.1. Animal Minds

I shall assume that most animals have minds much like our own. They have beliefs and desires, and engage in practical reasoning in the light of their beliefs and desires. (This is true even of some invertebrates, including bees and jumping spiders, I believe.) Many animals feel pain and fear, and (in some cases) an emotion much like grief. (For discussion of the evidence supporting these claims, see Carruthers, 2006, ch.2.) In short: most animals can *suffer*. Stronger still, I shall assume for these purposes that most animals undergo experiences and feelings that are *conscious*, having the same kind of rich phenomenology and inner "feel" as do our own conscious mental states.[1]

I shall also assume, however, that animals don't count as *rational agents* in the following (quite demanding) sense: A rational agent is a creature that is capable of governing its behavior in accordance with universal rules (such as "Don't tell lies") and that is capable of thinking about the costs and benefits of the general adoption of a given rule, to be obeyed by most members of a community that includes other rational agents. This assumption is quite obviously true in connection with most animals. I believe that it is also true (although this is slightly more controversial) in connection with members of other species of great ape, such as chimpanzees and gorillas. (If it should turn out that the members of some species of animal *do* count as rational agents in this sense, then those creatures will be accorded full moral standing, on the approach taken here.) Why the absence of rational agency should matter will emerge in the sections that follow.

1.2. Moral Theory

I shall assume that some or other version of contractualist moral theory is correct. (The problems with utilitarian theories are notorious, and well known. Forms of virtue theory are best pursued and accounted for within the framework of contractualism, I believe.) All contractualists agree that moral truths are, in a certain sense, human constructions, emerging out of some or other variety of hypothetical rational agreement concerning the basic rules to govern our behavior.

In one version of contractualism, moral rules are those that would be agreed upon by rational agents choosing, on broadly self-interested grounds, from behind a "veil of ignorance" (Rawls, 1972). On this account, we are to picture rational agents as attempting to agree on a set of rules to govern their conduct for their mutual benefit in full knowledge of all facts of human psychology, sociology, economics, and so forth, but in ignorance of any particulars about themselves—their own strengths, weaknesses, tastes, life plans, or position in society. All they are allowed to assume as goals when making their choice are the things that they will want *whatever* particular desires and plans they happen to have—namely, wealth, happiness, power, and self-respect. Moral rules are then the rules that would be agreed upon in this situation, provided that the agreement is made on rational grounds. The governing intuition behind this approach is that justice is fairness: Since the situation behind the veil of ignorance is fair (all rational agents are equivalently placed), the resulting agreement must also be fair.

In another version of contractualism, moral rules are those that no rational agent could reasonably reject who shared (as their highest priority) the aim of reaching free and unforced general agreement on the rules that are to govern their behavior (Scanlon, 1982, 1998). On this account, we start from agents who are allowed full knowledge of their particular qualities and circumstances (as well as of general truths of psychology and so forth). But we imagine that they are guided, above all, by the goal of reaching free and unforced agreement on the set of rules that are to govern everyone's behavior. Here each individual agent can be thought of as having a veto over the proposed rules. But it is a veto that will only be exercised if it doesn't derail the agreement process, making it impossible to find any set of rules that no one can reasonably reject.

It should be stressed that within a contractualist approach, as I shall understand it, rational agents aren't allowed to appeal to any moral beliefs as part of the idealized contract process.[2] Since moral truths are to be the output of the contract process, they cannot be appealed to at the start. Put differently: Since morality is to be constructed through the agreement of rational agents, it cannot be supposed to exist in advance of that agreement. It is also worth pointing out that on each of the previously mentioned approaches, some moral rules will be mere local conventions. This will happen whenever the contract process entails that there should be *some* moral rule governing a behavior or set of circumstances, but where there are no compelling grounds for selecting one candidate rule over the others.[3]

In what follows I shall often consider arguments from the perspective of *both* of these forms of contractualism. In that way we can increase our confidence that the conclusions are entailed by contractualist approaches as such, rather than by the specifics of some or other particular variety.

2. All Humans Have Standing

In the present section I shall argue that all human beings have moral standing, irrespective of their status as rational agents. I shall argue first that all rational agents have standing, and will then show that the same basic sort of standing should be accorded to human infants and senile (or otherwise mentally defective) adult humans.[4] Since these arguments don't extend to animals (as we will see in section 3), they constitute a reply to Singer's (1979) challenge. For Singer claims that contractualism can't consistently deny moral standing to animals without *also* withholding it from infants and mentally defective humans. This section and the one following will demonstrate that he is mistaken.

2.1. The Basic Case: Rational Agents Have Standing

The contractualist framework plainly entails that all rational agents should have the same moral standing. For moral rules are here conceived to be constructed *by* rational agents *for* rational agents. It is obvious that rational agents behind a veil of ignorance would opt to accord the same basic rights, duties, and protections to themselves (that is to say: to all rational agents, since they are choosing in ignorance of their particular identities). And likewise within Scanlon's framework: It is obvious that any proposed rule that would withhold moral standing from some subset of rational agents could reasonably be rejected by the members of that subset.

It should be stressed that contractualism accords the same basic moral standing to all rational agents as such, and not merely to the members of some actual group or society. On Rawls's approach, contracting agents don't even know which group or society they will turn out to be members of once the veil is drawn aside. And on Scanlon's account, although we are to picture rational agents seeking to agree on a framework of rules in full knowledge of who they are and the groups to which they belong, those rules can be vetoed by *any* rational agent, irrespective of group membership. It follows that if Mars should turn out to be populated by a species of rational agent, then contractualism will accord the members of that species full moral standing.

2.2. Nonrational Humans: The Argument from Social Stability

It seems that rational contractors wouldn't automatically cede moral standing to those human beings who are *not* rational agents (e.g., infants and senile old people), in the way that they must cede standing to each other. But there are considerations that should induce them to do so, nevertheless. The main one is this.[5] Notice that the basic goal of the contract process is to achieve a set of moral rules that will provide social stability and preserve the peace. This means that moral rules will have to be *psychologically supportable*, in the following sense: They have to be such that rational agents can, in general, bring themselves to abide by them without brainwashing. (Arguably, no rational agent would consent to the loss of autonomy involved in any form of the latter practice.) But now the contractors just have to reflect that, if anything counts as part of "human nature" (and certainly much does; see Pinker, 2002), then people's deep attachment to their infants and aged relatives surely belongs within it. In general, people care as deeply about their immediate relatives as they care about anything (morality included), irrespective of their relatives' status as rational agents. In which case contracting agents should accord moral standing to all human beings, and not just to those human beings who happen to be rational agents.

Consider what a society would be like that denied moral standing to infants and/or senile old people. The members of these groups would, at most, be given the same type of protection that gets accorded to items of private property, deriving from the legitimate concerns of the rational agents who care about them. But that would leave the state or its agents free to destroy or cause suffering to the members of these groups whenever it might be in the public interest to do so, provided that their relatives receive financial compensation. (For example, senile old people might be killed so that their organs can be harvested, or it might be particularly beneficial to use human infants in certain painful medical experiments.) We can see in advance that these arrangements would be highly unstable. Those whose loved ones were at risk would surely resist with violence, and would band together with others to so resist. Foreseeing this, contracting rational agents should agree that all human beings be accorded moral standing.[6]

2.3. A Reply from Anthropology

It might be replied against this argument that there have been many communities in the world where infanticide and the killing of the old have been sanctioned, without any of the predicted dire consequences for the stability of those societies. Thus in many traditional societies the smaller of a pair of twins, or any infant born deformed, might be abandoned by its mother to die (Hrdy, 1999). And some Inuit tribes are said to have had the practice of forsaking their old people to die in the snow when the latter became too infirm to travel.

One point to be made in response to this objection is that all of the communities in question were sustained and stabilized by systems of traditional belief (often religious belief: "The gods require it," might be the justification given). This is no longer possible for us in conditions of modernity, where it is acceptable for any belief, no matter how revered and long-standing, to be subjected to critical scrutiny. And plainly, the contract process envisaged by contractualism can't make appeal to such traditional beliefs, either.

Another point to be made in response to the objection is that all of the communities in question were teetering on the edge of survival for their members; or at the very least the costs to individuals for acting differently would have been *very* high. In which case it is far from obvious that the practices we are considering involve the denial of moral standing to infants and/or the old, anyway. For

notice that in these communities death occurs from failure to support, or from the withdrawal of aid, rather than by active killing. And we, too, accept that it can be permissible to withdraw support, allowing someone to die, when the costs to oneself become too great. Think, for example, of someone in the process of rescuing another person from drowning, who has to give up his effort when he realizes that the current is too strong, and that he himself is in danger of drowning.

2.4. Conclusion: All Humans Have Standing

We can conclude the following. If, as I claim, contractualism is the correct framework for moral theorizing, then it follows that all human beings—whether infant, child, adult, old, or senile—should be accorded the same basic structure of rights and protections. In section 3 I shall show, in contrast, that contractualism leaves all animals beyond the moral pale, withholding moral standing from them.

Before completing this section it is worth noting that infants and senile old people aren't by any means accorded "second-class moral citizenship" by contractualism. Although it is only rational agents who get to grant moral standing through the contract process, and although the considerations that should lead them to grant moral standing to humans who aren't rational agents are indirect ones (not emerging directly out of the structure of the contract process, as does the moral standing of rational agents themselves), this has no impact on the product. Although the considerations that demonstrate the moral standing of rational agents and of nonrational humans may differ from one another, the result is the same: Both groups have moral standing, and both should have similar basic rights and protections.

3. No Animals Have Standing

In this section I shall maintain, first, that the argument just given for according moral standing to all human beings doesn't extend to animals. Then, second, I shall consider two further attempts to secure moral standing for animals within contractualism, showing that they fail. The upshot can be captured in the slogan: "Humans in, animals out."

3.1. Social Stability Revisited

The argument of section 2.3 was that nonrational humans should be accorded moral standing in order to preserve social stability, since people's attachments to their infants and aged relatives are generally about as deep as it is possible to go. Someone might try presenting a similar argument to show that animals, too, should be accorded moral standing, citing the violence that has *actually* occurred in Western societies when groups of people (like members of the Animal Liberation Front) have acted in defense of the interests of animals. Such an argument fails, however, because members of these groups are acting, not out of attachments that are a normal product of human emotional mechanisms, but out of (what they take to be justified) moral beliefs.

Recall that rational agents engaging in the contract process are forbidden from appealing to any antecedent moral beliefs—whether their own or other people's. (This is because moral truth is to be the outcome of the contract, and shouldn't be presupposed at the outset.) So contracting rational agents should *not* reason that animals ought to be accorded moral standing on the grounds that some people have a moral belief in such standing, and may be prepared to kill or engage in other forms of violence in pursuit of their principles. The proper response is that such people aren't entitled to their belief in the moral standing of animals unless they can show that rational agents in the appropriate sort of contract situation would agree to it.

Many people come to care quite a bit about their pets, of course, and this is something that rational contractors might be expected to know. Could this give rise to a social-stability argument for moral standing? The answer is "no," for at least two distinct reasons.[7] One is that it is far from clear that the phenomenon of pet-keeping and attachment to pets is a human universal (in contrast with attachment to infants and aged relatives). It may be rather a product of local cultural forces operating in some societies but not others. And if the latter is the case, then such attachments aren't a "fixed point" of human nature, which should constrain rational contractors in their deliberations. They might appropriately decide, instead, that society should be arranged in such a way that people don't develop attachments that are apt to interfere with correct moral decision making.

A second problem with the suggestion is that attachment to pets is rarely so deep as attachments to relatives, in any case. Hence people should have little difficulty in coming to accept that pets can only be accorded the sorts of protections granted to other items of private property. Most of us would think that it would be foolish (indeed, reprehensible) to continue to keep a pet that threatens the life of a child (e.g., through severe allergic reactions). And when the state declares that the public interest requires that someone's dog be put down (e.g., because it is dangerous), it would surely be unreasonable to take up arms to defend the life of the animal, just as it would be unreasonable to kill to preserve a house that had been condemned for demolition.

3.2. Representing the Interests of Animals

While the argument from social stability doesn't show that animals should be accorded moral standing, other arguments could still be successful. One suggestion would be that some rational agents behind the veil of ignorance should be assigned to represent the interests of animals, much as a lawyer might be assigned to represent the interests of a pet in a court of law in a case involving a disputed will. If it was the job of those representatives to look out for the interests of animals in the formulation of the basic moral contract, then they might be expected to insist upon animals being granted moral standing.

This suggestion, however, is plainly at odds with the guiding idea of contractualism. For what possible motive could there be for assigning some agents to represent the interests of animals in the contract process, unless it were believed that animals *deserve* to have their interests protected? But that would be to assume a moral truth at the outset: the belief, namely, that animals deserve to be protected. We noted earlier, in contrast, that contractualism assumes that the contracting parties should come to the contract situation either without any moral beliefs at all, or setting aside (taking care not to rely upon) such moral beliefs as they do have.

The point is even easier to see in Scanlon's version of contractualism. Real individual agents with knowledge of their own particulars, but who either lack moral beliefs or have set aside their moral beliefs while trying to agree to rules that no one could reasonably reject, could have no reason to assign some of their number to represent the interests of animals. For to do so would be tantamount to insisting at the outset that animals should be accorded moral standing, preempting and usurping the constructive contract process.

3.3. Ignorance of Species

Another suggestion is that people behind the veil of ignorance should be selecting moral rules in ignorance of their species, just as they are ignorant of their life-plans, age, strength, intelligence, gender, race, position in society, and so on (Regan, 1984). Then just as rational agents might be expected to agree on rules to protect the weak, since for all they know they might end up to *be* weak, so, too, rational agents might be expected to agree on a system of fundamental rights for animals, since for all they know they might end up *being* an animal.

One problem with this suggestion is that Rawls's veil of ignorance is designed to rule out reliance upon factors that are widely agreed to be morally irrelevant. Amongst the intuitions that a good moral theory should preserve is the belief that someone's moral standing shouldn't depend upon such factors as their age, or gender, or race. In contrast we don't (or don't all) think that species is morally irrelevant. On the contrary, this is highly disputed, with (I would guess) a clear majority believing that differences of species (e.g., between human and dog) *can* be used to ground differential moral treatment.

The veil of ignorance is a theoretical device designed to ensure that deeply held moral beliefs about what is, or isn't, morally relevant should be preserved in the resulting theory. So although the contracting agents aren't allowed to appeal to any moral beliefs in the contract process, in effect the moral theorist has relied upon his prior moral beliefs

in designing the surrounding constraints. Scanlon's version of contractualism, in contrast, digs deeper. It has the capacity to *explain why* the properties mentioned in the veil of ignorance are morally irrelevant. This is because one should be able to see in advance as one approaches the contract situation that if one proposes a rule favoring men, then this will be vetoed by those rational agents who are women, and vice versa; and so on for differences of age, intelligence, strength, race, and so on. So if we are motivated by the goal of reaching free and unforced general agreement among rational agents, we should abjure proposals that might favor one group over another. For we can foresee that these would be vetoed, and that others could equally well suggest proposals favoring other groups, in any case, which *we* would need to veto. But in contrast there is no reason for us to abjure rules that favor humans over animal.

The idea of choosing rules in ignorance of one's species isn't even coherent within the framework of Scanlon's form of contractualism, in which agents are supposed to have full knowledge of their own particular qualities and circumstances, as well as of general truths of psychology, economics, and so forth. So there is no way to argue for the moral significance of animals from such a standpoint. Indeed, one should be able to see in advance that a proposed rule that would accord moral standing to animals would be vetoed by some, because of the costs and burdens that it would place on us.

3.4. Conclusion: No Animals Have Standing

I conclude that while the moral standing of all humans (including infants and senile old people) is entailed by contractualism, by the same token such standing should be denied to animals. Even if this position is theoretically impeccable, however, it faces a serious challenge. This is that most people believe very strongly indeed that it is possible to act wrongly in one's dealings with animals. And most people believe, too, that it is something about what is happening *to the animal* that warrants the moral criticism. These are intuitions that need to be explained, or explained away. This will form the topic of sections 4 and 5.

4. Forms of Indirect Moral Significance for Animals

Imagine that while walking in a city one evening you turn a corner to confront a group of teenagers who have caught a cat, doused it in kerosene, and are about to set it alight. Of course you would be horrified. You would think that the teenagers were doing something very wrong; and the vast majority of people would agree with you. It would be a serious black mark against contractualist moral theories in general, and against the line that I am pursuing in this essay in particular, if this intuition couldn't be accommodated.

4.1. Offense to Animal Lovers

One suggestion would be that we have *indirect* duties toward animals. These fail to have any corresponding rights on the part of the animal, but rather derive from a direct duty not to cause unnecessary offense to the feelings of animal lovers or animal owners. Compare the scenario just mentioned with this one: While walking through a city you come across a pair of young people, stark naked, making love on a park bench in broad daylight. Here, too, you would be horrified, and you would think that what they were doing was wrong. But the wrongness isn't, as it were, intrinsic to the activity. It is rather that the lovemaking is being conducted in a way that might be disturbing or distressing to other people: namely, in public. Likewise, it might be said, in the case of the teenagers setting light to the cat: What they are doing is wrong because it is likely to be disturbing or distressing to other people.

On the face of it this proposal isn't very promising. For while it can explain why the teenagers are wrong to set light to a cat in the street (since there is a danger that they might be observed), it can't so easily explain our intuition that it would be wrong of them to set light to the cat in the privacy of their own garage. Admittedly, there is some wiggle room here if one wanted to defend the proposal. For animals, having minds of their own, are apt to render public a suffering that was intended to remain private. The burning cat might escape from the garage, for example, or might emit such ear-piercing screams that the neighbors feel called upon

to investigate. But we can demonstrate the inadequacy of this whole approach through an example where such factors are decisively controlled for. This is the example of Astrid the astronaut.

You are to imagine that Astrid is an extremely rich woman who has become tired of life on Earth, and who purchases a space rocket for herself so that she can escape that life permanently. She blasts off on a trajectory that will eventually take her out of the solar system, and she doesn't even carry with her a radio or other means of communication. We can therefore know that she will never again have any contact with another human being. Now suppose that Astrid has taken with her a cat for company, but that at a certain point in the journey, out of boredom, she starts to use the cat for a dartboard, or does something else that would cause the cat unspeakable pain. Don't we think that what Astrid does is very wrong? But of course the ground of its wrongness can't be the danger that animal lovers will discover what she has done and be upset. For we know from the description of the case that there is no such danger.

4.2. Judging Acts by Character

Another approach, which I shall spend most of the remainder of this essay developing and defending, would be to claim that the action of torturing a cat is wrong because of what it shows about the moral character of the actor, not because it infringes any rights or is likely to cause distress to other people. Specifically, what the teenagers do in the street and what Astrid does on her space rocket show them to be *cruel*. And this would be our ground for saying that the actions themselves are wrong. In order for this account to work, however, it needs to be shown more generally that we sometimes judge actions by the qualities of moral character that they evince, irrespective of any morally significant harm that they cause, or of any rights that they infringe. I shall argue as much here, before briefly providing a contractualist rationale in section 5.

Return to the example of Astrid the astronaut. But now suppose that, in addition to a cat, she has taken with her another person. In one version of the story, this might be her beloved grandfather. In another version of the story (to avoid contaminating our intuitions with beliefs about family duties) it might be an employee whom she hires to work for her as a lifetime servant. Now at a certain point in the journey this other person dies. Astrid's response is to cut up the corpse into small pieces, thereafter storing them in the refrigerator and feeding them one by one to the cat.

Surely what Astrid does is wrong. But why? It causes no direct harm of a morally relevant sort. (Her companion, after all, is dead, and can't know or be upset.) And nor can any harm be caused indirectly to others. For in the nature of the case, no one else can ever know and be offended. Nor are any rights infringed. For even if one thinks that the dead have rights (which is doubtful), Astrid might know that her companion was an atheist who took not the slightest interest in ceremonies for the dead. Indeed, he might once have said to her, "Once I am dead I don't care what happens to my corpse; you can do what you like with it," thus waiving any rights that he might have in the matter. But still what Astrid does is very wrong.

Why is what Astrid does wrong? Surely this is because of what it shows about *her*. Just as her treatment of her cat shows her to be cruel, so her treatment of her dead companion displays a kind of disrespectful, inhuman, attitude toward humanity in general, and her companion in particular. (Note that practices for honoring the dead, and for treating corpses with respect, are a human universal. They are common to all cultures across all times.) And in each case we judge the action to be wrong because of the flaw that it evinces (both manifesting and further encouraging and developing) in her moral character.

Consider a different sort of example. Suppose that Lazy Jane is a doctor who is attending a conference of other medical professionals at a large hotel. She is relaxing in the bar during the evening, sitting alone with her drink in a cubicle. The bar is so arranged that there are many separate cubicles surrounding it, from each of which the bar itself is plainly visible, but the insides of which are invisible to each other. Jane is idly watching someone walk alone toward the bar when he collapses to the floor with all the signs of having undergone a serious heart attack. Jane feels no impulse to assist him, and continues calmly sipping her martini.

Plainly what Jane does (or in this case, doesn't do) is wrong. But why? For we can suppose that no harm is caused. Since the man collapses in plain view of dozens of medical personnel, expert help is swift in arriving; and she had every reason to believe that this would be so in the circumstances. And no rights are infringed. For even if there is such a thing as a general right to medical assistance when sick (which is doubtful), the man had no claim on *her* help in particular. If he had still been able to speak, he could have said, and (perhaps) said truly, "Someone should help me." But he certainly wouldn't have been correct if he had said, "Jane, in particular, should help me." Since our belief in the wrongness of Jane's inactivity survives these points, the explanation must be the one that we offered in connection with Astrid: It is wrong because of what it reveals about *her*. Specifically, it shows her to be callous and indifferent to the suffering of other people; or at least it shows that she lacks the sort of spontaneous, emotional, noncalculative concern for others that we think a good person should have.

My suggestion, then, is that our duties toward animals are indirect in the following way. They derive from the good or bad qualities of moral character that the actions in question would display and encourage; where those qualities *are* good or bad in virtue of the role that they play in the agent's interactions with other human beings. On this account, the most basic kind of wrongdoing toward animals is *cruelty*. A cruel action is wrong because it evinces a cruel character. But what makes a cruel character bad is that it is likely to express itself in cruelty toward *people*, which would involve direct violations of the rights of those who are caused to suffer.[8] Our intuition that the teenagers and Astrid all act wrongly is thereby explained, but explained in a way that is consistent with the claim that animals lack moral standing.

5. Contractualism, Virtue Ethics, and Animals

How, in general, do qualities of character acquire their significance within a contractualist moral framework? This question needs to be answered before the position sketched previously can be considered acceptable. And we need to investigate, too, in what ways cruelty to animals and cruelty to humans are linked to one another.

5.1. Contractualism and Character

Contracting rational agents should know in advance that human beings aren't calculating machines. We have limited time, limited memory, limited attention, and limited intellectual powers. In consequence, in everyday life we frequently have to rely on a suite of "quick and dirty" heuristics for decision making, rather than reasoning our way slowly and laboriously to the optimal solution (Gigerenzer et al., 1999). Contracting rational agents should realize, too, the vital role that motivational states and emotional reactions play in human decision making (Damasio, 1994). Hence they should do far more than agree on a framework of rules to govern their behavior. They should also agree to foster certain long-term dispositions of motivation and emotion that will make right action much more likely (especially when action is spontaneous, or undertaken under severe time constraints). That is to say: Contracting agents should agree on a duty to foster certain qualities of character, or *virtues*.

For example, contracting agents should agree on a duty to develop the virtue of *beneficence*. This is because they should foresee that more than merely rules of justice (which are for the most part negative in form: "don't steal, don't kidnap, don't kill, etc.") are necessary for human beings to flourish. People also need to develop positive attachments to the welfare of others, fostering a disposition and willingness to help others when they can do so at no important cost to themselves. For there are many ways in which people will inevitably, at some point in their lives, need the assistance of others if they are to succeed with their plans and projects, ranging from needing the kindness of a neighbor to jump-start one's car on a frosty morning, to needing someone on the river bank to throw one a life buoy or a rope when one is drowning.[9]

Rational contractors should also agree that people's actions can be judged (that is, praised or blamed) for the qualities of character they evince, independently of the harm caused, and independently of violations of right. This is because people *should possess*, or should develop, the required good qualities. Although these good qualities *are* good, in general, because of their effects on the welfare and rights of other people, their display on a given occasion can be independent of such effects. Hence we can, and should, evaluate the action in light of the qualities of character that it displays, independently of other considerations.

5.2. Cruelty to Animals and Cruelty to Humans

If the account given of the reasons that it is wrong for the teenagers to set light to a cat is to be successful, then cruelty to animals must be psychologically and behaviorally linked to cruelty to humans. To a first approximation, it must be the case that there is a single virtue of kindness, and a single vice of cruelty, that can be displayed toward either group. How plausible is this?

Certainly it would appear that attitudes toward the sufferings of animals and of humans are quite deeply linked in Western culture. For many of us have pets whom we treat as honorary family members, toward whom we feel filial obligations. And our practices of child-rearing make central use of animal subjects in moral education. Indeed, a child's first introduction to moral principles will frequently involve ones that are focused upon animals. A parent says, "Don't be cruel—you mustn't pull the whiskers out of the cat," "You must make sure that your pet gerbil has plenty of water," and so on and so forth. It would not be surprising, then, if attitudes toward the sufferings and welfare of animals and humans should thereafter be pretty tightly linked. This will warrant us in saying that the teenagers who are setting light to a cat are doing something wrong, not because the cat has moral standing, but because they are evincing attitudes that are likely to manifest themselves in their dealings with human beings (who do have moral standing, of course).

It seems possible, however, that the linkages that exist between attitudes to animal and to human suffering depend upon local cultural factors. For it seems implausible that these linkages should reflect properties of a universal human nature. In cultures where pets aren't kept, where people's interactions with animals are entirely pragmatic (e.g., through farming), and where animals aren't used as exemplars in moral education, it is possible that these attitudes are pretty cleanly separable. In which case, someone in such a culture who hangs a dog in a noose, strangling it to death slowly (perhaps because this is believed to make the meat taste better), won't be displaying cruelty, although someone in our culture who behaved likewise would be.

It may therefore be that our Western moral attitudes toward animals form part of the *conventional* content of our morality. If there is nothing in our human nature that links cruelty to animals with cruelty to humans, then contracting rational agents would have no reason to insist upon a rule forbidding cruelty to animals, or a rule mandating a virtue of kindness that extends to animals. But contracting agents have to settle upon some or other way of bringing up their children, and cultural practices (such as pet-keeping) may be adopted for reasons having nothing to do with the moral contract itself, but which nevertheless have an impact upon morals. Given such facts, we can become obliged not to be cruel to animals.

5.3. Acting for the Sake of the Animal

Notice that in our culture, someone with the right sort of kindly character who acts to prevent suffering to an animal will do so *for the sake of the animal.* For this is what having the right sort of sympathetic attitude consists in. It involves a spontaneous upwelling of sympathy at the sight or sound of suffering. Likewise it is something about the animal itself (its pain) that forms the immediate object of the emotion, and of the subsequent response. Certainly someone acting to ease the suffering of an animal won't be doing it to try to make himself into a better person! Nevertheless, the reason why this attitude is a virtue at all can be because of the way in which it is likely to manifest itself in the person's dealings with other human beings.

We can therefore *explain away* the commonsense intuition that when we are morally required to act to prevent the suffering of an animal, we are required to do so *for the sake of the animal,* where this is understood to mean that the animal itself has moral standing. As a theoretical claim about what grounds our duties toward animals, this is false, since animals lack standing. But as a psychological claim about the state of mind and motivations of the actor, who has acquired the right sort of kindly attitude, it is true. While agents should act as they do for the animal's sake (with the animal's interests in mind), the reason that they are required to do so doesn't advert to facts about the animal (which would require animals to have standing), but rather to wider effects on human beings.

6. Conclusion

I have argued in this essay that moral standing is possessed by all and only human beings (together with other rational agents, if there are any), who thus make direct moral claims upon us. Animals, in contrast, lack standing and make no direct claims upon us. Nevertheless, I have shown how there can be justified moral criticism for things that we do, or don't do, to an animal. This derives from the good or bad qualities of character that our actions evince. But these criticisms may have a conventional and culturally local quality, deriving from contingent facts about contemporary Western cultures. They aren't criticisms that are warranted by rules that no rational agents could reasonably reject (whatever their culture) when guided by facts about human nature.

Acknowledgments

The ideas in this essay develop and modify the position that I defended at much greater length in Carruthers (1992). I am grateful to many generations of skeptical students for helping me to think more clearly about these issues, and to Christopher Morris for his comments on an earlier draft of the essay.

Notes

1. I make this assumption because I believe that nothing of importance turns on it in the context of the present debate. Although I myself have defended a theory of consciousness that would probably deny conscious experiences to most if not all species of animal

(Carruthers, 2000), I have also argued that unconscious forms of pain and suffering are perfectly appropriate objects of sympathy and moral concern (Carruthers, 2005)—which isn't to say, I should stress, that sympathetic concern for animals is morally mandatory; that is the topic of the present essay.

2. Not all forms of contractualism satisfy this constraint. (Some allow the contracting agents to appeal to antecedent moral *values.*) Where they don't, their implications for the animals issue are much more difficult to discern. I believe that the constraint is justified by the goal of providing a comprehensive moral theory that will be naturalistically acceptable, requiring us to postulate no properties and processes that wouldn't be acceptable to science.

3. By way of analogy, think of the rule requiring us (in the United States) to drive on the right. Obviously there should be a rule requiring people to drive on one side of the road or the other, or chaos will ensue. But it doesn't much matter which side is chosen.

4. It is an interesting question what this and related arguments show about the moral status of abortion. I believe (although I shall not argue here) that they would show early (e.g., first trimester) abortions to be permissible, while ruling out most later forms of abortion.

5. For other arguments for the same conclusion, see Carruthers (1992), chapter 5.

6. This doesn't mean that all humans are accorded the same rights, however. While normal human adults might be given a right to autonomy, for example, it will make little sense to accord such a right to a human who isn't an autonomous agent.

7. A third problem is that moral standing would only be accorded, in any case, to those animals that are often kept as pets, such as dogs and cats. Animal species to whose members it is difficult to become emotionally attached would be left beyond the pale.

8. The United Kingdom's Royal Society for the Prevention of Cruelty to Animals claims on its Web site to have amassed voluminous evidence that people who are cruel to animals are also likely to engage in cruelty that involves human beings, and that the society's prosecutions for cruelty to animals are almost always built upon this premise. The ASPCA in the United States makes similar claims on its "information for professionals" Web site, citing a number of empirical studies.

9. Notice that this does *not* mean that actions undertaken out of generosity are really self-interested ones. (On the contrary, generous people are people who feel an impulse to help another simply because they can see that the other person needs it.) It only means that self-interest enters into the explanation of why generosity is a virtue. This is because self-interested rational agents attempting to agree on a framework of rules that no one could reasonably reject would agree on a duty to become a generous sort of person.

References

Carruthers, P. (1992). *The Animals Issue.* Cambridge University Press.

Carruthers, P. (2000). *Phenomenal Consciousness.* Cambridge University Press.

Carruthers, P. (2005). *Consciousness.* Oxford University Press.

Carruthers, P. (2006). *The Architecture of the Mind.* Oxford University Press.

Damasio, A. (1994). *Descartes' Error.* Papermac.

Gigerenzer, G., Todd, P., and the ABC Research Group. (1999). *Simple Heuristics That Make Us Smart.* Oxford University Press.

Hrdy, S. (1999). *Mother Nature.* Pantheon Press.

Pinker, S. (2002). *The Blank Slate.* Viking Press.

Rawls, J. (1972). *A Theory of Justice.* Oxford University Press.

Regan, T. (1984). *The Case for Animal Rights.* Routledge.

Scanlon, T. (1982). Contractualism and Utilitarianism. In A. Sen and B. Williams (eds.), *Utilitarianism and Beyond.* Cambridge University Press.

Scanlon, T. (1998). *What We Owe to Each Other.* Harvard University Press.

Singer, P. (1979). *Practical Ethics.* Cambridge University Press.

QUESTIONS

1. What is Carruthers's case against the moral standing of animals?
2. How does he seek to show that cruelty to animals is something that can be criticized? How can this be reconciled with his position that animals lack moral standing?

44. Puppies, Pigs, and People: Eating Meat and Marginal Cases

ALASTAIR NORCROSS

Alastair Norcross (1960–) is a British philosopher and teaches at the University of Colorado, Boulder. He publishes widely in ethics. One of his main aims is to defend consequentialist accounts of morality such as utilitarianism. He is the coeditor with B. Steinbock of an excellent collection, *Killing and Letting Die* (1994).

In this essay, Norcross tries to persuade readers that factory farming and similar mistreatment of animals is wrong. He does this by considering a number of analogies, starting with the horrific story of Fred.

1. Fred's Basement

Consider the story of Fred, who receives a visit from the police one day. They have been summoned by Fred's neighbors, who have been disturbed by strange sounds emanating from Fred's basement. When they enter the basement they are confronted by the following scene: Twenty-six small wire cages, each containing a puppy, some whining, some whimpering, some howling. The puppies range in age from newborn to about six months. Many of them show signs of mutilation. Urine and feces cover the bottoms of the cages and the basement floor. Fred explains that he keeps the puppies for twenty-six weeks, and then butchers them while holding them upside-down. During their lives he performs a series of mutilations on them, such as slicing off their noses and their paws with a hot knife, all without any form of anesthesia. Except for the mutilations, the puppies are never allowed out of the cages, which are barely big enough to hold them at twenty-six weeks. The police are horrified, and promptly charge Fred with animal abuse. As details of the case are publicized, the public is outraged. Newspapers are flooded with letters demanding that Fred be severely punished. There are calls for more severe penalties for animal abuse. Fred is denounced as a vile sadist.

Finally, at his trial, Fred explains his behavior, and argues that he is blameless and therefore deserves no punishment. He is, he explains, a great lover of chocolate. A couple of years ago, he was involved in a car accident, which resulted in some head trauma. Upon his release from hospital, having apparently suffered no lasting ill effects, he visited his favorite restaurant and ordered their famous rich dark chocolate mousse. Imagine his dismay when he discovered that his experience of the mousse was a pale shadow of its former self. The mousse tasted bland, slightly pleasant, but with none of the intense chocolaty flavor he remembered so well. The waiter assured him that the recipe was unchanged from the last time he had tasted it, just the day before his accident. In some consternation, Fred rushed out to buy a bar of his favorite Belgian chocolate. Again, he was dismayed to discover that his experience of the chocolate was barely even pleasurable. Extensive investigation revealed that his experience of other foods remained unaffected, but chocolate, in all its

From Alastair Norcross, "Puppies, Pigs, and People: Eating Meat and Marginal Cases," *Philosophical Perspectives 18, Ethics*, 2004, pp. 229–245. Reprinted by permission of Blackwell Publishing.

forms, now tasted bland and insipid. Desperate for a solution to his problem, Fred visited a renowned gustatory neurologist, Dr. T. Bud. Extensive tests revealed that the accident had irreparably damaged the godiva gland, which secretes cocoamone, the hormone responsible for the experience of chocolate. Fred urgently requested hormone replacement therapy. Dr. Bud informed him that, until recently, there had been no known source of cocoamone, other than the human godiva gland, and that it was impossible to collect cocoamone from one person to be used by another. However, a chance discovery had altered the situation. A forensic veterinary surgeon, performing an autopsy on a severely abused puppy, had discovered high concentrations of cocoamone in the puppy's brain. It turned out that puppies, who don't normally produce cocoamone, could be stimulated to do so by extended periods of severe stress and suffering. The research, which led to this discovery, while gaining tenure for its authors, had not been widely publicized, for fear of antagonizing animal welfare groups. Although this research clearly gave Fred the hope of tasting chocolate again, there were no commercially available sources of puppy-derived cocoamone. Lack of demand, combined with fear of bad publicity, had deterred drug companies from getting into the puppy torturing business. Fred appeals to the court to imagine his anguish, on discovering that a solution to his severe deprivation was possible, but not readily available. But he wasn't inclined to sit around bemoaning his cruel fate. He did what any chocolate lover would do. He read the research, and set up his own cocoamone collection lab in his basement. Six months of intense puppy suffering, followed by a brutal death, produced enough cocoamone to last him a week, hence the twenty-six cages. He isn't a sadist or an animal abuser, he explains. If there were a method of collecting cocoamone without torturing puppies, he would gladly employ it. He derives no pleasure from the suffering of the puppies itself. He sympathizes with those who are horrified by the pain and misery of the animals, but the court must realize that human pleasure is at stake. The puppies, while undeniably cute, are mere animals. He admits that he would be just as healthy without chocolate, if not more so. But this isn't a matter of survival or

health. His life would be unacceptably impoverished without the experience of chocolate.

End of story. Clearly, we are horrified by Fred's behavior, and unconvinced by his attempted justification. It is, of course, unfortunate for Fred that he can no longer enjoy the taste of chocolate, but that in no way excuses the imposition of severe suffering on the puppies. I expect near universal agreement with this claim (the exceptions being those who are either inhumanly callous or thinking ahead, and wish to avoid the following conclusion, to which such agreement commits them). No decent person would even contemplate torturing puppies merely to enhance a gustatory experience. However, billions of animals endure intense suffering every year for precisely this end. Most of the chicken, veal, beef, and pork consumed in the US comes from intensive confinement facilities, in which the animals live cramped, stress-filled lives and endure unanaesthetized mutilations.[1] The vast majority of people would suffer no ill health from the elimination of meat from their diets. Quite the reverse. The supposed benefits from this system of factory farming, apart from the profits accruing to agribusiness, are increased levels of gustatory pleasure for those who claim that they couldn't enjoy a meat-free diet as much as their current meat-filled diets. If we are prepared to condemn Fred for torturing puppies merely to enhance his gustatory experiences, shouldn't we similarly condemn the millions who purchase and consume factory-raised meat? Are there any morally significant differences between Fred's behavior and their behavior?

2. Fred's Behavior Compared with Our Behavior

The first difference that might seem to be relevant is that Fred tortures the puppies himself, whereas most Americans consume meat that comes from animals that have been tortured by others. But is this really relevant? What if Fred had been squeamish and had employed someone else to torture the puppies and extract the cocoamone? Would we have thought any better of Fred? Of course not.

Another difference between Fred and many consumers of factory-raised meat is that many, perhaps most, such consumers are unaware of the treatment of the animals, before they appear in neatly wrapped packages on supermarket shelves. Perhaps I should moderate my challenge, then. If we are prepared to condemn Fred for torturing puppies merely to enhance his gustatory experiences, shouldn't we similarly condemn those who purchase and consume factory-raised meat, in full, or even partial, awareness of the suffering endured by the animals? While many consumers are still blissfully ignorant of the appalling treatment meted out to meat, that number is rapidly dwindling, thanks to vigorous publicity campaigns waged by animal welfare groups. Furthermore, any meat-eating readers of this article are now deprived of the excuse of ignorance.

Perhaps a consumer of factory-raised animals could argue as follows: While I agree that Fred's behavior is abominable, mine is crucially different. If Fred did not consume his chocolate, he would not raise and torture puppies (or pay someone else to do so). Therefore Fred could prevent the suffering of the puppies. However, if I did not buy and consume factory-raised meat, no animals would be spared lives of misery. Agribusiness is much too large to respond to the behavior of one consumer. Therefore I cannot prevent the suffering of any animals. I may well regret the suffering inflicted on animals for the sake of human enjoyment. I may even agree that the human enjoyment doesn't justify the suffering. However, since the animals will suffer no matter what I do, I may as well enjoy the taste of their flesh.

There are at least two lines of response to this attempted defense. First, consider an analogous case. You visit a friend in an exotic location, say Alabama. Your friend takes you out to eat at the finest restaurant in Tuscaloosa. For dessert you select the house specialty, "Chocolate Mousse à la Bama," served with a small cup of coffee, which you are instructed to drink before eating the mousse. The mousse is quite simply the most delicious dessert you have ever tasted. Never before has chocolate tasted so rich and satisfying. Tempted to order a second, you ask your friend what makes this mousse so delicious. He informs you that the mousse itself is ordinary, but the coffee contains a concentrated dose of cocoamone, the newly discovered chocolate-enhancing hormone. Researchers at Auburn University have perfected a technique for extracting cocoamone from the brains of freshly slaughtered puppies, who have been subjected to lives of pain and frustration. Each puppy's brain yields four doses, each of which is effective for about fifteen minutes, just long enough to enjoy one serving of mousse. You are, naturally, horrified and disgusted. You will certainly not order another serving, you tell your friend. In fact, you are shocked that your friend, who had always seemed to be a morally decent person, could have both recommended the dessert to you and eaten one himself, in full awareness of the loathsome process necessary for the experience. He agrees that the suffering of the puppies is outrageous, and that the gain in human pleasure in no way justifies the appalling treatment they have to endure. However, neither he nor you can save any puppies by refraining from consuming cocoamone. Cocoamone production is now Alabama's leading industry, so it is much too large to respond to the behavior of one or two consumers. Since the puppies will suffer no matter what either of you does, you may as well enjoy the mousse.

If it is as obvious as it seems that a morally decent person, who is aware of the details of cocoamone production, couldn't order Chocolate Mousse à la Bama, it should be equally obvious that a morally decent person, who is aware of the details of factory farming, can't purchase and consume factory-raised meat. If the attempted excuse of causal impotence is compelling in the latter case, it should be compelling in the former case. But it isn't.

The second response to the claim of causal impotence is to deny it. Consider the case of chickens, the most cruelly treated of all animals raised for human consumption, with the possible exception of veal calves. In 1998, almost 8 billion chickens were slaughtered in the US,[2] almost all of them raised on factory farms. Suppose that there are 250 million chicken eaters in the US, and that each one consumes, on average, 25 chickens per year (this leaves a fair number of chickens slaughtered for nonhuman consumption, or for export). Clearly, if only one of those chicken eaters gave up eating chicken, the industry would not respond. Equally clearly, if they all gave up eating chicken, billions of chickens (approximately 6.25 billion per year) would not be bred, tortured, and killed. But there must also be some number of consumers, far short of 250 million, whose renunciation of chicken would cause the industry to reduce the number of chickens bred in factory farms. The industry may not be able to respond to each individual's behavior, but it must respond to the behavior of fairly large numbers. Suppose that the industry is sensitive to a reduction in demand for chicken equivalent to 10,000 people becoming vegetarians. (This seems like a reasonable guess, but I have no idea what the actual numbers are, nor is it important.) For each group of 10,000 who give up chicken, a quarter of a million fewer chickens are bred per year. It appears, then, that if you give up eating chicken, you have only a one in ten thousand chance of making any difference to the lives of chickens, unless it is certain that fewer than 10,000 people will ever give up eating chicken, in which case you have no chance. Isn't a one in ten thousand chance small enough to render your continued consumption of chicken blameless? Not at all. While the chance that your behavior is harmful may be small, the harm that is risked is enormous. The larger the numbers needed to make a difference to chicken production, the larger the difference such numbers would make. A one in ten thousand chance of saving 250,000 chickens per year from excruciating lives is morally and mathematically equivalent to the certainty of saving 25 chickens per year. We commonly accept that even small risks of great harms are unacceptable. That is why we disapprove of parents who fail to secure their children in car seats or with seat belts, who leave their small children unattended at home, or who drink or smoke heavily during pregnancy. Or consider commercial aircraft safety measures. The chances that the oxygen masks, the lifejackets, or the emergency exits on any given plane will be called on to save any lives in a given week, are far smaller than one in ten thousand. And yet we would be outraged to discover that an airline had knowingly allowed a plane to fly for a week with nonfunctioning emergency exits, oxygen masks, and lifejackets. So, even if it is true that your giving up factory raised chicken has only a tiny chance of preventing suffering, given that the amount of suffering that would be prevented is in inverse proportion to your chance of

preventing it, your continued consumption is not thereby excused.

But perhaps it is not even true that your giving up chicken has only a tiny chance of making any difference. Suppose again that the poultry industry only reduces production when a threshold of 10,000 fresh vegetarians is reached. Suppose also, as is almost certainly true, that vegetarianism is growing in popularity in the US (and elsewhere). Then, even if you are not the one, newly converted vegetarian, to reach the next threshold of 10,000, your conversion will reduce the time required before the next threshold is reached. The sooner the threshold is reached, the sooner production, and therefore animal suffering, is reduced. Your behavior, therefore, does make a difference. Furthermore, many people who become vegetarians influence others to become vegetarian, who in turn influence others, and so on. It appears, then, that the claim of causal impotence is mere wishful thinking, on the part of those meat lovers who are morally sensitive enough to realize that human gustatory pleasure does not justify inflicting extreme suffering on animals.

Perhaps there is a further difference between the treatment of Fred's puppies and the treatment of animals on factory farms. The suffering of the puppies is a necessary means to the production of gustatory pleasure, whereas the suffering of animals on factory farms is simply a by-product of the conditions dictated by economic considerations. Therefore, it might be argued, the suffering of the puppies is *intended as a means* to Fred's pleasure, whereas the suffering of factory raised animals is merely *foreseen* as a side-effect of a system that is a means to the gustatory pleasures of millions. The distinction between what is intended, either as a means or as an end in itself, and what is "merely" foreseen is central to the Doctrine of Double Effect. Supporters of this doctrine claim that it is sometimes permissible to bring about an effect that is merely foreseen, even though the very same effect could not permissibly be brought about if intended. (Other conditions have to be met in order for the Doctrine of Double Effect to judge an action permissible, most notably that there be an outweighing good effect.) Fred acts impermissibly, according to this line of argument, because he intends the suffering of the puppies as a means to his pleasure. Most meat eaters, on the other hand, even if aware of the suffering of the animals, do not intend the suffering.

In response to this line of argument, I could remind the reader that Samuel Johnson said, or should have said, that the Doctrine of Double Effect is the last refuge of a scoundrel.[3] I won't do that, however, since neither the doctrine itself, nor the alleged moral distinction between intending and foreseeing can justify the consumption of factory-raised meat. The Doctrine of Double Effect requires not merely that a bad effect be foreseen and not intended, but also that there be an outweighing good effect. In the case of the suffering of factory-raised animals, whatever good could plausibly be claimed to come out of the system clearly doesn't outweigh the bad. Furthermore, it would be easy to modify the story of Fred to render the puppies' suffering "merely" foreseen. For example, suppose that the cocoamone is produced by a chemical reaction that can only occur when large quantities of drain-cleaner are forced down the throat of a conscious, unanaesthetized puppy. The consequent appalling suffering, while not itself a means to the production of cocoamone, is nonetheless an unavoidable side-effect of the means. In this variation of the story, Fred's behavior is no less abominable than in the original.

One last difference between the behavior of Fred and the behavior of the consumers of factory-raised meat is worth discussing, if only because it is so frequently cited in response to the arguments of this paper. Fred's behavior is abominable, according to this line of thinking, because it involves the suffering of *puppies*. The behavior of meat-eaters, on the other hand, "merely" involves the suffering of chickens, pigs, cows, calves, sheep, and the like. Puppies (and probably dogs and cats in general) are morally different from the other animals. Puppies *count* (morally, that is), whereas the other animals don't, or at least not nearly as much.

So, what gives puppies a higher moral status than the animals we eat? Presumably there is some morally relevant property or properties possessed by puppies but not by farm animals. Perhaps puppies have a greater degree of rationality than farm animals, or a more finely developed moral sense, or at

least a sense of loyalty and devotion. The problems with this kind of approach are obvious. It's highly unlikely that any property that has even an outside chance of being ethically relevant[4] is both possessed by puppies and not possessed by any farm animals. For example, it's probably true that most puppies have a greater degree of rationality (whatever that means) than most chickens, but the comparison with pigs is far more dubious. Besides, if Fred were to inform the jury that he had taken pains to acquire particularly stupid, morally obtuse, disloyal and undevoted puppies, would they (or we) have declared his behavior to be morally acceptable? Clearly not. This is, of course, simply the puppy version of the problem of marginal cases (which I will discuss later). The human version is no less relevant. If their lack of certain degrees of rationality, moral sensibility, loyalty, devotion, and the like makes it permissible to torture farm animals for our gustatory pleasure, it should be permissible to do the same to those unfortunate humans who also lack those properties. Since the latter behavior isn't permissible, the lack of such properties doesn't justify the former behavior.

Perhaps, though, there *is* something that separates puppies, even marginal puppies (and marginal humans) from farm animals—our sympathy. Puppies count more than other animals, because we care more about them. We are outraged to hear of puppies abused in scientific experiments, but unconcerned at the treatment of laboratory rats or animals on factory farms. Before the 2002 World Cup, several members of the England team sent a letter to the government of South Korea protesting the treatment of dogs and cats raised for food in that country. The same players have not protested the treatment of animals on factory farms in England. This example, while clearly illustrating the difference in attitudes towards cats and dogs on the one hand, and farm animals on the other, also reveals one of the problems with this approach to the question of moral status. Although the English footballers, and the English (and US) public in general, clearly care far more about the treatment of cats and dogs than of farm animals, the South Koreans, just as clearly, do not. Are we to conclude that Fred's behavior would not be abominable were he living in

South Korea, where dogs and cats are routinely abused for the sake of gustatory pleasure? Such relativism is, to put it mildly, hard to swallow. Perhaps, though, we can maintain the view that human feelings determine the moral status of animals, without condoning the treatment of dogs and cats in South Korea (and other countries). Not all human feelings count. Only the feelings of those who have achieved exactly the right degree of moral sensibility. That just so happens to be those in countries like the US and Britain who care deeply for the welfare of dogs and cats, but not particularly for the welfare of cows, chickens, pigs, and other factory-raised animals. Dog and cat eaters in South Korea are insufficiently sensitive, and humane farming advocates in Britain and the US are overly so. But, of course, it won't do simply to insist that this is the right degree of moral sensibility. We need an explanation of why this is the right degree of sensibility. Moral sensibility consists, at least in part, in reacting differently to different features of situations, actions, agents, and patients. If the right degree of moral sensibility requires reacting differently to puppies and to farm animals, there must be a morally relevant difference between puppies and farm animals. Such a difference can't simply consist in the fact that (some) people do react differently to them. The appeal to differential human sympathy illustrates a purely descriptive psychological difference between the behavior of Fred and that of someone who knowingly consumes factory-raised meat. It can do no serious moral work.

I have been unable to discover any morally relevant differences between the behavior of Fred, the puppy torturer, and the behavior of the millions of people who purchase and consume factory-raised meat, at least those who do so in the knowledge that the animals live lives of suffering and deprivation. If morality demands that we not torture puppies merely to enhance our own eating pleasure, morality also demands that we not support factory farming by purchasing factory-raised meat.

3. The Texan's Challenge

Perhaps what I have said thus far is enough to convince many that the purchase and consumption of factory-raised meat is immoral. It is clear that the attribution of a different (and elevated) moral status to puppies from that attributed to farm animals is unjustified. But, one philosopher's *modus ponens*, as they say, is another Texan's *modus tollens*. Here is the *modus ponens* I have been urging:

(1) If it's wrong to torture puppies for gustatory pleasure, it's wrong to support factory farming.
(2) It is wrong to torture puppies for gustatory pleasure.
(3) Therefore it's wrong to support factory farming.

But some may be so convinced that supporting factory farming is not wrong that they may substitute that conviction for the second premise, and conclude that it is not wrong to torture puppies for gustatory pleasure. Thus we are confronted with the Texan's *modus tollens*:

(T1) If it's wrong to torture puppies for gustatory pleasure, then it's wrong to support factory farming.
(T2) It's not wrong to support factory farming.
(T3) Therefore it's not wrong to torture puppies for gustatory pleasure.

I'm not saying that there is a large risk that many people, even Texans, will start breeding puppies for food (outside of those countries where it is already accepted practice). What they may do (and have done when I have presented them with this argument) is explain their reluctance to do so as a mere sentimental preference, as opposed to a morally mandated choice. They may claim, in a somewhat Kantian spirit, that someone who can treat puppies like that may be more likely to mistreat humans. They may agree that all animals deserve equal consideration of their interests. They may then justify their different treatment of animals either on the grounds that they are simply giving some animals *more* than they deserve, or that they are attending to their own interests. If the former, they could claim that morality mandates minimal standards of conduct, but that nothing prevents us from choosing to go beyond the requirements of morality when we feel like it. If the latter, they could claim that their sentimental attachment to puppies, kittens, and the like, makes it in their own interests not to raise and kill them for food. Nonetheless, they may insist, in terms of moral status, there is a clear difference between humans and other animals. Humans have a moral status so far above that of other animals that we couldn't even consider raising humans for food (even humanely), or experimenting on them without their consent, even though we routinely do such things to other animals.

4. Humans' versus Animals' Ethical Status—The Rationality Gambit

For the purposes of this discussion, to claim that humans have a superior ethical status to animals is to claim that it is morally right to give the interests of humans greater weight than those of animals in deciding how to behave. Such claims will often be couched in terms of rights, such as the rights to life, liberty or respect, but nothing turns on this terminological matter. One may claim that it is generally wrong to kill humans, but not animals, because humans are rational, and animals are not. Or one may claim that the suffering of animals counts less than the suffering of humans (if at all), because humans are rational, and animals are not. These claims may proceed through the intermediate claim that the rights of humans are more extensive and stronger than those (if any) of animals. Alternatively, one may directly ground the judgment about the moral status of certain types of behavior in claims about the alleged natural properties of the individuals involved. Much of the debate over the moral status of abortion proceeds along these lines. Many opponents of abortion appeal to features that fetuses have in common with adult humans, in order to argue that it is, at least usually, just as seriously wrong to kill them as it is to kill us. For example, John Noonan claims that it is the possession of a full human genetic code that grounds the attribution to fetuses of this exalted ethical status. Such an argument may, but doesn't have to, proceed through the intermediate claim that anything that possesses a full human genetic code has a right to life. Many proponents of the moral permissibility of abortion, on the other hand, claim features such as self-consciousness or linguistic ability as necessary conditions of full moral status, and thus deny such status to fetuses.

What could ground the claim of superior moral status for humans? Just as the defender of a higher moral status for puppies than for farm animals needs to find some property or properties possessed by puppies but not by farm animals, so the defender of a higher moral status for humans needs to find some property or properties possessed by humans but not by other animals. The traditional view, dating back at least to Aristotle, is that rationality is what separates humans, both morally and metaphysically, from other animals. With a greater understanding of the cognitive powers of some animals, recent philosophers have often refined the claim to stress the kind and level of rationality required for moral reasoning. Let's start with a representative sample of three. Consider first these claims of Bonnie Steinbock:

> While we are not compelled to discriminate among people because of different capacities, if we can find a significant difference in capacities between human and non-human animals, this could serve to justify regarding human interests as primary. It is not arbitrary or smug, I think, to maintain that human beings have a different moral status from members of other species because of certain capacities which are characteristic of being human. We may not all be equal in these capacities, but all human beings possess them to some measure, and non-human animals do not. For example, human beings are normally held to be responsible for what they do. . . . Secondly, human beings can be expected to reciprocate in a way that non-human animals cannot . . . Thirdly, . . . there is the "desire for self-respect."[5]

Similarly, Mary Anne Warren argues that "the rights of persons are generally stronger than those of sentient beings which are not persons." Her main premise to support this conclusion is the following:

> [T]here is one difference [between human and non-human nature] which has a clear moral relevance: people are at least sometimes capable of being moved to action or inaction by the force of reasoned argument.[6]

Carl Cohen, one of the most vehement modern defenders of what Peter Singer calls "speciesism" states his position as follows:

Between species of animate life, however—between (for example) humans on the one hand and cats or rats on the other—the morally relevant differences are enormous, and almost universally appreciated. Humans engage in moral reflection; humans are morally autonomous; humans are members of moral communities, recognizing just claims against their own interest. Human beings do have rights, theirs is a moral status very different from that of cats or rats.[7]

So, the claim is that human interests and/or rights are stronger or more important than those of animals, because humans possess a kind and level of rationality not possessed by animals. How much of our current behavior towards animals this justifies depends on just how much consideration should be given to animal interests, and on what rights, if any, they possess. Both Steinbock and Warren stress that animal interests need to be taken seriously into account. Warren claims that animals have important rights, but not as important as human rights. Cohen, on the other hand, argues that we should actually *increase* our use of animals.

5. The Challenge of Marginal Cases

One of the most serious challenges to this defense of the traditional view involves a consideration of what philosophers refer to as "marginal cases." Whatever kind and level of rationality is selected as justifying the attribution of superior moral status to humans will either be lacking in some humans or present in some animals. To take one of the most commonly-suggested features, many humans are incapable of engaging in moral reflection. For some, this incapacity is temporary, as is the case with infants, or the temporarily cognitively disabled. Others who once had the capacity may have permanently lost it, as is the case with the severely senile or the irreversibly comatose. Still others never had and never will have the capacity, as is the case with the severely mentally disabled. If we base our claims for the moral superiority of humans over animals on the attribution of such capacities, won't we have to exclude many humans? Won't we then be forced to the claim that there is at least as much moral reason to use cognitively deficient humans in experiments and for food

as to use animals? Perhaps we could exclude the only temporarily disabled, on the grounds of potentiality, though that move has its own problems. Nonetheless, the other two categories would be vulnerable to this objection.

I will consider two lines of response to the argument from marginal cases. The first denies that we have to attribute different moral status to marginal humans, but maintains that we are, nonetheless, justified in attributing different moral status to animals who are just as cognitively sophisticated as marginal humans, if not more so. The second admits that, strictly speaking, marginal humans are morally inferior to other humans, but proceeds to claim pragmatic reasons for treating them, at least usually, *as if* they had equal status.

As representatives of the first line of defense. I will consider arguments from three philosophers, Carl Cohen, Alan White, and David Schmidtz. First, Cohen:

> [the argument from marginal cases] fails; it mistakenly treats an essential feature of humanity as though it were a screen for sorting humans. The capacity for moral judgment that distinguishes humans from animals is not a test to be administered to human beings one by one. Persons who are unable, because of some disability, to perform the full moral functions natural to human beings are certainly not for that reason ejected from the moral community. The issue is one of kind . . . What humans retain when disabled, animals have never had.[8]

Alan White argues that animals don't have rights, on the grounds that they cannot intelligibly be spoken of in the full language of a right. By this he means that they cannot, for example, claim, demand, assert, insist on, secure, waive, or surrender a right. This is what he has to say in response to the argument from marginal cases:

> Nor does this, as some contend, exclude infants, children, the feeble-minded, the comatose, the dead, or generations yet unborn. Any of these may be for various reasons empirically unable to fulfill the full role of right-holder. But . . . they are logically possible subjects of rights to whom the full language of rights can significantly, however falsely,

be used. It is a misfortune, not a tautology, that these persons cannot exercise or enjoy, claim, or waive, their rights or do their duty or fulfil their obligations.[9]

David Schmidtz defends the appeal to typical characteristics of species, such as mice, chimpanzees, and humans, in making decisions on the use of different species in experiments. He also considers the argument from marginal cases:

> Of course, some chimpanzees lack the characteristic features in virtue of which chimpanzees command respect as a species, just as some humans lack the characteristic features in virtue of which humans command respect as a species. It is equally obvious that some chimpanzees have cognitive capacities (for example) that are superior to the cognitive capacities of some humans. But whether every human being is superior to every chimpanzee is beside the point. The point is that we can, we do, and we should make decisions on the basis of our recognition that mice, chimpanzees, and humans are relevantly different *types*. We can have it both ways after all. Or so a speciesist could argue.[10]

There is something deeply troublesome about the line of argument that runs through all three of these responses to the argument from marginal cases. A particular feature, or set of features is claimed to have so much moral significance that its presence or lack can make the difference to whether a piece of behavior is morally justified or morally outrageous. But then it is claimed that the presence or lack of the feature in any *particular* case is not important. The relevant question is whether the presence or lack of the feature is *normal*. Such an argument would seem perfectly preposterous in most other cases. Suppose, for example, that ten famous people are on trial in the afterlife for crimes against humanity. On the basis of conclusive evidence, five are found guilty and five are found not guilty. Four of the guilty are sentenced to an eternity of torment, and one is granted an eternity of bliss. Four of the innocent are granted an eternity of bliss, and one is sentenced to an eternity of torment. The one innocent who is sentenced to torment asks why he, and not the fifth guilty person, must go to hell. Saint Peter replies, "Isn't it obvious Mr. Ghandi?

You are male. The other four men—Adolf Hitler, Joseph Stalin, George W. Bush, and Richard Nixon—are all guilty. Therefore the normal condition for a male defendant in this trial is guilt. The fact that you happen to be innocent is irrelevant. Likewise, of the five female defendants in this trial, only one was guilty. Therefore the normal condition for female defendants in this trial is innocence. That is why Margaret Thatcher gets to go to heaven instead of you."

As I said, such an argument is preposterous. Is the reply to the argument from marginal cases any better? Perhaps it will be claimed that a biological category such as a species is more "natural," whatever that means, than a category like "all the male (or female) defendants in this trial." Even setting aside the not inconsiderable worries about the conventionality of biological categories, it is not at all clear why this distinction should be morally relevant. What if it turned out that there were statistically relevant differences in the mental abilities of men and women? Suppose that men were, on average, more skilled at manipulating numbers than women, and that women were, on average, more empathetic than men. Would such differences in what was "normal" for men and women justify us in preferring an innumerate man to a female math genius for a job as an accountant, or an insensitive woman to an ultra-sympathetic man for a job as a counselor? I take it that the biological distinction between male and female is just as real as that between human and chimpanzee.

A second response to the argument from marginal cases is to concede that cognitively deficient humans really do have an inferior moral status to normal humans. Can we, then, use such humans as we do animals? I know of no-one who takes the further step of advocating the use of marginal humans for food (though R. G. Frey has made some suggestive remarks concerning experimentation). How can we advocate this second response while blocking the further step? Warren suggests that "there are powerful practical and emotional reasons for protecting non-rational human beings, reasons which are absent in the case of most non-human animals."[11] It would clearly outrage common human sensibilities, if we were to raise retarded children for food or medical experiments.[12] Here is Steinbock in a similar vein:

> I doubt that anyone will be able to come up with a concrete and morally relevant difference that would justify, say, using a chimpanzee in an experiment rather than a human being with less capacity for reasoning, moral responsibility, etc. Should we then experiment on the severely retarded? Utilitarian considerations aside, we feel a special obligation to care for the handicapped members of our own species, who cannot survive in this world without such care. . . . In addition, when we consider the severely retarded, we think, "That could be me." It makes sense to think that one might have been born retarded, but not to think that one might have been born a monkey. . . . Here we are getting away from such things as "morally relevant differences" and are talking about something much more difficult to articulate, namely, the role of feeling and sentiment in moral thinking.[13]

This line of response clearly won't satisfy those who think that marginal humans really do deserve equal moral consideration with other humans. It is also a very shaky basis on which to justify our current practices. What outrages human sensibilities is a very fragile thing. Human history is littered with examples of widespread acceptance of the systematic mistreatment of some groups who didn't generate any sympathetic response from others. That we do feel a kind of sympathy for retarded humans that we don't feel for dogs is, if true, a contingent matter. To see just how shaky a basis this is for protecting retarded humans, imagine that a new kind of birth defect (perhaps associated with beef from cows treated with bovine growth hormone) produces severe mental retardation, green skin, and a complete lack of emotional bond between parents and child. Furthermore, suppose that the mental retardation is of the same kind and severity as that caused by other birth defects that don't have the other two effects. It seems likely that denying moral status to such defective humans would not run the same risks of outraging human sensibilities as would the denial of moral status to other, less easily distinguished and more loved defective humans. Would these contingent empirical differences between our reactions to different sources of mental retardation justify us in ascribing different direct moral status to their subjects? The only difference between them is skin color and whether they are loved by others. Any theory that could ascribe moral relevance to differences such as these doesn't deserve to be taken seriously.[14]

Finally, perhaps we could claim that the practice of giving greater weight to the interests of all humans than of animals is justified on evolutionary grounds. Perhaps such differential concern has survival value for the species. Something like this may well be true, but it is hard to see the moral relevance. We can hardly justify the privileging of human interests over animal interests on the grounds that such privileging serves human interests!

6. Agent and Patient—The Speciesist's Central Confusion

Although the argument from marginal cases certainly poses a formidable challenge to any proposed criterion of full moral standing that excludes animals, it doesn't, in my view, constitute the most serious flaw in such attempts to justify the status quo. The proposed criteria are all variations on the Aristotelian criterion of rationality. But what is the moral relevance of rationality? Why should we think that the possession of a certain level or kind of rationality renders the possessor's interests of greater moral significance than those of a merely sentient being? In Bentham's famous words "The question is not, Can they reason? nor Can they talk? But, Can they suffer?"[15]

What do defenders of the alleged superiority of human interests say in response to Bentham's challenge? Some, such as Carl Cohen, simply reiterate the differences between humans and animals that they claim to carry moral significance. Animals are not members of moral communities, they don't engage in moral reflection, they can't be moved by moral reasons, *therefore* (?) their interests don't count as much as ours. Others, such as Steinbock and Warren, attempt to go further. Here is Warren on the subject:

> Why is rationality morally relevant? It does not make us "better" than other animals or more "perfect." . . . But it is morally relevant insofar as it

provides greater possibilities for cooperation and for the nonviolent resolution of problems.[16]

Warren is certainly correct in claiming that a certain level and kind of rationality is morally relevant. Where she, and others who give similar arguments, go wrong is in specifying what the moral relevance amounts to. If a being is incapable of moral reasoning, at even the most basic level, if it is incapable of being moved by moral reasons, claims, or arguments, then it cannot be a moral agent. It cannot be subject to moral obligations, to moral praise or blame. Punishing a dog for doing something "wrong" is no more than an attempt to alter its future behavior. So long as we are undeceived about the dog's cognitive capacities, we are not, except metaphorically, expressing any moral judgment about the dog's behavior. (We may, of course, be expressing a moral judgment about the behavior of the dog's owner, who didn't train it very well.) All this is well and good, but what is the significance for the question of what weight to give to animal interests? That animals can't be moral *agents* doesn't seem to be relevant to their status as moral *patients*. Many, perhaps most, humans are both moral agents and patients. Most, perhaps all, animals are only moral patients. Why would the lack of moral agency give them diminished status as moral patients? Full status as a moral patient is not some kind of reward for moral agency. I have heard students complain in this regard that it is *unfair* that humans bear the burdens of moral responsibility, and don't get enhanced consideration of their interests in return. This is a very strange claim. Humans are subject to moral obligations, because they are the kind of creatures who *can* be. What grounds moral agency is simply different from what grounds moral standing as a patient. It is no more unfair that humans and not animals are moral agents, than it is unfair that real animals and not stuffed toys are moral patients.

One other attempt to justify the selection of rationality as the criterion of full moral standing is worth considering. Recall the suggestion that rationality is important insofar as it facilitates cooperation. If we view the essence of morality as reciprocity, the significance of rationality is obvious. A certain twisted, but all-too-common, interpretation of the

Golden Rule is that we should "do unto others in order to get them to do unto us." There's no point, according to this approach, in giving much, if any, consideration to the interests of animals, because they are simply incapable of giving like consideration to our interests. In discussing the morality of eating meat, I have, many times, heard students claim that we are justified in eating meat, because "the animals would eat us, if given half a chance." (That they say this in regard to our practice of eating cows and chickens is depressing testimony to their knowledge of the animals they gobble up with such gusto.) Inasmuch as there is a consistent view being expressed here at all, it concerns self-interest, as opposed to morality. Whether it serves my interests to give the same weight to the interests of animals as to those of humans is an interesting question, but it is not the same question as whether it is *right* to give animals' interests equal weight. The same point, of course, applies to the question of whether to give equal weight to my interests, or those of my family, race, sex, religion, etc. as to those of other people.

Perhaps it will be objected that I am being unfair to the suggestion that the essence of morality is reciprocity. Reciprocity is important, not because it serves *my* interests, but because it serves the interests of all. Reciprocity facilitates cooperation, which in turn produces benefits for all. What we should say about this depends on the scope of "all." If it includes all sentient beings, then the significance of animals' inability to reciprocate is in what it tells us about *how* to give their interests equal consideration. It certainly can't tell us that we should give less, or no, consideration to their interests. If, on the other hand, we claim that rationality is important for reciprocity, which is important for cooperation, which is important for benefiting humans, which is the ultimate goal of morality, we have clearly begged the question against giving equal consideration to the interests of animals.

It seems that any attempt to justify the claim that humans have a higher moral status than other animals by appealing to some version of rationality as the morally relevant difference between humans and animals will fail on at least two counts. It will fail to give an adequate answer to the argument from marginal cases, and, more importantly, it will fail to make the case that such a difference is morally relevant to the status of animals as moral patients as opposed to their status as moral agents.

I conclude that our intuitions that Fred's behavior is morally impermissible are accurate. Furthermore, given that the behavior of those who knowingly support factory farming is morally indistinguishable, it follows that their behavior is also morally impermissible.[17]

Notes

1. For information on factory farms, see, for example, Jim Mason and Peter Singer, *Animal Factories*, 2d ed. (New York: Harmony Books, 1990), Karen Davis, *Prisoned Chickens, Poisoned Eggs: An Inside Look at the Modern Poultry Industry* (Summertown, TN: Book Publishing Co., 1996), John Robbins, *Diet for a New America* (Walpole, NH: Stillpoint, 1987).

2. *Livestock Slaughter 1998 Summary*, NASS, USDA (Washington, D.C.: March 1999), 2; and *Poultry Slaughter*, NASS, USDA (Washington, D.C.; February 2, 1999), 1f.

3. For a fine critique of the Doctrine of Double Effect, see Jonathan Bennett, *The Act Itself* (Oxford 1995), ch. 11.

4. If someone were to assert that "puppyishness" or simply "being a puppy" were ethically relevant, I could do no more than favor them with an incredulous stare.

5. Bonnie Steinbock, "Speciesism and the Idea of Equality," *Philosophy* 53, no. 204 (April 1978). Reprinted in *Contemporary Moral Problems,* 5th edition, James E. White (ed.) (West, 1997) 467–468.

6. Mary Anne Warren, "Difficulties with the Strong Animal Rights Position," *Between the Species* 2, no. 4, 1987. Reprinted in *Contemporary Moral Problems,* 5th edition, James E. White (ed.) (West, 1997), 482.

7. Carl Cohen. "The Case for the Use of Animals in Biomedical Research," *New England Journal of Medicine,* vol. 315, 1986. Reprinted in *Social Ethics*, 4th edition, Thomas A. Mappes and Jane S. Zembaty (eds.) (New York: McGraw-Hill, 1992), 463.

8. Cohen, op. cit. 461.

9. Alan White, *Rights* (OUP 1984). Reprinted in *Animal Rights and Human Obligations*, 2nd edition, Tom Regan and Peter Singer (eds.) (Prentice Hall, 1989), 120.

10. David Schmidtz, "Are All Species Equal?" *Journal of Applied Philosophy*, Vol. 15, no. 1 (1998), 61, my emphasis.

11. Warren, op. cit. 483.

12. For a similar argument, see Peter Carruthers, *The Animals Issue: Moral Theory in Practice* (Cambridge University Press, 1992).

13. Steinbock, op. cit. 469–470.

14. Certain crude versions of the so-called ethics of care do seem to entail that the mere fact of being loved gives a different ethical status.

15. Jeremy Bentham, *Introduction to the Principles of Morals and Legislation,* (Various) chapter 17.

16. Warren, op. cit. 482.

17. This paper, in various forms, has been presented in more places than I can remember, and has benefited from the comments of more people than I can shake a stick at. I particularly wish to thank, for their helpful comments, Doug Ehring, Mylan Engel, Mark Heller, and Steve Sverdlik.

QUESTIONS

1. What is the structure of Norcross's case against factory farming?
2. Is this argument effective?

IX

Suicide

I s it ever permissible to take one's own life? Many have thought that it is not. The question is important in its own right, but our interest in it is motivated in no small part for the implications it has for the ethics of euthanasia and assisted suicide. Were suicide always to be impermissible, it may be that euthanasia and assisted suicide would almost always be as well. Were traditional concerns about suicide insufficient to show that it is always impermissible, then this would have implications for euthanasia and assisted suicide too.

Suicide is the taking of one's own life. It is usually thought necessary to require that suicide involve the *intentional* taking of one's own life. *Accidentally* doing something that brings about one's death will not count as suicide. There is controversy about whether doing something that one merely *foresees* or *expects* to be fatal is suicide—for example, a soldier throwing himself on a grenade in order to save his fellows. The term *suicide bomber* is often used for insurgents or terrorists who blow themselves up with their targets. It is not clear in many of these cases that the person really aims at his or her own death. Normally we seem to think that suicides require the intentional taking of one's life, that this be an aim or purpose of the act. But much depends on how we understand these notions. We can initially think of an act of suicide as one of intentionally bringing about one's own death and see if this preliminary characterization is adequate.

There are a number of questions that need to be distinguished. The principal question for ethicists may be the permissibility or the moral status of suicide. But the first question has to be, more broadly, that of its rationality or intelligibility: Does it ever make sense to end one's life? If it does, then the question arises as to whether it is permissible to do so in these cases. More generally, do we have a right to commit suicide? And lastly there are questions to be asked about interfering with someone's suicide.

At least some suicides seem to be mistakes of some kind. Teenage suicides—one of the leading causes of death among young people—are rarely mentioned without the thought that something needs to be done to decrease them, the assumption being that they are regrettable or tragic. These cases raise special questions in addition to the examples that are usually considered in contemporary courses. Many readers of this text may have known someone young who took his or her life, and it may be difficult even to think about the incident. The type of case that we need to think about, however, is quite different from that of youthful suicide. We should think of someone in his or her adult years, perhaps at the end of a normal life, who faces a serious hardship that raises the question as to whether it might not be in his or her interest to die. Some think that one might reasonably prefer death to continuing to live when faced with a terminal disease that will bring only unremitting pain and suffering and that will also rob one of what dignity one has left. Many have taken their own lives out of a sense of honor as well. And consideration for others may also motivate a suicide (e.g., sparing others great hardships). The question is whether in situations like these it may be reasonable or it may make sense to take one's own life. If it is, the question of its permissibility then arises.

45. On the Proper Time to Slip the Cable

SENECA

Seneca (ca. 4 BC–65 AD), also Lucius Annaeus Seneca or Seneca the Younger, was a Roman playwright, orator, politician, and philosopher. He served as tutor to the young Nero, who retained Seneca as advisor when he became emperor. He was later accused (falsely?) of conspiring against Nero and ordered to take his own life.

He writes that "mere living is not a good, but living well. Accordingly, the wise man will live as long as he ought, not as long as he can." Making a case for taking one's own life when it is no longer worth living, he says that "it is not a question of dying earlier or later, but of dying well or ill. And dying well means escape from the danger of living ill."

After a long space of time I have seen your beloved Pompeii. I was thus brought again face to face with the days of my youth. And it seemed to me that I could still do, nay, had only done a short time ago, all the things which I did there when a young man. We have sailed past life, Lucilius, as if we were on a voyage, and just as when at sea, to quote from our poet Vergil, "Land and towns are left astern," even so, on this journey where time flies with the greatest speed, we put below the horizon first our boyhood and then our youth, and then the space which lies between young manhood and middle age and borders on both, and next, the best years of old age itself. Last of all, we begin to sight the general bourne of the race of man. Fools that we are, we believe this bourne to be a dangerous reef; but it is the harbor in his early years, he has no more right to complain than a sailor who has made a quick voyage. For some sailors, as you know, are tricked and held back by sluggish winds, and grow weary and sick of the slow-moving calm; while others are carried quickly home by steady gales.

You may consider that the same thing happens to us: life has carried some men with the greatest rapidity to the harbor, the harbor they were bound to reach even if they tarried on the way, while others it has fretted and harassed. To such a life, as you are aware, one should not always cling. For mere living is not a good, but living well. Accordingly, the wise man will live as long as he ought, not as long as he can. He will mark in what place, with whom, and how he is to conduct his existence, and what he is about to do. He always reflects concerning the quality not the quantity, of his life. As soon as there are many events in his life that give him trouble and disturb his peace of mind, he sets himself free. And this privilege is his, not only when the crisis is upon him, but as soon as Fortune seems to be playing him false; then he looks about carefully and sees whether he ought, or ought not, to end his life on that account. He holds that it makes no difference to him whether his taking-off be natural or self-inflicted, whether it comes later or earlier. He does not regard it with fear, as if it were a great loss; for no man can lose very much when but a driblet remains. It is not a question of dying earlier or later, but of dying well or ill. And dying well means escape from the danger of living ill.

From Seneca, *Moral Epistles*, trans. Richard M. Gummere (London: William Heinemann, 1918).

That is why I regard the words of the well-known Rhodian as most unmanly. This person was thrown into a cage by his tyrant, and fed here like some wild animal. And when a certain man advised him to end his life by fasting, he replied; "A man may hope for anything while he has life." This may be true; but life is not to be purchased at any price. No matter how great or how well-assured certain rewards may be, I shall not strive to attain them at the price of a shameful confession of weakness. Shall I reflect that Fortune has all power over one who lives, rather than reflect that she has no power over one who knows how to die? There are times nevertheless, when a man, even though certain death impends and he knows that torture in store for him, will refrain from lending a hand to his own punishment; to himself, however, he would lend a hand. It is folly to die through fear of dying. The executioner is upon you; wait for him. Why anticipate him? Why assume the management of a cruel task that belongs to another? Do you grudge your executioner his privilege, or do you merely relieve him of his task? Socrates might have ended his life by fasting; he might have died by starvation rather than poison. But instead of this he spent thirty days in prison awaiting death, not with the idea "everything may happen," or "so long an interval has room for many a hope" but in order that he might show himself submissive to the laws and make the last moments of Socrates an edification to his friends. What would have been more foolish than to scorn death, and yet fear poison?

Scribonia, a woman of the stern old type, was an aunt of Drusus Libo. This young man was as stupid as he was well born, with higher ambitions than anyone could have been expected to entertain in that epoch, or a man like himself in any epoch at all. When Libo had been carried away ill from the senate-house in his litter, though certainly with a very scanty train of followers,—for all his kinsfolk undutifully deserted him, when he was no longer a criminal but a corpse,—he began to consider whether he should commit suicide, or await for death. Scribonia said to him: "What pleasure do you find in doing another man's work?" But he did not follow her advice; he laid violent hands upon himself. And he was right, after all; for when a man is doomed to die in two or three days at his enemy's pleasure, he is really "doing another man's work" if he continues to live.

No general statement can be made, therefore, with regard to the question whether, when a power beyond our control threatens us with death, we should anticipate death, or await it. For there are many arguments to pull us in either direction. If one death is accompanied by torture, and the other is simple and easy, why not snatch the latter? Just as I shall select my ship when I am about to go on a voyage, or my house when I propose to take a residence, so I shall choose death when I am about to depart from life. Moreover, just as a long-drawn-out life does not necessarily mean a better one, so a long-drawn-out death necessarily means a worse one. There is no occasion when the soul should be humored more than at the moment of death. Let the soul depart as it feels itself impelled to go; whether it seeks the sword, or the halter, or some draught that attacks the veins, let it proceed and burst the bonds of its slavery. Every man ought to make his life acceptable to others besides himself alone. The best form of death is one we like. Men are foolish who reflect thus: "One person will say that my conduct was not brave enough; another, that I was too headstrong; a third that a particular kind of death would have betokened more spirit." What you should really reflect is: "I have under consideration a purpose with which the talk of men has no concern!" Your sole aim should be to escape from Fortune as speedily as possible; otherwise, there will be no lack of persons who will think ill of what you have done.

You can find men who have gone so far as to profess wisdom and yet maintain that one should not offer violence to one's own life, and hold it accursed for a man to be the means of his own destruction; we should wait, say they, for the end decreed by nature. But one who says this does not see that he is shutting off the path to freedom. The best thing which eternal law ever ordained was that it allowed to us one entrance into life, but many exits. Must I await the cruelty either of disease or of man, when I can depart through the midst of torture, and shake off my troubles? This is the one reason why we cannot complain of life: it keeps no one against his will. Humanity is well situated, because no man is unhappy except by his own fault. Live, if you so desire; if not, you may return to the place whence you came. You have often been cupped in order to relieve headaches. You have had veins cut for the purpose of reducing your weight. If you would pierce your heart, a gaping wound is not necessary; a lancet will open the way to that great freedom, and tranquility can be purchased at the cost of a pin-prick.

What, then, is it which makes us lazy and sluggish? None of us reflects that some day he must depart from his house of life; just so old tenants are kept from moving by fondness for a particular place and by custom, even in spite of ill-treatment. Would you be free from the restraint of your body? Live in it as if you were about to leave it. Keep thinking of the fact that some day you will be deprived of this tenure; then you will be more brave against the necessity of departing. But how will a man take though of his own end, if he craves all things without end? And yet there is nothing so essential for us to consider. For our training in other things is perhaps superfluous. Our souls have been made ready to meet poverty; but our riches have held out. We have armed ourselves to scorn pain; but we have had good fortune to possess sound and healthy bodies, and so have never been forced to put this virtue to the test. We have taught ourselves to endure bravely the loss of those we love; but Fortune has preserved to us all whom we loved. It is in this one matter only that the day will come which will require us to test our training.

You need not think that none but great men have had the strength to burst the bonds of human servitude; you need not believe that this cannot be done except by a Cato,—Cato, who with his hand dragged forth the spirit which he had succeeded in freeing by the sword. Nay, men of the meanest lot in life have by a mighty impulse escaped to safety, and when they were not allowed to die at their own convenience, or to suit themselves in their choice of the instruments of death, they have snatched up whatever was lying ready to hand, and by sheer strength have turned objects which were by nature harmless into weapons of their own. For example,

there was lately in a training-school for the wild-beast gladiators a German, who was making ready for the morning exhibition; he withdrew in order to relieve himself,—the only thing which he was allowed to do in secret and without the presence of a guard. While so engaged, he seized the stick of wood, tipped with a sponge, which was devoted to the vilest uses, and stuffed it, just as it was, down his throat; thus he blocked up his windpipe, and choked the breath from his body. That was truly to insult death! Yes, indeed; it was not a very elegant or becoming way to die; but was it more foolish than to be over-nice about dying? What a brave fellow! He surely deserved to be allowed to choose his fate! How bravely he would have wielded a sword! With what courage he would have hurled himself into the depths of the sea, or down a precipice! Cut off from resources on every hand, he yet found a way to furnish himself with death, and with a weapon for death. Hence you can understand that nothing but the will need postpone death. Let each man judge the deed of this most zealous fellow as he likes, provided we agree on this point,—that the foulest death is preferable to the fairest slavery.

Inasmuch as I began with an illustration taken from humble life, I shall keep on with that sort. For men will make greater demands upon themselves, if they see that death can be despised even by the most despised class of men. The Catos, the Scipios, and the others whose names we are wont to hear with admiration, we regard as beyond the sphere of imitation; but I shall now prove to you that the virtue of which I speak is found as frequently in the gladiators' training-school as among the leaders in a civil war. Lately a gladiator, who had been sent forth to the morning exhibition, was being conveyed in a cart along with the other prisoners; nodding as if he were heavy with sleep, he let his head fall over so far that it was caught in the spokes; then he kept his body in position long enough to break his neck by the revolution of the wheel. So he made his escape by means of the very wagon which was carrying him to his punishment.

When a man desires to burst forth and take his departure, nothing stands in his way. It is an open space in which Nature guards us. When our plight is such as to permit it, we may look about us for an easy exit. If you have many opportunities ready to hand, by means of which you may liberate yourself, you may make a selection and think over the best way of gaining freedom; but if a chance is hard to find, instead of the best, snatch the next best, even though it be something unheard of, something new. If you do not lack the courage, you will not lack the cleverness, to die. See how even the lowest class of slave, when suffering goads him on, is aroused and discovers a way to deceive even the most watchful guards! He is truly great who not only has given himself the order to die, but has also found the means.

I have promised you, however, some more illustration drawn from the same games. During the second event in a sham sea-flight one of the barbarians sank deep into his own throat a spear which had been given him use against his foe. "Why, oh why," he said, "have I not long ago escaped from all this torture and all this mockery? Why should I be armed and yet wait for death to come?" This exhibition was all the more striking because of the lesson men learn from it that dying is more honorable than killing.

What, then? If such a spirit is possessed by abandoned and dangerous men, shall it not be possessed also by those who have trained themselves to meet such contingencies by long meditation, and by reason, the mistress of all things? It is reason which teaches us that fate has various ways of approach, but the same end, and that it makes no difference at what point the inevitable event begins. Reason, too, advises us to die, if we may, according to our taste; if this cannot be, she advises us to die according to our ability, and to seize upon whatever means shall offer itself for doing violence to ourselves. It is criminal to "love by robbery"; but, on the other hand, it is most noble to "die by robbery." Farewell.

QUESTIONS
1. What is Seneca's case for taking one's own life?
2. Does Seneca address the question of the *permissibility* of taking one's own life?

46. Whether It Is Lawful to Kill Oneself?

THOMAS AQUINAS

For a description of the author and a note on the text, see chapter 2.

In this chapter Aquinas argues that taking one's own life is wrong. The objections are included as it is important to consider Aquinas's reply to them. In Roman and early Christian times, suicide was not generally considered to be wrong or misguided.

Thomas Aquinas, *Summa Theologica* (Benziger Bros. edition, 1947), translated by Fathers of the English Dominion Province.

Q64. Of Murder

Art. 5 Whether It Is Lawful to Kill Oneself?

Objection 1: It would seem lawful for a man to kill himself. For murder is a sin in so far as it is contrary to justice. But no man can do an injustice to himself, as is proved in Ethic. v, 11. Therefore no man sins by killing himself.

Objection 2: Further, it is lawful, for one who exercises public authority, to kill evil-doers. Now he who exercises public authority is sometimes an evil-doer. Therefore he may lawfully kill himself.

Objection 3: Further, it is lawful for a man to suffer spontaneously a lesser danger that he may avoid a greater: thus it is lawful for a man to cut off a decayed limb even from himself, that he may save his whole body. Now sometimes a man, by killing himself, avoids a greater evil, for example an unhappy life, or the shame of sin. Therefore a man may kill himself.

Objection 4: Further, Samson killed himself, as related in Judges 16, and yet he is numbered among the saints (Heb. 11). Therefore it is lawful for a man to kill himself.

Objection 5: Further, it is related (2 Mac. 14:42) that a certain Razias killed himself, "choosing to die nobly rather than to fall into the hands of the wicked, and to suffer abuses unbecoming his noble birth." Now nothing that is done nobly and bravely is unlawful. Therefore suicide is not unlawful.

On the contrary, Augustine says (De Civ. Dei i, 20): "Hence it follows that the words 'Thou shalt not kill' refer to the killing of a man—not another man; therefore, not even thyself. For he who kills himself, kills nothing else than a man."

I answer that, It is altogether unlawful to kill oneself, for three reasons. First, because everything naturally loves itself, the result being that everything naturally keeps itself in being, and resists corruptions so far as it can. Wherefore suicide is contrary to the inclination of nature, and to charity whereby every man should love himself. Hence suicide is always a mortal sin, as being contrary to the natural law and to charity. Secondly, because every part, as such, belongs to the whole. Now every man is part of the community, and so, as such, he belongs to the community. Hence by killing himself he injures the community, as the Philosopher declares (Ethic. v, 11). Thirdly, because life is God's gift to man, and is subject to His power, Who kills and makes to live. Hence whoever takes his own life, sins against God, even as he who kills another's slave, sins against that slave's master, and as he who usurps to himself judgment of a matter not entrusted to him. For it belongs to God alone to pronounce sentence of death and life, according to Dt. 32:39, "I will kill and I will make to live."

Reply to Objection 1: Murder is a sin, not only because it is contrary to justice, but also because it is opposed to charity which a man should have towards himself: in this respect suicide is a sin in relation to oneself. In relation to the community and to God, it is sinful, by reason also of its opposition to justice.

Reply to Objection 2: One who exercises public authority may lawfully put to death an evil-doer, since he can pass judgment on him. But no man is judge of himself. Wherefore it is not lawful for one who exercises public authority to put himself to death for any sin whatever: although he may lawfully commit himself to the judgment of others.

Reply to Objection 3: Man is made master of himself through his free-will: wherefore he can lawfully dispose of himself as to those matters which pertain to this life which is ruled by man's free-will. But the passage from this life to another and happier one is subject not to man's free-will but to the power of God. Hence it is not lawful for man to take his own life that he may pass to a happier life, nor that he may escape any unhappiness whatsoever of the present life, because the ultimate and most fearsome evil of this life is death, as the Philosopher states (Ethic. iii, 6). Therefore to bring death upon oneself in order to escape the other afflictions of this life, is to adopt a greater evil in order to avoid a lesser. In like manner it is unlawful to take one's own life on account of one's having committed a sin, both because by so doing one does oneself a very great injury, by depriving oneself of the time needful for repentance, and because it is not lawful to slay an evildoer except by the sentence of the public authority. Again it is unlawful for a woman to kill herself lest she be violated, because she ought not to commit on herself the very great sin of suicide, to avoid the lesser sin; of another. For she commits no sin in being violated by force, provided she does not consent, since "without consent of the mind there is no stain on the body," as the Blessed Lucy declared. Now it is evident that fornication and adultery are less grievous sins than taking a man's, especially one's own, life: since the latter is most grievous, because one injures oneself, to whom one owes the greatest love. Moreover it is most dangerous since no time is left wherein to expiate it by repentance. Again it is not lawful for anyone to take his own life for fear he should consent to sin, because "evil must not be done that good may come" (Rom. 3:8) or that evil may be avoided especially if the evil be of small account and an uncertain event, for it is uncertain whether one will at some future time consent to a sin, since God is able to deliver man from sin under any temptation whatever.

Reply to Objection 4: As Augustine says (De Civ. Dei i, 21), "not even Samson is to be excused that he crushed himself together with his enemies under the ruins of the house, except the Holy Ghost, Who had wrought many wonders through him, had secretly commanded him to do this." He assigns the same reason in the case of certain holy women, who at the time of persecution took their own lives, and who are commemorated by the Church.

Reply to Objection 5: It belongs to fortitude that a man does not shrink from being slain by another, for the sake of the good of virtue, and that he may avoid sin. But that a man take his own life in order to avoid penal evils has indeed an appearance of fortitude (for which reason some, among whom was Razias, have killed themselves thinking to act from fortitude), yet it is not true fortitude, but rather a weakness of soul unable to bear penal evils, as the Philosopher (Ethic. iii, 7) and Augustine (De Civ. Dei 22,23) declare.

QUESTIONS

1. How many arguments does Aquinas present against suicide? State each one.
2. Consider Aquinas's replies to the objections, especially the first and third. Are they cogent replies?

47. Of Suicide

DAVID HUME

David Hume (1711–1776) was a Scottish philosopher, historian, and economist and is a major influence on modern philosophy. His writings on ethics are especially influential today. Hume's major philosophical work is *A Treatise of Human Nature* (1739–1740), written when he was twenty-six.

Hume's essay must be the most famous defense of the permissibility of suicide. He argues that taking one's own life is not "a transgression of our duty, either to God, our neighbor, or ourselves."

One considerable advantage, that arises from philosophy, consists in the sovereign antidote, which it affords to superstition and false religion. All other remedies against that pestilent distemper are vain, or, at least, uncertain. Plain good-sense, and the practice of the world, which alone serve most purposes of life, are here found ineffectual: History, as well as daily experience, affords instances of men, endowed with the strongest capacity for business and affairs, who have all their lives crouched under slavery to the grossest superstition. Even gaiety and sweetness of temper, which infuse a balm into every other wound, afford no remedy to so virulent a poison; as we may particularly observe of the fair sex, who, tho' commonly possessed of these rich presents of nature, feel many of their joys blasted by this importunate intruder. But when sound philosophy has once gained possession of the mind, superstition is effectually excluded; and one may safely affirm, that her triumph over this enemy is more compleat than over most of the vices and imperfections, incident to human nature. Love or anger, ambition or avarice, have their root in the temper and affections, which the soundest reason is scarce ever able fully to correct. But superstition, being founded on false opinion, must immediately vanish, when true philosophy has inspired juster sentiments of superior powers. The contest is here more equal between the distemper and the medicine: And nothing can hinder the latter from proving effectual, but its being false and sophisticated.

It will here be superfluous to magnify the merits of philosophy, by displaying the pernicious tendency of that vice, of which it cures the human mind. The superstitious man, says *Tully*,[1] is miserable in every scene, in every incident of life. Even sleep itself, which banishes all other cares of unhappy mortals, affords to him matter of new terror; while he examines his dreams, and finds in those visions of the night, prognostications of future calamities. I may add, that, tho' death alone can put a full period to his misery, he dares not fly to this refuge, but still prolongs a miserable existence, from a vain fear, lest he offend his maker, by using the power, with which that beneficent being has endowed him. The presents of God and Nature are ravished from us by this cruel enemy; and notwithstanding that one step would remove us from the regions of pain and sorrow, her menaces still chain us down to a hated being, which she herself chiefly contributes to render miserable.

It is observed of such as have been reduced by the calamities of life to the necessity of employing this fatal remedy, that, if the unseasonable care of their friends deprive them of that species of death, which they proposed to themselves, they seldom venture upon any other, or can summon up so much resolution, a second time, as to execute their purpose. So great is our horror of death, that when it presents itself under any form, besides that to which a man has endeavoured to reconcile his imagination, it acquires new terrors, and overcomes his feeble courage. But when the menaces of superstition are joined to this natural timidity, no wonder it quite deprives men of all power over their lives; since even many pleasures and enjoyments, to which we are carried by a strong propensity, are torn from us by this inhuman tyrant. Let us here endeavour to restore men to their native liberty, by examining all the common arguments against Suicide, and shewing, that That action may be free from every imputation of guilt or blame; according to the sentiments of all the antient philosophers.

If Suicide be criminal, it must be a transgression of our duty, either to God, our neighbour, or ourselves.

To prove, that Suicide is no transgression of our duty to God, the following considerations may perhaps suffice. In order to govern the material world, the almighty creator has established general and immutable laws, by which all bodies, from the greatest planet to the smallest particle of matter, are maintained in their proper sphere and function. To govern the animal world, he has endowed all living creatures with bodily and mental powers; with senses, passions, appetites, memory, and judgment; by which they are impelled or regulated in that course of life, to which they are destined. These two distinct principles of the material and animal world continually encroach upon each other, and mutually retard or forward each other's operation. The powers of men and of all other animals are restrained and directed by the nature and qualities of the surrounding bodies; and the modifications and actions of these bodies are incessantly altered by the operation of all animals. Man is stopped by rivers in his passage over the surface of the earth; and rivers, when properly directed, lend their force to the motion of machines, which serve to the use of man. But tho' the provinces of the material and animal powers are not kept entirely separate, there result from thence no discord or disorder in the creation: On the contrary, from the mixture, union, and contrast of all the various powers of inanimate bodies and living creatures, arises that surprizing harmony and proportion, which affords the surest argument of supreme wisdom.

The providence of the deity appears not immediately in any operation, but governs every thing by those general and immutable laws, which have been established from the beginning of time. All events, in one sense, may be pronounced the action of the almighty: They all proceed from those powers, with which he has endowed his creatures. A house, which falls by its own weight, is not brought to ruin by his providence more than one destroyed by the hands of men; nor are the human faculties less his workmanship than the laws of motion and gravitation. When the passions play, when the judgment dictates, when the limbs obey; this is all the operation of God; and upon these animate principles, as well as upon the inanimate, has he established the government of the universe.

Every event is alike important in the eyes of that infinite being, who takes in, at one glance, the most distant regions of space and remotest periods of time. There is no one event, however important to us, which he has exempted from the general laws that govern the universe, or which he has peculiarly reserved for his own immediate action and operation. The revolutions of states and empires depend upon the smallest caprice or passion of single men; and the lives of men are shortened or extended by the smallest accident of air or diet, sunshine or tempest. Nature still continues her progress and operation; and if general laws be ever broke by particular volitions of the deity, 'tis after a manner which entirely escapes human observation. As on the one hand, the elements and other inanimate parts of the creation carry on their action without regard to the particular interest and situation of men; so men are entrusted to their own judgment and discretion in the various shocks of matter, and may employ every faculty, with which they are endowed, in order to provide for their ease, happiness, or preservation.

What is the meaning, then, of that principle, that a man, who, tired of life, and hunted by pain and misery, bravely overcomes all the natural terrors of death, and makes his escape from this cruel scene; that such a man, I say, has incurred the indignation of his creator, by encroaching on the office of divine providence, and disturbing the order of the universe? Shall we assert, that the Almighty has reserved to himself, in any peculiar manner, the disposal of the lives of men, and has not submitted that event, in common with others, to the general laws, by which the universe is governed? This is plainly false. The lives of men depend upon the same laws as the lives of all other animals; and these are subjected to the general laws of matter and motion. The fall of a tower or the infusion of a poison will destroy a man equally with the meanest creature: An inundation sweeps away every thing, without distinction, that comes within the reach of its fury. Since therefore the lives of men are for ever dependent on the general laws of matter and motion; is a man's disposing of his life criminal, because, in every case, it is criminal to encroach upon these laws, or disturb their operation? But this seems absurd. All animals are entrusted to their own prudence and skill for their conduct in the world, and have full authority, as far as their power extends, to alter all the operations of nature. Without the exercise of this authority, they could not subsist a moment. Every action, every motion of a man innovates in the order of some parts of matter, and diverts, from their ordinary course, the general laws of motion. Putting together, therefore, these conclusions, we find, *that* human life depends upon the general laws of matter and motion, and *that* 'tis no encroachment on the office of providence to disturb or alter these general laws. Has not every one, of consequence, the free disposal of his own life? And may he not lawfully employ that power with which nature has endowed him?

In order to destroy the evidence of this conclusion, we must shew a reason, why this particular case is excepted. Is it because human life is of so great importance, that it is a presumption for human prudence to dispose of it? But the life of man is of no greater importance to the universe than that of an oyster. And were it of ever so great importance, the order of nature has actually submitted it to human prudence, and reduced us to a necessity, in every incident, of determining concerning it.

Were the disposal of human life so much reserved as the peculiar province of the almighty that it were an encroachment on his right for men to dispose of their own lives; it would be equally criminal to act for the preservation of life as for its destruction. If I turn aside a stone, which is falling upon my head, I disturb the course of nature, and I invade the peculiar province of the almighty, by lengthening out my life, beyond the period, which, by the general laws of matter and motion, he had assigned to it.

A hair, a fly, an insect is able to destroy this mighty being, whose life is of such importance. Is it an absurdity to suppose, that human prudence may lawfully dispose of what depends on such insignificant causes?

It would be no crime in me to divert the *Nile* or *Danube* from its course, were I able to effect such purposes. Where then is the crime of turning a few ounces of blood from their natural chanels!

Do you imagine that I repine at providence or curse my creation, because I go out of life, and put a period to a being, which, were it to continue, would render me miserable? Far be such sentiments from me. I am only convinced of a matter of fact, which you yourself acknowledge possible, that human life may be unhappy, and that my existence, if farther prolonged, would become uneligible. But I thank providence, both for the good, which I have already enjoyed, and for the power, with which I am endowed, of escaping the ill that threatens me.[2] To you it belongs to repine at providence, who foolishly imagine that you have no such power, and who must still prolong a hated being, tho' loaded with pain and sickness, with shame and poverty.

Do you not teach, that when any ill befalls me, tho' by the malice of my enemies, I ought to be resigned to providence; and that the actions of men are the operations of the almighty as much as the actions of inanimate beings? When I fall upon my own sword, therefore, I receive my death equally from the hands of the deity, as if it had proceeded from a lion, a precipice, or a fever.

The submission, which you require to providence, in every calamity, that befalls me, excludes not human skill and industry; if possibly, by their means, I can avoid or escape the calamity. And why may I not employ one remedy as well as another?

If my life be not my own, it were criminal for me to put it in danger, as well as to dispose of it: Nor could one man deserve the appellation of *Hero,* whom glory or friendship transports into the greatest dangers, and another merit the reproach of *Wretch* or *Miscreant,* who puts a period to his life, from the same or like motives.

There is no being, which possesses any power or faculty, that it receives not from its creator; nor is there any one, which, by ever so irregular an action, can encroach upon the plan of his providence, or disorder the universe. Its operations are his work equally with that chain of events, which it invades; and which ever principle prevails, we may, for that very reason, conclude it to be most favoured by him. Be it animate or inanimate, rational or irrational, 'tis all a case: Its power is still derived from the supreme creator, and is alike comprehended in the order of his providence. When the horror of pain prevails over the love of life: When a voluntary action anticipates the effect of blind causes; it is only in consequence of those powers and principles, which he has implanted in his creatures. Divine providence is still inviolate, and placed far beyond the reach of human injuries.

It is impious, says the old *Roman* superstition,[3] to divert rivers from their course, or invade the prerogatives of nature. 'Tis impious, says the *French* superstition, to inoculate for the small-pox, or usurp the business of providence, by voluntarily producing distempers and maladies. 'Tis impious, says the modern *European* superstition, to put a period to our own life, and thereby rebel against our creator. And why not impious, say I, to build houses, cultivate the ground, and sail upon the ocean? In all these actions, we employ our powers of mind and body to produce some innovation in the course of nature; and in none of them do we any more. They are all of them, therefore, equally innocent or equally criminal.

But you are placed by providence, like a sentinel, in a particular station; and when you desert it, without being recalled, you are guilty of rebellion against your almighty sovereign, and have incurred his displeasure. I ask, why do you conclude, that Providence has placed me in this station? For my part, I find, that I owe my birth to a long chain of causes, of which many and even the principal, depended upon voluntary actions of men. *But Providence guided all these causes, and nothing happens in the universe without its consent and co-operation.* If so, then neither does my death, however voluntary, happen without it's consent; and whenever pain and sorrow so far overcome my patience as to make me tired of life, I may conclude, that I am recalled from my station, in the clearest and most express terms.

It is providence, surely, that has placed me at present in this chamber: But may I not leave it, when I think proper, without being liable to the imputation of having deserted my post or station? When I shall be dead, the principles, of which I am composed, will still perform their part in the universe, and will be equally useful in the grand fabric, as when they composed this individual creature. The difference to the whole will be no greater than between my being in a chamber and in the open air. The one change is of more importance to me than the other; but not more so to the universe.

It is a kind of blasphemy to imagine, that any created being can disturb the order of the world, or invade the business of providence. It supposes, that that being possesses powers and faculties, which it received not from its creator, and which are not subordinate to his government and authority. A man may disturb society, no doubt; and thereby incur the displeasure of the almighty: But the government of the world is placed far beyond his reach and violence. And how does it appear, that the almighty is displeased with those actions, that disturb society? By the principles which he has implanted in human nature, and which inspire us with a sentiment of remorse, if we ourselves have been guilty of such actions, and with that of blame and disapprobation, if we ever observe them in others. Let us now examine, according to the method proposed, whether Suicide be of this kind of actions, and be a breach of our duty to our *neighbour* and to society.

A man, who retires from life, does no harm to society. He only ceases to do good; which, if it be an injury, is of the lowest kind.

All our obligations to do good to society seem to imply something reciprocal. I receive the benefits of society, and therefore ought to promote its interest. But when I withdraw myself altogether from society, can I be bound any longer?

But allowing, that our obligations to do good were perpetual, they have certainly some bounds. I am not obliged to do a small good to society, at the expence of a great harm to myself. Why then should I prolong a miserable existence, because of some frivolous advantage, which the public may, perhaps, receive from me? If upon account of age and infirmities, I may lawfully resign any office, and employ my time altogether in fencing against these calamities, and alleviating, as much as possible, the miseries of my future life: Why may I not cut short these miseries at once by an action, which is no more prejudicial to society?

But suppose, that it is no longer in my power to promote the interest of the public: Suppose, that I am a burthen to it: Suppose, that my life hinders some person from being much more useful to the public. In such cases my resignation of life must not only be innocent but laudable. And most people, who lie under any temptation to abandon existence, are in some such situation. Those, who have health, or power, or authority, have commonly better reason to be in humour with the world.

A man is engaged in a conspiracy for the public interest; is seized upon suspicion; is threatened with the rack; and knows, from his own weakness, that the secret will be extorted from him: Could such a one consult the public interest better than by putting a quick period to a miserable life? This was the case of the famous and brave *Strozzi* of *Florence*.

Again, suppose a malefactor justly condemned to a shameful death; can any reason be imagined, why he may not anticipate his punishment, and save himself all the anguish of thinking on its dreadful approaches? He invades the business of providence no more than the magistrate did, who ordered his execution; and his voluntary death is equally advantageous to society, by ridding it of a pernicious member.

That Suicide may often be consistent with interest and with our duty to *ourselves*, no one can question, who allows, that age, sickness, or misfortune may render life a burthen, and make it worse even than annihilation. I believe that no man ever threw away life, while it was worth keeping. For such is our natural horror of death, that small motives will never be able to reconcile us to it. And tho' perhaps the situation of a man's health or fortune did not seem to require this remedy, we may at least be assured, that any one, who, without apparent reason, has had recourse to it, was curst with such an incurable depravity or gloominess of temper, as must poison all enjoyment, and render him equally miserable as if he had been loaded with the most grievous misfortunes.

If Suicide be supposed a crime, 'tis only cowardice can impel us to it. If it be no crime, both prudence and courage should engage us to rid ourselves at once of existence, when it becomes a burthen. 'Tis the only way, that we can then be useful to society, by setting an example, which, if imitated, would preserve to every one his chance for happiness in life, and would effectually free him from all danger of misery.[4]

Notes

1. *De Divin*. lib. ii.
2. *Agamus Deo gratias, quod nemo in vita teneri potest.* Seneca, *Epist.* xii.
3. *Tacit. Ann.* lib. i.
4. It would be easy to prove, that Suicide is as lawful under the *christian* dispensation as it was to the heathens. There is not a single text of scripture, which prohibits it. That great and infallible rule of faith and practice, which must controul all philosophy and human reasoning, has left us, in this particular, to our natural liberty. Resignation to providence is, indeed, recommended in scripture; but that implies only submission to ills, which are unavoidable, not to such as may be remedied by prudence or courage. *Thou shalt not kill* is evidently meant to exclude only the killing of others, over whose life we have no authority. That this precept like most of the scripture precepts, must be modified by reason and common sense, is plain from the practice of magistrates, who punish criminals capitally, notwithstanding the letter of this law. But were this commandment ever so express against Suicide, it could now have no authority. For all the law of *Moses* is abolished, except so far as it is established by the law of nature; and we have already endeavoured to prove, that Suicide is not prohibited by that law. In all cases, *Christians* and *Heathens* are precisely upon the same footing; and if *Cato* and *Brutus*, *Arria* and *Portia* acted heroically, those who now imitate their example ought to receive the same praises from posterity. The power of committing Suicide is regarded by *Pliny* as an advantage which men possess even above the deity himself. *Deus non sibi potest mortem consciscere, si velit, quod homini dedit optimum in tantis vitæ pœnis.* Lib. ii. Cap. 7.

QUESTIONS

1. What are Hume's arguments that suicide is not a violation of our duties to God, our neighbors, or ourselves? How many arguments does he make?
2. Hume claims that "no man ever threw away life, while it was worth keeping. For such is our natural horror of death, that small motives will never be able to reconcile us to it." Is this claim true?

Euthanasia

T here is considerable controversy about euthanasia and assisted suicide, in the United
States and elsewhere. There may also be considerable uncertainty about what exactly
the sources of controversy are. The Nazis deceptively used the term *euthanasia* for
their program started in 1939 to kill severely disabled people, sometimes described as "life
unworthy of life." And proponents of some forms of euthanasia are sometimes said to
support something favored by the Nazis.

The Greek roots of "euthanasia" suggest a good death. An act of euthanasia is one of
bringing about or assisting in someone's death for the sake of the person. As such it is meant
to be an act of kindness. Someone who kills for the benefit of others or meaning to harm the
victim cannot be said to be carrying out acts of euthanasia in this traditional sense of the term.

Does euthanasia involve *killing*? Sometimes euthanasia seems instead to involve
(merely) letting someone die—for example, withholding or withdrawing care. A distinction
is often made between *killing* and *letting die*, and there is considerable controversy about its
nature and merit. Euthanasia does seem to involve intending or at least expecting the
person's death, even if it is merely allowed to happen, say, by withholding care.[1] Some forms
of euthanasia are best thought of as assisted suicide.[2] Some of the questions raised here are
those raised by reasonable suicide (see section IX).

Our main question is when, if ever, is euthanasia morally permissible? It can be hard to
distinguish this question from another: When, if ever, should euthanasia be *legally* permitted? There has been considerable discussion of both for the last several decades in the
United States, Europe, and elsewhere. A consensus now exists in the United States that

---

1. A distinction between killing and letting die may be relevant to the debate about famine in
section IV.

2. See, for instance, the Death with Dignity law enacted in Oregon in 1997.

(competent) patients may refuse medical treatment, even if the reasons are thought to be poor. Sometimes it is said that patients have a right to refuse treatment. Health care providers are not normally thought to kill or to induce death by complying with the patient's wish to cease or to forgo treatment.

There is controversy about other cases that may be characterized as euthanasia. Indeed, almost all of the controversy concerns certain kinds of cases. As a result, it may be best to distinguish between different types of euthanasia. There are two sets of categories, the first concerning the voluntariness of euthanasia. A mercy killing can be voluntary, involuntary, or nonvoluntary. Voluntariness is quite difficult to characterize, but we can say that a voluntary act is roughly one that is freely done, while reasonably informed, by someone who is competent. The involuntary and the nonvoluntary need clearly to be distinguished. An *involuntary* act of euthanasia is one that is carried out *against* the person's will. Virtually always we consider such action as impermissible.[3] Nonvoluntary euthanasia would describe cases where the individual is unable to understand his or her condition or is unconscious. So euthanasia may be voluntary (e.g., the person wants to die and requests death), involuntary (e.g., the person wants to live, expresses a wish), or nonvoluntary (e.g., the person expresses no desire).

The second set of categories is simpler, even if less clear. A distinction is commonly made between "passive" and "active" euthanasia. The latter is supposed to cover acts such as administering drugs that kill someone, while the former is meant to cover acts that merely involve doing things that have as their consequence the death of the person. Sometimes the distinction is said to be between *doing* something (e.g., killing) and *refraining* from doing something (e.g., saving). On this understanding it is like the distinction between killing and letting die. Some of the controversy about euthanasia turns on the adequacy of this distinction. But it is so commonly deployed that it is worth using it to distinguish, at least provisionally, between different kinds of euthanasia.

Putting our categories together, then, we have six possible types of cases of euthanasia:

	Voluntary	Involuntary	Nonvoluntary
"Passive"	treatment withdrawn, withheld, or refused with consent	treatment withdrawn, withheld, or refused against the person's will	treatment withdrawn, withheld, or refused without consent
"Active"	death induced with consent	death induced against the person's will	death induced without consent

Using these categories we see that it is commonly thought that there are six general kinds of euthanasia. We can say that there is very little controversy about involuntary euthanasia, some controversy about some cases of nonvoluntary euthanasia, and a great deal of controversy about active voluntary euthanasia. Indeed, much of the debate consists of defenses of the permissibility of active voluntary euthanasia and criticisms.

---

3. It is very hard to think of cases where one might be tempted to kill someone, for their own sake, against their desire. In battle, retreating from the advance of a brutal and merciless adversary, one might be tempted to kill the wounded who could not be transported, knowing of the fate that would await them if captured alive.

48. The Tragedy of Euthanasia

JOHN PAUL II

For a description of the author, see chapter 4.

In another excerpt from the late pope's *Evangelium vitae*, he makes a case for the impermissibility of euthanasia, which he characterizes as "an action or omission which of itself and by intention causes death, with the purpose of eliminating all suffering." He argues that "depending on the circumstances, this practice involves the malice proper to suicide or murder."

64. At the other end of life's spectrum, men and women find themselves facing the mystery of death. Today, as a result of advances in medicine and in a cultural context frequently closed to the transcendent, the experience of dying is marked by new features. When the prevailing tendency is to value life only to the extent that it brings pleasure and well-being, suffering seems like an unbearable setback, something from which one must be freed at all costs. Death is considered "senseless" if it suddenly interrupts a life still open to a future of new and interesting experiences. But it becomes a "rightful liberation" once life is held to be no longer meaningful because it is filled with pain and inexorably doomed to even greater suffering.

Furthermore, when he denies or neglects his fundamental relationship to God, man thinks he is his own rule and measure, with the right to demand that society should guarantee him the ways and means of deciding what to do with his life in full and complete autonomy. It is especially people in the developed countries who act in this way: they feel encouraged to do so also by the constant progress of medicine and its ever more advanced techniques. By using highly sophisticated systems and equipment, science and medical practice today are able not only to attend to cases formerly considered untreatable and to reduce or eliminate pain, but also to sustain and prolong life even in situations of extreme frailty, to resuscitate artificially patients whose basic biological functions have undergone sudden collapse, and to use special procedures to make organs available for transplanting.

In this context the temptation grows to have recourse to euthanasia, that is, to take control of death and bring it about before its time, "gently" ending one's own life or the life of others. In reality, what might seem logical and humane, when looked at more closely is seen to be senseless and inhumane. Here we are faced with one of the more alarming symptoms of the "culture of death," which is advancing above all in prosperous societies, marked by an attitude of excessive preoccupation with efficiency and which sees the growing number of elderly and disabled people as intolerable and too burdensome. These people are very often isolated by their families and by society, which are organized almost exclusively on the basis of criteria of productive efficiency, according to which a hopelessly impaired life no longer has any value.

65. For a correct moral judgment on euthanasia, in the first place a clear definition is required.

From John Paul II, *Evangelium vitae*, 1995.

Euthanasia in the strict sense is understood to be an action or omission which of itself and by intention causes death, with the purpose of eliminating all suffering. "Euthanasia's terms of reference, therefore, are to be found in the intention of the will and in the methods used."[1]

Euthanasia must be distinguished from the decision to forego so-called "aggressive medical treatment," in other words, medical procedures which no longer correspond to the real situation of the patient, either because they are by now disproportionate to any expected results or because they impose an excessive burden on the patient and his family. In such situations, when death is clearly imminent and inevitable, one can in conscience "refuse forms of treatment that would only secure a precarious and burdensome prolongation of life, so long as the normal care due to the sick person in similar cases is not interrupted."[2] Certainly there is a moral obligation to care for oneself and to allow oneself to be cared for, but this duty must take account of concrete circumstances. It needs to be determined whether the means of treatment available are objectively proportionate to the prospects for improvement. To forego extraordinary or disproportionate means is not the equivalent of suicide or euthanasia; it rather expresses acceptance of the human condition in the face of death.[3]

In modern medicine, increased attention is being given to what are called "methods of palliative care," which seek to make suffering more bearable in the final stages of illness and to ensure that the patient is supported and accompanied in his or her ordeal. Among the questions which arise in this context is that of the licitness of using various types of painkillers and sedatives for relieving the patient's pain when this involves the risk of shortening life. While praise may be due to the person who voluntarily accepts suffering by forgoing treatment with painkillers in order to remain fully lucid and, if a believer, to share consciously in the Lord's Passion, such "heroic" behaviour cannot be considered the duty of everyone. Pius XII affirmed that it is licit to relieve pain by narcotics, even when the result is decreased consciousness and a shortening of life, "if no other means exist, and if, in the given circumstances, this does not prevent the carrying out of other religious and moral duties."[4] In such a case, death is not willed or sought, even though for reasonable motives one runs the risk of it: there is simply a desire to ease pain effectively by using the analgesics which medicine provides. All the same, "it is not right to deprive the dying person of consciousness without a serious reason":[5] as they approach death people ought to be able to satisfy their moral and family duties, and above all they ought to be able to prepare in a fully conscious way for their definitive meeting with God.

Taking into account these distinctions, in harmony with the Magisterium of my Predecessors[6] and in communion with the Bishops of the Catholic Church, I confirm that euthanasia is a grave violation of the law of God, since it is the deliberate and morally unacceptable killing of a human person. This doctrine is based upon the natural law and upon the written word of God, is transmitted by the Church's Tradition and taught by the ordinary and universal Magisterium.[7]

Depending on the circumstances, this practice involves the malice proper to suicide or murder.

66. Suicide is always as morally objectionable as murder. The Church's tradition has always rejected it as a gravely evil choice.[8] Even though a certain psychological, cultural and social conditioning may induce a person to carry out an action which so radically contradicts the innate inclination to life, thus lessening or removing subjective responsibility, suicide, when viewed objectively, is a gravely immoral act. In fact, it involves the rejection of love of self and the renunciation of the obligation of justice and charity towards one's neighbour, towards the communities to which one belongs, and towards society as a whole.[9] In its deepest reality, suicide represents a rejection of God's absolute sovereignty over life and death, as proclaimed in the prayer of the ancient sage of Israel: "You have power over life and death; you lead men down to the gates of Hades and back again" (Wis 16:13; cf. Tob 13:2).

To concur with the intention of another person to commit suicide and to help in carrying it out through so-called "assisted suicide" means to cooperate in, and at times to be the actual perpetrator of, an injustice which can never be excused, even if it is requested. In a remarkably relevant passage Saint Augustine writes that "it is never licit to kill another: even if he should wish it, indeed if he request it because, hanging between life and death, he begs for help in freeing the soul struggling against the bonds of the body and longing to be released; nor is it licit even when a sick person is no longer able to live."[10] Even when not motivated by a selfish refusal to be burdened with the life of someone who is suffering, euthanasia must be called a false mercy, and indeed a disturbing "perversion" of mercy. True "compassion" leads to sharing another's pain; it does not kill the person whose suffering we cannot bear. Moreover, the act of euthanasia appears all the more perverse if it is carried out by those, like relatives, who are supposed to treat a family member with patience and love, or by those, such as doctors, who by virtue of their specific profession are supposed to care for the sick person even in the most painful terminal stages.

The choice of euthanasia becomes more serious when it takes the form of a murder committed by others on a person who has in no way requested it and who has never consented to it. The height of arbitrariness and injustice is reached when certain people, such as physicians or legislators, arrogate to themselves the power to decide who ought to live and who ought to die. Once again we find ourselves before the temptation of Eden: to become like God who "knows good and evil" (cf. Gen 3:5). God alone has the power over life and death: "It is I who bring both death and life" (Dt 32:39; cf. 2 Kg 5:7; 1 Sam 2:6). But he only exercises this power in accordance with a plan of wisdom and love. When man usurps this power, being enslaved by a foolish and selfish way of thinking, he inevitably uses it for injustice and death. Thus the life of the person who is weak is put into the hands of the one who is strong; in society the sense of justice is lost, and mutual trust, the basis of every authentic interpersonal relationship, is undermined at its root.

Notes

1. Congregation for the Doctrine of the Faith, Declaration on Euthanasia *Iura et Bona* (5 May 1980), II: *AAS* 72 (1980), 546.
2. Ibid., IV: loc. cit., 551.
3. Cf. ibid.
4. Pius XII, Address to an International Group of Physicians (24 February 1957), III: *AAS* 49 (1957), 147; cf. Congregation for the Doctrine of the Faith, Declaration on Euthanasia *Iura et Bona*, III: *AAS* 72 (1980), 547–548.
5. Pius XII, Address to an International Group of Physicians (24 February 1957), III: *AAS* 49 (1957), 145.
6. Pius XII, Address to an International Group of Physicians (24 February 1957): loc. cit., 129–147; Congregation of the Holy Office, *Decretum de directa insontium occisione* (2 December 1940): *AAS* 32 (1940), 553–554; Paul VI, Message to French Television: "Every Life Is Sacred" (27 January 1971): *Insegnamenti* IX (1971), 57–58; Address to the International College of Surgeons (1 June 1972): *AAS* 64 (1972), 432–436; Second Vatican Ecumenical Council, Pastoral Constitution on the Church in the Modern World *Gaudium et Spes*, 27.
7. Cf. Second Vatican Ecumenical Council, Dogmatic Constitution on the Church *Lumen Gentium*, 25.
8. Cf. Saint Augustine, *De Civitate Dei* I, 20: CCL 47, 22; Saint Thomas Aquinas, *Summa Theologiae*, II-II, q. 6, a. 5.
9. Congregation for the Doctrine of the Faith, Declaration on Euthanasia *Iura et Bona* (5 May 1980), I: *AAS* 72 (1980), 545; *Catechism of the Catholic Church*, Nos. 2281–2283.
10. *Ep.* 204, 5: *CSEL* 57, 320.

QUESTIONS

1. What is the basis for the late pope's argument against euthanasia?
2. How is euthanasia distinguished from "aggressive medical treatment"?

49. Active and Passive Euthanasia

JAMES RACHELS

For a description of the author, see ch. 8.

In 1975 James Rachels published a defense of euthanasia in a famous article, "Active and Passive Euthanasia," published in the *New England Journal of Medicine*. There he argued that the common distinction between killing and letting die lacks the moral significance it is thought to have and that the case against active euthanasia cannot be made to depend on it. He claims that if we think passive euthanasia to be permissible, we must think the same of active euthanasia. This article has generated enormous controversy. In this chapter of his book, *The End of Life,* Rachels develops it and replies to critics.

As with all of these debates, students should pay attention to the manner in which Rachels and other writers frame the debate about euthanasia and the way in which they characterize the different kinds of euthanasia. There are different ways of understanding different kinds of euthanasia, and this affects the conclusions reached.

Killing and Letting Die

The idea that it is all right to allow patients to die is an old one. Four centuries before Christ Socrates said of a physician, with approval, "bodies which disease had penetrated through and through, he would not have attempted to cure . . . he did not want to lengthen out good-for-nothing lives." In the centuries that followed neither the Christians nor the Jews significantly altered this basic idea: both viewed allowing to die, in circumstances of hopeless suffering, as permissible. It was killing that was zealously opposed.

The morality of allowing people to die by not treating them has become more important as methods of treatment have become more sophisticated. By using such devices as respirators, heart-lung machines, and intravenous feeding, we can now keep almost anybody alive indefinitely, even after he or she has become a "human vegetable" without thought or feeling or hope of recovery. The maintenance of life by artificial means is, in such cases, sadly pointless. Virtually everyone who has thought about the matter agrees that it is morally all right, at some point, to cease treatment and allow such people to die. In our own time, no less a figure than the Pope has reaffirmed the permission: Pius XII emphasized in 1958 that we may "allow the patient who is virtually already dead to pass away in peace." The American Medical Association policy statements [. . .] are in this tradition: they condemn mercy-killing, but say it is permissible to "cease or omit treatment to let a terminally ill patient die."

Thus the medical community embraces, as part of its fundamental code, a distinction between active euthanasia and what we might call "passive euthanasia." By "active euthanasia" we mean taking some positive action designed to kill the patient; for example, giving a lethal injection of potassium

From James Rachels, *The End of Life* (1986), reprinted by permission of Oxford University Press.

chloride. "Passive euthanasia," on the other hand, means simply refraining from doing anything to keep the patient alive. In passive euthanasia we withhold medication or other life-sustaining therapy, or we refuse to perform surgery, and so on, and let the patient die "naturally" of whatever ills already afflict him. It is the difference between *killing people*, on the one hand, and merely *letting people die* on the other.

Many writers prefer to use the term "euthanasia" only in connection with active euthanasia. They use other words to refer to what I am calling "passive euthanasia"—for example, instead of "passive euthanasia" they may speak of "death with dignity." One reason for this choice of terms is the emotional impact of the words: it *sounds* so much better to defend "death with dignity" than to advocate "euthanasia" of any sort. And of course if one believes that there is a great moral difference between the two, one will prefer a terminology that puts as much psychological distance as possible between them. But nothing of substance depends on which label is used. I will stay with the terms "active euthanasia" and "passive euthanasia" because they are the most convenient; but other terms could be substituted without affecting my argument.

The belief that there is an important moral difference between active and passive euthanasia has obvious consequences for medical practice. It makes a difference to what doctors are willing to do. Consider this case: a patient dying from incurable cancer of the throat is in terrible pain that we can no longer satisfactorily alleviate. He is certain to die within a few days, but he decides that he does not want to go on living for those days since the pain is unbearable. So he asks the doctor to end his life now, and his family joins in the request.

One way the doctor might comply with this request is simply by killing the patient with a lethal injection. Most doctors would not do that, for all the reasons we have been considering. Yet, even so, the physician may sympathize with the dying patient's request and feel that it is reasonable for him to prefer death now rather than after a few more days of suffering. The active/passive euthanasia doctrine tells the doctor what to do: it says that although he may not administer the lethal injection—that would be active euthanasia, which is forbidden—he *may* withhold treatment and let the patient die sooner than he otherwise would. It is no wonder that this simple idea is so widely accepted, for it seems to give the doctor a way out of his dilemma without having to kill the patient, and without having to prolong the patient's agony.

I will argue, against the prevailing view, that active and passive euthanasia are morally equivalent—there is no moral difference between them. By this I mean that there is no reason to prefer one over the other as a matter of principle; the fact that one case of euthanasia is active, while another is passive, is not *itself* a reason to think one morally better than the other. My argument will not depend on assuming that either practice is acceptable or unacceptable. Here I will only argue that the two forms of euthanasia are morally equivalent: either both are acceptable or both are not. They stand or fall together. Of course, if you already think that passive euthanasia is all right, then you may conclude from this that active euthanasia must be all right, too. On the other hand, if you believe that active euthanasia is immoral, you may want to conclude that passive euthanasia is also immoral. Obviously, I prefer the former alternative; however, nothing in the argument of this chapter will depend on that.

Practical Consequences of the Traditional View

I will discuss the theoretical shortcomings of the traditional view at some length. However, I also want to emphasize the practical side of the issue. Employing the traditional distinction has serious adverse consequences for patients. Consider again the man with terminal cancer. Basically, the doctors have three options. First, they can end his life now by a lethal injection. Second, they can withhold treatment and allow him to die sooner than he otherwise would—this will take some time, however, so let us say that he would die in one day. And third, they could continue treatment and prolong his life as long as possible—say, for five days. (The exact numbers do not matter; they are merely for the purpose of illustration.) The traditional view says that the second, but not the first, option may be chosen.

As a practical matter, what is wrong with this? Remember that the justification for allowing the patient to die, rather than prolonging his life for a few more hopeless days, is that he is in horrible pain. One problem is that, if we simply withhold treatment, it will take him *longer* to die, and so he will suffer *more*, than if we administered the lethal injection. Why, if we have already decided to shorten his life because of the pain, should we prefer the option that involves more suffering? This seems, on the face of it, contrary to the humanitarian impulse that prompts the decision not to prolong his life in the first place. I think I can understand why some people oppose euthanasia in any form—the view that prefers option three is mistaken, in my opinion, but it has a certain kind of integrity. A preference for the first option is also understandable. But the view which makes option two the top choice is a "moderate" position that incorporates the worst, and not the best, of both extremes.

The cruelty lurking in the distinction between killing and letting die may also be illustrated by a very different kind of case. Down's syndrome (mongolism) is sometimes complicated by duodenal atresia (blocked intestine), and the unfortunate infant cannot obtain nourishment. In such cases, the parents and doctors have sometimes decided not to perform the surgery necessary to remove the blockage, and let the baby die. Here is one doctor's account of what happens then:

> When surgery is denied [the doctor] must try to keep the infant from suffering while natural forces sap the baby's life away. As a surgeon whose natural inclination is to use the scalpel to fight off death, standing by and watching a salvageable baby die is the most exhausting experience I know. It is easy at a conference, in a theoretical discussion, to decide that such infants should be allowed to die. It is altogether different to stand by in the nursery and watch as dehydration and infection wither a tiny being over hours and days. This is a terrible ordeal for me and the hospital staff—much more so than for the parents who never set foot in the nursery.

This is not the account of a doctor who opposes the practice he is describing. On the contrary, Dr. Anthony Shaw, the author of this account and

one of the most frequently cited writers on the subject, supports the morality of letting these infants die. He is troubled only by the "ordeal" he seems to think is necessary. But why is the ordeal necessary? Why must the hospital staff "stand by in the nursery and watch as dehydration and infection wither a tiny being over hours and days"? What is gained from this, when an injection would end its life at once? No matter what you think of the lives of such infants, there seems to be no satisfactory answer. If you think that the babies' lives are precious and should be protected, then of course you will oppose killing them *or* letting them die. On the other hand, if you think death is a permissible choice here, why shouldn't you think the injection at least as good as letting the infant "wither"?

Let me mention another, even more bizarre, practical consequence of the traditional doctrine. Duodenal atresia is not part of Down's syndrome; it is only a condition that sometimes *accompanies* it. When duodenal atresia is present, a decision might be made to let the baby die. But when there is no intestinal blockage (or other similar defect requiring surgery), other Down's babies live on. Let us focus on this fact: *some Down's infants, with duodenal atresia, die, while other Down's infants, without duodenal atresia, live.* This, I wish to suggest, is irrational.

To bring out the irrationality of this situation, we may first ask *why* the babies with blocked intestines are allowed to die. Clearly, it is not because they have blocked intestines. The parents do not despair, and opt for death, over this condition which often could easily be corrected. The reason surgery is not performed is, obviously, that the child is mongoloid and the parents and doctors judge that because of *that* it is better for the child not to survive. But notice that the other babies, without duodenal atresia, are *also* mongoloid—they have the very same condition which dooms the ones with the blocked intestines—and yet they live on.

This is absurd, no matter what view one takes of the lives and potentials of such infants. Again, if you think that the life of such an infant is worth preserving, then what does it matter if it needs a simple operation? Or, if you think Down's syndrome so terrible that such babies may be allowed to die, then what does it matter if some babies' intestinal tracts are *not* blocked? In either case, the matter of life and death is being decided on irrelevant grounds. It is the Down's syndrome, and not the intestines, that is the issue. The issue should be decided, if at all, on *that* basis, and not be allowed to depend on the essentially irrelevant question of whether the intestinal tract is blocked.

What makes this situation possible, of course, is the idea that there is a big moral difference between letting die and killing: when there is an intestinal obstruction we can "let the baby die," but when there is no such defect there is no choice to be made, for we must not "kill" it. The fact that this idea leads to such results as deciding life or death on irrelevant grounds is one reason, among others, why it should be rejected.

The Bare Difference Argument

The Equivalence Thesis, as I will call it, says that there is no morally important difference between killing and letting die; if one is permissible (or objectionable), then so is the other, and to the same degree. More precisely, it is a claim about what does, or does not, count as a morally good reason in support of a value judgement: the bare fact that one act is an act of killing, while another act is an act of "merely" letting someone die, is not a morally good reason in support of the judgement that the former is worse than the latter.

It is compatible with the Equivalence Thesis that there may be *other* differences between such acts that are morally significant. For example, the family of an irreversibly comatose hospital patient may want their loved one to be allowed to die, but not killed. In that case, we have at least one reason to let the patient die rather than to kill him—the reason is that the family prefers it that way. This does not mean, however, that the distinction between killing and letting die *itself* is important. What is important is respecting the family's wishes. (It is often right to respect people's wishes even when we think those wishes are based on false beliefs.) In another sort of case, a patient with a painful terminal illness may want to be killed rather than allowed to die because a slow, lingering death would be agonizing. Here we have reason to kill and not let die, but once again the reason is not that one course is intrinsically

preferable to the other. The reason is, rather, that the latter course would lead to more suffering.

I will argue that the Equivalence Thesis is true. It should be clear, however, that I will *not* be arguing that every act of letting die is equally as bad as every act of killing. There are lots of reasons, such as those I have just mentioned, why a particular act of killing may be morally inferior to a particular act of letting die, or vice versa. All I will argue is that, whatever reasons there may be for judging one act worse than another, the bare fact that one is killing, while the other is letting die, is not among them.

The Equivalence Thesis is one of those airy, abstract sorts of philosophical claims that may seem impossible to "prove" one way or the other. But I think it is possible to give some fairly convincing reasons for accepting it. The practical considerations adduced in the previous section should go some way towards making the thesis plausible; yet those considerations do not add up to a rigorous argument. What follows is an attempt to provide something more compelling.

In the sciences we often want to know what influence is exerted by one element of a complex situation. The familiar procedure is to isolate the element of interest by studying cases in which everything else is held constant, while that one element is varied. Children are taught this idea in school by having them perform simple experiments. For example, does the colour of a combustible material affect whether it will burn? Children can see that it does not by trying—and succeeding—to burn bits of paper of different colours. Does the presence of air affect combustion? Most of us will remember placing a candle in a bell-jar and watching it go out after the oxygen is consumed, while a similar candle outside the jar continues to burn. By varying one element, we see what difference it makes.

We may try a similar "experiment" with the distinction between killing and letting die. We may consider two cases which are exactly alike except that one involves killing where the other involves letting die. Then we can ask whether this difference makes any difference to our moral assessments. It is important that the cases be *exactly* alike except for this one difference, because otherwise we cannot be confident that it is *this* difference which accounts for any variation in the assessments. Consider, then, this pair of cases:

> Smith stands to gain a large inheritance if anything should happen to his six-year-old cousin. One evening while the child is taking his bath, Smith sneaks into the bathroom and drowns the child, and then arranges things so that it will look like an accident. No one is the wiser, and Smith gets his inheritance.

> Jones also stands to gain if anything should happen to his six-year-old cousin. Like Smith, Jones sneaks in planning to drown the child in the bath. However, just as he enters the bathroom Jones sees the child slip, hit his head, and fall face-down in the water. Jones is delighted; he stands by, ready to push the child's head back under if necessary, but it is not necessary. With only a little thrashing about, the child drowns all by himself, "accidentally," as Jones watches and does nothing. No one is the wiser, and Jones gets his inheritance.

Now Smith killed the child, while Jones "merely" let the child die. That is the only difference between them. Did either man behave better, from a moral point of view? Is there a moral difference between them? *If the difference between killing and letting die were itself a morally important matter, then we should say that Jones's behaviour was less reprehensible than Smith's.* But do we want to say that? I think not, for several reasons.

First, both men acted from the same motive—personal gain—and both had exactly the same end in view when they acted. We may infer from Smith's conduct that he is a bad man, although we may withdraw or modify that judgement if we learn certain other facts about him, for example, that he is mentally deranged. But would we not also infer the very same thing about Jones from his conduct? And would not the same further considerations also be relevant to any modification of that judgement?

Second, the *results* of their conduct were the same—in both cases, the cousin ended up dead and the villain ended up with the money.

Third, suppose Jones pleaded, in his defence, "After all, I didn't kill the child. I only stood there and let him die." Again, if letting die were in itself less bad than killing, this defence should have at least some weight. But—morally, at least —it does not. Such a "defence" can only be regarded as a grotesque perversion of moral reasoning.

Thus, it seems that when we are careful not to smuggle in any further differences which prejudice the issue, the bare difference between killing and letting die does not itself make any difference to the morality of actions concerning life and death. I will call this the "Bare Difference Argument."

Now it may be pointed out, quite properly, that the cases of euthanasia with which doctors are concerned are not like this at all. They do not involve personal gain or the destruction of normal, healthy children. Doctors are concerned only with cases in which the patient's life is of no further use to him, or in which the patient's life has become a positive burden. However, the point will be the same even in those cases: the difference between killing and letting die does not, *in itself*, make a difference, from the point of view of morality. If a doctor lets a patient die, for humane reasons, he is in the same moral position as if he had given the patient a lethal injection for humane reasons. If the decision was wrong—if, for example, the patient's illness was in fact curable—then the decision would be equally regrettable no matter which method was used to carry it out. And if the doctor's decision was the right one, then the method he used is not itself important.

Counter-Arguments

Our argument has brought us to this point: we cannot draw any moral distinction between active and passive euthanasia on the grounds that one involves killing while the other only involves letting someone die, because that is a difference that does not make a difference, from a moral point of view. Some people will find this hard to accept. One reason, I think, is that they fail to distinguish the question of whether killing is, in itself, worse than letting die, from the very different question of whether most actual cases of killing are more reprehensible than most actual cases of letting die. Most actual cases of killing are clearly terrible—think of the murders reported in the newspapers—and we hear of such cases almost every day. On the other hand, we hardly ever hear of a case of letting die, except for the actions of doctors who are motivated by humanitarian concerns. So we learn to think of killing in a much worse light than letting die; and we conclude, invalidly, that there must be something about killing which makes it *in itself* worse than letting die. But this does not follow, for it is not the bare difference between killing and letting die that makes the difference in these cases. Rather, it is the other factors—the murderer's motive of personal gain, for example, contrasted with the doctor's humanitarian motivation, or the fact that the murderer kills a healthy person while the doctor lets die a terminal patient racked with disease—that account for our different reactions to the different cases.

There are, however, some substantial arguments that may be advanced to oppose this conclusion. Here are three of them:

1. The first counter-argument focuses specifically on the concept of *being the cause of someone's death*. If we kill someone, then we are the cause of his death. But if we merely let someone die, we are not the cause; rather, he dies of whatever condition he already has. The doctor who gives the cancer patient a lethal injection will have caused his patient's death, whereas if he merely ceases treatment, the cancer and not the doctor is the cause of death. According to some thinkers, this is supposed to make a moral difference. Ramsey, for example, urges us to remember that "In omission no human agent causes the patient's death, directly or indirectly." And, writing in the *Villanova Law Review*, Dr. J. Russell Elkinton said that what makes the active/passive euthanasia distinction important is that in passive euthanasia "The patient does not die from the act [that is, the act of turning off a respirator] but from the underlying disease or injury."

This argument will not do, for two reasons. First, just as there is a distinction to be drawn between being and not being the cause of someone's death, there is also a distinction to be drawn between letting someone die and not letting anyone die. It is certainly desirable, in general, not to be the cause of anyone's death; but it is also desirable, in general, not to let anyone die when we can save them. (Doctors act on this precept every day.) Therefore, we cannot draw any special conclusion about the relative desirability of passive euthanasia just on these grounds.

Second, the reason we think it is bad to be the cause of someone's death is that we think death is a great evil—and so it is. However, if we have decided that euthanasia, even passive euthanasia, is desirable in a given case, then we have decided that in *this* instance death is no greater an evil than the patient's continued existence. And if this is true, then the usual reason for not wanting to be the cause of someone's death simply does not apply. To put the point just a bit differently: there is nothing wrong with being the cause of someone's death if his death is, all things considered, a good thing. And if his death is *not* a good thing, then *no* form of euthanasia, active or passive, is justified. So once again we see that the two kinds of euthanasia stand or fall together.

2. The second counter-argument appeals to a favourite idea of philosophers, namely that our duty not to harm people is generally more stringent than our duty to help them. The law affirms this when it forbids us to kill people, or steal their goods, but does not require us in general to save people's lives or give them charity. And this is said to be not merely a point about the law, but about morality as well. We do not have a strict moral duty to help some poor man in Ethiopia—although it might be kind and generous of us if we did—but we *do* have a strict moral duty to refrain from doing anything to harm him. Killing someone is a violation of our duty not to do harm, whereas letting someone die is merely a failure to give help. Therefore, the former is a more serious breach of morality than the latter; and so, contrary to what was said above, there is a morally significant difference between killing and letting die.

This argument has a certain superficial plausibility, but it cannot be used to show that there is a morally important difference between active and passive euthanasia. For one thing, it only seems that our duty to help people is less stringent than our duty not to harm them when we concentrate on certain sorts of cases: cases in which the people we would help are very far away, and are strangers to us; or cases in which it would be very difficult for us to help them, or in which helping would require a substantial sacrifice on our part. Many people feel that, in *these* types of cases, it may be kind and generous of us to give help, but we are not morally required to do so. Thus it is felt that when we give money for famine relief we are being especially big-hearted, and we deserve special praise—even if it would be immodest of us to seek such praise—because we are doing more than we are, strictly speaking, required to do.

However, if we think of cases in which it would be very easy for us to help someone who is close at hand and in which no great personal sacrifice is required, things look very different. Think again of the child drowning in the bathtub: *of course* anyone standing next to the tub would have a strict moral duty to help the child. Here the alleged asymmetry between the duty to help and the duty not to do harm vanishes. Since most of the cases of euthanasia with which we are concerned are of this latter type—the patient is close at hand, it is well within the professional skills of the physician to keep him alive, and so on—the alleged asymmetry has little relevance.

It should also be remembered, in considering this argument, that the duty of doctors towards their patients *is* precisely to help them; that is what doctors are supposed to do. Therefore, even if there were a general asymmetry between the duty to help and the duty not to harm—which I deny [. . .] —it would not apply in the special case of the relation between doctors and their patients.

Finally, it is not clear that killing such a patient *is* harming him, even though in other cases it certainly is a great harm to someone to kill him. For we are going under the assumption that the patient would be no worse off dead than he is now (otherwise, even *passive* euthanasia would be unthinkable); and if this is so, then killing him is not harming him. For the same reason we should not classify letting such a patient die as a failure to help. Therefore, even if we grant that our duty to help people is less stringent than our duty not to harm them, nothing follows about our duties with respect to killing and letting die in the special case of euthanasia.

3. The third counter-argument appeals to a consideration that has often been mentioned by doctors. Allowing a patient to die is, normally, a rather impersonal thing, in the sense that the physician does not feel "involved" in the death—the cancer, or whatever, causes the death, and the doctor has nothing to do with it. So, there is no reason for him to feel guilty or responsible for the death. But if the physician were to give a lethal injection, *he* would be responsible, and feelings of guilt would be inevitable.

I do not wish to minimize the importance of the psychological situation in which doctors and other health-care professionals may find themselves. No doubt, many people who are comfortable enough letting die would find it psychologically impossible to kill—they just couldn't bring themselves to do it, and if they did, they would be haunted by feelings of remorse. But, important as this is for the people involved, we should be careful not to infer too much from it. We are trying to figure out whether mercy-killing is *wrong,* and whether it is *morally different* from letting die. So, we should ask: If someone feels guilty about mercy-killing, is that evidence that it is wrong? Or, if someone feels guiltier about mercy-killing than about letting die, is that evidence that it is worse?

Guilt feelings may, of course, be irrational. Someone may *feel* guilty even when he has not done anything wrong. Thus, we should not conclude that something is bad simply because someone feels, or would feel, guilty about it. We must *first* decide whether the conduct is wrong, on the basis of objective reasons; and then, if it is wrong, we may view feelings of guilt as justified. But if it is not wrong, the feelings of guilt are irrational and we may encourage the person suffering them not to feel so bad. At any rate, feelings of guilt and the judgement of real guilt are different matters, and we cannot validly argue that a form of conduct *is* wrong, or that one type of behaviour *is* worse than another, because of feelings of guilt or innocence. That gets things the wrong way round.

The Physician's Commitments

Some people find it especially difficult to accept the idea of *physicians* engaging in active euthanasia. Doctors, they remind us, are dedicated to protecting and preserving life; that is their special task. Thus we should not expect *them* to kill, regardless of whatever might be right for the rest of us. Passive euthanasia, however, is another matter; since it only involves withholding pointless treatment, there is nothing in the physician's special position to rule it out.

This idea has been used by some philosophers as the basis for a qualified defence of the active/passive euthanasia distinction. It is said that the distinction is important for doctors, because of their special role, regardless of whether it is important for anyone else. We need to ask, then, whether there is anything in the doctor's position that makes it impossible for him to accept active euthanasia. According to this argument, the doctor has some sort of special commitment, which the rest of us do not have, which makes the ethics of his position different.

Is this true? Everything turns on the nature of the physician's commitment. Exactly what kind of commitment is it? It might be a moral commitment—a matter of what physicians believe to be morally right—or it might be some sort of professional commitment, having to do with their role in society. Professional commitments and moral commitments are very different, and so we should consider them separately. Therefore, let's look at them one at a time.

Moral Commitments

Many doctors certainly do believe that active euthanasia is immoral. Indeed, that is one reason the medical community so firmly rejects the practice. However, we should remember that anyone, including doctors, might have moral beliefs that are mistaken. To discover the truth, we must look at the arguments that can be given for and against active euthanasia; if better reasons can be given against it, it is wrong regardless of what anyone thinks. But the fact that someone believes something is wrong never entails, by itself, that it *is* wrong. And so the fact that doctors *believe* active euthanasia to be wrong cannot, by itself, justify the conclusion that it is wrong for them to practice it.

When thinking about this point, it is easy to fall into a certain confusion. Suppose someone mistakenly believes that something is wrong—he believes it is wrong, when in fact it is perfectly all right. If he goes ahead and does that thing, even though he believes it is wrong, he is certainly open to criticism—you may think him in some sense a morally defective person, for he should not have done what he thought was wrong. This is where the confusion can slip in. When we say "He should not have done

it" we do not mean that what he did was wrong. In *fact,* what he did was perfectly all right. Despite this, he behaved badly because he did what he *thought* was wrong. Thus, if doctors believe active euthanasia is wrong, we can say that, in this sense, they shouldn't practise it. But this will not mean that, if they did practise it, they would be doing the wrong thing.

What doctors believe is also relevant in another way. It is in general true that, other things being equal, people should be allowed to follow their own consciences. We should not, without very strong reasons, compel people to do what they think is wrong *even if their beliefs are mistaken.* Otherwise we do not respect their autonomy as rational beings. Thus, if a doctor believes that something is wrong, he should be permitted to refrain from it. For example, many doctors believe that abortion is immoral, and so they should not be (and in fact they are not) required to perform abortions, even though the procedure is legal and accepted by other doctors without qualm. The same might be true of active euthanasia: those physicians who disapprove of it should not have to engage in it. But it does not follow that other doctors, who take a different view, should be forbidden, and so it does not follow that it would be wrong for the medical profession in general.

Therefore, if we focus on the question of *moral* commitment, the argument we are considering fails. There is nothing in the idea of a doctor's moral commitments to support the notion that doctors are precluded from accepting active euthanasia—unless, that is, active euthanasia is objectively wrong, in which case *everyone's* moral commitments ought to forbid it.

Professional Commitments

There are two ways in which doctors might be professionally committed against active euthanasia. First, it might be that doctors pledge themselves to shun it, by subscribing to an explicit professional code of conduct. For a long time the Hippocratic Oath was taken to be such a code, although now it seems to have become more a historical relic than an actual guide. (The oath forbids abortion, for example.) More recently, the American Medical

Association's policy statements have condemned active euthanasia—but it is not the purpose of those statements to bind physicians, and as we have noted, various of their provisions are regularly ignored in hospitals. Therefore, if the "professional commitment" against mercy-killing is supposed to be in virtue of a pledge to an explicit code, there doesn't seem to be such a code. (And even if there were, advocates of active euthanasia could argue that the code should be changed.)

There is, however, another possibility. Perhaps physicians are committed to certain things, not by having taken a specific pledge, but *simply in virtue of being physicians*. Roger Rigterink, a philosopher who defends the general argument we are considering, suggests this when he says, "*The point of medicine is to preserve human life whenever it occurs*," and "*A profession can hardly authorize an activity that is antithetical to its basic function*" (italics added). The idea is that there is something in the very conception of what it is to be a physician that rules out killing patients.

To evaluate this suggestion, let us consider a parallel argument drawn from another area of life. Suppose someone argued that, while it can sometimes be right to destroy an automobile, it can never be right *for a mechanic* to do such a thing. After all, the whole point of automobile mechanics is to repair cars and make them serviceable. In destroying a car, a mechanic would be going against the very nature of his profession. So, if an automobile is beyond salvaging, it may be acceptable for the owner to junk it, but he cannot expect the mechanic to have any part of such a thing.

Obviously, this is a silly argument. But why? It isn't because there is something less noble about automobile mechanics than there is about doctors; nor is it silly because cars lack special moral worth. (There is no "sanctity of automotive life.") It is a bad argument because the concept of a profession cannot be used to show that it is wrong for a professional to do something that falls outside the concept. Mechanics fix cars when they can be fixed; if, in consigning a jalopy to the junk-heap, he isn't acting "as a mechanic," what of it? Similarly, if a doctor, in practicing active euthanasia, wasn't acting "as a doctor," what of it?

It might be objected that, in engaging in mercy-killing, the physician isn't merely doing something *outside* his professional rule; he is doing something *incompatible* with it. However, the same can be said about the auto mechanic. If the point of that profession is "to repair cars and make them serviceable"—and isn't that its point?—then it is equally incompatible with auto mechanics to junk cars. Nevertheless, we would think it very strange for a mechanic to insist that he can do nothing to help us junk cars without violating his calling.

Suppose, however, we admit for purposes of argument that the nature of medicine does somehow imply that those engaged in it cannot be involved in mercy-killing. Would that mean we must meekly accept the implied conclusion? No, for consider this: we can define a *different* profession, very much like medicine, but called (perhaps) "smedicine." Smedicine, as we will define it, is the profession which does everything it can to treat illness, cure disease, and repair the human body, so long as there is any point to it; but, when the possibility of a meaningful life is gone, smedicine helps to make the passage to death as easy as possible. We could argue that medicine, which (we are assuming) precludes this latter kind of help, is morally defective, and should be abandoned, to be replaced by the better practice of smedicine. If I thought that the concept of medicine precluded mercy-killing, that is exactly what I would argue, for "medicine," thus conceived, would be forbidding its practitioners from doing what is in many instances the morally right thing.

There is, therefore, nothing in the physician's commitments that leads to the conclusion that the active/passive euthanasia distinction is somehow valid "for him." If it is in general an unsound distinction, then it is as much unsound for him as for anyone.

Thomson's Objection

The Bare Difference Argument relies on a certain method of reasoning, and some philosophers have suggested that this method is not sound. Judith Jarvis Thomson has urged that *something* must be wrong with this way of reasoning, because it leads to patently absurd conclusions. To demonstrate this, she offers an argument that is parallel to the one involving Smith and Jones, but which is obviously unsound:

> Alfrieda knows that if she cuts off Alfred's head he will die, and wanting him to die, cuts it off; Bertha knows that if she punches Bert in the nose he will die—Bert is in peculiar physical condition—and, wanting him to die, punches him in the nose. But what Bertha does is surely every bit as bad as what Alfrieda does. So cutting off a man's head isn't worse than punching a man in the nose.

She concludes that, since this absurd argument doesn't prove anything, the Smith-and-Jones argument doesn't prove anything either.

If Thomson were right, we would have to scuttle the Bare Difference Argument and look elsewhere for support for the Equivalence Thesis. But I don't think she is right: the Alfrieda-and-Bertha argument is not absurd, as strange as it is. A little analysis shows that it is a sound argument and that its conclusion is true. The analysis is a bit tedious, but it is worth doing, for it clarifies the nature of the Bare Difference Argument and confirms its soundness.

We need first to notice that the reason it is wrong to chop someone's head off is, obviously, that this causes death. (I am setting aside secondary reactions having to do with messiness.) The act is objectionable because of its consequences. Thus, a different act with the same consequences may be equally objectionable. In Thomson's example, punching Bert in the nose has the same consequences as chopping off Alfred's head; and, indeed, the two actions are equally bad.

Now the Alfrieda-and-Bertha argument presupposes a distinction between the act of chopping off someone's head, and the results of that act, the victim's death. (It is stipulated that, except for the fact that Alfrieda chops off someone's head, while Bertha punches someone in the nose, the two acts are "in all other respects alike." The "other respects" include the act's consequence, the victim's death.) This is not a distinction we would normally think to make, since we cannot in fact cut off someone's head without killing him. Yet in thought the distinction can be

drawn. The question raised in the argument, then, is whether, *considered apart from their consequences*, head-chopping is worse than nose-punching. And the answer to *this* strange question is No, just as the argument says it should be.

The conclusion of the argument should be constructed like this: the bare fact that one act is an act of head-chopping, while another act is an act of nose-punching, is not a reason for judging the former to be worse than the latter. At the same time—and this is perfectly compatible with the argument—the fact that one act causes death, while another does not, *is* a reason for judging the former to be worse. Thomson has specified, however, that in the cases of Alfrieda and Bertha there is no difference in this regard either; and so their acts turn out to be morally equivalent. So be it.

The parallel construal of the conclusion to the Smith-and-Jones argument is: the bare fact that one act is an act of killing, while another act is an act of letting die, is not a reason for judging the former to be worse than the latter. At the same time—and this is perfectly compatible with that argument—the fact that an act (of killing, for example) prevents suffering, while another act (of letting die, for example) does not, is a reason for preferring the former. So once we see exactly how the Alfrieda-and-Bertha argument *is* parallel to the Smith-and-Jones argument, we find that Thomson's argument is, surprisingly, quite all right. Therefore, it provides no reason for doubting the soundness of the style of reasoning employed in the Bare Difference Argument.

The Compromise View

Some philosophers concede that, in the case of Smith and Jones, there is no moral difference between killing and letting die; but they continue to maintain that in the euthanasia cases the distinction *is* morally important. Thus, it is suggested that the Bare Difference Argument commits an elementary fallacy—the fallacy of hasty generalization. It leaps from one example, in which the distinction appears to be unimportant, to the general conclusion that the distinction is *never* important. But why should this be so? Why should the only options be that the distinction is *always* important, or *never* important?

Perhaps the truth is simply that the difference between killing and letting die is sometimes morally important, and sometimes not, depending on the particular case you choose to think about.

I will call this the Compromise View. It is the most appealing alternative to the view I am defending, and of all possible views of the matter it most closely conforms to our pre-reflective intuitions. The Compromise View allows us to look at cases one at a time, and decide in each case whether the difference between killing and letting die is significant. What could be more reasonable?

In fact, I will argue, such a procedure is not reasonable at all. Logic requires that the distinction be always, or never, important. There is no middle ground. This may sound unattractively dogmatic. Nevertheless, it follows from some inescapable principles of reasoning.

The crucial question is this: Is it possible for a fact sometimes to count as a good reason in support of a moral judgement, sometimes not? Imagine what it would be like if this were possible. I tell you that John is a bad man because he is stingy and a liar; you then observe that Frank is also a stingy liar, and so you conclude that he is a bad man as well. But I object, and say that although stinginess and dishonesty count against John, the same does not apply to Frank. Frank, I say, is a splendid fellow. I am *not* saying that, despite being a stingy liar, Frank has other qualities that compensate for this. I am saying something much more radical—I take the fact that John is stingy and dishonest to be a good reason for judging him to be a bad man; but I do not take the fact that Frank has these qualities to be a reason for judging him badly. I am holding these qualities against John, but I am not holding these very same qualities against Frank at all, not even as something that needs to be compensated for.

Or, to take a different example: I say that you ought to vote for Brown, a candidate for public office, because she favours gun control. You point out that Black, her opponent, also favours gun control; therefore you say that I have not given any reason for preferring Brown over Black. But again, I object, and say that Brown's position is a reason in her favour, but Black's identical position is not a reason in Black's favour.

Surely, in both these cases, I am inconsistent. It would be perfectly all right to argue that Brown, but not Black, should be elected for other reasons. Perhaps we know more about them than that they both favour gun control: perhaps we also know that both candidates are strong supporters of affirmative action programmes, and that Brown has greater experience in dealing with governmental matters. Then we might tabulate what we know like this:

Reasons for Voting for Brown
Brown favours gun control.
Brown supports affirmative action programmes.
Brown has greater experience.

Reasons for Voting for Black
Black favours gun control.
Black supports affirmative action programmes.

We certainly may conclude that, all things considered, one ought to vote for Brown. In every respect save one, they are equally good candidates; and in the one respect in which they differ, Brown has the edge. So she is the candidate of choice, at least on this information. What we *cannot* do, without violating the requirement of consistency, is say that Brown's position on gun control (or her position on affirmative action) goes on the list in her favour, but that Black's position doesn't even go on the list.

There is a formal principle of reasoning involved here; "formal" because it is a principle of logic that everyone must accept regardless of the content of his or her particular moral code. Let *A* and *B* stand for any actions, and let *P* stand for any property of actions. Then:

> *Principle I*
> If the fact that *A* has *P* is a morally good reason in support of the judgement that *A* ought (or ought not) to be done, and *B* also has *P*, then that is also a reason, of equal weight, for the judgement that *B* ought (or ought not) to be done.

The act "voting for Brown" has the property "being a vote for someone who favours gun control," and the act "voting for Black" has the same property; so, if this provides a reason for voting for Brown, it also provides a reason for voting for Black.

The following corollary covers cases in which the merits of two acts are being compared:

> *Principle II*
> If the fact that A has P and B has Q is a morally good reason for preferring A over B, then if C has P and D has Q, that is a reason of equal weight for preferring C over D.

Thus, if we say that Brown's experience as compared with Black's is a reason for preferring Brown, then in any other similar election between an experienced and an inexperienced candidate, we must say this is a reason for preferring the former.

Superficially, there appear to be some counter-examples to this principle—that is, examples which show the principle to be unsound. Suppose we prefer Brown's experience over Black's in one election, but in another election we think it important to bring in a candidate from outside the government—"fresh blood," as it is called. Doesn't this mean that, in one instance, we are taking experience as desirable, and in another instance taking it as undesirable—and can't this be all right? Of course this is all right—it certainly isn't irrational—but that does not violate the principle. It only appears that we have violated the principle because we have not specified the reasons accurately. The reason we sometimes prefer an "inexperienced" candidate is not that he is inexperienced. It is because we think it likely that he will have a fresher approach, be more open to new ideas and be less bound by the mistakes of the past. And these are *always* good qualities in a candidate. Other apparent counter-examples to the principle may be explained away in a similar manner.

Now, with these principles in mind, let us return to the distinction between killing and letting die. You will recall that the Equivalence Thesis is a thesis about what does, or what does not, count as a morally good reason in support of a value judgement. It says: the fact that one act is an act of killing, while another act is an act of letting someone die, is not a morally good reason in support of the judgement that either act is preferable to the other. The Compromise View, on the other hand, says that in some cases the distinction may be important, while in other cases it is not. In other words, the Compromise View implies this:

> In some cases, the fact that A is letting die, while B is killing, is a morally good reason for preferring A over B. But in other cases, the fact that C is letting die, while D is killing, may *not* be a morally good reason for preferring C over D.

And this violates Principle II. This is what I meant when I said that the Compromise View is inconsistent with sound principles of moral reasoning. The reasonable-sounding compromise offered by this view is not tenable; and so we are stuck with the radical-sounding alternatives: either the distinction between killing and letting die is always important, or it never is.

What do advocates of the Compromise View actually say? Philippa Foot proposes a version of the Compromise View. She asks, "When is this distinction morally relevant?" and answers "in cases in which rights are in question." It may violate a person's rights to kill him, she says, even when in the same circumstances it would not violate his rights to let him die. She adds that "permission may make all the difference in such a case . . . if someone gives us the right to kill him, for his own good, by seriously consenting to the action, it then makes no moral difference whether we do kill him or rather allow him to die."

Foot thinks that it is "obvious" that there is sometimes a moral difference between killing and letting die, especially "when one thinks about the crucial question of rights." She suggests that those who defend the Equivalence Thesis are confused about what they are denying; they "seem simply to have misunderstood the position of their opponents."

It would not be surprising if there were some misunderstanding here. Often, when people take sides on complex issues, and are determined to defend their views, misunderstanding occurs. People become more interested in scoring debating points, and proving themselves right, than in patiently analysing issues. Rather than being immune from this tendency, philosophers often seem to be among the worst offenders.

I can think of one way to bring the two sides on this issue a little closer together. I (and other defenders of the Equivalence Thesis) can easily concede that, in some cases, it may be permissible to let die but not to kill. Likewise, in other cases it may be permissible to kill but not to let die. This is perfectly compatible with the Equivalence Thesis. All the Equivalence Thesis requires is that, in such a case, it is some *other* feature of the case that makes the difference.

Permission may, indeed, be a crucial matter, as Foot says. Suppose I give you permission to let me die, but say that I do not want to be killed. Then it might be all right for you to let me die but not to kill me. (If it is the other way round—I give permission to be killed, but don't want to be allowed to die—the reverse may be true.) However, the *reason* one is permissible, but not the other, will not be that one is killing and the other is letting die. The reason will be, simply, that I permitted one but not the other.

Perhaps the Equivalence Thesis is misunderstood by those who reject it. Foot emphasizes that "If one may, in particular circumstances, allow a man to die it does not *follow* that one may also kill him, even for his own good." She apparently thinks this is a telling point against those of us on the other side of the issue. But it isn't; this is something we all agree on. Suppose, again, that someone wants to be allowed to die but does not want to be killed. In those "particular circumstances," one may allow him to die; but, as she says, "it does not *follow* that one may also kill him." The Equivalence Thesis does not imply otherwise. The Equivalence Thesis only says that the reason one course, but not the other, is permissible, isn't simply the intrinsic "moral importance" of the difference between killing and letting die. In this case that difference is *correlated* with another difference (between permission and objection) and this other difference is, indeed, morally important.

I do not know whether clearing away such misunderstandings, and exposing areas of common ground, will lead to agreement. It should at least reduce the extent of the disagreement, and clarify the differences that remain. Complete agreement is probably too much to hope for; that is rare in any branch of philosophy, and even rarer when philosophical theses lie so close to moral practice.

QUESTIONS

1. How does Rachels understand the relation between the distinction between killing and letting die and the distinction between passive and active euthanasia?
2. How does Rachels defend the Equivalence Thesis?
3. What is the basic argument for thinking that if passive euthanasia is permissible, so must be active euthanasia?

50. A Right to Choose Death? A Moral Argument for the Permissibility of Euthanasia and Physician-Assisted Suicide

FRANCES M. KAMM

Frances M. Kamm is professor of philosophy at Harvard University. She writes about normative and practical ethics, especially about questions of life and death. She is the author of *Creation and Abortion* (1992), *Morality, Mortality*, vol. 1: *Death and Whom to Save from It* (1993), *Morality, Mortality*, vol. 2: *Rights, Duties, and Status* (1996), and *Intricate Ethics: Rights, Responsibilities, and Permissible Harm* (2007).

In this article Kamm constructs an argument for the permissibility of euthanasia and physician-assisted suicide. Her argument depends on the proposal that in treating a medical patient, we may intend lesser evils to her, for the sake of her greater good. If administering morphine will ease the patient's pain but also bring about death, it may be thought permissible as long as we don't intend (or aim at) the patient's death. Kamm questions the thought that the physician's duty to save the patient's life always outweighs other aims, such as furthering the patient's greater good of dying when this is the only way to end great pain. This article is difficult, but the essential argument is found in the second section.

Do people have a right to choose death? More particularly, are *euthanasia* and *physician-assisted suicide* morally permissible? To clarify terms: Euthanasia involves a death that is intended to benefit the person who dies, and requires a final act by some other person (for example, a doctor); physician-assisted suicide, which requires a final act by the patient, can also be undertaken for the good of that patient, and I will confine my attention to cases in which it is. The essential point is that both involve *intentionally* ending a human life: In voluntary euthanasia, the patient and doctor both intend the death; in physician-assisted suicide, the patient intends the death and the doctor may.[1] But how, some ask, can we ever permit people to intentionally end human lives (even their own lives) without degrading human life? How, others ask, can we simply prevent people from deciding when to end their own lives without denying people the autonomy so essential to the value of a human life? As this pair of questions suggests, the debate about the right to choose death may appear to present a stand-off between people who endorse life's intrinsic value, and those who think life's value depends on the interests, judgments, and choices of the person whose life it is.

This picture of irreconcilable moral conflict is, I believe, too despairing about the powers of moral argument. To make headway, however, we may need to pay closer attention to the complexities of cases

From F. M. Kamm, "A Right to Choose Death? A Moral Argument for the Permissibility of Euthanasia and Physician-Assisted Suicide," *Boston Review* (Summer 1997), pp. 20–23. Reprinted by permission of the author.

and the specific moral terrain they occupy: to think about people on medication, being treated by physicians, sometimes relying on technical means to stay alive, trying to decide how to live out what remains of their lives. I will explore this terrain in *moral*, not legal, terms: I will be asking you to consult your moral judgments about cases, and follow out the implications of those judgments. Though this moral argument bears on constitutional argument and on appropriate legislation, I will not propose laws or rules for judges, doctors, or hospital administrators to consult, or worry about slippery slopes created by legally hard cases. The moral landscape affords firmer footing, and does not, I will suggest, permit a blanket ban on euthanasia and physician-assisted suicide: Though both involve intentionally ending human lives, both are sometimes morally permissible. I will conclude by discussing a different argument for such permissibility offered by a distinguished group of moral philosophers in a recent *amicus* brief to the Supreme Court.

I. Logical Troubles?

Before getting to the issue of moral permissibility, we need to overcome a preliminary hurdle. I said that euthanasia and physician-assisted suicide are intended to benefit the patient. Some may object that these ideas make no sense. How is it possible for death to benefit the person who dies? Death eliminates the person—how can we produce a benefit if we eliminate the potential beneficiary?

To see how, consider the parallel question about death as a harm: Can a person be harmed by her own death even though death means that she is no longer around to suffer the harm? Suppose Schubert's life would have included even greater musical achievement had he not died so young. Because musical achievement is an important good, Schubert had a less good life overall than he would have had if he lived longer. But living a less good life is a harm. By excluding those achievements, then, Schubert's death harmed him: it prevented the better life. Now come back to the original concern about how death might be a benefit. Suppose a person's life would go on containing only misery and pain with no compensating goods. That person will be better off living a shorter life containing fewer

such uncompensated-for bad things rather than a longer one containing more of them. But living a better life is a benefit. By interfering with the important bads, the person's death benefits him: it prevents the worse life.

It is possible, in short, to benefit a person by ending his life. The concept of euthanasia is, therefore, at least not simply logically confused; similarly for the idea that physician-assisted suicide may be aimed at the good of the patient. But conceptual coherence does not imply moral permissibility. So let's turn now to the moral question: Is it ever morally permissible to benefit a person by hastening his death, even when he requests it?

II. A Right to Choose

Suppose a doctor is treating a terminally ill patient in severe pain. Suppose, too, that the pain can only be managed with morphine, but that giving the morphine is certain to hasten the patient's death. With the patient's consent, the doctor may nevertheless give the morphine. Why so? Because, in this particular case, the greater good for the patient is relief of pain, and the lesser evil is loss of life: after all, the patient is terminally ill, and in severe pain, so life would end soon anyway and is not of very good quality. So the patient is overall benefited by having a shorter pain-free life rather than a longer, even more painful life. (Notice that this could be true even if the morphine put the patient in a deep unconscious state from which he never awoke, so that he never consciously experienced pain-free time.)

In giving morphine to produce pain relief, the doctor foresees with certainty (let's assume) that the patient will die soon. Still, death is a side-effect of the medication, not the doctor's goal or reason for giving it: the doctor, that is, is not *intending* the patient's death, and would give the medication even if he thought death would not result. (If I have a drink to soothe my nerves and foresee a hangover, it does not follow that I intend the hangover.) Because the intended death is not present, we don't yet have a case of euthanasia or physician-assisted suicide. At the same time, in giving morphine for pain relief, the doctor is not simply letting the patient die as the disease runs its course; he administers a drug which causes death. So I think this should be understood as a case of killing, even though the doctor does not intend the death. (In other cases we have no trouble seeing that it is possible to kill without intending death: consider a driver who runs someone over while speeding.)

Now suppose the morphine loses its power to reduce the intensity of the patient's pain, but that administering it would still shorten the patient's life and thus limit the duration of his pain. Suppose, too, that the patient requests the morphine; fully aware of its effects, he wants to take it so that it will end his pain by killing him. In short, we now have a case of *morphine for death* rather than *morphine for pain relief*. Is it still morally permissible to give the morphine? Some people say that we may not kill in this case. They do not deny that relief of pain is still the greater good and death the lesser evil: they know that the consequences are essentially the same as in the case of morphine for pain relief. The problem, they say, lies in a difference of intent. In the case of giving morphine for pain relief, we intend the pain relief, and merely foresee the death; but in the case of giving morphine for death, we intend the death (which is the lesser evil): we would not give the morphine if we did not expect the death. But some people think it is impermissible to act with the intent to produce an evil. They support what is called the *Doctrine of Double Effect*, according to which there is a large moral difference between acting with the foresight that one's conduct will have some evil consequence and acting with the intent to produce that same evil (even as part of or means to a greater good). So whereas killing the patient by giving morphine for pain relief is permissible, killing the patient by giving morphine for death is impermissible.

The distinction between intending an evil and merely foreseeing it sometimes makes a moral difference. But does it provide a reason to refrain from performing euthanasia or assisting in suicide? I think not. On many occasions already, doctors (with a patient's consent) *intend the lesser evil* to a person in order *to produce his own greater good*. For example, a doctor may intentionally amputate a healthy leg (the lesser evil) in order to get at and remove a cancerous tumor, thereby saving the patient's life (the greater good). Or, he may intentionally cause blindness in a patient if seeing would somehow, for

example, destroy the patient's brain, or cause him to die. Furthermore, he may intentionally cause someone pain, thereby acting contrary to a duty to relieve suffering, if this helps to save the person's life. The duty to save life sometimes just outweighs the other duty. Why then is it impermissible for doctors to intend death when it is the lesser evil, in order to produce the greater good of no pain; why is it morally wrong to benefit the patient by giving her a shorter, less painful life rather than having her endure a longer, more painful one? Recall that in the case of morphine for pain relief, it was assumed that death would be the lesser evil and pain relief the greater good. That was one reason we could give the morphine. Why is it wrong, then, for doctors sometimes to act against a duty to preserve life in order to relieve pain, just as they could sometimes act against a duty not to intend pain in order to save a life?

To summarize, I have constructed a three-step argument for physician-assisted suicide and euthanasia. Assuming patient consent:

1. We may permissibly cause death as a side effect if it relieves pain, because sometimes death is a lesser evil and pain relief a greater good.
2. We may permissibly intend other lesser evils to the patient, for the sake of her greater good.
3. Therefore, when death is a lesser evil, it is sometimes permissible for us to intend death in order to stop pain.

Thus, suppose we accept that it is sometimes permissible to *knowingly* shorten a life by giving pain-relieving medication, and agree, too, that it is sometimes permissible for a doctor to *intend* a lesser evil in order to produce a greater good. How, then, can it be wrong to *intentionally* shorten a life when that will produce the greater good?[2]

I don't expect that everyone will immediately find this argument compelling. I suspect that many—including some who are inclined to agree with the conclusion—will feel that death is different, so to speak. While they agree that we may intend pain, if it is a lesser evil, in order to save a life, they think it is impermissible to intentionally hasten death in order to relieve pain. I will address this concern later. But first I want to add another set of considerations that support euthanasia and physician-assisted suicide.

III. An Argument for Duty

According to the three-step argument, a doctor is *permitted* to give morphine for pain relief, even though he knows it will expedite the patient's death, if death is the lesser evil. But I think we can say more. Suppose, as I have stipulated, that giving morphine is the only way for a doctor to relieve a patient's suffering. A doctor, I assume, has a duty to relieve suffering. I conclude that the doctor has a *duty* to relieve suffering by giving the morphine, if the patient requests this. He cannot refuse to give the morphine on the ground that he will be a killer if he does.

If doctors have a duty to relieve pain, and even being a killer does not override this duty when the patient requests morphine for pain relief, then perhaps they also have a duty, not merely a permission, to kill their patients, or aid in their being killed, intending their deaths in order to relieve suffering. Now we have a new argument. Assuming patient consent:

1. There is a duty to treat pain even if it foreseeably makes one a killer, when death is the lesser evil and no pain is the greater good.
2. There is a duty to intend the other lesser evils (e.g., amputation) for a patient's own greater good.
3. There is a duty to kill the patient, or assist in his being killed, intending his death when this is the lesser evil and pain relief the greater good.

I think this argument, too, is compelling, but will concentrate here on the case for permissibility.

IV. Is Killing Special?

As I indicated earlier, a natural rejoinder to the three-step argument for euthanasia and physician-assisted suicide is to emphasize that "death is different." But how precisely is it different, and why is the difference morally important?

Perhaps it will be said, simply, that the doctor who intends the death of his patient is *killing*. Even if

intending a lesser evil for a greater good is often permissible, it might be condemned when it involves killing. Killing, it might be said, is not on a par with other lesser evils.

But this does not suffice to upset the three-step argument. For giving a lethal injection of morphine to relieve pain also involves killing, and we approve of giving the morphine. To be sure, a patient's right to life includes a right not to be killed. But that right gives us a protected option whether to live or die, an option with which others cannot legitimately interfere; it does not give one a duty to live. If a patient decides to die, he is waiving his right to live. By waiving his right, he releases others (perhaps a specific other person) from a duty not to kill him, at least insofar as that duty stems from his right to live.[3] The duty not to kill him may also stem from their duty not to harm him, even if he so wishes; but I have stipulated that the doctor is to kill only when death is the lesser evil.

A more compelling version of the objection is, however, waiting in the wings. This one points not merely to the fact of killing, but to intentional killing. It claims that there is something distinctive about intending death, and that this distinction makes a large moral difference. In particular, acting with the intention to bring about death as a lesser evil requires that we treat ourselves or other persons as available to be used for achieving certain goods—in particular, the reduction of suffering. In euthanasia and physician-assisted suicide, we intentionally terminate a being with a rational nature—a being that judges, aims at goals, and evaluates how to act.[4] We have no such intention to use a person as a mere means when we aim at such lesser evils as destruction of a leg. Indeed, one of the things that seems odd about killing someone only if he is capable of voluntarily deciding in a reasonable way to end his life is that one is thereby ensuring that what is destroyed is a reasoning, thinking being, and therefore a being of great worth. This will not be so if the person is unconscious or vegetative or otherwise no longer functioning as a rational being. Obviously, people take control of their lives and devote their rational natures to the pursuit of certain goals within those lives; but, it is claimed, when this is appropriate, they do not aim to interfere with or destroy their personhood but set it in one direction or another.

The idea that there are limits on what we may do to ourselves as persons derives from Immanuel Kant. In his moral writings, Kant said that rational humanity, as embodied in ourselves and others, is—and should be treated as—*an end in itself, and not a mere means* to happiness or other goals. The fact that one is a judging, aiming, evaluating rational agent has worth in itself. To have this value as a person is more like an honor to us (Kant called it "dignity") than a benefit that answers to some interest of ours. Thus my life may have worth, even if my life is not a benefit to me (and my death would benefit me) because goods *other than* being a person are outweighed by bads. The worth of my life is not measured solely by its worth to me in satisfying my desires, or its worth to others in satisfying theirs. According to Kant, then, it is wrong for others to treat me as a mere means for their ends, but equally wrong for me to treat myself as a mere means for my own ends: As others should respect my dignity as a person by not using me merely as a means for their purposes, I should have proper regard for my own dignity as a person, and not simply use myself as a means for my own purposes. But that is precisely what I do when I aim at my own death as a way to eliminate pain. So I ought not to pursue that aim, and therefore ought not to consent to a morphine injection aiming at death, or give one to a patient who has consented.

Before assessing this Kantian argument, I want to justify focusing it on intentional killing rather than other ways of intentionally contributing to a death. Consider a patient who intends his own death and therefore wants life support of any sort removed. Suppose, for the sake of argument, that we disapprove of this intention. Suppose, too, that we disapprove of a doctor's agreeing to remove treatment because he also intends this patient's death. But while we may disapprove of the intentions and conduct, acting on that disapproval would require us to *force* life support on the patient, and he has a right that we not do this. Our opposition to his intentions and the doctor's is trumped by our opposition to forced invasion of the patient. So we permit the patient and doctor to act—to remove treatment—intending death. Consider, in contrast, a patient who intends his own death and, therefore, requests a lethal injection or pills. Suppose, once more, that we disapprove of this intention. Acting on our opposition would require us to refrain from invading him with a lethal injection or refuse the pills. But it seems clear that the right not to be invaded with treatment against one's will is stronger than the right simply to be invaded (with a lethal injection) or given pills. So the fact that we must terminate treatment, even when the patient and doctor intend the patient's death, does not show that it is permissible to kill the patient or assist him in killing when he and his doctor intend his death. Correspondingly, an objection to intentional killing need not imply an objection to terminating treatment for someone who intends his own death.[5]

I turn now to the Kantian-style argument against aiming at one's death (or aiming at another's death with his consent). In assessing this argument, we must distinguish three different ways in which one may treat a person as a mere means:

1. Calculating the worth of living on in a way which gives insufficient weight to the worth of being a person.
2. Treating the nonexistence of persons as a means to a goal (e.g., no pain).
3. Using persons in order to bring about their own end.

The first idea is that being a person has worth in itself and is not merely a means to an overall balance of other goods over evils in the person's life. On this interpretation, we treat persons as a mere means if we give inadequate weight in our decisions to the value of our existence as persons; if we do, then death may seem a lesser evil. But even when there are few goods in life besides the capacity to be a rational agent, the loss of life—and therefore the loss of that capacity—may still be a greater evil than pain.

Though I do not doubt that this idea has force, it can equally well be given as a reason for not terminating a course of treatment, even when one merely foresees one's death. Because this way of treating a person as a mere means does not distinguish the *morality of intending death* from the *morality of merely foreseeing death*, it cannot be used to explain why intentional killing in particular is impermissible.[6]

It might be said that this observation should prompt us to rethink the permissibility of killing in, for example, the case of morphine for pain relief, where death is foreseeable but not intended. For it might be said that the concern to treat people as ends and not mere means can be met only by giving *overriding* weight to the value of rational humanity, and that this requires that we refrain from acting in ways that we foresee as leading to death, and not simply from intentional killing. This response seems unjustified. Suppose life involves such unbearable pain that one's whole life is focused on that pain. In such circumstances, one could, I believe, decline the honor of being a person. In so doing, we need not treat our life as mere means to a balance of good over evil. We might acknowledge the great (and normally overriding) value of being a person, and believe it is right to go on in life even if it has more pain than other goods besides rational agency: though we reject the thought that rational agency is merely a means to happiness, we allow that some bad conditions may overshadow its very great value.

What, then, about the second and third interpretations of the idea of using persons as mere means? To see the difference between them, consider an analogy: My radio is a device for getting good sounds and filtering out bad sounds. It is a means to a balance of good sounds over bad ones. Suppose it stops performing well, that it only produces static, but cannot be turned off. I can wait until its batteries run down and not replace them, or I can smash it now, thus using the radio itself to stop the noise it produces. Either way, I would see its death as I saw its life, as a means to a better balance of good over bad sounds. While I have always seen my radio as a mere means to an end, if I smash it, I use it as a means to its end (termination): This is sense (3).[7] If I let the radio run down, intending its demise, but do not smash it—I see it wasting away and do not replace its parts—then I do not see it as a means to its own end, but I do see *its end as a means* to a better balance of sounds. This is sense (2).

Active suicide is analogous to smashing the radio: the person uses himself as a means to his own death. Some people find this complete taking control of one's life particularly morally inappropriate, perhaps because they think our bodies belong to God and that we have no right to achieve the goal of our own death by manipulating a "tool" that is not ours (or intending that others manipulate it). This objection is not present if—here we have sense (2)—we terminate medical assistance with the intention that the system run down, aiming at its death. For then we achieve the goal of death by interfering with what is ours (the medication), not God's. Here we have another reason why someone may object to killing but not to terminating treatment, even if accompanied by the intention that the system run down: unlike intentional killing, terminating treatment does not involve using persons to bring about their own end. Some say, though, that this way of using persons as means is also more objectionable than merely foreseeing the death. They say that if we terminate medical assistance, intending death, we do not merely treat our life as a means to greater good over bad, but treat *our death* (*the end of our life*) as a means to greater good over bad.

How much weight, then, should be placed on the second and third senses of "using a person as a means"? Should they really stand in our way? I believe not. It cannot be argued, at least in secular moral terms, that one's body belongs to someone else and that one cannot, therefore, use it as a means to achieve death. Notice also that if your body belonged to someone else, it isn't clear why you should be permitted to use it by administering morphine to stop your pain when you merely foresee that this will destroy the body. We aren't usually permitted to treat other people's property in this way either. Nor does it seem that treating one's death as available for one's purposes (i.e., being rid of pain) is necessarily a morally inappropriate attitude to take to oneself—so long as there is no failure to properly value the importance of just being a person. If this is right, then, at least sometimes, a patient would do no wrong in intending or causing his death. At least sometimes, a doctor who helped him by giving pills would also do no wrong merely because he killed, or assisted killing, aiming at death.

The strongest case for such conduct can be made, I believe, if the overriding aim is to end physical pain. The need to do this may be rare with modern techniques of pain control, but still the patient has a "disjunctive" right: either to adequate pain control or the assistance in suicide of a willing doctor. Psychological suffering which is a reaction to one's knowledge or beliefs about a state of affairs is a weaker case. The test I suggest here is: Would we give a drug to treat psychological suffering if we *foresaw* that it would rapidly kill as a side effect? If not, then giving pills to a patient intending that they kill him in order to end psychological suffering would not be permissible. This same test can be applied to other reasons that might be offered for seeking death by euthanasia or physician-assisted suicide. For example, would we allow a patient to use a drug that will rapidly cause death (rather than a safer one) if it will save him money? If not, then we may not perform euthanasia or physician-assisted suicide to stop the drain on his family finances. Would we give a demented patient a drug that unraveled the tangled neurons that caused his dementia but which we foresaw would rapidly kill him as a side effect? If not, then why should we be permitted to give him pills, intending his death? Of course, the application of this test may yield positive responses rather than negative ones to these questions.

V. A Philosopher's Brief

I have argued that if it is permissible to treat someone in his best interests though we *foresee* that this treatment will rapidly cause death, it is permissible to kill or assist in killing someone *intending* his death when this is in his best interest. (Consent is required in both cases.) In their recent "philosophers' brief," Ronald Dworkin, Thomas Nagel, Robert Nozick, John Rawls, Thomas Scanlon, and Judith Jarvis Thomson[8] also reject a blanket ban on physician-assisted suicide, but their strategy of argument (and some of their conclusions) differ from mine. They argue from the premise that it is permissible to omit or terminate treatment with the intention that the patient die to the conclusion that it is permissible to assist in the killing of the patient intending death. I think this approach neglects the moral force of the distinction between killing a person and letting her die.

Dworkin et al. wrote as *amici curiae* in the "assisted suicide cases" that the Supreme Court heard this past January.[9] The cases came on appeal from two circuit courts, which had both ruled that government cannot simply prohibit doctors from prescribing medication that would hasten the death of patients who request such medication. The philosophers urge the Supreme Court to uphold those decisions. One part of their argument builds on the Court's 1990 decision in *Cruzan v. Missouri*, in which the Court majority assumed (if only for the sake of argument) that patients have a constitutional right to refuse life-preserving treatment.[10] According to Dworkin et al., the existence of a right to refuse treatment also implies a right to assistance in suicide: if, as *Cruzan* indicates, it is permissible for doctors to let a patient die (even when patient and doctor intend the patient's death), then it is permissible for doctors to assist in killing. In a preface to the philosophers' brief written after the Supreme Court heard oral arguments on the case, Ronald Dworkin notes that several justices rejected this link between *Cruzan* and the assisted suicide cases. They sought to distinguish them by reference to a "common-sense distinction" between the moral significance of acts and omissions: assisting suicide is an act, and thus requires a compelling moral justification; in contrast, not providing treatment is an omission, a matter of "letting nature take its course," and can be justified more easily. Dworkin says that "the brief insists that such suggestions wholly misunderstand the 'common-sense' distinction, which is not between acts and omissions, but between acts or omissions that are designed to cause death and those that are not."

I agree that the *act/omission* distinction will not bear much moral weight in this setting: When a doctor removes treatment by pulling a plug, she acts, though she does not necessarily kill. If the doctor is terminating aid she (or an organization she is part of) started, then I think she does not kill the patient but lets him die. Consider an analogy: I am saving someone from drowning and decide to stop. Even if I have to push a button to make myself stop, I do not kill the person but let him die. When the doctor gives morphine to ease pain, foreseeing it also causes death, she also acts and even kills. But I part company with these philosophers when they argue that, once a patient has consented, we can always move from the permissibility of removing treatment while intending the patient's death to the permissibility of assisted suicide. Killing is not on a moral par with letting die. Let me explain by reference to some cases.

In the first, doctors act *against* their patients' wishes to live. Dworkin et al. agree that a doctor may permissibly deny an organ to a patient in order to give it to another, but *not* kill a patient to get his organ for another. This is not, they say, because of a moral difference between letting a patient die and killing him, but because the doctor merely foresees death in the first case, whereas he intends it in the second. If this showed, however, that killing made no moral difference, it would imply that it is permissible for a doctor, in order to transplant an organ into a patient, to use a chemical that he *foresees* will seep into the next room where another patient lies, killing that patient. For in this case, the doctor does not intend to kill the patient in the other room, but only foresees his death as a side-effect of the chemical. Presumably, though, transplanting with this effect is wrong because it is a killing, albeit foreseeable rather than intended. So in cases in which we merely foresee death, killing may be wrong, even if letting die is not.

Killing can also be a significant factor in cases where a patient does not want to die because letting die with the intention that death occur might be permissible even if killing with such intention is not. It is true, as the brief says, that a doctor who lets his patient die of infection against the patient's will, intending that he die so that his organs are available, has done something wrong, as has a doctor who kills the same sort of patient, intending him to die. In both cases, the doctors aim against the welfare of their patients and violate their rights. The first doctor violates a right to treatment; the second doctor violates a right against being killed. But this does not always imply, as Dworkin et al. think, that "a doctor violates his patient's rights whether the doctor acts or refrains from acting against the patient's wishes in a way that is designed to cause death." For example, suppose that someone does not want to die but it would be in his interest to die. If a treatment is experimental, or in general something to which the patient has no positive right, it may be permissible

to deny it to him because death would be in his own best interest. I do not believe the patient acquires a right to have the experimental therapy merely because the doctor's reason for refusing it is that he aims at the patient's death. Still, it would be morally wrong to kill the patient if he did not want to die, even if it were in his interest to die.

Consider next the type of case in which the patient wants death. Here, the distinction between killing and letting die makes a moral difference when deciding on the scope of permissible refusal of treatment versus permissible assistance to killing. Dworkin et al. seem to suggest the scope should be the same, saying that if a doctor can turn off a respirator, he can prescribe pills. But a mentally competent patient may legally refuse treatment, intending to die, even when it is not in his best interest to do so and, on many occasions, even when he could be cured. Presumably, in many of these cases, he could also insist on terminating treatment, even if his intention is to die. Furthermore, even if the doctor in these cases improperly intends that the patient die, the treatment must be terminated. *This is because the alternative to letting the patient die is forcing treatment on him.* We think a competent patient's right not to be physically invaded against his will is typically stronger than our interest in his well-being (though this right is, to be sure, not absolute and can sometimes be overridden by considerations of public safety). But if he asks for assistance in killing himself when it is not in his interest to be killed, it might well be morally impermissible to kill him. Contrary to what Dworkin et al. say, therefore, a doctor might in some cases be permitted and even required to turn off a respirator but not permitted to give pills.[11]

The alternative to letting die, then, has such a morally objectionable feature—forcing treatment which he has a right we not do—that even if we think the patient's and doctor's goals are wrong, we must terminate aid. In contrast, the alternative to assisted suicide may simply be leaving the patient alone; this often does not violate any of his rights against us, and so we can, and sometimes we should be required to, refuse to help because we disapprove of his goals. Many people—including the Supreme Court justices Dworkin et al. cite—might, then, reasonably distinguish refusing treatment and thus letting a patient die from assisting in a suicide. The move from *Cruzan*'s right to refuse treatment to the permissibility of assisted suicide is, therefore, not generally available. Still, my discussion here indicates that we may have other reasons to accept the fundamental moral conclusion: that assisted suicide (and euthanasia) are sometimes morally permissible.[12]

Notes

1. Only "may," because some doctors aim simply to give patients a choice whether to live or die.

2. I first presented this argument in *Creation and Abortion* (New York: Oxford University Press, 1992), pp. 33–35, and again in *Morality, Mortality*, vol. II (New York: Oxford University Press, 1996), pp. 194–98.

3. Notice that this waiver seems to be morally necessary even when the doctor wishes to give morphine that will kill as a foreseen side effect. This means doctors should get permission for giving the morphine for pain relief as well as for giving it to deliberately kill. (I do not believe they always do so.)

4. We also terminate human life considered independently of whether it is the life of a rational being. It may seem harder to justify destroying a person than a human life that lacks qualities required for personhood—for example, a functioning brain. But I will assume that one could substitute "human life" for "person" in the argument I give against intentional killing and in my response to that argument.

5. In contrast, suppose that a patient who intends his own death is also suffering great pain that only morphine will stop. He asks for the morphine, not because it will stop the pain, but because he knows it will kill him. If it would not kill him, he would not ask for it. Does he have a right that the doctor give him the morphine? If he does, then the doctor is not at liberty to refuse simply because of the *patient's*

intention, any more than he could refuse to terminate treatment because of the patient's intention. Indeed we might not be permitted to interfere with the doctor's giving morphine in this case even if he gave it only because *he* intended death. I owe this case to Timothy Hall.

6. Kant thought we had a duty to actively preserve rational humanity and hence we should not too lightly do what we foresee will lead to its end. Still, he allows that we may sometimes engage in conduct though we foresee it will result in our deaths, but we may never aim at our deaths.

7. If I see someone else destroy it and do not interfere, I may be intending its use as a means to its own end, though I do not myself use it.

8. *New York Review of Books*, March 27, 1997.

9. *State of Washington et al. v. Glucksberg et al.* and *Vacco et al. v. Quill et al.*

10. *Cruzan v. Missouri*, 497 U.S. 261 (1990). The Court did not, however, agree that Nancy Cruzan had clearly decided, before an automobile accident that left her in a persistent vegetative state, that she would refuse treatment.

11. It seems to me that the lower court in the Washington case also overlooked this point when they said that whether we assist killing or let die is not morally or legally crucial. For even that court was concerned to limit the doctor's right to assist in killing the patient to cases where the patient's life is going to end shortly anyway and when death is not against his interests. But the right to refuse treatment and have it terminated applies much more broadly. If, however, the distinction between killing and letting die as such makes no moral or legal difference, then refusing treatment should be permitted no more broadly than assisting killing. See *Compassion in Dying v. Washington* 79 F.3d 790 (9th Cir. 1996).

12. I am grateful to Joshua Cohen, Timothy Hall, and Seana Shiffrin for their comments.

QUESTIONS

1. Restate Kamm's argument. What needs to be added to her summary in section II to make the argument clearer?

2. Is death "different"?

51. Against the Right to Die

DAVID VELLEMAN

*D*avid Velleman (1952–) is professor of philosophy at New York University and an important contemporary moral thinker. His books include *The Possibility of Practical Reason* (2000), *Self to Self* (2006), and *How We Get Along* (2009).

In this article Velleman argues against institutionalizing a right to die, in law or the norms governing medical practice. He thinks there are important reasons not to give certain options at the end of life, reasons having to do with features of our culture. For the most part the articles in this reader focus on moral controversies without considering the ways in which our political or legal institutions should address them. But with some controversies it is hard to abstract away from all institutional considerations.

Velleman also raises a possible option when considering questions of policies and practices. He says that the "best public policy of euthanasia, I sometimes think, is no policy at all." In a political culture that is rather legalistic, we sometimes think that the resolution of moral problems ought to be mirrored in our laws. Perhaps that is not always best.

In this paper I offer an argument against establishing an institutional right to die, but I do not consider how my argument fares against countervailing considerations, and so I do not draw any final conclusion on the subject. The argument laid out in this paper has certainly inhibited me from favoring a right to die, and it has also led me to recoil from many of the arguments offered for such a right. But I am very far from an all-things-considered judgment.

My argument is addressed to a question of public policy—namely, whether the law or the canons of medical practice should include a rule requiring, under specified circumstances, that caregivers honor a patient's request to be allowed or perhaps even helped to die. This question is distinct from the question whether anyone is ever morally entitled to be allowed or helped to die. I believe that the answer to the latter question is yes, but I doubt whether our moral obligation to facilitate some people's deaths is best discharged through the establishment of an institutional right to die.

I

Although I believe in our obligation to facilitate some deaths, I want to dissociate myself from some of the arguments that are frequently offered for such an obligation. These arguments, like many arguments in medical ethics, rely on terms borrowed from Kantian moral theory—terms such as "dignity" and "autonomy." Various kinds of life-preserving treatment are said to violate a patient's dignity or to detain him in an undignified state; and the patient's right of autonomy is said to require that we respect his competent and considered wishes, including a wish to die. There may or may not be some truth in each of these claims. Yet when we evaluate such claims, we must take care not to assume that terms like "dignity" and "autonomy" always express the

Published by permission of the author.

same concepts, or carry the same normative force, as they do in a particular moral theory.

When Kant speaks, for example, of the dignity that belongs to persons by virtue of their rational nature, and that places them beyond all price (Kant, 1964, p. 102), he is not invoking anything that requires the ability to walk unaided, to feed oneself, or to control one's bowels. Hence the dignity invoked in discussions of medical ethics—a status supposedly threatened by physical deterioration and dependency—cannot be the status whose claim on our moral concern is so fundamental to Kantian thought. We must therefore ask whether this other sort of dignity, whatever it may be, embodies a value that's equally worthy of protection.

My worry, in particular, is that the word "dignity" is sometimes used to dignify, so to speak, our culture's obsession with independence, physical strength, and youth. To my mind, the dignity defined by these values—a dignity that is ultimately incompatible with *being cared for* at all—is a dignity not worth having.[1]

I have similar worries about the values expressed by the phrase "patient autonomy"; for there are two very different senses in which a person's autonomy can become a value for us. On the one hand, we can obey the categorical imperative, by declining to act for reasons that we could not rationally propose as valid for all rational beings, including those who are affected by our action, such as the patient. What we value in that ease is the patent's *capacity* for self-determination, and we value it in a particular way—namely, by according it *respect*. We respect the patient's autonomy by regarding the necessity of sharing our reasons with him, among others, as a constraint on what decisions we permit ourselves to reach.

On the other hand, we can value the patient's autonomy by making it our goal to maximize his effective options. What we value, in that case, is not the patient's capacity but his *opportunities* for self-determination—his having choices to make and the means with which to implement them; and we value these opportunities for self-determination by regarding them as *goods*—as objects of desire and pursuit rather than respect.

These two ways of valuing autonomy are fundamentally different. Respecting people's autonomy, in the Kantian sense, is not just a matter of giving them effective options. To make our own decisions only for reasons that we could rationally share with others is not necessarily to give *them* decisions to make, nor is it to give them the means to implement their actual decisions.[2]

As with the term "dignity," then, we must not assume that the term "autonomy" is always being used in the sense made familiar by Kantian moral theory; and we must therefore ask ourselves what sort of autonomy is being invoked, and whether it is indeed something worthy of our moral concern. I believe that, as with the term "dignity," the answer to the latter question may be no in some cases, including the case of the right to die.

II

Despite my qualms about the use of Kantian language to justify euthanasia, I do believe that euthanasia can be justified, and on Kantian grounds. In particular, I believe that respect for a person's dignity, properly conceived, can require us to facilitate his death when that dignity is being irremediably compromised. I also believe, however, that a person's dignity can be so compromised only by circumstances that are likely to compromise his capacity for fully rational and autonomous decisionmaking. So although I do not favor euthanizing people against their wills, of course, neither do I favor a policy of euthanizing people for the sake of deferring to their wills, since I think that people's wills are usually impaired in the circumstances required to make euthanasia permissible. The sense in which I oppose a right to die, then, is that I oppose treating euthanasia as a protected option for the patient.

One reason for my opposition is the associated belief (also Kantian) that so long as patients would be fully competent to exercise an option of being euthanized, their doing so would be immoral, in the majority of cases, because their dignity as persons would still be intact. I discuss this argument elsewhere, but I do not return to it in the present paper.[3] In this paper I discuss a second reason for opposing euthanasia as a protected option for the patient. This reason, unlike the first, is consequentialist.

What consequentialist arguments could there be against giving the option of euthanasia to patients?

One argument, of course, would be that giving this option to patients, even under carefully defined conditions, would entail providing euthanasia to some patients for whom it would be a harm rather than a benefit (Kamisar, 1970). But the argument that interests me does not depend on this strategy. My consequentialist worry about the right to die is not that some patients might mistakenly choose to die when they would be better off living.

In order to demonstrate that I am not primarily worried about mistaken request to die, I shall assume, from this point forward, that patients are infallible, and that euthanasia would therefore be chosen only by those for whom it would be a benefit. Even so, I believe, the establishment of a right to die would harm many patients, by increasing their autonomy in a sense that is not only un-Kantian but also very undesirable.

This belief is sometimes expressed in public debate, although it is rarely developed in any detail. Here, for example, is Yale Kamisar's argument against "Euthanasia Legislation":

> Is this the kind of choice . . . that we want to offer a gravely ill person? Will we not sweep up, in the process, some who are not really tired of life, but think others are tired of them; some who do not really want to die, but who feel they should not live on, because to do so when there looms the legal alternative of euthanasia is to do a selfish or a cowardly act? Will not some feel an obligation to have themselves "eliminated" . . . ? (Kamisar, 1970)

Note that these considerations do not, strictly speaking, militate against euthanasia itself. Rather, they militate against a particular decision procedure for euthanasia—namely, the procedure of placing the choice of euthanasia in the patient's hands. What Kamisar is questioning in this particular passage is, not the practice of helping some patients to die, but rather the practice of asking them to choose whether to die. The feature of legalized euthanasia that troubles him is precisely its being an option offered to patients—the very feature for which it's touted, by its proponents, as an enhancement of the patients' autonomy. Kamisar's remarks thus betray the suspicion that this particular enhancement of one's autonomy is not to be welcomed.

But what exactly is the point of Kamisar's rhetorical questions? The whole purpose of giving people choices, surely, is to allow those choices to be determined by their reasons and preferences rather than ours. Kamisar may think that finding one's life tiresome is a good reason for dying whereas thinking that others find one tiresome is not. But if others honestly think otherwise, why should we stand in their way? Whose life is it anyway?

IV

A theoretical framework for addressing this question can be found in Thomas Schelling's book *The Strategy of Conflict* (1960), and in Gerald Dworkin's paper "Is More Choice Better Than Less?" (1982). These authors have shown that our intuitions about the value of options are often mistaken, and their work can help us to understand the point of arguments like Kamisar's.

We are inclined to think that, unless we are likely to make mistakes about whether to exercise an option (as I am assuming we are not), the value of having the option is as high as the value of exercising it and no lower than zero. Exercising an option can of course be worse than nothing, if it causes harm. But if we are not prone to mistakes, then we will not exercise a harmful option; and we tend to think that simply *having* the unexercised option cannot be harmful. And insofar as exercising an option would make us better off than we are, having the option must have made us better off than we were before we had it—or so we tend to think.

What Schelling showed, however, is that having an option can be harmful even if we do not exercise it and—more surprisingly—even if we exercise it and gain by doing so. Schelling's examples of this phenomenon were drawn primarily from the world of negotiation, where the only way to induce one's opponent to settle for less may be by proving that one doesn't have the option of giving him more. Schelling pointed out that in such circumstances, a lack of options can be an advantage. The union leader who cannot persuade his membership to approve a pay-cut, or the ambassador who cannot contact his head-of-state for a change of brief, negotiates from a position of strength; whereas the negotiator for whom all concessions are possible deals from weakness.

If the rank-and-file give their leader the option of offering a pay-cut, then management may not settle for anything less, whereas they might have settled for less if he hadn't had the option of making the offer. The union leader will then have to decide whether to take the option and reach an agreement or to leave the option and call a strike. But no matter which of these outcomes would make him better off, choosing it will still leave him worse off than he would have been if he had never had the option at all.

Dworkin has expanded on Schelling's point by exploring other respects in which options can be undesirable. Just as options can subject one to pressure from an opponent in negotiation, for example, they can subject one to pressure from other sources as well. The night cashier in a convenience store doesn't want the option of opening the safe—and not because he fears that he'd make mistakes about when to open it. It is precisely because the cashier would know when he'd better open the safe that his having the option would make him an attractive target for robbers; and it's because having the option would make him a target for robbers that he'd be better off without it. The cashier who finds himself opening the safe at gunpoint can consistently think that he's doing what's best while wishing that he'd never been given the option of doing it.

Options can be undesirable, then, because they subject one to various kinds of pressure; but they can be undesirable for other reasons, too. Offering someone an alternative to the status quo makes two outcomes possible for him, but neither of them is the outcome that was possible before. He can now choose the status quo or choose the alternative, but he can no longer *have* the status quo without *choosing* it. And having the status quo by default may have been what was best for him, even though choosing the status quo is now worst. If I invite you to a dinner party, I leave you the possibilities of choosing to come or choosing to stay away; but I deprive you of something that you otherwise would have had—namely, the possibility of being absent from my table by default, as you are on all other occasions. Surely, preferring to accept an invitation is consistent with wishing you had never received it. These attitudes are consistent because refusing to attend a party is a different outcome from *not* attending without

having to refuse; and even if the former of these outcomes is worse than attending, the latter may still have been better. Having choices can thus deprive one of desirable outcomes whose desirability depends on their being unchosen.

The offer of an option can also be undesirable because of what it expresses. To offer a student the option of receiving remedial instruction after class is to imply that he is not keeping up. If the student needs help but doesn't know it, the offer may clue him in. But even if the student does not need any help, to begin with, the offer may so undermine his confidence that he will need help before long. In the latter case, the student may ultimately benefit from accepting the offer, even though he would have been better off not receiving it at all.

Note that in each of these cases, a person can be harmed by having a choice even if he chooses what's best for him. Once the option of offering a concession has undermined one's bargaining position, once the option of opening the safe has made one the target of a robbery, once the invitation to a party has eliminated the possibility of absence by default, once the offer of remedial instruction has implied that one needs it—in short, once one has been offered a problematic choice—one's situation has already been altered for the worse, and choosing what's best cannot remedy the harm that one has already suffered. Choosing what's best in these cases is simply a way of cutting one's losses.

Note, finally, that we cannot always avoid burdening people with options by offering them a second-order option as to which options they are to be offered. If issuing you an invitation to dinner would put you in an awkward position, then asking you whether you want to be invited would usually do so as well; if offering you the option of remedial instruction would send you a message, then so would asking you whether you'd like that option. In order to avoid doing harm, then, we are sometimes required, not only to withhold options, but also to take the initiative for withholding them.

V

Of course, the options that I have discussed can also be unproblematic for many people in many circumstances. Sometimes one has good reason to welcome a dinner invitation or an offer of remedial instruction. Similarly, some patients will welcome the option of euthanasia, and rightly so. The problem is how to offer the option only to those patients who will have reason to welcome it. Arguments like Kamisar's are best understood, I think, as warning that the option of euthanasia may unavoidably be offered to some who will be harmed simply by having the option, even if they go on to choose what is best.

I think that the option of euthanasia may harm some patients in all of the ways canvassed above; but I will focus my attention on only a few of those ways. The most important way in which the option of euthanasia may harm patients, I think, is that it will deny them the possibility of staying alive by default.

Now, the idea of surviving by default will be anathema to existentialists, who will insist that the choice between life and death is a choice that we have to make every day, perhaps every moment.[4] Yet even if there is a deep, philosophical sense in which we do continually choose to go on living, it is not reflected in our ordinary self-understanding. That is, we do not ordinarily think of ourselves or others as continually rejecting the option of suicide and staying alive by choice. Thus, even if the option of euthanasia won't alter a patient's existential situation, it will certainly alter the way in which his situation is generally perceived. And changes in the perception of a patient's situation will be sufficient to produce many of the problems that Schelling and Dworkin have described, since those problems are often created not just by *having* options but by *been seen* to have them.

Once a person is given the choice between life and death, he will rightly be perceived as the agent of his own survival. Whereas his existence is ordinarily viewed as a given for him—as a fixed condition with which he must cope—formally offering him the option of euthanasia will cause his existence thereafter to be viewed as his doing.

The problem with this perception is that if others regard you as choosing a state of affairs, they will hold you responsible for it; and if they hold you responsible for a state of affairs, they can ask you to justify it. Hence if people ever come to regard you as existing by choice, they may expect you to justify your continued existence. If your daily arrival in the office is interpreted as meaning that you have once again declined to kill yourself, you may feel obliged to arrive with an answer to the question "Why not?"

I think that our perception of one another's existence as a given is so deeply ingrained that we can hardly imagine what life would be like without it. When someone shows impatience or displeasure with us, we jokingly say, "Well, excuse me for living!" But imagine that it were no joke; imagine that living were something for which one might reasonably be thought to need an excuse. The burden of justifying one's existence might make existence unbearable—and hence unjustifiable.

VI

I assume that people care, and are right to care, about whether they can justify their choices to others. Of course, this concern can easily seem like slavishness or neurotic insecurity; but it should not be dismissed too lightly. Our ability to justify our choices to the people around us is what enables us to sustain the role of rational agent in our dealings with them; and it is therefore essential to our remaining, in their eyes, an eligible partner in cooperation and conversation, or an appropriate object of respect.

Retaining one's status as a person among others is especially important to those who are ill or infirm. I imagine that when illness or infirmity denies one the rewards of independent activity, then the rewards of personal intercourse may be all that make life worth living. To the ill or infirm, then, the ability to sustain the role of rational person may rightly seem essential to retaining what remains of value in life. Being unable to account for one's choices may seem to entail the risk of being perceived as unreasonable—as not worth reasoning with—and consequently being cut off from meaningful intercourse with others, which is life's only remaining consolation.

Forcing a patient to take responsibility for his continued existence may therefore be tantamount to confronting him with the following prospect: unless he can explain, to the satisfaction of others, why he chooses to exist, his only remaining reasons for existence may vanish.

VII

Unfortunately, our culture is extremely hostile to any attempt at justifying an existence of passivity and dependence. The burden of proof will lie heavily on the patient who thinks that his terminal illness or chronic disability is not a sufficient reason for dying.

What is worse, the people with whom a patient wants to maintain intercourse, and to whom he therefore wants to justify his choices, are often in a position to incur several financial and emotional costs from any prolongation of his life. Many of the reasons in favor of his death are therefore likely to be exquisitely salient in their minds. I believe that some of these people may actively pressure the patient to exercise the option of dying. (Students who hear me say this usually object that no one would ever do such a thing. My reply is that no one would ever do such a thing as abuse his own children or parents—except that many people do.)

In practice, however, friends and relatives of a patient will not have to utter a word of encouragement, much less exert any overt pressure, once the option of euthanasia is offered. For in the discussion of a subject so hedged by taboos and inhibitions, the patient will have to make some assumptions about what they think and how they feel, irrespective of what they say (see Schelling, 1984). And the rational assumption for him to make will be that they are especially sensible of the considerations in favor of his exercising the option.

Thus, even if a patient antecedently believes that his life is worth living, he may have good reason to assume that many of the people around him do not, and that his efforts to convince them will be frustrated by prevailing opinions about lives like his, or by the biases inherent in their perspective. Indeed, he can reasonably assume that the offer of euthanasia is itself an expression of attitudes that are likely to frustrate his efforts to justify declining it. He can therefore assume that his refusal to take the option of euthanasia will threaten his standing as rational person in the eyes of friends and family, thereby threatening the very things that make his life worthwhile. This patient may rationally judge that he's better off taking the option of euthanasia, even though he would have been best off not having the option at all.

Establishing a right to die in our culture may thus be like establishing a right to duel in a culture obsessed with personal honor.[5] If someone defended the right to duel by arguing that a duel is a private transaction between consenting adults, he would have missed the point of laws against dueling. What makes it rational for someone to throw down or pick up a gauntlet may be the social costs of choosing not to, costs that result from failing to duel only if one fails to duel by choice. Such costs disappear if the choice of dueling can be removed. By eliminating the option of dueling (if we can), we eliminate the reasons that make it rational for people to duel in most cases. To restore the option of dueling would be to give people reasons for dueling that they didn't previously have. Similarly, I believe, to offer the option of dying may be to give people new reasons for dying.

VIII

Do not attempt to refute this argument against the right to die by labeling it paternalistic. The argument is not paternalistic—at last, not in any derogatory sense of the word. Paternalism, in the derogatory sense, is the policy of saving people from self-inflicted harms, by denying them options that they might exercise unwisely. Such a policy is distasteful because it expresses a lack of respect for others' ability to make their own decisions.

But my argument is not paternalistic in this sense. My reason for withholding the option of euthanasia is not that others cannot be trusted to exercise it wisely. On the contrary, I have assumed from the outset that patients will be infallible in their deliberations. What I have argued is—not that people to whom we offer the option of euthanasia might harm themselves—but rather that in offering them this option, *we* will do them harm. My argument is therefore based on a simple policy of non-malfeasance rather than on the policy of paternalism. I am arguing that we must not harm others by giving them choices, not that we must withhold the choices from them lest they harm themselves.

Of course, harming some people by giving them choices may be unavoidable if we could not withhold those choices from them without unjustly withholding the same choices from others. If a significant number of patients were both competent and morally entitled to choose euthanasia, then we might be obligated to make that option available even if, in doing so, we would inevitably give it to some who would be harmed by having it. Consider here a closely related option.[6] People are morally entitled to refuse treatment, because they are morally entitled not to be drugged, punctured, or irradiated against their wills—in short, not to be assaulted. Protecting the right not to be assaulted entails giving some patients what amounts to the option of ending their lives. And for some subset of these patients, having the option of ending their lives by refusing treatment may be just as harmful as having the option of electing active euthanasia. Nevertheless, these harms must be tolerated as an inevitable byproduct of protecting the right not to be assaulted.

Similarly, if I believed that people had a moral right to end their lives, I would not entertain consequentialist arguments against protecting that right. But I don't believe in such a moral right, for reasons to which I have briefly alluded but cannot fully expound in this essay. My willingness to entertain the arguments expounded here thus depends on reasons that are explained elsewhere.[7]

IX

I have been assuming, in deference to existentialists, that a right to die would not alter the options available to a patient but would, at most, alter the social perception of his options. What would follow, however, if we assumed that death was not ordinarily a genuine option? In that case, offering someone the choice of euthanasia would not only cause his existence to be perceived as his responsibility; it would actually cause his existence to become his responsibility for the first time. And this new responsibility might entail new and potentially burdensome obligations.

That options can be undesirable because they entail obligations is a familiar principle in one area of everyday life—namely, the practice of offering, accepting, and declining gifts and favors. When we decline a gift or a favor that someone has spontaneously offered, we deny him an option, the option of providing us with a particular benefit. And our reason for declining is often that he could not have the option of providing the benefit without being obligated to exercise that option. Indeed, we sometimes feel obligated, on our part, to decline a benefit precisely in order to prevent someone from being obligated, on his part, to provide it.[8] We thus recognize that giving or leaving someone the option of providing a benefit to us may be a way of harming him, by burdening him with an obligation.

When we decline a gift or favor, our would-be benefactor sometimes protests in language similar to that used by proponents of the right to die. "I know what I'm doing," he says, "and no one is twisting my arm. It's my money [or whatever], and I want you to have it." If he's unaware of the lurking allusion, he might even put it like this: "Whose money is it, anyway?"

Well, it is his money (or whatever); and we do believe that he's entitled to dispose of his money as he likes. Yet his right of personal autonomy in disposing of his money doesn't always require that we let him dispose of it on us. We are entitled—and, as I have suggested, sometimes obligated—to restrict his freedom in spending his money for our benefit, insofar as that freedom may entail burdensome obligations.

The language in which favors are declined is equally interesting as that in which they are offered. What we often say when declining a favor is, "I can't let you do that for me: it would be too much to ask." The phrase "too much to ask" is interesting because it is used only when we haven't in fact asked for anything. Precisely because the favor in question would be too much to ask, we haven't asked for it, and now our prospective benefactor is offering it spontaneously. Why, then, do we give our reason for not having solicited the favor as a reason for declining when it's offered unsolicited?

The answer, I think, is that we recognize how little distance there is between permitting someone to do us a favor and asking him to do it. Because leaving someone the option of doing us a favor can place him under an obligation to do it, it has all the consequences of asking for the favor. To say "I'm leaving you the option of helping me but I'm not asking you to help" is to draw a distinction without a difference, since options can be just as burdensome as requests.

X

Clearly, a patient's decision to die will sometimes be a gift or a favor bestowed on loved ones whose financial or emotional resources are being drained by his condition. And clearly, death is the sort of gift that one might well want to decline, by denying others the option of giving it. Yet protections for the option of euthanasia would in effect protect the option of giving this gift, and they would thereby prevent the prospective beneficiaries from declining it. Establishing a right to die would thus be tantamount to adopting the public policy that death is never too much to ask.

I don't pretend to understand fully the ethics of gifts and favors. It's one of those subjects that gets neglected in philosophical ethics, perhaps because it has more to do with the supererogatory than the obligatory. One question that puzzles me is whether we are permitted to restrict people's freedom to benefit us in ways that require no active participation on our part. Someone cannot successfully give us a gift, in most cases, unless we cooperate by taking it into our possession; and denying someone the option of giving us a gift usually consists of refusing to do our part in the transaction. But what about cases in which someone can do us a good turn without any cooperation from us? To what extent are we entitled to decline the favor by means of restrictions on his behavior rather than omissions in ours?

Another question, of course, is whether we wouldn't, in fact, play some part in the deaths of patients who received socially sanctioned euthanasia. Would a medically assisted or supervised death be a gift that we truly took no part in accepting? What if "we"—the intended beneficiary of the gift—were society as a whole, the body that established the right to die and trained physicians in its implementation? Surely, establishing the right to die is tantamount to saying, to those who might contemplate dying for the social good, that such favors will never be refused.

These considerations, inconclusive though they are, show how the theoretical framework developed by Schelling and Dworkin might support remarks like Kamisar's about patients' "obligation to have themselves 'eliminated.'" The worry that a right to die would become an obligation to die is of a piece with other worries about euthanasia, not in itself, but as a problematic option for the patient.

XI

As I have said, I favor euthanasia in some cases. And of course, I believe that euthanasia must not be administered on competent patients without their consent. To that extent, I think that the option of dying will have to be presented to some patients, so that they can receive the benefit of a good death.

On the basis of the foregoing arguments, however, I doubt whether policymakers can formulate a general definition that distinguishes the circumstances in which the option of dying would be beneficial from those in which it would be harmful. The factors that make an option problematic are too subtle and too various to be defined in a statute or regulation. How will the option of euthanasia be perceived by the patient and his loved ones? How will it affect the relations among them? Is he likely to fear being spurned for declining the option? Would he exercise the option merely as a favor to them? And are they genuinely willing to accept that favor? Sensitivity to these and related questions could never be incorporated into an institutional rule defining conditions under which the option must be offered.

Insofar as I am swayed by the foregoing arguments, then, I am inclined to think that society should at most permit, and never require, health professionals to offer the option of euthanasia or to grant patients' requests for it. We can probably define some conditions under which the option should never be offered; but we are not in a position to define conditions under which it should always be offered; and so we can at most define a legal permission rather than a legal requirement to offer it. The resulting rule would leave caregivers free to withhold the option whenever they see fit, even if it is explicitly and spontaneously requested. And so long as caregivers are permitted to withhold the option of euthanasia, patients will not have a right to die.

XII

The foregoing arguments make me worry even about an explicitly formulated permission for the practice of euthanasia, since an explicit law or regulation to this effect would already invite patients, and hence potentially pressure them, to request that the permission be exercised in their case. I feel most comfortable with a policy of permitting euthanasia by default—that is, by a tacit failure to enforce the institutional rules that currently serve as barriers to justified euthanasia, or a gradual elimination of those rules without fanfare. The best public policy of euthanasia, I sometimes think, is no policy at all.

This suggestion will surely strike some readers as scandalous, because of the trust that it would place in the individual judgment of physicians and patients. But I suspect that to place one's life in the hands of another person, in the way that one does today when placing oneself in the care of a physician, may simply be to enter a relationship in which such trust is essential, because it cannot be replaced or even underwritten by institutional guarantees. Although I do not share the conventional view that advances in medical technology have outrun our moral understanding of how they should be applied, I am indeed tempted to think they have outrun the capacity of institutional rules to regulate their application. I am therefore tempted to think that public policy regulating the relation between physician and patient should be weak and vague by design; and that insofar as the aim of medical ethics is to strengthen or sharpen such policy, medical ethics itself is a bad idea.

Notes

This is a revised version of a paper that was originally published in *The Journal of Medicine and Philosophy* (1992). That paper began as a comment of a paper by Dan Brock, presented at the Central Division of the APA in 1991. See his "Voluntary Active Euthanasia" (Brock, 1992). I received help in writing that paper from: Dan Brock, Elizabeth Anderson, David Hills, Yale Kamisar, and Patricia White. The present version of the paper replaces sections II and III of the original paper with a new and substantially different section II.

1. Here I echo some excellent remarks on the subject by Felicia Ackerman (Ackerman, 1990). I discuss the issue of "dying with dignity" in (Velleman, 1999a).
2. I discuss this issue further in (Velleman, 1999b), pp. 356–58, esp. nn. 69, 72.
3. See (Velleman, 1999a).

4. The *locus classicus* for this point is of course Camus's essay "The Myth of Sisyphus" (Camus, 1955).
5. For this analogy, see (Stell, 1979). Stell argues—implausibly, in my view—that one has the right to die for the same reason that one has a right to duel.
6. The analogy is suggested, in the form of an objection to my arguments, by Dan Brock in (Brock, 1992).
7. See my 1999a.
8. Of course, there are many other reasons for declining gifts and favors, such as pride, embarrassment, or a desire not to be in someone else's debt. My point is simply that there are cases in which these reasons are absent and a very different reason is present—namely, our desire not to burden someone else with obligations.

References

Ackerman, Felicia: 1990, "No, Thanks. I Don't Want to Die with Dignity," *Providence Journal-Bulletin*, April 19, 1990.

Brock, Dan: 1992, "Voluntary Active Euthanasia," *Hastings Center Report* 22, pp. 10–22; reprinted in *Life and Death; Philosophical Essays in Biomedical Ethics* (Cambridge: Cambridge University Press, 1993).

Camus, Albert: 1955, "The Myth of Sisyphus," in *The Myth of Sisyphus and Other Essays*, tr. Justin O'Brien, Vintage Books, New York.

Dworkin, Gerald: 1982, "Is More Choice Better Than Less?" *Midwest Studies in Philosophy* 7, pp. 47–61.

Kamisar, Yale: 1970, "Euthanasia Legislation: Some Non-Religious Objections," in A. B. Downing (ed.), *Euthanasia and the Right to Die*, Humanities Press, New York. pp. 85–133.

Kant, I.: 1964, *Groundwork of the Metaphysic of Morals*, trans. H. J. Paton, Harper and Row, New York.

Schelling, Thomas: 1960, *The Strategy of Conflict*, Harvard University Press, Cambridge, Massachusetts.

Schelling, Thomas: 1984, "Strategic Relationships in Dying," in *Choice and Consequence*, Harvard University Press, Cambridge, Massachusetts.

Stell, Lance K.: 1979, "Dueling and the Right to Life," *Ethics* 90, pp. 7–26.

Velleman, J. David: 1991, "Well-Being and Time," *Pacific Philosophical Quarterly* 72, pp. 48–77.

Velleman, J. David: 1999a, "A Right of Self-Termination?" *Ethics* 109, pp. 606–28.

Velleman, J. David: 1999b, "Love as a Moral Emotion," *Ethics* 109, pp. 338–74.

QUESTIONS

1. Why does Velleman think we ought not to have a right to die?
2. If one still wishes to institutionalize a right to die, are there measures that can be taken to address the concerns that Velleman raises?

---

52. Intending Death: The Structure of the Problem and Proposed Solutions

ALLEN BUCHANAN

Allen Buchanan (1948–) is professor of philosophy at Duke University. He has published extensively in many areas of practical philosophy, including bioethics, the theory of justice, political philosophy, Marxism, and economic systems. He has also served in a number of advisory positions, including staff philosopher for the President's Commission for the Study of Ethical Problems in Medicine and Behavioral and Biomedical Research (1982), staff consultant to the President's Advisory Committee on Human Radiation Experiments (1994), consultant to the Transitional Government of Ethiopia (1993), and consultant to the European High Commissioner on National Minorities in the Hague (1996). He also served on the Advisory Council for the National Human Genome Research Institute (1997–2000).

Most of the controversies in this reader are about killing and, in particular, intentional killing. And some of the clearest formulations of our principles against killing prohibit the intentional killing of innocent beings (with moral standing). But suicide, (forms of) euthanasia, and assisted suicide all seem to be intentional killings of the innocent. Allen Buchanan addresses the tension that results when we recognize, if we do, that some intentional killings of the innocent are permissible. Buchanan considers the options available to us, the different ways we can think about our views and principles. He suggests that understanding the wrongness of killing in terms of the victim's right to life may provide the best account of the wrong involved in intentional killings. This essay presupposes familiarity with the controversies surrounding euthanasia and related debates, as well as some elements of moral theory.

From Allen Buchanan, "Intending Death: The Structure of the Problem and Proposed Solutions," in *Intending Death: The Ethics of Assisted Suicide and Euthanasia*, ed. Tom L. Beauchamp (Prentice-Hall, 1996), pp. 23–41. Reprinted by permission of Pearson Education.

The Problem of Intending Death

Intending death may be a special problem in medicine, but controversies over the moral status of intentional killing reach far beyond medicine. The prohibition against intentionally taking human life is so deeply ingrained—so morally primal—that the killing of heinous criminals and aggressors in wars is rejected by some persons of undoubted moral integrity. Indeed, even those who find capital punishment and the killing of aggressors acceptable usually do so with a sense of profound moral loss and feel obliged to articulate and refine moral justifications for such exceptions to the general prohibition. To take intentionally an innocent person's life may seem like the very paradigm of an immoral act. One is tempted to say: if anything is wrong, *that* is wrong.

Virtually every moral code and ethical theory, religious or secular, includes the general prohibition against intentionally taking innocent human life.[1] This prohibition lies at the heart of the criminal law as well: not only is murder the most serious offense,[2] but the consent of the victim himself is not recognized as a defense in homicide. Even more strikingly, the criminal law's requirement of *mens rea* (guilty state of mind) is interpreted so as to be compatible with the life-taker acting from a good motive. The fact that a person kills another with the intent to benefit this person—say by ending this person's misery—neither excuses nor justifies.[3] It is the intention to kill, not the motive in killing, that constitutes the *mens rea* required for the crime of homicide.[4]

The legal prohibition against intentional killing is not limited to the killing of another. Until this century suicide was a crime, and to this day assisted suicide is a felony in almost half the jurisdictions of this country.[5] The legal definition of *suicide* is simply the intentional bringing about of one's own death.[6] Neither the means of achieving death nor the motive in seeking it are part of the definition. And as with homicide generally, the former crime of suicide and the present crime of assisted suicide admit of no defense on grounds of good motive.

The criminalization of suicide is the most extreme legal expression of the prohibition against the intentional taking of life. While the law's refusal to recognize consent as a defense in the killing of another implies that the right to life cannot be waived so that others are released from their obligation not to kill an individual, the prohibitions against suicide and assisted suicide go further still in the direction of absolutism, amounting to a denial that the person has the authority to take his or her own life.

A series of landmark "right to die" cases, from *Quinlan* to *Conroy*, provide still more evidence of the depth of the law's commitment to the prohibition. In each instance the courts found it necessary to declare an important state interest in preventing suicide—and then to argue, quite unconvincingly, that refusal of life-support was not suicide.[7]

Codes of medical ethics, from the Hippocratic Oath to resolutions adopted by the American Medical Association, usually forbid physicians from killing patients, even from the best of motives and with the patient's consent or direction.[8] Especially for those who identify themselves as healers and savers of lives, the idea that it is permissible for them to kill patients—let alone the claim that respect for patient autonomy may require them to do so—may seem utterly unacceptable, even repugnant.

Yet there is an equally firm conviction, one that seems to be growing in this country, that in some instances intentionally taking the life of an innocent person is morally permissible, at least in certain medical contexts. It is true that those who hold this conviction sometimes disagree among themselves either as to which cases of intending death are permissible or as to which cases are instances in which the death that occurs was intended. Nevertheless, there are some cases that clearly are instances of intending death and which many find justifiable. The following are two of the most compelling types of cases.

Case 1: Active Voluntary Euthanasia

The competent, well-informed, terminally ill patient is in severe pain. Adequate pain relief is either unattainable or would so impair the patient's cognitive abilities and his capacity for interacting with others that he finds this option incompatible with his conception of personal dignity and of a fitting end to his life. He rejects the proposal that he be allowed to die of dehydration or to succumb to an infection, saying that this would be too hard on his family, both emotionally and financially. Merely withdrawing other forms of life-support would result in prolonged suffering. His physician finally agrees to give him a lethal injection.

Case 2: Assisted Suicide

Jones is a competent, well-informed patient suffering from a terminal, incurable, degenerative disease that will soon rob him of his cognitive capacities, then his ability to act, and finally his life. He is living at home, where he can freely interact with family and friends, and is adamant that he not be rehospitalized. After much reflection and discussion with those he loves and respects, he decides to end his life quickly and painlessly, before further loss of capacities occurs. Because he finds some methods distasteful and fears that he may be unable to achieve his goal with certainty if he acts alone, he asks a friend to help him administer a drug intravenously and to make sure it works. The friend agrees.

The problem about intending death, then, is the apparent contradiction between allegiance to the prohibition against intentionally taking innocent human life, on the one hand, and the conviction that, at least in cases such as these, intentionally killing is permissible. But since the prohibition against intentional killing is deeply entrenched in the fabric of our society, resolving the problem may require more than a mere change in belief. It may necessitate changes in our institutions and in social roles as well. There are two questions to answer. First, "How, if at all, can the apparent contradiction be resolved?" and second, "What changes, if any, will its resolution require in our institutions and in our conception of what it is to be a physician—or, if assisted suicide for the terminally ill becomes widely accepted, in our conception of what it is to be a friend?"

In this essay I begin the task of answering the first question by articulating the main strategies for resolving the apparent contradiction. Although I will not attempt to provide a conclusive evaluation of their respective merits, I will indicate which of them I think is most promising. In the end, an adequate response to the problem of intending death

will require an act of moral self-consciousness so fundamental that it is rarely even contemplated, much less performed: we must make explicit the nature of the wrong we do, when we do wrong, in intentionally killing a human being.

The Strategies

Assuming, at least provisionally, that it is not an acceptable option to abandon entirely the prohibition against intentionally killing, there are five strategies for resolving the contradiction between the general prohibition and conflicting intuitions in particular cases.

Strategy 1

Acknowledge that intentionally ending the life of an innocent human being is always wrong, but then argue that what appear to be cases of justifiably intending death are not, because the individual is already dead. On this view, intentionally bringing about the death of an anencephalic infant or of an older patient who is permanently unconscious is only bringing about the death of a system of organs, not of a human being. Call this the "they're already dead strategy."

Strategy 2

Defend the general prohibition, but only on the condition that its application is restricted to human beings that have interests. Then argue that some living human beings lack the rudimentary capacities for pleasure and pain required for having interests and are, therefore, not covered by the general prohibition. Call this the "no interests, no right to life strategy."

Strategy 3

Affirm the general prohibition without exception, but argue that in all the cases in which bringing about the death of an innocent person is justifiable, the death was foreseen but not intended. Or argue that the doctrine of double effect adds so much support to the prohibition against intentional killing that we should revise those intuitions that conflict with it. Call this the "double effect strategy."

Strategy 4

Acknowledge that even though in principle intentionally bringing about the death of an innocent human being is sometimes permissible, there are a number of considerations which, taken together, show that morally sound public policy should not allow any exceptions to the prohibition, at least in medical contexts. These include the fallibility of human judgment, the dangers of abuse, the erosion of patient trust, and the tendency to descend a slippery slope toward morally unacceptable practices concerning death. Call this the "prudent public policy strategy."

Strategy 5

Show that the intuitively justifiable cases of intending death are principled exceptions to the general prohibition, supported by widely held and plausible moral values, including those that ground the general prohibition itself. Call this the "principled exception strategy." The principled exception strategy has two main variants: a moderate version which contends that only cases in which the one to be killed consents to being killed are justifiable exceptions to the general prohibition; and a radical version which allows the possibility of justifiable nonvoluntary intentional killing.

The first (they're already dead) and fourth (prudent public policy) strategies have this in common: both accept the prohibition and acknowledge no exceptions to it. The second (no interests, no right to life) and fifth (principled exception) strategies both seek to resolve the contradiction by acknowledging genuine exceptions to the prohibition.

The first and second strategies may be quickly dismissed if presented as complete solutions to the problem of intending death. Each does reconcile the prohibition against intended death with some intuitions about the justifiability of intending death, and in that sense both the first and second strategies offer partial solutions to the problem. But neither comes close to providing a reconciliation across the whole range of intuitively justifiable cases. If either of the two cases described above presents an apparent conflict with the general prohibition, then neither the first nor the second strategy solves the problem of intending death, since they say nothing about such cases. In neither Case 1 nor Case 2 is the patient dead according to any plausible conception of death and in both the patient clearly has substantial interests.[9]

Foreseen but Not Intended: The Double Effect Strategy

The distinction is between what is intended, either as an end or as a means toward something else that is an end, and what is foreseen but intended neither as a means nor as an end. The doctrine of double effect holds that (1) it is sometimes permissible to bring about a death that one foresees without intending, when to bring that death about intentionally would be wrong.[10] There is some disagreement among those who endorse the doctrine as to what the conditions are which together make a case of killing in which death is merely foreseen a justifiable killing. There does seem to be agreement that a condition of proportionality must be satisfied: "the good effect must be sufficiently desirable to compensate for the allowing of the bad effect" or "there [must] be a proportionately grave reason for permitting the evil effect."[11] Thesis (1) must be distinguished from another, namely, that (2) it is never permissible to bring about an innocent person's death intentionally, but sometimes permissible to bring it about if one foresees but does not intend it. Thesis (1) does not entail thesis (2): (1) is compatible with there being some cases of intentionally bringing about death being permissible.[12]

Neither principle (1) nor (2), even when supplemented with appropriate conditions for justifiable foreseen killings, can provide a resolution to the problem of intending death unless at least those cases, such as 1 and 2, which seem to be the most compelling counter-examples to the prohibition against intentional killing, can be shown to be cases in which the death is merely foreseen but not intended. The difficulty is that there seems to be no good reason—aside from the desire to describe the cases so that the doctrine can be invoked—to characterize either cases of type 1 or type 2 as not being cases of intentional killing. In Case 1 it is quite natural to say that the physician intentionally kills the patient, at the patient's request. In Case 2 it is equally natural to say that the patient intentionally kills himself with the help of his friend.

A desperate dedication to the doctrine has led some to attempt to redescribe such cases as follows: The patient's intention—or as courts in the right to die cases cited above said, his "specific intention"—was not to die but only to avoid futile suffering. That this is so is shown by a counterfactual test: If he could have avoided the futile suffering without dying he would have done so.

This attempt at redescription is sheer sophistry. From the fact that one would prefer another means to an end if that other means were available, it does not follow that one isn't doing what one is doing, namely, intentionally performing the act in question as a means toward one's end. Analogously, from the fact that what a bank robber really wants is a large sum of money and that he wouldn't rob if it were given to him or if he won it in a lottery, it doesn't follow that when he robs a bank to get the money he didn't rob it intentionally.

Those who find the doctrine congenial point out that its invocation does resolve or avoid some painful moral dilemmas, by distinguishing cases of justifiable and unjustifiable killing. More specifically, the doctrine of double effect enables us to take consequences into account without falling into a purely consequentialist ethic. For example, the doctrine can explain why it would be permissible for an engineer to steer a runaway train down one track, where one will be killed, to avoid going down another, where five would be killed, while it would be wrong for a judge to have one innocent person executed to save five others. The explanation is that though the engineer kills a person, he does not intend that person's death, while the judge would be intentionally killing one to save five. We are told that the doctrine has another advantage: it frees us from the power of moral blackmailers. For example, if a ruthless tyrant or terrorist tells you to kill one innocent person or he will kill five, you can avoid feeling obliged to comply, if you console yourself with the fact that the deaths that result from your refusal are merely foreseen, but not intended by you.

For those who have more consequentialist intuitions these may be dubious benefits. But the main point is that there are other ways of avoiding pure consequentialism. Each of the examples just described can be accommodated by a distinction between positive and negative duties, along with a set of principles for resolving conflicts of duties.[13] For instance, the trolley case can be seen as a conflict of negative duties, with the governing principle being: when basic negative duties, that is, those of the same seriousness or moral importance, conflict, do the least harm. In the case of the judge, killing an innocent person to save others would be impermissible, according to the principle that when basic negative and positive duties conflict, negative duties override. And the same principle enables us to avoid moral blackmail: in the case of basic duties, the negative duty not to harm the one innocent person overrides the positive duty to save the lives of the five.[14]

A Kantian interpretation of the doctrine of double effect has been suggested by Warren Quinn.[15] According to this view, the doctrine is based on respect for persons as rational beings, which in turn requires not treating them as mere means. The idea is that at least in some instances, intending a person's death (either as one's end or as a means towards it) would be treating the person as a mere means, not as an end in oneself, while acting in such a way that his or her death is merely foreseen, but not intended, would not be treating him or her as a mere means.

For three reasons, a Kantian interpretation of the doctrine of double effect holds little promise as a solution to the problem of intending death. First, it limits the applicability of the doctrine to persons in the Kantian sense–rational beings capable of self-determination. Yet the general prohibition is against killing innocent human beings, including those who lack the capacity for rational self-determination.

Second, and more important, it makes good sense, on Kantian grounds, to say that when an autonomous agent freely consents to being killed (or freely requests that one kill him or her or help him or her do so) one is not treating this person as a mere means. But if this is so, then it will be the notion of consent, not the distinction between intended and merely foreseen consequences, that provides a resolution to the problem of intending death.

Third, one can fail to treat a person as an end by killing him or her, even though one only foresees and does not intend the death. For example, if my intention is to fire a round into the bull's eye of a target and I do so knowing that a person is resting against the other side of the target, I have in a very concrete sense not treated this person as an end. Instead, I have acted as if this person was a mere thing, like the target. What this suggests is that the distinction between treating persons as persons, or ends in themselves, and failing to treat them as such, is not congruent with the distinction between merely foreseeing and intending death.[16]

The appeal of the doctrine of double effect is that it allows us to hold fast to the absolute prohibition against intentional killing while still being able, at least in some cases, to take consequences into account, even if doing so requires killing—but without collapsing into pure consequentialism. In other words, at least for those who find pure consequentialism unacceptable, the doctrine *lowers the moral cost of adherence to the absolute prohibition* by allowing us to take consequences into account (as when we steer down the track with one person rather than five), yet without determining our conduct solely by what will produce the most good or avoid the most harm. And this brings us to the second, indirect, way in which the doctrine of double effect might be thought to resolve the conflict between our allegiance to the prohibition against intentional killing and our intuitions that it is permissible in cases such as 1 and 2. By lowering the moral cost of adherence to the prohibition against intentional killing, the doctrine might be thought to lend independent support to the prohibition itself. And if this support made the prohibition sufficiently attractive, we might then even be led to revise our intuitions concerning cases of types 1 and 2—indeed to overrule them, as it were. We would then bring our responses to such cases in line with the prohibition rather than modifying or abandoning the prohibition.

However, as we have seen, there are other ways of taking consequences into account without collapsing into pure consequentialism that seem to do the job as well or better than the doctrine of double effect. So, reliance on the doctrine lends no significant independent support to the prohibition against

intentional killing. But if that is so, and if cases like 1 and 2 are troubling apparent counter-examples to the prohibition, then the doctrine of double effect does not weaken their force significantly.

The inadequacy of the doctrine runs much deeper than this, however. What is most striking and disturbing is that the doctrine itself is utterly blind to the whole question of consent. Surely consent must at least be morally relevant in some cases of intentional killing, even if it should turn out not to be decisive as a justification. Any view, including the doctrine of double effect, which considers consent to be irrelevant to the question of whether intentional killing can be justified faces a painful dilemma. Either one must say that consent is relevant to the justifiability of withholding life-support, but not relevant to the justifiability of intentional killing; or one must say that consent is irrelevant in both cases.

The latter alternative is clearly untenable. Embracing it would amount to a denial of the competent patient's right to refuse life-sustaining treatment. The former alternative is scarcely more attractive: if consent is not only relevant, but morally decisive in cases of terminating life-support, how could it be the case that it is never of any moral consequence in any case of killing? It will not do, of course, to reply that in the latter case one is intentionally killing and that this is always wrong. This reply simply begs the question against those who argue, as I shall in the final section of this paper, that there are principled exceptions to the prohibition against intentional killing.

There is, however, an even more serious flaw in any attempt to escape the dilemma by admitting that consent can sometimes justify terminating life-support, while denying that consent can ever justify intentional killing: some cases of justified withdrawal of life-support are intentional killings. There are cases in which physicians kill patients by withdrawing life-support, and do so deliberately, with sound moral justification, and with increasing support from the law, ethical theory, and public opinion.

A familiar example will illustrate this important point. Suppose Smith, who is connected to a ventilator and will die without it, competently decides he does not wish to live in such a state of dependency, and convinces his physician to withdraw this means of life-support. However, before the physician can do so, Smith's wicked nephew, Brown, steals into Smith's room and shuts off the ventilator. When his foul deed is discovered, Brown lamely protests, with all the feigned indignation he can muster: "I didn't kill him, the disease did!"

The usual moral drawn from such examples is that killing is itself no worse than letting die.[17] But the hollowness of Brown's protest shows that we may draw a different conclusion. Withdrawing life-support can be killing in a straightforward sense: an act which results in death. And if the act is done with the intention of bringing about death—whether as a means to getting a fortune or as a means to relieving futile suffering—it is an act of intentional killing.

Those who use such examples to show that killing itself is not worse than letting die do us a great service by focusing on the real moral issues: whether a person is responsible for a death and whether, if responsible, he is culpable. But they concede too much. The proper conclusion to be drawn is that one can kill by withdrawing care, and that some cases of killing are justifiable and recognized as being justifiable, even if we do not always recognize them as cases of killing. And if some instances of withdrawing life-support are killings, then a defender of the doctrine of double effect cannot argue that consent is relevant for the justification of withdrawing life-support, but never relevant for killing because intentional killing is wrong even if there is consent. To argue in this way is both to beg the question against those who hold that there are principled exceptions against the prohibition on intentional killing and to assume, quite falsely, that no instances of withdrawing life-support are killings.

The next strategy for solving the problem of intentional killing fares better than the doctrine of double effect in this respect. It does answer the question, "Why is consent morally relevant in cases of terminating life-support, but not in cases of intentional killing?" The answer is that sound public policy should strictly prohibit intentional killing in medicine, while allowing that the competent patient's consent can justify withholding life-support.

The Prudent Public Policy Argument

This strategy acknowledges the validity of our intuitions in cases such as 1 and 2, without attempting to deny that these are cases of intending death. Instead, it is argued that even if there are cases, considered in isolation, in which intentional killing would be justified, the moral costs of a public policy that allowed intentional killing, including active voluntary euthanasia or assisted suicide, would be unacceptable. There are two versions of the prudent public policy argument. One contends that an exceptionless prohibition against voluntary active euthanasia and assisted suicide should extend to everyone, regardless of professional role. The other restricts the prohibition to members of the medical (and/or nursing) profession.

The first version, in its most plausible form, would begin by cataloguing the moral costs of a policy of permitting active voluntary euthanasia and assisted suicide, list the moral benefits of such a policy, and provide an assessment that shows the former to outweigh the latter. Unfortunately, most proponents of the argument, in either variant, at best execute the first step, while omitting an impartial consideration of the benefits of the policy they oppose—and leap to an ill-founded assessment that the costs are unacceptable.

The main possible moral costs of allowing voluntary active euthanasia and/or assisted suicide are these: (1) individuals who did not really wish to be killed would succumb to family or social pressure (because of the drive to contain costs); (2) in some cases outright murder might occur and be disguised as active voluntary euthanasia or assisted suicide; and (3) allowing even these limited instances of intentional killing would "weaken the reverence for life."[18]

The second version of the argument builds on the first, noting that there are additional special costs for a policy that allows physicians (or nurses) to kill patients. (4) If physicians (or nurses) were permitted to kill, then the fundamental trust on which so much that is good depends in the physician-patient (or nurse-patient) relationship would be damaged if not utterly destroyed.

Advocates of intentional killing in medicine are quick to emphasize the other side of the ledger. The chief moral values that would be served by allowing active voluntary euthanasia and/or assisted suicide are: (1) patient self-determination; and (2) patient well-being. It is these same two values that provide the foundation of the legal and moral doctrine that the competent patient has the right to accept or refuse care.[19] While not denying the possibility that serious moral costs may arise if physicians or others are allowed to kill, those who believe that intentional killing is sometimes justifiable contend that appropriate institutional safeguards would keep these costs within acceptable limits. To make their case they must also argue that the adoption and effective implementation of such safeguards is sufficiently likely to justify whatever moral risks would remain.

The difficulty in assessing the debate between the advocates of the prudent public policy argument and those who would permit some forms of intentional killing in medicine is the uncertainty of the predictions on both sides and the abstractness of the discussion about possible institutional safeguards. One great benefit of the current experiment with active euthanasia in the Netherlands is that it at least provides a concrete focus for debate.[20]

I will make no effort here to supply a conclusive assessment of the prudent public policy argument. Instead, I will only emphasize two considerations which significantly undercut its force. First, the stronger of the two versions of the argument, which appeals not only to general moral costs but also to those special costs that allowing physicians to kill might involve, mistakenly assumes that physicians *are not already killing patients* and that their doing so is not compatible with adequate patient trust. Second, those who assume that the moral costs of allowing active voluntary euthanasia or assisted suicide would be too great fail to appreciate that the case for allowing these forms of intentional killing rests on *the very values that support the general prohibition* against intentional killing, values that can both guide the development of appropriate safeguards and motivate us to implement them. Let us say that an account of exceptions to a general moral principle shows these exceptions to be deeply principled if it shows the exceptions to be justified by the same basic values that support the general principle itself.

When I say that physicians are already killing patients I do not mean simply that some physicians are already engaging in what is ordinarily considered to be active voluntary euthanasia and assisted suicide—as in Cases 1 and 2—in which the physician administers or helps the patient administer a lethal injection. Instead, what I have in mind is the point made in the preceding section of this paper, namely, that there are many more cases in which physicians *kill patients by withdrawing life-support*, and do so deliberately, with sound moral justification, and with increasing support from the law, ethical theory, and public opinion.

If withdrawing life-support can count as killing, and if, as is now widely agreed, the withdrawal of life-support is compatible with being a good physician, then it is hard to see why the same cannot be true for those other forms of killing, voluntary active euthanasia and assisted suicide. Including the permissibility of voluntary active euthanasia or assisted suicide within our conception of the role of physician does not require repudiating or even supplementing the basic values which underlie that role as it is now conceived, and which already support withdrawal of life-support. Nor does it even require a transition from a situation in which physicians do not kill patients to one in which they do, if I am right in holding that they do kill patients when they withhold care in order to end life.

This is not the whole story, however. The strong resistance to voluntary active euthanasia and assisted suicide that some physicians express will not simply dissipate in the light of philosophical analysis. It has other sources than a failure to recognize that withdrawing life-support can be killing and that the same values of self-determination and well-being that support it can support more direct forms of killing as well. In part, physicians' opposition to voluntary active euthanasia and assisted suicide may stem from a very understandable uneasiness, not about what they will be permitted to do, but rather about what they may be required to do.[21]

With some simplification it can be said that we have witnessed in the past 15 years or so, not just the recognition of a right to die, but the transformation of that right from a purely negative right against intrusive medical procedures to a positive right to determine the manner of one's dying.[22] It is true that advance directives were first developed as mechanisms for ensuring that the negative right against intrusion was not violated by over aggressive physicians. But the emphasis on patient self-determination which was invoked to establish the negative right inevitably pointed toward the need for giving patients more positive control over the dying process. Not without reason, therefore, physicians may fear that an expansive, positive right to die may result in a redefinition of the physician's role to include the idea that he is obligated to perform voluntary active euthanasia or to assist the patient in committing suicide. Physicians may fear that what began as a struggle to free patients from unwanted control by physicians will result in patients exercising excessive control over physicians.

This fear, though understandable, does not provide a reason for refusing to allow further, responsible, institutionally safe-guarded exceptions to the prohibition against intentional killing by physicians—to allow killing by lethal injection, for example, in addition to killing by removal of life-support. The proper conclusion to be drawn, rather, is that any sound public policy allowing intentional killing in medicine must recognize the patient's right of self-determination is not a right of unlimited, nonconsensual authority over others.

A morally acceptable public policy allowing intentional killing in medicine would have to be based on clear distinctions among the following rights: (1) the patient's right of self-determination, as a right against unwanted medical intrusions; (2) the patient's right to seek voluntary active euthanasia or assistance in suicide (subject to appropriate safeguards) without interference from the law or medical personnel; and (3) the physician's right to refuse to participate in intentional killings (other than withdrawal of care) that are recognized as legitimate by sound public policy.

The first right carries a corresponding obligation on the part of the physician, but only a negative one—the obligation not to subject the patient to unwanted intrusions. Fulfilling this negative obligation, however, can require positive actions, such as killing by withdrawing life-support, as well as allowing to die by not starting life-support.

The second right carries no obligation on the part of the physician to participate in voluntary active euthanasia or assisted suicide. All it guarantees is that those patients who seek these forms of intentional killing and those physicians who agree to participate will not be interfered with or held liable (so long as they operate within prescribed institutional safeguards).

The third right, which might be called a physician autonomy right or a right of conscientious refusal, allows the physician to limit his role in patient care so as to exclude voluntary active euthanasia or assisted suicide. Physicians who fear the imposition of an obligation to kill should take heart from the fact that there is already widespread recognition of a right of conscientious refusal in at least two other areas of medicine having to do with life and death decisions: the right of a physician not to participate in abortions and the right not to participate in some forms of withdrawal of care, in particular, termination of feeding and hydration. Effective institutionalization of all three of these rights is a necessary condition for a morally acceptable public policy allowing intentional death in medicine, at least for our society at this time.[23] Whether such a policy can be morally justified will depend on whether an adequate account of principled exceptions to the fundamental legal and moral prohibition against intentionally killing human beings can be articulated. In the next and final section such an account will be sketched.

Principled Exceptions to the Prohibition on Intentional Killing or Replacement of the Prohibition?

The last strategy for dealing with the conflict between our deeply felt allegiance to the prohibition on intentionally killing human beings and the growing conviction that there are some cases in which voluntary active euthanasia and assisted suicide are morally justifiable is to affirm the prohibition, but then provide a convincing, principled account of legitimate exceptions to it in such a way as to accommodate our most confident intuitions concerning justified intentional killing. The chief outlines of such an account have already been drawn: the same fundamental values of individual self-determination and well-being whose recognition have led to the acknowledgment of the right to refuse life-support also speak in favor of allowing voluntary active euthanasia and assisted suicide.

As Cases 1 and 2 show, there are circumstances in which these values will not be served adequately by the right to refuse life-support. First, there are situations where merely not starting or withdrawing life-support will not enable the patient to avoid futile pain. Although the number of cases in which adequate pain relief cannot be achieved if the best available techniques for pain control are employed may not be great, such cases do occur. Moreover, it is a sad fact that many patients do not receive the best pain control that is technically available. Further, our ability to ameliorate suffering does not match our technology for pain control. People who are faced with an incurable degenerative disease experience what they find to be intolerable suffering—severe psychological distress—even if they are not in extreme pain, and even the best psychiatric care may not provide adequate relief, at least in the eyes of the sufferer himself. This is not surprising, especially in cases in which the individual cannot be comforted with the thought that the condition causing the psychological distress will only be a transient phase. Consequently, even if it were true that in virtually all cases adequate pain control is possible, this would not solve the problem of suffering. A second, and much more frequently occurring situation is one in which pain can be controlled, but at the price of rendering the patient virtually unconscious, and the patient regards the prolongation of life in such a condition unacceptable. The third case in which the values of individual well-being and self-determination speak in favor of allowing intentional killing, if the patient requests it, is where the patient, though not choosing between extreme pain and virtual unconsciousness, nevertheless concludes that he no longer wishes to live, because continued care will be a great burden on his family or on public resources, and because he finds no compensating benefit to offset that burden, given his impaired condition. (This may well describe the condition of the woman with Alzheimer's dementia whose suicide was assisted by Dr. Kevorkian in Michigan.) In each of these three types of situations the values of individual self-determination and well-being support intentional killing—if the legitimate concerns about fallibility and abuse stressed by the prudent public policy argument are addressed by adequate safeguards.

In some instances, as continuing controversies over the justifiability of paternalism attest, self-determination and well-being conflict. They often do not conflict, however, chiefly because, at least for competent, informed individuals, the individual is likely to be the best judge of his or her interests, especially an interest in sustaining an acceptable quality of life. This (albeit imperfect) congruence between the competent, informed individual's well-being and one's own judgement concerning what is conducive to it is due to two factors: the likelihood that the individual will be more highly motivated to preserve his or her own good and more concretely aware of his or her own wants and needs and the conditions for their satisfaction, and the fact that, especially with regard to the question of the quality of one's own life, well-being is to some extent subjective, that is, constituted in part by the individual's own conception of what life has been and what it should be. For these reasons, regardless of whether we view self-determination and well-being as distinct, coordinate values, or view self-determination as being valuable only because it tends to promote well-being, we will best promote both values if the competent, informed patient is allowed to determine whether to continue living.

It should now be clear that the justifications given for intentional killing in the preceding sorts of cases do not apply in the cases of intentional killing which we all regard as morally unacceptable and against which the prohibition on intentional killing is at least primarily directed. Nonetheless, to make a convincing case that allowing voluntary active euthanasia or assisted suicide in such cases would constitute principled exceptions to the general prohibition, it is necessary to provide an account of what is morally wrong with intentional killing when it is wrong, and then show that the features that constitute the moral wrong do not exist in the exceptional cases. The justification for the exceptions will be especially strong if the same values that are shown to support the exceptions also support the general prohibition itself.

They do. At least in a secular account of what is wrong with intentional killing, the values of individual self-determination and well-being must be paramount. What makes killing a human being morally bad, in the first instance at least, quite aside from indirect consequences, is that it deprives the person of any form of well-being and puts an end to self-determination. Furthermore, most intentional killings are not committed with consent and hence cannot be viewed as promoting self-determination.

A plausible secular interpretation of the reverence for human life, as distinct for a reverence for mere physiological life, is that it consists at least in large part in concern for individual well-being and self-determination. In that sense it is true that the prohibition on intentional killing expresses a reverence for life.

Some religious interpretations of the prohibition against intentional killing would take a different stance. Human beings would be thought of as being under a strict injunction from their creator to refrain from intentionally killing themselves or their fellows—an injunction which cannot be waived by the consent or request of a mere human being. This, in fact, has been a prominent strain in Christian religious ethics, one that has been invoked to condemn suicide, assisted suicide, and voluntary active euthanasia. On one construal, this is the idea that in killing ourselves or other human beings we are destroying god's property. On a less demeaning interpretation—one that does not see human beings as things owned by God—it is the view that God alone has the rightful authority to decide when we may "quit our stations." There are two serious difficulties with invoking any such notion to justify a strict prohibition on intentional killing in medicine. First, the religious view justifies too much: not only a ban on destroying God's property or quitting one's station by killing, but by refusing or withdrawing life-support as well. In other words, if it is wrong for a human being to decide to shorten one's life by killing or having another person do the killing, why is it not wrong deciding to shorten life by refusing life-support? Or, conversely, if respect for God's property in us or authority over us is compatible with our shortening our life by refusing life-support, why is it not also compatible with shortening our lives by taking

a lethal injection? In either case we take it on ourselves to decide when to end our lives, and either we have a right to make such a decision or we do not. Some proponents of a religious interpretation of the prohibition against intentional killing might contend that neither the God's property view nor the God's authority view is the true basis of their belief that consent can never justify intentional killing. Instead, they would hold that there are certain types of actions—intentional killing of innocent human beings being one of them—that are wrong in themselves and that if the action in itself is wrong, then the fact that it is consented cannot alter its moral status. It seems to me that such a stance faces a dilemma. If asked to justify the claim that such actions are wrong in themselves, those who hold this view can either appeal to revelation, saying that God has decreed these actions to be wrong in themselves; or they can attempt to give a substantive account of why these actions are wrong in themselves. The former reply not only faces all the familiar epistemological objections to appeals to alleged divinely revealed truths generally, but also runs counter to the assumption that we must confine ourselves to a secular, public ethical discourse suitable for a pluralistic society. The latter strategy seems unpromising as well. As I have argued, the most plausible substantive account of what is wrong with intentional killing (when it is wrong) relies on broadly accepted values of self-determination and well-being, and those values support not only withdrawing care but voluntary active euthanasia and assisted suicide as well, if adequate institutional safeguards are in place.

What makes intentionally killing a human being a moral wrong for which the killer is to be condemned is that the killer did this morally bad thing not inadvertently or even negligently, but with conscious purpose—with eyes open and a will directed toward that very object. But if a particular instance of intentional killing does not deprive a person of well-being, but rather relieves that person of what deprives of well-being, and is an exercise of autonomy, rather than a thwarting of it, then there is no basis for saying that this act was morally bad, at least in terms of the values of individual self-determination and well-being. And if the act is not morally bad, then it is hard to see how the fact that it is done intentionally can make it a wrong.

Of course, this qualifier "in the first instance" is extremely important. As proponents of the prudent public policy argument rightly note, certain types of acts, some instances of which are not wrong, nevertheless ought sometimes to be prohibited because a policy of allowing this type of act will lead to unacceptable consequences either for those directly involved or for others. But given the fundamental character of the values that speak in favor of allowing exceptions to the prohibition on intentional killing— the *same values that are the primary justification for the prohibition itself*, at least in public, secular moral discourse—the burden of argument to be borne by the prudent public policy argument is onerous. For reasons indicated earlier, I do not believe that this burden has been successfully borne. The case against allowing limited instances of intentional killing in medicine is greatly weakened as soon as these three points are acknowledged. First, since physicians already justifiably engage in intentional killing by withdrawing life-support in some cases, intentional killing per se is not incompatible with a proper conception of the physician's role. Second, merely allowing physicians to perform voluntary active euthanasia or to assist with suicide in certain cases does not place an obligation on physicians to engage in such practices. Third, the principled exceptions to the prohibition against intentional killing are deeply principled, that is, they spring from the same basic values that support the prohibition itself.[24]

There is, however, a more radical conclusion to be drawn from these reflections on principled exceptions to the prohibition against intentionally killing innocent persons. We might conclude, not that there are valid exceptions to the principle that it is wrong intentionally to kill innocent human beings, but that the principle itself ought to be abandoned, not qualified, and replaced with one that makes clearer the nature of the wrong that is committed in those cases in which intentional killing is wrong. The principled exception strategy's emphasis on consent points toward this other principle, and in doing so points beyond itself to a replacement for the prohibition against intentional killing, rather than to a qualification of it.

My suggestion is that the best account of the nature of the wrong that we do when we do wrong in intentionally killing is that we *violate an innocent human being's right to life*.[25] This enables us to explain why cases in which there is consent to being killed are justifiable: the right has been waived by the act of consenting. More important, perhaps, including a principle that articulates a right to life, rather than one which prohibits intentional killing, focuses on *the individual who is killed*, and this better accords with the secular account of why intentional killing is wrong when it is wrong, an account which, as I have suggested, is based on respect for the individual's self-determination and concern for well-being. In contrast, the principle that intentional killing is wrong makes no connection with any features of the victim at all, much less any which could serve to justify the prohibition.[26] In other words, the principle that it is wrong intentionally to kill innocent persons suggests that the wrongness of the act is to be understood by reference to the perpetrator, not the victim.

Reliance on the principle that intentional killing is wrong makes more sense, then, in an ethical theory that views the prohibition as an *agent-centered constraint* on action, while the principle that innocent human beings have a right to life fits better into an ethical theory that is *subject-centered* and takes certain features of individuals, namely their capacities for well-being and self-determination, as the source of moral constraints on the agency of others. Thus, we might conclude that the best solution to the problem of intentional killing—the one that makes the structure of the morality of intentional killing most perspicuous—is one which resolves the conflict between allegiance to the general prohibition and the conviction that some cases of intentional killing are justified by abandoning the prohibition and replacing it with the principle that innocent persons have a right to life.[27]

Notes

1. It is instructive to note that the First Commandment is "Thou shalt not kill," not "Thou shalt not kill an innocent person," or "Thou shalt not kill except under such and such circumstances."

2. Treason is a possible exception.

3. For the distinction between excuse and justification, see H. L. A. Hart, *Punishment and Responsibility.* Oxford: Oxford University Press, 1968, pp. 28–53.

4. More specifically, all that may be needed in second degree murder is intention to do the act, with a high degree of foreseeability that a death may result. Wayne R. LaFave and Austin W. Scott, Jr., *Substantive Criminal Law,* vol. 1. St. Paul: West Publishing, 1986, pp. 303–305.

5. LaFave and Scott, vol. 2, pp. 248–251.

6. By one who is sane and over the age of legal discretion. LaFave and Scott, vol. 2, p. 246.

7. Sanford Kadish, "Authorizing Death," in Jules Coleman and Allen Buchanan, eds. *In Harm's Way.* New York: Cambridge University Press, 1993.

8. For a useful presentation of a number of official ethical statements by various health care professional groups, see *Ethics in Emergency Medicine,* Iserson et al., eds. Baltimore: Williams & Wilkens, 1986, pp. 240–262.

9. However, even if they are not powerful enough to solve the problem of intending death, these two approaches are not without moral implications. Under certain conditions, each would reduce the scope of the contradiction between the general prohibition and intuitions concerning particular cases. If a cognitivist conception of death came to be accepted, the first strategy would provide a clear and uncontroversial justification for administering lethal injections to anencephalics or permanently unconscious patients, without in any way restricting the generality of the prohibition against intentionally killing human beings. Similarly, if, as the second strategy advocates, we restrict the scope of the prohibition against intending death to human beings who have interests, and if the idea that those who are permanently bereft of all awareness lack interests, then killing such beings would not offend against the prohibition.

Whether either of the changes that would be needed to give the first and second strategies moral bite will occur is a matter of speculation. In my opinion, wide acceptance of the view that basic moral principles generally apply only to human beings with interests and that the permanently unconscious have no interests is much more likely, at least in the near term, than the adoption of a cognitivist conception of death. However, the former change might well be a way-station on the path to the second. Quite independently of these possible developments, the first and second strategies are worth at least a brief consideration, if only because both point toward what is really at issue in the problem of intending death: What is it about a life—about the quality or character of life—that makes intentionally ending a life wrong, when it is wrong?

10. P. Foot, "The Problem of Abortion and the Doctrine of the Double Effect," *Oxford Review* 5; 1967: 5–15, reprinted in Bonnie Steinbock, ed. *Killing and Letting Die.* Englewood City, NJ: Prentice Hall, 1980, pp. 156–165.

11. Both versions of the conditions are cited in Donald B. Marquis, "Four Versions of Double Effect," *The Journal of Medicine and Philosophy,* 16; 1991: 516–517.

12. Nor do either (1) or (2), singly or in conjunction, entail that (3) It is always permissible to bring about a death, so long as it is merely foreseen and not intended. The latter principle, of course, is patently unacceptable, as a familiar example clearly shows. Suppose an unscrupulous merchant intends to make a profit by selling poison oil to unsuspecting customers. He merely foresees their deaths and does not intend them, either as an end or as a means. His action is still wrong.

13. Foot, Ibid 157–160.

14. This is not to say that such a view and, indeed, any view that relies heavily on a distinction between positive and negative duties, is without problems of its own. In particular, it must develop an adequate account of "levels" of duties, distinguishing basic from nonbasic duties, if the ordering principles noted are to be at all plausible. For example, it would not do to say that negative duties, no matter whether they are basic or not, always override positive ones. This would commit one to the wrongheaded view that the negative duty not to lie could never be overridden by a positive duty, for example, the duty to help save millions of lives.

15. Warren Quinn, "Reply to Boyle's 'Who Is Entitled to Double-Effect?'" *The Journal of Medicine and Philosophy,* 16; 1991: 511–514.

16. This example is due to Dan Brock. It might be argued, of course, that once we add other conditions, such as proportionality, that is, that there is a good effect of such importance as to justify the evil, then the doctrine of double effect will only permit foreseen deaths in just those cases in which the Kantian injunction to treat persons as ends in themselves would permit

them. I am not convinced that the addition of such conditions would produce a perfect congruence, but even if it did, it seems that the use of the doctrine of double effect would be redundant. If the point is to treat persons as ends in themselves, why should one think that it is either necessary or permissible to explicate this fundamentally anticonsequentialist notion in terms of apparently consequentialist considerations such as the proportionality between the magnitude of the evil that is foreseen and the good that is intended?

17. James Rachels, "Active and Passive Euthanasia," reprinted in *Contemporary Issues in Bioethics*, Tom L. Beauchamp and LeRoy Walters, eds. Encino, CA: Dickenson, 1978, pp. 291–294; also reprinted in Bonnie Steinbock, ed. *Killing and Letting Die*. Englewood Cliffs, NJ: Prentice-Hall, 1980; pp. 63–68. Originally appeared in *The New England Journal of Medicine*, 292, no. 2; 1975: 78–80.

18. My discussion of the positive and negative consequences of a policy of allowing some forms of intentional killing has benefitted from a more detailed analysis of these issues by Dan W. Brock, "Voluntary Active Euthanasia," *Hastings Center Report*, 22, no. 2; 1992: 10.

19. See Allen Buchanan, Dan W. Brock, *Deciding For Others*. Cambridge: Cambridge University Press, 1989, pp. 29–40.

20. This is not to assume that the same institutional arrangements that would work there simply could be transferred to other cultures.

21. This fear is not merely speculative. In totalitarian regimes, physicians have become executioners, as in Hitler's "euthanasia" program.

22. Daniel Wikler makes this point as well (personal communication).

23. This is not to say that including an *obligation* to perform voluntary active euthanasia or to assist in suicide is incompatible with the role of physician—an essence, as it were, of physicianhood, a universal set of normative components of the role, valid for all times and places. What the proper normative constitution of a social role is can only be determined by complex moral reasoning that takes into account not only basic moral values but also the nature of the concrete social conventions and above all the social division of labor in a given historical setting. My suggestion is only that at this time, in our society, acknowledging the physician's right of conscientious

refusal is morally and practically necessary, both as a matter of respecting the autonomy of physicians as individuals and in order to secure their cooperation in devising and effectively implementing adequate safeguards for voluntary active euthanasia and assisted suicide.

24. A more comprehensive discussion of the desiderata for a sound public policy allowing voluntary active euthanasia and assisted suicide would have to address the issue of the context in which such actions would be deemed legitimate. My opinion is that the strongest case for the claim that adequate safeguards can be developed will require that voluntary active euthanasia and physician-assisted suicide take place within medical institutions. It is an important feature of modern medical institutions that decisionmaking within them is to a large extent (a) public and (b) collective. These two features serve as significant constraints on decisionmaking and provide a foothold for adequate procedural safeguards and other checks on abuse and error. To put the same point differently, the prudent public policy argument is much more powerful against a policy that allows extrainstitutional voluntary active euthanasia and assisted suicide, than against a policy that allows them only within appropriate institutional contexts.

25. My own view is that rights principles are conclusions to be supported by complex arguments whose premises include reference to a plurality of fundamental values, such as individual well-being and self-determination, and contingent empirical assumptions about social institutions, some features of which are substantially conventional. In other words, accepting the proposal to replace the prohibition on intentional killing with a principle that human beings or innocent human beings have a right to life does not commit oneself either to a rights-based or a consequentialist ethical theory.

26. Albert Jonsen has pointed out to me that the prohibition, at least as it is stated in Catholic moral theology, always includes the qualification that the individual is innocent and that the traditional notion of innocence identifies it with harmlessness rather than lack of guilt. If this is so, then the prohibition, at least in those versions that include the qualifier "innocent," does point toward something about the victim that can be relevant to the wrongness of the act. However, by so doing, the prohibition opens itself to demands for an account of why

innocence alone—as opposed say, to innocence and absence of consent—is the only feature of the victim that is morally relevant.

27. I am indebted to Dan Brock and Albert Jonsen for their perceptive comments on an earlier version of this paper.

QUESTIONS

1. What is "the apparent contradiction" that motivates Buchanan's inquiry?
2. What are the options or strategies he thinks we have?
3. Why think that explaining the wrongness of intentional killing in terms of the right to life may offer the best account?

When Do We Die?

There has been a debate for several decades now about "the definition of death." As we noted earlier in the introduction to section II, this characterization of the debate is misleading. For typically it has not been the *definition* of death that has been in question but the choice of *criteria* for ascertaining *when* death has occurred. For various reasons traditional criteria such as cessation of heartbeat and breathing have proved inadequate in some medical and legal contexts, and others have been proposed. Considerable controversy has ensued. The debate here is not unconnected to that about the definition or nature of death. Death is the end of life (in this world); our death is the end of our life. But who are *we*? The answer to this question matters to the question of when we die.

We might say that we are organisms of a certain kind, human animals. We would then inquire when organisms of this kind die. But consider someone who suffers serious, irreversible dementia; after some time this individual cannot remember anything, does not respond to others, seems to be unaware of his or her surroundings, and the like. Or think of someone in an irreversible coma. We often say in such cases that she or he "has left us"; she or he may be said to have died before the death of the organism. In this case we would be denying that *we* are to be thought of as organisms, as human animals. What are we then? Some philosophers say that we are minds or persons, beings with certain forms of consciousness. There are two versions of this view worth distinguishing, the first focusing on consciousness (we are minds), the second on self-consciousness (we are persons). The three views—we are organisms, we are minds, we are persons—yield different views about our persistence over time: We persist over time insofar as we are the same human animal, as we remain the same conscious mind, and as we retain certain psychological features.

If we think of ourselves as organisms of a certain kind, then our death occurs with the irreversible cessation of the functioning of the organism as a whole. A criterion or standard for determining when that has happened would be the traditional cardiopulmonary one, cessation of heartbeat and breathing. But with the development of assisted respiration, which can keep someone breathing even though his or her entire brain is irreversibly nonfunctional, this criterion has been replaced by a brain-death criterion, "the whole-brain standard." By this criterion we are dead when our entire brain, including the brainstem, irreversibly stops functioning.

If we think of ourselves as conscious or self-conscious beings, then another brain-death criterion may be more plausible. We need to distinguish between the "higher brain," the *cerebrum* (needed for consciousness) and the *cerebellum* (controlling muscle movements), and the "lower brain," or brainstem (which includes a lot of parts and controls spontaneous respiration). Someone in a "persistent vegetative state" still has a functioning brainstem, and a permanently comatose person has partial brainstem functioning. By the whole-brain criterion, these people are still alive. But if we are conscious or self-conscious beings, then they are not. If one thinks we are not organisms but conscious beings of a kind, then higher-brain criteria are more plausible.

The question of when we die, then, turns out to be quite complicated. We need to know *what* we are in the first place.

53. Defining Death

PRESIDENT'S COMMISSION

In 1981, a Presidential Commission issued its report after studying how we should determine when death has occurred. The full report of the commission is available at http://www.bioethics.georgetown.edu/pcbe/reports/past_commissions/defining_death.pdf. The opening chapter reports on the different criteria that exist for determining the onset of death.

In the United States these sorts of commissions are appointed by the president to investigate a particular subject or controversy and then issue a report. The second chapter of the 1981 report, which explains the different criteria for determining the time of death, is reprinted here. Consider this background material for the two essays that follow in this section. Included as well are the commission's conclusions and recommendations.

Until the past few decades, comatose patients fairly rapidly either improved or died. If no other complication supervened and the patient did not improve, death followed from starvation and dehydration within days; pneumonia, apnea, or effects of the original disease typically brought on death even more quickly. Before such techniques as intravenous hydration, nasogastric feeding, bladder catheterization and respirators, no patient continued for long in deep coma.

With the aid of modern medicine, some comatose patients can be kept from a rapid death. Many, however, become permanently and totally unresponsive. In other words, their appearance resembles that of the dead as traditionally perceived: they no longer respond to their environment by sensate and intellectual activity. But their appearance also differs from that traditionally associated with the dead because mechanical support generates breathing, heartbeat, and the associated physical characteristics (e.g., warm, moist skin) of life.

The ever more sophisticated capabilities developed by biomedical practitioners during the past quarter century to support or supplant certain vital functions have thus created new problems in diagnosing death. If these diagnostic problems were the only consequence of medicine's new capabilities, those who developed and employed them might well be criticized for having opened a Pandora's Box of troubles for physicians and for society. But, as witnesses told the Commission, in a portion of the cases the armamentarium of resuscitative medicine brings comatose patients back from the brink of death by supporting their breathing and blood flow during a period of acute need.

Since the witnesses and existing medical literature lacked information on the relative proportion of comatose, respirator-assisted patients who survive versus those who die (as determined by either brain-based or heart/lung-based tests), the Commission sponsored a small study. This study was not intended to generate definitive data on the incidence of such outcomes but rather to provide a rough estimate of the extent of the various outcomes. The study examined the experience over a period ranging from two months to one year at seven hospitals serving major metropolitan areas.

At the four acute care centers from which such data were available, 2–4 cases of irreversible loss of all brain functions arose each month, a figure consistent with other data.[1] These figures convey a useful, if limited, perspective on the frequency with which the medicolegal dilemma of determining death in comatose, respirator-assisted cases arises at such hospitals.

The social and legal as well as medical consequences attached to a determination of death make it imperative that the diagnosis be incontrovertible. One must be certain that the functions of the entire brain are irreversibly lost and that respiration and circulation are, therefore, solely artifacts of mechanical intervention. Indeed, though suspicious that their interventions may be doing nothing more than masking what would otherwise manifestly be death by the traditional measures, physicians are concerned about doing anything—such as removing a respirator—that would hinder the recovery of a patient whose loss of brain functioning might be only partial or reversible.[2]

Development of the Concept of "Brain Death"

The concept of "brain death" and efforts to refine criteria to identify that condition have been developing during the last two decades, concomitant with the spread of life support systems in clinical medicine. In 1959, several French neurophysiologists published results of research they had conducted on patients in extremely deep coma receiving respirator assistance, a condition they termed "coma dépassé."[3] Multiple tests showed these patients lacked reflexes and electrophysiologic activity. The investigators concluded that the patients had suffered permanent loss of brain functions—they were, in other words, "beyond coma." Postmortem examinations of those patients revealed extensive destruction (necrosis and autolysis) of the brain—a phenomenon that has since been called the "respirator brain."[4]

With the advent of transplant surgery employing cadaver donors—first with kidney transplantation in the 1950's and later, and still more dramatically, with heart transplantation in the

1960's—interest in "brain death" took on a new urgency.[5] For such transplants to be successful, a viable, intact organ is needed. The suitability of organs for transplantation diminishes rapidly once the donor's respiration and circulation stop. The most desirable organ donors are otherwise healthy individuals who have died following traumatic head injuries and whose breathing and blood flow are being artifically maintained. Yet even with proper care, the organs of these potential donors will deteriorate. Thus, it became important for physicians to be able to determine when the brains of mechanically-supported patients irretrievably ceased functioning.

Yet, the need for viable organs to transplant does not account fully for the interest in diagnosing irreversible loss of brain functions. The Commission's study illustrates this point; of 36 comatose patients who were declared dead on the basis of irreversible loss of brain functions, only six were organ donors. Other studies also report that organs are procured in only a small percentage of cases in which brain-based criteria might be applied.[6] Thus, medical concern over the determination of death rests much less with any wish to facilitate organ transplantation than with the need both to render appropriate care to patients and to replace artificial support with more fitting and respectful behavior when a patient has become a dead body. Another incentive to update the criteria for determining death stems from the increasing realization that the dedication of scarce and expensive intensive care facilities to bodies without brain functions may not only prolong the uncertainty and suffering of grieving families but also preclude access to the facilities for patients with reversible conditions.[7]

The Emergence of a Medical Consensus

Medical concern over making the proper diagnosis in respirator-supported patients led to the development of criteria which reliably establish permanent loss of brain functions. A landmark in this process was the publication in 1968 of a report by an ad hoc committee of the Harvard Medical School which became known as the "Harvard criteria."[8] The Committee's report described the following characteristics of a permanently nonfunctioning brain, a condition it referred to as "irreversible coma":

1. *Unreceptivity and unresponsitivity.* The patient shows a total unawareness to externally applied stimuli and inner need, and complete unresponsiveness, even when intensely painful stimuli are applied.
2. *No movements or breathing.* All spontaneous muscular movement, spontaneous respiration, and response to stimuli such as pain, touch, sound or light are absent.
3. *No reflexes.* Among the indications of absent reflexes are: fixed, dilated pupils; lack of eye movement even when the head is turned or ice water is placed in the ear; lack of response to noxious stimuli; and generally, unelicitable tendon reflexes.

In addition to these three criteria, a flat electro-encephalogram (EEG), which shows that there is no discernible electrical activity in the cerebral cortex, was recommended as a confirmatory test, when available. All tests were to be repeated at least 24 hours later without showing change. Drug intoxication (e.g., barbiturates) and hypothermia (body temperature below 90°F), which can cause a reversible loss of brain functions, also had to be excluded before the criteria could be used.

The "Harvard criteria" have been found to be quite reliable. Indeed, no case has yet been found that met these criteria and regained any brain functions despite continuation of respirator support. Criticisms of the criteria have been of five kinds. First, the phrase "irreversible coma" is misleading as applied to the cases at hand. "Coma" is a condition of a living person, and a body without any brain functions is dead and thus beyond any coma. Second, the writers of these criteria did not realize that the spinal cord reflexes actually persist or return quite commonly after the brain has completely and permanently ceased functioning. Third, "unreceptivity" is not amenable to testing in an unresponsive body without consciousness. Next, the need adequately to test brainstem reflexes, especially apnea, and to exclude drug and metabolic intoxication as possible causes of the coma, are not made sufficiently explicit and precise. Finally, although all

individuals that meet "Harvard criteria" are dead (irreversible cessation of all functions of the entire brain), there are many other individuals who are dead but do not maintain circulation long enough to have a 24-hour observation period. Various other criteria have been proposed since 1968 that attempt to ameliorate these deficiencies.[9]

As the Harvard Committee noted, permanent loss of brain functions can also be confirmed by absence of circulation to the brain. The brain necessarily ceases functioning after a short period without intracranial circulation, unless it is protected by hypothermia or drug induced depression of neuronal metabolism. In recent years, several procedures have been developed to test for absence of intracranial blood flow, including radioisotope cerebral angiography by bolus or static imaging and four vessel intracranial contrast angiography.[10]

Clinical research has emphasized the development of procedures that can be performed reliably at a patient's bedside, so as to interfere as little as possible with treatment and not to risk harming the patient when recovery may still be possible. The aim of the tests is to reduce mistaken diagnoses that a patient is still alive, without incurring risks of erroneous diagnoses that a patient lacks all brain functioning when such functions actually remain or could recur. This is achieved by establishing first that all brain functions have ceased and then ascertaining that the cessation is irreversible. To do this, the cause of coma must be established and this may require, in addition to history and physical examination, such tests as computerized axial tomography, electroencephalography and echoencephalography.[11] The cause of the cessation of functions must be sufficient to explain the individual's clinical status and must be demonstrated to be permanent during a period of observation.[12]

The studies that document the adequacy of criteria have followed one of two general formats. Some define a group of subjects who have met the proposed criteria and demonstrate that in all such cases the heart soon stopped beating despite intensive therapy.[13] Other studies identify a group of subjects who met the proposed criteria and demonstrate widespread brain necrosis at autopsy, providing the body has remained on a respirator for sufficient time for necrosis to occur.[14] All the studies focus on patients with deep coma including absence of spontaneous breathing (apnea): in addition, some require known and sufficient cause for the absence of brain functions, isoelectric electroencephalogram, dilated pupils, or absent circulation shown by angiography. The published criteria for determining cessation of brain functions have been uniformly successful in diagnosing death. The differences among criteria often arise from differing assessments of the technical skill and instrumentation available to the physician. Experts now generally agree that careful clinical assessment (including identification of a cause of the damage to the brain which is sufficient to explain the clinical findings) is the sine qua non of a diagnosis.

The role of confirmatory tests such as electroencephalography or circulation tests beyond such bedside judgments in establishing either the cessation of brain functions or the irreversibility of such cessation has been the subject of considerable discussion.[15] For example, the Conference of Royal Colleges and Faculties in Britain focused on the function of the brainstem alone to diagnose death.[16] Since the brainstem's retricular activating formation is essential to generating consciousness and its transmittal of motor and sensation impulses is essential to these functions, loss of brainstem functions precludes discernable functioning of the cerebral hemispheres. In addition, the brainstem is the locus of homeostatic control, cranial nerve reflexes, and control of respiration. Thus, if the brainstem completely lacks functions, the brain as a whole cannot function. American physicians, however, judge the reliability of brainstem testing to be incomplete. Therefore they endorse the appropriate use of cerebral blood flow testing or electroencephalography in order to confirm the completeness of injury and the irreversibility of conditions that have led to cessation of brain functions.[17] The published data support the reliability of both approaches.

The prevailing British viewpoint on the neurologic diagnosis of death is closer to a *prognostic* approach (that a "point of no return"[18] has been reached in the process of dying), while the American approach is more *diagnostic* in seeking to determine that all functions of the brain have irreversibly ceased at the time of the declaration of death. Also, the British diagnose brain death almost entirely where irremediable structural injury has occured while the American concept has encompassed all etiologies that may lead to irreversible loss of brain functions in respirator-maintained patients.

The British criteria resemble the American, however, in holding that death has been established when "all functions of the brain have permanently and irreversibly ceased."[19] In measuring *functions*, physicians are not concerned with mere *activity* in cells or groups of cells if such activity (metabolic, electrical, etc.) is not manifested in some way that has significance for the organism as a whole. The same is true of the cells of the heart and lungs; they too may continue to have metabolic and electrical activity after death has been diagnosed by cardiopulmonary standards. Tests that measure cellular activity are thus relevant to the determination of death only when they forecast whether missing functions may reappear.

Translating Medical Knowledge into Policy

Knowledgeable physicians agree that, when used in appropriate combinations, available procedures for diagnosing death by brain criteria are at least as accurate as the customary cardiopulmonary tests. Indeed, medical experts testified to the Commission that the risk of mistake in a competently performed examination was infinitesimal. Plainly, the results depend on the personal knowledge, judgment and care of the physicians who apply them. Expert witnesses before the Commission pointed out that many physicians (including some neurologists and neurosurgeons) are not sufficiently familiar with the criteria (much less the detailed tests) by which the cessation of total brain functions is assessed. As one step toward professional education, a group of physicians, working with the encouragement of the Commission, has developed a summary of currently accepted medical practices. [...] Such criteria—particularly as they relate to diagnosing death on neurological grounds—will be continually revised by the biomedical community in light of clinical experience and new scientific knowledge.

At present, the accepted norm is that the tests will be employed by a physician who has specialized knowledge of their use. Consultation with another appropriately trained physician is typically undertaken to confirm a brain-based diagnosis in an artificially supported individual before any decisions are made on whether to discontinue support.

Particular care must be exercised to establish the cause of the patient's condition and especially to rule out conditions (such as drug intoxication or treatable brain lesions) that can give the misleading appearance that brain functions have stopped irreversibly. (Research is currently underway to test whether hypothermia and large doses of barbiturates might be used to reduce brain injury after trauma or surgery. This will complicate the diagnosis of death in these patients.)

The Commission concludes that reliable means of diagnosis are essential for determinations of death and that the medical community has developed such means. Insistence that determinations of death accord with "accepted medical standards" would thus, in the opinion of the Commission, bring to bear all the usual stimuli for assuring accuracy in medical diagnosis: the testing of practices through biomedical research and the dissemination of the results of such research; the continuing education of physicians and other health care personnel; the conscientious application of professional skills and knowledge; and the encouragement of due care provided by professional standards and by state civil and criminal laws. In the Commission's view, it is not necessary—indeed, it would be a mistake—to enshrine any particular medical criteria, or any requirements for procedure or review, as part of a statute.

Summary of Conclusions and Recommended Statute

The enabling legislation for the President's Commission directs it to study "the ethical and legal implications of the matter of defining death, including the advisability of developing a uniform definition of death."[20] In performing its mandate, the Commission has reached conclusions on a series of questions which are the subject of this Report. In summary, the central conclusions are:

1. That recent developments in medical treatment necessitate a restatement of the standards traditionally recognized for determining that death has occurred.
2. That such a restatement ought preferably to be a matter of statutory law.
3. That such a statute ought to remain a matter for state law, with federal action at this time being limited to areas under current federal jurisdiction.
4. That the statutory law ought to be uniform among the several states.
5. That the "definition" contained in the statute ought to address general physiological standards rather than medical criteria and tests, which will change with advances in biomedical knowledge and refinements in technique.
6. That death is a unitary phenomenon which can be accurately demonstrated either on the traditional grounds of irreversible cessation of heart and lung functions or on the basis of irreversible loss of all functions of the entire brain.
7. That any statutory "definition" should be kept separate and distinct from provisions governing the donation of cadaver organs and from any legal rules on decisions to terminate life-sustaining treatment.

To embody these conclusions in statutory form the Commission worked with the three organizations which had proposed model legislation on the subject, the American Bar Association, the American Medical Association, and the National Conference of Commissioners on Uniform State Laws. These groups have now endorsed the following statute, in place of their previous proposals:

> Uniform Determination of Death Act
> An individual who has sustained either (1) irreversible cessation of circulatory and respiratory functions, or (2) irreversible cessation of all functions of the entire brain, including the brain stem, is dead. A determination of death must be made in accordance with accepted medical standards.

The Commission recommends the adoption of this statute in all jurisdictions in the United States.

Notes

1. Ake Grenvik, David J. Powner, James V. Snyder, Michael S. Jastremski, Ralph A. Babcock and Michael G. Loughhead, "Cessation of Therapy in Terminal Illness and Brain Death," 6 *Critical Care Med.* 284 (1978).

2. Accordingly, in the procedures for diagngsing death set forth by the Commission's medical consultants, the test for apnea involves elevating the level of circulating oxygen before turning off the respirator and allowing the level of carbon dioxide to rise as a stimulus for spontaneous respiration. The high level of oxygen protects the brain cells (if any remain active) from further damage.

3. P. Mollaret and M. Goulon, "Le Coma Depasse," 101 *Rev. Neural.* 3 (1959).

4. A. Earl Walker, E. L. Diamond and John Moseley, "The Neuropathological Findings in Irreversible Coma; A Critique of the Respirator Brain," 34 *J. Neuropath. Exp. Neurol.* 295 (1975); John I. Moseley, Gaetano F. Molinari and A. Earl Walker, "Respirator Brain: Report of a Survey and Review of Current Concepts," 100 *Arch. Pathol. Lab. Med.* 61 (1976).

5. See, e.g., Renée C. Fox and Judith P. Swazey, *The Courage to Fail: A Social View of Organ Transplantation and Dialysis*, University of Chicago Press, Chicago (1978); Francis D. Moore, *Give and Take: The Biology of Tissue Transplantation*, W. B. Sanders, Co., Philadelphia, Pa. (1964).

6. See e.g., Howard H. Kaufman, John D. Hutchton, Megan M. McBride, Carolyn A. Beardsley and Barry D. Kahan, "Kidney Donation: Needs and Possibilities," 5 *Neurosurg.* 237 (1979); K. J. Bart, "The Prevalance of Cadaveric Organs for Transplantation" in S. W. Sell, U. P. Perry and M. M. Vincent (eds.) *Proceedings of the 1977 Annual Meeting of American Association Tissue Banks*, American Association of Tissue Banks, Rockville, Md. (1977) at 124–130; A. Earl Walker, "The Neurosurgeon's Responsibility for Organ Procurement," 44 *J. Neurosurg.* 1 (1976).

7. B. D. Colen, "Medical Examiner's Solution to Life and Death Problem," January 28, 1978, *Wash Post* §A at 8, col. 1, describing the attempts of Dr. Ron Wright, deputy chief medical examiner for Dade County Florida, to have medical interventions ceased for bodies declared dead on the basis of brain-oriented criteria. (Florida did not enact a statute on the subject until 1980.) "Wright was able to get a judge to hold a special Sunday morning hearing at the hospital—with reporters and photographers in attendance—at which he successfully argued that the family was being forced to pay $2,000 a day to keep a dead body in the intensive care unit." Patricia H. Butcher, "Management of the Relatives of Patients with Brain Death" in Ronald V. Trubuhovich (ed). *Management of Acute Intracranial Disasters*, Little, Brown and Company, Boston, Mass. (1979) at 327.

8. Ad Hoc Committee of the Harvard Medical School to Examine the Definition of Brain Death, "A Definition of Irreversible Coma," 205 *J.A.M.A.* 337 (1968).

9. David J. Pawner, James V. Snyder, and Ake Grenvik, "Brain Death Certification: A Review," 5 *Crit. Care Med.* 230 (1977); Julius Korein, "Brain Death," in J. Cottrell and H. Turndorf (eds.) *Anesthesia and Neurosurgery* (1980) at 282; Peter McL. Black, "Brain Death" 299 *N.E.J.M.* 338 & 393 (1978).

10. See, e.g., Julius Korein (ed.), *Brain Death: Interrelated Medical and Social Issues*, 315 *Ann. N.Y. Acad. Sci.* 62–214 (1978); Julius Korein, Phillip Braunstein, Ajax George, Melvin Wichter, Irving Kricheff, Abraham Lieberman and John Pearson, "Brain Death: I. Angiographic Correlation with the Radioisotopic Bolus Technique for Evaluation of Critical Deficit of Cerebral Blood Flow," 2 *Ann. Neural.* 206 (1977); Andrew J. K. Smith and A. Earl Walker, "Cerebral Blood Flow and Brain Metabolism as Indicators of Cerebral Death: A Review," 133 *Johns Hopkins Med. J.* 107 (1973); Julius M. Goodman and Larry I. Heck, "Confirmation of Brain Death by Bedside Isotope Angiography," 238 *J.A.M.A.* 966 (1977).

11. See, e.g., Gian Emilio Chatrian, "Electrophysiologic Evaluation of Brain Death: A Critical Appraisal," in M. J. Aminoff (ed.) *Electrodiagnosis in Clinical Neurology*, Churchill Livingstone, New York (1980); Donald R. Bennett, Julius Korein, John R. Hughes, Jerome K. Merlis and Cary Suter, *Atlas of Electroencephalography in Coma and Cerebral Death*, Raven Press, New York (1976); Fred Plum and Jerome B. Posner, op. cit.; Stuart A. Schneck, "Brain Death and Prolonged State of Impaired Responsiveness," 58 *Denver L.J.* 609. 612–613 (1981).

12. See, e.g., U.S. Department of Health and Human Services, *The NINCDS Collaborative Study of Brain Death*, N.I.H. Publication No. 81-2286, U.S. Government

Printing Office (1980), reported in, "An Appraisal of the Criteria of Cerebral Death. A Summary Statement. A Collaborative Study," 237 *J.A.M.A.* 982 (1977); Peter McL. Black, op. cit; Pamela F. Prior, "Brain Death" 1980(i) *Lancet* 1142.

13. See, e.g., Bryan Jennett, John Gleave and Peter Wilson, "Brain Death in Three Neurosurgical Units" 282 *Brit. Med. J.* 533 (1981).

14. See, e.g., U.S. Department of Health and Human Services, The NINCDS Collaborative Study of Brain Death, op. cit.

15. Peter McL. Black, op. cit.

16. Conference of Royal Colleges and Faculties of the United Kingdom, "Memorandum on the Diagnosis of Death" (January 1979), in Working Party of the United Kingdom Health Departments, *The Removal of Cadaveric Organs for Transplantation: A Code of Practice* (1979) at 32–36.

17. See Peter McL. Black op. cit; Julius Korein, "Brain Death" op. cit.

18. Conference of Royal Colleges and Faculties, op. cit. at 35. "Medicine and the Media," 281 *Brit. Med. J* 1064 (1980). See also A. Mohandas and Shelley Chou, "Brain Death: A Clinical and Pathological Study," 35 *J. Neurosurg.* 211, 215 (1971) (authors of so-called "Minnesota criteria" hold that "the state of irreversible damage to the brain-stem . . . is the point of no return"). The more typical contrast between the American and British approaches is illustrated by the criteria employed at the University of Pittsburgh School of Medicine where "brain death" is defined as the "irreversible cessation of all brain function," as demonstrated by coma of established cause, absence of movements and brainstem reflexes, and an isoelectric EEG. David J. Powner and Ake Grenvik, "Triage in Patient Care: From Expected Recovery to Brain Death," 8 *Heart & Lung* 1103 (1979). The British rely instead on another observation, confirmed by the University of Pittsburgh, that *"prognosis* appears to be *similarly hopeless* for those patients who have clinical findings consistent with brain death but who have a nonisoelectric EEG." Id. at 1107 (emphasis added) (cited by British neurologist Christopher Pallis in lecture at Conference on Brain Death, Boston, Mass., April 4, 1981).

19. Conference of Royal Colleges and Faculties, op. cit. at 36.

20. See also 142 D.S.C. §1802 (1978).

QUESTIONS

1. What is "brain death"?
2. What is the Uniform Determination of Death Act?
3. Why is clarity about when we die of importance?

54. Biology, Consciousness, and the Definition of Death

DAVID DeGRAZIA

*D*avid DeGrazia (1962–) is professor of philosophy at George Washington University. He writes about a number of topics in practical ethics, including the status of animals, abortion, and death. In an important book, *Human Identity and Bioethics* (2005), he investigates the importance of understanding our identity in order to resolve contemporary practical controversies. His books include *Animal Rights: A Very Short Introduction* (2002) and *Human Identity and Bioethics* (2005).

The "whole-brain death" criterion is widely accepted today: The irreversible cessation of all functions of the entire brain signals death. A question now raised is whether this criterion should be replaced by a "higher-brain" criterion, one that points to the cessation of those parts of the brain needed for consciousness. Someone in a permanent coma would be dead according to the higher-brain criterion but not the whole-brain one. DeGrazia examines this controversy and argues against replacing the whole-brain standard. He contrasts two conceptions of human death: that of the human *organism* and that of the human *person*. DeGrazia raises a number of objections to the second view.

When does a human life end? This question used to be answered quite easily. According to the traditional standard, which has only recently been questioned, a human being is dead when her heart and lungs have irreversibly ceased to function. In some cases, permanent loss of consciousness may precede cardiopulmonary failure. But the interval between these two events has typically been a matter of hours or days, and the traditional standard regards only the latter event as definitive.

Today, however, the development of mechanical respirators, electronic pacemakers, and other medical technologies has created the possibility of a greater temporal separation between various system failures—a patient may lose consciousness a decade or more before his heart and lungs fail, for example.

Meanwhile, interest in the availability of transplantable organs has provided an incentive not to delay unnecessarily in determining that a person has died. (Current law, it need hardly be said, embraces the so-called "dead-donor rule": organs necessary for life may not be procured before donors are dead, since the removal of such organs would otherwise *cause* death—that is, kill the donors—violating laws against homicide.)

Two landmark reports helped to generate a movement away from exclusive reliance on the traditional standard: the 1968 report of the Harvard Medical School Ad Hoc Committee and a 1981 presidential commission report, *Defining Death*. This second document included what became the Uniform Determination of Death Act

From David DeGrazia, "Biology, Consciousness, and the Definition of Death," *Philosophy & Public Policy Quarterly*, Vol. 18, Nos. 1–2 (Winter/Spring 1998), pp. 18–22. Reprinted with permission of the author.

(UDDA). Today all fifty states and the District of Columbia follow the UDDA in recognizing *whole-brain death*—irreversible cessation of all functions of the entire brain—as a legal standard of death. The UDDA doesn't jettison the cardiopulmonary standard, however. Instead, it holds that death occurs whenever *either* standard (whichever applies first) is met. One important consequence of this change is that an individual can be legally dead even if her cardiopulmonary system continues to function. If a patient's entire brain is nonfunctioning, so that breathing and heartbeat are maintained only by artificial life-supports, that patient meets the whole-brain standard of death.

Some philosophers and scientists have argued that the whole-brain standard does not go far enough. Several leading authors on the subject have advocated a *higher-brain* standard, according to which death is the irreversible cessation of the capacity for consciousness. This standard is often met prior to whole-brain death, which includes death of the brainstem—that part of the brain which allows spontaneous respiration and heartbeat but is insufficient for consciousness. Thus, a patient in a permanent coma or permanent vegetative state (PVS) meets the higher-brain, but not the whole-brain, standard of death.

Should society embrace the higher-brain standard? Should laws be changed so that permanently unconscious patients can legally be declared dead? This essay offers both conceptual and pragmatic grounds for rejecting such a change. However, it will also argue that the linkage between definitions of death and policies regarding life-supports and organ procurement is less strict than some observers might suppose. In other words, a rejection of the higher-brain standard does not imply an endorsement of policies that would prolong life at any cost.

A Biological Perspective

One way to approach the issue of defining death is to consider it from a biological perspective. The concept of death applies not only to humans, but also to nonhuman animals and plants; it is a biological fact that all organisms live and die. In asking what death

is, then, it seems logical to ask what is common to all instances of death. The answer will provide the core meaning of the term "death."

What happens when a human, dog, squid, bee, or tulip dies? In each case, the organism breaks down in a fundamental way. Particular systems may break down before others, and the events from the first major system failure to eventual putrefaction clearly involve a process. But somewhere in the continuum that includes both dying and disintegration, the organism as a whole ceases to function. Charles Culver and Bernard Gert have helpfully defined death as "the permanent cessation of functioning of the organism as a whole." The phrase "organism as a whole" does not mean literally the entire organism (since loss of a limb or spleen, say, is compatible with life); it refers to the integrated functioning of most or all of the important subsystems (organ subsystems, in the case of all but the most primitive animals). This, roughly, is the core meaning of "death" as seen from a biological perspective.

Both of the currently recognized standards of death are arguably compatible with this organismic concept. Under the cardiopulmonary standard, death occurs when a patient's heart and lungs have permanently ceased to function—that is to say, when they no longer support each other or other organ systems. Under the whole-brain standard, a patient is dead when her brainstem no longer orchestrates her vital functions. In either case, the appeal is to the role of a particular organ or system in the functioning of the organism as a whole.

In contrast, the higher-brain standard is clearly not compatible with the organismic concept of death. Consider a patient in a permanent vegetative state. Her mind is gone, but her brainstem continues to function. Her heart beats spontaneously, maintaining normal blood pressure. Body temperature continues to be regulated, and other organ systems function as usual. From a biological standpoint, it would appear that this organism continues to function as a whole, despite her permanent unconsciousness. Thus, from this standpoint, the higher-brain standard of death appears incorrect. It must receive support from a different perspective, to which we now turn.

A Person-Based Perspective

Higher-brain theorists contend that human death cannot be adequately understood by assimilating it to organismic death in general. This claim can be defended in two different ways.

First, it might be argued that there *is* no core meaning shared by all correct applications of the term "death." The various uses of the term, on this view, bear only a "family resemblance" to one another. In a family, a certain characteristic feature (e.g., above-average height) may be shared by most but not all members, while another common feature (e.g., brown eyes) is shared by a different set of family members, and so on, without any single, definable family "look" being shared by all. Similarly, there might be no essence common to the deaths of all organisms that can be invoked in an effort to illuminate human death.

Second, it might be argued that even if there is a core meaning of "death" applying to all organisms, a *reconstruction* of the term may be justified in the human case. Sometimes the original meaning of a term is justifiably extended or reshaped to fit certain practical interests or changing circumstances. The original meaning of "conversation," for example, may have required that two individuals be able to hear or at least see each other. But the rapid exchange made possible at great distances by e-mail seems to justify applying the term "conversation" in this context. Perhaps a reconstruction of the term "death" is justified in its application to the special case of human beings.

From the present perspective, then, the core-meaning argument does not settle the question of the nature of human death. A more promising approach, on this view, is to take seriously the fact that we are not only organisms; we are also *persons*. According to one prominent argument for the higher-brain standard, the capacity for consciousness is *essential* to persons—essential in the strict philosophical sense of being necessary: Any being lacking this capacity is not a person. It follows that when someone permanently loses the capacity for consciousness, there is no longer a person associated with the body. The person who was, is no more—that is to say, she is dead. Thus, the argument goes, *human* death is captured by the higher-brain standard.

While this essentialist argument may represent the most prominent case for the higher-brain view, there is also an important value-based alternative, which runs as follows. Human persons value consciousness as necessary for any meaningful existence. When we permanently lose consciousness, we lose all possibility of such an existence: We can no longer think or feel, enjoy relationships with loved ones, pursue projects, or act at all. When we no longer know we exist, there is no point to existing; when we are not aware of life, life has no meaning for us. Because human beings regard consciousness as a precondition for all meaning and value, the permanent loss of the capacity for consciousness is rightly regarded as human death.

Problems with the Person-Based Approach

We have seen that human death can be conceptualized from a biological perspective and from a person-based perspective, with only the latter supporting the higher-brain standard. Can we reasonably select between these two approaches? The case for favoring the biological concept of death begins with a critique of the person-based approach.

First of all, it is an approach that faces certain unresolvable tensions. Here is one example. Since human beings *are* organisms as well as persons, the concept of organismic death clearly applies in the human case. (This, I should say, is a fact acknowledged by some higher-brain theorists, even though it undermines the "family resemblance" thesis.) As we have seen, however, permanent unconsciousness is not definitive of organismic death. Thus, if the higher-brain standard is correct, then in PVS cases there are *two* deaths—one of the person and a later death of the organism—for a single human being. This is somewhat odd, since we are accustomed to believing that there is just one death associated with every human being. The oddity is reflected in the phraseology of Tristam Engelhardt, a higher-brain theorist, who describes the permanently unconscious as "biologically living corpses."

A difficulty that faces the essentialist argument in particular concerns its appeal to the concept of a person. The capacity for consciousness is held to be necessary for personhood. But this capacity cannot be *sufficient*, since many animals that clearly are not persons (e.g., other mammals, birds) have the capacity for consciousness, too. So what other capacities are necessary? The philosophical tradition that requires consciousness for personhood traces back at least to Locke, who held that persons also possess the traits of self-awareness over time and rationality. This tradition, recently championed by Derek Parfit, consistently requires some psychological capacities beyond mere consciousness to distinguish persons from such conscious nonpersons as gerbils and blue jays. Thus Parfit holds that a person must be "self-conscious, aware of its identity and continued existence over time," while Engelhardt states that "[w]hat distinguishes persons is their capacity to be self-conscious, rational, and concerned with worthiness of blame and praise." (It may be tempting to say that a person is any *Homo sapiens* with the capacity for consciousness. But this move has been consistently rejected as chauvinistic; we may reasonably ask whether individuals outside our species—such as *Homo erectus,* the Great Apes, the computer HAL in *2001,* and God—were or are persons.)

Where is the problem? The essentialist argument assumes not just that persons are essentially beings with the capacity for consciousness, but also that *we are essentially (necessarily) persons.* Without this second assumption, one could hold that we continue to exist, to live, after losing personhood (including the capacity for consciousness)—the very point that the higher-brain theorists wish to deny. Now the assumption that we are essentially persons, combined with the point that personhood requires psychological capacities in addition to consciousness (say, rationality and self-awareness), has a peculiar implication. Since newborns lack the psychological capacities in question, newborns are, strictly speaking, not persons (even if we often casually refer to them as persons). But if we are essentially persons, meaning we cannot exist as nonpersons, then *we* did not exist as newborns; the newborns in question were our organismic predecessors. This is a strange result, since we all believe that we were born.

The greatest difficulty with the essentialist argument is that the way it reasons about death is pernicious. By assuming that we are essentially persons, and defining death as loss of personhood, the argument logically invites an expansion of those humans to be counted as dead. Again, analyses of personhood standardly require more than the capacity for consciousness, so the present line of reasoning suggests that some highly subnormal *yet conscious* human beings—for example, the most severely demented individuals—are actually dead.

The value-based alternative to the essentialist argument also has its vulnerabilities. First, in its effort to define meaninglessness as death, it conflates two concepts whose distinctness cannot simply be erased by definitional fiat. One might agree that a future of permanent unconsciousness would be devoid of meaning and value, but that doesn't show that one wouldn't be alive in such a state. The higher-brain theorist might reply that, even so, the fact that existing in a permanently unconscious state would be meaningless is sufficient reason to *regard* that state as death. But this, too, turns out to be a pernicious way to argue. For while it is reasonable to think that a meaningful existence requires the capacity for consciousness, it is no less reasonable to hold that the former requires a modicum of self-awareness and some ability to socialize with others (or at least the prospect of developing these, as with newborns). The fact that some severely disabled individuals are neither self-aware nor able to socialize casts doubt on this whole way of thinking about life and death.

Finally, any effort to base a standard for human death on "our" values confronts the problem of value pluralism. While liberal intellectuals, and perhaps a majority of Americans, are likely to regard a future of permanent unconsciousness as meaningless, many people—some of them religious fundamentalists—would disagree. For the dissenters, biological life in PVS or permanent coma is at least *life* and therefore valuable (perhaps infinitely so). For at least some of these people, such a state is meaningful because it is a gift from God, a gift that must not be thrown away through active killing—or defined away with a new definition of death.

Definitions and Policy

Since the higher-brain standard might be viewed as a basis for enacting liberal policies regarding end-of-life medical care and organ donation, rejecting this standard may seem tantamount to embracing conservative policies. This is not so.

It is firmly established, both in case law and in medical ethics, that competent adult patients have the right to refuse life-supporting medical treatments, even artificial nutrition and hydration. By the same token, an appropriate surrogate can refuse life-supports on behalf of the legally incompetent if there is sufficient reason to believe the patient would have refused treatment in the present circumstances. Because of this broad legal and moral right to refuse treatment, life-supports that are unwanted or are considered unhelpful—including life-supports for permanently unconscious patients—can be terminated without first declaring the patient dead.

What if a family or another surrogate requests life-supports for a patient who has become permanently unconscious? Would not honoring such requests necessitate major expenditures on care that many people believe to be futile? It would, but the public need not fund such care. While there are compelling arguments for the thesis that society should ensure all citizens access to health care (an obligation our society sadly fails to meet), there is no support for the claim that the public must fund *all* desired care. What is owed is some basic package of health care benefits, and it is reasonable to include in such a publicly funded package only care that everyone can agree is beneficial. Thus, treatment that is arguably futile, including life-supports for the permanently unconscious, need not be covered.

On the other hand, if a patient's family is willing to pay for such care, or subscribes to a private insurance scheme that covers it, it should be provided (at least if there is no shortage of available hospital beds and other critical supplies). In such a case, the family or insurance company does *not* consider the treatment futile—no doubt because it successfully prolongs the patient's life (which the family or insurance company considers a substantial benefit) without causing any suffering.

Rejecting the higher-brain standard entails neither forcing patients to have treatment they don't want or need, nor making the public pay for care that many consider futile. But since permanent unconsciousness often precedes death as determined by an organismic standard (whole-brain or cardiopulmonary), doesn't rejecting the higher-brain approach mean that we must often delay before procuring donor organs?

Not necessarily, because in principle this issue can be addressed at another level. Without adopting the higher-brain standard, we *could* obtain organs from the permanently unconscious if we allowed an exception to the dead-donor rule in this sort of case. However, permitting any exception to the rule would provoke legitimate slippery-slope concerns. That is, if we were to allow one exception, predictably there would be pressures —economic and otherwise—to make additional exceptions.

How one reacts to this prospect depends both on one's ethical judgments about such possible exceptions and on one's degree of trust in the medical profession, legislators, and the broader public. I, for one, am not inclined to abandon the dead-donor rule, even for a class of patients who are permanently unconscious. However, prospective organ donors can already (through advance medical directives, for example) refuse life-supports, including nutrition and hydration. This means that even if we retain the dead-donor rule, the practical loss of rejecting the higher-brain standard of death—not getting some organs quite as soon as we otherwise might—is very modest indeed. And as we have seen, several considerations, both conceptual and pragmatic, favor this position.

QUESTIONS

1. What are the reasons for favoring the higher-brain criterion of death?
2. What are the reasons for favoring the older, whole-brain criterion?

55. Endings

JEFF McMAHAN

For a description of the author, see chapter 6.

The second of three excerpts from his book *The Ethics of Killing*, here McMahan distinguishes between two conceptions of death and of being alive. If we are organisms, we die when our organism dies; if we are persons, we die when we permanently lose the capacity for consciousness. In his book McMahan argues that we are essentially embodied minds. The loss of the capacity for consciousness thus signals our end. McMahan, unlike DeGrazia in the previous chapter, is critical of the organismic conception. Only a few pages of the chapter are included here; in the remaining pages McMahan has many critical things to say about our understanding of brain death.

When Do We Die, or Cease to Exist?

1.1. Two Concepts of Death

I have argued that the view that best captures our intuitions about our own survival and persistence is that we are essentially embodied minds. If that is right, we begin to exist when our brains begin to support the existence of a mind—that is, when they develop the capacity to generate consciousness and mental activity. Since the capacity for consciousness is the defining essential property of a mind, we must cease to exist when we lose the capacity for consciousness in a way that is in principle irreversible.

It is quite commonly believed that we cease to exist, or at least cease to exist *here*, in association with our organisms, when our brains lose the capacity to support consciousness. When the body of Nancy Cruzan died in 1990, after spending almost eight years in a persistent vegetative state (PVS), her family, who had gone to the Supreme Court in their efforts to terminate the body's life support, engraved on her tombstone: "DEPARTED JAN 11, 1983 / AT PEACE DEC 26, 1990."[1] This is not an isolated phenomenon. In the late 1960s and early 1970s, the highly successful efforts to persuade medical bodies and legislatures that brain death marks the death of a human being focused largely on the fact that brain death is sufficient for the irreversible loss of the capacity for consciousness. Thus Alan Shewmon, a pediatric neurologist who has written extensively on brain death, observes that "the introducers of the concepts [of brain death] intended to *redefine* death in terms of unconsciousness rather than diagnose it as the cessation of biological life of the human organism."[2] Significantly, the title of the report that was most influential in gaining support for the concept of brain death was "A Definition of Irreversible Coma," implying that what the tests for brain death actually test for is not death but the irreversible loss of the capacity for consciousness—that is, that brain death indicates when a coma is genuinely irreversible.[3] For death and coma are mutually exclusive states.

Perhaps initially many people believed that only with a diagnosis of brain death could one be confident that an individual had lost the capacity for consciousness irreversibly.[4] It soon became obvious,

From *The Ethics of Killing: Problems at the Margins of Life* (Oxford, 2002). By permission of Oxford University Press.

however, that in certain conditions there is a near certainty that the capacity for consciousness has been destroyed even though brain death has not occurred. Most neurologists agree, for example, that this is true in most instances of PVS. Some of those who had been motivated to accept brain death as the criterion of death therefore obeyed the promptings of consistency by rejecting brain death and embracing instead a criterion that they took to be more tightly connected with the irreversible loss of the capacity for consciousness. Some contended that the proper criterion of death is *neocortical death*, defined by the neurologist Julius Korein as "the destruction of cortical neurons bilaterally while deep structures of the cerebral hemispheres such as the thalamus and basal ganglia may be intact along with the brainstem and cerebellum."[5] Others, slightly more conservative in their estimation of what is sufficient for the irreversible loss of the capacity for consciousness, defended the notion of *cerebral death*, defined by Korein as the "irreversible destruction of both cerebral hemispheres exclusive of the brainstem and cerebellum."[6] According to these views, a person dies when he or she suffers the destruction of those areas of the brain in which consciousness is realized, whether these areas are confined to the cortex, as some believe, or include other parts of the cerebral hemispheres as well.

These revisionist proposals for a "higher-brain" criterion of death continue to enjoy strong support in certain quarters, but they have been unsuccessful in dislodging brain death as the orthodox criterion of death in most parts of the world.[7] The main reason why this is so is that both cerebral death and neocortical death are compatible with the survival and continued functional integrity of the brainstem, and thus with continued spontaneous respiration and heartbeat in the organism. A human organism that has suffered neocortical death or cerebral death can continue to breathe and to maintain other vital functions with a minimum of external support—in some cases with little more than intravenous nutrition and hydration and basic nursing care. It has seemed to most observers to be preposterous to say of such an organism that it is *dead*.

We can escape this impasse if we accept that we are not identical with our organisms. Recognition that we are embodied minds distinct from our organisms allows us to embrace the intuition behind the revisionist higher-brain proposals—namely, that we cease to exist when we irreversibly lose the capacity for consciousness—while at the same time recognizing that an organism that has suffered neocortical or cerebral death is nevertheless a living organism. For if we are not identical with our organisms, one of us can cease to exist even if his or her organism remains in existence and, indeed, even if it remains alive.

If a person and his organism are distinct substances, and if both can die or cease to be alive, it seems that we need two concepts of death—one for the person and one for the organism. Following most writers in the area, I accept that the death of a human organism is a biological phenomenon that consists in the irreversible cessation of integrated functioning in the major organs and subsystems (respiratory, circulatory, immune, and so on) of the body. Perhaps this is not exactly right; I do not pretend to any particular expertise in the matter.[8] But for our purposes it is close enough. If we were human organisms, it might be important to be able to determine precisely what the death of an organism essentially involves, and to be able to identify precisely when it occurs. But we are not organisms. We die or cease to exist when our brains lose the capacity for consciousness in a way that is in principle irreversible.

Many people believe that the concept of death is univocal and belongs to biology. Charles M. Culver and Bernard Gert, for example, assert that "death is a biological concept. Thus in a literal sense, death can he applied directly only to biological organisms and not to persons. We do not object to the phrase 'death of a person,' but the phrase in common usage actually means the death of the organism which was the person."[9] This view is echoed by David Lamb, who claims that "the concept of 'death' can only be applied to organisms, not persons."[10] As the passage quoted indicates, Culver and Gert take "person" to be a phase sortal rather than a substance sortal. It is therefore unsurprising that they believe that a person can die only in a way that is supervenient upon the death of an organism. A person dies only if an organism dies while it is a person, just as a child dies only if an organism dies during its childhood phase.

Just as no child dies when an organism ceases to he a child by becoming an adult, so no one dies when a living organism ceases to be a person by losing certain psychological attributes that are constitutive of personhood.

While it is often asserted that death is a univocal biological concept, the assertion is never, to my knowledge, argued for. People seem to have no difficulty in understanding the idea that I may die before my organism does. I have been telling my students this for years and am pretty confident that they have not suspected me of talking nonsense. Even if the primary sense of the notion of death is biological, people are able to grasp an extended sense in which a person—a psychological rather than a biological substance—dies when he loses the capacity for consciousness. For it is entirely natural to say that a person dies when he ceases to exist, even if his organism remains alive. (Thus James Rachels quotes the wife of a man who some years previously had lapsed into a PVS: "He died back in 1970. We know that.")[11] A person who is first alive and then ceases to exist thereby also ceases to be alive; and normally ceasing to be alive is a sufficient condition of dying. (There are exceptions. An amoeba ceases to exist when it divides but arguably does not die. Similarly, two embryos in the same womb may fuse, thereby also ceasing to exist but not necessarily dying.) In any case, I propose to say that when a person ceases to exist by losing the capacity for consciousness, he dies. If this is a technical sense of the notion of death, so be it.

The two concepts of death correspond to two concepts of life, or of being alive. To say that a human organism is alive is just to say that its various organs and subsystems are functioning together in a coordinated and harmonious way. To say that a person is alive is just to say that she exists—for which, at present, it is a necessary but not a sufficient condition that her organism be biologically alive.

These two concepts of life should not be confused with the distinction James Rachels has drawn between *being alive,* which involves only life in the biological sense, and *having a life,* which involves life "in the biographical sense" and requires a conscious subject.[12] Rachels believes that in the normal case both types of life, biological and biographical, can be predicated of one and the same tiling: the human organism or human being. Thus he also believes that there are cases—for example, cases of PVS—in which a human being ceases to have a life in the biographical sense but does not die because he remains alive in the biological sense. In my view, by contrast, the organism is the primary bearer of biological life, and only the mind (or self or person) has a biography. Thus most of the cases that, according to Rachels, involve an individual's remaining alive only in the biological sense are, in my view, cases in which the self or conscious subject dies (and thus has no life of any sort) while his or her organism continues to live.

Notes

1. Cited in Singer (1994), p. 62. Similar claims by relatives of other people who lapsed into PVS are quoted in Rachels (1986), p. 55.
2. Shewmon (1997), p. 81. Emphasis in the original.
3. Ad Hoc Committee of the Harvard Medical School (1968).
4. For discussion, see Bartlett and Youngner (1988), pp. 201–3.
5. Quoted in Gervais (1986), p. 11.
6. Ibid.
7. Higher-brain criteria are defended by Green and Wikler (1980), Gervais (1986), Bartlett and Youngner (1988), Veatch (1988), and by others whose essays are included in Zaner (1988).
8. For some challenges to certain standard analyses of the death of an organism, see Feldman (1992), ch. 7.
9. Culver and Gert (1982), p. 183.
10. Lamb (1985), p. 93. Also compare Bernat (1998), pp. 15–16.
11. Rachels (1986), p. 55.
12. Rachels (1986), pp. 5–6 and 24–27.

References

Ad Hoc Committee of the Harvard Medical School. 1968. "A Definition of Irreversible Coma." *Journal of the American Medical Association* 205: 337–40.
Bartlett, Edward T., and Youngner, Stuart J. 1988. "Human Death and the Destruction of the Neocortex." Pp. 199–215 in Zaner (1988).
Bernat, James L. 1998. "A Defense of the Whole-Brain Concept of Death." *Hastings Center Report* 28: 14–23.

Culver, Charles M., and Gert, Bernard. 1982. *Philosophy in Medicine*. New York: Oxford University Press.

Feldman, Fred. 1992. *Confrontations with the Reaper*. New York: Oxford University Press.

Gervais, Karen Grandstand. 1986, *Redefining Death*. New Haven: Yale University Press.

Green, Michael B., and Wikler, Daniel. 1980. "Brain Death and Personal Identity." *Philosophy and Public Affairs* 9: 105–33.

Lamb, David. 1985. *Death, Brain Death, and Ethics* Albany: State University of New York Press.

Rachels, James. 1986. *The End of Life: Euthanasia and Morality*. Oxford: Oxford University Press.

Shewmon, D. Alan. 1997. "Recovery from 'Brain Death': A Neurologist's Apologia." *Linacre Quarterly* 64: 30–96.

Singer, Peter. 1994. *Rethinking Life and Death: The Collapse of Our Traditional Ethics*. New York: St. Martin's Press.

Veatch, Robert M. 1988. "Whole-brain Neocortical, and Higher Brain Related Concepts." Pp. 171–186 in Zaner (1988).

QUESTION

1. Is it possible for someone to die *before* his or her organism dies? What implications do the answer have for the question as to whether we are organisms or persons?

Abortion

Abortion has been controversial for a long time. But the debate about its permissibility has been especially heated in the United States since the Supreme Court's landmark decision, *Roe v. Wade*, in 1973. This decision made most restrictions on abortion in American states illegal. Specifically, the Court ruled that states may not restrict first-trimester abortion, that they may regulate second-trimester abortions for the health of the mother, and that they may regulate postviability abortion for sake of "the potentiality of human life," subject to constraints (preserving the life or health of mother). The political reaction to legalization is still being felt today. Many people strongly object to the Court's decision, both to the ruling and to the legal reasoning supporting it.

Since 1973 more than 45 million abortions have been performed in the United States.[1] The number of abortions performed annually peaked in 1990 (more than 1.4 million) and has been dropping ever since (about 820,000 in 2005). Most abortions take place in the first trimester of gestation: Almost 90 percent of abortions in the United States are performed before the thirteenth week, 54 to 58 percent before the ninth week. One to 1.5 percent take place after the twentieth week, and .01 percent take place in the third trimester.[2]

The controversy over abortion reflects a large set of concerns, all squeezed into one apparent debate. There are concerns about life, homicide, women, work, children, family, and politics, and it can be hard to separate them. Disagreement seems to be deep, and it is hard to see what room there might be for compromise. It is difficult to make progress in adjudicating the debate, and many have given up.

The abortion controversy turns out to be remarkably complex, and it is important to proceed slowly. Our interests in this reader are largely in the central ethical questions raised by abortion, and many of the important social and political questions will be neglected. The

---

1. A source of the statistical information is the Centers for Disease Control. See http://www.cdc.gov/mmwr/PDF/ss/ss5713.pdf.

2. See http://en.wikipedia.org/wiki/File:US_abortion_by_gestational_age_2004_histogram.svg.

initial cause of the controversy lies in the facts of human reproduction. For humans there is a relatively long period of gestation during which the "unborn" human depends on the mother.[3] In the case of an unwanted pregnancy, there is a conflict between the life of the unborn and the autonomy or well-being of the woman; both cannot be served (or so it appears). There is a conflict of interests or goals. The question then is how to address this conflict.

There are a number of questions that need to be distinguished. There is first a set of questions about the moral status of abortion and the different parties involved. In particular, there is the question about the moral status of the human embryo or fetus. Depending on how that question is addressed, there is the problem of the conflicting claims or interests of the unborn and its mother. The second set of questions concerns policy: What legal and social policies should we adopt given the answers to the first set of questions? Popular debate sometimes suggests that there are essentially two policies, permissive or restrictive. But in fact there is a full range of possibilities. Current U.S. law, contrary to the impression often given, is not as permissive as it could be. And few people in fact recommend that abortion be made illegal in all circumstances. Our interest in this reader will focus on the first set of questions, but attention will have to be paid to the second as well.

There are reasons that the debate over abortion is as complex and acrimonious as it is. The moral questions posed by abortion are in fact quite difficult. We often reason by analogy when thinking about ethical problems, but it is hard to reason analogically with regard to abortion. As a medical procedure it is unique. And the relationship between the mother and the unborn is unique, unlike other similar relations. Add in our complicated attitudes toward children, family, the role of women, and other matters, and the controversy about abortion becomes very hard to resolve.

It is usually assumed, at least in popular presentations of the topic, that there are two dominant positions: the antiabortion or pro-life (or "conservative") position and the pro-choice (or "liberal") position. This is a gross oversimplification, as there are a number of intermediate or moderate positions. But it is worth examining the disagreement between these two (families of) positions. The antiabortion position usually views abortion as the killing of a human being, and consequently morally wrong and something that ought to be illegal. By contrast, the pro-choice position is often premised on the belief that abortion is essentially a private act, something that has the status of a simple medical procedure, and consequently not morally wrong, and something that should be legally permissible. Framed in this way the core disagreement between these parties concerns the status of the unborn human.

In the introductory remarks to section VIII, we introduced the basic idea of moral standing. Something has *moral standing* if it is owed moral consideration, for instance duties are owed *to* it. The core ethical question about abortion seems to be that of the moral status of the unborn: Does it have moral standing? Do we have duties not to kill or otherwise harm it? We assume that virtually all humans of a certain age have moral standing and are protected by duties owed to them. The question is whether unborn humans have a similar status. Answering this question need not settle the debate. If the unborn have no moral standing, then it is likely that abortion will then have the status of a normal medical procedure. But if the unborn have some moral standing, then there is still the question of how to resolve conflicts in case of unwanted pregnancies.

---

3. Since almost everything about abortion is controversial, I note that the term *unborn human* is meant to be neutral between competing accounts of the moral and legal status of human embryos and fetuses. In this sense of the term, something is human if it is a member of the species homo sapiens. Other senses of *human* are not preempted.

56. The Unspeakable Crime of Abortion

JOHN PAUL II

For a description of the author, see chapter 4.

In this excerpt from the *Evangelium vitae*, the late pope condemns abortion. His case relies on the humanity of the unborn: "The one eliminated is a human being at the very beginning of life. No one more absolutely innocent could be imagined." He claims that "human life is sacred and inviolable at every moment of existence, including the initial phase which precedes birth."

58. Among all the crimes which can be committed against life, procured abortion has characteristics making it particularly serious and deplorable. The Second Vatican Council defines abortion, together with infanticide, as an "unspeakable crime."[1]

But today, in many people's consciences, the perception of its gravity has become progressively obscured. The acceptance of abortion in the popular mind, in behaviour and even in law itself, is a telling sign of an extremely dangerous crisis of the moral sense, which is becoming more and more incapable of distinguishing between good and evil, even when the fundamental right to life is at stake. Given such a grave situation, we need now more than ever to have the courage to look the truth in the eye and to call things by their proper name, without yielding to convenient compromises or to the temptation of self-deception. In this regard the reproach of the Prophet is extremely straightforward: "Woe to those who call evil good and good evil, who put darkness for light and light for darkness" (Is 5:20). Especially in the case of abortion there is a widespread use of ambiguous terminology, such as "interruption of pregnancy," which tends to hide abortion's true nature and to attenuate its seriousness in public opinion. Perhaps this linguistic phenomenon is itself a symptom of an uneasiness of conscience. But no word has the power to change the reality of things: procured abortion is the deliberate and direct killing, by whatever means it is carried out, of a human being in the initial phase of his or her existence, extending from conception to birth.

The moral gravity of procured abortion is apparent in all its truth if we recognize that we are dealing with murder and, in particular, when we consider the specific elements involved. The one eliminated is a human being at the very beginning of life. No one more absolutely innocent could be imagined. In no way could this human being ever be considered an aggressor, much less an unjust aggressor! He or she is weak, defenceless, even to the point of lacking that minimal form of defence consisting in the poignant power of a newborn baby's cries and tears. The unborn child is totally entrusted to the protection and care of the woman carrying him or her in the womb. And yet sometimes it is precisely the mother herself who makes the decision and asks for the child to be eliminated, and who then goes about having it done.

It is true that the decision to have an abortion is often tragic and painful for the mother, insofar as the decision to rid herself of the fruit of conception

From John Paul II, *Evangelium vitae*, 1995.

is not made for purely selfish reasons or out of convenience, but out of a desire to protect certain important values such as her own health or a decent standard of living for the other members of the family. Sometimes it is feared that the child to be born would live in such conditions that it would be better if the birth did not take place. Nevertheless, these reasons and others like them, however serious and tragic, can never justify the deliberate killing of an innocent human being.

59. As well as the mother, there are often other people too who decide upon the death of the child in the womb. In the first place, the father of the child may be to blame, not only when he directly pressures the woman to have an abortion, but also when he indirectly encourages such a decision on her part by leaving her alone to face the problems of pregnancy:[2] in this way the family is thus mortally wounded and profaned in its nature as a community of love and in its vocation to be the "sanctuary of life." Nor can one overlook the pressures which sometimes come from the wider family circle and from friends. Sometimes the woman is subjected to such strong pressure that she feels psychologically forced to have an abortion: certainly in this case moral responsibility lies particularly with those who have directly or indirectly obliged her to have an abortion. Doctors and nurses are also responsible, when they place at the service of death skills which were acquired for promoting life.

But responsibility likewise falls on the legislators who have promoted and approved abortion laws, and, to the extent that they have a say in the matter, on the administrators of the health-care centres where abortions are performed. A general and no less serious responsibility lies with those who have encouraged the spread of an attitude of sexual permissiveness and a lack of esteem for motherhood, and with those who should have ensured—but did not—effective family and social policies in support of families, especially larger families and those with particular financial and educational needs. Finally, one cannot overlook the network of complicity which reaches out to include international institutions, foundations and associations which systematically campaign for the legalization and spread of abortion in the world. In this sense abortion goes beyond the responsibility of individuals and beyond the harm done to them, and takes on a distinctly social dimension. It is a most serious wound inflicted on society and its culture by the very people who ought to be society's promoters and defenders. As I wrote in my Letter to Families, "we are facing an immense threat to life: not only to the life of individuals but also to that of civilization itself."[3] We are facing what can be called a "structure of sin" which opposes human life not yet born.

60. Some people try to justify abortion by claiming that the result of conception, at least up to a certain number of days, cannot yet be considered a personal human life. But in fact, "from the time that the ovum is fertilized, a life is begun which is neither that of the father nor the mother; it is rather the life of a new human being with his own growth. It would never be made human if it were not human already. This has always been clear, and . . . modern genetic science offers clear confirmation. It has demonstrated that from the first instant there is established the programme of what this living being will be: a person, this individual person with his characteristic aspects already well determined. Right from fertilization the adventure of a human life begins, and each of its capacities requires time—a rather lengthy time—to find its place and to be in a position to act."[4] Even if the presence of a spiritual soul cannot be ascertained by empirical data, the results themselves of scientific research on the human embryo provide "a valuable indication for discerning by the use of reason a personal presence at the moment of the first appearance of a human life: how could a human individual not be a human person?"[5]

Furthermore, what is at stake is so important that, from the standpoint of moral obligation, the mere probability that a human person is involved would suffice to justify an absolutely clear prohibition of any intervention aimed at killing a human embryo. Precisely for this reason, over and above all scientific debates and those philosophical affirmations to which the Magisterium has not expressly committed itself, the Church has always taught and continues to teach that the result of human procreation, from the first moment of its existence, must be guaranteed that unconditional respect which is morally due to the human being in his or her totality and unity as body and spirit: "The human being is to be respected and treated as a person from the moment of conception; and therefore from that same moment his rights as a person must be recognized, among which in the first place is the inviolable right of every innocent human being to life."[6]

61. The texts of Sacred Scripture never address the question of deliberate abortion and so do not directly and specifically condemn it. But they show such great respect for the human being in the mother's womb that they require as a logical consequence that God's commandment "You shall not kill" be extended to the unborn child as well.

Human life is sacred and inviolable at every moment of existence, including the initial phase which precedes birth. All human beings, from their mothers' womb, belong to God who searches them and knows them, who forms them and knits them together with his own hands, who gazes on them when they are tiny shapeless embryos and already sees in them the adults of tomorrow whose days are numbered and whose vocation is even now written in the "book of life" (cf. Ps 139: 1, 13–16). There too, when they are still in their mothers' womb—as many passages of the Bible bear witness[7]—they are the personal objects of God's loving and fatherly providence.

Christian Tradition—as the Declaration issued by the Congregation for the Doctrine of the Faith points out so well[8]—is clear and unanimous, from the beginning up to our own day, in describing abortion as a particularly grave moral disorder. From its first contacts with the Greco-Roman world, where abortion and infanticide were widely practised, the first Christian community, by its teaching and practice, radically opposed the customs rampant in that society, as is clearly shown by the Didache mentioned earlier.[9] Among the Greek ecclesiastical writers, Athenagoras records that Christians consider as murderesses women who have recourse to abortifacient medicines, because children, even if they are still in their mother's womb, "are already under the protection of Divine Providence."[10] Among the Latin authors, Tertullian affirms: "It is anticipated murder to prevent someone from being born; it makes little difference whether one kills a soul already born or

puts it to death at birth. He who will one day be a man is a man already."[11]

Throughout Christianity's two thousand year history, this same doctrine has been constantly taught by the Fathers of the Church and by her Pastors and Doctors. Even scientific and philosophical discussions about the precise moment of the infusion of the spiritual soul have never given rise to any hesitation about the moral condemnation of abortion.

62. The more recent Papal Magisterium has vigorously reaffirmed this common doctrine. Pius XI in particular, in his Encyclical Casti Connubii, rejected the specious justifications of abortion.[12] Pius XII excluded all direct abortion, i.e., every act tending directly to destroy human life in the womb "whether such destruction is intended as an end or only as a means to an end."[13] John XXIII reaffirmed that human life is sacred because "from its very beginning it directly involves God's creative activity."[14] The Second Vatican Council, as mentioned earlier, sternly condemned abortion: "From the moment of its conception life must be guarded with the greatest care, while abortion and infanticide are unspeakable crimes."[15]

The Church's canonical discipline, from the earliest centuries, has inflicted penal sanctions on those guilty of abortion. This practice, with more or less severe penalties, has been confirmed in various periods of history. The 1917 Code of Canon Law punished abortion with excommunication.[16] The revised canonical legislation continues this tradition when it decrees that "a person who actually procures an abortion incurs automatic (latae sententiae) excommunication."[17] The excommunication affects all those who commit this crime with knowledge of the penalty attached, and thus includes those accomplices without whose help the crime would not have been committed.[18] By this reiterated sanction, the Church makes clear that abortion is a most serious and dangerous crime, thereby encouraging those who commit it to seek without delay the path of conversion. In the Church the purpose of the penalty of excommunication is to make an individual fully aware of the gravity of a certain sin and then to foster genuine conversion and repentance.

Given such unanimity in the doctrinal and disciplinary tradition of the Church, Paul VI was able to declare that this tradition is unchanged and unchangeable.[19] Therefore, by the authority which Christ conferred upon Peter and his Successors, in communion with the Bishops—who on various occasions have condemned abortion and who in the aforementioned consultation, albeit dispersed throughout the world, have shown unanimous agreement concerning this doctrine—I declare that direct abortion, that is, abortion willed as an end or as a means, always constitutes a grave moral disorder, since it is the deliberate killing of an innocent human being. This doctrine is based upon the natural law and upon the written Word of God, is transmitted by the Church's Tradition and taught by the ordinary and universal Magisterium.[20]

No circumstance, no purpose, no law whatsoever can ever make licit an act which is intrinsically illicit, since it is contrary to the Law of God which is written in every human heart, knowable by reason itself, and proclaimed by the Church.

63. This evaluation of the morality of abortion is to be applied also to the recent forms of intervention on human embryos which, although carried out for purposes legitimate in themselves, inevitably involve the killing of those embryos. This is the case with experimentation on embryos, which is becoming increasingly widespread in the field of biomedical research and is legally permitted in some countries. Although "one must uphold as licit procedures carried out on the human embryo which respect the life and integrity of the embryo and do not involve disproportionate risks for it, but rather are directed to its healing, the improvement of its condition of health, or its individual survival,"[21] it must nonetheless be stated that the use of human embryos or fetuses as an object of experimentation constitutes a crime against their dignity as human beings who have a right to the same respect owed to a child once born, just as to every person.[22]

This moral condemnation also regards procedures that exploit living human embryos and fetuses—sometimes specifically "produced" for this purpose by in vitro fertilization—either to be used as "biological material" or as providers of organs or tissue for transplants in the treatment of certain diseases. The killing of innocent human creatures, even if carried out to help others, constitutes an absolutely unacceptable act.

Special attention must be given to evaluating the morality of prenatal diagnostic techniques which enable the early detection of possible anomalies in the unborn child. In view of the complexity of these techniques, an accurate and systematic moral judgment is necessary. When they do not involve disproportionate risks for the child and the mother, and are meant to make possible early therapy or even to favour a serene and informed acceptance of the child not yet born, these techniques are morally licit. But since the possibilities of prenatal therapy are today still limited, it not infrequently happens that these techniques are used with a eugenic intention which accepts selective abortion in order to prevent the birth of children affected by various types of anomalies. Such an attitude is shameful and utterly reprehensible, since it presumes to measure the value of a human life only within the parameters of "normality" and physical well-being, thus opening the way to legitimizing infanticide and euthanasia as well.

And yet the courage and the serenity with which so many of our brothers and sisters suffering from serious disabilities lead their lives when they are shown acceptance and love bears eloquent witness to what gives authentic value to life, and makes it, even in difficult conditions, something precious for them and for others. The Church is close to those married couples who, with great anguish and suffering, willingly accept gravely handicapped children. She is also grateful to all those families which, through adoption, welcome children abandoned by their parents because of disabilities or illnesses.

Notes

1. Second Vatican Ecumenical Council, Pastoral Constitution on the Church in the Modern World *Gaudium et Spes*, 51, "Abortus necnon infanticidium nefanda sunt crimina."
2. Cf. John Paul II, Apostolic Letter *Mulieris Dignitatem* (15 August 1988), 14: *AAS* 80 (1988), 1686.
3. No. 21: *AAS* 86 (1994), 920.
4. Congregation for the Doctrine of the Faith, *Declaration on Procured Abortion* (18 November 1974), Nos. 12–13: *AAS* 66 (1974), 738.

5. Congregation for the Doctrine of the Faith, Instruction on Respect for Human Life in Its Origin and on the Dignity of Procreation *Donum Vitae* (22 February 1987), I, No. 1: *AAS* 80 (1988), 78–79.

6. Ibid., loc. cit., 79.

7. Hence the Prophet Jeremiah: "The word of the Lord came to me saying: 'Before I formed you in the womb I knew you, and before you were born I consecrated you; I appointed you a prophet to the nations'" (1:4–5). The Psalmist, for his part, addresses the Lord in these words: "Upon you I have leaned from my birth; you are he who took me from my mother's womb" (Ps 71:6; cf. Is 46:3; Job 10:8–12; Ps 22:10–11). So too the Evangelist Luke—in the magnificent episode of the meeting of the two mothers, Elizabeth and Mary, and their two sons, John the Baptist and Jesus, still hidden in their mothers' wombs (cf. 1:39–45)—emphasizes how even before their birth the two little ones are able to communicate: the child recognizes the coming of the Child and leaps for joy.

8. Cf. *Declaration on Procured Abortion* (18 November 1974), No. 7: *AAS* 66 (1974), 740–747.

9. "You shall not kill a child by abortion nor shall you kill it once it is born": V, 2: *Patres Apostolici*, ed. F. X. Funk, I, 17.

10. *Apologia on behalf of the Christians*, 35: PG 6, 969.

11. *Apologeticum*, IX, 8: CSEL 69, 24.

12. Cf. Encyclical Letter *Casti Connubii* (31 December 1930), II: *AAS* 22 (1930), 562–592.

13. Address to the Biomedical Association "San Luca" (12 November 1944): *Discorsi e Radiomessaggi*, VI (1944–1945), 191; cf. Address to the Italian Catholic Union of Midwives (29 October 1951), No. 2: *AAS* 43 (1951), 838.

14. Encyclical Letter *Mater et Magistra* (15 May 1961), 3: *AAS* 53 (1961), 447.

15. Pastoral Constitution on the Church in the Modern World *Gaudium et Spes*, 51.

16. Canon 2350, § 1.

17. *Code of Canon Law*, canon 1398; cf. *Code of Canons of the Eastern Churches*, canon 1450, § 2.

18. Cf. ibid., canon 1329; also *Code of Canons of the Eastern Churches*, canon 1417.

19. Cf. Address to the National Congress of Italian Jurists (9 December 1972): *AAS* 64 (1972), 777; Encyclical Letter *Humanae Vitae* (25 July 1968), 14: *AAS* 60 (1968), 490.

20. Second Vatican Ecumenical Council, Dogmatic Constitution on the Church *Lumen Gentium*, 25.

21. Congregation for the Doctrine of the Faith, Instruction on Respect for Human Life in Its Origin and on the Dignity of Procreation *Donum Vitae* (22 February 1987), I, 3: *AAS* 80 (1988), 80.

22. *Charter of the Rights of the Family* (22 October 1983), article 4b: Vatican Polyglot Press, 1983.

QUESTIONS

1. Why is the unborn's humanity—it being a human—relevant to John Paul's argument for the impermissibility of abortion? Does he say?

2. How is an unborn innocent? "In no way could this human being ever be considered an aggressor . . ." Is that true?

57. A Defense of Abortion

JUDITH JARVIS THOMSON

Judith Jarvis Thomson (1929–) is professor of philosophy emeritus at the Massachusetts Institute of Technology. She is an influential philosopher, well known for her views about abortion. The following famous and very influential essay must be one of the most anthologized today. She has written extensively on topics in ethics, political philosophy, and metaphysics. Her books include *Rights, Restitution, and Risk* (1986), *The Realm of Rights* (1990), *Moral Relativism and Moral Objectivity* (1996), *Goodness and Advice* (2003), and *Normativity* (2008).

Here Judith Thomson asks what follows from "the premise that the fetus is a human being, a person, from the moment of conception." She also grants that the unborn has a right to life. She argues that it does not follow that abortion is always wrong. It is important to note that she grants, for the sake of the inquiry, her opponent's central premise. At the time that Thomson wrote this article, in the early 1970s, many opponents of abortion favored a blanket prohibition, with few, if any, exceptions (e.g., rape, the life or health of the mother). Today most antiabortion or pro-life positions allow for some exceptions, where abortion is permissible.

One of the reasons the abortion debate is so difficult is that there are few analogies to the relation between the unborn and its mother. Thomson makes up one—the famous example of the kidnapped violinist—and reasons about it. Much of her argument depends on the aptness of the analogy, as well as the value of contrived analogies of this kind (sometimes called "science-fiction" cases).

Some of the ideas or doctrines Thomson appeals to, it is interesting to note, figure in discussions of other controversies in this volume, for instance, the ethics of war, of self-defense, and of responsibility.

Most opposition to abortion relies on the premise that the fetus is a human being, a person, from the moment of conception. The premise is argued for, but, as I think, not well. Take, for example, the most common argument. We are asked to notice that the development of a human being from conception through birth into childhood is continuous; then it is said that to draw a line, to choose a point in this development and say "before this point the thing is not a person, after this point it is a person" is to make an arbitrary choice, a choice for which in the nature of things no good reason can be given. It is concluded that the fetus is, or anyway that we had better say it is, a person from the moment of conception. But this conclusion does not follow. Similar things might be said about the development of an

From Judith Jarvis Thomson, "A Defense of Abortion," *Philosophy and Public Affairs,* Vol. 1, No. 1. (Autumn, 1971), pp. 47–66. Reprinted by permission of Blackwell Publishing.

acorn into an oak tree, and it does not follow that acorns are oak trees, or that we had better say they are. Arguments of this form are sometimes called "slippery slope arguments"—the phrase is perhaps self-explanatory—and it is dismaying that opponents of abortion rely on them so heavily and uncritically.

I am inclined to agree, however, that the prospects for "drawing a line" in the development of the fetus look dim. I am inclined to think also that we shall probably have to agree that the fetus has already become a human person well before birth. Indeed, it comes as a surprise when one first learns how early in its life it begins to acquire human characteristics. By the tenth week, for example, it already has a face, arms and legs, fingers and toes; it has internal organs, and brain activity is detectable.[1] On the other hand, I think that the premise is false, that the fetus is not a person from the moment of conception. A newly fertilized ovum, a newly implanted clump of cells, is no more a person than an acorn is an oak tree. But I shall not discuss any of this. For it seems to me to be of great interest to ask what happens if, for the sake of argument, we allow the premise. How, precisely, are we supposed to get from there to the conclusion that abortion is morally impermissible? Opponents of abortion commonly spend most of their time establishing that the fetus is a person, and hardly any time explaining the step from there to the impermissibility of abortion. Perhaps they think the step too simple and obvious to require much comment. Or perhaps instead they are simply being economical in argument. Many of those who defend abortion rely on the premise that the fetus is not a person, but only a bit of tissue that will become a person at birth; and why pay out more arguments than you have to? Whatever the explanation, I suggest that the step they take is neither easy nor obvious, that it calls for closer examination than it is commonly given, and that when we do give it this closer examination we shall feel inclined to reject it.

I propose, then, that we grant that the fetus is a person from the moment of conception. How does the argument go from here? Something like this, I take it. Every person has a right to life. So the fetus has a right to life. No doubt the mother has a right to decide what shall happen in and to her body; everyone would grant that. But surely a person's right to life is stronger and more stringent than the mother's right to decide what happens in and to her body, and so outweighs it. So the fetus may not be killed; an abortion may not be performed.

It sounds plausible. But now let me ask you to imagine this. You wake up in the morning and find yourself back to back in bed with an unconscious violinist. A famous unconscious violinist. He has been found to have a fatal kidney ailment, and the Society of Music Lovers has canvassed all the available medical records and found that you alone have the right blood type to help. They have therefore kidnapped you, and last night the violinist's circulatory system was plugged into yours, so that your kidneys can be used to extract poisons from his blood as well as your own. The director of the hospital now tells you, "Look, we're sorry the Society of Music Lovers did this to you—we would never have permitted it if we had known. But still, they did it, and the violinist now is plugged into you. To unplug you would be to kill him. But never mind, it's only for nine months. By then he will have recovered from his ailment, and can safely be unplugged from you." Is it morally incumbent on you to accede to this situation? No doubt it would be very nice of you if you did, a great kindness. But do you *have* to accede to it? What if it were not nine months, but nine years? Or longer still? What if the director of the hospital says, "Tough luck, I agree, but you've now got to stay in bed, with the violinist plugged into you, for the rest of your life. Because remember this. All persons have a right to life, and violinists are persons. Granted you have a right to decide what happens in and to your body, but a person's right to life outweighs your right to decide what happens in and to your body. So you cannot ever be unplugged from him." I imagine you would regard this as outrageous, which suggests that something really is wrong with that plausible-sounding argument I mentioned a moment ago.

In this case, of course, you were kidnapped; you didn't volunteer for the operation that plugged the violinist into your kidneys. Can those who oppose abortion on the ground I mentioned make an exception for a pregnancy due to rape? Certainly. They can say that persons have a right to life only if they didn't come into existence because of rape; or they can say that all persons have a right to life, but that some have less of a right to life than others, in particular, that those who came into existence because of rape have less. But these statements have a rather unpleasant sound. Surely the question of whether you have a right to life at all, or how much of it you have, shouldn't turn on the question of whether or not you are the product of a rape. And in fact the people who oppose abortion on the ground I mentioned do not make this distinction, and hence do not make an exception in case of rape.

Nor do they make an exception for a case in which the mother has to spend the nine months of her pregnancy in bed. They would agree that would be a great pity, and hard on the mother; but all the same, all persons have a right to life, the fetus is a person, and so on. I suspect, in fact, that they would not make an exception for a case in which, miraculously enough, the pregnancy went on for nine years, or even the rest of the mother's life.

Some won't even make an exception for a case in which continuation of the pregnancy is likely to shorten the mother's life; they regard abortion as impermissible even to save the mother's life. Such cases are nowadays very rare, and many opponents of abortion do not accept this extreme view. All the same, it is a good place to begin: a number of points of interest come out in respect to it.

1. Let us call the view that abortion is impermissible even to save the mother's life "the extreme view." I want to suggest first that it does not issue from the argument I mentioned earlier without the addition of some fairly powerful premises. Suppose a woman has become pregnant, and now learns that she has a cardiac condition such that she will die if she carries the baby to term. What may be done for her? The fetus, being a person, has a right to life, but as the mother is a person too, so has she a right to life. Presumably they have an equal right to life. How is it supposed to come out that an abortion may not be performed? If mother and child have an equal right to life, shouldn't we perhaps flip a coin? Or should we add to the mother's right to life her right to decide what happens in and to her body, which everybody seems to be ready to

grant—the sum of her rights now outweighing the fetus' right to life?

The most familiar argument here is the following. We are told that performing the abortion would be directly killing[2] the child, whereas doing nothing would not be killing the mother, but only letting her die. Moreover, in killing the child, one would be killing an innocent person, for the child has committed no crime, and is not aiming at his mother's death. And then there are a variety of ways in which this might be continued. (1) But as directly killing an innocent person is always and absolutely impermissible, an abortion may not be performed. Or, (2) as directly killing an innocent person is murder, and murder is always and absolutely impermissible, an abortion may not be performed.[3] Or, (3) as one's duty to refrain from directly killing an innocent person is more stringent than one's duty to keep a person from dying, an abortion may not be performed. Or, (4) if one's only options are directly killing an innocent person or letting a person die, one must prefer letting the person die, and thus an abortion may not be performed.[4]

Some people seem to have thought that these are not further premises which must be added if the conclusion is to be reached, but that they follow from the very fact that an innocent person has a right to life.[5] But this seems to me to be a mistake, and perhaps the simplest way to show this is to bring out that while we must certainly grant that innocent persons have a right to life, the theses in (1) through (4) are all false. Take (2), for example. If directly killing an innocent person is murder, and thus is impermissible, then the mother's directly killing the innocent person inside her is murder, and thus is impermissible. But it cannot seriously be thought to be murder if the mother performs an abortion on herself to save her life. It cannot seriously be said that she *must* refrain, that she *must* sit passively by and wait for her death. Let us look again at the case of you and the violinist. There you are, in bed with the violinist, and the director of the hospital says to you, "It's all most distressing, and I deeply sympathize, but you see this is putting an additional strain on your kidneys, and you'll be dead within the month. But you *have* to stay where you are all the same. Because unplugging you would be directly killing an innocent violinist, and that's murder, and that's impermissible." If anything in the world is true, it is that you do not commit murder, you do not do what is impermissible, if you reach around to your back and unplug yourself from that violinist to save your life.

The main focus of attention in writings on abortion has been on what a third party may or may not do in answer to a request from a woman for an abortion. This is in a way understandable. Things being as they are, there isn't much a woman can safely do to abort herself. So the question asked is what a third party may do, and what the mother may do, if it is mentioned at all, is deduced, almost as an afterthought, from what it is concluded that third parties may do. But it seems to me that to treat the matter in this way is to refuse to grant to the mother that very status of person which is so firmly insisted on for the fetus. For we cannot simply read off what a person may do from what a third party may do. Suppose you find yourself trapped in a tiny house with a growing child. I mean a very tiny house, and a rapidly growing child—you are already up against the wall of the house and in a few minutes you'll be crushed to death. The child on the other hand won't be crushed to death; if nothing is done to stop him from growing he'll be hurt, but in the end he'll simply burst open the house and walk out a free man. Now I could well understand it if a bystander were to say, "There's nothing we can do for you. We cannot choose between your life and his, we cannot be the ones to decide who is to live, we cannot intervene." But it cannot be concluded that you too can do nothing, that you cannot attack it to save your life. However innocent the child may be, you do not have to wait passively while it crushes you to death. Perhaps a pregnant woman is vaguely felt to have the status of house, to which we don't allow the right of self-defense. But if the woman houses the child, it should be remembered that she is a person who houses it.

I should perhaps stop to say explicitly that I am not claiming that people have a right to do anything whatever to save their lives. I think, rather, that there are drastic limits to the right of self-defense. If someone threatens you with death unless you torture someone else to death, I think you have not the right, even to save your life, to do so. But the case under consideration here is very different. In our case there are only two people involved, one whose life is threatened, and one who threatens it. Both are innocent: the one who is threatened is not threatened because of any fault, the one who threatens does not threaten because of any fault. For this reason we may feel that we bystanders cannot intervene. But the person threatened can.

In sum, a woman surely can defend her life against the threat to it posed by the unborn child, even if doing so involves its death. And this shows not merely that the theses in (1) through (4) are false; it shows also that the extreme view of abortion is false, and so we need not canvass any other possible ways of arriving at it from the argument I mentioned at the outset.

2. The extreme view could of course be weakened to say that while abortion is permissible to save the mother's life, it may not be performed by a third party, but only by the mother herself. But this cannot be right either. For what we have to keep in mind is that the mother and the unborn child are not like two tenants in a small house which has, by an unfortunate mistake, been rented to both: the mother *owns* the house. The fact that she does adds to the offensiveness of deducing that the mother can do nothing from the supposition that third parties can do nothing. But it does more than this: it casts a bright light on the supposition that third parties can do nothing. Certainly it lets us see that a third party who says "I cannot choose between you" is fooling himself if he thinks this is impartiality. If Jones has found and fastened on a certain coat, which he needs to keep him from freezing, but which Smith also needs to keep him from freezing, then it is not impartiality that says "I cannot choose between you" when Smith owns the coat. Women have said again and again "This body is *my* body!" and they have reason to feel angry, reason to feel that it has been like shouting into the wind. Smith, after all, is hardly likely to bless us if we say to him, "Of course it's your coat, anybody would grant that it is. But no one may choose between you and Jones who is to have it."

We should really ask what it is that says "no one may choose" in the face of the fact that the body that houses the child is the mother's body. It may be simply a failure to appreciate this fact. But it may be something more interesting, namely the sense that one has a right to refuse to lay hands on people, even where it would be just and fair to do so, even where justice seems to require that somebody do so. Thus justice might call for somebody to get Smith's coat back from Jones, and yet you have a right to refuse to be the one to lay hands on Jones, a right to refuse to do physical violence to him. This, I think, must be granted. But then what should be said is not "no one may choose," but only "*I* cannot choose," and indeed not even this, but "*I* will not *act*," leaving it open that somebody else can or should, and in particular that anyone in a position of authority, with the job of securing people's rights, both can and should. So this is no difficulty. I have not been arguing that any given third party must accede to the mother's request that he perform an abortion to save her life, but only that he may.

I suppose that in some views of human life the mother's body is only on loan to her, the loan not being one which gives her any prior claim to it. One who held this view might well think it impartiality to say "I cannot choose." But I shall simply ignore this possibility. My own view is that if a human being has any just, prior claim to anything at all, he has a just, prior claim to his own body. And perhaps this needn't be argued for here anyway, since, as I mentioned, the arguments against abortion we are looking at do grant that the woman has a right to decide what happens in and to her body.

But although they do grant it, I have tried to show that they do not take seriously what is done in granting it. I suggest the same thing will reappear even more clearly when we turn away from cases in which the mother's life is at stake, and attend, as I propose we now do, to the vastly more common cases in which a woman wants an abortion for some less weighty reason than preserving her own life.

3. Where the mother's life is not at stake, the argument I mentioned at the outset seems to have a much stronger pull. "Everyone has a right to life, so the unborn person has a right to life." And isn't the child's right to life weightier than anything other than the mother's own right to life, which she might put forward as ground for an abortion?

This argument treats the right to life as if it were unproblematic. It is not, and this seems to me to be precisely the source of the mistake.

For we should now, at long last, ask what it comes to, to have a right to life. In some views having a right to life includes having a right to be given at least the bare minimum one needs for continued life. But suppose that what in fact *is* the bare minimum a man needs for continued life is something he has no right at all to be given? If I am sick unto death, and the only thing that will save my life is the touch of Henry Fonda's cool hand on my fevered brow, then all the same, I have no right to be given the touch of Henry Fonda's cool hand on my fevered brow. It would be frightfully nice of him to fly in from the West Coast to provide it. It would be less nice, though no doubt well meant, if my friends flew out to the West Coast and carried Henry Fonda back with them. But I have no right at all against anybody that he should do this for me. Or again, to return to the story I told earlier, the fact that for continued life that violinist needs the continued use of your kidneys does not establish that he has a right to be given the continued use of your kidneys. He certainly has no right against you that *you* should give him continued use of your kidneys. For nobody has any right to use your kidneys unless you give him such a right; and nobody has the right against you that you shall give him this right—if you do allow him to go on using your kidneys, this is a kindness on your part, and not something he can claim from you as his due. Nor has he any right against anybody else that *they* should give him continued use of your kidneys. Certainly he had no right against the Society of Music Lovers that they should plug him into you in the first place. And if you now start to unplug yourself, having learned that you will otherwise have to spend nine years in bed with him, there is nobody in the world who must try to prevent you, in order to see to it that he is given something he has a right to be given.

Some people are rather stricter about the right to life. In their view, it does not include the right to be given anything, but amounts to, and only to, the right not to be killed by anybody. But here a related difficulty arises. If everybody is to refrain from killing that violinist, then everybody must refrain from doing a great many different sorts of things. Everybody must refrain from slitting his throat, everybody must refrain from shooting him—and everybody must refrain from unplugging you from him. But does he have a right against everybody that they shall refrain from unplugging you from him? To refrain from doing this is to allow him to continue to use your kidneys. It could be argued that he has a right against us that *we* should allow him to continue to use your kidneys. That is, while he had no right against us that we should give him the use of your kidneys, it might be argued that he anyway has a right against us that we shall not now intervene and deprive him of the use of your kidneys. I shall come back to third-party interventions later. But certainly the violinist has no right against you that *you* shall allow him to continue to use your kidneys. As I said, if you do allow him to use them, it is a kindness on your part, and not something you owe him.

The difficulty I point to here is not peculiar to the right to life. It reappears in connection with all the other natural rights; and it is something which an adequate account of rights must deal with. For present purposes it is enough just to draw attention to it. But I would stress that I am not arguing that people do not have a right to life—quite to the contrary, it seems to me that the primary control we must place on the acceptability of an account of rights is that it should turn out in that account to be a truth that all persons have a right to life. I am arguing only that having a right to life does not guarantee having either a right to be given the use of or a right to be allowed continued use of another person's body—even if one needs it for life itself. So the right to life will not serve the opponents of abortion in the very simple and clear way in which they seem to have thought it would.

4. There is another way to bring out the difficulty. In the most ordinary sort of case, to deprive someone of what he has a right to is to treat him unjustly. Suppose a boy and his small brother are jointly given a box of chocolates for Christmas. If the older boy takes the box and refuses to give his brother any of the chocolates, he is unjust to him, for the brother has been given a right to half of them. But suppose that, having learned that otherwise it means nine years in bed with that violinist, you unplug yourself from him. You surely are not being unjust to him, for you gave him no right to use your kidneys, and no one else can have given him any such right. But we have to notice that in unplugging yourself, you are killing him; and violinists, like everybody else, have a right to life, and thus in the view we were considering just now, the right not to be killed. So here you do what he supposedly has a right you shall not do, but you do not act unjustly to him in doing it.

The emendation which may be made at this point is this: the right to life consists not in the right not to be killed, but rather in the right not to be killed unjustly. This runs a risk of circularity, but never mind: it would enable us to square the fact that the violinist has a right to life with the fact that you do not act unjustly toward him in unplugging yourself, thereby killing him. For if you do not kill him unjustly, you do not violate his right to life, and so it is no wonder you do him no injustice.

But if this emendation is accepted, the gap in the argument against abortion stares us plainly in the face: it is by no means enough to show that the fetus is a person, and to remind us that all persons have a right to life—we need to be shown also that killing the fetus violates its right to life, i.e., that abortion is unjust killing. And is it?

I suppose we may take it as a datum that in a case of pregnancy due to rape the mother has not given the unborn person a right to the use of her body for food and shelter. Indeed, in what pregnancy could it be supposed that the mother has given the unborn person such a right? It is not as if there were unborn persons drifting about the world, to whom a woman who wants a child says "I invite you in."

But it might be argued that there are other ways one can have acquired a right to the use of another person's body than by having been invited to use it by that person. Suppose a woman voluntarily indulges in intercourse, knowing of the chance it will issue in pregnancy, and then she does become pregnant; is she not in part responsible for the presence, in fact the very existence, of the unborn person inside her? No doubt she did not invite it in. But doesn't her partial responsibility for its being there itself give it a right to the use of her body?[6] If so, then her aborting it would be more like the boy's taking away the chocolates, and less like your unplugging yourself from the violinist—doing so would be depriving it of what it does have a right to, and thus would be doing it an injustice.

And then, too, it might be asked whether or not she can kill it even to save her own life: If she voluntarily called it into existence, how can she now kill it, even in self-defense?

The first thing to be said about this is that it is something new. Opponents of abortion have been so concerned to make out the independence of the fetus, in order to establish that it has a right to life, just as its mother does, that they have tended to overlook the possible support they might gain from making out that the fetus is *dependent* on the mother, in order to establish that she has a special kind of responsibility for it, a responsibility that gives it rights against her which are not possessed by any independent person—such as an ailing violinist who is a stranger to her.

On the other hand, this argument would give the unborn person a right to its mother's body only if her pregnancy resulted from a voluntary act, undertaken in full knowledge of the chance a pregnancy might result from it. It would leave out entirely the unborn person whose existence is due to rape. Pending the availability of some further argument, then, we would be left with the conclusion that unborn persons whose existence is due to rape have no right to the use of their mothers' bodies, and thus that aborting them is not depriving them of anything they have a right to and hence is not unjust killing.

And we should also notice that it is not at all plain that this argument really does go even as far as it purports to. For there are cases and cases, and the details make a difference. If the room is stuffy, and I therefore open a window to air it, and a burglar climbs in, it would be absurd to say, "Ah, now he can stay, she's given him a right to the use of her house— for she is partially responsible for his presence there, having voluntarily done what enabled him to get in, in full knowledge that there are such things as burglars, and that burglars burgle." It would be still more absurd to say this if I had had bars installed outside my windows, precisely to prevent burglars from getting in, and a burglar got in only because of a defect in the bars. It remains equally absurd if we imagine it is not a burglar who climbs in, but an innocent person who blunders or falls in. Again, suppose it were like this: people-seeds drift about in the air like pollen, and if you open your windows, one may drift in and take root in your carpets or upholstery. You don't want children, so you fix up your windows with fine mesh screens, the very best you can buy. As can happen, however, and on very, very rare occasions does happen, one of the screens is defective; and a seed drifts in and takes root. Does the person-plant who now develops have a right to the use of your house? Surely not—despite the fact that you voluntarily opened your windows, you knowingly kept carpets and upholstered furniture, and you knew that screens were sometimes defective. Someone may argue that you are responsible for its rooting, that it does have a right to your house, because after all you *could* have lived out your life with bare floors and furniture, or with sealed windows and doors. But this won't do—for by the same token anyone can avoid a pregnancy due to rape by having a hysterectomy, or anyway by never leaving home without a (reliable!) army.

It seems to me that the argument we are looking at can establish at most that there are *some* cases in which the unborn person has a right to the use of its mother's body, and therefore *some* cases in which abortion is unjust killing. There is room for much discussion and argument as to precisely which, if any. But I think we should sidestep this issue and leave it open, for at any rate the argument certainly does not establish that all abortion is unjust killing.

5. There is room for yet another argument here, however. We surely must all grant that there may be cases in which it would be morally indecent to detach a person from your body at the cost of his life. Suppose you learn that what the violinist needs is not nine years of your life, but only one hour: all you need do to save his life is to spend one hour in that bed with him. Suppose also that letting him use your kidneys for that one hour would not affect your health in the slightest. Admittedly you were kidnapped. Admittedly you did not give anyone permission to plug him into you. Nevertheless it seems to me plain you *ought* to allow him to use your kidneys for that hour—it would be indecent to refuse.

Again, suppose pregnancy lasted only an hour, and constituted no threat to life or health. And suppose that a woman becomes pregnant as a result of rape. Admittedly she did not voluntarily do anything to bring about the existence of a child. Admittedly she did nothing at all which would give the unborn person a right to the use of her body. All the same it might well be said, as in the newly emended violinist story, that she *ought* to allow it to remain for that hour—that it would be indecent in her to refuse.

Now some people are inclined to use the term "right" in such a way that it follows from the fact that you ought to allow a person to use your body for the hour he needs, that he has a right to use your body for the hour he needs, even though he has not been given that right by any person or act. They may say that it follows also that if you refuse, you act unjustly toward him. This use of the term is perhaps so common that it cannot be called wrong; nevertheless it seems to me to be an unfortunate loosening of what we would do better to keep a tight rein on. Suppose that box of chocolates I mentioned earlier had not been given to both boys jointly, but was given only to the older boy. There he sits, stolidly eating his way through the box, his small brother watching enviously. Here we are likely to say "You ought not to be so mean. You ought to give your brother some of those chocolates." My own view is that it just does not follow from the truth of this that the brother has any right to any of the chocolates. If the boy refuses to give his brother any, he is greedy, stingy, callous—but not unjust. I suppose that the people I have in mind will say it does follow that the brother has a right to some of the chocolates, and thus that the boy does act unjustly if he refuses to give his brother any. But the effect of saying this is to obscure what we should keep distinct, namely the difference between the boy's refusal in this case and the boy's refusal in the earlier case, in which the box was given to both boys jointly, and in which the small brother thus had what was from any point of view clear title to half.

A further objection to so using the term "right" that from the fact that A ought to do a thing for B, it follows that B has a right against A that A do it for him, is that it is going to make the question of whether or not a man has a right to a thing turn on how easy it is to provide him with it; and this seems not merely unfortunate, but morally unacceptable.

Take the case of Henry Fonda again. I said earlier that I had no right to the touch of his cool hand on my fevered brow, even though I needed it to save my life. I said it would be frightfully nice of him to fly in from the West Coast to provide me with it, but that I had no right against him that he should do so. But suppose he isn't on the West Coast. Suppose he has only to walk across the room, place a hand briefly on my brow—and lo, my life is saved. Then surely he ought to do it, it would be indecent to refuse. Is it to be said "Ah, well, it follows that in this case she has a right to the touch of his hand on her brow, and so it would be an injustice in him to refuse"? So that I have a right to it when it is easy for him to provide it, though no right when it's hard? It's rather a shocking idea that anyone's rights should fade away and disappear as it gets harder and harder to accord them to him.

So my own view is that even though you ought to let the violinist use your kidneys for the one hour he needs, we should not conclude that he has a right to do so—we should say that if you refuse, you are, like the boy who owns all the chocolates and will give none away, self-centered and callous, indecent in fact, but not unjust. And similarly, that even supposing a case in which a woman pregnant due to rape ought to allow the unborn person to use her body for the hour he needs, we should not conclude that he has a right to do so; we should conclude that she is self-centered, callous, indecent, but not unjust, if she refuses. The complaints are no less grave; they are just different. However, there is no need to insist on this point. If anyone does wish to deduce "he has a right" from "you ought," then all the same he must surely grant that there are cases in which it is not morally required of you that you allow that violinist to use your kidneys, and in which he does not have a right to use them, and in which you do not do him an injustice if you refuse. And so also for mother and unborn child. Except in such cases as the unborn person has a right to demand it—and we were leaving open the possibility that there may be such cases—nobody is morally *required* to make large sacrifices, of health, of all other interests and concerns, of all other duties and commitments, for nine years, or even for nine months, in order to keep another person alive.

6. We have in fact to distinguish between two kinds of Samaritan: the Good Samaritan and what we might call the Minimally Decent Samaritan. The story of the Good Samaritan, you will remember, goes like this:

> A certain man went down from Jerusalem to Jericho, and fell among thieves, which stripped him of his raiment, and wounded him, and departed, leaving him half dead.
>
> And by chance there came down a certain priest that way; and when he saw him, he passed by on the other side.
>
> And likewise a Levite, when he was at the place, came and looked on him, and passed by on the other side.
>
> But a certain Samaritan, as he journeyed, came where he was; and when he saw him he had compassion on him.
>
> And went to him, and bound up his wounds, pouring in oil and wine, and set him on his own beast, and brought him to an inn, and took care of him.
>
> And on the morrow, when he departed, he took out two pence, and gave them to the host, and said unto him, "Take care of him; and whatsoever thou spendest more, when I come again, I will repay thee." (Luke 10:30–35)

The Good Samaritan went out of his way, at some cost to himself, to help one in need of it. We are not told what the options were, that is, whether or not the priest and the Levite could have helped by doing less than the Good Samaritan did, but assuming they could have, then the fact they did nothing at all shows they were not even Minimally Decent Samaritans, not because they were not Samaritans, but because they were not even minimally decent.

These things are a matter of degree, of course, but there is a difference, and it comes out perhaps most clearly in the story of Kitty Genovese, who, as you will remember, was murdered while thirty-eight people watched or listened, and did nothing at all to help her. A Good Samaritan would have rushed out to give direct assistance against the murderer. Or perhaps we had better allow that it would have been a Splendid Samaritan who did this, on the ground that it would have involved a risk of death for himself. But the thirty-eight not only did not do this, they did not even trouble to pick up a phone to call the police. Minimally Decent Samaritanism would call for doing at least that, and their not having done it was monstrous.

After telling the story of the Good Samaritan, Jesus said "Go, and do thou likewise." Perhaps he meant that we are morally required to act as the Good Samaritan did. Perhaps he was urging people to do more than is morally required of them. At all events it seems plain that it was not morally required of any of the thirty-eight that he rush out to give direct assistance at the risk of his own life, and that it is not morally required of anyone that he give long stretches of his life—nine years or nine months—to sustaining the life of a person who has no special right (we were leaving open the possibility of this) to demand it.

Indeed, with one rather striking class of exceptions, no one in any country in the world is *legally* required to do anywhere near as much as this for anyone else. The class of exceptions is obvious. My main concern here is not the state of the law in respect to abortion, but it is worth drawing attention to the fact that in no state in this country is any man compelled by law to be even a Minimally Decent Samaritan to any person; there is no law under which charges could be brought against the thirty-eight who stood by while Kitty Genovese died. By contrast, in most states in this country women are compelled by law to be not merely Minimally Decent Samaritans, but Good Samaritans to unborn persons inside them. This doesn't by itself settle anything one way or the other, because it may well be argued that there should be laws in this country—as there are in many European countries—compelling at least Minimally Decent Samaritanism.[7] But it does show that there is a gross injustice in the existing state of the law. And it shows also that the groups currently working against liberalization of abortion laws, in fact working toward having it declared unconstitutional for a state to permit abortion, had better start working for the adoption of Good Samaritan laws generally, or earn the charge that they are acting in bad faith.

I should think, myself, that Minimally Decent Samaritan laws would be one thing, Good Samaritan laws quite another, and in fact highly improper.

But we are not here concerned with the law. What we should ask is not whether anybody should be compelled by law to be a Good Samaritan, but whether we must accede to a situation in which somebody is being compelled—by nature, perhaps—to be a Good Samaritan. We have, in other words, to look now at third-party interventions. I have been arguing that no person is morally required to make large sacrifices to sustain the life of another who has no right to demand them, and this even where the sacrifices do not include life itself; we are not morally required to be Good Samaritans or anyway Very Good Samaritans to one another. But what if a man cannot extricate himself from such a situation? What if he appeals to us to extricate him? It seems to me plain that there are cases in which we can, cases in which a Good Samaritan would extricate him. There you are, you were kidnapped, and nine years in bed with that violinist lie ahead of you. You have your own life to lead. You are sorry, but you simply cannot see giving up so much of your life to the sustaining of his. You cannot extricate yourself, and ask us to do so. I should have thought that—in light of his having no right to the use of your body—it was obvious that we do not have to accede to your being forced to give up so much. We can do what you ask. There is no injustice to the violinist in our doing so.

7. Following the lead of the opponents of abortion, I have throughout been speaking of the fetus merely as a person, and what I have been asking is whether or not the argument we began with, which proceeds only from the fetus' being a person, really does establish its conclusion. I have argued that it does not.

But of course there are arguments and arguments, and it may be said that I have simply fastened on the wrong one. It may be said that what is important is not merely the fact that the fetus is a person, but that it is a person for whom the woman has a special kind of responsibility issuing from the fact that she is its mother. And it might be argued that all my analogies are therefore irrelevant—for you do not have that special kind of responsibility for that violinist, Henry Fonda does not have that special kind of responsibility for me. And our attention might be drawn to the fact that men and women both *are* compelled by law to provide support for their children.

I have in effect dealt (briefly) with this argument in section 4 above; but a (still briefer) recapitulation now may be in order. Surely we do not have any such "special responsibility" for a person unless we have assumed it, explicitly or implicitly. If a set of parents do not try to prevent pregnancy, do not obtain an abortion, and then at the time of birth of the child do not put it out for adoption, but rather take it home with them, then they have assumed responsibility for it, they have given it rights, and they cannot *now* withdraw support from it at the cost of its life because they now find it difficult to go on providing for it. But if they have taken all reasonable precautions against having a child, they do not simply by virtue of their biological relationship to the child who comes into existence have a special responsibility for it. They may wish to assume responsibility for it, or they may not wish to. And I am suggesting that if assuming responsibility for it would require large sacrifices, then they may refuse. A Good Samaritan would not refuse—or anyway, a Splendid Samaritan, if the sacrifices that had to be made were enormous. But then so would a Good Samaritan assume responsibility for that violinist; so would Henry Fonda, if he is a Good Samaritan, fly in from the West Coast and assume responsibility for me.

8. My argument will be found unsatisfactory on two counts by many of those who want to regard abortion as morally permissible. First, while I do argue that abortion is not impermissible, I do not argue that it is always permissible. There may well be cases in which carrying the child to term requires only Minimally Decent Samaritanism of the mother, and this is a standard we must not fall below. I am inclined to think it a merit of my account precisely that it does *not* give a general yes or a general no. It allows for and supports our sense that, for example, a sick and desperately frightened fourteen-year-old schoolgirl, pregnant due to rape, may *of course* choose abortion, and that any law which rules this out is an insane law. And it also allows for and supports our sense that in other cases resort to abortion is even positively indecent. It would be indecent in the woman to request an abortion, and indecent in a doctor to perform it, if she is in her seventh month,

and wants the abortion just to avoid the nuisance of postponing a trip abroad. The very fact that the arguments I have been drawing attention to treat all cases of abortion, or even all cases of abortion in which the mother's life is not at stake, as morally on a par ought to have made them suspect at the outset.

Secondly, while I am arguing for the permissibility of abortion in some cases, I am not arguing for the right to secure the death of the unborn child. It is easy to confuse these two things in that up to a certain point in the life of the fetus it is not able to survive outside the mother's body; hence removing it from her body guarantees its death. But they are importantly different. I have argued that you are not morally required to spend nine months in bed, sustaining the life of that violinist; but to say this is by no means to say that if, when you unplug yourself, there is a miracle and he survives, you then have a right to turn round and slit his throat. You may detach yourself even if this costs him his life; you have no right to be guaranteed his death, by some other means, if unplugging yourself does not kill him. There are some people who will feel dissatisfied by this feature of my argument. A woman may be utterly devastated by the thought of a child, a bit of herself, put out for adoption and never seen or heard of again. She may therefore want not merely that the child be detached from her, but more, that it die. Some opponents of abortion are inclined to regard this as beneath contempt—thereby showing insensitivity to what is surely a powerful source of despair. All the same, I agree that the desire for the child's death is not one which anybody may gratify, should it turn out to be possible to detach the child alive.

At this place, however, it should be remembered that we have only been pretending throughout that the fetus is a human being from the moment of conception. A very early abortion is surely not the killing of a person, and so is not dealt with by anything I have said here.

Notes

I am very much indebted to James Thomson for discussion, criticism, and many helpful suggestions.

1. Daniel Callahan, *Abortion: Law, Choice and Morality* (New York, 1970), p. 373. This book gives a fascinating survey of the available information on abortion. The Jewish tradition is surveyed in David M. Feldman, *Birth Control in Jewish Law* (New York, 1968), Part 5, the Catholic tradition in John T. Noonan, Jr., "An Almost Absolute Value in History," in *The Morality of Abortion*, ed. John T. Noonan, Jr. (Cambridge, Mass., 1970).

2. The term "direct" in the arguments I refer to is a technical one. Roughly, what is meant by "direct killing" is either killing as an end in itself, or killing as a means to some end, for example, the end of saving someone else's life. See note 5, below, for an example of its use.

3. Cf. *Encyclical Letter of Pope Pius XI on Christian Marriage*, St. Paul Editions (Boston, n.d.), p. 32: "however much we may pity the mother whose health and even life is gravely imperiled in the performance of the duty allotted to her by nature, nevertheless what could ever be a sufficient reason for excusing in any way the direct murder of the innocent? This is precisely what we are dealing with here." Noonan (*The Morality of Abortion*, p. 43) reads this as follows: "What cause can ever avail to excuse in any way the direct killing of the innocent? For it is a question of that."

4. The thesis in (4) is in an interesting way weaker than those in (1), (2), and (3): they rule out abortion even in cases in which both mother *and* child will die if the abortion is not performed. By contrast, one who held the view expressed in (4) could consistently say that one needn't prefer letting two persons die to killing one.

5. Cf. the following passage from Pius XII, *Address to the Italian Catholic Society of Midwives*: "The baby in the maternal breast has the right to life immediately from God.—Hence there is no man, no human authority, no science, no medical, eugenic, social, economic or moral 'indication' which can establish or grant a valid juridical ground for a direct deliberate disposition of an innocent human life, that is a disposition which looks to its destruction either as an end or as a means to another end perhaps in itself not illicit.—The baby, still not born, is a man in the same degree and for the same reason as the mother" (quoted in Noonan, *The Morality of Abortion*, p. 45).

6. The need for a discussion of this argument was brought home to me by members of the Society for Ethical and Legal Philosophy, to whom this paper was originally presented.

7. For a discussion of the difficulties involved, and a survey of the European experience with such laws, see *The Good Samaritan and the Law*, ed. James M. Ratcliffe (New York, 1966).

QUESTIONS

1. Reconstruct the main argument for the permissibility of abortion. In what circumstances is abortion permissible according to this argument?
2. Are Thomson's conclusions "a defense of abortion"? Is the title of her essay misleading in any way?
3. What ideas or doctrines would one have to give up in order to resist Thomson's conclusions?

58. On the Moral and Legal Status of Abortion (and Postscript on Infanticide, 1982)

MARY ANN WARREN

Mary Ann Warren (1946–2010) was professor of philosophy emeritus at San Francisco State University. She is well-known for her writings on abortion, the treatment of animals, and other topics in practical ethics. She is the author of *Gendercide: The Implications of Sex Selection* (1985) and *Moral Status: Obligations to Persons and Other Living Things* (2000).

This article is also an early discussion of abortion, published shortly after Thomson's essay. It attempts to give a much more general defense of abortion. Warren introduces the notion of "the moral community," a notion very much like that of moral standing used in the contemporary literature. To be a member of the moral community—to have moral standing—something needs to be a person. Warren offers a general characterization of personhood, one that can be used for other debates in this reader.

Reprinted with the original 1973 article is a 1982 postscript, responding to criticism that her defense of abortion has unacceptable implications.

The question which we must answer in order to produce a satisfactory solution to the problem of the moral status of abortion is this: How are we to define the moral community, the set of beings with full and equal moral rights, such that we can decide whether a human fetus is a member of this community or not? What sort of entity, exactly, has the inalienable rights to life, liberty, and the pursuit of happiness? Jefferson attributed these rights to all *men*, and it may or may not be fair to suggest that he intended to attribute

From Mary Ann Warren, "On the Moral and Legal Status of Abortion," *Monist* 57, 1 (1973), pp. 43–61. Copyright © 1973 *The Monist: An International Quarterly Journal of General Philosophical Inquiry*, Peru, Illinois, USA, 61354. Reprinted by permission.

them *only* to men. Perhaps he ought to have attributed them to all human beings. If so, then we arrive, first, at [John] Noonan's problem of defining what makes a being human, and, second, at the equally vital question which Noonan does not consider, namely, What reason is there for identifying the moral community with the set of all human beings, in whatever way we have chosen to define that term?

1. On the Definition of "Human"

One reason why this vital second question is so frequently overlooked in the debate over the moral status of abortion is that the term "human" has two distinct, but not often distinguished, senses. This fact results in a slide of meaning, which serves to conceal the fallaciousness of the traditional argument that since (1) it is wrong to kill innocent human beings, and (2) fetuses are innocent human beings, then (3) it is wrong to kill fetuses. For if "human" is used in the same sense in both (1) and (2) then, whichever of the two senses is meant, one of these premises is question-begging. And if it is used in two different senses then of course the conclusion doesn't follow.

Thus, (1) is a self-evident moral truth,[1] and avoids begging the question about abortion, only if "human being" is used to mean something like "a full-fledged member of the moral community." (It may or may not also be meant to refer exclusively to members of the species *Homo sapiens*.) We may call this the *moral* sense of "human." It is not to be confused with what we will call the *genetic* sense, i.e., the sense in which *any* member of the species is a human being, and no member of any other species could be. If (1) is acceptable only if the moral sense is intended, (2) is non-question-begging only if what is intended is the genetic sense.

In "Deciding Who Is Human," Noonan argues for the classification of fetuses with human beings by pointing to the presence of the full genetic code, and the potential capacity for rational thought.[2] It is clear that what he needs to show, for his version of the traditional argument to be valid, is that fetuses are human in the moral sense, the sense in which it is analytically true that all human beings have full moral rights. But, in the absence of any argument showing that whatever is genetically human is also

morally human, and he gives none, nothing more than genetic humanity can be demonstrated by the presence of the human genetic code. And, as we will see, the *potential* capacity for rational thought can at most show that an entity has the potential for *becoming* human in the moral sense.

2. Defining the Moral Community

Can it be established that genetic humanity is sufficient for moral humanity? I think that there are very good reasons for not defining the moral community in this way. I would like to suggest an alternative way of defining the moral community, which I will argue for only to the extent of explaining why it is, or should be, self-evident. The suggestion is simply that the moral community consists of all and only *people*, rather than all and only human beings;[3] and probably the best way of demonstrating its self-evidence is by considering the concept of personhood, to see what sorts of entity are and are not persons, and what the decision that a being is or is not a person implies about its moral rights.

What characteristics entitle an entity to be considered a person? This is obviously not the place to attempt a complete analysis of the concept of personhood, but we do not need such a fully adequate analysis just to determine whether and why a fetus is or isn't a person. All we need is a rough and approximate list of the most basic criteria of personhood, and some idea of which, or how many, of these an entity must satisfy in order to properly be considered a person.

In searching for such criteria, it is useful to look beyond the set of people with whom we are acquainted, and ask how we would decide whether a totally alien being was a person or not. (For we have no right to assume that genetic humanity is necessary for personhood.) Imagine a space traveler who lands on an unknown planet and encounters a race of beings utterly unlike any he has ever seen or heard of. If he wants to be sure of behaving morally toward these beings, he has to somehow decide whether they are people, and hence have full moral rights, or whether they are the sort of thing which he need not feel guilty about treating as, for example, a source of food.

How should he go about making this decision? If he has some anthropological background, he might look for such things as religion, art, and the manufacturing of tools, weapons, or shelters, since these factors have been used to distinguish our human from our prehuman ancestors, in what seems to be closer to the moral than the genetic sense of "human." And no doubt he would be right to consider the presence of such factors as good evidence that the alien beings were people, and morally human. It would, however, be overly anthropocentric of him to take the absence of these things as adequate evidence that they were not, since we can imagine people who have progressed beyond, or evolved without ever developing, these cultural characteristics.

I suggest that the traits which are most central to the concept of personhood, or humanity in the moral sense, are, very roughly, the following:

1. consciousness (of objects and events external and/or internal to the being), and in particular the capacity to feel pain;
2. reasoning (the *developed* capacity to solve new and relatively complex problems);
3. self-motivated activity (activity which is relatively independent of either genetic or direct external control);
4. the capacity to communicate, by whatever means, messages of an indefinite variety of types, that is, not just with an indefinite number of possible contents, but on indefinitely many possible topics;
5. the presence of self-concepts, and self-awareness, either individual or racial, or both.

Admittedly, there are apt to be a great many problems involved in formulating precise definitions of these criteria, let alone in developing universally valid behavioral criteria for deciding when they apply. But I will assume that both we and our explorer know approximately what (1)–(5) mean, and that he is also able to determine whether or not they apply. How, then, should he use his findings to decide whether or not the alien beings are people? We needn't suppose that an entity must have *all* of these attributes to be properly considered a person; (1) and (2) alone may well be sufficient for personhood, and quite probably (1)–(3) are sufficient. Neither do we need to insist that any one of these

criteria is *necessary* for personhood, although once again (1) and (2) look like fairly good candidates for necessary conditions, as does (3) if "activity" is construed so as to include the activity of reasoning.

All we need to claim, to demonstrate that a fetus is not a person, is that any being which satisfies *none* of (1)–(5) is certainly not a person. I consider this claim to be so obvious that I think anyone who denied it, and claimed that a being which satisfied none of (1)–(5) was a person all the same, would thereby demonstrate that he had no notion at all of what a person is—perhaps because he had confused the concept of a person with that of genetic humanity. If the opponents of abortion were to deny the appropriateness of these five criteria, I do not know what further arguments would convince them. We would probably have to admit that our conceptual schemes were indeed irreconcilably different, and that our dispute could not be settled objectively.

I do not expect this to happen, however, since I think that the concept of a person is one which is very nearly universal (to people), and that it is common to both proabortionists and antiabortionists, even though neither group has fully realized the relevance of this concept to the resolution of their dispute. Furthermore, I think that on reflection even the antiabortionists ought to agree not only that (1)–(5) are central to the concept of personhood, but also that it is a part of this concept that all and only people have full moral rights. The concept of a person is in part a moral concept; once we have admitted that *x* is a person we have recognized, even if we have not agreed to respect, *x*'s right to be treated as a member of the moral community. It is true that the claim that *x is a human being* is more commonly voiced as part of an appeal to treat *x* decently than is the claim that *x* is a person, but this is either because "human being" is here used in the sense which implies personhood, or because the genetic and moral senses of "human" have been confused.

Now if (1)–(5) are indeed the primary criteria of personhood, then it is clear that genetic humanity is neither necessary nor sufficient for establishing that an entity is a person. Some human beings are not people, and there may well be people who are not human beings. A man or woman whose consciousness has been permanently obliterated but who remains alive is a human being which is no longer a person; defective human beings, with no appreciable mental capacity, are not and presumably never will be people; and a fetus is a human being which is not yet a person, and which therefore cannot coherently be said to have full moral rights. Citizens of the next century should be prepared to recognize highly advanced, self-aware robots or computers, should such be developed, and intelligent inhabitants of other worlds, should such be found, as people in the fullest sense, and to respect their moral rights. But to ascribe full moral rights to an entity which is not a person is as absurd as to ascribe moral obligations and responsibilities to such an entity.

3. Fetal Development and the Right to Life

Two problems arise in the application of these suggestions for the definition of the moral community to the determination of the precise moral status of a human fetus. Given that the paradigm example of a person is a normal adult human being, then (1) How like this paradigm, in particular how far advanced since conception, does a human being need to be before it begins to have a right to life by virtue, not of being fully a person as of yet, but of being *like* a person? and (2) To what extent, if any, does the fact that a fetus has the *potential* for becoming a person endow it with some of the same rights? Each of these questions requires some comment.

In answering the first question, we need not attempt a detailed consideration of the moral rights of organisms which are not developed enough, aware enough, intelligent enough, etc., to be considered people, but which resemble people in some respects. It does seem reasonable to suggest that the more like a person, in the relevant respects, a being is, the stronger is the case for regarding it as having a right to life, and indeed the stronger its right to life is. Thus we ought to take seriously the suggestion that, insofar as "the human individual develops biologically in a continuous fashion . . . the rights of a human person might develop in the same way."[4] But we must keep in mind that the attributes which are relevant in determining whether or not an entity is enough like a person to be regarded as having some

of the same moral rights are no different from those which are relevant to determining whether or not it is fully a person—i.e., are no different from (1)–(5)— and that being genetically human, or having recognizably human facial and other physical features, or detectable brain activity, or the capacity to survive outside the uterus, are simply not among these relevant attributes.

Thus it is clear that even though a seven- or eight-month fetus has features which make it apt to arouse in us almost the same powerful protective instinct as is commonly aroused by a small infant, nevertheless it is not significantly more personlike than is a very small embryo. It is *somewhat* more personlike; it can apparently feel and respond to pain, and it may even have a rudimentary form of consciousness, insofar as its brain is quite active. Nevertheless, it seems safe to say that it is not fully conscious, in the way that an infant of a few months is, and that it cannot reason, or communicate messages of indefinitely many sorts, does not engage in self-motivated activity, and has no self-awareness. Thus, in the *relevant* respects, a fetus, even a fully developed one, is considerably less personlike than is the average mature mammal, indeed the average fish. And I think that a rational person must conclude that if the right to life of a fetus is to be based upon its resemblance to a person, then it cannot be said to have any more right to life than, let us say, a newborn guppy (which also seems to be capable of feeling pain), and that a right of that magnitude could never override a woman's right to obtain an abortion, at any stage of her pregnancy.

There may, of course, be other arguments in favor of placing legal limits upon the stage of pregnancy in which an abortion may be performed. Given the relative safety of the new techniques of artificially inducing labor during the third trimester, the danger to the woman's life or health is no longer such an argument. Neither is the fact that people tend to respond to the thought of abortion in the later stages of pregnancy with emotional repulsion, since mere emotional responses cannot take the place of moral reasoning in determining what ought to be permitted. Nor, finally, is the frequently heard argument that legalizing abortion, especially late in the pregnancy, may erode the level of respect for human life, leading, perhaps, to an increase in unjustified euthanasia and other crimes. For this threat, if it is a threat, can be better met by educating people to the kinds of moral distinctions which we are making here than by limiting access to abortion (which limitation may, in its disregard for the rights of women, be just as damaging to the level of respect for human rights).

Thus, since the fact that even a fully developed fetus is not personlike enough to have any significant right to life on the basis of its personlikeness shows that no legal restrictions upon the stage of pregnancy in which an abortion may be performed can be justified on the grounds that we should protect the rights of the older fetus, and since there is no other apparent justification for such restrictions, we may conclude that they are entirely unjustified. Whether or not it would be *indecent* (whatever that means) for a woman in her seventh month to obtain an abortion just to avoid having to postpone a trip to Europe, it would not, in itself, be *immoral,* and therefore it ought to be permitted.

4. Potential Personhood and the Right to Life

We have seen that a fetus does not resemble a person in any way which can support the claim that it has even some of the same rights. But what about its *potential*, the fact that if nurtured and allowed to develop naturally it will very probably become a person? Doesn't that alone give it at least some right to life? It is hard to deny that the fact that an entity is a potential person is a strong prima facie reason for not destroying it: but we need not conclude from this that a potential person has a right to life, by virtue of that potential. It may be that our feeling that it is better, other things being equal, not to destroy a potential person is better explained by the fact that potential people are still (felt to be) an invaluable resource, not to be lightly squandered. Surely, if every speck of dust were a potential person, we would be much less apt to conclude that every potential person has a right to become actual.

Still, we do not need to insist that a potential person has no right to life whatever. There may well be something immoral, and not just imprudent, about wantonly destroying potential people, when doing so isn't necessary to protect anyone's rights. But even if a potential person does have some prima facie right to life, such a right could not possibly outweigh the right of a woman to obtain an abortion, since the rights of any actual person invariably outweigh those of any potential person, whenever the two conflict. Since this may not be immediately obvious in the case of a human fetus, let us look at another case.

Suppose that our space explorer falls into the hands of an alien culture, whose scientists decide to create a few hundred thousand or more human beings, by breaking his body into its component cells, and using these to create fully developed human beings, with, of course, his genetic code. We may imagine that each of these newly created men will have all of the original man's abilities, skills, knowledge, and so on, and also have an individual self-concept, in short that each of them will be a bona fide (though hardly unique) person. Imagine that the whole project will take only seconds, and that its chances of success are extremely high, and that our explorer knows all of this, and also knows that these people will be treated fairly. I maintain that in such a situation he would have every right to escape if he could, and thus to deprive all of these potential people of their potential lives; for his right to life outweighs all of theirs together, in spite of the fact that they are all genetically human, all innocent, and all have a very high probability of becoming people very soon, if only he refrains from acting.

Indeed, I think he would have a right to escape even if it were not his life which the alien scientists planned to take, but only a year of his freedom, or indeed, only a day. Nor would he be obligated to stay if he had gotten captured (thus bringing all these people-potentials into existence) because of his own carelessness, or even if he had done so deliberately, knowing the consequences. Regardless of how he got captured, he is not morally obligated to remain in captivity for *any* period of time for the sake of permitting any number of potential people to come into actuality, so great is the margin by which one actual person's right to liberty outweighs whatever right to life even a hundred thousand potential people have. And it seems reasonable to conclude that the rights of a woman will outweigh by a similar margin whatever right to life a fetus may have by virtue of its potential personhood.

Thus, neither a fetus's resemblance to a person, nor its potential for becoming a person provides any basis whatever for the claim that it has any significant right to life. Consequently, a woman's right to protect her health, happiness, freedom, and even her life,[5] by terminating an unwanted pregnancy, will always override whatever right to life it may be appropriate to ascribe to a fetus, even a fully developed one. And thus, in the absence of any overwhelming social need for every possible child, the laws which restrict the right to obtain an abortion, or limit the period of pregnancy during which an abortion may be performed, are a wholly unjustified violation of a woman's most basic moral and constitutional rights.[6]

6. Postscript on Infanticide

Since the publication of this article, many people have written to point out that my argument appears to justify not only abortion, but infanticide as well. For a newborn infant is not significantly more personlike than an advanced fetus, and consequently it would seem that if the destruction of the latter is permissible so too must be that of the former. Inasmuch as most people, regardless of how they feel about the morality of abortion, consider infanticide a form of murder, this might appear to represent a serious flaw in my argument.

Now, if I am right in holding that it is only people who have a full-fledged right to life, and who can be murdered, and if the criteria of personhood are as I have described them, then it obviously follows that killing a newborn infant isn't murder. It does *not* follow, however, that infanticide is permissible, for two reasons. In the first place, it would be wrong, at least in this country and in this period of history, and other things being equal, to kill a newborn infant, because even if its parents do not want it and would not suffer from its destruction, there are other people who would like to have it, and would, in all probability, be deprived of a great deal of pleasure by its destruction. Thus, infanticide is wrong for reasons analogous to those which make it wrong to wantonly destroy natural resources, or great works of art.

Secondly, most people, at least in this country, value infants and would much prefer that they be preserved, even if foster parents are not immediately available. Most of us would rather be taxed to support orphanages than allow unwanted infants to be destroyed. So long as there are people who want an infant preserved, and who are willing and able to provide the means of caring for it, under reasonably humane conditions, it is ceteris paribus, wrong to destroy it.

But, it might be replied, if this argument shows that infanticide is wrong, at least at this time and in this country, doesn't it also show that abortion is wrong? After all, many people value fetuses, are disturbed by their destruction, and would much prefer that they be preserved, even at some cost to themselves. Furthermore, as a potential source of pleasure to some foster family, a fetus is just as valuable as an infant. There is, however, a crucial difference between the two cases: so long as the fetus is unborn, its preservation, contrary to the wishes of the pregnant woman, violates her rights to freedom, happiness, and self-determination. Her rights override the rights of those who would like the fetus preserved, just as if someone's life or limb is threatened by a wild animal, his right to protect himself by destroying the animal overrides the rights of those who would prefer that the animal not be harmed.

The minute the infant is born, however, its preservation no longer violates any of its mother's rights, even if she wants it destroyed, because she is free to put it up for adoption. Consequently, while the moment of birth does not mark any sharp discontinuity in the degree to which an infant possesses the right to life, it does mark the end of its mother's right to determine its fate. Indeed, if abortion could be performed without killing the fetus, she would never possess the right to have the fetus destroyed, for the same reasons that she has no right to have an infant destroyed.

On the other hand, it follows from my argument that when an unwanted or defective infant is born into a society which cannot afford and/or is not willing to care for it, then its destruction is permissible. This conclusion will, no doubt, strike many people as heartless and immoral; but remember that the very existence of people who feel this way, and who are willing and able to provide care for unwanted infants, is reason enough to conclude that they should be preserved.

Notes

1. Of course, the principle that it is (always) wrong to kill innocent human beings is in need of many other modifications, e.g., that it may be permissible to do so to save a greater number of other innocent human beings, but we may safely ignore these complications here.

2. John Noonan, "Deciding Who Is Human," *Natural Law Forum*, 13 (1968), 135.

3. From here on, we will use "human" to mean genetically human, since the moral sense seems closely connected to, and perhaps derived from, the assumption that genetic humanity is sufficient for membership in the moral community.

4. Thomas L. Hayes, "A Biological View," *Commonweal*, 85 (March 17, 1967), 677–78; quoted by Daniel Callahan, in *Abortion: Law, Choice and Morality* (London: Macmillan & Co., 1970).

5. That is, insofar as the death rate, for the woman, is higher for childbirth than for early abortion.

6. My thanks to the following people, who were kind enough to read and criticize an earlier version of this paper: Herbert Gold, Gene Glass, Anne Lauterbach, Judith Thomson, Mary Mothersill, and Timothy Binkley.

QUESTIONS

1. What is Warren's argument for her "alternative way of defining the moral community"?
2. Is this argument successful?
3. Is her reply to critics in the postscript successful?

59. Why Abortion Is Immoral

DONALD MARQUIS

Donald Marquis (1935–) is professor of philosophy at the University of Kansas. He writes about abortion, death, and other topics in bioethics.

Most of the discussions of abortion assume that the central questions require a judgment about the moral status of the fetus. Don Marquis takes a different tack and argues that we should instead consider the reasons that it is wrong to kill people like us. The answer to that question, he thinks, will enable us to determine that abortion is presumptively wrong.

The view that abortion is, with rare exceptions, seriously immoral has received little support in the recent philosophical literature. No doubt most philosophers affiliated with secular institutions of higher education believe that the anti-abortion position is either a symptom of irrational religious dogma or a conclusion generated by seriously confused philosophical argument. The purpose of this essay is to undermine this general belief. This essay sets out an argument that purports to show, as

From Don Marquis, "Why Abortion Is Immoral," *Journal of Philosophy* 86:4 (April 1989): 183–202. Reprinted by permission of the *Journal of Philosophy* and of the author.

well as any argument in ethics can show, that abortion is, except possibly in rare cases, seriously immoral, that it is in the same moral category as killing an innocent adult human being.

The argument is based on a major assumption. Many of the most insightful and careful writers on the ethics of abortion—such as Joel Feinberg, Michael Tooley, Mary Anne Warren, H. Tristram Engelhardt, Jr., L. W. Sumner, John T. Noonan, Jr., and Philip Devine[1]—believe that whether or not abortion is morally permissible stands or falls on whether or not a fetus is the sort of being whose life it is seriously wrong to end. The argument of this essay will assume, but not argue, that they are correct.

Also, this essay will neglect issues of great importance to a complete ethics of abortion. Some anti-abortionists will allow that certain abortions, such as abortion before implantation or abortion when the life of a woman is threatened by a pregnancy or abortion after rape, may be morally permissible. This essay will not explore the casuistry of these hard cases. The purpose of this essay is to develop a general argument for the claim that the overwhelming majority of deliberate abortions are seriously immoral.

I.

A sketch of standard anti-abortion and pro-choice arguments exhibits how those arguments possess certain symmetries that explain why partisans of those positions are so convinced of the correctness of their own positions, why they are not successful in convincing their opponents, and why, to others, this issue seems to be unresolvable. An analysis of the nature of this standoff suggests a strategy for surmounting it.

Consider the way a typical anti-abortionist argues. She will argue or assert that life is present from the moment of conception or that fetuses look like babies or that fetuses possess a characteristic such as a genetic code that is both necessary and sufficient for being human. Anti-abortionists seem to believe that (1) the truth of all of these claims is quite obvious, and (2) establishing any of these claims is sufficient to show that abortion is morally akin to murder.

A standard pro-choice strategy exhibits similarities. The pro-choicer will argue or assert that fetuses are not persons or that fetuses are not rational agents or that fetuses are not social beings. Pro-choicers seem to believe that (1) the truth of any of these claims is quite obvious, and (2) establishing any of these claims is sufficient to show that an abortion is not a wrongful killing.

In fact, both the pro-choice and the anti-abortion claims do seem to be true, although the "it looks like a baby" claim is more difficult to establish the earlier the pregnancy. We seem to have a standoff. How can it be resolved?

As everyone who has taken a bit of logic knows, if any of these arguments concerning abortion is a good argument, it requires not only some claim characterizing fetuses, but also some general moral principle that ties a characteristic of fetuses to having or not having the right to life or to some other moral characteristic that will generate the obligation or the lack of obligation not to end the life of a fetus. Accordingly, the arguments of the anti-abortionist and the pro-choicer need a bit of filling in to be regarded as adequate.

Note what each partisan will say. The anti-abortionist will claim that her position is supported by such generally accepted moral principles as "It is always prima facie seriously wrong to take a human life" or "It is always prima facie seriously wrong to end the life of a baby." Since these are generally accepted moral principles, her position is certainly not obviously wrong. The pro-choicer will claim that her position is supported by such plausible moral principles as "Being a person is what gives an individual intrinsic moral worth" or "It is only seriously prima facie wrong to take the life of a member of the human community." Since these are generally accepted moral principles, the pro-choice position is certainly not obviously wrong. Unfortunately, we have again arrived at a standoff.

Now, how might one deal with this standoff? The standard approach is to try to show how the moral principles of one's opponent lose their plausibility under analysis. It is easy to see how this is possible. On the one hand, the anti-abortionist will defend a moral principle concerning the wrongness of killing which tends to be broad in scope in order that even fetuses at an early stage of pregnancy will fall under it. The problem with broad principles is that they often embrace too much. In this particular instance, the principle "It is always prima facie wrong to take a human life" seems to entail that it is wrong to end the existence of a living human cancer-cell culture, on the grounds that the culture is both living and human. Therefore, it seems that the anti-abortionist's favored principle is too broad.

On the other hand, the pro-choicer wants to find a moral principle concerning the wrongness of killing which tends to be narrow in scope in order that fetuses will *not* fall under it. The problem with narrow principles is that they often do not embrace enough. Hence, the needed principles such as "It is prima facie seriously wrong to kill only persons" or "It is prima facie wrong to kill only rational agents" do not explain why it is wrong to kill infants or young children or the severely retarded or even perhaps the severely mentally ill. Therefore, we seem again to have a standoff. The anti-abortionist charges, not unreasonably, that pro-choice principles concerning killing are too narrow to be acceptable; the pro-choicer charges, not unreasonably, that anti-abortionist principles concerning killing are too broad to be acceptable.

Attempts by both sides to patch up the difficulties in their positions run into further difficulties. The anti-abortionist will try to remove the problem in her position by reformulating her principle concerning killing in terms of human beings. Now we end up with: "It is always prima facie seriously wrong to end the life of a human being." This principle has the advantage of avoiding the problem of the human cancer-cell culture counterexample. But this advantage is purchased at a high price. For although it is clear that a fetus is both human and alive, it is not at all clear that a fetus is a human *being*. There is at least something to be said for the view that something becomes a human being only after a process of development, and that therefore first trimester fetuses and perhaps all fetuses are not yet human beings. Hence, the anti-abortionist, by this move, has merely exchanged one problem for another.[2]

The pro-choicer fares no better. She may attempt to find reasons why killing infants, young children,

and the severely retarded is wrong which are independent of her major principle that is supposed to explain the wrongness of taking human life, but which will not also make abortion immoral. This is no easy task. Appeals to social utility will seem satisfactory only to those who resolve not to think of the enormous difficulties with a utilitarian account of the wrongness of killing and the significant social costs of preserving the lives of the unproductive.[3] A pro-choice strategy that extends the definition of "person" to infants or even to young children seems just as arbitrary as an anti-abortion strategy that extends the definition of "human being" to fetuses. Again, we find symmetries in the two positions and we arrive at a standoff.

There are even further problems that reflect symmetries in the two positions. In addition to counterexample problems, or the arbitrary application problems that can be exchanged for them, the standard anti-abortionist principle "It is prima facie seriously wrong to kill a human being," or one of its variants, can be objected to on the grounds of ambiguity. If "human being" is taken to be a *biological* category, then the anti-abortionist is left with the problem of explaining why a merely biological category should make a moral difference. Why, it is asked, is it any more reasonable to base a moral conclusion on the number of chromosomes in one's cells than on the color of one's skin?[4] If "human being," on the other hand, is taken to be a *moral* category, then the claim that a fetus is a human being cannot be taken to be a premise in the anti-abortion argument, for it is precisely what needs to be established. Hence, either the anti-abortionist's main category is a morally irrelevant, merely biological category, or it is of no use to the anti-abortionist in establishing (noncircularly, of course) that abortion is wrong.

Although this problem with the anti-abortionist position is often noticed, it is less often noticed that the pro-choice position suffers from an analogous problem. The principle "Only persons have the right to life" also suffers from an ambiguity. The term "person" is typically defined in terms of psychological characteristics, although there will certainly be disagreement concerning which characteristics are most important. Supposing that this matter can be settled, the pro-choicer is left with the problem of explaining why *psychological* characteristics should make a *moral* difference. If the pro-choicer should attempt to deal with this problem by claiming that an explanation is not necessary, that in fact we do treat such a cluster of psychological properties as having moral significance, the sharp-witted anti-abortionist should have a ready response. We do treat being both living and human as having moral significance. If it is legitimate for the pro-choicer to demand that the anti-abortionist provide an explanation of the connection between the biological character of being a human being and the wrongness of being killed (even though people accept this connection), then it is legitimate for the anti-abortionist to demand that the pro-choicer provide an explanation of the connection between psychological criteria for being a person and the wrongness of being killed (even though that connection is accepted).[5]

Feinberg has attempted to meet this objection (he calls psychological personhood "commonsense personhood"):

> The characteristics that confer commonsense personhood are not arbitrary bases for rights and duties, such as race, sex or species membership; rather they are traits that make sense out of rights and duties and without which those moral attributes would have no point or function. It is because people are conscious; have a sense of their personal identities; have plans, goals, and projects; experience emotions; are liable to pains, anxieties, and frustrations; can reason and bargain, and so on—it is because of these attributes that people have values and interests, desires and expectations of their own, including a stake in their own futures, and a personal well-being of a sort we cannot ascribe to unconscious or nonrational beings. Because of their developed capacities they can assume duties and responsibilities and can have and make claims on one another. Only because of their sense of self, their life plans, their value hierarchies, and their stakes in their own futures can they be ascribed fundamental rights. There is nothing arbitrary about these linkages. (op. cit., p. 270)

The plausible aspects of this attempt should not be taken to obscure its implausible features. There is a great deal to be said for the view that being a psychological person under some description is a necessary condition for having duties. One cannot have a duty unless one is capable of behaving morally, and a being's capability of behaving morally will require having a certain psychology. It is far from obvious, however, that having rights entails consciousness or rationality, as Feinberg suggests. We speak of the rights of the severely retarded or the severely mentally ill, yet some of these persons are not rational. We speak of the rights of the temporarily unconscious. The New Jersey Supreme Court based their decision in the Quinlan case on Karen Ann Quinlan's right to privacy, and she was known to be permanently unconscious at that time. Hence, Feinberg's claim that having rights entails being conscious is, on its face, obviously false.

Of course, it might not make sense to attribute rights to a being that would never in its natural history have certain psychological traits. This modest connection between psychological personhood and moral personhood will create a place for Karen Ann Quinlan and the temporarily unconscious. But then it makes a place for fetuses also. Hence, it does not serve Feinberg's pro-choice purposes. Accordingly, it seems that the pro-choicer will have as much difficulty bridging the gap between psychological personhood and personhood in the moral sense as the anti-abortionist has bridging the gap between being a biological human being and being a human being in the moral sense.

Furthermore, the pro-choicer cannot any more escape her problem by making person a purely moral category than the anti-abortionist could escape by the analogous move. For if person is a moral category, then the pro-choicer is left without the resources for establishing (noncircularly, of course) the claim that a fetus is not a person, which is an essential premise in her argument. Again, we have both a symmetry and a standoff between pro-choice and anti-abortion views.

Passions in the abortion debate run high. There are both plausibilities and difficulties with the standard positions. Accordingly, it is hardly surprising that partisans of either side embrace with fervor the moral generalizations that support the conclusions they preanalytically favor, and reject with disdain the moral generalizations of their opponents as being subject to inescapable difficulties. It is easy to believe that the counterexamples to one's own moral principles are merely temporary difficulties that will dissolve in the wake of further philosophical research, and that the counterexamples to the principles of one's opponents are as straightforward as the contradiction between *A* and *O* propositions in traditional logic. This might suggest to an impartial observer (if there are any) that the abortion issue is unresolvable.

There is a way out of this apparent dialectical quandary. The moral generalizations of both sides are not quite correct. The generalizations hold for the most part, for the usual cases. This suggests that they are all *accidental* generalizations, that the moral claims made by those on both sides of the dispute do not touch on the *essence* of the matter.

This use of the distinction between essence and accident is not meant to invoke obscure metaphysical categories. Rather, it is intended to reflect the rather atheoretical nature of the abortion discussion. If the generalization a partisan in the abortion dispute adopts were derived from the reason why ending the life of a human being is wrong, then there could not be exceptions to that generalization unless some special case obtains in which there are even more powerful countervailing reasons. Such generalizations would not be merely accidental generalizations; they would point to, or be based upon, the essence of the wrongness of killing, what it is that makes killing wrong. All this suggests that a necessary condition of resolving the abortion controversy is a more theoretical account of the wrongness of killing. After all, if we merely believe, but do not understand, why killing adult human beings such as ourselves is wrong, how could we conceivably show that abortion is either immoral or permissible?

II.

In order to develop such an account, we can start from the following unproblematic assumption concerning our own case: it is wrong to kill *us*. Why is it wrong? Some answers can be easily eliminated. It might be said that what makes killing us wrong is that a killing brutalizes the one who kills. But the brutalization consists of being inured to the performance of an act that is hideously immoral; hence, the brutalization does not explain the immorality. It might be said that what makes killing us wrong is the great loss others would experience due to our absence. Although such hubris is understandable, such an explanation does not account for the wrongness of killing hermits, or those whose lives are relatively independent and whose friends find it easy to make new friends.

A more obvious answer is better. What primarily makes killing wrong is neither its effect on the murderer nor its effect on the victim's friends and relatives, but its effect on the victim. The loss of one's life is one of the greatest losses one can suffer. The loss of one's life deprives one of all the experiences, activities, projects, and enjoyments that would otherwise have constituted one's future. Therefore, killing someone is wrong, primarily because the killing inflicts (one of) the greatest possible losses on the victim. To describe this as the loss of life can be misleading, however. The change in my biological state does not by itself make killing me wrong. The effect of the loss of my biological life is the loss to me of all those activities, projects, experiences, and enjoyments which would otherwise have constituted my future personal life. These activities, projects, experiences, and enjoyments are either valuable for their own sakes or are means to something else that is valuable for its own sake. Some parts of my future are not valued by me now, but will come to be valued by me as I grow older and as my values and capacities change. When I am killed, I am deprived both of what I now value which would have been part of my future personal life, but also what I would come to value. Therefore, when I die, I am deprived of all of the value of my future. Inflicting this loss on me is ultimately what makes killing me wrong. This being the case, it would seem that what makes killing *any* adult human being prima facie seriously wrong is the loss of his or her future.[6]

How should this rudimentary theory of the wrongness of killing be evaluated? It cannot be faulted for deriving an "ought" from an "is," for it does not. The analysis assumes that killing me (or you, reader) is prima facie seriously wrong. The point of the analysis is to establish which natural property ultimately explains the wrongness of the killing, given that it is wrong. A natural property will ultimately explain the wrongness of killing, only if (1) the explanation fits with our intuitions about the matter and (2) there is no other natural property that provides the basis for a better explanation of the wrongness of killing. This analysis rests on the intuition that what makes killing a particular human or animal wrong is what it does to that particular human or animal. What makes killing wrong is some natural effect or other of the killing. Some would deny this. For instance, a divine–command theorist in ethics would deny it. Surely this denial is, however, one of those features of divine–command theory which renders it so implausible.

The claim that what makes killing wrong is the loss of the victim's future is directly supported by two considerations. In the first place, this theory explains why we regard killing as one of the worst of crimes. Killing is especially wrong, because it deprives the victim of more than perhaps any other crime. In the second place, people with AIDS or cancer who know they are dying believe, of course, that dying is a very bad thing for them. They believe that the loss of a future to them that they would otherwise have experienced is what makes their premature death a very bad thing for them. A better theory of the wrongness of killing would require a different natural property associated with killing which better fits with the attitudes of the dying. What could it be?

The view that what makes killing wrong is the loss to the victim of the value of the victim's future gains additional support when some of its implications are examined. In the first place, it is incompatible with the view that it is wrong to kill only beings who are biologically human. It is possible that there exists a different species from another planet whose members have a future like ours. Since having a future like that is what makes killing someone wrong, this theory entails that it would be wrong to kill members of such a species. Hence, this theory is opposed to the claim that only life that is biologically human has great moral worth, a claim which many anti-abortionists have seemed to adopt. This opposition, which this theory has in common with personhood theories, seems to be a merit of the theory.

In the second place, the claim that the loss of one's future is the wrong-making feature of one's being killed entails the possibility that the futures of some actual nonhuman mammals on our own planet are sufficiently like ours that it is seriously wrong to kill them also. Whether some animals do have the same right to life as human beings depends on adding to the account of the wrongness of killing some additional account of just what it is about my future or the futures of other adult human beings which makes it wrong to kill us. No such additional account will be offered in this essay. Undoubtedly, the provision of such an account would be a very difficult matter. Undoubtedly, any such account would be quite controversial. Hence, it surely should not reflect badly on this sketch of an elementary theory of the wrongness of killing that it is indeterminate with respect to some very difficult issues regarding animal rights.

In the third place, the claim that the loss of one's future is the wrong-making feature of one's being killed does not entail, as sanctity of human life theories do, that active euthanasia is wrong. Persons who are severely and incurably ill, who face a future of pain and despair, and who wish to die will not have suffered a loss if they are killed. It is, strictly speaking, the value of a human's future which makes killing wrong in this theory. This being so, killing does not necessarily wrong some persons who are sick and dying. Of course, there may be other reasons for a prohibition of active euthanasia, but that is another matter. Sanctity-of-human-life theories seem to hold that active euthanasia is seriously wrong even in an individual case where there seems to be good reason for it independently of public policy considerations. This consequence is most implausible, and it is a plus for the claim that the loss of a future of value is what makes killing wrong that it does not share this consequence.

In the fourth place, the account of the wrongness of killing defended in this essay does straightforwardly entail that it is prima facie seriously wrong to kill children and infants, for we do presume that they have futures of value. Since we do believe that it is wrong to kill defenseless little babies, it is important that a theory of the wrongness of killing easily account for this. Personhood theories of the wrongness of killing, on the other hand, cannot straightforwardly account for the wrongness of killing infants and young children.[7] Hence, such theories must add special ad hoc accounts of the wrongness of killing the young. The plausibility of such ad hoc theories seems to be a function of how desperately one wants such theories to work. The claim that the primary wrong-making feature of a killing is the loss to the victim of the value of its future accounts for the wrongness of killing young children and infants directly; it makes the wrongness of such acts as obvious as we actually think it is. This is a further merit of this theory. Accordingly, it seems that this value of a future-like-ours theory of the wrongness of killing shares strengths of both sanctity-of-life and personhood accounts while avoiding weaknesses of both. In addition, it meshes with a central intuition concerning what makes killing wrong.

The claim that the primary wrong-making feature of a killing is the loss to the victim of the value of its future has obvious consequences for the ethics of abortion. The future of a standard fetus includes a set of experiences, projects, activities, and such which are identical with the futures of adult human beings and are identical with the futures of young children. Since the reason that is sufficient to explain why it is wrong to kill human beings after the time of birth is a reason that also applies to fetuses, it follows that abortion is prima facie seriously morally wrong.

This argument does not rely on the invalid inference that, since it is wrong to kill persons, it is wrong to kill potential persons also. The category that is morally central to this analysis is the category of having a valuable future like ours; it is not the category of personhood. The argument to the conclusion that abortion is prima facie seriously morally wrong proceeded independently of the notion of person or potential person or any equivalent. Someone may wish to start with this analysis in terms of the value of a human future, conclude that abortion is, except perhaps in rare circumstances, seriously morally wrong, infer that fetuses have the right to life, and then call fetuses "persons" as a result of their having the right to life. Clearly, in this case, the category of person is being used to state the *conclusion* of the analysis rather than to generate the *argument* of the analysis.

The structure of this anti-abortion argument can be both illuminated and defended by comparing it to what appears to be the best argument for the wrongness of the wanton infliction of pain on animals. This latter argument is based on the assumption that it is prima facie wrong to inflict pain on me (or you, reader). What is the natural property associated with the infliction of pain which makes such infliction wrong? The obvious answer seems to be that the infliction of pain causes suffering and that suffering is a misfortune. The suffering caused by the infliction of pain is what makes the wanton infliction of pain on me wrong. The wanton infliction of pain on other adult humans causes suffering. The wanton infliction of pain on animals causes suffering. Since causing suffering is what makes the wanton infliction of pain wrong and since the wanton infliction of pain on animals causes suffering, it follows that the wanton infliction of pain on animals is wrong.

This argument for the wrongness of the wanton infliction of pain on animals shares a number of structural features with the argument for the serious prima facie wrongness of abortion. Both arguments start with an obvious assumption concerning what it is wrong to do to me (or you, reader). Both then look for the characteristic or the consequence of the wrong action which makes the action wrong. Both recognize that the wrong–making feature of these immoral actions is a property of actions sometimes directed at individuals other than postnatal human beings. If the structure of the argument for the wrongness of the wanton infliction of pain on animals is sound, then the structure of the argument for the prima facie serious wrongness of abortion is also sound, for the structure of the two arguments is the same. The structure common to both is the key to the explanation of how the wrongness of abortion can be demonstrated without recourse to the category of person. In neither argument is that category crucial.

This defense of an argument for the wrongness of abortion in terms of a structurally similar argument for the wrongness of the wanton infliction of pain on animals succeeds only if the account regarding animals is the correct account. Is it? In the first place, it seems plausible. In the second place, its major competition is Kant's account. Kant believed that we do not have direct duties to animals at all, because they are not persons. Hence, Kant had to explain and justify the wrongness of inflicting pain on animals on the grounds that "he who is hard in his dealings with animals becomes hard also in his dealing with men."[8] The problem with Kant's account is that there seems to be no reason for accepting this latter claim unless Kant's account is rejected. If the alternative to Kant's account is accepted, then it is easy to understand why someone who is indifferent to inflicting pain on animals is also indifferent to inflicting pain on humans, for one is indifferent to what makes inflicting pain wrong in both cases. But, if Kant's account is accepted, there is no intelligible reason why one who is hard in his dealings with animals (or crabgrass or stones) should also be hard in his dealings with men. After all, men are persons: animals are no more persons than crabgrass or stones. Persons are Kant's crucial moral category. Why, in short, should a Kantian accept the basic claim in Kant's argument?

Hence, Kant's argument for the wrongness of inflicting pain on animals rests on a claim that, in a world of Kantian moral agents, is demonstrably false. Therefore, the alternative analysis, being more plausible anyway, should be accepted. Since this alternative analysis has the same structure as the anti-abortion argument being defended here, we have further support for the argument for the immorality of abortion being defended in this essay.

Of course, this value of a future-like-ours argument, if sound, shows only that abortion is prima facie wrong, not that it is wrong in any and all circumstances. Since the loss of the future to a standard fetus, if killed, is, however, at least as great a loss as the loss of the future to a standard adult human being who is killed, abortion, like ordinary killing, could be justified only by the most compelling reasons. The loss of one's life is almost the greatest misfortune that can happen to one. Presumably abortion could be justified in some circumstances, only if the loss consequent on failing to abort would be at least as great. Accordingly, morally permissible abortions will be rare indeed unless, perhaps, they occur so early in pregnancy that a fetus is not yet definitely an individual. Hence, this argument should be taken as showing that abortion is presumptively very seriously wrong, where the presumption is very

strong—as strong as the presumption that killing another adult human being is wrong.

III.

How complete an account of the wrongness of killing does the value of a future-like-ours account have to be in order that the wrongness of abortion is a consequence? This account does not have to be an account of the necessary conditions for the wrongness of killing. Some persons in nursing homes may lack valuable human futures, yet it may be wrong to kill them for other reasons. Furthermore, this account does not obviously have to be the sole reason killing is wrong where the victim did have a valuable future. This analysis claims only that, for any killing where the victim did have a valuable future like ours, having that future by itself is sufficient to create the strong presumption that the killing is seriously wrong.

One way to overturn the value of a future-like-ours argument would be to find some account of the wrongness of killing which is at least as intelligible and which has different implications for the ethics of abortion. Two rival accounts possess at least some degree of plausibility. One account is based on the obvious fact that people value the experience of living and wish for that valuable experience to continue. Therefore, it might be said, what makes killing wrong is the discontinuation of that experience for the victim. Let us call this the *discontinuation account.*[9] Another rival account is based upon the obvious fact that people strongly desire to continue to live. This suggests that what makes killing us so wrong is that it interferes with the fulfillment of a strong and fundamental desire, the fulfillment of which is necessary for the fulfillment of any other desires we might have. Let us call this the *desire account.*[10]

Consider first the desire account as a rival account of the ethics of killing which would provide the basis for rejecting the anti-abortion position. Such an account will have to be stronger than the value of a future-like-ours account of the wrongness of abortion if it is to do the job expected of it. To entail the wrongness of abortion, the value of a future-like-ours account has only to provide a sufficient, but not a necessary, condition for the wrongness of killing. The desire account, on the other hand, must provide us also with a necessary condition for the wrongness of killing in order to generate a pro-choice conclusion on abortion. The reason for this is that presumably the argument from the desire account moves from the claim that what makes killing wrong is interference with a very strong desire to the claim that abortion is not wrong because the fetus lacks a strong desire to live. Obviously, this inference fails if someone's having the desire to live is not a necessary condition of its being wrong to kill that individual.

One problem with the desire account is that we do regard it as seriously wrong to kill persons who have little desire to live or who have no desire to live or, indeed, have a desire not to live. We believe it is seriously wrong to kill the unconscious, the sleeping, those who are tired of life, and those who are suicidal. The value-of-a-human-future account renders standard morality intelligible in these cases; these cases appear to be incompatible with the desire account.

The desire account is subject to a deeper difficulty. We desire life, because we value the goods of this life. The goodness of life is not secondary to our desire for it. If this were not so, the pain of one's own premature death could be done away with merely by an appropriate alteration in the configuration of one's desires. This is absurd. Hence, it would seem that it is the loss of the goods of one's future, not the interference with the fulfillment of a strong desire to live, which accounts ultimately for the wrongness of killing.

It is worth noting that, if the desire account is modified so that it does not provide a necessary, but only a sufficient, condition for the wrongness of killing, the desire account is compatible with the value of a future-like-ours account. The combined accounts will yield an anti-abortion ethic. This suggests that one can retain what is intuitively plausible about the desire account without a challenge to the basic argument of this paper.

It is also worth noting that, if future desires have moral force in a modified desire account of the wrongness of killing, one can find support for an anti-abortion ethic even in the absence of a value of a future-like-ours account. If one decides that a morally relevant property, the possession of which is sufficient to make it wrong to kill some individual, is the desire at some future time to live—one might decide to justify one's refusal to kill suicidal teenagers on these grounds, for example—then, since typical fetuses will have the desire in the future to live, it is wrong to kill typical fetuses. Accordingly, it does not seem that a desire account of the wrongness of killing can provide a justification of a pro-choice ethic of abortion which is nearly as adequate as the value of a human-future justification of an anti-abortion ethic.

The discontinuation account looks more promising as an account of the wrongness of killing. It seems just as intelligible as the value of a future-like-ours account, but it does not justify an anti-abortion position. Obviously, if it is the continuation of one's activities, experiences, and projects, the loss of which makes killing wrong, then it is not wrong to kill fetuses for that reason, for fetuses do not have experiences, activities, and projects to be continued or discontinued. Accordingly, the discontinuation account does not have the anti-abortion consequences that the value of a future-like-ours account has. Yet, it seems as intelligible as the value of a future-like-ours account, for when we think of what would be wrong with our being killed, it does seem as if it is the discontinuation of what makes our lives worthwhile which makes killing us wrong.

Is the discontinuation account just as good an account as the value of a future-like-ours account? The discontinuation account will not be adequate at all, if it does not refer to the *value* of the experience that may be discontinued. One does not want the discontinuation account to make it wrong to kill a patient who begs for death and who is in severe pain that cannot be relieved short of killing. (I leave open the question of whether it is wrong for other reasons.) Accordingly, the discontinuation account must be more than a bare discontinuation account. It must make some reference to the positive value of the patient's experiences. But, by the same token, the value of a future-like-ours account cannot be a bare future account either. Just having a future surely does not itself rule out killing the above patient. This account must make some reference to the value of the patient's future experiences and projects also.

Hence, both accounts involve the value of experiences, projects, and activities. So far we still have symmetry between the accounts.

The symmetry fades, however, when we focus on the time period of the value of the experiences, etc., which has moral consequences. Although both accounts leave open the possibility that the patient in our example may be killed, this possibility is left open only in virtue of the utterly bleak future for the patient. It makes no difference whether the patient's immediate past contains intolerable pain, or consists in being in a coma (which we can imagine is a situation of indifference), or consists in a life of value. If the patient's future is a future of value, we want our account to make it wrong to kill the patient. If the patient's future is intolerable, whatever his or her immediate past, we want our account to allow killing the patient. Obviously, then, it is the value of that patient's future which is doing the work in rendering the morality of killing the patient intelligible.

This being the case, it seems clear that whether one has immediate past experiences or not does no work in the explanation of what makes killing wrong. The addition the discontinuation account makes to the value of a human future account is otiose. Its addition to the value-of-a-future account plays no role at all in rendering intelligible the wrongness of killing. Therefore, it can be discarded with the discontinuation account of which it is a part.

IV.

The analysis of the previous section suggests that alternative general accounts of the wrongness of killing are either inadequate or unsuccessful in getting around the anti-abortion consequences of the value of a future-like-ours argument. A different strategy for avoiding these anti-abortion consequences involves limiting the scope of the value of a future argument. More precisely, the strategy involves arguing that fetuses lack a property that is essential for the value-of-a-future argument (or for any anti-abortion argument) to apply to them.

One move of this sort is based upon the claim that a necessary condition of one's future being valuable is that one values it. Value implies a valuer. Given this one might argue that, since fetuses cannot value their futures, their futures are not valuable to them. Hence, it does not seriously wrong them deliberately to end their lives.

This move fails, however, because of some ambiguities. Let us assume that something cannot be of value unless it is valued by someone. This does not entail that my life is of no value unless it is valued by me. I may think, in a period of despair, that my future is of no worth whatsoever, but I may be wrong because others rightly see value—even great value—in it. Furthermore, my future can be valuable to me even if I do not value it. This is the case when a young person attempts suicide, but is rescued and goes on to significant human achievements. Such young people's futures are ultimately valuable to them, even though such futures do not seem to be valuable to them at the moment of attempted suicide. A fetus's future can be valuable to it in the same way. Accordingly, this attempt to limit the anti-abortion argument fails.

Another similar attempt to reject the anti-abortion position is based on Tooley's claim that an entity cannot possess the right to life unless it has the capacity to desire its continued existence. It follows that, since fetuses lack the conceptual capacity to desire to continue to live, they lack the right to life. Accordingly, Tooley concludes that abortion cannot be seriously prima facie wrong (op. cit., pp. 46/7).

What could be the evidence for Tooley's basic claim? Tooley once argued that individuals have a prima facie right to what they desire and that the lack of the capacity to desire something undercuts the basis of one's right to it (op. cit., pp. 44/5). This argument plainly will not succeed in the context of the analysis of this essay, however, since the point here is to establish the fetus's right to life on other grounds. Tooley's argument assumes that the right to life cannot be established in general on some basis other than the desire for life. This position was considered and rejected in the preceding section of this paper.

One might attempt to defend Tooley's basic claim on the grounds that, because a fetus cannot apprehend continued life as a benefit, its continued life cannot be a benefit or cannot be something it has a right to or cannot be something that is in its interest.

This might be defended in terms of the general proposition that, if an individual is literally incapable of caring about or taking an interest in some X, then one does not have a right to X or X is not a benefit or X is not something that is in one's interest.[11]

Each member of this family of claims seems to be open to objections. As John C. Stevens[12] has pointed out, one may have a right to be treated with a certain medical procedure (because of a health insurance policy one has purchased), even though one cannot conceive of the nature of the procedure. And, as Tooley himself has pointed out, persons who have been indoctrinated, or drugged, or rendered temporarily unconscious may be literally incapable of caring about or taking an interest in something that is in their interest or is something to which they have a right, or is something that benefits them. Hence, the Tooley claim that would restrict the scope of the value of a future-like-ours argument is undermined by counterexamples.[13]

Finally, Paul Bassen[14] has argued that, even though the prospects of an embryo might seem to be a basis for the wrongness of abortion, an embryo cannot be a victim and therefore cannot be wronged. An embryo cannot be a victim, he says, because it lacks sentience. His central argument for this seems to be that, even though plants and the permanently unconscious are alive, they clearly cannot be victims. What is the explanation of this? Bassen claims that the explanation is that their lives consist of mere metabolism and mere metabolism is not enough to ground victimizability. Mentation is required.

The problem with this attempt to establish the absence of victimizability is that both plants and the permanently unconscious clearly lack what Bassen calls "prospects" or what I have called "a future life like ours." Hence, it is surely open to one to argue that the real reason we believe plants and the permanently unconscious cannot be victims is that killing them cannot deprive them of a future life like ours; the real reason is not their absence of present mentation.

Bassen recognizes that his view is subject to this difficulty, and he recognizes that the case of children seems to support this difficulty, for "much of what we do for children is based on prospects." He argues, however, that, in the case of children and in other

such cases, "potentiality comes into play only where victimizability has been secured on other grounds" (ibid., p. 333).

Bassen's defense of his view is patently question-begging, since what is adequate to secure victimizability is exactly what is at issue. His examples do not support his own view against the thesis of this essay. Of course, embryos can be victims: when their lives are deliberately terminated, they are deprived of their futures of value, their prospects. This makes them victims, for it directly wrongs them.

The seeming plausibility of Bassen's view stems from the fact that paradigmatic cases of imagining someone as a victim involve empathy, and empathy requires mentation of the victim. The victims of flood, famine, rape, or child abuse are all persons with whom we can empathize. That empathy seems to be part of seeing them as victims.[15]

In spite of the strength of these examples, the attractive intuition that a situation in which there is victimization requires the possibility of empathy is subject to counterexamples. Consider a case that Bassen himself offers: "Posthumous obliteration of an author's work constitutes a misfortune for him only if he had wished his work to endure" (op cit., p. 318). The conditions Bassen wishes to impose upon the possibility of being victimized here seem far too strong. Perhaps this author, due to his unrealistic standards of excellence and his low self-esteem, regarded his work as unworthy of survival, even though it possessed genuine literary merit. Destruction of such work would surely victimize its author. In such a case, empathy with the victim concerning the loss is clearly impossible.

Of course, Bassen does not make the possibility of empathy a necessary condition of victimizability; he requires only mentation. Hence, on Bassen's actual view, this author, as I have described him, can be a victim. The problem is that the basic intuition that renders Bassen's view plausible is missing in the author's case. In order to attempt to avoid counterexamples, Bassen has made his thesis too weak to be supported by the intuitions that suggested it.

Even so, the mentation requirement on victimizability is still subject to counterexamples. Suppose a severe accident renders me totally unconscious for a month, after which I recover. Surely killing me while I am unconscious victimizes me, even though I am incapable of mentation during that time. It follows that Bassen's thesis fails. Apparently, attempts to restrict the value of a future-like-ours argument so that fetuses do not fall within its scope do not succeed.

V.

In this essay, it has been argued that the correct ethic of the wrongness of killing can be extended to fetal life and used to show that there is a strong presumption that any abortion is morally impermissible. If the ethic of killing adopted here entails, however, that contraception is also seriously immoral, then there would appear to be a difficulty with the analysis of this essay.

But this analysis does not entail that contraception is wrong. Of course, contraception prevents the actualization of a possible future of value. Hence, it follows from the claim that futures of value should be maximized that contraception is prima facie immoral. This obligation to maximize does not exist, however; furthermore, nothing in the ethics of killing in this paper entails that it does. The ethics of killing in this essay would entail that contraception is wrong only if something were denied a human future of value by contraception. Nothing at all is denied such a future by contraception, however.

Candidates for a subject of harm by contraception fall into four categories: (1) some sperm or other, (2) some ovum or other, (3) a sperm and an ovum separately, and (4) a sperm and an ovum together. Assigning the harm to some sperm is utterly arbitrary, for no reason can be given for making a sperm the subject of harm rather than an ovum. Assigning the harm to some ovum is utterly arbitrary, for no reason can be given for making an ovum the subject of harm rather than a sperm. One might attempt to avoid these problems by insisting that contraception deprives both the sperm and the ovum separately of a valuable future like ours. On this alternative, too many futures are lost. Contraception was supposed to be wrong, because it deprived us of one future of value, not two. One might attempt to avoid this problem by holding that contraception deprives the combination of

sperm and ovum of a valuable future like ours. But here the definite article misleads. At the time of contraception, there are hundreds of millions of sperm, one (released) ovum and millions of possible combinations of all of these. There is no actual combination at all. Is the subject of the loss to be a merely possible combination? Which one? This alternative does not yield an actual subject of harm either. Accordingly, the immorality of contraception is not entailed by the loss of a future-like-ours argument simply because there is no nonarbitrarily identifiable subject of the loss in the case of contraception.

VI.

The purpose of this essay has been to set out an argument for the serious presumptive wrongness of abortion subject to the assumption that the moral permissibility of abortion stands or falls on the moral status of the fetus. Since a fetus possesses a property, the possession of which in adult human beings is sufficient to make killing an adult human being wrong, abortion is wrong. This way of dealing with the problem of abortion seems superior to other approaches to the ethics of abortion, because it rests on an ethics of killing which is close to self-evident, because the crucial morally relevant property clearly applies to fetuses, and because the argument avoids the usual equivocations on "human life," "human being," or "person." The argument rests neither on religious claims nor on Papal dogma. It is not subject to the objection of "speciesism." Its soundness is compatible with the moral permissibility of euthanasia and contraception. It deals with our intuitions concerning young children.

Finally, this analysis can be viewed as resolving a standard problem—indeed, *the* standard problem—concerning the ethics of abortion. Clearly, it is wrong to kill adult human beings. Clearly, it is not wrong to end the life of some arbitrarily chosen single human cell. Fetuses seem to be like arbitrarily chosen human cells in some respects and like adult humans in other respects. The problem of the ethics of abortion is the problem of determining the fetal property that settles this moral controversy. The thesis of this essay is that the problem of the ethics of abortion, so understood, is solvable.

Notes

1. Feinberg, "Abortion," in *Matters of Life and Death: New Introductory Essays in Moral Philosophy*, Tom Regan, ed. (New York: Random House, 1986), pp. 256–293; Tooley, "Abortion and Infanticide," *Philosophy and Public Affairs*, II, 1 (1972):37–65; Tooley, *Abortion and Infanticide* (New York: Oxford, 1984); Warren, "On the Moral and Legal Status of Abortion," *The Monist*, i.VII, 1 (1973):43–61; Engelhardt, "The Ontology of Abortion," *Ethics*, i.XXXIV, 3 (1974):217–234; Sumner, *Abortion and Moral Theory* (Princeton: Princeton University Press, 1981); Noonan, "An Almost Absolute Value in History," in *The Morality of Abortion: Legal and Historical Perspectives*, Noonan, ed. (Cambridge: Harvard, 1970); and Devine, *The Ethics of Homicide* (Ithaca: Cornell, 1978).

2. For interesting discussions of this issue, see Warren Quinn, "Abortion: Identity and Loss," *Philosophy and Public Affairs*, XIII, 1 (1984):24–54; and Lawrence C. Becker, "Human Being: The Boundaries of the Concept," *Philosophy and Public Affairs*, IV, 4 (1975):334–359.

3. For example, see my "Ethics and the Elderly: Some Problems," in Stuart Spicker, Kathleen Woodward, and David Van Tassel, eds., *Aging and the Elderly: Humanistic Perspectives in Gerontology* (Atlantic Highlands, NJ: Humanities, 1978), pp. 341–355.

4. See Warren, op. cit., and Tooley, "Abortion and Infanticide."

5. This seems to be the fatal flaw in Warren's treatment of this issue.

6. I have been most influenced on this matter by Jonathan Glover, *Causing Death and Saving Lives* (New York: Penguin, 1977), ch. 3; and Robert Young, "What Is So Wrong with Killing People?" *Philosophy*, I.IV, 210 (1979):515–528.

7. Feinberg, Tooley, Warren, and Engelhardt have all dealt with this problem.

8. "Duties to Animals and Spirits," in *Lectures on Ethics*, Louis Infeld, trans. (New York: Harper, 1963), p. 239.

9. I am indebted to Jack Bricke for raising this objection.

10. Presumably a preference utilitarian would press such an objection. Tooley once suggested that his account has such a theoretical underpinning. See his "Abortion and Infanticide," pp. 44/5.

11. Donald VanDeVeer seems to think this is self-evident. See his "Whither Baby Doe?" in *Matters of Life and Death*, p. 233.

12. "Must the Bearer of a Right Have the Concept of That to Which He Has a Right?" *Ethics*, XCV, 1 (1984):68–74.

13. See Tooley again in "Abortion and Infanticide," pp. 47–49.

14. "Present Sakes and Future Prospects: The Status of Early Abortion," *Philosophy and Public Affairs*, XI, 4 (1982):322–326.

15. Note carefully the reasons he gives on the bottom of p. 316.

QUESTIONS

1. What is Marquis's argument for the impermissibility of abortion?
2. Why does Marquis think we can determine the morality of abortion without first taking up the question of the moral status of the unborn?
3. Is the argument for the wrongness of abortion successful?

60. Beginnings

JEFF McMAHAN

For a description of the author, see chapter 6.

In this excerpt from his book, Jeff McMahan considers the morality of abortion. According to the view he defends in the book, we are essentially embodied minds. Thus, "we do not begin to exist until our organisms develop the capacity to generate consciousness. Only then is there *someone* present rather than merely *something*." An early abortion, before the time when the fetal brain develops the capacity to support consciousness, "will not kill anyone; it merely prevents someone from coming into existence." The life that is ended by virtually all abortions will be that of a human organism, in its early stages of development.

Much of this excerpt is a treatment of late abortion and of Don Marquis's article (see the previous chapter); it is much more difficult reading than the short first section.

1. Early Abortion

The Embodied Mind Account of Identity has immediate implications for the morality of abortion. For, according to that account, we do not begin to exist until our organisms develop the capacity to generate consciousness. Only then is there *someone* present rather than merely *something*. Let us define an *early abortion* as an abortion that is performed prior to that point—that is, the point at which the fetal brain acquires the capacity to support consciousness and at which one of us consequently begins to exist in association with the fetal organism. If the Embodied Mind Account is right, there is no one to be affected for better or worse by an early abortion other than the pregnant woman, her partner, and anyone else who might care about her or her possible progeny. An early abortion does not kill anyone; it merely prevents someone from coming into existence. In this respect, it is relevantly like contraception and wholly unlike the killing of a person. For there is, again, no one there to be killed.

It is not known with certainty at what point during gestation the fetal brain develops the capacity to generate consciousness. Most neurologists accept that the earliest point at which consciousness is possible is around the twentieth week of pregnancy, which is when synaptic connections begin to form among the cortical neurons. It is, however, unlikely that consciousness becomes possible until after at least another month—that is, until around the sixth month. Neurologist Julius Korein offers a representative sketch of the relevant aspects of fetal brain development:

Neurons in the cortical plate first begin to form cortical synapses at about 20 weeks. These neurons then form synaptic connections between other intracerebral structures such as the thalamus and the brain stem, resulting in sensory reception and more patterned spontaneous and induced motor activity. Cortical EEG activity can be first recorded at about 21–22 weeks after fertilization; the blink-startle response, with eyes opening, to auditory

From *The Ethics of Killing: Problems at the Margins of Life* (Oxford, 2002). By permission of Oxford University Press.

stimuli can be demonstrated at 24 weeks; and *cortical sensory evoked potentials* appear at about 25–27 weeks. . . . Major components of cerebral function including aspects of consciousness (sentience) are unequivocally present in the fetus after 28 weeks of fetal age. The onset of the fundamental core of brain function . . . can be identified between the limits of about 20 to 28 weeks.[1]

Let us assume that the fetal brain develops the capacity to generate consciousness some time between the twentieth and the twenty-eighth week of gestation. It was during this period that each of us began to exist. This is, of course, a broad period in which to locate the beginning of our existence, but it does not seem possible as yet to be more specific by identifying a narrower interval. There are various reasons for this, not least of which is that our understanding of the neural basis of consciousness is still comparatively rudimentary. We do not, moreover, have a clear understanding of the nature of consciousness at lower levels. We are not even clear about what constitutes evidence of its presence at these levels, as is clear from the fact that there is no consensus, even among scientists who study the matter, whether houseflies or other insects are conscious. But, even if our understanding of these matters were considerably more advanced than it is, it would still be unlikely that we could determine with precision when the capacity for consciousness first arises. One reason for this is that the fetal organism may develop the *capacity* to generate consciousness before there is any actual consciousness. Thus, as Michael Lockwood has observed, we might begin to exist in a state of dreamless sleep—capable of consciousness but not yet actually conscious.[2] If so, we may begin to exist before there is any behavioral evidence that we are there. There may, moreover, be some genuine indeterminacy about when consciousness becomes possible. Assuming that consciousness is not possible in the absence of substantial synaptic connections among the cortical neurons, there must be some minimum degree of connectivity necessary for consciousness to occur. But it does not follow that there must be some precise number of synaptic connections such that the formation of only one more synapse would make consciousness possible where before it was not.

Our inability to identify a precise point at which we begin to exist is, I believe, of comparatively little practical significance. [. . .] Let us pretend, for convenience of exposition, that there *is* an exact point at which we begin to exist—say, to make the most conservative assumption, at twenty weeks, or roughly five months after conception. An early abortion, therefore, is an abortion performed prior to twenty weeks. This is significant, for approximately 99 percent of all abortions in the United States are performed prior to twenty weeks.[3] If the Embodied Mind Account of Identity is right, these abortions merely prevent someone like you or me from existing. There is no one there to be killed.

There is, however, some*thing* that is killed in an early abortion—namely, a developing human organism. (I will assume for the present that abortion involves killing, though there are reasons to believe that some abortion techniques do not kill but merely allow the fetus to die.) [. . .] How significant, in moral terms, is the killing of an unoccupied human organism? Three grounds of objection have been advanced. I will mention each briefly and suggest in a general way why I think it is mistaken. [. . .]

First, some people believe that a fetal organism has a special sanctity or intrinsic value simply by virtue of being alive and human. I believe that this view is "speciesist"—that is, that it groundlessly attributes greater value to a *human* organism than to an otherwise comparable organism belonging to another biological species. [. . .]

Second, many people claim that the fetal organism, even if it is not one of us, nevertheless has the potential to become one of us (or, as it is more commonly put, to become a person). This, it is held, makes it seriously wrong to kill the fetal organism, even if one is not thereby killing someone like you or me. But the claim that the fetal organism has the potential to become one of us is ambiguous. Understood in one way, the claim is true but has little or no moral significance. Understood in another way, it is false, though it would have great moral significance *if* it were true. [. . .]

Third and finally, it might be contended that the fetal organism merits protection because it is the vehicle through which someone like you or me, whose life would be worth living, may be brought into existence. The problem with this contention, however, is that it applies equally to any pair of sperm and egg.

In short, if the Embodied Mind Account is correct and the early fetal organism is not identical with the person who will later exist in association with it, it is hard to see how the organism can have a special moral status sufficient to make it seriously wrong to kill it. Apart from any effects it might have on the pregnant woman or on other preexisting people, an early abortion is morally indistinguishable from contraception. (I stress, again, that not all the argumentation for this conclusion has yet been given. It remains to be shown that the early fetal organism— that is, the organism prior to twenty weeks—cannot have a special sanctity that otherwise comparable nonhuman organisms lack and that it does not have the relevant sort of potential to become a person. [. . .])

2. Late Abortion

According to the Embodied Mind Account of Identity, an entity of our kind—one of us—begins to exist when a human organism develops the capacity to generate consciousness. If we assume that the capacity for consciousness arises at approximately twenty weeks after conception (an assumption that probably errs on the side of caution by a month or more), it follows that an abortion performed later than twenty weeks after conception involves the killing of some*one* rather than merely some*thing*. It involves the killing of one of us. Let us call such an abortion a *late abortion* and let us refer to the individual who is killed by a late abortion as the *developed fetus*—bearing in mind that the developed fetus is a distinct individual from the fetal organism that supports its existence. For, if we are not identical with our organisms, the developed fetus, being one of us, cannot be either.

How are we to understand the morality of killing a developed fetus? Before advancing the view that seems to me most plausible, I will briefly outline some of the other positions that might be defended. According to some views, late abortion is like early abortion in being morally indistinguishable from contraception. For example [. . .] the Psychological Account of Identity implies that we do not begin to exist until some time after birth, for only then does

the mental life generated by the brain become sufficiently rich for there to be psychological continuity over time, and psychological continuity is, on this view, the criterion of our identity. If this view of our identity were correct, any abortion, whether performed early or late in the course of fetal gestation, would merely prevent one of us from existing. Of course, even on this view, an early abortion might be objectionable on the ground that the fetal organism would have a special sanctity, and a late abortion might be objectionable on the ground that it would frustrate the time-relative interest that the conscious pre-person might have in the future life of the person whose existence the abortion would prevent. But I will not pursue these possibilities here, since [. . .] I reject this account of personal identity.

One influential approach to abortion appeals to an understanding of the morality of killing that is very like what I have called the Harm-Based Account. This approach has been defended by Don Marquis. Although he does not invoke the concept of harm, he claims that what is essentially wrong with or objectionable about killing people is that it deprives the victim of a future that would have contained a great deal of good. He then notes that the killing of a human fetus normally has the same effect. "The future of a standard fetus," he writes, "includes a set of experiences, projects, activities, and such which are identical with the futures of adult human beings and are identical with the futures of young children. Since the reason that is sufficient to explain why it is wrong to kill human beings after the time of birth is a reason that also applies to fetuses, it follows that abortion is prima facie seriously morally wrong."[4] In short, the harm that killing inflicts on the fetus—namely, the loss or deprivation of all that future good—is sufficient to make the killing seriously wrong.

Marquis's argument is carefully qualified. He does not claim that it is a necessary condition of an act of killing being wrong that it should deprive the victim of a future that would have contained a great deal of good. There might, he concedes, be other reasons why killing is morally objectionable. Nor does he explicitly embrace or even consider what [. . .] I called the assumption of correlative variation—that is, the assumption that the wrongness of killing varies with the degree of harm caused to the victim. Thus the view he articulates does not imply that it is permissible to kill people whose futures cannot be expected to contain more good than evil; nor does it imply that, because the deprivation that an animal suffers in being killed is less, it is less objectionable to kill animals than it is to kill people. What Marquis does claim is that the fundamental reason why killing people is seriously wrong applies at least equally in the case of the fetus; hence abortion, which involves killing the fetus, must be seriously wrong, other things being equal.

There are at least three important objections to this argument, the first of which is that, because Marquis assumes that we begin to exist at conception, it fails to distinguish between early and late abortions. If, as I have argued, we do not begin to exist until approximately twenty weeks after conception, Marquis's argument does not apply to abortions performed before that point. But his position can, of course, be adjusted to accommodate the view that we begin to exist only after twenty weeks. It would then hold that only late abortions are wrong. For only in the case of a late abortion is there a victim who is deprived of a future like ours.

Revised in this way, Marquis's argument offers a distinctive view of the morality of late abortion. But it remains vulnerable to two other objections. The first is based on the claim that Marquis's position cannot remain noncommittal about the assumption of correlative variation. His understanding of the wrongness of killing requires an explanation of why it is more objectionable to deprive people of future goods through killing than it is to cause them lesser deprivations in nonlethal ways. And it should offer an explanation of why killing an animal is normally less objectionable than killing a person. The natural solution is to adopt the assumption of correlative variation. With that assumption, his view has an explanation of why killing a person is more seriously objectionable than either stealing his wallet or killing an animal: namely, the deprivation or loss inflicted is greater.

But if Marquis's view incorporates an assumption of correlative variation, it implies that a late abortion is more seriously wrong, if other things are equal, than the killing of an older child or adult. For in losing its future, the developed fetus suffers a greater loss—the whole of a human life. But scarcely anyone really accepts that the killing of a fetus is worse. On the contrary, even most opponents of abortion appear to accept that even an abortion performed relatively late in pregnancy is less seriously wrong than the killing of an older child or adult. If people really believed that the developed fetus has the same moral status as a normal adult, it would be difficult to explain why even most of those who are in general opposed to abortion are willing to recognize certain exceptions to what they regard as the general impermissibility of abortion—for example, in the case of pregnancies that result from rape or incest, or in cases involving fetal deformity, or when the continuation of the pregnancy poses a serious threat to the pregnant woman's life or health. It would also be difficult to explain why even most opponents of abortion strongly disapprove of the killing of abortionists and the bombing of abortion clinics. For if even the proportionally rather small number of late abortions performed each year were morally comparable to the murder of innocent children or adults, there would be a strong case for the permissibility of defending further innocent victims by violent means. The shootings and bombings might be reasonable responses to a practice of widespread, legally sanctioned murder.

Part of the reason why Marquis's view leads naturally to an implausibly strong condemnation of late abortion is that it presupposes that identity is what matters, both prudentially and morally. It presupposes that our moral concern should be with what is better or worse for individuals, taking account of their lives as wholes. It evaluates a late abortion in terms of its effect on the fetus's life as a whole, and thus finds no difference between the deprivation that abortion inflicts on a developed fetus and that which killing inflicts on an adult, except that the former is quantitatively greater. It fails, in short, to take account of the differences in the ways that fetuses and adults are related to their own future selves. This is the third objection to the view.

I will assume that these objections are decisive. I will also assume, from here on, that the Embodied Mind Account of Identity is correct and thus that there is no one present in the womb to be affected for the worse by an early abortion but that, after twenty weeks, there is someone present who would be killed by a late abortion. If this is the metaphysical situation, what should we believe about the morality of a late abortion? I suspect that many people would conclude that, while early abortion is innocuous because it merely prevents a person from existing, late abortion is murder because it involves the intentional killing of someone like you or me. It is not uncommon, after all, for people to want to draw a sharp line before which abortion is supposed to be permissible but after which it is not. The idea that the onset of the capacity for consciousness at twenty weeks marks the point at which one of us begins to exist offers a line that seems (in contrast to previously favored lines such as viability and quickening) to have obvious moral significance.

On reflection, however, it seems hardly plausible to suppose that there could be a sharp dividing line of this sort. Twenty weeks is 140 days. Is it really acceptable to suppose that an abortion performed 139 days after conception would be perfectly innocuous while an abortion performed a day later would be gravely wrong? Certainly it seems odd to suppose that abortion could go from being innocuous to being murder just as a result of the establishment of a few more synaptic connections in the fetal brain. As opponents of abortion often observe, fetal development is a smoothly continuous process in which it seems impossible to identify an event that is significant enough to make the difference between permissible killing and murder. Intuitively, the extent to which abortion seems morally objectionable increases slowly and gradually over time in a way that corresponds to the process of fetal maturation.

Of course, if I am right that the onset of the capacity for consciousness marks the beginning of the existence of an entirely new individual, the impression that fetal development is a process of merely incremental change is an illusion. For the onset of the capacity for consciousness is a momentous event, both metaphysically and, it seems, morally. Still, I find it difficult to believe that the moral status of abortion could shift radically overnight—or even (if there is genuine indeterminacy in the onset of the capacity for consciousness) over a

period of a week or month. We should want, I think, an account of the morality of abortion that captures the sense that most people have, on reflection, that abortion becomes a morally more serious matter the later it is performed.

It is difficult for an account that assigns the developed fetus the same moral status as a normal adult to deliver that desired implication. For example, the Harm-Based Account, of which Marquis's view is a variant, draws a sharp line: before twenty weeks, no one suffers the loss of a future like ours; after twenty weeks, someone does. There will also be a radical moral difference between early and late abortion if the developed fetus comes within the scope of the morality of respect. For given that assumption, the killing of the developed fetus would be just as wrong as the killing of any adult person, if other things were equal. Yet an early abortion would not violate any requirement of respect, for, given that the early fetus is not one of us but is instead a mere unoccupied organism, it is uncontroversially not the sort of being that commands respect.

Is it reasonable to suppose that the developed fetus comes within the scope of the morality of respect? [. . .] I [have] remained somewhat agnostic about the basis of the worth that demands respect. It is nevertheless possible to reach a conditional conclusion about whether the developed fetus is owed respect. The basis of respect must be some intrinsic property or set of intrinsic properties. These properties are what relevantly differentiate persons like you and me from animals. While many people believe that what distinguishes us from animals is that we but not they have souls—souls that are, perhaps, made in the image of God—I [have] argued [. . .] that this view is indefensible. The most plausible remaining candidates for the basis of respect are certain psychological capacities, such as self-consciousness, rationality, and autonomy. Our possession of these capacities does seem to distinguish us from animals in an importantly relevant way. But if the possession of certain psychological capacities is what relevantly distinguishes us from animals and so is the basis of respect, the developed fetus must fall outside the scope of the morality of respect, for it clearly does not possess the capacities that distinguish persons from animals.

There are, in fact, only two respects in which the developed fetus differs from an animal that might be thought to elevate the developed fetus above the threshold of respect while leaving the animal below it. One is the developed fetus's membership in the human species. But while many people believe that mere membership in the human species is a significant basis of moral status. I [have] argued [. . .] that this is a mistake. The other difference between the developed fetus and an animal is that the former, but not the latter, has the potential to develop the psychological capacities that distinguish us from animals. Although the developed fetus does not now have the capacities for self-consciousness, rationality, and autonomy, it will acquire these capacities during the normal course of its development. This, it might be claimed, is a sufficient basis for the worth that commands respect.

I will not pause here to consider whether the developed fetus's potential might be sufficient to bring it within the scope of the morality of respect. [. . .] My conclusion [is] that potential alone cannot be a basis for respect. [. . .] I will proceed on the assumption that the developed fetus lies below the threshold of respect.

It would, in fact, be rather problematic if the developed fetus did come within the scope of the morality of respect. For if that were the case, late abortion would be morally equivalent to the killing of a person, other things being equal. And while this is less implausible than the implication of the Harm-Based Account that late abortion is *more* seriously wrong than the killing of an adult, it is, as I suggested earlier, not what most people believe. Even most of those who believe that late abortion is wrong implicitly accept that it is less seriously wrong than the killing of an adult normally is.

It may, of course, be that the relation between a pregnant woman and the fetus she carries is such that abortion is relevantly different from, and substantially less objectionable than, paradigm instances of murder, even if the developed fetus has the same moral status as an innocent adult. It might be, for example, that abortion can be justified as a matter of self-defense, or that it is permissible for a pregnant woman to kill the developed fetus if that is the only way she can prevent it from appropriating her body

as an instrument of life support. There are arguments that attempt to defend the permissibility of abortion on these grounds that grant that the fetus (and a fortiori the developed fetus) has the same intrinsic moral status as an innocent adult. [. . .] It is sufficient to note that it is unlikely that the considerations identified in these arguments can explain the almost universal sense that even late abortion is quite different morally from the killing of an older child or adult. The main reason why this is so is that the vast majority of those who intuitively regard abortion as morally different from the killing of an adult have never thought of abortion in the ways suggested by these arguments. So, for example, if one has never conceived of pregnancy as a state in which a woman is compelled by the fetus's presence to submit to her body's being used as a means of life support, one is very unlikely to believe that abortion is different from murder *because* one believes that a woman has a right to prevent herself from being forcibly used as a source of life support for another person. Moreover, even if one of these arguments can explain how a late abortion could be permissible even if the developed fetus has the same moral status as an innocent adult, it cannot fully explain or support the common intuition that a late abortion becomes morally more serious the later it is performed. It is, of course, possible to argue that a later abortion is harder to justify because the burden to the pregnant woman of carrying the fetus to term diminishes as pregnancy progresses. But this fails to capture our intuitive sense that the explanation of why a later abortion is worse is that the fetus has by then undergone morally important changes. Only a view that recognizes that the developed fetus's moral status evolves along with its biological or psychological development can adequately explain and justify the common belief that a late abortion becomes morally more problematic the later it is performed.

It seems, therefore, that most people implicitly recognize that, even if the developed fetus is one of us, its moral status is different in certain critical respects from that of an adult. There are several possible views of late abortion that attempt to capture that recognition. One holds that, although the developed fetus is one of us, it is not harmed or affected for the worse by being killed. According to this view, an individual cannot have an interest in continuing to live, and therefore cannot be harmed by dying, unless it is capable of desiring to continue to live.[5] Call this the *Capacity Condition*. According to this view, although I once existed as a developed fetus, it would not have been bad for me to have died or to have been killed at that age. If we combine the claim that the developed fetus cannot have an interest in continuing to live with the Harm-Based Account of the wrongness of killing, we get the conclusion that, if there is any objection at all to a late abortion, it must have to do with the effects on individuals other than the fetus itself.

The Capacity Condition is vulnerable to a powerful objection, which is that there is a sense in which death would clearly be worse for a developed fetus even though the fetus is incapable of desiring to continue to live. If a developed fetus's future life would be worth living, the truncated life it will have if it dies will be a less good life than the longer life it will have if it does not die. Death would therefore be worse for it because it would cause it to have the less good of two possible lives. This insight of the Life Comparative Account seems undeniable; therefore a capacity to desire continued life is not necessary in order for death to be bad for an individual. We have seen, however, that while the Life Comparative Account states an obvious truth, it nevertheless gives a distorted account of the badness of death. It presupposes that identity is what matters and thus implies that the death of a developed fetus is worse, other things being equal, than the death of an adult. But fetal death seems less bad; somehow the loss does not seem fully ascribable to the fetus. One can interpret the Capacity Condition as a crude attempt to explain this intuition. It holds that what is missing in the case of the developed fetus is desire: only through desire can the goods of an individual's future have value for it now. We have seen, however, that the Time-Relative Interest Account offers a subtler and more plausible explanation. What matters is not all-or-nothing (that is, the presence or absence of a capacity to desire continued life); it is, rather, the extent to which the various prudential unity relations would hold. Desire is only one of many elements that relevantly bind an individual to its own future.

The Capacity Condition and the Time-Relative Interest Account both offer an explanation of why the death of a developed fetus is less bad. But the Capacity Condition implies that it is not bad at all. And it implies that death becomes bad for a human being abruptly, when that individual develops the capacity to conceive of and to desire its own future. The Time-Relative Interest Account, by contrast, has the more plausible implication that death becomes a more serious misfortune gradually as a human being's psychological capacities mature and it becomes more closely related to its future self in the ways that ground egoistic concern. [. . .]

Another view that is perhaps more plausible than the Capacity Condition and seems to be more widely accepted is that, although the developed fetus is one of us, and although it suffers a significant loss in being killed, its loss matters less because the developed fetus as yet lacks the sort of status that would make it a proper subject of serious moral concern. According to a prominent variant of this view, personhood is the foundation of the high moral status that each of us now enjoys. But when we began to exist, and for some time thereafter, we were not yet persons. During that time—that is, before we became persons—our moral status was significantly lower. Our interests mattered less because we were not persons, in much the way that many people believe that the interests of animals matter less, not because they are lesser interests but simply because they are the interests *of animals*. So, even if our interest in not being killed was strong before we became persons, it would not have been as seriously wrong for someone to have killed one of us before he or she became a person.

This view is correct in claiming that it is significant that the developed fetus is not a person. But it misidentifies the significance of this fact. It is not that, because the fetus lacks the moral status of a person, its interests matter less. Rather, its not being a person means that it falls outside of the scope of the morality of respect, so that it is *only* its interests—or rather its time-relative interests—that significantly constrain our treatment of it. In short, it means that the morality of killing a developed fetus is governed by the Time-Relative Interest Account. [. . .]

According to the Time-Relative Interest Account, what is fundamentally wrong about killing is that it thwarts or frustrates the victim's time-relative interest in continuing to live; and the degree to which an act of killing is wrong varies, other things being equal, with the strength of the victim's time-relative interest in continuing to live. The strength of an individual's time-relative interest in continuing to live is itself a function of two factors: first, the amount of future good that the individual may rationally anticipate in an egoistic way, and second, the degree to which the prudential unity relations would hold between the individual now and itself in the future when the goods it may egoistically anticipate would occur. In the case of a developed fetus, the amount of good that lies in prospect is normally very great. But the prudential unity relations would hold only very weakly between the fetus and itself in the future. The developed fetus cannot envisage or contemplate its future and hence cannot have future-directed psychological states, such as intentions; it would, if it were to become a person, be unable to recall its life as a fetus; and it now has no psychological architecture—no beliefs, desires, or dispositions of character—to carry forward into the future. It is, in short, psychologically cut off or severed or isolated from itself in the future. Its future is, figuratively speaking, relevantly like someone else's future. It is for this reason that, despite the great good in prospect for it, the developed fetus has only a comparatively weak time-relative interest in continuing to live.

It is important to remember that the Time-Relative Interest Account is not a complete account of the morality of killing, but is instead just one component of the more comprehensive Two-Tiered Account. According to the Two-Tiered Account, the wrongness of killing beings who are above the threshold of respect is governed by a requirement of respect. Thus even if a person has a very weak time-relative interest in continuing to live because the amount of good in prospect for him is quite small, it would nevertheless be just as wrong to kill him as it would be to kill any other person, if other things are equal. For his worth as a person is a function of his intrinsic nature and is unaffected by the amount of good the future holds in prospect. It is only in the

case of beings that fall below the threshold of respect that the morality of killing is governed by the Time-Relative Interest Account. Given the provisional assumption that the developed fetus is below that threshold, the morality of a late abortion should come within the scope of the Time-Relative Interest Account.

It is, I think, reasonable to believe that an act of killing that violates a requirement of respect for the victim must be more seriously wrong than an act of killing that merely frustrates the victim's time-relative interest in continuing to live. So a late abortion is in an altogether different moral category from an act of killing an older child or adult. There are forms of justification that are largely or wholly ruled out within the morality of respect but may be acceptable within the area of morality governed by the Time-Relative Interest Account. For example, it is generally held to be unacceptable intentionally to sacrifice one person for the greater good of others. But this constraint does not seem to operate below the threshold of respect. Thus even most of those who believe that animals matter morally accept that it may be permissible to kill an animal if that is necessary to prevent a greater amount of harm to people or other animals. If that is right, there will be a range of justifications for late abortion that appeal to considerations capable of outweighing the developed fetus's time-relative interest in continuing to live—for example, the interests of the pregnant woman.

The idea that the morality of a late abortion is governed by the Time-Relative Interest Account also supports the common view that a late abortion becomes increasingly morally objectionable the later it is performed. According to the Time-Relative Interest Account, the wrongness of killing varies with the strength of the victim's time-relative interest in continuing to live. As the developed fetus matures, its psychological capacities become more advanced, and the degree to which it would be psychologically continuous with itself in the future increases correspondingly. Assuming that its life in the womb contains little or no good, the amount of good in its future remains effectively constant until birth. Therefore, because the amount of good in prospect remains constant while the extent to which it would be relevantly related to itself in the future gradually increases, the developed fetus's time-relative interest in continuing to live becomes stronger as gestation progresses. And this means that killing it becomes increasingly objectionable, if other things are equal.

I claimed earlier that it may not be important, for practical purposes, to identify with precision when we begin to exist. I can now explain the basis for that claim. Note that, immediately after the developed fetus begins to exist and for some time thereafter, its mental life, such as it is, is confined entirely to the present: its mental states do not refer forward or backward in time and there are no elements of its mental life, such as beliefs or desires, that persist over time. It is psychologically locked in the present. It has no psychological connections whatever to itself in the future. If it is right that psychological continuity is among the prudential unity relations, it seems reasonable to conclude that the developed fetus's time-relative interest in continuing to live is extremely weak, despite the amount of good its future can be expected to contain. According to the Time-Relative Interest Account, therefore, the moral objection to killing the developed fetus immediately after it begins to exist should be very weak. Thus there is no radical shift in the morality of abortion when the developed fetus begins to exist. It is not the case that, as soon as abortion comes to have a *victim* (that is, when the developed fetus appears), it shifts abruptly from being innocuous to being seriously objectionable. Rather, the moral status of abortion changes only incrementally. An early abortion, if it is morally objectionable at all, is objectionable only because of its effects on individuals other than the fetus. When the developed fetus begins to exist, there is then a victim who is affected for the worse by abortion, but the relevant effect, according to the Time-Relative Interest Account of the wrongness of killing, is minimal. At least initially, the developed fetus's time-relative interest in continuing to live is extremely weak and the moral objection to abortion is therefore correspondingly weak. As the pregnancy progresses and the developed fetus's time-relative interest in continuing to live increases in strength, a late abortion gradually becomes increasingly morally objectionable.

It is because the moral status of abortion changes incrementally over time that our inability to determine with precision when we begin to exist has relatively little practical significance. I have suggested that we begin to exist at some time between the twentieth and the twenty-eighth week of pregnancy, but that it is not at present possible to be much more precise than that. Just prior to twenty weeks, there is no one there to be affected by an abortion. After twenty-eight weeks, the developed fetus is definitely present and would be affected for the worse by an abortion. How strong its time relative interest in continuing to live is at twenty-eight weeks depends on how long the developed fetus has existed. It will be stronger if the developed fetus began to exist shortly after twenty weeks and weaker if it began to exist closer to twenty-eight weeks. But unless the developed fetus matures psychologically at a rapid rate, it should not make a very great difference to the strength of its time-relative interest in continuing to live whether it is only a few days old or whether it is almost a couple of months old. Therefore the degree to which an abortion at twenty-eight weeks would be morally objectionable will be substantially the same whether the developed fetus began to exist at twenty weeks or closer to twenty-eight weeks.

If this is right, of course, it implies that the moral gravity of a late abortion does not substantially increase between the time that the developed fetus begins to exist and the time of birth. While a late abortion becomes a morally more serious matter as pregnancy progresses, the increase in gravity over the last three or four mouths of pregnancy cannot be very great. To suppose otherwise, one must (if one is being guided by the Time-Relative Interest Account) assume that the developed fetus's psychological capacities develop rapidly over that period, so that by the end of pregnancy its potential psychological connections to itself in the future would be significantly stronger than they were when it first began to exist. But this seems an unrealistic assumption.

Thus far I have sought to defend the common view that late abortion is morally less objectionable than the killing of an older child or adult by appealing to two claims: first, that the developed fetus's time-relative interest in continuing to live is comparatively weak, and second, that, because the developed fetus falls below the threshold of respect, the morality of late abortion is governed by the Time-Relative Interest Account of the wrongness of killing. There is, however, an alternative but closely related defense of this common view that appeals to a different understanding of the status of the developed fetus. It attributes to the developed fetus a rather peculiar metaphysical status. Because the metaphysical claims underlying this view are obscure, my sketch of the view, though sympathetic, will be noncommittal.

When we note [. . .] that the death of a developed fetus is intermediate between nonconception and the death of a person, the intuition we are seeking to capture is that there is somehow less of a victim than there is when a person dies. The developed fetus seems too insubstantial—too psychologically insubstantial—to be a victim in the same way that a person would be. The idea that there is less of a victim may seem a figurative way of articulating the sense that the loss matters less; but there is also a quite literal understanding of this idea. It may be that the developed fetus is not a fully real or fully existing individual of our kind.

Warren Quinn, to whose views on these matters I am much indebted, defends a *gradualist* understanding of the coming into existence of entities of certain kinds. According to gradualism, "the coming to be of substantial individuals may be a genuine process in time in the course of which the prospective individual comes into existence gradually, entering the world by degrees. The ontology in question thus involves the idea of the extent to which an individual has at a given time become fully actual or real—or . . . the degree to which it already fully exists."[6] Quinn cites as an example the building of a house. Materials are gathered, the foundation is laid, a wooden skeleton is erected, plumbing and electrical wiring are installed, bricks are laid, and so on until the house is completed. But in all this there is no point at which a house suddenly begins to exist. Instead, the house seems genuinely to come into existence gradually. During much of the process by which the house is erected, the existence of the house is only *partial*. The degree to which it exists increases as the work progresses.

According to Quinn, it is plausible to take an analogous gradualist view about the beginning of our own existence. We may defensibly believe that we are essentially human beings and that the fetus is a human being in the process of becoming—that is, a partially real or partially existing human being. This view does not, he notes, have the absurd implication that the fetus is in any way empirically indeterminate, or that its existence is somehow ghostly or flickering. Again, the case of the house is illuminating: "A house under construction can, at a given moment, be characterized with every bit as much precision as a fully built house. Its incompleteness lies only in its relation to the special sortal that best indicates the kind of thing it is, namely 'house.' Thus there is no reason in the kind of full empirical reality that the fetus possesses to reject the claim that it is the human being in the making ."[7]

Quinn does not say what he takes the essential properties of a human being to be or how he thinks a human being differs from a human organism. (He concedes that "a fetus is indeed a full-fledged organism, but this is quite consistent with the claim that such a full-fledged organism is not a fully real individual."[8] In the same way, a house in the making may be a full-fledged *construction* but not a fully real house.) According to the Embodied Mind Account of Identity, the substance sortal that provides the criteria of our identity is not "human being" but "mind" or "self." But a parallel gradualist account of the coming into existence of a mind or self can be given. There are, it might be claimed, the beginnings of a mind around the twentieth week of pregnancy, when (we are assuming) the capacity for consciousness first appears, but as the various psychological capacities characteristic of a human mind are being developed, the mind is relevantly like a house under construction: it is not yet fully present; it is only partially though increasingly present.

The gradualist view may be intuitively more compelling when applied to certain cases involving the ceasing to exist rather than the beginning to exist of a mind. In cases involving Alzheimer's disease or other forms of progressive dementia, for example, it is quite natural to think of the person as going out of existence gradually as the mind is increasingly eroded, with its constituent psychological states and capacities disappearing as the tissues of the brain atrophy and die. On this view, dying is not so much a process that occurs within life but an extended transition between life and total nonexistence in which the *existence* of the person gradually diminishes until it is extinguished altogether. [. . .]

Suppose that the gradualist view is plausible and that the process by which we come into existence begins around the twentieth week of pregnancy. If we are essentially embodied minds, it seems reasonable to suppose that this process continues at least until birth and perhaps until some time after. If that is right, the developed fetus is not fully one of us; it is not a fully realized mind or self but a self in the process of becoming. It is a partially existing entity of the sort that you and I essentially are.

Recall the claim that the death of a newborn infant, and by extension the death of a developed fetus, is, intuitively, intermediate between the death of a person and nonconception, or the failure of a person to come into existence. That claim makes perfect sense if the developed fetus, and perhaps the newborn infant as well, is an only partially existing entity of our sort.

There are two ways in which the claim that the developed fetus is a partially existing member of our kind might support the permissibility of a late abortion. One appeals to the principle that the more fully real an individual is as a member of our kind, the higher its moral *status* must be, other things being equal. Quinn's view seems to be of this sort. He writes that because "the morally binding force of humane considerations varies according to various dimensions in which the object affected is nearer to or further from us, the fact that the fetus is to some extent already a human being, already to some extent one of us, can only make its loss, however qualified, count for more. And as the fetus becomes more fully human the seriousness of aborting it will approach that of infanticide."[9] According to this view, the more like one of us the fetus becomes, the stronger its rights will be.

The other approach, which seems to me more plausible, is to claim that the developed fetus's ontological status means that its loss in dying must be less than that which is normally suffered by a person

who dies. For according to the gradualist view, the developed fetus is not fully identical with the person who will be the subject of future good if an abortion is not performed. (On the gradualist view, it seems that identity as well as existence must be a matter of degree.) The subject of the good that will be lost if the abortion is performed does not yet fully exist. The victim of that loss exists now only partially in the form of the developed fetus. Therefore the loss of future good that would be caused by a late abortion is only partially ascribable to the developed fetus. It is in this sense that the developed fetus is not a victim of loss in the same way as a person who dies is. The loss that is ascribable to it is less because the future that is lost is not fully *its* future (or, alternatively, it is not fully the same individual as the one who would have been the subject of the goods that are lost).

Is the gradualist view ultimately plausible? I will not attempt to judge. I mention it because it offers a particularly bold and striking way of accounting for our sense that, when a late abortion is performed and the whole of a human life is thereby lost, the developed fetus is nevertheless not a victim of loss in quite the same way that a person is when he or she dies or is killed.

Notes

1. Korein (1997), pp. 25–26. For a similar view, see Glover and Fisk (1999).
2. Lockwood (1985), p. 212, note 18.
3. Steinbock (1992), p. 87.
4. Marquis (1989), p. 192.
5. Among those who have defended the Capacity Condition are Singer (1993a), chs. 4 and 5, Harris (1995), p. 9, Cigman (1981), and Velleman (1991).
6. Quinn (1984), p. 34.
7. Ibid., p. 39.
8. Ibid.
9. Ibid., p. 54.

References

Cigman, Ruth. 1981. "Death, Misfortune, and Species Inequality." *Philosophy and Public Affairs* 10: 47–64.

Glover, Vivette, and Fisk, Nicholas M. 1999. "Fetal Pain: Implications for Research and Practice." *British Journal of Obstetrics and Gynaecology* 106: 881–86.

Harris, John. 1995. "Euthanasia and the Value of Life." Pp. 6–22 in Keown (1995).

Keown, John. ed. 1995. *Euthanasia Examined: Ethical, Clinical, and Legal Perspectives.* Cambridge: Cambridge University Press.

Korein, Julius. 1997. "Ontogenesis of the Brain in the Human Organism: Definitions of Life and Death of the Human Being and Person." *Advances in Bioethics* 2: 1–74.

——. 1985. "When Does a Life Begin?" Pp. 9–31 in Michael Lockwood, ed., *Moral Dilemmas in Modern Medicine.* Oxford: Oxford University Press.

Marquis, Don. 1989. "Why Abortion Is Immoral." *Journal of Philosophy* 86: 183–203.

Quinn, Warren. 1984. "Abortion: Identity and Loss." *Philosophy and Public Affairs* 13: 24–54.

Singer, Peter. 1993a. *Practical Ethics.* 2d edition. Cambridge: Cambridge University Press.

Steinbock, Bonnie. 1992. *Life Before Birth: The Moral and Legal Status of Embryos and Fetuses.* New York: Oxford University Press.

Velleman, J. David. 1991. "Well-Being and Time." *Pacific Philosophical Quarterly* 72: 48–77.

QUESTIONS

1. Does McMahan's embodied minds conceptions of us settle the morality of most abortions?
2. Consider McMahan's critical examination of Marquis's position. What questions does he raise for Marquis's account, and can they be answered?

61. The Egg and I: Conception, Identity, and Abortion

EUGENE MILLS

Eugene Mills (1956–) is professor of philosophy at Virginia Commonwealth University. His interests are very broad, and he has published on a variety of topics, including personal identity, mental causation, justification, and the liar paradox.

In this essay Mills asks when we come into existence. The question turns out to be very difficult to answer and of some importance to the abortion controversy. He argues that we do not originate at conception, but either before or after. He uses this conclusion to criticize a number of pro-life positions, including that of Marquis.

Mills's essay is quite difficult, and students might first (or only) read sections I–II and VI. Section V contains an extended criticism of Marquis.

From "The Egg and I: Conception, Identity, and Abortion," *Philosophical Review* 117 (2008), 323–48.

I. The Metaphysics and Morality of Origination

When did I come into existence, and why should you care? Take the second question first. You should care because what goes for me goes for all human persons: we aren't all the same age, but we all came into existence at the same stage of biological development. This fact bears on the morality of abortion. I assume—without argument but for its sake— that you care about *this*.

The answer to the first question may hinge partly on the answer to a different question: what kind of thing am I? I'll suppose for the sake of argument, except where explicitly stated otherwise, that the true, relevant, and known answer is that I'm a "human being" in the sense of a human *animal*, a member of the genus *Homo*.[1] Given this supposition, I'll argue first and foremost that I originated not at the moment of my biological conception, but either before or after. This metaphysical point carries moral freight. I'll argue secondarily that if any familiar "pro-life" moral principle raises moral qualms about the permissibility of zygotic abortion,[2] these qualms apply equally (or at least almost equally) to the permissibility of contraception and abstinence.

Although I think my primary, metaphysical argument is strong, a related but weaker argument will serve for most of my moral purposes. I hope that even if I don't convince you that I originated either before or after conception, I'll at least convince you that it's at least reasonably doubtful that I originated at conception. And if you're convinced of even this much, I'll argue, my primary moral arguments should convince you as well.

Regardless of your moral attitude toward abortion, you probably hold that human biological conception—the fertilization of the egg—creates a new being. You probably hold that this being is at least a candidate for being or becoming a living human being. If you lean one way on abortion's moral status, you probably deny that this being is a person or a "human being" in a moral sense while allowing that it may eventually become one. You may deny that it has moral standing, while allowing that it may eventually gain it. Still, you probably affirm that

conception results in *a new being* (even if you think this being a constituent part of the pregnant woman). If you lean the other way on abortion, you're more likely to insist that this new being has moral standing; you may, though you needn't, hold that it's a person right from the start. Whichever way you lean, you probably hold that from conception on, but not before, a being exists that probably will, absent abortion or mishap, become a normal adult human being.

From the retrospective first-person perspective, this shared assumption amounts to the view that I—the human animal that I'm assuming is me—originated with the fertilization of an egg. I'll argue that this assumption is mistaken. "Conception" has an ontological sense on which it's analytic that conception is origination. It's not analytic, though, that *biological* conception is origination. I'll argue that it's not even true; biological conception creates no new being.

I'll then draw out some consequences for abortion. Pro-life arguments typically involve two main premises. The first assigns to the human organism *in utero* some salient metaphysical status. Candidates for this status include: person, potential person, being with the potential for a valuable future, sentient being, and living human being. The second premise is a moral principle to the effect that (at least generally, at least presumptively) it's wrong to kill beings with the metaphysical status in question. I focus here on the metaphysical rather than the moral premise and mainly on the question *at what stage of development* is the salient metaphysical status attained? I argue that there's no good reason to think, for any standard candidate, that biological conception—hereafter, just "conception"—is the point of attainment.

I don't debate whether any sound principle leads from the metaphysical status of beings who could survive[3] to normal adulthood to the presumptive wrongness of abortion.[4] I argue that any such principle of familiar stripe, if true, either renders contraception and sexual abstinence presumptively wrong, or else does *not* rule presumptively wrong zygotic abortion.

"Morning-after pills" destroy zygotes. Though my argument renders no categorical verdict on the permissibility of such destruction, it does show that no familiar basis for condemning morning-after pills while condoning contraception and abstinence can succeed. Given the current public debate over the moral status of morning-after pills, my argument thus has a practical upshot of contemporary relevance.

Here's a sketch of the coming argument. Common sense holds, and I assume for convenience,[5] that an organism existing at one time may be numerically identical to an organism existing at another time, though it grows and otherwise changes in the interim. When I say truly that "I existed ten years ago," I say that I (now) am identical with an organism that existed ten years ago. I argue in section 2 that, given this view, I didn't come into existence at conception. I consider objections in section 3. In section 4, I consider the only two plausible candidates for my origination, neither of which is my conception. In sections 5 and 6, I trace some consequences of my metaphysical argument for the morality of abortion.

II. The Egg and I

Suppose, again, that I'm a human animal—a member of the genus *Homo*. When did I originate?

I'm intimately related to a zygote that inhabited my mother's womb when she was pregnant with me. Either the intimate relation connecting me with the zygote is identity, or it isn't. If it's identity, then I (now) and the zygote (then) are the same being at different stages of development. If it isn't identity, then our intimate relation consists in my having "developed out of" the zygote in a distinctive way. In either case, I'll argue, I didn't originate at conception.

Suppose I'm not identical with the zygote from which I developed. Now, temporally gappy existence may be possible. (Dismantle a car, scatter its parts, and then recover and reassemble them. Perhaps the car has gappy existence.) Whether or not existence *can* be gappy, though, my actual existence clearly isn't.[6] So if I was never a zygote, then I didn't exist before or during the existence of the zygote to which I'm intimately related. Conception occurred either before or during the existence of that zygote. Hence if I was never a zygote, then I existed neither before conception nor for some time after. Thus I originated

sometime after conception. So if I was never a zygote, I didn't originate at conception.

Suppose on the other hand that I once was a zygote. A zygote is a fertilized egg. A fertilized egg doesn't pop into existence upon fertilization; it exists, unfertilized, before its encounter with the fertilizing sperm. So if I was once a fertilized egg, then I was once an unfertilized egg. The fertilization of the egg is (biological) conception. Hence if I was once an unfertilized egg, then I existed before conception. So if I was once a fertilized egg—a zygote—then I did not originate at conception.

In sum: whether or not I was once a zygote, I did not originate at conception.

III. Some Objections Considered

I expect that the first horn of my dilemma—that if I was never a zygote, then my conception wasn't my origination—will raise no eyebrows. I expect that the crucial claim of the second horn—that if I was once a zygote, then I was once an unfertilized egg—will inspire incredulity. I now consider some objections to it.

One objection to my argument for the second horn is as follows. A fertilized egg is not, contrary to my suggestion, an egg—just as a crowned prince is not a prince, a victorious candidate not a candidate. So I wrongly claim that a zygote is an egg that was once unfertilized and then became fertilized.

I note that despite my forthcoming concession of this point for argument's sake, it's utterly implausible. You can buy fertilized hen's eggs in grocery stores. I see no license in common sense, biology, ontology or agribusiness for the claim that they aren't really eggs.

The main point, though, is that my argument doesn't require that a fertilized human egg be an *egg*, it's enough that it's an organism (or, in fact, a *thing*). It would indeed be a mistake to say that a crowned prince is a prince who was once uncrowned and then became crowned. It would be no mistake, though, to say that a crowned prince is a thing that was once uncrowned and then became crowned. What matters is that the crowned prince is identical with—the very same being as—the uncrowned prince, not that this being is a prince at both times under consideration. Similarly, it suffices for my argument that a fertilized egg—a zygote—is a thing that existed before fertilization and then became fertilized.

Let me reinforce this claim. If I was once a fertilized egg but never an unfertilized one, then the organism that's the fertilized egg didn't exist before its union with a sperm. More accurately, it didn't exist before its predecessor's union with a sperm: the organism that is the fertilized egg never joined with a sperm, on the suggestion I now consider, since on that suggestion the joining precedes the existence of that organism. If this is true, then eggs can't survive fertilization. Eggs never *become fertilized*; nothing is at one time an unfertilized egg and later a zygote. Fertilization annihilates one organism and creates another.

The problem with this suggestion is that it seems plainly false, notwithstanding its wide uncritical acceptance. Review some sex education materials; watch, via microscope, the fertilization of an egg. You see an unfertilized oocyte—the one-celled human egg. A sperm approaches and, after traversing the corona radiata and zona pellucida, contacts the egg's cell wall. The sperm breaches that wall, enters, and dissolves, discharging its contents. The breach in the cell wall is immediately sealed.[7] The most natural description of these events is that you've watched one egg *become fertilized*, not the annihilation of one organism and the creation of another.

I offer no principle of organismic identity over time—no conjunction of nontrivial necessary and sufficient conditions. Even without such a principle, we recognize clear cases of the persistence (or failure of persistence) of organisms through change, just as we need no principle of (say) chair-identity over time to recognize clear cases of the persistence (or failure of persistence) of chairs through change. A concrete look at the events involved in conception reveals what seems a clear case of organismic persistence through change—a clearer case, certainly, than we find in many other cases that we take as *uncontroversial* cases of organismic persistence. The description of the case as one of persistence—of an egg undergoing and surviving fertilization—rather than annihilation is, as I say, natural. There is, I will argue, no good reason to reject it.

I'll argue this by surveying the most likely sources of rejection and showing of each that it fails. This procedure isn't ironclad; perhaps there's some good reason that I don't consider. If you can produce it, well and good. Otherwise, the mere possibility of such a reason is no rebuttal of my argument.

If you insist that fertilization annihilates the egg, then tell me: at what point does the unfertilized egg cease to exist and a new organism come into existence? In response, you might identify the relevant point, or you might demur while arguing that your demurral doesn't concede the point at issue. I consider these two responses in turn.

Suppose you identify the relevant point. I don't know where you might put it, but the most likely candidates are the moments when (a) the sperm breaches the cell wall of the egg, and (b) the paternal genetic material is fully incorporated into the nucleus of the egg. I'll discuss these two possibilities, confident that no candidate with dimmer prospects will succeed.

Suppose it's the first: the egg blinks out when the sperm breaches its cell wall. *Why* would you think this? Cells don't generally suffer annihilation when their outer layers are breached. If a cell can't survive a breach, then an amoeba can't survive a meal; but this is absurd. With respect to cross-time identity, no relevant difference separates an amoeba's absorbing its food and an egg's absorbing a fertilizing sperm. So an egg doesn't cease to exist (whether or not it ceases to be an egg) when a sperm breaches its cell wall.

Suppose, then, that the unfertilized egg ceases to exist when it has fully incorporated the sperm's genetic material into its own genetic makeup. This occurs after the sperm has dissolved and the breach in the egg has been sealed. On the suggestion now under consideration, what would naturally be described as an internal rearrangement of parts in a persisting organism would naturally be *mis*described. In fact, when the genetic material is finally sorted out—when the haploid oocyte becomes diploid—the unicellular organism that was an unfertilized oocyte *ceases to exist,* and a new organism is created.

This seems once again absurd. The egg is a living cell. Throughout the process of fertilization, there's just a single living cell relevantly in view. After the absorption of the spermatic material, this cell undergoes rearrangement of its internal parts, and in particular of its genetic material. If you accept this description of the situation, you *already* reject the suggestion that the conversion from haploid to diploid status marks a simultaneous annihilation and creation. For if it did, there would be nothing of which we could truly say that *it* underwent rearrangement of its internal parts. There's simply no basis in ordinary views of cross-time organismic identity for the idea that full absorption of spermatic genetic material extinguishes the oocyte.

So much for identifying the moment of the zygote's creation. Turn to demurral. You might invoke vagueness: it's a vague matter when one egg blinks out of existence and a new one blinks in. Still, you say, we can be sure that the (unfertilized) egg that precedes fertilization is distinct from the (fertilized) egg that follows it.

I gladly allow that if there's good reason to think that the unfertilized egg is an organism distinct from the zygote, then it's a vague matter when one vanishes and the other appears. I grant, that is, that if there's good reason to think that there's a relevant transition, then it's a vague one. In standard cases of vagueness, we rightly grant the vagueness of a transition (say, between something's being red and being orange) because we have good reason to believe that the transition must have occurred, even if we can't pinpoint its occurrence. In the case of conception, I claim, there's no good reason to think that any relevant transition occurs. There's no basis for the view that there are two successive organisms here rather than one that undergoes significant changes—changes that pale, of course, in comparison with those distinguishing a fetus from the adult with which it's identical, or a caterpillar from the butterfly with which it's identical.

Some philosophers might invoke genetic essentialism to defend the view that conception is origination. I have my doubts about genetic essentialism, but I won't press them here. For such an invocation would be confused, even granting genetic essentialism. Kripke, for example, defends the necessity of origin and apparently infers from it that Queen Elizabeth's conception couldn't have involved an egg *or* sperm different from those actually involved.[8] This inference hinges, however, on the unargued—indeed, unacknowledged—assumption that Elizabeth originated at conception. Everything I say here is compatible with the thesis of the necessity of origin and also with the thesis that a being's original genetic endowment is essential to its existence. (It is compatible, that is, with the thesis that a being could not have existed with an original genetic endowment different from its actual one. No one, I hope, will advocate that a being cannot survive *changes*, including additions, to its genetic endowment. I wouldn't cease to exist if I became the first victim of adult-onset Down's syndrome.) These theses entail the necessity of spermatic ancestry, however, only when wedded to the question-begging assumption that conception is *origin*. There's nothing in the theses of necessity of origin or of original genetic endowment to suggest that the Queen couldn't be identical with an unfertilized oocyte. Both theses are perfectly compatible with the view that oocytes survive fertilization.

You might plump for the conception-as-origination thesis on the following, related grounds. A particular genus-membership is an essential property of that which has it; I am a member of *Homo*; so if I first acquired that membership at conception, then I must have originated at conception. I accept this argument for argument's sake. (If you prefer to cast it in terms of species- rather than genus-membership, go right ahead.) But to move from its conclusion to the conception-as-origination thesis, you must justify the antecedent of that conclusion: the claim that I *did* first acquire my genus-membership at conception.

This claim is, by itself, neutral on genus-essentialism. You might deploy it in arguments concerning abortion's permissibility even if you decouple it from genus-essentialism. Discussion of it thus fits naturally into a discussion of metaphysical features *other* than origination that might bear on the permissibility of abortion, and I will discuss these below. To avoid redundancy, I issue here a promissory note: I'll argue below (in section 6) that there's no good basis for marking conception as the moment at which I became a member of *Homo*. I'll assume here the success of the lengthier argument to come later.

I expect another objection. It's commonly claimed that sperm and egg contribute equally to conception. If the zygote is identical with the unfertilized egg, then it seems that it must also be identical with the preconception sperm. But the sperm and the egg are numerically distinct, so my claim violates the transitivity of identity. It's absurd, too, that both the sperm and the oocyte still exist after conception, when there's only one relevant organism in view. Given their equal status and the problem with transitivity, we should conclude that both the sperm and the oocyte cease to exist at conception, and the zygote is a fresh creation. So goes the objection.

I answer that the sperm and the unfertilized oocyte are equal in some senses but not in the one that matters for the issue at hand. They're equal insofar as they contribute equal amounts of nuclear genetic material to the zygote. (Mitochondrial DNA, all maternal, is another matter.) They're equal insofar as they're both needed (causally, at least normally, at least in humans)[9] for the survival of the oocyte and its transformation into a zygote. They're roughly equal insofar as they contribute roughly equally to many salient traits of the later adult. They're not equal, however, in surviving conception.

To repeat: the sperm breaches the egg's cell wall, enters, and *dissolves*. Its dissolution is its death. The sperm "lives on" as we live on in our children, our works, and the compost our bodies eventually become: that is, figuratively. The sperm doesn't literally exist after conception. The oocyte does. Life is unfair.

You might just insist that fertilization is different from all other processes involving the absorption of extracellular material or the internal rearrangement of parts. One way or another, fertilization *must* mark the beginning of a new being.

This insistence is as ad hoc and unjustified as it is common and unquestioned. Its wide acceptance gives it no support but does call for diagnostic explanation, and I offer one speculative but plausible such explanation. (Whether it's the correct explanation is an empirical matter that exceeds my expertise.) Long before the biology of human reproduction was understood, the clear sign that a new being had been brought into being was a baby. Sex was the salient

recognizable link in the causal chain leading to babies: abstinence prevents them, indulgence produces them. (I ignore in-vitro fertilization and the like because these technologies can't be responsible for the common attitudes that predate their existence.) Given their background knowledge, our ancestors had no reason to think that any human beings existed except those that either had been born or were growing inside pregnant women. So it's easy to understand why our ancestors would believe that sex initiated a causal process that resulted in the creation of a new being, and it's easy to understand how such a belief might become entrenched. Biological conception was later found to be the salient concomitant of sex: babies result only when conception occurs, and conception, when it occurs, is an effect of sex. (Again, I ignore alternatives only recently rendered medically possible.) These simple facts are enough to account for the prevailing belief that conception marks the beginning of existence: that belief would result from combining two independently reasonable beliefs. That the resulting conjunctive belief contradicts another, far more reasonable, belief concerning identity over time is something easily and understandably overlooked.

The relevant beliefs of biologists need no diagnostic explanation, for biologists don't *have* the false belief in question. (They don't have it, at least, when wearing their biologist-hats. They can change headgear as well as anyone else.) You'll look in vain in the embryology literature for any hint that conception is anything other than an important event punctuating—not originating—the life of a single being.[10]

Fertilization resembles other cellular processes in this respect. Consider bacteria. Here's an account whose substance is wholly unremarkable in the biological literature:

> Among bacteria, genetic information transfer occurs without reproduction: one bacterium transmits genetic information directly to another by DNA transfer through the cell walls. *The receiver mating organism remains, with a changed genetic constitution, but no new offspring organism is formed* [my emphasis]. Bacteria reproduce without sex, by dividing and creating two organisms exactly like the original.[11]

Bacteria, which like oocytes are single cells, routinely survive the alteration of their genetic material. Oocytes can surely do the same.

There's no good reason to affirm and good reason to deny that I came into existence at my biological conception. I hope you agree; but even if you don't, reason requires that—absent some compelling argument to the contrary—you should at least hold, in light of my discussion so far, that it's unjustified to think I *did* come into existence at my conception. (Perhaps you think you should simply withhold judgment.) I'll take my stronger claim as established and trace its moral consequences, but I'll argue eventually that the most compelling of those consequences attend even the weaker claim.

IV. How Old Am I?

The moral consequences of separating my conception from my origination depend in part on when origination occurred. If I didn't originate at conception, then when? Only two times are plausible candidates, corresponding to the two horns of my main dilemma—corresponding, that is, to whether I was or wasn't once a zygote.

Suppose, first, that I was once a zygote. Then, as I've argued, I was once an unfertilized egg. I didn't exist *before* that unfertilized egg did. Hence I came into existence when it did.

If I originated when the egg did, then I'm probably several decades older than I am on the conventional reckoning of age that starts the clock at birth. (If you peg my conception as my origin, you'll say that I'm about nine months older than on the conventional reckoning.) The received view is that all the oocytes a mammalian female ever harbors originate while she's a fetus. A recent study suggests that some oocytes may develop later,[12] but it remains likely that the unfertilized egg that was me (if I was once a zygote) originated while my mother was a fetus. I came into existence, on this view, decades before my conception, and I don't look my age.

Suppose, then, that I was never a zygote. I was once a baby; that baby was once a fetus; that fetus, an embryo. Adults, babies, fetuses, and embryos are organisms, and there's no denying that in the normal course of development, a single organism is first an embryo, then a fetus, then a baby, child, and adult. So while the embryo that was I developed from a zygote, the embryo (-organism) was never the zygote (-organism). Hence if I was never a zygote, I came into existence at or after the demise of the zygote and at or before the first presence of an embryo.

You might grant this conditional but take it as a reductio of its antecedent. For just as there's no denying that an embryo is identical with the fetus that it becomes, you might insist, there's equally no denying that a zygote is identical with the embryo that *it* becomes.

I needn't rebut you. Grasp this horn of my dilemma, and you thereby commit yourself to my having once been an unfertilized egg. This is fine with me. The other horn is, however, at least prima facie defensible, so I want to see where it leads.

First, let me buttress my claim of prima facie defensibility. Here's why it isn't silly to deny that the zygote and embryo are identical. The zygote is a single cell. It cleaves into two distinct blastomeres, also single cells. Let "Z" name the zygote; "B1" and "B2," the two blastomeres into which it cleaves. What identity relations hold among Z, B1, and B2? We encounter here a familiar problem of cross-time identity in the face of fission.

B1 isn't identical with B2 since their properties differ. Since identity is transitive, it can't be that $Z = B1$ and $Z = B2$.

Perhaps $Z = B1$ or $Z = B2$. You might think that exactly one of these identity relations holds, though we can't tell which it is. Suppose you're right. Suppose that (unbeknownst to us) $Z = B1$. Each blastomere divides in turn; B1 divides into B1a and B1b. The fission puzzle recurs. Presumably you say that B1 is either B1a or B1b but not both. (If not, what distinguishes this fission case from the first one?) Suppose it's B1b. Then $Z = B1b$. As pregnancy proceeds, on this picture, the zygote survives, but always as a single cell. So while the zygote coexists with the embryo, it's not identical with it. Instead it's a single cell in the embryo's body[13] (or in the placenta, given further facts of embryology). So on the view that a fission-ancestor survives as exactly one of its fission-descendants, the zygote isn't identical with the embryo.

On the other hand, there's considerable intuitive pull to the idea that given the similarities between B1 and B2, Z is identical either with both of them or with neither; and since it can't be identical with both, it must be identical with neither. Because there's nothing with which it might be identical *other* than the blastomeres, it must be that, in this case, the organism that is the zygote ceases to exist when the zygote divides, and each blastomere is a fresh creation.

You might avoid this conclusion by denying that there's nothing with which the zygote might be identical after its division except for the blastomeres. For (you might say) the blastomeres compose something distinct from either of them. There's no reason why the zygote can't be identical with a two-celled object, composed by the blastomeres, and there's no reason why that object can't be identical with the later embryo, fetus, and so on.

If you say this, you say something questionable (though perhaps true). For if the zygote is identical with an object composed by the blastomeres, then an object may be a cell at one time and a noncell at another. There's nothing problematic, of course, about a child (or a tinker, or a tailor) continuing to exist while ceasing to be a child (tinker, tailor). There's some plausibility, though, to the view that *being a cell*, unlike *being a child*, is a property possessed essentially if at all. I don't say that this view is true. (If it is, then I was never a zygote—a claim on which I'm explicitly neutral.) My claim about its plausibility springs merely from two failures on my part: a failure to imagine a situation of which I think it would be clearly true, rather than simply unclear, that a cell persisted while losing its cellhood; and a failure to discern any clearly unacceptable consequence of denying it. I note two things about this view. First, denying it constitutes once again a reversion to the first horn of my dilemma: if the zygote is the same organism as the embryo that is me, then I was once an unfertilized egg. Second, to whatever degree it's intuitively plausible, it supports my claim that the second horn of the dilemma is at least prima facie defensible to the same degree. But again, it won't faze me if you find one horn or the other indefensible; if one doesn't catch you, the other one will.

Return to the line of thought on which the zygote ceases to exist when it divides. Do the two blastomeres compose an organism? If so, then (it seems reasonable that) this compound organism can survive further cellular division and eventual transformation into an embryo (fetus, baby, adult). So if the two blastomeres compose an organism, then (it's reasonable to think that) I am that organism, and hence that I came into existence when the zygote first divided.

Perhaps, though, the blastomeres compose nothing, or perhaps they compose an object that isn't an organism. (Multicellular organisms aren't mere colonies of unicellular ones.) Given the further details of embryology, which I won't recite here, it seems likely that *if* the blastomeres compose something, it's not an organism. It doesn't follow that they don't compose me: perhaps I who am now an organism once existed as a nonorganism. It's at least not obviously mistaken, though, to maintain both that I came into existence when the embryo did, and also that the embryo came into existence after the blastomeres did and so some time after the destruction of the zygote. I'm content, though, to leave this matter unsettled, for I'm not sure how to settle it, and anyway I've accomplished my stated goal. I've shown that if I was never a zygote, then I didn't exist until at least such time as the zygote ceased to exist.

V. Origination and the Morality of Abortion

I didn't originate, then, at conception. This fact makes trouble of various kinds for some standard pro-life positions. The trouble may be surmountable, but it must be and hasn't been surmounted.

Perhaps the most philosophically prominent pro-life position is that of Don Marquis.[14] Marquis argues that it's seriously wrong to deprive any being of the potential for certain kinds of valuable future experiences—of a "future like ours" (FLO). (By "seriously wrong," Marquis means "seriously presumptively wrong." I'll follow his lead.) Since abortion typically deprives the fetus of an FLO, Marquis says, it is typically seriously wrong.

Marquis considers the objection that on his account, contraception and abstinence are seriously wrong because they deprive a being of an FLO.[15]

To take this as an *objection* is to presuppose, as Marquis seems to do, that contraception and abstinence aren't seriously wrong. It's worth noting that even if contraception and abstinence *do* deprive a being of an FLO, they needn't be equally wrong even by Marquis's lights. If you plump for a morally relevant distinction between acts and omissions, you might well see abstinence as less wrong than contraception and both, perhaps, as less wrong than abortion. For abstinence looks like a (mere?) failure to rescue—though the rescue is in most cases an easy and pleasant one—whereas contraception looks like a more odious active interference with a rescue. You might even think that active interference with a rescue is not, unlike abortion, a matter of active killing, and so you might think it less odious than abortion. I don't endorse this hypothetical parsing of moral gravity, but if you do, no matter. What I'm concerned with is the question whether, given Marquis's assumptions, there's something seriously wrong with abstinence or contraception, not with whether they must be equally wrong or *as* wrong as abortion. If actively depriving something of an FLO is seriously wrong, then surely failing to prevent such deprivation, when prevention is easy, is at least very significantly wrong.

You might pin your hopes on the gap, if there is one, between very significant wrongs and serious ones. You might say, that is, that while actively killing a being with an FLO is seriously wrong, failure to perform an easy rescue of such a being isn't. This surely isn't Marquis's view; if it were, he would have said so in response to the objection at issue. In any case, the view looks desperate and ad hoc on its face. (This isn't to deny, of course, that some serious wrongs are worse than others.) I'll take for granted that if abstinence and contraception deprive a being of an FLO, then they are seriously wrong by Marquis's lights. If you want to insist that they are only very significantly but not seriously wrong, go right ahead.

The question for Marquis is this: which being is deprived of an FLO by contraception or abstinence? Marquis surveys the candidates

in order of the increasing number of individuals harmed: (1) The single harmed individual might be the combination of the particular sperm and the particular egg that would have united to form a zygote if contraception had not been used. (2) The two harmed individuals might be the particular sperm itself, and, in addition, the ovum itself that would have physically combined to form the zygote. . . . (3) The many harmed individuals might be the millions of *combinations* of sperm and the released ovum whose (small) chances of having an FLO were reduced by the successful contraception. (4) The even larger class of harmed individuals (larger by one) might be the class consisting of all of the individual sperm in an ejaculate and, in addition, the individual ovum released at the time of the successful contraception. (1) through (4) are all candidates for being the subject(s) of harm in the case of successful contraception or abstinence from sex. Which should be chosen? Should we hold a lottery? There seems to be no non-arbitrarily determinate subject of harm in the case of successful contraception. But if there is no such subject of harm, then no determinate thing was harmed.[16]

Marquis is mistaken. There is a single, nonarbitrarily determinate subject of harm in a case of contraception or abstinence: the unique oocyte that would (or could)[17] otherwise have been fertilized. When a woman ovulates, only one oocyte is (typically) ripe for fertilization. If it's fertilized, *it* survives to become a zygote, and nothing else does. Deprive it of fertilization, and you deprive it of an FLO—if, that is, the zygote is identical with the fetus that it becomes.[18] If I was once a zygote, then, Marquis has no adequate defense against the objection that abstinence and contraception are (by his lights) seriously wrong.

Marquis might allow, in light of this point, that I was never a zygote. Suppose I wasn't. Then the zygote from which I developed didn't survive to fetushood, and its failure to survive is a matter of at least nomological necessity. So that zygote lacked the potential for an FLO. It was hardly unique in this respect: if I was never a zygote, then no human zygote has the potential for an FLO. So killing a zygote doesn't deprive it of an FLO. Hence Marquis's argument, even if otherwise sound, does nothing to show the serious wrongness of killing a zygote.

This point might not ruffle Marquis. He allows that "during the first fourteen days after conception . . . there is an argument that the fetus is not definitely an individual,"[19] and so he allows that perhaps abortion isn't seriously wrong during those two weeks. (Marquis uses "fetus" to encompass zygote, embryo, and fetus proper.) I don't know what argument Marquis has in mind, but this allowance is confused on its face since if there's anything that is *the fetus*, then that thing is ipso facto an individual. The view that Marquis might more plausibly mean to countenance is that during the first two weeks, there's nothing that would be identical with the later fetus were the pregnancy to progress normally. Hence there's no individual during the first fourteen days that abortion would deprive of an FLO.

It may seem, then, that my argument should resolve Marquis's apparent indecision about whether his argument applies from the moment of conception. He ought, by his own lights and absent some other argument, to view early abortion as no worse than contraception and abstinence, and he seems to view these as not seriously (or even significantly) wrong.

If all of this is right, it's a substantial result. For Marquis leaves it open whether his argument applies to zygotes, whereas the foregoing considerations clinch the case that it doesn't, at least if contraception and abstinence aren't seriously wrong.

Things aren't so simple, though, and the upshot of my argument may be more substantial still. As I've said, it's a murky question whether zygotes are identical with the fetuses that they become. (I've offered prima facie reasons for thinking they aren't, but these aren't conclusive.) Murky questions of identity can raise flags of moral caution. Absent moral certainty that zygotes aren't identical with later fetuses, moral caution requires us to act as though they are and thus to treat abstinence and contraception as seriously wrong, given Marquis's principles.[20] Perhaps Marquis has the requisite moral certainty. I don't.

I don't say that moral caution forbids abstinence or contraception. I say that it forbids them *by Marquis's lights,* absent moral certainty about metaphysical murk. I lack that moral certainty,[21] and I expect you do, too. *If* you're justified in thinking abstinence and contraception permissible, then Marquis's lights don't illuminate. That is, if you're justified in thinking

contraception and abstinence permissible, but you aren't certain that you were never a zygote, then you can't justifiably hold that deprivation of an FLO suffices for the serious wrongness of abortion. If, on the other hand, you buy Marquis's explanation for the wrongness of abortion and share my epistemic modesty, then you should think that we ought to treat contraception and abstinence as seriously wrong.

You may question my application of moral caution to the case at hand for more than one reason. You might have misgivings about applying moral caution (only) when relevant doubts are "metaphysical."[22] These misgivings are baseless. Whether moral caution applies hinges on whether genuine doubt is reasonable in the circumstances, not on whether the point at issue is metaphysical. Whether something is a person or a paper target *is* a question about its metaphysical status; the juror who asks whether the defendant is *identical with* the criminal is asking a metaphysical question of cross-time identity. A philosopher's worries would, of course, rightly be laughed out of court. ("An evil genius may be fooling you into thinking that my client is guilty" or "The problem of temporary intrinsics raises reasonable doubt about my client's guilt.") This isn't because such worries raise "metaphysical doubts," however, but because they raise no actual, relevant doubts at all; or if they do, as they may for the mentally ill, those doubts are unreasonable. Skepticism (for example) raises deep, hard philosophical challenges, but not by inducing *reasonable, actual doubt* about relevant metaphysical claims (as opposed to doubt about various claims of metaphysical, epistemic, or normative theory). But if they really do induce reasonable doubt in you, then you'd be unreasonable to ignore that doubt and throw moral caution to the wind.

One sort of doubt deserves special mention.[23] You might doubt that there's any fact of the matter whether zygotes are identical with later fetuses; you might doubt, that is, that the proposition that they are so identical is either true or false.[24] Such doubt might be both actual and (at least initially) reasonable. The grim consequences of denying the principle of bivalence render such doubt ultimately indefensible, in my view, but fortunately, I needn't argue this here. For doubt of this sort is grist for my mill. If you lack moral certainty whether there's any relevant fact in the neighborhood, then you lack moral certainty that there *isn't* such a fact and (presumably) that it isn't a fact of the sort that requires the safe moral choice. In this case, my invocation of moral caution proceeds as before. If, on the other hand, you're morally certain *that there is no relevant fact*, then you're faced with deciding the moral status of an action X such that (a) X is morally wrong if and only if X has property F, but (b) you're morally certain that there's no fact of the matter whether X is F. I know of no one with pro-life leanings who will embrace the combination of theses necessary in this case to yield the result that abortion is seriously wrong but abstinence and contraception aren't. Those with such leanings will want to resist, not endorse, the thought that there's no fact of the matter whether the zygote is identical with the later fetus.

I'm supposing for argument's sake, once again, that I'm a human animal and that I *know* that I'm a human animal. Drop this supposition, and the scope of moral caution changes. If I'm convinced that I'm an immaterial soul rather than a human animal, then I'll see moral caution as bearing on (at least, though probably not only) my uncertainty concerning the moment of ensoulment. If I'm sure I'm material but unsure which materialist account is correct, or if I'm simply unsure whether I'm material or immaterial—never mind the details of this or that account—then the proper scope of moral caution will have to widen and bend to follow the contours of my uncertainty. I won't try to trace these permutations here, sticking instead to the assumption that I know that I'm a human animal.

Some other candidates for *morally relevant metaphysical status* follow the same pattern as Marquis's. Suppose you think that abortion is seriously wrong on the ground that the aborted being is a *potential person*. (I bypass standard objections to this view.) If I was never a zygote, then zygotes aren't potential people, so your ground says nothing about the moral status of zygotic abortion. If I was once a zygote, though, then unfertilized eggs are potential people, and your principle would make contraception and abstinence seriously wrong. Either way, moral caution would once again coun-

sel treating contraception and abstinence as wrong if your principle were true, barring moral certainty about whether zygotes are identical with the fetuses they become.

You might think that the morally relevant status is not that of being a potential person but simply that of being a person: abortion is seriously wrong because (or when) it kills a person. The question, then, is: at what point does personhood appear? One standard view is that being a person is a matter of having at least some of certain capacities, such as the capacity to reason, to use language, to have a self-concept, or to make or understand moral claims. There's no serious debate that zygotes (and embryos and fetuses, not to mention newborns) lack all these capacities, so if you hold the capacity-view of persons, then personhood can't ground the wrongness of zygotic abortion. Robert Larner has argued, however, that personhood requires having not the *capacity* for reason (or whatever) but merely the *potential* for it.[25] On this view, embryos are people, not just potential people. I don't engage the merits of Larner's argument. I merely point out that if having the relevant potentials suffices for personhood and I was once a zygote, then unfertilized eggs are people, too. In that case, contraception and abstinence are once again thrown into moral jeopardy. If I was never a zygote, on the other hand, then the view now in play yields nothing morally problematic about zygotic abortion. Moral caution plays its usual role.

The moral caution to which I've appealed so far stems from moral uncertainty whether I was once a zygote, taking it as established that I didn't originate at conception. A second moral uncertainty might, however, underlie a second application of moral caution. I think I've shown that I didn't originate at conception. It isn't necessary for all of my moral purposes, however, that I've convinced you of this. It's enough that I've made you morally uncertain that I *did* originate then. For if you aren't morally certain that I originated at conception, then you shouldn't be morally certain that abstinence and conception are permissible while zygotic abortion isn't. If I've convinced you of this much, I'm content; moral caution will do the rest. Analogous points about moral caution apply, mutatis mutandis, to all my arguments still to come; to avoid tedium, I won't rehearse them.

VI. Acquiring Humanity and the Morality of Abortion

Consider next the claim that what matters is *being a living human being*. If "human being" is used with a sense that includes personhood, see the previous section. If not, matters are more interesting.

It may seem platitudinous that every living biological organism belongs to some species or other. It's nevertheless false if "belonging" is a matter of *membership*. Some living organisms are members of no species. Consider a particular living cell that's now a constituent of my liver—call it "Liv." A living cell is paradigmatically a living organism, and Liv is a living cell. Yet Liv is not a member of the genus *Homo*; Liv is not a "human being" on the usual meaning of that term. Liv isn't a *member* of any genus at all.

Liv is, however, a *human* liver cell, distinct in biological kind from (say) a canine liver cell. Since Liv is a being, and Liv is human, there's a sense in which Liv is a "human being."

We can, then, distinguish two purely biological senses of "human being," in addition to the sense that includes psychological personhood. Let's say that something is a "human-being-1" if and only if it's a *member* of the genus *Homo*. (This is, I think, the normal biological sense of "human being.") Let's say that something is a "human-being-2" if and only if it's an organism that is a (not necessarily proper) part of a human-being-1.[26] Liv is a human-being-2 but not a human-being-1.

The unfertilized egg is, it seems, a human-being-2,[27] but not a human-being-1. A baby is a human-being-1. The suggestion I'm now considering is that biological conception marks the acquisition of the property of *being a human-being-1*.[28]

If you've bought my argument thus far, you'll agree that the question concerns the acquisition of this property *by a preexisting being*. You might still hold out hope, though, for the conception-as-origination thesis, on the grounds that particular genus-membership is an essential property of that which has it; if I first acquired membership in *Homo* at conception, then I must have originated then. Here, then, I'll make good on the promissory note I issued earlier.

Is it true, then, that I first acquired my genus-membership at conception?

If we defer to biologists, we'll take the answer as a clear *no*. When biologists take population censuses, they count only beings that have been born. They certainly allow that unborn human fetuses and their biological predecessors (embryos, zygotes, unfertilized eggs, and so on) are human, just as Liv is human, but they don't count them as *members* of the genus *Homo*. They don't count them, that is, as human-beings-1.

I don't assume, though, that we should defer to biologists on this matter. Suppose conception marks the point at which something becomes a human-being-1. Suppose, too, that I was never a zygote. Then for every live human birth, two human-beings-1 die: the one born (who typically dies many years after birth) and the zygote from which that being developed (which dies soon after conception). The zygote from which I developed ceased to exist before the subsequent embryo came into existence. If the zygote and embryo were both human-beings-1, then conception caused something that was not a human-being-1 both to become one and then to die. The oocyte dies no matter what (if I was never a zygote). It dies different deaths, though, depending on whether it's fertilized, and only if it's fertilized is its death the death of a human-being-1. So if it's the killing *of a human-being-1* that is seriously presumptively wrong, then on this view *conception* must be seriously wrong. Perhaps overriding considerations make conception permissible in some cases—if it's necessary to the survival of the species, perhaps—but it always comes with a huge moral cost. If you nod at this result, you're beyond my reach.

Is there, then, any good reason for holding that I became a human-being-1 at the moment of conception and that I *was* once a zygote? The defender of the conception-suggestion can't defend that suggestion on the basis of genetic endowment. An unfertilized oocyte is clearly *human*—it is at least a human-being-2. It has fewer chromosomes than it will have after fertilization. But I now have fewer chromosomes than I would have were I to suffer the first case of adult-onset Down's syndrome, and I could certainly survive such an affliction. As my earlier discussion of genetic essentialism suggests, though, there's no principled basis for denying that every human-being-1—every member of the genus *Homo*—simply has two genotypic stages, one before fertilization and one after. Given the difficulties I've pointed out with the hypothesis that conception marks the dawn of a new individual, this two-stage claim seems vastly *more* plausible than its denial if the zygote is a human-being-1.

One sort of principled reason you might oppose to this appearance is a moral one. Suppose you have a good argument that abortion is seriously presumptively wrong from the moment of conception and not earlier. This argument might then contribute somehow to a larger argument that we ought to count conception as the moment at which something becomes a human-being-1 (and that I was once a zygote).

I don't mind the idea that we might properly reach metaphysical conclusions from moral premises.[29] But if a moral premise concerning the permissibility of abortion offers the only route to these metaphysical conclusions, then it would be viciously circular to argue from the metaphysical claims about genus-membership or cross-time identity to a moral conclusion concerning abortion that's presupposed by the premise.

If the unfertilized oocyte is debarred from being a human-being-1 on the ground that it, like Liv, is a proper constituent of a human-being-1, then the zygote is debarred as well. For fertilization does not, on any standard view, cause an egg to go from being a proper constituent to not being a proper constituent of a human-being-1. So if a zygote is a human-being-1, there's no good reason to deny that an unfertilized oocyte is one as well.

John Noonan Jr. argues that conception marks the point at which there is a new "human being,"[30] and he seems to mean that it is the point at which something *becomes* a human-being-1. In some respects his argument echoes, and shares the fate of, Marquis's defense against the contraception-objection that I've already discussed. Noonan also says something new (238):

The positive argument for conception as the decisive moment of humanization is that at conception the new being receives the genetic code. It is this

genetic information which determines his characteristics, which is the biological carrier of the possibility of human wisdom, which makes him a self-evolving being.

Unfortunately, this argument collapses under scrutiny. Leave aside for a moment the bald claim that at conception a *new being* receives a genetic code. It's false that the genetic information encoded in a (male) fertilized egg determines "his characteristics" if this means that it determines *all* the traits he'll have at maturity. (I suppose temporarily for argument's sake, as Noonan supposes in fact, that the fertilized egg is identical with the human adult into which it develops.) A zygote's genetic endowment determines some of the adult's traits (ceteris paribus) and not others; some are determined by later genetic alteration, parenting, education, nutrition, and so on. The same goes for the genetic endowment of the unfertilized oocyte: it determines some adult traits (ceteris paribus) and not others. The only truth in the neighborhood is an impotent truism: the diploid genetic information bestowed by conception determines some of a being's characteristics—namely those determined by that diploid genetic information. These aren't all of the being's characteristics, though, and it's an equally impotent truism that the haploid genetic information contained in the unfertilized oocyte determines some of a being's characteristics—namely those determined by that haploid genetic information.

Noonan suggests that a zygote's having a distinctively human diploid genetic endowment is a biologically necessary condition for the eventual development of human wisdom. Suppose this is right. It's equally true that an unfertilized egg's having a distinctively human haploid genetic endowment is a biologically necessary condition for the eventual development of human wisdom. In both cases, we have a biologically necessary condition for the possibility of human wisdom. In neither case do we have a sufficient one. Again, there's no basis here for the view that conception marks the acquisition of being a human-being-1.

What lies behind Noonan's fallacious argument concerning the acquisition of "humanness" seems pretty clearly to be the explicit, unargued, and untenable assumption that biological conception is in fact *ontological* conception. It may not be silly to think—though it's also far from obvious—that whenever a new being appears that will someday be an uncontroversial human-being-1, it's a human-being-1 from the beginning. You argue in a tight, vicious circle, however, if you invoke the thesis that conception confers genus-membership to support the conception-as-origination thesis, and then offer that very thesis as the sole reason for thinking that conception confers genus-membership. As I've shown, there's no good reason to think that a new being appears at conception. It doesn't follow that conception *doesn't* mark the first moment of something's being a human-being-1. I claim merely that no plausible reason for thinking that it *does* has been articulated.

I've been supposing for argument's sake that I'm a human organism. Suppose instead that I'm an immaterial being, or a compound of body and soul, or a material being numerically if not mereologically distinct from any human organism. Can ontological revision rescue the view that conception is ontologically or morally salient? It's hard to see how; it seems, in fact, to put this view farther out of reach. You might argue that conception is the moment at which a preexisting organism becomes (for example) ensouled, or at which a material being distinct from but colocated with the zygote comes into existence. It's hard to see how any such argument might succeed, but I await with interest attempts in this direction.

Nothing I've said here precludes the possibility of a compelling argument that abortion is presumptively wrong after conception but not before. Current arguments to this effect fail, though, and defenders of this view have their work cut out for them.

Notes

I'm grateful to Anthony Ellis, Gayla Mills, Allen Thompson, Mikhail Valdman, and an anonymous referee for helpful comments and suggestions.

1. I suppose this—merely for argument's sake—for two reasons. First, it's now the default (though not the unanimous) materialist view of the self; for one forceful presentation, see Eric Olson, *The Human Animal* (New York: Oxford University Press, 1997). Second, it forms the chief support for a moral position on which my coming metaphysical argument bears. That argument has some commonalities with, and some bearing on, recent attempts to establish moral conclusions about abortion via the metaphysics of personal identity. See David Boonin, *A Defense of Abortion* (Cambridge: Cambridge University Press, 2002); Jeff McMahan, *The Ethics of Killing: Problems at the Margins of Life* (Oxford: Oxford University Press, 2002); and David DeGrazia, "Identity, Killing, and the Boundaries of Our Existence," *Philosophy and Public Affairs* 31 (2003): 413–42. I don't assume, though, that persons are *essentially* persons, and my argument, which is less ambitious than those of Boonin and McMahan, rests on considerations of cross-time identity that needn't involve *personal* identity at all.

2. Pregnancies are reckoned medically as starting with (not conception but) the implantation of the zygote into the womb. I stipulate that by "zygotic abortion" I mean the killing of a zygote as a means or as a consequence of preventing or aborting the pregnancy that does or would consist in a woman's being pregnant with that zygote.

3. I stipulate that I use "survive" so that, necessarily, if a being survives from one time to another, then *it* exists at both times. I don't deny the intelligibility of views according to which "survival" doesn't require identity; my use of "survive" is mere shorthand.

4. If Judith Jarvis Thomson's famous defense of abortion convinces you, then you may doubt that there's any such true principle or think that if there is one, the presumption of wrongness is typically defeated. See Thomson, "A Defense of Abortion," *Philosophy and Public Affairs* 1 (1971): 47–66. In that case you may see my argument as having little practical force. Note three points. First, even if Thomson's argument succeeds, its applicability remains controversial over many actual cases, given the circumstances and methods of actual abortions; second, Thomson's argument clearly does *not* apply to some medically possible (and probably actual) cases of abortion to which my argument *does* apply; and third, my argument carries philosophical interest independent of its practical upshot.

5. "For convenience": thus do I gloss over matters of bitter metaphysical controversy. This is not because I think these matters unimportant but because my

coming argument adapts smoothly to fit all standard views of cross-time identity, including those that cash it out in terms of genidentity or sortal identity, endurance or perdurance. For reasons of space, I merely assert this here rather than show it, but I invite you to confirm it for yourself.

6. Assuming, again, that I'm an organism. On some psychologistic views of personal identity, I cease existing when I cease thinking—say, during dreamless sleep—and resume existing when I resume thinking. On such views, however, I'm no organism.

7. For details, see any standard textbook of embryology, for example, Felix Beck, David Burns Moffat, and John Benjamin Lloyd, *Human Embryology and Genetics* (Oxford: Blackwell, 1973). A concise account with animated depiction may be found at Clovis Neves and Roberto Mueller, "Teleeducation: Fertilization," www.cenapad.ufmg.br/~teleeduc/fer.html (accessed August 25, 2005).

8. Saul Kripke, *Naming and Necessity* (Cambridge, MA: Harvard University Press, 1980), 112–13.

9. Parthenogenesis is common in invertebrates. Recent work suggests that unfertilized eggs might be induced to mature even in humans; see Sylvia Westphal, "Virgin Birth Method Could Found Stem Cell Dynasties," *New Scientist*, April 26, 2003, 17.

10. Harold Morovitz and James Trefil, writing for a popular audience in *The Facts of Life: Science and the Abortion Controversy* (New York: Oxford University Press, 1992), get the main point right while displaying the tenacity of the confusion infecting the received view. They say (46–47):

When biologists object to statements about life beginning at conception, they are not splitting hairs or being pedantic. There is no time in the sequence [of events including and flanking conception] where new life is created. In fact, from the point of view of the biologist, *at conception, two previously existing living things come together to form another living thing.*

The (false) italicized statement flatly contradicts the (true) sentence preceding it unless somehow the formation of a new living thing might not bring the creation of new life.

11. Ernest Callenbach, *Ecology: A Pocket Guide* (Berkeley: University of California Press, 1998), 104.

12. Joshua Johnson, Jacqueline Canning, Tomoko Kaneko, James K. Pru, and Jonathan L. Tilly, "Germ-line Stem Cells and Follicular Renewal in the Postnatal Mammalian Ovary," *Nature*, March 11, 2004, 145–50, suggests some postnatal production of oocytes in mice. What goes for mice may go as well for humans, though it has yet to be shown.

13. That is, there's a single cell in the embryo's body that *was* once a zygote.

14. Don Marquis, "An Argument That Abortion Is Wrong," in *Contemporary Moral Problems*, 6th ed, ed. James White (Belmont, CA: Wadsworth. 2000), 164–75. This article is a revised version of "Why Abortion Is Immoral," *Journal of Philosophy* 86 (1989): 183–202.

15. I ignore many other criticisms of Marquis's argument; see, for example, Gerald Paske, "Abortion and the Neo-Natal Right to Life," in *Life and Death*, 2nd ed., ed. Louis Pojman (Belmont, CA: Wadsworth, 2000), 293–301; reprinted from Louis Pojman and Frank Beckwith, eds., *The Abortion Controversy* (Boston: Jones and Bartlett, 1994), 343–53.

16. Marquis, "An Argument That Abortion Is Wrong," 174.

17. Fertilization might fail. But it's no excuse for not attempting an easy rescue that your attempt *might* have failed.

18. A can "become B" both in cases in which A is identical with B and in cases in which it isn't. The boy can become, and be identical with, the man; the man can become dust, by ceasing to exist and undergoing decomposition.

19. Marquis, "An Argument That Abortion Is Wrong," 164.

20. "Is that a person or a paper target in the distance? It's unclear, so I'll shoot." Suppose you're lucky and it's a paper target. Luck doesn't justify your action or make it "permissible" in an internalist sense, even if the act is "permissible" in an externalist sense. Articulating a clear and true *principle* of moral caution is no trivial task, and I don't attempt it here. We can see a clear role for moral caution in some cases absent such a principle, though, and this case is one of them. I use "moral certainty" to pick out whatever epistemic relation is appropriate for moral caution—perhaps mere epistemic justification, perhaps more.

21. Remember my background supposition: strictly speaking, I lack moral certainty that *if* I'm a human organism, then I was never a zygote.

22. As some readers of earlier versions of this article have done.

23. I thank an anonymous referee for *Philosophical Review* for raising this point.

24. These may be distinct and independent doubts, depending on your view of the relation between factuality and truth. The doubt about truth-value is the crucial one here; I'll treat the doubt about factuality as equivalent to it, recognizing that on some views these are different matters.

25. "Abortion, Personhood, and the Potential for Consciousness," *Journal of Applied Philosophy* 12 (1995): 241–51.

26. These senses aren't exhaustive. A cell biologically indistinguishable from Liv but living in a petri dish is as much a human liver cell as Liv is, intuitively, even though it's a constituent of no human-being-1. The two senses given suffice, though, for present purposes. Roger Wertheimer hints at the distinction they capture in "Understanding the Abortion Argument," *Philosophy and Public Affairs* 1 (1971): 67–95; see pp. 69–70, though he blurs the distinction between a human-being-1 and a psychological person.

27. This appearance isn't beyond argument. Some living beings within living human-beings-1 (for example, the bacteria that live in our guts) are not human-beings-2; there's more to parthood than interiority, and perhaps oocytes aren't parts of the human-beings-1 that harbor them. Still, an unfertilized oocyte is certainly a living being, and there's some intuitively clear sense in which it's "human." Whether this sense is what's captured by "human-being-2" isn't important for present purposes—see previous note—so long as it's *not* what's captured by "human-being-1."

28. Wertheimer, "Understanding the Abortion Argument," 79, gives several reasons for thinking that "one can't go back further" than conception in tracing the life of a human being; if you've followed me so far, you'll recognize all of them as either false or irrelevant. He also says that "*no one* is inclined to call . . . an [unfertilized] egg a human life," and what he means by "a human life" is the life of something that is at least (though not merely) a human-being-1. He admits that "At one time people were so inclined, but only because they thought the sperm merely triggered the development of the egg and hence the egg was a human being." I take no stand on whether an unfertilized egg is a human-being-1; I do think, as should be clear, that the sperm triggers the development of the egg, though I wouldn't say it does "merely" this. I note, however, that even if (a) the sperm does merely trigger the development of the egg, (b) the zygote is a human-being-1, and (c) the zygote is identical with the unfertilized egg, it doesn't follow that the unfertilized egg is a human-being-1. So the diagnostic explanation Wertheimer offers for old inclinations doesn't render those inclinations reasonable, even given the background biological beliefs.

29. Michael Thompson argues, in effect, that normative considerations play a role in fixing matters of biological taxonomy in "The Representation of Life," in *Virtues and Reasons*, ed. Rosalind Hursthouse, Gavin Lawrence, and Warren Quinn (Oxford: Oxford University Press, 1995): 247–97. He may be right; his account of species-membership is wholly consistent with all of my suppositions here.

30. Noonan, "An Almost Absolute Value in History," in *Contemporary Moral Problems,* 6th ed., ed. James White (Belmont, CA: Wadsworth, 2000), 136–41; reprinted from John T. Noonan Jr., ed., *The Morality of Abortion* (Cambridge, MA: Harvard University Press), 51–59.

QUESTIONS

1. Reconstruct the argument against our originating at conception.
2. Consider the objections in section II and determine whether Mills's replies to them are cogent.

62. Abortion and the Morality of Nurturance

PAUL GOMBERG

*P*aul Gomberg (1943–) is professor of philosophy at Chicago State University. He has written essays on a wide variety of topics in ethics and political philosophy and recently a book, *How to Make Opportunity Equal: Race and Contributive Justice* (2007).

In this article Gomberg raises the question whether the abortion controversy derives in large part because of questions having to do with parental duties of nurturance. Instead of—or in addition to—asking about killing other persons, we might ask about duties to offspring. "The paradigm of someone protected by the principle prohibiting the killing of another is an adult with developed capabilities. The paradigm of one protected by the morality of nurturance is precisely the undeveloped, vulnerable, and dependent being biologically related to us. One reason that our babies have a moral claim on our care is precisely that they are not developed beings." Gomberg thinks that "the greatest advantage of interpreting the abortion controversy as a dispute centering on the morality of nurturance is that it allows us to understand what issues separate conservatives and liberals."

I

The moral problem of abortion seemed simple to describe, if not resolve. There was consensus that at least some methods of birth control—avoiding or preventing the development of a conceptus—were not wrong. There was consensus that it was wrong to kill another person like ourselves. The problem seemed to be this: when in the development toward adult life does it become wrong to prevent or terminate that development? The conservatives said, "from conception." Liberals said that it became wrong after viability, or after birth, or after early infancy. Some moderate liberals have argued that there is an intermediate stage where stopping the development of a fetus is wrong—but not the same as killing a person—because of the fetus's similarity to or potential to become a person. While all agree on the moral principle that it is wrong to kill another person, there has been little progress toward agreement on how this principle applies to the fetus.[1]

The present paper explores a different approach. Perhaps the abortion controversy derives less from disagreement about how to apply the principle prohibiting the killing of another person and more from the part of our morality that concerns parental duties of nurturance to the young: what are our duties to our offspring? when do those duties take hold?[2]

The proposal that the abortion controversy is a dispute about the morality of nurturance brings a number of issues into focus: it gives a better articulation of the objection to abortion than the claim that abortion is murder; it allows us to understand

From Paul Gomberg, "Abortion and the Morality of Nurturance," *Canadian Journal of Philosophy* 21, 4 (December 1991), pp. 513–524. Reprinted by permission of the University of Calgary Press and of the author.

why many believe that later abortions are morally more problematic than earlier ones; it puts the issue of abortion in the context of the morality that governs family life; and, most important, it allows us to understand why there is, on the one hand, a connection between conservatism on abortion and traditional women's roles and, on the other, a connection between liberalism and affirmation of equality between men and women.

II The Morality of Nurturance

The central norm of the morality of nurturance is that it is the duty of parents to nurture their offspring, to provide them with sustenance and guidance until they reach self-sufficiency.[3] Evidence that we accept this norm is found in laws requiring child support and punishing child neglect and in our moral condemnation of those who abandon or neglect, and particularly those who abuse their children. The norm applies in the first instance to biological parents and to others only by special arrangement. I am concerned with this norm as an important component of the morality of our culture, although I suspect that *some* principle regarding care of the young is part of the moral norms of every human society.

It may seem that the application of this principle to the fetus raises essentially the same problems as applying the principle prohibiting the killing of another person: in one case we must decide when something is a person, in the other when something is "one's offspring." But while the problems are parallel in many ways, they are different. The paradigm of someone protected by the principle prohibiting the killing of another is an adult with developed capabilities. The paradigm of one protected by the morality of nurturance is precisely the undeveloped, vulnerable, and dependent being biologically related to us. One reason that our babies have a moral claim on our care is precisely that they are not developed beings.

There are other significant differences between the two principles. It is during the transition from infancy to adulthood that we come to regard someone as a person, but, as I will argue in this section, it is *during pregnancy* that we come to regard something as our baby to be protected and nurtured. And, as we shall see in the next section, while both the concept of a person and that of an offspring are ones that we come to apply as a being acquires more and more characteristics paradigmatic of the concept, in borderline cases our conception of women's roles may be decisive in determining when we should regard something as our offspring.

Duties of nurturance, at least as they are understood in our society, apply paradigmatically to newborns.[4] By a natural extension of principles specifying our nurturing duties toward children, we condemn abuse of the fetus with drugs or alcohol. (Of course, moral condemnation of *addicts* may be pointless and inappropriate.) Well before birth we come to believe we are bound by a responsibility to care for the fetus and its future. We may feel obligated to give up cigarettes, alcohol, prescription drugs, and aspirin and to maintain a well balanced diet including adequate vitamins. We may take walks or swim. (These changes usually apply more particularly to the mother; others may apply equally to both parents.) We may take out insurance, stop picking up hitchhikers, sell the motorcycle, and try to drive more carefully. We may find a new place to live, paying particular attention to the schools in the neighborhood. If a rift has developed with the family of one of the parents, there may be an effort to repair it. We do these things because we believe ourselves responsible to a developing life; we are coming to regard the fetus as our offspring and ourselves as parents.

Neither our sense of responsibility toward the fetus nor a corresponding loving attitude springs suddenly into existence. As Rawls has stressed, there is a connection between the development of natural attitudes and of moral responsibilities: the attitudes entail moral commitments and among the commitments are to have certain attitudes.[5] It is our responsibility to love this child because without this love she cannot be properly nurtured.

As soon as we accept our pregnancy, we cultivate feelings which will allow this child to develop. We may personify the fetus, giving the fetus a name, not the name it will bear as a separate person, but a whimsical fetal name. The parents stroke the abdomen of the expectant mother, talking to and about the fetus. As the fetus grows, the personification of the fetus becomes more intense: we may scold it for taking up too much room, moving about and kicking, or getting the hiccups.[6]

I have described here how the morality of nurturance takes hold when we accept our pregnancy. But when a woman becomes aware that she is pregnant, she may not accept her pregnancy. She may, in fact, regard the thing developing inside her as alien.[7] Accordingly, she may seek to terminate the pregnancy if she can find a way to do so. It is true that in accepting a pregnancy, we begin to accept responsibility to nurture that fetus, to regard it as an offspring, and to develop the corresponding attitudes. But are we morally required to accept the pregnancy? I will turn to this question shortly.

III Nurturance, Abortion, and Women's Roles

Once it is accepted that a fetus is an offspring protected by the central norm of the morality of nurturance, it is easy to derive a condemnation of abortion. Recall the widely displayed photograph of the feet of an eight week fetus held in the fingers of an adult hand. We are supposed to respond, "It's a miniature *baby*!". To destroy that is to destroy what we should nurture. By showing us an enlarged picture of tiny feet, appeals such as this try to convince us that the fetus is already an offspring.

The suggestion of this paper is that the morality of nurturance is central to the abortion debate. If this suggestion is correct, then the arguments of Warren, Tooley, and many others that the fetus lacks those characteristics that make one a full-fledged person, a member of the moral community, may be correct, but fail to respond to objections to abortion derived from the morality of nurturance. *Of course* the fetus is not a full-fledged person; it is, after all, a baby, or becoming one, and in need of our care if it is to become a full-fledged person. The duties of nurturance are strongest

precisely when the one to be nurtured lacks developed human capacities.

But Warren, Tooley, and the others were in fact only responding to the way the issue was defined by the conservatives on abortion. It was Noonan and others who argued that abortion is the taking of a human life comparable with the life of the mother. If this were true, then legal penalties for abortion should be comparable to those for any other murder. Few opponents of legal abortion are willing to accept the full consequences of the view that abortion is murder.[8]

If the morality of nurturance is the hidden issue in the abortion debate, then the condemnation of abortion is not condemnation of it as murder, a term whose paradigmatic application is to the morality between adults. As a violation of nurturing duties, abortion is less and more than murder. It is more than murder just as stuffing a newborn baby into a garbage can shocks us in a special way: we wonder what kind of monster could kill its own child.[9] What shocks us about infanticide is that it violates the morality of nurturance. Yet abortion and infanticide both are significantly less than murder. We are appalled by infanticide, but many human societies have tolerated it at the same time as they condemned murder.[10] The suggestion of this paper is that we accept Tooley's claim that abortion and infanticide are akin but recognize that there are serious objections to both based on duties of nurturance. If this is correct, the concession that abortion is not murder does not end the argument about tolerating it. If the morality of nurturance can generate a condemnation of infanticide or abandonment of an infant, then it may also generate a condemnation of abortion.

So the condemnation of abortion within the morality of nurturance is not the same as the condemnation of murder, but carries comparable emotional and moral weight. Earlier I said that once we accept a pregnancy, the morality of nurturance begins to take hold: we come to regard the fetus as an offspring and come to believe ourselves responsible for its care. I earlier set aside the question whether we are morally required to accept our pregnancies. Now we must deal with that question.

The morality of nurturance requires us to care for our offspring, but when does something become "our offspring"? Just as we gradually acquire the characteristics of personhood, so also, at an earlier stage of our development, the ovum, zygote, blastocyst, embryo, and fetus gradually acquire the characteristics of an offspring. By the time a pregnancy has reached the ninth month, the fetus is an offspring of its parents. The facts speak too clearly for there to be room for dispute. We have duties to nurture the nine month fetus. But earlier in the pregnancy there is room for argument, just as, in the case of personhood, any decision that "now this is a person" seems arbitrary, so also any judgment that "now this is your baby and you must care for it" also will seem arbitrary. So, at least in the case of the early fetus, the morality of nurturance cannot tell us that now something is our offspring and that a pregnancy must be accepted.

Because the fetus gradually becomes more and more like a baby, most of us believe that later abortions are morally and emotionally more problematic. Even if there is no precise point at which it is clear that the morality of nurturance must apply to the fetus, it is clear that the longer we wait to abort, the more like a baby is the thing we destroy. Conversely, for most of us early abortions seem consistent with the morality of nurturance. But not everyone would agree. For some people there are *other* considerations that lead them to apply the morality of nurturance to the early fetus. These people believe that all pregnancies must be accepted.

It is part of a traditional conception of a woman's role that a sexually active woman should bear and nurture children. On this conception a pregnancy is a fulfillment of one's role. Combining this traditional conception of a woman's role with the morality of nurturance generates a condemnation of abortion: it is our duty to accept our pregnancies and to nurture developing human life. The traditional morality of a woman's role leads us to apply the morality of nurturance to the early fetus (and even to earlier forms). It thus leads us to classify the early fetus as an offspring and hence generates the condemnation of even early abortions as akin to infanticide.[11]

IV Explaining the Abortion Controversy

The greatest advantage of interpreting the abortion controversy as a dispute centering on the morality of nurturance is that it allows us to understand what issues separate conservatives and liberals. The morality of nurturance generates a condemnation of all abortions when combined with a traditional conception of women's roles. This suggests that there are two foci of the dispute about abortion: (1) what does the morality of nurturance require of us, and (2) what is the proper role of women? These are in fact two major issues that separate conservatives and liberals.

If the abortion controversy really centers on the morality of nurturance, then one would expect that conservatives would see themselves as defenders of children and would perceive liberals as failing to appreciate our nurturing duties toward children. This is precisely what we find. Kristin Luker's study of activists is a rich source of data on (and useful interpretations of) the outlooks of both conservatives and liberals.[12]

We can draw the following (oversimplified) portrait of the conservative attitude toward duties of nurturance: duties of nurturance represent the highest expression of human morality, making women (the defenders of nurturance) morally superior to men (163). Children need to be looked upon more positively, the responsibilities of raising children being a full-time job (170, 161). Liberals tend to value money and material possessions too highly, with the consequence that they view children as an obstacle to good things that money can buy (168). Money is not important to proper nurturance, and those who think that the rearing of children requires that they be provided with expensive possessions are misguided (206–7). The unconditioned love of parent for child "where none of us has a price tag" is the highest expression of human morality, and those who value children for their potential for achievement and would abort embryos that are defective have a bad morality (207–8). (The conservative activists Luker interviewed were for the most part of very modest means and generally less affluent than the liberal activists.)

Conservatives regard the nurturing role as the *main life role* of sexually active people, particularly women. "Women who choose to be in the public world of work should eschew the role of wife and mother, or, if they marry, should be prepared to put the public world of work second to their role as wife and mother" (169). "To try to balance a number of competing commitments—especially when parenthood gets shuffled into second or fourth place—is . . . morally wrong" (170). Hence, given only the qualification of sexual activity, those who oppose abortion express an ideal of life, particularly for women, where nurturing is the responsibility that takes priority over every other responsibility. If a woman fulfils her highest role in life by being a mother, then if she discovers she is pregnant, she should continue the pregnancy, not end it. So we can see how the anti-abortion position can be derived from a conception that the woman's role is to be a mother and uphold the morality of nurturance.

Those who uphold abortion rights might reply in two ways. First, they might deny the moral ideal of a woman's role as being to have and nurture children above all other duties. Second, they might reply, within the morality of nurturance, that nurturing the children one already has or preparing oneself to nurture children properly in the future may require, when other contraceptive means fail, availing oneself of abortion. Both replies are found both in the philosophical literature and in Luker's survey of activists.

Martha Bolton objects to the conservative conception of women's roles:

> I think it is also central to the life of a morally responsible person that he/she develop abilities which make him/her a useful, productive, contributing member of the community. Doing so often requires large commitments of a person's time, thought, and other personal resources; such commitments are liable to conflict with the activity of nurturing a fetus and raising a child.[13]

Bolton's view is echoed among abortion rights activists. According to Luker, they argue that "*control* over reproduction is essential for women to be able to live up to their full human potential."

Women's reproductive and family roles are "potential barriers to full equality" (176; cf. 92). Hence, there are weighty moral reasons why the nurturing role cannot have absolute predominance, and abortion must be allowed where other means of birth control fail.

The second argument, within the morality of nurturance, that responsible parents must sometimes abort, is also made by both philosophers and activists. Bolton points out that development of the fetus and care of it may be in conflict with a woman's other commitments and may undermine her ability to fulfil responsibilities to others who are dependent on her.[14] From the context it is clear that commitments to living children are among those she has in mind. The people Luker interviewed gave a slightly different argument: that commitment to any children one might bear requires that we have the emotional and financial resources to give them the best possible life, and that this in turn requires control of fertility and, where other methods might fail, the availability of abortion (181–2). This argument is in direct conflict with the conservatives' views that it is natural to be a parent (and hence we need no special preparation for it) and that material things are not very significant for proper nurturance.[15]

V Conclusion

The purpose of most papers on abortion is to make practical recommendations about the legality of abortions. My purpose has been different, one step removed: to argue that the arguments, in the philosophical literature, for the past twenty years have focused on the wrong set of issues, trying to judge the morality of abortion by moral concepts more appropriate to relations between adults.

Nevertheless, the proposal that conservatives have misarticulated their objection to abortion, that, at worst, abortion violates the morality of nurturance rather than the prohibition on killing a person, has practical consequences. Early abortions seem consistent with the morality of nurturance unless we take the conservative view of women's roles. Conservative objections to early abortions derive from the norm, based on traditional women's roles, that sexually active women should accept their pregnancies and regard the early fetus as a baby. Hence, it seems, our view of the morality of abortion depends in part on our view of women's roles.

If objections to abortion are based on the morality of nurturance, there is a second issue: what is the connection between abortion and our concern for children? Is there any justice to the conservatives' claims that liberalism about abortion is linked to indifference to children or excessive valuation of material things?

Let us deal first with the relation between abortion and the welfare of children. In our society we condemn infanticide rather strongly, and legally it is homicide. Yet even infanticide, where it has been practiced, has often coexisted with nurturing attitudes toward children. So it is doubtful that the conservatives can argue that widespread practice of abortion will undermine nurturing attitudes generally.

Still, our psychology sets limits to our morality. Wherever infanticide is practiced it seems to create emotional and moral difficulties, presumably because nurturing attitudes and morality take hold before birth.[16] This means that cavalier attitudes toward abortions and the insistence that late abortions are innocuous might undermine the morality of nurturance if these attitudes were widely held. I have in mind here Warren's remarks that abortion ought to be regarded as morally innocuous, like cutting one's hair, and that there is no moral wrong in aborting a seven month fetus to avoid postponing a trip to Europe. If such attitudes were widespread, would we develop a proper sense of our duties of nurturance toward our children? It is hard to be unaware that one is considering aborting what one might raise to an adult.[17]

The conservatives also claim that the liberals incorrectly identify proper nurturance with material wealth. This claim may contain a grain of truth, but no more. Generally, the conservatives show a pollyannish disregard for the difficulties many face in trying to provide proper nurturance for children. In our society, the conflict between what a woman must do to function adequately and the responsibilities of a pregnancy carried to term are real.

The issue of women's roles is much clearer. Women's labor in capitalist society has been demeaned: jobs stereotyped as women's jobs have received low pay and low status. Women are demeaned by sexist epithets; in the workplace they are routinely called "honey" and referred to by their bosses as "my girl." The demeaning of women is linked ideologically to their role as mothers and childbearers: it is implied that women are good for this role and little else and that the things women can do have little value. Thus the conservatives' claim that women are morally superior is hypocritical, for they accept these traditional roles and their demeaned status. If the conservatives believed their own claim that women are morally superior because they are more committed to nurturance, then they would attempt to cultivate nurturing attitudes equally among men.

The liberals are right that equality between men and women requires that women be able to control their reproduction. Of all the moral issues implied in the abortion controversy the issue of equality of men and women is the clearest and the most favorable to the liberals. But even here I would add a qualification. The conservatives argue that if women as much as men pursue high status and success in our present business and academic environments, we will all be worse off, for the competitive environments of these worlds subordinate commitment to people to pursuit of status and success (Luker, 163). Even if this is, as I believe, one of their stronger arguments, the solution is not to advocate that women be confined to a demeaned status as servants of men and nannies to children. The conservatives glorify servility by calling it morality.

Let me suggest a twofold solution. First, instead of allowing the communism of the family to be undermined by the competitiveness of the capitalist order, the egalitarianism and commitment to others that characterize family relations at their best should be spread to the larger world. Second, nurturing attitudes can represent morality rather than servility in a world where they are cultivated equally among all adults; the duties of nurturance must fall equally on men. But where much of our social life is governed by market imperatives, it becomes impossible to share nurturing equally among men and women. This suggests that a satisfactory solution to the problems surrounding the abortion issue will require changing the economic structures of our society. The moral problems of abortion are really social problems of capitalist society.[18]

Notes

1. The conservative position on abortion is stated by John T. Noonan, Jr., "An Almost Absolute Value in History," in Noonan, ed., *The Morality of Abortion* (Cambridge, MA: Harvard University Press 1970) 1–59. The last several pages are frequently reprinted. A more developed argument for the conservative view is given by Baruch Brody, *Abortion and the Sanctity of Human Life* (Cambridge, MA: MIT Press 1975). A widely discussed presentation of an extremely liberal position (defending the innocuousness of infanticide) is Michael Tooley, "Abortion and Infanticide," *Philosophy and Public Affairs* 2 (1972) 37–65. Tooley amplifies his argument in *Abortion and Infanticide* (Oxford: Clarendon Press 1983). Mary Anne Warren defends a similar position, but tries to back off on the issue of infanticide, in "On the Moral and Legal Status of Abortion," *The Monist* 57 (1973) 43–61. Martha Brandt Bolton, "Responsible Women and Abortion Decisions," in Onora O'Neill and William Ruddick, eds., *Having Children* (New York: Oxford University Press 1979), puts the issue of abortion in the context of the array of moral responsibilities that may be part of a woman's life. The papers by Noonan, Warren, and Bolton are reprinted in Ronald Munson, ed., *Intervention and Reflection*, 3rd ed. (Belmont, CA: Wadsworth Publishing 1988).

   I use the terms "conservative" and "liberal" for what are sometimes called the "pro-life" and "pro-choice" positions because I believe the latter terms are politically more loaded and less accurate. As I will argue, the former terms capture the essence of much of the political difference between the two camps.

2. Carol Gilligan, *In a Different Voice* (Cambridge, MA: Harvard University Press 1982), suggests that women's orientations toward moral problems are often different from those of men. She does not suggest what is proposed here: that both men and women have within their repertoires of moral competence both the morality of relations between adults and the morality of nurturance. Also the morality of nurturance is not the same as what she calls ethic of care, which is a fully developed orientation toward moral problems. Still, this work is relevant to the discussion at hand. For the morality of relations between adults is the morality that governs the relations between agents in the world of business and commerce in capitalist societies, a domain of social life traditionally dominated by men. The morality of nurturance, in contrast, is an important component of the morality that governs family relations, where women have traditionally concentrated their concerns.

3. The suggestion of this paper is that this norm is part of the morality of our culture. I doubt that the morality of nurturance is derivable from principles governing moral relations between adults, the principle prohibiting killing of another person being paradigmatic of morality between adults. Hence I doubt the significance of both the attempts to derive a prohibition on abortion from potential to become an adult like ourselves, and the vindications of abortion which rely on criticisms of such arguments. For the latter see Tooley, *Abortion and Infanticide*, 178–83. Since the purpose of the present paper is only to understand the abortion debate, I adopt, methodologically, a moral inflationism which articulates the moral imperatives commonly accepted in our culture.

4. I would speculate that our abhorrence of infanticide is related to the development of the technology of birth control. Societies that have had to limit population but have not had contraceptive technologies (all human societies throughout most of human prehistory) almost certainly had to practice infanticide. However emotionally difficult such a practice may have been, it was probably not severely condemned morally. The present controversy over abortion is probably partly due to the availability of pre-conceptive means of population control.

5. John Rawls, *A Theory of Justice* (Cambridge, MA: Harvard University Press 1971), 453–512 ("The Sense of Justice"), esp. 485–90.

6. For a published description of the personification of the fetus in late pregnancy see Barbara Katz Rothman, *Recreating Motherhood* (New York: Norton 1989), 97–105.

7. The idea that accepting a pregnancy is a crucial stage was suggested to me by a discussion with Charlotte Jackson. Laura Coleman pointed out to me that one can carry to term and never accept the pregnancy or develop a nurturing attitude. See Sandy Robey, "Weighing the Mother Load," *Chicago Tribune,* May 14, 1989, Sect. 6, 1 for an account of a decision to accept a pregnancy. In that case, however, it seemed that nurturing attitudes were already at work in that decision. This suggests that the physical development of the fetus, combined with our awareness of what it will become, can cause us to accept a pregnancy.

8. But see Brody (63) for an attempt to explain why we might treat this particular instance of murder differently. I assume here that the conservatives are wrong, that abortion is not murder and that Warren and Tooley are correct. Otherwise there is no need for an alternative conception of the objection to abortion.

9. Of course, someone who does this is not necessarily a monster, but someone who, for whatever reason, did not develop a nurturing attitude toward this baby.

10. Infanticide is a common form of birth control when there are few other ways to limit births. See, for example, Marvin Harris, *Cultural Anthropology* (New York: Harper and Row 1983), 56–7. Killing of children may be murder *and* a violation of the morality of nurturance.

11. This conception of women's roles *by itself* is enough to generate a condemnation of abortion, but not as akin to infanticide. That is, this conception of women's roles does not by itself explain the focus on the fetus by the opponents of abortion.

   If I am right about the importance of the conceptions of women's roles to the abortion dispute, then the issue of abortion was raised in a more forthright way in the nineteenth century when, according to Linda Gordon, the criminalization of abortion was justified on the grounds that "abortion was a sign of women's selfishness in evading their prescribed destiny as mothers." See Linda Gordon, review of Barbara Katz Rothman, *Recreating Motherhood, New York Times Book Review,* April 16, 1989.

12. *Abortion and the Politics of Motherhood* (Berkeley: University of California Press 1984). Page references to Luker's study are in the text.

13. Bolton in Munson, 99.

14. Ibid.

15. Many complexities of Luker's study are omitted or inadequately covered here. She gives a sensitive account of how the conservatives' views on abortion are tied to their conceptions of sexuality, spirituality, birth control, relations between husbands and wives, and human relationships generally. Most important, she shows how the dispute about abortion is an attempt by women whose lives exemplify different conceptions of women's roles to defend the dignity and value of their lives.

16. On the difficulty of infanticide see Robert F. Spencer, *The North Alaskan Eskimo: A Study in Ecology and Society, Smithsonian Institution Bureau of American Ethnology Bulletin 171* (Washington, DC: US Government Printing Office 1959), 94, also 87–8, 92–3. On secrecy about infanticide, a secrecy that seems to indicate shame, see Richard Lee, *The Kung San* (Cambridge: Cambridge University Press 1979), 451–2.

17. Two friends have reported to me that they have raised children that they considered aborting. They were explaining why they could not take abortion lightly. See also Robey (cited in n. 7).

18. I am indebted to many who contributed their ideas to this paper but who may not agree with my formulations and conclusions. I learned much from discussions with Charlotte Jackson, Laura Coleman, Donda West, and Maureen Ruder. Bonnie Bluestein and Michael Davis criticized an early draft; Mary Gomberg offered sharp criticisms of several later drafts. An anonymous editor and two anonymous referees for the *Canadian Journal of Philosophy* made extensive criticisms of a late draft. I have tried to answer or incorporate all that I have learned from these many criticisms.

QUESTIONS

1. Why think that the abortion controversy might be clarified by considering it from the standpoint of the ethics of nurturance?

2. Is Gomberg right in thinking that his perspective illuminates the contemporary debate about abortion?

Making People: Cloning

XIII

Recent advances in biology and biotechnology have made cloning human beings a genuine possibility. In 1996 a sheep named Dolly was born, the first mammal cloned from a somatic cell of an adult sheep. The controversy over cloning humans has since been heated. There is the prospect of *reproductive cloning*, the production of a child for parents otherwise unable to have children. The prospect of *therapeutic cloning*, the creation of embryos for medical purposes, creates different hopes and fears. If successful, cloning could be enormously beneficial; it could provide cells for transplantation, in particular stem cells, with the prospect of treating a wide number of diseases. Such cells would be genetically identical and thus would not trigger an autoimmune response on the part of the recipient.

The concerns about both reproductive and therapeutic cloning are multiple. There is general concern that cloning is contrary to human dignity,[1] as well as a general unease about the prospect of "meddling" with nature and the production of humans. Many who object worry specifically about interfering with God's creation. There are specific objections to therapeutic cloning and the production of human organisms in order to provide parts for others. Some worries seem to be based on misunderstandings. For instance, it is sometimes said that clones would be mere replicas of the original and that it would not be possible to distinguish them, but clones are no more identical than identical twins.

Cloning also holds out the prospect not only of improved medical treatment for disease but also for improving, as it were, the capacities of people. The prospect of "designer babies," with improved abilities, is alarming to many.

---

1. UNESCO's *Universal Declaration on the Human Genome and Human Rights* (1997), Article 11.

63. Preventing a Brave New World

LEON KASS

Leon Kass (1939–) is professor in the Committee on Social Thought at the University of Chicago and fellow at the American Enterprise Institute in Washington, D.C. His doctoral degree is in biochemistry, but his interests are broadly humanistic and philosophical. He was chair of the President's Council on Bioethics, which issued its report, *Human Cloning and Human Dignity: An Ethical Inquiry*, in 2002.

Human cloning, the process of creating a genetically identical copy of another human (alive or deceased), raises many ethical questions. Kass worries about the possibility and its implications: "We are compelled to decide nothing less than whether human procreation is going to remain human, whether children are going to be made to order rather than begotten, and whether we wish to say yes in principle to the road that leads to the dehumanized hell of *Brave New World*." Kass notes our repugnance at the prospect of human cloning and thinks that "we are repelled by the prospect of cloning human beings not because of the strangeness or the novelty of the undertaking, but because we intuit and we feel, immediately and without argument, the violation of things we rightfully hold dear. We sense that cloning represents a profound defilement of our given nature as pro-creative beings, and of the social relations built on this natural ground." He offers a number of arguments in support of his reaction.

The urgency of the great political struggles of the twentieth century, successfully waged against totalitarianisms first right and then left, seems to have blinded many people to a deeper and ultimately darker truth about the present age: all contemporary societies are traveling briskly in the same utopian direction. All are wedded to the modern technological project; all march eagerly to the drums of progress and fly proudly the banner of modern science; all sing loudly the Baconian anthem, "Conquer nature, relieve man's estate." Leading the triumphal procession is modern medicine, which is daily becoming ever more powerful in its battle against disease, decay, and death, thanks especially to astonishing achievements in biomedical science and technology—achievements for which we must surely be grateful.

Yet contemplating present and projected advances in genetic and reproductive technologies, in neuroscience and psychopharmacology, and in the development of artificial organs and computer-chip implants for human brains, we now clearly recognize new uses for biotechnical power that soar beyond the traditional medical goals of healing disease and relieving suffering. Human nature itself lies on the operating table, ready for alteration, for eugenic and psychic "enhancement," for wholesale re-design. In leading laboratories, academic and industrial, new creators are confidently amassing their powers and quietly honing their skills, while

From Leon Kass, "Preventing a Brave New World," *Human Life Review* (Summer 2001), pp. 14–35 (originally published in the *New Republic* [21 May 2001]). Reprinted by permission of the author.

on the street their evangelists are zealously prophesying a post-human future. For anyone who cares about preserving our humanity, the time has come to pay attention.

Some transforming powers are already here. The Pill. In vitro fertilization. Bottled embryos. Surrogate wombs. Cloning. Genetic screening. Genetic manipulation. Organ harvesting. Mechanical spare parts. Chimeras. Brain implants. Ritalin for the young, Viagra for the old, Prozac for everyone. And, to leave this vale of tears, a little extra morphine accompanied by Muzak.

Years ago Aldous Huxley saw it coming. In his charming but disturbing novel, *Brave New World* (it appeared in 1932 and is more powerful on each re-reading), he made its meaning strikingly visible for all to see. Unlike other frightening futuristic novels of the past century, such as Orwell's already dated *Nineteen Eighty-Four,* Huxley shows us a dystopia that goes with, rather than against, the human grain. Indeed, it is animated by our own most humane and progressive aspirations. Following those aspirations to their ultimate realization, Huxley enables us to recognize those less obvious but often more pernicious evils that are inextricably linked to the successful attainment of partial goods.

Huxley depicts human life seven centuries hence, living under the gentle hand of humanitarianism rendered fully competent by genetic manipulation, psychoactive drugs, hypnopaedia, and high-tech amusements. At long last, mankind has succeeded in eliminating disease, aggression, war, anxiety, suffering, guilt, envy, and grief. But this victory comes at the heavy price of homogenization, mediocrity, trivial pursuits, shallow attachments, debased tastes, spurious contentment, and souls without loves or longings. The Brave New World has achieved prosperity, community, stability, and nigh-universal contentment, only to be peopled by creatures of human shape but stunted humanity. They consume, fornicate, take "soma," enjoy "centrifugal bumble-puppy," and operate the machinery that makes it all possible. They do not read, write, think, love, or govern themselves. Art and science, virtue and religion, family and friendship are all passé.

What matters most is bodily health and immediate gratification: "Never put off till tomorrow the fun you can have today." Brave New Man is so dehumanized that he does not even recognize what has been lost.

Huxley's novel, of course, is science fiction. Prozac is not yet Huxley's "soma"; cloning by nuclear transfer or splitting embryos is not exactly "Bokanovskification"; MTV and virtual-reality parlors are not quite the "feelies"; and our current safe and consequenceless sexual practices are not universally as loveless or as empty as those in the novel. But the kinships are disquieting, all the more so since our technologies of bio-psycho-engineering are still in their infancy, and in ways that make all too clear what they might look like in their full maturity. Moreover, the cultural changes that technology has already wrought among us should make us even more worried than Huxley would have us be.

In Huxley's novel, everything proceeds under the direction of an omnipotent—albeit benevolent—world state. Yet the dehumanization that he portrays does not really require despotism or external control. To the contrary, precisely because the society of the future will deliver exactly what we most want—health, safety, comfort, plenty, pleasure, peace of mind and length of days—we can reach the same humanly debased condition solely on the basis of free human choice. No need for World Controllers. Just give us the technological imperative, liberal democratic society, compassionate humanitarianism, moral pluralism, and free markets, and we can take ourselves to a Brave New World all by ourselves—and without even deliberately deciding to go. In case you had not noticed, the train has already left the station and is gathering speed, but no one seems to be in charge.

Some among us are delighted, of course, by this state of affairs: some scientists and biotechnologists, their entrepreneurial backers, and a cheering claque of sci-fi enthusiasts, futurologists, and libertarians. There are dreams to be realized, powers to be exercised, honors to be won, and money—big money—to be made. But many of us are worried, and not, as the proponents of the revolution self-servingly claim, because we are either ignorant of science or afraid of the unknown. To the contrary, we can see all too clearly where the train is headed, and we do not like the destination. We can distinguish cleverness about means from wisdom about ends, and we are loath to entrust the future of the race to those who cannot tell the difference. No friend of humanity cheers for a post-human future.

Yet for all our disquiet, we have until now done nothing to prevent it. We hide our heads in the sand because we enjoy the blessings that medicine keeps supplying, or we rationalize our inaction by declaring that human engineering is inevitable and we can do nothing about it. In either case, we are complicit in preparing for our own degradation, in some respects more to blame than the bio-zealots who, however misguided, are putting their money where their mouth is. Denial and despair, unattractive outlooks in any situation, become morally reprehensible when circumstances summon us to keep the world safe for human flourishing. Our immediate ancestors, taking up the challenge of their time, rose to the occasion and rescued the human future from the cruel dehumanizations of Nazi and Soviet tyranny. It is our more difficult task to find ways to preserve it from the soft dehumanizations of well-meaning but hubristic biotechnical "recreationism"—and to do it without undermining biomedical science or rejecting its genuine contributions to human welfare. [. . .]

Not the least of our difficulties in trying to exercise control over where biology is taking us is the fact that we do not get to decide, once and for all, for or against the destination of a post-human world. The scientific discoveries and the technical powers that will take us there come to us piecemeal, one at a time and seemingly independent from one another, each often attractively introduced as a measure that will "help [us] not to be sick." But sometimes we come to a clear fork in the road where decision is possible, and where we know that our decision will make a world of difference—indeed, it will make a permanently different world. Fortunately, we stand now at the point of such a momentous decision. Events have conspired to provide us with a perfect opportunity to seize the initiative and to gain some control of the biotechnical project. I refer to the prospect of human cloning, a practice absolutely central to Huxley's fictional world. Indeed, creating and manipulating life in the laboratory is the gateway to a Brave New World, not only in fiction but also in fact.

"To clone or not to clone a human being" is no longer a fanciful question. Success in cloning sheep, and also cows, mice, pigs, and goats, makes it perfectly clear that a fateful decision is now at hand: whether we should welcome or even tolerate the cloning of human beings. If recent newspaper reports are to be believed, reputable scientists and physicians have announced their intention to produce the first human clone in the coming year. Their efforts may already be under way.

The media, gawking and titillating as is their wont, have been softening us up for this possibility by turning the bizarre into the familiar. In the four years since the birth of Dolly the cloned sheep, the tone of discussing the prospect of human cloning has gone from "Yuck" to "Oh?" to "Gee whiz" to "Why not?" The sentimentalizers, aided by leading bioethicists, have downplayed talk about eugenically cloning the beautiful and the brawny or the best and the brightest. They have taken instead to defending clonal reproduction for humanitarian or compassionate reasons: to treat infertility in people who are said to "have no other choice," to avoid the risk of severe genetic disease, to "replace" a child who has died. For the sake of these rare benefits, they would have us countenance the entire practice of human cloning, the consequences be damned.

But we dare not be complacent about what is at issue, for the stakes are very high. Human cloning, though partly continuous with previous reproductive technologies, is also something radically new in itself and in its easily foreseeable consequences—especially when coupled with powers for genetic "enhancement" and germline genetic modification that may soon become available, owing to the recently completed Human Genome Project. I exaggerate somewhat, but in the direction of the truth: we are compelled to decide nothing less than whether human procreation is going to remain human, whether children are going to be made to order rather than begotten, and whether we wish to say yes in principle to the road that leads to the dehumanized hell of *Brave New World*.

In 1997 I addressed this subject in the *New Republic*, trying to articulate the moral grounds of our repugnance at the prospect of human cloning ("The Wisdom of Repugnance," June 2, 1997). Subsequent events have only strengthened my conviction that cloning is a bad idea whose time should not come; but my emphasis this time is more practical. To be sure, I would still like to persuade undecided readers that cloning is a serious evil, but I am more interested in encouraging those who oppose human cloning but who think that we are impotent to prevent it, and in mobilizing them to support new and solid legislative efforts to stop it. In addition, I want readers who may worry less about cloning and more about the impending prospects of germline genetic manipulation or other eugenic practices to realize the unique practical opportunity that now presents itself to us.

For we have here a golden opportunity to exercise some control over where biology is taking us. The technology of cloning is discrete and well defined, and it requires considerable technical know-how and dexterity; we can therefore know by name many of the likely practitioners. The public demand for cloning is extremely low, and most people are decidedly against it. Nothing scientifically or medically important would be lost by banning clonal reproduction; alternative and non-objectionable means are available to obtain some of the most important medical benefits claimed for (non-reproductive) human cloning. The commercial interests in human cloning are, for now, quite limited; and the nations of the world are actively seeking to prevent it. Now may be as good a chance as we will ever have to get our hands on the wheel of the runaway train now headed for a post-human world and to steer it toward a more dignified human future.

II

What is cloning? Cloning, or asexual reproduction, is the production of individuals who are genetically identical to an already existing individual. The procedure's name is fancy—"somatic cell nuclear transfer"—but its concept is simple. Take a mature but unfertilized egg; remove or deactivate its nucleus; introduce a nucleus obtained from a specialized (somatic) cell of an adult organism. Once the egg begins to divide, transfer the little embryo to a woman's uterus to initiate a pregnancy. Since almost all the hereditary material of a cell is contained within its nucleus, the re-nucleated egg and the individual into which it develops are genetically identical to the organism that was the source of the transferred nucleus.

An unlimited number of genetically identical individuals—the group, as well as each of its members, is called "a clone"—could be produced by nuclear transfer. In principle, any person, male or female, newborn or adult, could be cloned, and in any quantity; and because stored cells can outlive their sources, one may even clone the dead. Since cloning requires no personal involvement on the part of the person whose genetic material is used, it could easily be used to reproduce living or deceased persons without their consent—a threat to reproductive freedom that has received relatively little attention.

Some possible misconceptions need to be avoided. Cloning is not Xeroxing: the clone of Bill Clinton, though his genetic double, would enter the world hairless, toothless, and peeing in his diapers, like any other human infant. But neither is cloning just like natural twinning: the cloned twin will be identical to an older, existing adult; and it will arise not by chance but by deliberate design; and its entire genetic makeup will be pre-selected by its parents and/or scientists. Moreover, the success rate of cloning, at least at first, will probably not be very high: the Scots transferred two hundred seventy-seven adult nuclei into sheep eggs, implanted twenty-nine clonal embryos, and achieved the birth of only one live lamb clone.

For this reason, among others, it is unlikely that, at least for now, the practice would be very popular; and there is little immediate worry of mass-scale production of multicopies. Still, for the tens of thousand of people who sustain more than three hundred assisted-reproduction clinics in the United States and already avail themselves of in vitro fertilization and other techniques, cloning would be an option with virtually no added fuss. Panos Zavos, the Kentucky reproduction specialist who has announced his plans to clone a child, claims that he has already received thousands of e-mailed requests from people eager to clone, despite the known risks of failure and damaged offspring. Should commercial interests develop in "nucleus-banking," as they have in sperm-banking and egg-harvesting; should famous athletes or other celebrities decide to market their DNA the way they now market their autographs and nearly everything else; should techniques of embryo and germline genetic testing and manipulation arrive as anticipated, increasing the use of laboratory assistance in order to obtain "better" babies—should all this come to pass, cloning, if it is permitted, could become more than a marginal practice simply on the basis of free reproductive choice.

What are we to think about this prospect? Nothing good. Indeed, most people are repelled by nearly all aspects of human cloning: the possibility of mass production of human beings, with large clones of look-alikes, compromised in their individuality; the idea of father-son or mother-daughter "twins"; the bizarre prospect of a woman bearing and rearing a genetic copy of herself, her spouse, or even her deceased father or mother; the grotesqueness of conceiving a child as an exact "replacement" for another who has died; the utilitarian creation of embryonic duplicates of oneself, to be frozen away or created when needed to provide homologous tissues or organs for transplantation; the narcissism of those who would clone themselves, and the arrogance of others who think they know who deserves to be cloned; the Frankensteinian hubris to create a human life and increasingly to control its destiny; men playing at being God. Almost no one finds any of the suggested reasons for human cloning compelling, and almost everyone anticipates its possible misuses and abuses. And the popular belief that human cloning cannot be prevented makes the prospect all the more revolting.

Revulsion is not an argument; and some of yesterday's repugnances are today calmly accepted—not always for the better. In some crucial cases, however, repugnance is the emotional expression of deep wisdom, beyond reason's power completely to articulate it. Can anyone really give an argument fully adequate to the horror that is father-daughter incest (even with consent), or bestiality, or the mutilation of a corpse, or the eating of human flesh, or the rape or murder of another human being? Would anybody's failure to give full rational justification for his revulsion at those practices make that revulsion ethically suspect?

I suggest that our repugnance at human cloning belongs in this category. We are repelled by the prospect of cloning human beings not because of the strangeness or the novelty of the undertaking, but because we intuit and we feel, immediately and without argument, the violation of things that we rightfully hold dear. We sense that cloning represents a profound defilement of our given nature as pro-creative beings, and of the social relations built on this natural ground. We also sense that cloning is a radical form of child abuse. In this age in which everything is held to be permissible so long as it is freely done, and in which our bodies are regarded as mere instruments of our autonomous rational will, repugnance may be the only voice left that speaks up to defend the central core of our humanity. Shallow are the souls that have forgotten how to shudder.

III

Yet repugnance need not stand naked before the bar of reason. The wisdom of our horror at human cloning can be at least partially articulated, even if this is finally one of those instances about which the heart has its reasons that reason cannot entirely know. I offer four objections to human cloning: that it constitutes unethical experimentation; that it threatens identity and individuality; that it turns procreation into manufacture (especially when understood as the harbinger of manipulations to come); and that it means despotism over children and perversion of parenthood. Please note: I speak only about so-called reproductive cloning, not about the creation of cloned embryos for research. The objections that may be raised against creating (or using) embryos for research are entirely independent of whether the research embryos are produced by cloning. What is radically distinct and radically new is reproductive cloning.

Any attempt to clone a human being would constitute an unethical experiment upon the resulting child-to-be. In all the animal experiments, fewer than two to three percent of all cloning attempts succeeded. Not only are there fetal deaths and still-born infants, but many of the so-called "successes" are in fact failures. As has only recently become clear, there is a very high incidence of major disabilities and deformities in cloned animals that attain live birth. Cloned cows often have heart and lung problems; cloned mice later develop pathological obesity; other live-born cloned animals fail to reach normal developmental milestones.

The problem, scientists suggest, may lie in the fact that an egg with a new somatic nucleus must re-program itself in a matter of minutes or hours (whereas the nucleus of an unaltered egg has been prepared over months and years). There is thus a greatly increased likelihood of error in translating the genetic instructions, leading to developmental defects some of which will show themselves only much later. (Note also that these induced abnormalities may also affect the stem cells that scientists hope to harvest from cloned embryos. Lousy embryos, lousy stem cells.) Nearly all scientists now agree that attempts to clone human beings carry massive risks of producing unhealthy, abnormal, and malformed children. What are we to do with them? Shall we just discard the ones that fall short of expectations? Considered opinion is today nearly unanimous, even among scientists: attempts at human cloning are irresponsible and unethical. We cannot ethically even get to know whether or not human cloning is feasible.

If it were successful, cloning would create serious issues of identity and individuality. The clone may experience concerns about his distinctive identity not only because he will be, in genotype and in appearance, identical to another human being, but because he may also be twin to the person who is his "father" or his "mother"—if one can still call them that. Unaccountably, people treat as innocent the homey case of intra-familial cloning—the cloning of husband or wife (or single mother). They forget about the unique dangers of mixing the twin relation with the parent-child relation. (For this situation, the relation of contemporaneous twins is no precedent; yet even this less problematic situation teaches us how difficult it is to wrest independence

from the being for whom one has the most powerful affinity.) Virtually no parent is going to be able to treat a clone of himself or herself as one treats a child generated by the lottery of sex. What will happen when the adolescent clone of Mommy becomes the spitting image of the woman with whom Daddy once fell in love? In case of divorce, will Mommy still love the clone of Daddy, even though she can no longer stand the sight of Daddy himself?

Most people think about cloning from the point of view of adults choosing to clone. Almost nobody thinks about what it would be like to be a cloned child. Surely his or her new life would constantly be scrutinized in relation to that of the older version. Even in the absence of unusual parental expectations for the clone—say, to live the same life, only without its errors—the child is likely to be ever a curiosity, ever a potential source of déjà-vu. Unlike "normal" identical twins, a cloned individual—copied from whomever—will be saddled with a genotype that has already lived. He will not be fully a surprise to the world: people are likely always to compare his doings in life with those of his alter ego, especially if he is a clone of someone gifted or famous. True, his nurture and his circumstances will be different; genotype is not exactly destiny. But one must also expect parental efforts to shape this new life after the original—or at least to view the child with the original version always firmly in mind. For why else did they clone from the star basketball player, the mathematician, or the beauty queen—or even dear old Dad—in the first place?

Human cloning would also represent a giant step toward the transformation of begetting into making, of procreation into manufacture (literally, "hand-made"), a process that has already begun with in vitro fertilization and genetic testing of embryos. With cloning, not only is the process in hand, but the total genetic blueprint of the cloned individual is selected and determined by the human artisans. To be sure, subsequent development is still according to natural processes; and the resulting children will be recognizably human. But we would be taking a major step into making man himself simply another one of the man-made things.

How does begetting differ from making? In natural procreation, human beings come together to give existence to another being that is formed exactly as we were, by what we are—living, hence perishable, hence aspiringly erotic, hence procreative human beings. But in clonal reproduction, and in the more advanced forms of manufacture to which it will lead, we give existence to a being not by what we are but by what we intend and design.

Let me be clear. The problem is not the mere intervention of technique, and the point is not that "nature knows best." The problem is that any child whose being, character, and capacities exist owing to human design does not stand on the same plane as its makers. As with any product of our making, no matter how excellent, the artificer stands above it, not as an equal but as a superior, transcending it by his will and creative prowess. In human cloning, scientists and prospective "parents" adopt a technocratic attitude toward human children: human children become their artifacts. Such an arrangement is profoundly dehumanizing, no matter how good the product.

Procreation dehumanized into manufacture is further degraded by commodification, a virtually inescapable result of allowing baby-making to proceed under the banner of commerce. Genetic and reproductive biotechnology companies are already growth industries, but they will soon go into commercial orbit now that the Human Genome Project has been completed. "Human eggs for sale" is already a big business, masquerading under the pretense of "donation." Newspaper advertisements on elite college campuses offer up to $50,000 for an egg "donor" tall enough to play women's basketball and with SAT scores high enough for admission to Stanford; and to nobody's surprise, at such prices there are many young coeds eager to help shoppers obtain the finest babies money can buy. (The egg and womb-renting entrepreneurs shamelessly proceed on the ancient, disgusting, misogynist premise that most women will give you access to their bodies, if the price is right.) Even before the capacity for human cloning is perfected, established companies will have invested in the harvesting of eggs from ovaries obtained at autopsy or through ovarian surgery, practiced embryonic genetic alteration, and initiated the stockpiling of prospective donor tissues. Through the rental of surrogate-womb services, and through the buying and selling of tissues and embryos priced according to the merit of the donor, the commodification of nascent human life will be unstoppable.

Finally, the practice of human cloning by nuclear transfer—like other anticipated forms of genetically engineering the next generation—would enshrine and aggravate a profound misunderstanding of the meaning of having children and the parent-child relationship. When a couple normally chooses to procreate, the partners are saying yes to the emergence of new life in its novelty—are saying yes not only to having a child, but also to having whatever child this child turns out to be. In accepting our finitude, in opening ourselves to our replacement, we tacitly confess the limits of our control.

Embracing the future by procreating means precisely that we are relinquishing our grip in the very activity of taking up our own share in what we hope will be the immortality of human life and the human species. This means that our children are not our children: they are not our property, they are not our possessions. Neither are they supposed to live our lives for us, or to live anyone's life but their own. Their genetic distinctiveness and independence are the natural foreshadowing of the deep truth that they have their own, never-before-enacted life to live. Though sprung from a past, they take an uncharted course into the future.

Much mischief is already done by parents who try to live vicariously through their children. Children are sometimes compelled to fulfill the broken dreams of unhappy parents. But whereas most parents normally have hopes for their children, cloning parents will have expectations. In cloning, such overbearing parents will have taken at the start a decisive step that contradicts the entire meaning of the open and forward-looking nature of parent-child relations. The child is given a genotype that has already lived, with full expectation that this blueprint of a past life ought to be controlling the life that is to come. A wanted child now means a child who exists precisely to fulfill parental wants. Like all the more precise eugenic manipulations that will follow in its wake, cloning is thus inherently despotic, for it seeks to make one's children after one's own image (or an image of one's choosing) and their future according to one's will.

Is this hyperbolic? Consider concretely the new realities of responsibility and guilt in the households of the cloned. No longer only the sins of the parents, but also the genetic choices of the parents, will be visited on the children—and beyond the third and fourth generations; and everyone will know who is responsible. No parent will be able to blame nature or the lottery of sex for an unhappy adolescent's big nose, dull wit, musical ineptitude, nervous disposition, or anything else that he hates about himself. Fairly or not, children will hold their cloners responsible for everything, for nature as well as for nurture. And parents, especially the better ones, will be limitlessly liable to guilt. Only the truly despotic souls will sleep the sleep of the innocent.

IV

The defenders of cloning are not wittingly friends of despotism. Quite the contrary. Deaf to most other considerations, they regard themselves mainly as friends of freedom: the freedom of individuals to reproduce, the freedom of scientists and inventors to discover and to devise and to foster "progress" in genetic knowledge and technique, the freedom of entrepreneurs to profit in the market. They want large-scale cloning only for animals, but they wish to preserve cloning as a human option for exercising our "right to reproduce"—our right to have children, and children with "desirable genes." As some point out, under our "right to reproduce" we already practice early forms of unnatural, artificial, and extra-marital reproduction, and we already practice early forms of eugenic choice. For that reason, they argue, cloning is no big deal.

We have here a perfect example of the logic of the slippery slope. The principle of reproductive freedom currently enunciated by the proponents of cloning logically embraces the ethical acceptability of sliding all the way down: to producing children wholly in the laboratory from sperm to term (should it become feasible), and to producing children whose entire genetic makeup will be the product of

parental eugenic planning and choice. If reproductive freedom means the right to have a child of one's own choosing by whatever means, then reproductive freedom knows and accepts no limits.

Proponents want us to believe that there are legitimate uses of cloning that can be distinguished from illegitimate uses, but by their own principles no such limits can be found. (Nor could any such limits be enforced in practice: once cloning is permitted, no one ever need discover whom one is cloning and why.) Reproductive freedom, as they understand it, is governed solely by the subjective wishes of the parents-to-be. The sentimentally appealing case of the childless married couple is, on these grounds, indistinguishable from the case of an individual (married or not) who would like to clone someone famous or talented, living or dead. And the principle here endorsed justifies not only cloning but also the future artificial attempts to create (manufacture) "better" or "perfect" babies.

The "perfect baby," of course, is the project not of the infertility doctors, but of the eugenic scientists and their supporters, who, for the time being, are content to hide behind the skirts of the partisans of reproductive freedom and compassion for the infertile. For them, the paramount right is not the so-called right to reproduce, it is what the biologist Bentley Glass called, a quarter of a century ago, "the right of every child to be born with a sound physical and mental constitution, based on a sound genotype . . . the inalienable right to a sound heritage." But to secure this right, and to achieve the requisite quality control over new human life, human conception and gestation will need to be brought fully into the bright light of the laboratory, beneath which the child-to-be can be fertilized, nourished, pruned, weeded, watched, inspected, prodded, pinched, cajoled, injected, tested, rated, graded, approved, stamped, wrapped, sealed, and delivered. There is no other way to produce the perfect baby.

If you think that such scenarios require outside coercion or governmental tyranny, you are mistaken. Once it becomes possible, with the aid of human genomics, to produce or to select for what some regard as "better babies"—smarter, prettier, healthier, more athletic—parents will leap at the opportunity to "improve" their offspring. Indeed, not to do so will be socially regarded as a form of child neglect. Those who would ordinarily be opposed to such tinkering will be under enormous pressure to compete on behalf of their as yet unborn children—just as some now plan almost from their children's birth how to get them into Harvard. Never mind that, lacking a standard of "good" or "better," no one can really know whether any such changes will truly be improvements.

Proponents of cloning urge us to forget about the science-fiction scenarios of laboratory manufacture or multiple-copy clones, and to focus only on the sympathetic cases of infertile couples exercising their reproductive rights. But why, if the single cases are so innocent, should multiplying their performance be so off-putting? (Similarly, why do others object to people's making money from that practice if the practice itself is perfectly acceptable?) The so-called science-fiction cases—say *Brave New World*—make vivid the meaning of what looks to us, mistakenly, to be benign. They reveal that what looks like compassionate humanitarianism is, in the end, crushing dehumanization.

V

Whether or not they share my reasons, most people, I think, share my conclusion: that human cloning is unethical in itself and dangerous in its likely consequences, which include the precedent that it will establish for designing our children. Some reach this conclusion for their own good reasons, different from my own: concerns about the distributive justice in access to eugenic cloning; worries about the genetic effects of asexual "inbreeding"; aversion to the implicit premise of genetic determinism; objections to the embryonic and fetal wastage that must necessarily accompany the efforts; religious opposition to "man playing God." But never mind why: the overwhelming majority of our fellow Americans remain firmly opposed to cloning human beings.

For us, then, the real questions are: What should we do about it? How can we best succeed? These questions should concern everyone eager to secure deliberate human control over the powers that could re-design our humanity, even if cloning is not the issue over which they would choose to make their stand. And the answer to the first question seems pretty plain. What we should do is work to prevent human cloning by making it illegal.

We should aim for a global legal ban, if possible, and for a unilateral national ban at a minimum—and soon, before the fact is upon us [. . .]

Some have argued that cloning is almost certainly going to remain a marginal practice, and that we should therefore permit people to practice it. Such a view is shortsighted. Even if cloning is rarely undertaken, a society in which it is tolerated is no longer the same society—any more than is a society that permits (even small-scale) incest or cannibalism or slavery. A society that allows cloning, whether it knows it or not, has tacitly assented to the conversion of procreation into manufacture and to the treatment of children as purely the projects of our will. Willy-nilly, it has acquiesced in the eugenic re-design of future generations. The humanitarian superhighway to a Brave New World lies open before this society.

But the present danger posed by human cloning is, paradoxically, also a golden opportunity. In a truly unprecedented way, we can strike a blow for the human control of the technological project, for wisdom, for prudence, for human dignity. The prospect of human cloning, so repulsive to contemplate, is the occasion for deciding whether we shall be slaves of unregulated innovation, and ultimately its artifacts, or whether we shall remain free human beings who guide our powers toward the enhancement of human dignity. The humanity of the human future is now in our hands.

QUESTIONS

1. Do you share Kass's repugnance at human cloning? Why or why not?
2. How many arguments does Kass offer? How successful are they?

64. Human Cloning and Human Dignity

ROBERT GEORGE (JOINED BY ALFONSO GÓMEZ-LOBO)

Robert George (1955–) is professor of jurisprudence at Princeton University. He writes widely on topics in politics and legal philosophy, and his is one of the names associated with the revival of natural law theory in the English-speaking world. His books include *Making Men Moral: Civil Liberties and Public Morality* (1995), *In Defense of Natural Law* (1999), *The Clash of Orthodoxies: Law, Religion and Morality in Crisis* (2001), and *Embryo: A Defense of Human Life*, with C. Tollefsen (2008).

Alfonso Gómez-Lobo (1940–) is professor of metaphysics and moral philosophy at Georgetown University.

In one of the thirteen personal statements in the appendix to the report of the President's Council on Bioethics, Robert George and Alfonso Gómez-Lobo argue that cloned human embryos "ought to be treated as having the same moral status as other human embryos." Reviewing the process of their creation, George and Gómez-Lobo concluded they are complete organisms, just like the embryos created by ordinary sexual reproduction. "But does this not mean that the human embryo is a human being deserving of full moral respect such that it may not legitimately be used as a mere means to benefit others?" They argue later that "since human beings are intrinsically valuable and deserving of full moral respect in virtue of what they are, it follows that they are intrinsically valuable from the point at which they come into being."

The subject matter of the present report is human cloning, the production of a human embryo by means of somatic cell nuclear transfer (SCNT) or similar technologies. Just as fertilization, if successful, generates a human embryo, cloning produces the same result by combining what is normally combined and activated in fertilization, that is, the full genetic code plus the ovular cytoplasm. Fertilization produces a new and complete, though immature, human organism. The same is true of successful cloning. Cloned embryos therefore ought to be treated as having the same moral status as other human embryos.

A human embryo is a whole living member of the species homo sapiens in the earliest stage of his or her natural development. Unless denied a suitable environment, an embryonic human being will by directing its own integral organic functioning develop himself or herself to the next more mature developmental stage, i.e., the fetal stage. The embryonic, fetal, infant, child, and adolescent stages are stages in the development of a determinate and enduring entity—a human being—who comes into existence as a single cell organism and develops, if all goes well, into adulthood many years later.[1]

From the appendix to the President's Council on Bioethics, *Human Cloning and Human Dignity: An Ethical Inquiry*, 2002.

Human embryos possess the epigenetic primordia for self-directed growth into adulthood, with their determinateness and identity fully intact. The adult human being that is now you or me is the same human being who, at an earlier stage of his or her life, was an adolescent, and before that a child, an infant, a fetus, and an embryo. Even in the embryonic stage, you and I were undeniably whole, living members of the species homo sapiens. We were then, as we are now, distinct and complete (though in the beginning we were, of course, immature) human organisms; we were not mere parts of other organisms.

Consider the case of ordinary sexual reproduction. Plainly, the gametes whose union brings into existence the embryo are not whole or distinct organisms. They are functionally (and not merely genetically) identifiable as *parts* of the male or female (potential) parents. Each has only half the genetic material needed to guide the development of an immature human being toward full maturity. They are destined either to combine with an oocyte or spermatozoon to generate a new and distinct organism, or simply die. Even when fertilization occurs, they do not survive; rather, their genetic material enters into the composition of a new organism.

But none of this is true of the human embryo, from the zygote and blastula stages onward. The combining of the chromosomes of the spermatozoon and of the oocyte generates what every authority in human embryology identifies as a new and distinct organism. Whether produced by fertilization or by SCNT or some other cloning technique, the human embryo possesses all of the genetic material needed to inform and organize its growth. Unless deprived of a suitable environment or prevented by accident or disease, the embryo is actively developing itself to full maturity. The direction of its growth is *not extrinsically determined,* but is in accord with the genetic information *within* it.[2] The human embryo is, then, a whole (though immature) and distinct human organism—a human being.

If the embryo were not a complete organism, then what could it be? Unlike the spermatozoa and the oocytes, it is not a part of the mother or of the father. Nor is it a disordered growth such as a hydatidiform mole or teratoma. (Such entities lack the internal resources to actively develop themselves to the next more mature stage of the life of a human being.) Perhaps someone will say that the early embryo is an intermediate form, something that regularly emerges into a whole (though immature) human organism but is not one yet. But what could cause the emergence of the whole human organism, and cause it with regularity? It is clear that from the zygote stage forward, the major development of this organism is *controlled and directed from within*, that is, by the organism itself. So, after the embryo comes into being, no event or series of events occur that could be construed as the production of a new organism; that is, nothing extrinsic to the developing organism itself acts on it to produce a new character or new direction in development.

But does this mean that the human embryo is a human being deserving of full moral respect such that it may not legitimately be used as a mere means to benefit others?

To deny that embryonic human beings deserve full respect, one must suppose that not every whole living human being is deserving of full respect. To do that, one must hold that those human beings who deserve full respect deserve it not in virtue of *the kind of entity they are*, but, rather, in virtue of some acquired characteristic that some human beings (or human beings at some stages) have and others do not, and which some human beings have in greater degree than others.[3]

We submit that this position is untenable. It is clear that one need not be *actually* conscious, reasoning, deliberating, making choices, etc., in order to be a human being who deserves full moral respect, for it is clear that people who are asleep or in reversible comas deserve such respect. So, if one denied that human beings are intrinsically valuable in virtue of what they are, but required an additional attribute, the additional attribute would have to be a capacity of some sort, and, obviously a capacity for certain mental functions. Of course, human beings in the embryonic, fetal, and early infant stages lack immediately exercisable capacities for mental functions characteristically carried out (though intermittently) by most (not all—consider cases of severely retarded children and adults and comatose persons) human beings at later stages of maturity. Still, they possess in radical (= root) form these very capacities. Precisely by virtue of *the kind of entity they are*, they are from the beginning actively developing themselves to the stages at which these capacities will (if all goes well) be immediately exercisable. In this critical respect, they are quite unlike cats and dogs—even adult members of those species. As humans, they are members of a natural kind—the human species—whose embryonic, fetal, and infant members, if not prevented by some extrinsic cause, develop in due course and by intrinsic self-direction the immediately exercisable capacity for characteristically human mental functions. Each new human being comes into existence possessing the internal resources to develop immediately exercisable characteristically human mental capacities—and only the adverse effects on them *of other causes* will prevent their full development. In this sense, even human beings in the embryonic, fetal, and infant stages have the *basic natural* capacity for characteristically human mental functions.

We can, therefore, distinguish two senses of the "capacity" (or what is sometimes referred to as the "potentiality") for mental functions: an immediately exercisable one, and a basic natural capacity, which develops over time. On what basis can one require for the recognition of full moral respect the first sort of capacity, which is an attribute that human beings acquire (if at all) only in the course of development (and may lose before dying), and that some will have in greater degree than others, and not the second, which is possessed by human beings as such? We can think of no good reason or nonarbitrary justification.

By contrast, there are good reasons to hold that the second type of capacity is the ground for full moral respect.

First, someone entertaining the view that one deserves full moral respect only if one has immediately exercisable capacities for mental functions should realize that the developing human being does not reach a level of maturity at which he or she performs a type of mental act that other animals do not perform—even animals such as dogs and cats—until at least several months after birth. A six-week-old baby lacks the *immediately exercisable* capacity to perform characteristically human mental functions.

So, if full moral respect were due only to those who possess immediately exercisable capacities for characteristically human mental functions, it would follow that six-week-old infants do not deserve full moral respect. If one further takes the position that beings (including human beings) deserving less than full moral respect may legitimately be dismembered for the sake of research to benefit those who are thought to deserve full moral respect, then one is logically committed to the view that, subject to parental approval, the body parts of human infants, as well as those of human embryos and fetuses, should be fair game for scientific experimentation.

Second, the difference between these two types of capacity is merely a difference between stages along a continuum. The proximate, or immediately exercisable, capacity for mental functions is only the development of an underlying potentiality that the human being possesses simply by virtue of the kind of entity it is. The capacities for reasoning, deliberating, and making choices are gradually developed, or brought toward maturation, through gestation, childhood, adolescence, and so on. But the difference between a being that deserves full moral respect and a being that does not (and can therefore legitimately be dismembered as a means of benefiting others) cannot consist only in the fact that, while both have some feature, one has more of it than the other. A mere *quantitative* difference (having more or less of the same feature, such as the development of a basic natural capacity) cannot by itself be a justificatory basis for treating different entities in *radically* different ways. Between the ovum and the approaching thousands of sperm, on the one hand, and the embryonic human being, on the other hand, there *is* a clear difference in kind. But between the embryonic human being and that same human being at any later stage of its maturation, there is only a difference in degree.

Third, being a whole human organism (whether immature or not) is an either/or matter—a thing either is or is not a whole human being. But the acquired qualities that could be proposed as criteria for personhood come in varying and continuous degrees: there is an infinite number of degrees of the relevant developed abilities or dispositions, such as for self-consciousness, intelligence, or rationality.

So, if human beings were worthy of full moral respect only because of such qualities, and not in virtue of the kind of being they are, then, since such qualities come in varying degrees, no account could be given of why basic rights are not possessed by human beings in varying degrees. The proposition that all human beings are created equal would be relegated to the status of a superstition. For example, if developed self-consciousness bestowed rights, then, since some people are more self-conscious than others (that is, have developed that capacity to a greater extent than others), some people would be greater in dignity than others, and the rights of the superiors would trump those of the inferiors where the interests of the superiors could be advanced at the cost of the inferiors. This conclusion would follow no matter which of the acquired qualities generally proposed as qualifying some human beings (or human beings at some stages) for full respect were selected. Clearly, developed self-consciousness, or desires, or so on, are arbitrarily selected degrees of development of capacities that all human beings possess in (at least) radical form from the coming into being of the organism until his or her death. So, it cannot be the case that *some* human beings and *not others* are intrinsically valuable, by virtue of a certain degree of development. Rather, human beings are intrinsically valuable *in virtue of what (i.e., the kind of being) they are*; and *all* human beings—not just some, and certainly not just those who have advanced sufficiently along the developmental path as to be able to exercise their capacities for characteristically human mental functions—are intrinsically valuable.

Since human beings are intrinsically valuable and deserving of full moral respect in virtue of what they are, it follows that they are intrinsically valuable from the point at which they come into being. Even in the embryonic stage of our lives, each of us was a human being and, as such, worthy of concern and protection. Embryonic human beings, whether brought into existence by union of gametes, SCNT, or other cloning technologies, should be accorded the status of inviolability recognized for human beings in other developmental stages.

Three arguments have been repeatedly advanced in the course of our Council's deliberations in an effort to cast doubt on the proposition that human embryos deserve to be accorded such status.

(1) Some have claimed that the phenomenon of monozygotic twinning shows that the embryo in the first several days of its gestation is not a human individual. The suggestion is that as long as twinning can occur, what exists is not yet a unitary human being but only a mass of cells—each cell is totipotent and allegedly independent of the others.

It is true that *if a cell or group of cells is detached from the whole* at an early stage of embryonic development, then what is detached can sometimes become a distinct organism and has the potential to develop to maturity as distinct from the embryo from which it was detached (this is the meaning of "totipotent"). But this does nothing to show that before detachment the cells within the human embryo constituted only an incidental mass. Consider the parallel case of division of a flatworm. Parts of a flatworm have the potential to become a whole flatworm when isolated from the present whole of which they are part. Yet no one would suggest that prior to the division of a flatworm to produce two whole flatworms the original flatworm was not a unitary individual. Likewise, at the early stages of human embryonic development, before specialization by the cells has progressed very far, the cells or groups of cells can become whole organisms if they are divided and have an appropriate environment after the division. But that fact does not in the least indicate that prior to such an extrinsic division the embryo is other than a unitary, self-integrating, actively developing human organism. It certainly does not show that the embryo is a mere clump of cells.

In the first two weeks, the cells of the developing embryonic human being already manifest a degree of specialization or differentiation. From the very beginning, even at the two-cell stage, the cells differ in the cytoplasm received from the original ovum. Also they are differentiated by their position within the embryo. In mammals, even in the unfertilized ovum, there is already an "animal" pole (from which the nervous system and eyes develop)[4] and a "vegetal" pole (from which the future "lower" organs and the gut develop). After the initial cleavage, the cell coming from the "animal" pole is probably the primordium of the nervous system and the other senses, and the cell coming from the "vegetal" pole is probably the primordium of the digestive system. Moreover, the relative position of a cell from the very beginning (that is, from the first cleavage) has an impact on its functioning. Monozygotic twinning usually occurs at the blastocyst stage, in which there clearly is a differentiation of the inner cell mass and the trophoblast that surrounds it (from which the placenta develops).[5]

The orientation and timing of the cleavages are species specific, and are therefore genetically determined, that is, determined from within. Even at the two-cell stage, the embryo begins synthesizing a glycoprotein called "E-cadherin" or "uvomorulin," which will be instrumental in the compaction process at the eight-cell stage, the process in which the blastomeres (individual cells of the embryo at the blastocyst stage) join tightly together, flattening and developing an inside-outside polarity.[6] And there is still more evidence, but the point is that from the zygote stage forward, the embryo, as well as maintaining homeostasis, is internally integrating various processes to direct them in an overall growth pattern toward maturity.[7]

But the clearest evidence that the embryo in the first two weeks is not a mere mass of cells but is a unitary organism is this: *if the individual cells within the embryo before twinning were each independent of the others, there would be no reason why each would not regularly develop on its own. Instead, these allegedly independent, noncommunicating cells regularly function together to develop into a single, more mature member of the human species.* This fact shows that interaction is taking place between the cells from the very beginning (even within the zona pellucida, before implantation), restraining them from individually developing as whole organisms and directing each of them to function as a relevant part of a single, whole organism continuous with the zygote. Thus, prior to an extrinsic division of the cells of the embryo, these cells together do constitute a single organism. So, the fact of twinning does not show that the embryo is a mere incidental mass of cells. Rather, the evidence clearly indicates that the human embryo, from the zygote stage forward, is a unitary, human organism.

(2) The second argument we wish to address suggests that since people frequently do not grieve, or do not grieve intensely, for the loss of an embryo early in pregnancy, as they do for the loss of a fetus late in pregnancy or of a newborn, we are warranted in concluding that the early embryo is not a human being worthy of full moral respect.

The absence of grieving is sometimes a result of ignorance about the facts of embryogenesis and intrauterine human development. If people are told (as they still are in some places) that there simply is no human being until "quickening"—a view which is preposterous in light of the embryological facts—then they are likely not to grieve (or not to grieve intensely) at an early miscarriage. But people who are better informed, and women in particular, very often *do* grieve even when a miscarriage occurs early in pregnancy.

Granted, some people informed about many of the embryological facts are nevertheless indifferent to early miscarriages; but this is often due to a reductionist view according to which embryonic human beings are misdescribed as mere "clumps of cells," "masses of tissue," etc. The *emotional* attitude one has toward early miscarriages is typically and for the most part *an effect* of what one thinks—rightly or wrongly—about the humanity of the embryo. Hence it is circular reasoning to use the indifference of people who deny (wrongly, in our view) that human beings in the embryonic stage deserve full moral respect as an argument for not according such respect.

Moreover, the fact that people typically grieve less in the case of a miscarriage than they do in the case of an infant's death is partly explained by the simple facts that they do not actually see the baby, hold her in their arms, talk to her, and so on. The process of emotional bonding is typically completed after the child is born—sometimes, and in some cultures, months after the child is born. However, a child's right not to be killed plainly does not depend on whether her parents or anyone else has formed an emotional bond with her. Every year—perhaps every day—people die for whom others do not grieve. This does not mean that they lacked the status of human beings who were worthy of full moral respect.

It is simply a mistake to conclude from the fact that people do not grieve, or grieve less, at early miscarriage that the embryo has in herself less dignity or worth than older human beings.

(3) We now turn to the third argument. Some people, apparently, are moved to believe that embryonic human beings are not worthy of full moral respect because a high percentage of embryos formed in natural pregnancies fail to implant or spontaneously abort. Again, we submit that the inference is fallacious.

It is worth noting first, as the standard embryology texts point out, that many of these unsuccessful pregnancies are really due to incomplete fertilizations. So, in many cases, what is lost is not actually a human embryo. To be a complete human organism (a human being), the entity must have the epigenetic primordia for a functioning brain and nervous system, though a chromosomal defect might only prevent development to maximum functioning (in which case it would be a human being, though handicapped). If fertilization is not complete, then what is developing is not an organism with the active capacity to develop itself to the mature (even if handicapped) state of a human.

Second, the argument here rests upon a variant of the naturalistic fallacy. It supposes that what happens in "nature," i.e., with predictable frequency without the intervention of human agency, must be morally acceptable when deliberately caused. Since embryonic death in early miscarriages happens with predictable frequency without the intervention of human agency, the argument goes, we are warranted in concluding that the deliberate destruction of human beings in the embryonic stage is morally acceptable.

The unsoundness of such reasoning can easily be brought into focus by considering the fact that historically, and in some places even today, the *infant* mortality rate has been very high. If the reasoning under review here were sound, it would show that human infants in such circumstances could not be full human beings possessing a basic right not to be killed for the benefit of others. But that of course is surely wrong. The argument is a *non sequitur*.

In conclusion, we submit that law and public policy should proceed on the basis of full moral

respect for human beings irrespective of age, size, stage of development, or condition of dependency. Justice requires no less. In the context of the debate over cloning, it requires, in our opinion, a ban on the production of embryos, whether by SCNT or other processes, for research that harms them or results in their destruction. Embryonic human beings, no less than human beings at other developmental stages, should be treated as subjects of moral respect and human rights, not as objects that may be damaged or destroyed for the benefit of others. We also hold that cloning-to-produce-children ought to be legally prohibited. In our view, such cloning, even if it could be done without the risk of defects or deformities, treats the child-to-be as a product of manufacture, and is therefore inconsistent with a due respect for the dignity of human beings. Still, it is our considered judgment that cloning-for-biomedical-research, inasmuch as it involves the deliberate destruction of embryos, is morally worse than cloning-to-produce-children. Thus we urge that any ban on cloning-to-produce-children be a prohibition on the practice of cloning itself, and not on the implantation of embryos. Public policy should protect embryonic human beings and certainly not mandate or encourage their destruction. An effective ban on cloning-to-produce-children would be a ban on all cloning.[8]

Although an optimal policy would permanently ban all cloning, we join in this Council's call for a permanent ban on cloning-to-produce-children combined with a four-year ban (or "moratorium") on cloning-for-biomedical-research for the reasons set forth by Gilbert Meilaender in his personal statement. It is our particular hope that a four-year period will provide time for a careful and thorough public debate about the moral status of the human embryo. This is a debate we welcome.

Notes

1. A human embryo (like a human being in the fetal, infant, child, or adolescent stage) is not properly classified as a "prehuman" organism with the mere potential to become a human being. No human embryologist or textbook in human embryology known to us presents, accepts, or remotely contemplates such a view. The testimony of all leading embryology textbooks is

that a human embryo is—already and not merely potentially—a human being. His or her potential, assuming a sufficient measure of good health and a suitable environment, is to develop by an internally directed process of growth through the further stages of maturity on the continuum that is his or her life.

2. The timing of the first two cleavages seems to be controlled by the maternal RNA within the embryo rather than by its new DNA (see Ronan O'Rahilly and Fabiola Mueller, *Human Embryology and Teratology* [New York: John Wiley & Sons, 1992], 23). Still, these cleavages do not occur if the embryo's nucleus is not present, and so the nuclear genes also control these early changes.

3. A possible alternative, though one finding little support in current discussions, would be to argue that what I am, or you are, is not a human organism at all, but rather a nonbodily consciousness or spirit merely inhabiting or somehow "associated with" a body. The problem with this argument is that it is clear that we are bodily entities-organisms, albeit of a particular type, namely, organisms of a rational nature. A living thing that performs bodily actions is an organism, a bodily entity. But it is immediately obvious in the case of the human individual that it is *the same subject* that perceives, walks, and talks (which are bodily actions), and that understands, deliberates, and makes choices—what everyone, including anyone who denies he is an organism, refers to as "I." It must be the same entity that perceives these words on a page, for example, and understands them. Thus, what each of us refers to as "I" is identically the physical organism that is the subject both of bodily actions, such as perceiving and walking, and of mental activities, such as understanding and choosing. Therefore, you and I are physical organisms, rather than consciousnesses that merely inhabit or are "associated with" physical organisms. And so, plainly, *we* came to be when the physical organism we are came to be; *we* once were embryos, then fetuses, then infants, and so on.

4. Werner A. Muller, *Developmental Biology* (New York: Springer Verlag, 1997), 12f; Scott Gilbert, *Developmental Biology,* 5th edition (Sunderland, Mass.: Sinnauer Associates, 1997); O'Rahilly and Mueller, *Human Embryology and Teratology,* 23–24.

5. O'Rahilly and Mueller, *Human Embryology and Teratology,* 30–31.

6. Ibid., 23–24; Keith Moore and T. V. N. Persaud, *Before We Are Born: Essentials of Embryology and Birth Defects* (Philadelphia: W. B. Saunders, 1998), 41; William J. Larson, *Human Embryology,* 3rd edition (New York: Churchill Livingstone, 2001), 18–21.

7. Gilbert, *Developmental Biology,* 12f; 167f. Also see O'Rahilly and Mueller, *Human Embryology and Teratology,* 23–24.

8. A ban on implantation of an existing embryo or class of embryos would be subject to constitutional as well as moral objections. Such a ban would certainly be challenged, and the challenge would likely come from a powerful coalition of "pro-life" and "pro-choice" forces. A prohibition of the production of embryos by cloning would have a far better likelihood of withstanding constitutional challenge than would a ban on implantation.

QUESTIONS

1. Reconstruct the argument that George and Gómez-Lobo use to establish that cloned human embryos are as deserving of full moral respect as other humans.

2. Is the argument persuasive?

65. The Moral Status of Cloning

MICHAEL TOOLEY

*M*ichael Tooley (1941–) is professor of philosophy at the University of Colorado, Boulder. His interests in philosophy are broad, and he has published on topics in ethics, metaphysics, and the philosophy of religion. His books include the well-known defense of abortion, *Abortion and Infanticide* (1983), as well as *Causation: A Realist Approach* (1987), *Time, Tense, and Causation* (1997), and *Knowledge of God*, with A. Plantinga (2008).

Tooley defends cloning. His overall conclusion "is that the cloning of human beings, both to produce mindless organ banks, and to produce human persons, is both morally acceptable in principle, and potentially very beneficial for society." The moral questions about the first possibility, the creation of mindless clones for organ banks, are similar to those about abortion, and Tooley rehearses those debates. Focusing on the case of cloning human persons, he examines first two major arguments against doing so, finding both wanting, and then considers a number of benefits of cloning.

Is the cloning of human beings morally acceptable, or not? If it is acceptable, are there any significant benefits that might result from it? In this essay, I shall begin by distinguishing between two radically different cases in which a human being might be cloned—one where the aim is to produce a mindless human organism that will serve as a living organ bank, and the other where the aim is to produce a person. I shall then go on to discuss the moral status of each.

My discussion of the first sort of case will be very brief, for the moral issues that arise in that case are precisely those that arise in connection with abortion. The second sort of case, on the other hand, raises very different issues, and it will be the main focus of my discussion. I shall argue that cloning of this second sort is in principle morally unobjectionable, and that, in addition, there are a number of ways in which such cloning would be beneficial.

1. Cloning: Persons, Human Beings, Organs, and Tissue

Cloning, in the broad sense, can be applied to very different things. One might, for example, clone a person's bone marrow, in order to use it in a transplant operation to treat a disease from which the person in question is suffering. Or one might, perhaps, clone some organ—though whether this is really possible in the case of structurally complex organs, such as the heart, is far from clear. In any case, such uses of cloning are both morally unproblematic, and obviously beneficial.

From Michael Tooley, "The Moral Status of the Cloning of Humans," in *Human Cloning, Biomedical Ethics Reviews*, edited by James M. Humber and Robert F. Almeder (Humana Press, 1998), pp. 65–101. Reprinted by permission of Humana Press.

Most people would also think, I believe, that the cloning of non-human animals is not in itself problematic. Whether this is true for all animals is, however, not entirely clear. If, as some philosophers have argued, some non-human animals are persons, with a capacity, say, for thought and self-consciousness, then the moral status of cloning in the case of such animals would, presumably, be very closely related to the status of cloning in the case of humans.

Let us focus, however, upon humans. Here it is crucial to distinguish two different cases of cloning, since they give rise to very different moral issues. First, there is the case where a human being is cloned to produce another human with the same genetic makeup as the original individual, and where the human being thus produced is to serve as an organ bank, so that if the original individual loses an arm in an accident, or winds up with cancer of the liver, appropriate spare parts will be available. If the second human being were a person, it would, of course, be wrong to take parts from him or her to repair the damage to the original individual. The idea, however, is that something will be done to the brain of the human that is produced so that the human organism in question *never* acquires the capacity for consciousness, let alone the capacities that make something a person—such as the capacity for thought and self-consciousness.

Secondly, there is the case of cloning where the goal is to produce a person, not a mindless organ bank. It is this latter type of cloning that is going to be the main focus of my discussion. Before turning to it, however, let me briefly touch upon the former sort.

What objections might be directed against cloning that is done with the goal of producing an organ bank for some person? One objection might be that if one were to use those organs, one would be using what belonged to someone else. Or, depending on what organs one was harvesting, one might even be bringing about the death of a human being. But here it is natural to reply that there is no person to whom the organs belong, or who is destroyed if the organism in question is killed. So no one's property is being taken from him or her, and no person is being killed.

How might one support this reply? The most familiar way of doing so is by appealing to cases where a normal adult suffers brain damage that ensures that there will never again be any mental states at all associated with the human organism in question. Perhaps there is complete destruction of the upper brain, or perhaps all of the individual's brain has been destroyed, and the organism in question is now being maintained on a life support system. In such cases, would it be seriously wrong to terminate life processes in the organism in question? The vast majority of people seem to think that it would not be. But if that view is right, then it would seem that one needs to distinguish between something like the death of a person—the death of an individual who enjoys a certain sort of mental life—and the death of a human organism.

It is possible to maintain, of course, that the intuitions in question rest upon an unsound view of human nature. Perhaps humans have immaterial, immortal souls that are the basis both of all their mental capacities, and of the states that make for personal identity. In that case, upper brain death, or even whole brain death, would not mean that there was no longer any person associated with the human body in question.

This is a possible view. But it is also a deeply implausible one, since there are facts about human beings, and other animals, that provide strong evidence for the hypothesis that the basis for all mental capacities lies in the brain. Thus, in the first place, there are extensive correlations between the behavioral capacities of different animals and the neural structures present in their brains. Secondly, the gradual maturation of the brain of a human being is accompanied by a corresponding increase in his or her intellectual capabilities. Thirdly, damage to the brain, due either to external trauma, or to stroke, results in impairment of one's cognitive capacities, and the nature of the impairment is correlated with the part of the brain that was damaged. These facts, and others, receive a very straightforward explanation given the hypothesis that mental capacities have as their basis appropriate neutral circuitry, whereas, on the other hand, they would be both unexplained, and deeply puzzling, if mental capacities had their basis not in the brain, but in some immaterial substance.

In addition, it is worth remarking, as a number of Catholic writers such as Karl Rahner and Joseph Donceel have pointed out,[1] that the hypothesis that an immaterial soul is added at the point of conception has, at least within Christianity, a very problematic implication, since most conceptions result, it seems, not in live births, but in miscarriages, and so the theological question arises as to the fate of those human beings who are never born. It seems unfair that they should wind up in hell. But equally, if they automatically went to heaven, that would seem unfair to humans who are born, and who, according to the New Testament, are more likely to wind up in hell than in heaven.[2] The traditional solution involves postulating a third after-life destiny—limbo—which, though originally rather unattractive, subsequently came to be conceived of as a place of perfect natural happiness. Even so, the idea that the majority of the human race never have a chance of eternal life in heaven seems ethically rather troubling.

How do things stand if one sets aside, as implausible, the idea that an immaterial, immortal soul enters the body at conception? The answer is that, first, the distinction between a human organism and a person then becomes a very important one. But, secondly, that distinction does not in itself suffice to show that there is nothing problematic about cloning that is aimed at producing a mindless organ bank, since this still leaves the possibility of arguing that what is seriously wrong here is not the killing of a mindless human being, but the earlier act of permanently preventing the organism in question from developing a functioning brain.

What reasons might be offered for holding that the latter act is morally wrong? One possibility would be to appeal to an idea just considered, and rejected as implausible—namely, the idea that every human organism involves an immaterial immortal soul. For if that were so, then there would be someone whose interests might well be harmed—depending upon exactly what happens to a soul in such a body—by the act of preventing the development of the brain of the organism in question. There is, however, a very different line of argument that one can offer, and one which does not involve the implausible assumption that humans involve immaterial souls, since one can claim instead that what is wrong about ensuring that a human organism can never develop a functioning brain is not that one is harming a person, but that one is thereby destroying a potentiality for personhood.

But is it morally wrong to destroy a potentiality for personhood? The following argument shows, I believe, that it is not. Compare the following two actions, the first of which involves two steps: (i) One modifies an unfertilized human egg cell, or else a spermatozoon, or both, in such a way that if the egg cell is fertilized by the spermatozoon, the result will be a member of our species which lacks an upper brain, and thus which will never enjoy any mental states whatsoever; (ii) One then brings about fertilization, and implants the resulting embryo. What about the second action? It involves taking a fertilized human egg cell, and changing it in such a way that it suffers from precisely the same defect as the fertilized egg cell that results from the first action. The argument now proceeds as follows. The person who holds that it is wrong to destroy a potentiality for personhood will certainly claim that the second action possesses a wrongmaking property—that of being an act of destroying a potentiality for personhood—which the first action does not possess. In response, it might be claimed that one is, in a sense, destroying a potentiality for personhood in the case of the first action as well as the second, and thus that, since the first action is not morally wrong, neither is the second. To this, however, one reply that one needs to distinguish between active potentialities and merely passive potentialities: one has a passive potentiality for personhood when one has a situation that, if acted upon in appropriate ways, will give rise to a person, whereas one has an active potentiality for personhood if one has a situation that will give rise to a person as long as it is not interfered with. The conclusion will then be that the first action involves the destruction of only a passive potentiality for personhood, whereas the second action involves the destruction of an active potentiality for personhood, and that it is only the latter that is wrong.

It may seem, then, that the defender of the view that it is wrong to destroy a potentiality for personhood has escaped the objection by reformulating the claim in terms of *active* potentiality. It turns out, however, that this response will not really do. In the first place, a fertilized human egg cell, *on its own*, does not involve an active potentiality for personhood: if left alone, it will simply die. If it is to develop into a person, it needs to be placed in an environment that will supply it with warmth, nutrients, etc.

But, secondly, even if one waived this point, the above response still could not provide a satisfactory response to the above argument. The reason is that one can bring in a third sort of action, which is as follows. Suppose that artificial wombs have been perfected, and that there is a device that contains an unfertilized human egg cell, and a human spermatozoon, and where the device is such that if it is not interfered with, it will bring about fertilization, and then transfer the fertilized human egg cell to an artificial womb, from which will emerge, in nine months' time, a healthy newborn human. Now one has a situation that involves not merely an almost active potentiality for personhood, as in the case of the fertilized human egg cell on its own, but, rather, a fully active potentiality for personhood. To turn off this device, then, and to allow the unfertilized egg cell to die, would involve the destruction of an active potentiality for personhood, and so that action would have to be wrong if the above, active potentiality principle were correct. But the action of turning off the device is not morally wrong, and so it follows that it is not wrong to destroy an active potentiality for personhood.

This argument could be countered if one had reasons for holding that human mental capacities, rather than being based upon structures present in the brain, were dependent upon the existence of an immaterial soul that God added to a fertilized human egg cell, since then one could hold that it was really only after the addition of such an immaterial entity that an active potentiality for personhood was present. However, as we have seen, there is very strong evidence against the view that mental capacities have their basis, not in

neural circuitry in the brain, but, instead, in some immaterial substance.

The terrain that we have just traversed, rather quickly, is very familiar, of course, from discussions of the moral status of abortion. Thus, discussions of abortion—or at least popular discussions—often begin with the claim that abortion is wrong because it involves the killing of an innocent member of our species. The objection is then that there are cases where an innocent member of our species is killed, but where no injustice is done—namely, cases where either the upper brain, or the brain as a whole, has already been destroyed. And so it is suggested that what is really wrong about killing, when it is wrong, is that *a person* is being destroyed. But if this is right, then one can argue that abortion is not wrong because the humans that are killed by abortion have not developed to the point where one has a person. This then typically leads—at least in the case of philosophically informed opponents of abortion—to the response that while it is wrong to kill innocent persons, it is also wrong to destroy an active potentiality for personhood. And then, finally, one can then reply, as above, that the potentiality principle in question cannot be correct, since it is exposed to counterexamples. For there are cases where the destruction of an active potentiality for personhood is not morally wrong.

To conclude. The creation of mindless human organisms would be wrong if it harmed a person who inhabited, at some point, the human body in question, or if the destruction of an active potentiality for personhood were wrong. But there are good reasons for thinking that neither of these things is the case. In the absence of some other line of argument, then, one is justified in concluding that there is no sound moral argument against the use of cloning to produce mindless human organisms to serve as organ banks.

2. Cloning in the Present Context

Let us now turn to the question of the moral status of cloning when the objective is that of producing a person. I shall be arguing that cloning with that goal in mind is in principle morally acceptable. This, however, is not to say that such cloning would be morally unproblematic at the present time. And, indeed, I believe that there are good reasons why cloning, aimed at producing persons, should not be done at present.

To see why, let us begin by considering what was involved in the successful attempt by Ian Wilmut and his coworkers to clone a sheep from the cell of an adult animal:

> The investigators started their experiments with 434 sheep oocytes. Of those, 157 failed to fuse with the transplanted donor cells and had to be discarded. The 277 successfully fused cells were grown in culture, but only twenty-nine embryos lived long enough to be transferred to surrogate mothers. During gestation the investigators detected twenty-one fetuses with ultrasound scanning, but gradually all were lost except Dolly.[3]

Given these statistics, it seems clear that the idea of producing persons via cloning would not be a rational undertaking at present. What is irrational need not, of course, be morally problematic. But in the present case, one is considering an action that affects other people, and so one needs to ask whether it would be acceptable to encourage more than 200 women to be surrogate mothers in a situation where it is likely that very few, if any, will have a successful pregnancy. And the situation is even worse if one is proposing cloning as a way of treating infertility: given the present state of technology, the result will, in all probability, be enormous frustration and emotional suffering.

In response, it might be said that you pay your money, and you take your chances: if an infertile couple desperately wants a child that will be a clone of someone, how can it be immoral to allow them to try? But this argument could also be used in other cases, such as that of providing those who are depressed, and who would like to commit suicide, with the means to do so. What I want to say, accordingly, is that if some course of action is very irrational—as, it seems to me, the attempt to have a child by cloning would be at present—then one may very well be acting immorally if one provides a person with the opportunity of performing that action.

But there are also other reasons for holding that the attempt to clone persons at the present time is morally objectionable—reasons that concern the individual who may result if the attempt is successful. In the first place, the fact that only one out of 277 pregnancies were successful in the case of the sheep suggests that something is seriously wrong with the procedure at present, and that in turns raises the question of whether there may not be a very significant chance, in the case of humans, that the outcome might be a seriously defective child, possibly born premature, but saved via intensive care. The attempt to clone a person given the present state of the art would seem to be wrong, therefore, because of the impaired quality of life that may be enjoyed by the resulting person.

Secondly, there is the unanswered question of how cloned individuals will fare when it comes to aging. For there is an important theory of aging that suggests that Dolly may very well have a significantly reduced life expectancy, as a result of having developed from the nucleus of a six-year-old sheep. Here is the basis of the worry:

> As early as the 1930s investigators took note of pieces of noncoding DNA—DNA that does not give rise to protein—at the ends of each chromosome, which they called telomeres (from the Greek words for "end" and "part"). When the differentiated cells of higher organisms undergo mitosis, the ordinary process of cell division, not all of the DNA in their nuclei is replicated. The enzyme that copies DNA misses a small piece at the ends of each chromosome, and so the chromosomes get slightly shorter each time a cell divides. As long as each telomere remains to buffer its chromosome against the shortening process, mitosis does not bite into any genes (remember that the telomeres are noncoding, much like the leaders at the ends of a reel of film). Eventually, however, the telomeres get so short that they can no longer protect the vital parts of the chromosome. At that point the cell usually stops dividing and dies.[4]

The question, accordingly, is whether Dolly started life with cells whose chromosomes have telomeres whose length is comparable to those in the cells of a six-year-old sheep. Perhaps not, since it may be that once a nucleus has been transplanted into an egg from which the nucleus has been removed, there is some mechanism that will produce an enzyme—called telomerase—that can create full-length telomeres. But the risk is surely a very serious one, and this provides strong grounds, I suggest, for holding that one should not at this point attempt to produce people by cloning.

The last two reasons also support a stronger conclusion—namely, that there are grounds for a temporary, legal prohibition on the cloning of humans where the goal is to produce persons. For the risk that is involved in such cloning is that one will bring into existence a person who will age prematurely, or who will suffer from other defects, and so what is at stake are potential violations of an individual's rights, and thus something that justifies the introduction of appropriate legislation.

The qualification here perhaps needs to be emphasized: this conclusion applies only to cloning that is directed at producing a person, since if one's goal were instead to produce a mindless human organism to serve as an organ bank, the above considerations would not apply.

3. Is It Intrinsically Wrong to Produce a Person by Cloning?

Let us now turn to the question of whether the use of cloning to produce a person is in principle morally acceptable or not. In this section, I shall focus upon the question of whether cloning, so used, is intrinsically wrong. Then, in a later section, I shall consider whether cloning to produce persons necessarily has consequences that render it morally wrong.

How might one attempt to argue that the production of persons via cloning is intrinsically wrong? Here it seems to me that Dan Brock is right when he suggests that there are basically two lines of argument that deserve examination.[5] First, there is an argument that appeals to what might initially be described as the right of a person to be a unique individual, but which, in the end, must be characterized instead as the right of a person to a genetically unique nature. Secondly, there is an argument that appeals to the idea that a person has a right to a future that is, in a certain sense, open.

3.1 Does a Person Have a Right to a Genetically Unique Nature?

Many people feel that being a unique individual is important, and the basic thrust of this first attempt to show that cloning is intrinsically wrong involves the idea that the uniqueness of individuals would be in some way impaired by cloning. In response, I think that one might very well question whether uniqueness is important. If, for example, it turned out that there was, perhaps on some distant planet, an individual that was qualitatively identical to oneself, down to the last detail, both physical and psychological, would that really make one's own life less valuable, less worth living?

In thinking about this issue, it may be important to distinguish two different cases: first, the case where the two lives are qualitatively identical due to the operation of deterministic causal laws; secondly, the case where it just happens that both individuals are always in similar situations in which they freely decide upon the same actions, have the same thoughts and feelings, and so on. The second of these scenarios, I suggest, is not troubling. The first, on the other hand, may be. But if it is, is it because there is a person who is qualitatively indistinguishable from oneself, or, rather, because one's life is totally determined?

I am inclined to question, accordingly, the perhaps rather widely held view that uniqueness is an important part of the value of one's life. Fortunately, however, one need not settle that issue in the present context, since cloning does not, of course, produce a person who is qualitatively indistinguishable from the individual who has been cloned, for, as is shown by the case of identical twins, two individuals with the same genetic makeup, even if raised within the same family at the same time, will differ in many respects, due to the different events that make up their life histories.

How great are those differences? The result of one study was as follows:

On average, our questionnaires show that the personality traits of identical twins have a 50 percent correlation. The traits of fraternal twins, by contrast, have a correlation of 25 percent, non-twin siblings a correlation of 11 percent and strangers a correlation of close to zero.[6]

Consequently, the personality traits of an individual and his or her clone should, on average, exhibit no more than a 50 percent correlation, and, presumably, the correlation will generally be even less, given that an individual and his or her clone will typically be raised at different times, and in generations that may differ quite substantially in terms of basic beliefs and fundamental values.

The present argument, accordingly, if it is to have any chance, must shift from an appeal to the claim that a person has a right to absolute uniqueness to an appeal to the very different claim that a person has a right to a genetically unique nature. How, then, does the argument fare when reformulated in that way?

An initial point worth noticing is that any appeal to a claimed right to a genetically unique nature poses a difficulty for a theist: if there is such a right, why has God created a world where identical twins can arise? But there are, of course, many features of the world that are rather surprising if our world is one that was created by an omnipotent, omniscient, and morally perfect person, and so the theist who appeals to a right to a genetically unique nature may simply reply that the presence of twins is just another facet of the general problem of evil.

How can one approach the question of whether persons have a right to a genetically unique nature? Some writers, I think, are content to rest with a burden of proof approach. Here the idea is that although it may be the case that many people do think that being a unique individual in the sense of not being qualitatively identical with anyone else is an important part of what is valuable about being a person, the idea that persons have a right to a genetically unique identity is one that, by contrast, has been introduced only recently, and so those who advance the latter claim really need to offer some reason for thinking that it is true.

There are, however, other ways of approaching this question that involve offering positive arguments against the claim. One possibility, for example, is to appeal to the intuitions that one has upon reflection. Thus, one can consider the case of identical twins, and ask oneself whether, upon reflection, one thinks that it would be prima facie wrong to reproduce if one somehow knew that doing so would result in identical twins. I think it would be surprising if many people felt that this was so.

Another way of approaching the issue is by appealing to some plausible general theory of rights. Thus, for example, I am inclined to think that rights exist where there are serious, self-regarding interests that deserve to be protected. If some such view is correct, then one can approach the question of whether persons have a right to a genetically unique nature by asking whether one has some serious, self-regarding interest that would be impaired if one were a clone. Is the latter the case? The initial reason for thinking that it is not is that the existence of a clone does not seem to impinge upon a person in the way in which being prevented from performing some action that harms no one, or being tortured, or being killed, do: a distant clone might have no impact at all upon one's life.

In response, it might be argued that while the mere existence of a clone need have no impact upon, and so need not impair in any way, one's self-regarding interests, the situation might be very different if one knew of the existence of the clone, since that knowledge might, for example, be damaging to one's sense of individuality. But why should this be so, given that individuals can differ greatly, while sharing the same genetic makeup? It seems to me that if the knowledge that a clone of oneself exists were disturbing to one, this would probably be because of the presence of some relevant, false belief—such as a belief in genetic determinism. But if this is so, then the question arises as to whether rights exist when the interests that they protect are ones that will be harmed only if the potential subjects of the harm have certain false, and presumably irrational, beliefs. My own feeling is that the responsibility for such harm is properly assigned to an individual who has acquired the irrational beliefs whose presence is necessary if there is to be any harm. Consequently, it seems to me that the actions of others should not be constrained in order to prevent such harm from occurring, and thus that there is no right that is violated in such a case.

A third way of thinking about this question of whether there is a right to a genetically unique nature is to consider a scenario in which individuals with the same genetic makeup are very common indeed, and to consider whether such a world would, for example, be inferior to the present world. Imagine, for example, that it is the year 4004 BC, and God is contemplating creating human beings. He has already considered the idea of letting humans come into being via evolution, but has rejected that plan on the grounds that a lottery approach to such a vital matter as bringing humans into existence hardly seems appropriate. He also considers creating an original human pair that are genetically distinct, and who will then give rise to humans who will be genetically quite diverse. Upon reflection, however, that idea also seems flawed, since the random shuffling of genes will result in individuals who may be physically impaired, or disposed to unpleasant diseases, such as cancer, that will cause them enormous suffering, and lead to premature deaths. In the end, accordingly, the Creator decides upon a genetic constitution with the following two properties. First, it will not lead to serious physical handicaps and diseases, and it will allow an individual, who makes wise choices, to grow in mind and spirit. Secondly, all of the genes involve identical alleles. God then creates one person with that genetic makeup—call her Eve—and a second individual—Adam—whose only genetic difference is that he has an X chromosome, and a funky Y chromosome, where Eve has two X chromosomes. The upshot will then be that when Adam and Eve reproduce, they will breed true, because of the fact that they have, aside from the one difference, the same genetic makeup, with identical alleles for every inherited character, and so all of their descendants will be genetically identical to either Adam or Eve.

How would such a world compare with the actual world? If one were choosing from behind the Rawlsian veil of ignorance, would it be rational to prefer the actual world, or the alternative world? This is not, perhaps, an easy question. But it is clear that there would be some significant pluses associated with the alternative world. First, unlike the actual world, one would be assured of a genetic makeup that would be free of dispositions to various unwelcome and life-shortening diseases, or to other debilitating conditions such as depression, schizophrenia, etc. Secondly, inherited traits would be distributed in a perfectly equitable fashion, and no one would start out, as is the case in the actual world, severely disadvantaged, and facing an enormous uphill battle. Thirdly, aside from the differences between men and women, everyone would be physically the same, and so people would differ only with regard to the quality of their souls, and thus one would have a world where judgments of people might well have a less superficial basis than is often the case in the actual world. So there would seem to be some serious reasons for preferring the alternative world over the actual world.

The third advantage just mentioned also points, of course, to an obvious practical drawback of the alternative world: knowing who was who would be a rather more difficult matter than it is in the actual world. But this problem can be dealt with by variants on the above scenario. One variant, for example, would involve having identity of genetic makeup except with regard to the genes that determine the appearance of face and hair. Then one would be able to identify individuals in just the way that one typically does in the actual world. This change would mean, of course, that one was no longer considering an alternative world where there was widespread identity with respect to genetic makeup. Nevertheless, if this other alternative world would be preferable to the actual world, I think that it still provides an argument against the view that individuals have a right to a unique genetic makeup. For, first of all, the preferability of this other alternative world strongly suggests that genetic difference, rather than being desirable in itself, is valuable only to the extent that it is needed to facilitate the easy identification of people. Secondly, is it plausible to hold that while genetic uniqueness is crucial, a very high degree of genetic similarity is not? But in the alternative world we are considering here, the degree of genetic similarity between any two individuals would be extraordinarily high. Thirdly, the alternative world is one where the genes that determine the initial structure of one's *brain* are not merely very similar, but absolutely the same in all individuals. But, then, can one plausibly hold that genetic uniqueness is morally crucial, while conceding that a world in which individuals do not differ with regard to the genes that determine the initial nature of their brains might be better than the actual world?

These three consequences, I suggest, provide good reasons for holding that one cannot plausibly maintain that individuals have a right to a genetically unique nature without also holding that the actual world is to be preferred to the alternative world just described. The identification problem can, however, also be addressed without shifting to a world where people differ genetically, since one could instead suppose that a different mechanism for identifying other people is built into human beings. God could, for example, incorporate special circuitry into the human brain, which both broadcasts one's name, and appropriate identifying information about one, and which picks up the information that is broadcast by other humans within one's perceptual field. The information is then checked against a memory bank containing information about everyone one knows, and if it turns out that one is in perceptual contact with some person with whom one is acquainted, and if one would like to know who the person in question is, one will automatically find oneself in possession of the relevant information to one, informing one.

The result will be a world where all individuals will have exactly the same genetic makeup, aside from an X and a Y chromosome, and all of the attractive features of the original alternative world will be present, without there being any problem of determining who was who. One can then ask how this world compares with the actual world, and whether, in particular, the fact that all people in this alternative world would have essentially the same genetic makeup really seems to be, upon reflection, a reason for preferring the actual world.

3.2 The Open Future Argument

Dan Brock mentions a second argument for the view that cloning which aims at producing persons is intrinsically wrong.[7] The argument—which is based upon ideas put forward by Joel Feinberg, who speaks of a right to an open future,[8] and by Hans Jonas, who refers to a right to ignorance of a certain

sort[9]—is essentially as follows. One's genetic makeup may very well determine to some extent the possibilities that lie open to one, and so it may constrain the course of one's future life. If there is no one with the same genetic makeup, or if there is such a person, but one is unaware of the fact, or, finally, if there is such a person, but the person is either one's contemporary, or someone who is younger, then one will not be able to observe the course of the life of someone with the same genetic makeup as oneself. But what if one does know of a genetically identical person whose life precedes one's own? Then one could have knowledge that one might well view as showing that certain possibilities were not really open to one, and so one would have less of a sense of being able to choose the course of one's life.

To see why this argument is unsound, one needs to ask about the reasoning that might be involved if someone, observing the earlier life of someone with the same genetic makeup, concludes that his or her own life is subject to certain constraints. One possibility is that one may have observed someone striving very hard, over a long period of time, to achieve some goal and failing to get anywhere near it. Perhaps the earlier, genetically identical individual wanted to be the first person to run the marathon in under two hours, and after several years of intense and well-designed training, attention to diet, etc., never got below two and a half hours. One would then surely be justified in viewing that particular goal as not really open to one. But would that knowledge be a bad thing, as Jonas seems to be suggesting? I would think that, on the contrary, such knowledge would be valuable, since it would make it easier for one to choose goals that one could successfully pursue.

A very different possibility is that one might observe the course of the life of the genetically identical individual, and conclude that no life significantly different from that life could really be open to one. Then one would certainly feel that one's life was constrained to a very unwelcome extent. But in drawing the conclusion that one's life could not be significantly different from that of the other individual, one would be drawing a conclusion for which there is no evidence, but one that there is excellent evidence against: the lives of identical twins demonstrate that very different lives indeed are possible, given the same genetic makeup.

In short, the idea that information about the life of a person genetically identical to oneself would provide grounds for concluding that only a narrow range of alternatives was open to one would only be justified if genetic determinism, or a close approximation thereto, was correct. But nothing like genetic determinism is true. This second argument for the view that cloning with the goal of producing persons is intrinsically wrong is, accordingly, unsound.

4. Considerations in Support of the Cloning of Persons

Whether it is desirable to produce persons by cloning depends, as we noticed earlier, upon the outcome of an issue that is not yet decided: the aging question. Here, however, I shall simply assume that it will become possible to clone an adult individual in such a way that one winds up with a cell whose chromosomes have full-length telomeres, so that the individual who results will have a normal life expectancy. Given that assumption, I want to argue that there are a number of important benefits that may result from the cloning of humans that is done with the goal of producing persons.

In setting out what I take to be benefits of cloning, I shall not address possible objections. These will be discussed, instead, in section 5.

4.1 Scientific Knowledge: Psychology and the Heredity versus Environment Issue

A crucial theoretical task for psychology is the construction of a satisfactory theory that will explain the acquisition of traits of character, and central to the development of such a theory is information about the extent to which various traits are (a) inherited, (b) dependent upon aspects of the environment that are controllable, or (c) dependent upon factors, either in the brain, or in the environment, that have a chancy quality. But such knowledge is not just theoretically crucial to psychology. Knowledge of the contributions that are, and are not, made to the individual's development by his or her genetic makeup, by the environment in which

he or she is raised, and by chance events, will enable one to develop approaches to childrearing that will increase the likelihood that one can raise people with desirable traits, people who will have a better chance of realizing their potentials, and of leading happy and satisfying lives. So this knowledge is not merely of great theoretical interest: it is also potentially very beneficial to society.

In the attempt to construct an adequate theory of human development, one thing that has been very important, and that has generated considerable information on the nature/nurture issue, is the study of identical twins. But adequate theories still seem rather remote. Cloning would provide a powerful way of speeding up scientific progress in this area, since society could produce a number of individuals with the same genetic makeup, and then choose adoptive parents who would provide those individuals with good, but significantly different environments, in which to mature.

4.2 Cloning to Benefit Society

One very familiar suggestion is that one might benefit mankind by cloning individuals who have made very significant contributions to society. In the form in which it is usually put, where it is assumed that if, for example, one had been able to clone Albert Einstein, the result would be an individual who would also make some very significant contribution to science, the suggestion is surely unsound. In the first place, whether an individual will turn out to do highly creative work, rather than being determined simply by his or her genetic makeup, surely depends upon traits whose acquisition is a matter of the environment in which the individual is raised. But could it not be argued in response that one could control the environment as well—raising a clone of Einstein, for example, in an environment that was as close as possible to the sort of environment in which Einstein was raised? That, of course, might prove difficult. But even if it could be done, it is not clear that it would be sufficient, for there is a second point that can be made here—namely, that great creative achievements may depend upon things that are to some extent accidental, and whose occurrence is not ensured by the combination of a certain genetic makeup and a certain general sort of environment. Many great mathematicians, for example, have developed an intense interest in numbers at an early age. Is there good reason to think that, had one been able to clone Carl Friedrich Gauss, and reared that person in an environment similar to Gauss's, that person would have developed a similar interest in numbers, and gone on to achieve great things in mathematics? Or is it likely that a clone of Einstein, raised in an environment similar to that in which Einstein was raised, would have wondered, as Einstein did, what the world would look like if one could travel as fast as light, and then gone on to reflect upon the issues that fascinated Einstein, and that led ultimately to the development of revolutionary theories in physics?

I think that there are, then, some serious problems with the present suggestion in the form in which it is usually put. On the other hand, I'm not convinced that a slightly more modest version cannot be sustained. Consider, for example, the Polgar sisters. There we have a case where the father of three girls succeeded in creating an environment in which all three of his daughters became very strong chess players, and one of them—Judit Polgar—is now the strongest female chess player who has ever lived. Is it not reasonable to think that if one were to make a number of clones of Judit Polgar, and then raise them in an environment very similar to that in which the Polgar sisters were raised, the result would be a number of very strong chess players?

More generally, I think it is clear that there is a strong hereditary basis for intelligence,[10] and I also believe that there is good reason for thinking that other traits that may play a crucial role in creativity—such as extreme persistence, determination, and confidence in one's own abilities—are such as are likely to be produced by the right combination of heredity and environment. So while the chance that the clone of an outstandingly creative individual will also achieve very great things is perhaps, at least in many areas, not especially high, I think that there is reason for thinking that, given an appropriate environment, the result will be an individual who is likely to accomplish things that may benefit society in significant ways.

4.3 Happier and Healthier Individuals

A third benefit of cloning is that it should make it possible to increase the likelihood that the person that one is bringing into existence will enjoy a healthy and happy life. For to the extent that one's genetic constitution has a bearing upon how long one is likely to live, upon what diseases, both physical and mental, one is likely to suffer from, and upon whether one will have traits of character or temperament that make for happiness, or for unhappiness, by cloning a person who has enjoyed a very long life, who has remained mentally alert, and not fallen prey to Alzheimer's disease, who has not suffered from cancer, arthritis, heart attacks, stroke, high blood pressure, etc., and who has exhibited no tendencies to depression, or schizophrenia, etc., one is increasing the chances that the individual that one is producing will also enjoy a healthy and happy life.

4.4 More Satisfying Childrearing: Individuals with Desired Traits

Many couples would prefer to raise children who possess certain traits. In some cases they may want children who have a certain physical appearance. In other cases they might like to have children who have the physical abilities that would enable them to have a better chance of performing at a high level in certain physical activities. Or they might prefer to have children who would have the intellectual capabilities that would enable them to enjoy mathematics, or science. Or they might prefer to have children who possess traits that would enable them to engage in, and enjoy, various aesthetic pursuits. Some of the traits that people might like their children to have presumably have a very strong hereditary basis, while others are such as a child, given both the relevant genes, and the right environment, would be very likely to acquire. To the extent that the traits in question fall in either of these categories, the production of children via cloning would enable more couples to raise children with traits that they judge to be desirable.

4.5 More Satisfying Childrearing: Using Self-Knowledge

There is a second way in which cloning could make childrearing more satisfying, and it emerges if one looks back on one's own childhood. Most people, when they do this, remember things that they think were good, and other things that they think would have been better if they had been different. In some cases, of course, one's views may be unsound, and it may be that some of the things that one's parents did, and which one did not like, actually had good effects on one's development. On the whole, however, it seems plausible that most people have reasonably sound views on which features of the way in which they were raised had good effects overall, and which did not.

The idea, then, is that if a couple raises a child who is a clone of one of the parents, the knowledge that the relevant parent has of the way in which he or she was raised can be used to bring up the child in a way that fits better with the individual psychology of the child. In addition, given the greater psychological similarity that will exist between the child and one of his parents in such a case, the relevant parent will better be able, at any point, to appreciate how things look from the child's point of view. So it would seem that there is a good chance both that such a couple will find childrearing a more rewarding experience, and that the child will have a happier childhood through being better understood.

4.6 Infertility

Since the successful cloning that resulted in Dolly, at least one person has expressed the intention of pushing ahead with the idea of using cloning to help infertile couples. For reasons that emerged in section 2, the idea that cloning should be so used in the near future seems morally very problematic. In principle, however, the general idea would seem to have considerable merit. One advantage, for example, as Dan Brock and others have pointed out, is

that "cloning would allow women who have no ova or men who have no sperm to produce an offspring that is biologically related to them."[11] Another advantage, also noted by Brock, is that "embryos might be cloned, either by nuclear transfer or embryo splitting, in order to increase the number of embryos for implantation and improve the chances of successful conception."[12]

4.7 Children for Homosexual Couples

Many people, especially in the United States, believe that homosexuality is deeply wrong, and that homosexuals should not be allowed either to marry or to raise children. These opinions, however, would be rejected, I think, by most philosophers, who would hold, on the contrary, that homosexuality is not morally wrong, that homosexuals should be allowed both to marry, and to raise children. Assume, for the sake of the present discussion, that the latter views are correct. Then, as Philip Kitcher and others have noted, cloning would seem to be a promising method of providing a homosexual couple with children that they could raise, since, in the case of a gay couple, each child could be a clone of one person, while in the case of a lesbian couple, every child could, in a sense, be biologically connected with both people:

> A lesbian couple wishes to have a child. Because they would like the child to be biologically connected to each of them, they request that a cell nucleus from one of them be inserted into an egg from the other, and that the embryo be implanted in the uterus of the woman who donated the egg.[13]

4.8 Cloning to Save Lives

A final possibility is suggested by the well-known case of the Ayala parents in California, who decided to have another child in the hope—which turned out to be successful—that the resulting child would be able to donate bone marrow for a transplant operation that would save the life of their teenage daughter, who was suffering from leukemia. If cloning had been possible at the time, a course of action would have been available to them that, unlike having another child in the normal way, would not have been chancy: if they could have cloned the child who was ill, a tissue match would have been certain.

5. Objections to the Cloning of Humans

5.1 The Cloning of Mindless Organ Banks

Certain objections to the cloning of humans to produce mindless human organisms that will serve as a source of organs for others are perfectly intelligible. If someone objects to this idea on the grounds that one is destroying a person, the concern that is being expressed here is both completely clear, and serious. The same is true if the objection is instead that such cloning is seriously wrong since, in preventing a human organism from developing a functioning brain, one is depriving an immaterial soul associated with the organism in question of the possibility of experiencing life in this world. And finally, the same is also true if someone holds that such cloning would be wrong because it involves the destruction of an active potentiality for personhood.

The problem with these objections, accordingly, is not that they are in any way incoherent. Nor is it the case that the points raised are unimportant. The problem is simply that all of these objections are, in the end, unsound, for reasons that emerged earlier. Thus, the problem with the first objection is that there are excellent reasons for holding that human embryos do not possess those capacities—such as the capacity for thought and self-consciousness—that something must have, at some point, if it is to be a person. The problem with the second objection is that there are strong reasons for holding that the ontological basis for the capacities involved in consciousness, self-consciousness, thought, and other mental processes resides in the human brain, and not in any immaterial soul. Finally, the problem with the third objection lies in the assumption that the destruction of an active potentiality for personhood is morally wrong, for that claim is, on the one hand, unsupported by any satisfactory argument, and, on the other, exposed to decisive objections—one of which was set out earlier.

Often, however, it seems that people who would agree that the above objections are unsound, and who, moreover, do not view abortion as morally problematic, still express uneasiness about the idea of producing mindless human organ banks. Such uneasiness is rarely articulated, however, and it usually takes the form simply of describing the idea of mindless organ banks as a "ghoulish" scenario. This sort of dismissal of the use of cloning to produce organ banks is very puzzling. For what we are considering here is a way in which lives can be saved, and so if one rejects this use of cloning, one is urging a course of action that will result in the deaths of innocent people. To do this on the grounds that mindless organ banks strike one as ghoulish seems morally irresponsible in the extreme: if this use of cloning is to be rejected, serious moral argument is called for.

5.2 The Cloning of Humans to Produce Persons

5.2.1 Violation of Rights Objections

Some people oppose cloning that is done with the goal of producing a person on the grounds that such cloning involves a violation of some right of the person who is produced. The most important versions of this first sort of objection are those considered earlier, namely, that there is a violation either of a person's right to be a unique individual—or, more accurately, to be a genetically unique individual—or, alternatively, of a person's right to enjoy an open future that is not constrained by knowledge of the course of the life of some individual with the same genetic makeup. But for the reasons set out earlier, neither of these objections is sound.

5.2.2 Brave New World Style Objections

Next, there is a type of objection which is not frequently encountered in scholarly discussions, but which is rather common in the popular press, and which involves scenarios where human beings are cloned in large numbers to serve as slaves, or as enthusiastic soldiers in a dictator's army. Such scenarios, however, do not seem very plausible. Is it really at all likely that, were cloning to become available, society would decide that its rejection of slavery had really been a mistake? Or that a dictator who was unable to conscript a satisfactory army from the existing citizens would be able to induce people to undertake a massive cloning program, in order that, eighteen years or so down the line, he would finally have the army he had always wanted?

5.2.3 Psychological Distress

This objection is closely related to the earlier, violation of rights objections, as the idea is that, even if cloning does not violate a person's right to be a unique individual, or to have a unique genetic makeup, or to have an open and unconstrained future, nevertheless, people who are clones may *feel* that their uniqueness is compromised, or that their future is constrained, and this may cause substantial psychological harm and suffering.

There are two reasons for rejecting this objection as unsound. The first arises once one asks what one is to say about the beliefs in question—that is, the belief that one's uniqueness is compromised by the existence of a clone, and the belief that one's future is constrained if one has knowledge of the existence of a clone. Both beliefs are, as we have seen, false. But, in addition, it also seems clear that such beliefs would be, in general, irrational, since it is hard to see what grounds one could have for accepting either belief, other than something like genetic determinism—against which, as we saw earlier, there is conclusive evidence.

Once it is noted that the feelings that may give rise to psychological distress are irrational, one can appeal to the point that I made earlier, when we considered the question of whether knowledge of the existence of a clone might, for example, be damaging to one's sense of individuality, and whether, if this were so, such damage would be grounds for holding that there was a corresponding right that would be violated by cloning. What I argued at that point was that harm to an individual that arises because the individual has an irrational belief has a different moral status from harm that is not dependent upon the presence of an irrational belief, and that, in particular, the possibility of the former sort

of harm should not be taken as morally constraining others. The responsibility for such harm should, instead, be assigned to the individual who has the irrational belief, and the only obligation that falls upon others is to point out to the person in question why the belief is an irrational one.

The second reason why the present objection cannot be sustained is also connected with the fact that the feelings in question are irrational, since the irrationality of the feelings means that they would not be likely to persist for very long, once cloning had become a fairly familiar occurrence. For suppose that John feels that he is no longer a unique individual, or that his future is constrained, given that he is a clone of some other individual. Mary may also be a clone of some individual, and she may point out to John that she is very different from the person with whom she is genetically identical, and that she has not been constrained by the way the other person lived her life. Will John then persist in his irrational belief? This does not really seem very likely. If so, any distress that is produced will not be such as is likely to persist for any significant period of time.

5.2.4 Failing to Treat Individuals as Ends in Themselves

A fourth objection is directed, not against the cloning of persons in general, but against certain cases—such as those where parents clone a child who is suffering from some life-threatening condition in order to produce another child who will be able to save the first child's life—and the thrust of this objection is that such cases involve a failure to view individuals as ends in themselves. Thus Philip Kitcher, referring to such cases, says that "a lingering concern remains," and he goes on to ask whether such scenarios "can be reconciled with Kant's injunction to 'treat humanity, whether in your own person or in the person of another, always at the same time as an end and never simply as a means.'"[14]

What is one to say about this objection? In thinking about it, it may be important to be explicit about what sacrifices the child who is being produced is going to have to make to save his or her sibling. When I set out this sort of case in section 4.8, I assumed that what was involved was a bone marrow transplant. Kitcher, in his formulation, assumes that it will be a kidney transplant. I think that one might well be inclined to take different views of these two cases, given that in the kidney donation case, but not the bone marrow case, the donor is making a sacrifice that may have unhappy consequences for that person in the future.

To avoid this complicating factor, let us concentrate, then, on the bone marrow case. In such a case, would there be a violation of Kant's injunction? There could be—if the parents were to abandon, or not really to care for the one child, once he or she had provided bone marrow to save the life of the other child. But this, surely, would be a very unlikely occurrence. After all, the history of the human race is the history of largely unplanned children, often born into situations where the parents are anything but well off, and yet typically those children are deeply loved by their parents.

In short, though this sort of case is by hypothesis one where the parents decide to have a child with a goal in mind that has nothing to do with the well being of that child, this is no reason for supposing that they are therefore likely to treat that child merely as a means, and not also as an end in itself. Indeed, surely there is good reason to think, on the contrary, that such a child will be raised in no less loving a way than is normally the case.

5.2.5 Interfering with Personal Autonomy

The final objection that I shall consider is also one that has been advanced by Philip Kitcher, and he puts it as follows: "If the cloning of human beings is undertaken in the hope of generating a particular kind of person, then cloning is morally repugnant. The repugnance arises not because cloning involves biological tinkering but because it interferes with human autonomy."[15]

This objection would not apply to all of the cases that I mentioned in section 4 as ones where the cloning of a person would be justified. It does, however, apply to many of them. Is the objection sound? I cannot see that it is. First, notice that in some cases where one's goal is to produce "a particular kind of person," what one is aiming at is simply a person

who will have certain potentialities. Parents might, for example, want to have children who are capable of enjoying intellectual pursuits. The possession of the relevant capacities does not force the children to spend their lives engaged in such pursuits, and so it is hard to see how cloning that is directed at that goal would interfere with human autonomy.

Secondly, consider cases where the goal is not to produce a person who will be *capable* of doing a wider range of things, but an individual who will be *disposed* in certain directions. Perhaps it is this sort of case that Kitcher has in mind when he speaks of interfering with human autonomy. But is it really morally problematic to attempt to create persons who will be disposed in certain directions, and not in others? To answer this question, one needs to consider concrete cases. Consider, in particular, the sorts of cases that I mentioned earlier. Is it morally wrong, for example, to attempt to produce, via cloning, individuals who will, because of their genetic makeup, be disposed not to suffer from conditions that may cause considerable pain, such as arthritis, or from life-threatening diseases, such as cancer, high blood pressure, strokes, and heart attacks? Or to attempt to produce individuals who will have a cheerful temperament, or who will not be disposed to depression, to anxiety, to schizophrenia, or to Alzheimer's disease?

It seems unlikely that Kitcher, or others, would want to say that attempting to produce individuals who will be constitutionally disposed in the ways just indicated is a case of interfering with human autonomy. But then what are the traits that are such that attempting to create a person with those traits is a case of interfering with human autonomy? Perhaps Kitcher, when he speaks about creating a particular kind of person, is thinking not just of any properties that persons have, but, more narrowly, of such things as personality traits, or traits of character, or the having of certain interests? But again one can ask whether there is anything morally problematic about attempting to create persons with such properties. Some personality traits are desirable, and parents typically encourage their children to develop those traits. Some character traits are virtues, and others are vices, and both parents and society attempt to encourage the acquisition of the former, and to discourage the acquisition of the latter. Finally, many interests—in music, art, mathematics, science, games, physical activities—can add greatly to the quality of one's life, and once again, parents typically expose their children to relevant activities, and help their children to achieve levels of proficiency that will enable them to enjoy those pursuits.

The upshot is that if cloning that aimed at producing people who would be more likely to possess various personality traits, or traits of character, or who would be more likely to have certain interests was wrong because it was a case of interfering with personal autonomy, then the childrearing practices of almost all parents would stand condemned on precisely the same grounds. But such a claim, surely, is deeply counterintuitive.

In addition, however, one need not rest content with an appeal to intuitions here. The same conclusion follows on many high order moral theories. Suppose, for example, that one is once again behind the Rawlsian veil of ignorance, and that one is deciding among societies that differ with regard to their approaches to the rearing of children. Would it be rational to choose a society where parents did not attempt to encourage their children to develop personality traits that would contribute to the latter's happiness? Or a society where parents did not attempt to instill in their children a disposition to act in ways that are morally right? Or one where parents made no attempt to develop various interests in their children? It is, I suggest, hard to see how such a choice could be a rational one, given that one would be opting, it would seem, for a society where one would be likely to have a life that, on average, would be less worth living.

I conclude, therefore, that contrary to what Philip Kitcher has claimed, it is not true that most cloning scenarios are morally repugnant, and that, in particular, there is, in general, nothing morally problematic about aiming at creating a child with specific attributes.

Summing Up

In this essay, I have distinguished between two very different cases involving the cloning of a human being—one which aims at the production of mindless human organisms that are to serve as organ banks for the people who are cloned, and the other of which aims at the creation of persons. As regards the former, the objections that can be advanced are just the objections that can be directed against abortion, and, for reasons that I briefly outlined above, those objections can be shown to be unsound.

Very different objections arise in the case of cloning whose aim is the production of persons. With regard to this second sort of cloning, I argued that it is important to distinguish between the question of whether such cloning is in principle morally acceptable, and whether it is acceptable at the present time. As regards the latter question, I argued that the present use of cloning to produce persons would be morally problematic. By contrast, as regards the question of whether such cloning is in principle morally acceptable, I argued, first, that such cloning is not intrinsically wrong; secondly, that there are a number of reasons why the cloning of persons would be desirable; and thirdly, that the objections that have been directed against such cloning cannot be sustained.

My overall conclusion, in short, is that the cloning of human beings, both to produce mindless organ banks, and to produce persons, is both morally acceptable in principle, and potentially very beneficial for society.

Notes

1. Joseph F. Donceel, S.J., "Immediate Animation and Delayed Hominization," *Theological Studies,* 31 (1970), 76–105, at p. 100–1. Donceel refers to Karl Rahner, *Schriften zur Theologie* 8 (Einsiedeln, 1967), 287. The figure of 50% may seem high, since the percentage of miscarriages is often given as about 15%. The latter figure refers, however, only to miscarriages that women are aware of, whereas the argument advanced by Donceel and Rahner is concerned with the total number of spontaneous abortions as a whole. As regards the latter, Moore (1993) says: "The frequency of early abortions is difficult to establish because they often occur before women are aware that they are pregnant." Estimates of the total number of spontaneous abortions are referred to, however, in Sadler (1995), who says: "Estimates suggest that as many as 50% of all pregnancies end

in spontaneous abortion and that half of these losses are due to chromosomal abnormalities."

2. See, for example, *Matthew* 7:13–14 and 22:13–14.

3. Marie A. Di Berardino and Rovert G. McKinnell, "Backward Compatible," *The Sciences* 37/5, September/October 1997, 32–7, at p. 37.

4. Ronald Hart, Angelo Turturro, and Julian Leakey, "Born Again," *The Sciences* 37/5, September/October 1997, 47–51, at p. 48.

5. Dan W. Brock, "Cloning Human Beings: An Assessment of the Ethical Issues Pro and Con," forthcoming in *Clones and Clones*, edited by Martha C. Nussbaum and Cass R. Sunstein (New York: W. W. Norton and Company, 1998). See the section entitled "Would the Use of Human Cloning Violate Important Human Rights?"

6. Thomas J. Bouchard Jr., "Whenever the Twain Shall Meet," *The Sciences* 37/5, September/October 1997, 52–57, at p. 54.

7. Dan Brock, op cit., in the section entitled "Would the Use of Human Cloning Violate Important Human Rights?"

8. Joel Feinberg, "The Child's Right to an Open Future," in *Whose Child? Children's Rights, Parental Authority, and State Power*, edited by W. Aiken and H. LaFollette (Totowa, NJ: Rowan and Littlefield, 1980).

9. Hans Jonas, *Philosophical Essay: From Ancient Creed to Technological Man* (Englewood Cliffs, NJ: Prentice-Hall, 1974).

10. See, for example, the discussion of this issue by Thomas J. Bouchard Jr. in "Whenever the Twain Shall Meet," pp. 55–6.

11. Dan Brock, op cit., in the subsection entitled "Human cloning would be a new means to relieve the infertility some persons now experience."

12. Ibid.

13. Philip Kitcher, "Whose Self Is It, Anyway?" *The Sciences* 37/5, September/October 1997, 58–62, at p. 61. It should be noted that although Kitcher mentions this idea as initially attractive, in the end he concludes that it is problematic, for a reason that will be considered in section 5.2.

14. Ibid., p.61.

15. Ibid., p.61.

References

Bilger, Burkhard, "Cell Block," *The Sciences* 37/5, September/October 1997, 17–19.

Bouchard, Thomas J., Jr., "Whenever the Twain Shall Meet," *The Sciences* 37/5, September/October 1997, 52–57.

Brock, Dan W., "Cloning Human Beings: An Assessment of the Ethical Issues Pro and Con," forthcoming in *Clones and Clones*, edited by Martha C. Nussbaum and Cass R. Sunstein (New York: W. W. Norton and Company, 1998).

Callahan, Daniel, "Perspective on Cloning: A Threat to Individual Uniqueness," *Los Angeles Times,* November 12, 1993: B7.

Di Berardino, Marie A., and Robert G. McKinnell, "Backward Compatible," *The Sciences* 37/5, September/October 1997, 32–7.

Donceel, Joseph F., S.J., "Immediate Animation and Delayed Hominization," *Theological Studies,* 31 (1970), 76–105.

Feinberg, Joel, "The Child's Right to an Open Future," in *Whose Child? Children's Rights, Parental Authority, and State Power*, edited by W. Aiken and H. LaFollette (Totowa, NJ: Rowan and Littlefield, 1980).

Fletcher, Joseph, *The Ethics of Genetic Control* (Garden City, NY: Anchor Books, 1974).

Gurdon, J. B., "The Birth of Cloning," *The Sciences* 37/5, September/October 1997, 26–31.

Hart, Ronald, Angelo Turturro, and Julian Leakey, "Born Again?" *The Sciences* 37/5, September/October 1997, 47–51.

Jonas, Hans, *Philosophical Essay: From Ancient Creed to Technological Man* (Englewood Cliffs, NJ: Prentice-Hall, 1974).

Kitcher, Philip, "Whose Self Is It, Anyway?" *The Sciences* 37/5, September/October 1997, 58–62.

Macklin, Ruth, "Splitting Embryos on the Slippery Slope: Ethics and Public Policy," *Kennedy Institute of Ethics Journal* 4 (1994), 209–26.

Meade, Harry M., "Dairy Gene," *The Sciences* 37/5, September/October 1997, 20–5.

Moore, Keith L., *Before We Are Born—Basic Embryology and Birth Defects*, 2nd edition, (Philadelphia: W. B. Saunders Company, 1983), ch. 2.

Moore, Keith L., *The Developing Human; Clinically Oriented Embryology*, 5th edition, (Philadelphia: W. B. Saunders Company, 1993), ch. 3, pp. 48–52.

Robertson, John A., *Children of Choice: Freedom and the New Reproductive Technologies* (Princeton: Princeton University Press, 1994).

Robertson, John A., "The Question of Human Cloning," *Hastings Center Report* 24 (1994), 6–14.

Sadler, T. W., *Langman's Medical Embryology*, 7th edition (Baltimore: Williams & Wilkins, 1995), ch. 2, pp. 34–36.

Wilmut, Ian, "Sheep Cloned by Nuclear Transfer from a Cultured Cell Line," *Nature* 380 (1996), 64–6.

QUESTIONS

1. Consider Tooley's case for creating mindless clones for organ banks. Is it persuasive?
2. Consider his more complicated case for cloning human persons. Is it persuasive?

XIV

Future Generations

Future generations, that is, people who will exist in the near or distant future, do not yet exist. Yet we often say that we have obligations to them. There are a number of theoretically important and interesting questions surrounding future generations.

Suppose we leave our planet in such a mess that a couple of hundred of years from now the humans that inhabit it will be quite miserable and their standard of living will be that of most people a thousand years ago. That seems wrong. Indeed it seems we would have wronged *them*, the people who inherit our earth. But had we acted more thoughtfully and not despoiled the earth, *these* people would not inherit our planet; some others would. Why? Because were we to have acted differently, the course of events would have been quite different. Some people who would have had children would not have even met. Indeed, some people who would have met and had children would have had different children, perhaps conceived on different days. After some time no one who would have inherited our earth had we despoiled it would exist were we to have acted more responsibly. This is because very small changes will affect who is conceived and born. Many policy decisions will change who exists in the future. It is hard to see how we could have duties *to* members of future generations, even if we have duties *regarding* or *concerning* them. (See the introductory remarks to section VIII for the distinction between duties *to* and *regarding* someone.)

And there are other puzzles as well.

66. The Paradox of Future Individuals

GREGORY S. KAVKA

Gregory S. Kavka (1947–1994) was professor of philosophy at the University of California, Irvine. His interests in moral and political philosophy ranged widely. He wrote about the seventeenth-century philosopher Thomas Hobbes, puzzles of rationality, decision theory, nuclear deterrence and war, and a number of topics in practical ethics. He published two books, *Hobbesian Moral and Political Theory* (1986) and *Moral Paradoxes of Nuclear Deterrence* (1988). A volume of essays written in his honor was published after his death (*Rational Commitment and Social Justice: Essays for Gregory Kavka*, ed. Jules L. Coleman and Christopher W. Morris [Cambridge University Press, 1998]).

In this fascinating article Kavka raises some questions concerning our moral relations to future generations given the contingencies of our existence. This remarkable contingency leads to some very odd conclusions, which Kavka finds paradoxical. The facts of the remarkable contingency of our existence are clear. Suppose that your parents never met, or suppose that the telephone rang shortly before you were conceived. Suppose almost anything different with the conditions of your creation or the environment in which your parents lived or were raised. Then the particular sperm and egg cells that created you would not have joined; then *you* would not have been conceived. Someone else might have existed, but that person would no more be you than a sibling—even your twin brother—is you. Why does this fact lead to a puzzle about obligations to future generations? Because any policy or program that would affect the conditions for conception in the world—and virtually anything does— would over time lead to a completely different set of people coming into existence than otherwise would. Many of our ordinary principles will yield counterintuitive conclusions as a consequence.

I have heard a rumor, from a reliable source, that I was conceived in New Brunswick, New Jersey. Had my father been on duty at Camp Kilmer that fateful weekend, or had there been an earthquake in central New Jersey at the wrong moment, or had any of innumerable other possible events occurred, the particular sperm and egg cells from which I developed would never have joined, and I would never have existed. This observation about the precariousness of my origin reflects a basic fact about identity and existence that seriously complicates attempts to understand our moral relationship to future generations. Which *particular* future people will exist is highly dependent upon the conditions under which we and our descendants procreate, with the slightest difference in the conditions of conception being sufficient, in a particular case, to insure the creation of a different future person.

From Gregory S. Kavka, "The Paradox of Future Individuals," *Philosophy and Public Affairs*, Vol. 11, No. 2 (Spring, 1982), pp. 93–112. Reprinted by permission of Blackwell Publishing.

This fact forms the basis of a surprising argument, discovered independently by Robert M. Adams, Derek Parfit, and Thomas Schwartz,[1] to the effect that we have no moral obligation to future generations—beyond, at most, the next few—to promote their well-being. The argument goes as follows. Let us assume that sameness of genetic structure is, for practical purposes, a necessary condition of personal identity.[2] Then any event that affects the conditions under which a particular conception takes place (that is, any event that influences which particular sperm and egg cells come together under favorable conditions) will influence *who* exists. As a result, any proposed policy that would directly or indirectly affect conditions for conception (that is, who mates with whom, and when) on a worldwide scale over a significant period of time would result in an entirely different set of human individuals coming into existence than otherwise would.[3] Now suppose, as seems reasonable, that the various broad-ranging policies designed to promote better living conditions for future generations (for example, population control[4] or resource conservation) would, if practiced, affect conditions for conception worldwide. Further, let us allow that if we do not practice these policies, future people will not be so badly off that it would have been better for them never to have existed.

Granted these assumptions, are we obligated to practice controlled growth policies in order to bring about better living conditions for future people? No, for we harm no one if we follow an alternative policy, call it laissez faire. Consider the individuals in the overcrowded world that would result from laissez faire. They are not worse off than if we had acted to bring about the less crowded state of the world, for in that case they would not have existed. And, by hypothesis, their existence is not worse than never having existed. But these people are all the people there *are,* if we practice laissez faire. Thus, in doing so, we make no one worse off (than he otherwise would be) and hence do nothing wrong. We are therefore under no moral obligation to future people to pursue controlled growth policies in order to promote their well-being.[5]

This argument poses a paradox. It moves by a correct route from plausible premises about biology, personal identity, and moral obligation to a strongly counterintuitive conclusion.[6] I dub this the Paradox of Future Individuals and shall explore it to see what can be learned from it. First, the view about moral obligation that the paradox presupposes is laid out. Then this view is discussed in light of our intuitions about certain hypothetical situations involving the creation of persons.

I. Two Obligation Principles

The following principle, which states a necessary condition for having a moral obligation, is a key premise in the Paradox of Future Individuals. It provides the transition to the paradoxical conclusion from the observation that if we practiced the laissez-faire policy, no individual would be worse off.

> *Obligation Principle*: One can have an obligation to choose act or policy A rather than alternative B only if it is the case that if one chose B, some particular person would exist and be worse off than if one had chosen A.

To clarify the meaning of this principle, it should be pointed out that both "existence" and "being worse off" are to be construed in a timeless sense. Thus, the relevant class of particular persons consists of all persons who would *at some time* exist if act B were performed. And their being worse off, in the relevant sense, consists in their lives as a whole being worse (for them) than what (if anything) their lives as a whole would have been had act A been performed.[7] Interpreting the principle in this timeless fashion does not threaten the derivation of our paradox. For if we practice laissez faire, those possible people that would have existed had we done otherwise never exist at *any* time and would not fall within the scope of the principle.

The Obligation Principle will seem extremely plausible to those who believe that morality is solely concerned with the protection and promotion of the well-being of human individuals. Thus, many utilitarians, and others in the broader class of theorists called welfarists by Amartya Sen,[8] might rally around it. And even some apparently nonwelfarist[9] writers, such as Thomas Schwartz and Jonathan Bennett, have endorsed the principle, or flirted with variants of it. One reason for accepting the principle is that it is the conclusion of this simple and tempting argument: One is obligated to do A (rather than alternative B) only if it would be wrong not to do it. But it is wrong to do A (rather than B) only if someone would thereby be harmed. But a person is harmed by the doing of A (rather than B) only if he is thereby rendered worse off than he would have been had B been done instead. Hence, one is obligated to perform act A rather than B only when the condition laid down in the Obligation Principle is satisfied.

This argument, however, contains an error. It may sometimes be possible to act wrongly by wronging someone without harming him. One may do this by acting in a way that promotes his interests, on balance, but violates his rights. Two examples from medical ethics, which involve, respectively, the right to autonomy and the right to be told the truth, are: killing a terminally ill patient who (correctly) admits he would be better off dying now, but who refuses to give his permission to be killed; and not revealing, to a patient who wants to know his true condition, the fact that he is terminally ill because of one's (correct) assessment that informing him would deprive him of happiness during his few remaining weeks of life.

Now it may be doubted whether this weakness in the underpinnings of the Obligation Principle has any bearing on the Paradox of Future Individuals. For it is not immediately obvious that, or how, we might wrong future people, other than by making them worse off than they otherwise might have been. Surely we cannot now do to them the objectionable things done to the patients in the above examples—deceive them, or override their express wishes about matters of vital concern to them. Later, in Section III, I shall argue that we can act wrongly toward them in other respects. To pave the way for those arguments, we may begin by examining some hypothetical cases involving acts that determine who shall exist.

Imagine a society choosing between heavy investment in either solar energy systems or nuclear fission power plants in order to meet its projected energy needs over the next few centuries. Monetary investment costs per unit of output will be slightly lower if the nuclear option is pursued. However, there is no storage or disposal system for nuclear wastes that is expected to contain them safely for more than a few generations. Hence, if the nuclear plan is pursued, there would very likely be radioactive leakage that would cause the deaths of thousands of people in future generations. Intuitively, it is clear that it would be wrong to build the nuclear plants rather than the solar energy systems, as doing the former would lead to the premature demise of thousands. But, because the choice of the nuclear plan would affect conditions for conception nationwide (relative to the selection of the solar plan), these thousands of individuals would never have existed had the solar energy option been pursued instead. Hence, if we assume that living a life shortened by exposure to radiation is not worse than never having existed at all, it would be permissible—according to the Obligation Principle—to select the nuclear option.[10]

A parallel example on a smaller scale envisions a pill that, when taken just before sexual relations, has two effects. It heightens the pilltaker's sexual pleasure a tiny bit and insures that any child conceived would be mildly handicapped. As pausing to take the pill would change who is conceived, and as existence with a mild handicap is not bad on the whole, no one would be rendered worse off if a prospective parent not using contraceptive devices were to take the pill before sex. But, surely, taking it would be wrong.[11]

Why does the Obligation Principle yield incorrect verdicts when applied to these hypothetical cases and the choice between controlled and uncontrolled growth? One suggestion is that the principle allows one to leave out of account entirely the *good* results that would come about only if you do *not* perform the acts in question, for example, the happiness of the healthy child you could have, and the full lives future people would live if the nuclear plants were not built. It might be thought that these should be treated as opportunity costs of the respective acts of taking the pill and building the plants, for they are benefits enjoyed only if these acts are foregone. Admittedly, these are potential benefits to *merely possible* people—that is, people who will exist only if the acts in question are not performed. But it appears such benefits must be figured into the moral equation if we are to come out with the correct answer in such cases.

Reasoning in this way, we might replace our original Obligation Principle with one that proposes a disjunctive necessary condition for being obligated to perform an action.

> *Extended Obligation Principle*: One can have an obligation to choose act or policy A rather than alternative B *only if* it is the case that either (i) if one chose B, some particular person would exist and be worse off than if one had chosen A, or (ii) if one chose A, some particular person would exist and be better off than if one had chosen B.[12]

The second clause in this principle allows for the possibility that we may be obligated to control growth in order to provide benefits for the future people who would exist if we controlled growth. Thus, the principle blocks the above argument to the conclusion of the Paradox of Future Individuals.

However, even aside from doubts about whether opportunity costs for possible people should be allowed to determine our obligations, there is a serious difficulty with the Extended Obligation Principle. It states only a necessary condition of having an obligation and is far too weak to establish our desired conclusions. It allows, for example, that one may be obligated to refrain from the pleasure pill in order to benefit the healthy child. But it equally allows that one may be obligated to take the pill in order to benefit the handicapped child by bestowing the "gift of life" on it. To conclude that it is obligatory to refrain, one must supplement the Extended Obligation Principle with further principles. The most obvious choice as a supplementary principle would be a maximizing principle that requires weighing the potential benefits to different (actual and) possible people and choosing the act that produces the greater net benefit.[13] However, this maximizing principle yields counterintuitive results when applied to certain cases of procreation. We do not, for example, feel normal prospective parents to be under an obligation to procreate even if this would maximize social utility. And if they do choose to have a child, they are not obligated to take genetic-enhancement pills if this would insure the production of a (different but) "better" child—one that would be happier or contribute more to others' happiness. Such people might justifiably prefer to reproduce naturally, without such interference. Yet the maximizing principle would seem to imply the opposite. To be plausible then, it must be restricted so that it normally entails neither a duty to reproduce nor one to produce the happiest child one could.

It turns out, however, that if we so restrict our maximizing principle, the Extended Obligation Principle will not yield a solution to the Paradox of Future Individuals. For, as we shall see in the next section, there are cases of procreation that these two principles are not able to handle.

II. The Case of the Slave Child

In a society in which slavery is legal, a couple that is planning to have no children is offered $50,000 by a slaveholder to produce a child to be a slave to him. They want the money to buy a yacht. Should they sign the agreement, accept the money, and produce the child?[14] On the assumption that life as a slave is better than never existing, their doing so would not harm the child. For if they turned down the slaveholder, they would either produce no children or—if they later changed their minds about becoming parents—produce *other* children.[15] Thus, all involved—themselves, the slaveholder, and the slave child they would produce—would benefit from the arrangement. Therefore, by the Extended Obligation Principle, the couple would not have an obligation to remain childless, rather than to produce a slave child. Nor would a duly restricted version of our maximizing principle imply that they are obligated to produce a nonslave child in preference to both alternatives.[16] Hence, according to the principles we have so far considered, the deal with the slaveholder would be permissible. And if, years later, the slave child were to visit the couple on their yacht to complain that they had acted wrongly, they could correctly deny this on the grounds that they could not have bestowed a better lot on *him* (or *her*).

But acting in this manner is outrageous. Surely it would be wrong for the couple to produce a slave child and to attempt to justify their action in this way. The fact that the Extended Obligation Principle, supplemented by an appropriately restricted maximizing principle, does not imply that it would be wrong suggests that we must look for additional principles if we are to understand the morality of procreation. However, before considering what such principles might be like, we must examine two objections to the above judgment on the case of the slave child. Both involve the claim that there is nothing inherently wrong with the (complex) *action* of contracting to produce, and then producing, the slave child, and that it is some other aspect of the case that our intuitions condemn.

According to the first objection, it is the couple's surrender of the child, once it exists, to the slaveholder that is wrong and condemnable, for this violates their parental duty to do as well by their children as they can. To deal with this objection, it suffices to describe a version of the case in which it is clear that the couple has acted wrongly even though they do their very best for the child once it exists. Imagine then that the couple signs the contract, knowing they will be unable to break or evade it, and produces the child. Upon seeing the live child, they attempt to keep it from the slaveholder's hands by hiding it, challenging the contract in court, and so forth. But, as they foresaw, these efforts are futile. They have done their best for their child once it exists. But, given that they knew that their best would not be good enough, this does not contravene our judgment that they acted wrongly in signing away and producing the child.

The second objection to be considered is that it is the couple's motives, selfishness and greed, that our intuitions condemn, and not their actions, which are permissible since they harm no one.[17] It appears, however, that selfish motives are not the only morally questionable elements of the slave child case. This can be seen by altering the case so that the couple's selfish motive—to obtain a yacht—is replaced by a benevolent one—to obtain $50,000 to donate to a worthy charity. Even with this change in motive, the intuitive reaction that the couple has acted wrongly remains strong. They have no right to produce a slave child (when they could produce a free child or none at all), even to aid the deserving poor.

What of benevolence directed toward the slave child itself? This is, after all, the sort of motive suggested by the observation that the slave child is not harmed, but rather is benefited, by the couple's actions. Suppose this were the couple's sole motive. Would their actions then be permissible, or at least excusable? Fortunately, we need not resolve this puzzling question on which people's intuitions may well differ. For our purposes, it suffices to note two things. First, given what we know about human psychology, it seems highly improbable that our couple's motives would be solely, or even primarily, of this kind. Second, ascribing the motive of "benevolence toward *the* slave child" to the couple seems to presuppose that there is a unique (potential) individual, in the metaphysical sense, that is (or will be) the slave child, and that the couple knows enough of the features it will possess to have grounds for being more benevolently disposed toward it than toward other potential children they might produce. The first condition is unlikely to be satisfied, for even if the couple accepted the slaveholder's offer, they could produce a variety of different slave children depending upon when, and under what conditions, they had sexual relations.[18] And, given the current limitations of the science of genetics, our couple could know little, if anything, of interest about the features that would be possessed by (potential) children of theirs conceived under various circumstances. Hence, the second condition could hardly be satisfied.[19]

How does all this bear on the Paradox of Future Individuals? The case of the slave child shows that individualistic principles of obligation—the Obligation Principle and even the Extended Obligation Principle—cannot be relied on to yield correct results when applied to cases involving the creation of persons. The objection currently under consideration purposes that these principles may be validly applicable to such cases when the agents' motive is to promote the well-being of the particular individuals they create. In the context of the Paradox of Future Individuals, this amounts to saying that we may be blameless for not controlling growth if we do so solely to promote the interests of the particular potential individuals who would come into existence as a result of this policy.

Now it is clearly implausible to suppose that many of us, in contributing to uncontrolled growth, are thus motivated. Moreover, we have seen that the existence of such motivation is possible only if the potential individuals in question are both metaphysically determinate and epistemically determinate with respect to us. But they appear to be neither. They are not metaphysically determinate, for the various different world-futures that could result from the general policy of not controlling growth have different and largely nonoverlapping sets of individuals in them. Nor, turning to epistemic matters, do we know much about the individuals who would inhabit crowded and polluted world-futures that could ground a reasonable desire to provide them, rather than potential individuals in other world-futures, with the "gift of life." Hence, the various considerations about motives advanced in this section do not provide a defense of the conclusion of the Paradox of Future Individuals, and the principles of obligation it is based on, from the slave child counterexample. We must seek alternative principles of obligation to account for our moral convictions about examples like the case of the slave child.

III. Restricted Lives and the Misuse of Reproduction

Does act-utilitarianism explicate our beliefs about the ethics of creation? An act-utilitarian principle of maximization, interpreted (in the spirit of the Extended Obligation Principle) so as to take the utilities of potential people into account, seems to produce the right results when applied to the cases we have discussed. It appears to require our yacht-desiring couple to produce a nonslave child and to require us to control growth for the benefit of future generations even at substantial cost to our own generation. There are, however, serious problems with an act-utilitarian approach to the ethics of creating people. The vexed problem of whether average or total utility maximization is the appropriate goal remains unsolved.[20] And, as noted above, act-utilitarianism has strongly counterintuitive implications in some familiar situations involving the creation of persons. It implies an obligation to procreate in many cases in which we regard this as nonobligatory.

Further, it seems to imply that if a couple has decided to have a child, they are obligated to produce the "best" child they can. But, provided they could expect to produce a reasonably normal child in any case, it is wrong to suppose that they have an obligation to produce the "best." Thus, act-utilitarian maximizing principles must be restricted to avoid these unacceptable results. But, as we have seen, if so restricted, they seem unable to deal with the case of the slave child. A search for alternative solutions to that case (and others like it) appears to be in order.[21]

One such alternative appeals to the intrinsic moral desirability (or undesirability) of the existence of certain conditions of society or the world, with this not being reducible solely to the well-being of the individuals partaking in these conditions.[22] On this view, for example, one reason it is wrong for our couple to produce the slave child is that it contributes to an undesirable state or feature of their society—being a slaveholding society. Similarly, our obligation to control growth derives from the fact that an overcrowded society (world) is an inherently worse society (world) than a less crowded one.

One approach to evaluating the desirability of states of society seems especially promising, in the present context. Let us introduce the notion of a *restricted* life, a life that is significantly deficient in one or more of the major respects that generally make human lives valuable and worth living.[23] Thus, the life of a slave is restricted in this sense, owing to the slave's lack of liberty. Clearly, the lives of persons significantly handicapped, either mentally or physically, from birth and of those struck down in the prime of life by illnesses caused by radioactivity are also restricted. So, for a variety of reasons, are the lives of many living in a very overcrowded world.

Now, suppose that we adopt the principle that, other things being equal, conditions of society or the world are intrinsically undesirable from a moral point of view to the extent that they involve people living restricted lives. Then we can derive the intuitively correct verdicts in the cases involving the slave child, nuclear power, the pleasure pill, and controlled growth. For, in each case, the morally wrong act can be condemned on the grounds that it foreseeably leads to (states of the world containing) restricted lives.[24] At the same time, the stated principle is consistent with our belief that prospective parents have no obligation to produce the "best" child they can. And it gains plausibility from its affinity with a frequently invoked canon of social justice: that high priority should be given to providing all with the means to live at least a minimally decent life and engage in the major activities of human and community living.[25] Our principle says to prevent restricted lives, this canon says to prevent lives from being restricted. Both seem to derive from the common intuition that there is something seriously wrong with people living restricted lives, which makes it incumbent upon others to stop this from happening if they can. Perhaps this intuition depends, in turn, on a fundamental belief in the dignity of human beings, conjoined with the observation that, given human nature, many people living restricted lives are likely to be treated by others, or to treat themselves, with less than the full respect that they deserve. In any case, it is an intuition that many of us share and that may serve as a provisional grounding for our principle concerning restricted lives.

I am confident that this principle or some variant of it underlies our reactions to many cases involving the creation of persons. Yet it constitutes only a partial explication of our beliefs on these matters. For there is another principle, representing a different approach to dealing with the case of the slave child, that must be taken into account to explain our judgments on that and similar cases. According to this approach, what is wrong with our yacht-desiring couple's action is that they are misusing their reproductive powers. They exploit their unearned position of control over life for others to, in a sense, "extort" an unfair price for the exercise of those powers. But, because the benefit they provide—life itself—is greater than the unearned price they exact, their actions do not appear immoral when assessed by the standards embodied in our previously stated Obligation Principles.

This account of the immorality of the couple's behavior is best explained by considering a series of similar cases that successively approximate the case of the slave child. First, imagine a member of a drought stricken tribe who, purely by luck, discovers a substantial underground source of water. Keeping its location a secret, he trades buckets of water at a very high price to those and only those who can afford to pay with useful goods. He grows enormously rich, while many die who would have lived had he disclosed the water source or sold his water at a reasonable price. Though his selling water at monopolistic prices renders no one worse off than they would have been had he left them alone, we would condemn his use of the natural danger to his fellows' lives to extract riches from them as a form of extortion.

A second case concerns a future society that has developed a technique for freezing people's bodies immediately after death and rejuvenating some of them later. In this society, a new fatal disease begins to strike down people in the prime of life. The government allows victims of the disease to opt for being frozen immediately after death, and it plans to resuscitate them when a cure is found. A "rejuvenation trust," consisting of an initial grant of government funds together with whatever money each victim contributes, is established for each victim who wishes to be frozen. Trustees are appointed to manage these trusts and to use the accumulated funds to pay for the revitalization and cure of the frozen bodies when a cure for the disease is found. No cure is found for many years, and scientists warn that, owing to gradual deterioration of the frozen corpses, they will soon be unable to bring them back to life. Then, while going over the scientific notes of his late uncle, a young man discovers a formula for a drug to cure the disease. He is able to produce the drug, and he enriches himself by selling doses of it only to those very few rejuvenation trustees able to pay his enormous monopolistic price. This too seems immoral.[26]

Finally, consider a future slaveholding society in which many individual sperm and egg cells from married couples are isolated. Fertilization is allowed if and only if the couple agrees to it and to having the zygote implanted in the mother's womb. For reasons that need not concern us, the society appoints guardians to advance and protect—by legal means—the (potential) interests of some individual potential persons represented by particular sperm-egg pairs. A couple that has produced one such sperm-egg pair forces its guardian to approve their selling the potential child to a slaveholder for $50,000 as a condition of their allowing and facilitating the production of the child. This is a third case of immoral extortion.

These three cases and the case of the slave child share several important features. First, there is a certain benefit E (that is, *existence*) which some person (or couple) A is in a position to provide for some group of potential recipients. Second, none of the potential recipients is entitled to receive E from A. That is, A is under no contractual or quasi-contractual obligation to provide E to any individual or group of the potential recipients. Third, A has *not* in any way earned (for example, by foresight, effort, or meritorious service) his being in a position of control over E. Fourth, because E is so valuable, any potential recipient would pay practically any price he could to obtain it. And any representative of a potential recipient, acting in that recipient's best interests, would commit the recipient to pay practically any price in order to obtain the benefit for him. Fifth, A exacts an extremely high price (compared, for example, to the costs he has incurred and to the market value of similar ways of providing E to recipients) from those to whom he provides E or from their representatives.

A's actions in such cases strike us as wrong because he extorts an excessive (and unearned) price from those to whom he provides the benefit of existence or from their representatives. (The water finder, for example, charges monopolistic prices for his buckets of water.) In so doing, he improperly treats human life as a commodity to be passed out to the highest bidder.

There are, of course, some disanalogies between the case of the slave child and the case of the drought. Two of these are especially noteworthy, but neither seems to vitiate the above conclusion. The first concerns the fact that the benefit being doled out in the latter is continued existence for already existing persons, while in the former it is a beginning of existence for as yet only potential persons. Does this difference imply that different principles or intuitions underlie our judgments about the cases? Consideration of the case of the rejuvenation, which is intermediate between the two, suggests not. Our view of the drug-selling nephew is much like our view of the water seller, though the former withholds (or asks an enormous price for) future life from persons who are not now alive. And it is hard to see why the fact that they *were once alive* should (given the assumption of metaphysical determinateness in both cases) make the morally relevant considerations in this case essentially different from those operating in the case of the slave child or the guardian.[27] I am inclined, then, to believe that the potential recipient's existence or nonexistence at the time of the provision of the benefit is largely irrelevant to our moral evaluation of cases having the outlined structure.[28]

A second difference between the cases of the drought and the slave child is that there is, in the latter, no one acting on the recipient's behalf from whom a high price is directly extorted. The slave child pays a price, by being born a slave, but he is not forced into making an expensive bargain as are the water buyers in the case of the drought. But, again, it is doubtful that this difference greatly affects the moral substance of the case. To see that it does not, one need only compare the case of the slave child and the very similar case of the guardian, which does contain an act of extortion. Our inclination to regard these latter two cases as involving like moral offenses suggests that the presence of a direct act of extortion is not necessary for us to condemn treating life as an exploitable commodity in such contexts. Another way to put the point is this. For the couple to *both* sell their prospective child into slavery *and* justify this act on the grounds that the child benefits may be viewed as similar to an act of indirect extortion. To offer such a justification is tantamount to saying, "This is a bargain that the child or its guardian would have agreed to, hence there is nothing wrong with the corresponding act." But as the case of the guardian indicates, the fact that such agreement would have been forthcoming under such coercive circumstances does not imply that the agreement is a fair one.[29] Nor may the couple act, in the absence of such an agreement, as though one existed and was fair.

This analysis of the case of the slave child can, I think, be applied directly to the Paradox of Future

Individuals. For our generation to procreate, consume, and pollute to our heart's content, *and to justify doing so* on the grounds that future individuals are benefited (or not harmed), would be analogous to what the slave child's parents do. Such purported justification derives a good part of its initial plausibility from implicit appeal to the argument that "future individuals (or their representatives) would agree to what we are doing, hence it is morally permissible." But, as we have seen, the special context in which such agreement may be presumed to take place vitiates the inference from "an act that would be agreed to" to "morally permissible act." This inference would be valid only if human existence, and the power to create it, were commodities that may be sold for whatever the market will bear. But they are not.

The spirit of this analysis may be expressed in the form of a small, but significant, proposed modification of the second form of Kant's Categorical Imperative. The modified imperative would forbid treating rational beings *or their creation* (that is, their being brought into existence) as a means only, rather than as ends in themselves. This principle directly condemns the couple's actions in the case of the slave child, for they use the creation of the slave child solely as a means to their ends.

The notion of using a person's creation as a means must be interpreted more broadly, however, if the case of the pleasure-pill and the Paradox of Future Individuals are to be encompassed within the scope of the modified imperative. For, in each of these cases, the acts of creating persons likely to live restricted lives are side effects of the parties acting to attain ends such as sexual pleasure or a high material standard of living, rather than means to these ends. What is objectionable in these cases is the attempt to justify (or excuse) acts whose immorality would otherwise be evident because they lead to the creation of restricted lives, on the grounds that those created are benefited (or not harmed).[30] In the case of the slave child, the act of creation is a means to the parent's end. But here the *fact* of creation is used as a means of cancelling the prima facie moral prohibition on the acts in question that derives from their undesirable effects. It is as though the agents in these cases claim a moral credit for the benefit of life they bestow on those whose existence results from their actions, which they may then draw against to justify the actions that they carry out for their own reasons. But, as our discussion of the cases involving the drought, rejuvenation, and the guardian indicated, this is to treat human life as a commodity, and it constitutes misuse of the agents' power over the existence of future individuals.

Our modified categorical imperative is ambiguous, then, in that the component notion of "treating the creation of rational beings as a means" has two rather distinct meanings. As the ambiguity has been explicitly noted, this should cause no serious difficulties. In addition, however, the modified imperative is vague, as is its parent principle. Is it so vague that it cannot usefully be applied to significant cases involving the creation of persons? I think not. It applies in a rather straightforward way, and yields plausible results, when brought to bear on certain cases of creation beyond those so far considered.

Imagine, for example, the following minor variant of an actual case from the medical literature.[31] A couple, who otherwise do not want a child, contemplate producing one so that the father may receive a needed kidney transplant from the infant. Here is a clear case of using the creation of a person solely as a means to an end. And it does seem that the act would be wrong, for that reason—this, in spite of the fact that if the child were produced and its kidney transplanted, the child would receive a net benefit, for it would not have existed otherwise. So, in a quite realistic case, we find the modified categorical imperative the apparent victor in a clear and direct conflict with the initially plausible Obligation Principles of Section I.

We have thus uncovered two independent and intuitively appealing moral principles—the modified categorical imperative and the above-stated limitation on creating restricted lives—that provide grounds for rejecting the conclusion of the Paradox of Future Individuals. These principles reveal the limits of plausible application of the Obligation Principle that produces this paradox. And a systematic justification of either principle, perhaps as part of a comprehensive rule-utilitarian or Kantian normative theory, might take us some way toward laying the paradox to rest.

Notes

An earlier version of this paper was presented at the California State University at Fullerton Philosophy Symposium in February 1980. I have received helpful discussion and comments from participants in that symposium, the Editors of *Philosophy & Public Affairs*, Robert M. Adams, Thomas E. Hill Jr., Derek Parfit (who provided extensive advice and who records some points of disagreement below), Ernest Partridge, Thomas Schwartz, and Virginia L. Warren.

1. Robert M. Adams, "Existence, Self-Interest, and the Problem of Evil," *Nous* 13 (1979): 57. Derek Parfit, "On Doing the Best for Our Children," in *Ethics and Population*, ed. Michael Bayles (Cambridge, MA: Schenkman, 1976), pp. 100–102. Thomas Schwartz, "Obligations to Posterity," in *Obligations to Future Generations*, ed. Richard Sikora and Brian Barry (Philadelphia: Temple University Press, 1978).

2. A few genes might vary without negating identity, if the history of the world, the early life of the person in question, and the lives of his ancestors were essentially the same. Schwartz's remarks on pp. 4–5 show that this qualification does not affect the argument. Obviously, sameness of genetic structure is not a *sufficient* condition of personal identity, else identical twins would be a single person.

3. At least, beyond the first few generations. See Schwartz, pp. 4–6.

4. In addition to the paradox discussed here, population control policies pose special moral problems concerning the comparison of alternative world futures in which different numbers of future people exist. These problems are not dealt with here.

5. Variants of this argument pose difficulties for the entitlement theory of justice presented in Robert Nozick, *Anarchy, State and Utopia* (New York: Basic Books, 1974). I discuss this in an unpublished paper titled "An Internal Critique of Nozick's Entitlement Theory."

6. The conclusion is not quite as shocking as it first appears for it leaves open the possibility that we have an obligation to our ancestors, our contemporaries, or our *immediate* descendants to sacrifice in order to promote future people's well-being. As it is not my purpose to argue for conservation policies, but rather to deal with certain theoretical issues, I only discuss whether, and why, laissez faire might be wrong irrespective of what we may owe to these groups.

7. Interpreted in this way, the Obligation Principle allows us to account for the wrongness of murder, which typically renders its once existent victim's life less valuable to him by shortening it.

8. In "Utilitarianism and Welfarism," *Journal of Philosophy* 76 (September 1979): 463–89, Amartya Sen defines welfarism as follows: "The judgment of the relative goodness of alternative states of affairs must be based exclusively on, and taken as an increasing function of, the respective collections of individual utilities in these states" (468). The Obligation Principle is entailed by (but does not entail) the conjunction of act-consequentialism and the form of welfarism that Sen calls Paretianism.

9. Strictly speaking, what Bennett and Schwartz seem to deny is the conjunction of welfarism and consequentialism. I infer this from sections 7 and 8 of Bennett's "On Maximizing Happiness," in Sikora and Barry, and from Schwartz's unpublished "Human Welfare: What It Is Not," in which he argues that welfare is essentially different from "utility" (the notion used in Sen's definition of welfarism), and that "if there is some value that individual actions and public choices should maximize, it is more akin to aggregate welfare than to aggregate utility." Bennett's forthcoming book on consequences, and Schwartz's on social choice theory, should provide the basis for a more definitive classification of their positions. (Bennett's endorsement of something like the Obligation Principle occurs in section 2 of "On Maximizing.")

10. I leave aside complications concerning the possible deaths, due to radioactivity, of immigrants or foreigners.

11. This case is essentially the same as one discussed by Parfit ("On Doing," pp. 100–101), save that it requires the additional, but surely correct, assumption that fertilization of the same egg by a different sperm of the father would produce a different individual.

12. As in the Obligation Principle, "existence" and "being worse/better off" are to be construed timelessly.

13. A principle that takes distribution as well as amounts of benefit into account might serve as well. For purposes of this paper, I ignore both distributive considerations and whether the principles in question concern maximizing total or per capita benefits. Obviously, a full discussion of the ethics of creation

and population would have to pay serious attention to these matters.

14. Parallel, and more realistic, examples involve couples producing (surrogate mothers carrying), for money, children for adoptive (genetic) parents that would seriously mistreat it, or would have to raise it in such poverty-stricken circumstances that its life would barely be worth living.

15. It is enormously improbable that the couple, if they turned down the slaveholder, could succeed in producing the same child they would have produced had they accepted, even if they tried. For it is unlikely that they could arrange conditions of conception similar enough to "what would have been" to ensure that the very same sperm would fertilize the same egg.

16. This assumes the following plausible transitivity principle for moral permissibility: If it would be permissible to do A if A and B were the alternatives, and would be permissible to do B if B and C were the alternatives, then it is permissible to do A if A, B, and C are the alternatives.

17. Even if this objection were correct, it would not save those now living from moral condemnation for not controlling growth. For selfishness and greed, in the form of desires for numerous children and a higher material standard of living, seem to be among our primary motives for allowing growth to go unchecked.

18. This does not contradict the point made in note 15. The fact that *neither* of the two phrases "the child they would have if they accepted the offer" and "the child they would have if they rejected the offer" refers to a specific determinate individual does not imply that both phrases refer to the same individual.

19. Future scientific advances may allow parents to know about the features of their various potential offspring. Benevolence toward particular potential children might then make sense. But, as the next two paragraphs in the text indicate, the couple's choice would not, under those circumstances, be analogous to our choice between controlled and uncontrolled growth.

20. See, for example, my "Rawls on Average and Total Utility," *Philosophical Studies* 27 (April 1975): 237–53. Peter Singer's recent attempt to solve the problem highlights its difficulty. See his "A Utilitarian Population Principle," in Bayles, and Parfit's criticisms in "On Doing."

21. These considerations do not preclude a rule-utilitarian solution. In fact, either or both of the principles introduced below might be incorporated into a rule-utilitarian normative system.

22. This is, in effect, suggested in Adams, "Existence," pp. 57–59.

23. To avoid misunderstanding, it should be emphasized that (i) restricted lives typically will be worth living, on the whole, for those who live them, (ii) some restricted lives will be more worth living than some (many) unrestricted lives, and (iii) an individual's restricted life may be better than the life he would have lived had he not had the restriction. Our characterization does imply, however, that, on average, restricted lives are less rewarding than unrestricted ones.

24. One apparent difficulty with the proposed principle is that it seems to imply that it is wrong for slaves to have children, because their children, being slaves, would live restricted lives. This implication may reasonably be avoided by supposing that the absence of the opportunity for a couple (or a society or a generation) to produce people with unrestricted lives constitutes other things not being equal, and thus blocks the conclusion that restricted lives may not be brought about knowingly. Is the conclusion that the couples (or surrogate mothers) in the cases mentioned in note 14 act wrongly blocked in the same way? Not necessarily. For it is not implausible to assume that couples have a moral right to "have" (some) children, which is a right to produce their own children if they are capable of doing so, and to raise the children they produce. It is the existence of this right which sanctions the production of children by enslaved parents. As this right does not entail the right to raise children produced by others, it does not imply that the couples (or surrogate mothers) described in note 14 may produce children who would live restricted lives.

25. See, for example, S. I. Benn and R. S. Peters, *Social Principles and the Democratic State* (London: Allen & Unwin, 1959), pp. 141–48.

26. Compare the proposed moral verdicts on these two cases with the treatment of similar cases in Nozick, pp. 180–81.

27. Perhaps the view that, other things being equal, the (past) desires of dead people should be satisfied contributes to our judgment that the nephew acts

wrongly. But, by itself, it is not a sufficiently weighty consideration to ground the strong moral condemnation that seems appropriate here.

28. In speaking of *"our"* moral evaluation," I refer to those who share my judgment that in all three cases, A (the "extortionist") acts in a seriously wrong manner. No doubt, there are some whose intuitions about the permissibility of taking advantage of one's control over others' (actual or potential) existence will be substantially different, and their verdicts on these three cases will vary accordingly.

29. Thomas Nagel makes a similar observation:

> When one justifies a policy on the ground that the affected parties would have (or even have) agreed to it, much depends on the reasons for their agreement. If it is motivated by ignorance or fear or helplessness or a defective sense of what is reasonable, then actual or possible prior agreement does not sanction anything. ("Rawls on Justice," *Philosophical Review* 82 [April 1973]: 224)

30. This is not to say that if the parties in these situations simply act, but make no attempt to justify their acts to themselves or others, they have acted permissibly. The point is that their acts are prima facie wrong, and that considerations of the sort mentioned cannot legitimately be regarded as overriding reasons on the other side of the moral ledger.

31. Mary Anne Warren, Daniel Maguire, and Carol Levine, "Can the Fetus Be an Organ Farm?" *Hastings Center Report* 8 (October 1978): 23–25.

QUESTIONS

1. State what the paradox is, and explain why exactly it is paradoxical.
2. How successfully is Kavka able to reject the conclusion of the paradox?

XV

Moral Theories

In addition to the theoretical reflections introduced in the chapters, students may want to become more familiar with traditional and contemporary "moral theories," that is, systematic accounts of the nature and content of morality. Some of these theories have been appealed to, implicitly or explicitly, by some of the authors. But this reader has not introduced them to this point. Some instructors wish to have students consider moral theories as they reflect on controversies of practical ethics; others prefer to leave the traditional moral theories to later.

67. A Moral Theory Primer

MARK TIMMONS

Mark Timmons (1951–) is professor of philosophy at the University of Arizona. His interests are in ethics, especially meta-ethics and Kant's moral philosophy. He has published a number of important papers in these areas and several books, including *Morality without Foundations* (1998) and *Moral Theory: An Introduction* (2002).

Many of the articles or book excerpts in this reader make reference to famous moral philosophers, ethical traditions, and moral theories. The topics and controversies covered in this reader can be discussed intelligently without the student having been exposed to much philosophy or moral philosophy in particular. And it is often best to gain an understanding of different controversies and of one's reactions to them before studying moral philosophy. But many students and instructors will want to bring in moral theories at different points in a course. Timmons's masterful explanation of what a moral theory is and his presentation of six principal theories will be helpful to many students working through the material in this reader. The six theories are moral consequentialism (e.g., utilitarianism), natural law theory (e.g., Thomas Aquinas), Kantian moral theory, rights-based moral theory, virtue ethics (e.g., Aristotle), and the ethics of prima facie duties.

In 1998, Dr. Jack Kevorkian helped Thomas Youk end his life by giving him a lethal injection of drugs—an incident that was videotaped and later broadcast on CBS's *60 Minutes*.[1] Youk had been suffering from amyotrophic lateral sclerosis (often called Lou Gehrig's disease), a progressive neurodegenerative disease that attacks nerve cells in the brain and spinal cord, eventually leading to death. In the later stages of the disease, its victims are completely paralyzed, as was Youk at the time of his death.

Kevorkian's killing Youk was a case of euthanasia, which is defined as the act of killing (or allowing to die) on grounds of mercy for the victim. In this case, because Youk consented to his own death and because Kevorkian brought about Youk's death by an act of lethal injection, Kevorkian's action was an instance of voluntary active euthanasia. Kevorkian was eventually tried and convicted of second degree murder for his active role in bringing about Youk's death. But even if Kevorkian did violate the law, was his action morally wrong? Youk's immediate family and many others saw nothing morally wrong with Youk's decision or with Kevorkian's act. They argued, for example, that proper respect for an individual's freedom of choice means that people in Youk's situation have a moral right to choose to die and that, therefore, Kevorkian was not acting immorally in helping Youk end his life. Of course, many others disagreed, arguing, for example, that euthanasia is morally wrong because of its possible bad effects over time on society, including the possibility that the practice of euthanasia could be abused, and vulnerable persons might be put to death without their consent. Which side of this moral dispute is correct?

From *Disputed Moral Issues: A Reader* (Oxford, 2007). By permission of Oxford University Press.

Is euthanasia at least sometimes morally right, or is this practice morally wrong?

Disputes over moral issues are a fact of our social lives. Most people, through television, the Internet, magazines, and conversing with others, are familiar with some of the general contours of such disputes—disputes, for example, over the death penalty, the ethical treatment of animals, human cloning, abortion. The same sort of moral question raised about the actions of Kevorkian can be raised about these and other moral issues. Thinking critically about such moral issues is where philosophy becomes especially important.

A *philosophical* approach to moral issues has as its guiding aim arriving at correct or justified answers to questions about the morality of the death penalty, the ethical treatment of animals, human cloning, abortion, and other issues of moral concern. Given the contested nature of such practices as cloning and abortion, one needs to be able to defend one's position with *reasons*. Just as those who dispute questions about, say, science or history are expected to give reasons for the scientific and historical beliefs they hold, those who seriously dispute moral questions are expected to give reasons for whatever moral position they take on a certain issue. If we examine how philosophers go about providing reasons for the moral positions they take on certain issues, we find that very often they appeal to a **moral theory**. That is, in arguing for a particular position on the topic of, say, euthanasia, philosophers often make their case by applying a moral theory to the practice of euthanasia. Applying moral theory to issues of practical concern—practical issues—is one dominant way in which reasoning in ethics proceeds, and this way of tackling moral issues by applying theory to cases is featured in this book of readings.

But what is a moral theory? What are its guiding aims? What moral theories are there? How is a moral theory used in reasoning about disputed moral issues? These are the main questions of concern in this moral theory primer.

1. What is a Moral Theory?

According to philosopher John Rawls, "The two main concepts of ethics are those of the right and the good. . . . The structure of an ethical theory is,

then, largely determined by how it defines and connects these two basic notions."[2]

In explaining what a moral theory is, then, the place to begin is by clarifying the two main concepts featured in such a theory.

The Main Concepts: The Right and the Good

In ethics, the terms "right" and "wrong" are used primarily to evaluate the morality of actions, and in this chapter we are mainly concerned with moral theories that address the nature of right and wrong action (or right action, for short). Here, talk of right action in contrast to wrong action involves using the term "right" broadly to refer to actions that aren't wrong. Used in this broad sense, to say of an action that it is right is to say that it is "all right" (not wrong) to perform, and we leave open the question of whether the act, in addition to being all right, is an action that we morally ought to perform—an obligation or duty. But we sometimes find "right" being used narrowly to refer to actions that are "the" morally right action for one to perform, and when so used, it refers to actions that are morally required or obligatory (one's obligation or duty). Actions that are all right to perform (right in the sense of merely being not wrong) and that are also not one's moral obligation to perform—actions that are all right to perform and all right not to perform—are morally optional. So, we have three basic categories of moral evaluation into which an action may fall: an action may be morally obligatory (something one morally ought to do, is morally required to do, is one's duty), or morally optional, or morally wrong. To help keep this terminology straight, I have summarized what I have been saying in Figure 1.

Again, in ethics, the terms "good" and "bad" are used primarily in assessing the value of persons (their character) as well as experiences, things, and states of affairs. Philosophers distinguish between something's having **intrinsic value** (that is, being intrinsically good or bad) and something's having **extrinsic value** (that is, being extrinsically good or bad). Something has intrinsic value when its value depends on features that are *inherent* to it, whereas something is extrinsically good when its goodness is a matter of how it is related to something else that

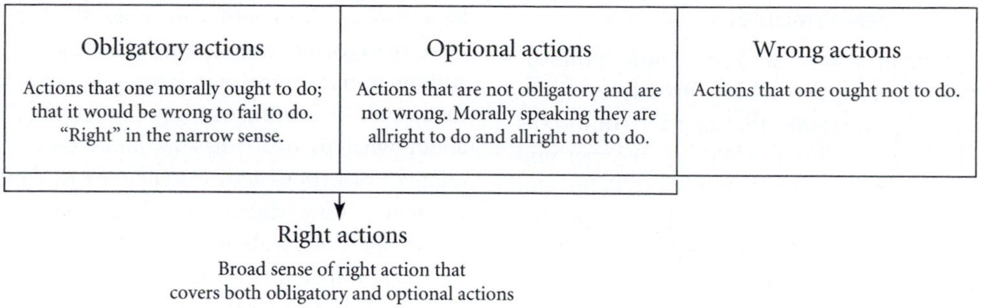

Obligatory actions	Optional actions	Wrong actions
Actions that one morally ought to do; that it would be wrong to fail to do. "Right" in the narrow sense.	Actions that are not obligatory and are not wrong. Morally speaking they are allright to do and allright not to do.	Actions that one ought not to do.

Right actions

Broad sense of right action that
covers both obligatory and optional actions

Figure 1. Basic Categories of Right Conduct

is intrinsically good. For instance, some philosophers maintain that happiness is intrinsically good—its goodness depends on the inherent nature of happiness—and that things like money and power, while not intrinsically good, are nevertheless extrinsically good (valuable) because they can be used to bring about or contribute to happiness. Thus, the notion of intrinsic value is the more basic of the two notions, and so philosophical accounts of value are concerned with the nature of intrinsic value. And here we can recognize three basic value categories: the *intrinsically good,* the *intrinsically bad* (also referred to as the intrinsically *evil*), and what we may call the *intrinsically value-neutral*—that is, the category of all those things that are neither intrinsically good nor bad (though they may have extrinsic value).[3]

A moral theory, then, is a theory about the nature of the right and the good and about the proper method for making correct or justified moral decisions. Accordingly, here are some of the main questions that a moral theory attempts to answer:

1. What *makes* an action right or wrong—what *best explains why* right acts are right and wrong acts are wrong?
2. What *makes* something good or bad—what *best explains why* intrinsically good things are intrinsically good (and similarly for things that are intrinsically bad or evil)?
3. What is the *proper method* (supposing there is one) for reasoning our way to correct or justified moral conclusions about the rightness and wrongness of actions and the goodness and

badness of persons, and other items of moral evaluation?

In order to understand more fully what a moral theory is and how it attempts to answer these questions, let us relate what has just been said to the two guiding aims of moral theory.

Two Main Aims of a Moral Theory

Corresponding to the first two questions about the nature of the right and the good is what we may call the theoretical aim of a moral theory:

The **theoretical aim** of a moral theory is to discover those underlying features of actions, persons, and other items of moral evaluation that *make* them right or wrong, good or bad and thus *explain why* such items have the moral properties they have. Features of this sort serve as *moral criteria* of the right and the good.

Our third main question about proper methodology in ethics is the basis for the practical aim of a moral theory:

The **practical aim** of a moral theory is to offer *practical guidance* for how we might arrive at correct or justified moral verdicts about matters of moral concern—verdicts which we can then use to help guide choice.

Given these aims, we can evaluate a moral theory by seeing how well it satisfies them. We will return to the issue of evaluating moral theories in section 3. For the time being, we can gain a clearer understanding of these aims by considering the role that principles typically play in moral theories.

The Role of Moral Principles

In attempting to satisfy these two aims, philosophers typically propose **moral principles**—very general moral statements that specify conditions under which an action is right (or wrong) and something is intrinsically good (or bad). Principles that state conditions for an action's being right (or wrong) are **principles of right conduct,** and those that specify conditions under which something has intrinsic value are **principles of value.** Here is an example of a principle of right conduct (where "right" is being used in its broad sense to mean "not wrong"):

> P An action is right if and only if (and because) it would, if performed, likely bring about at least as much overall happiness as would any available alternative action.[4]

This principle, understood as a moral criterion of right action, purports to reveal the underlying nature of right action—what *makes* a right action right. According to P, facts about how much overall happiness an action would bring about were it to be performed are what determine whether it is morally right. Although P addresses the rightness of actions, it has implications for wrongness as well. From P, together with the definitional claim that if an action is not morally right (in the broad sense of the term) then it is morally wrong, we may infer the following:

> P* An action is wrong if and only if (and because) it would, if performed, likely not bring about at least as much overall happiness as would some available alternative action.

Since, as we have just seen, principles about moral wrongness can be derived from principles of rightness, I shall, in explaining a moral theory's account of right and wrong, simply formulate a theory's principles (there may be more than one) for right action.

In addition to serving as moral criteria, principles like P are typically intended to provide some practical guidance for coming to correct or justified moral verdicts about particular issues, thus addressing the practical aim of moral theory. The idea is that if P is a correct moral principle, then we should be able to use it to guide our moral deliberations in coming to correct conclusions about the rightness of actions, thus serving as a basis for moral decision making. In reasoning our way to moral conclusions about what to do, P has us focus on the consequences of actions and instructs us to consider in particular how much overall happiness actions would likely bring about.

To sum up, a moral theory can be understood as setting forth moral principles of right conduct and value that are supposed to explain what makes an action or other object of evaluation right or wrong, good or bad (thus satisfying the theoretical aim), as well as principles that can be used to guide moral thought in arriving at correct or justified decisions about what to do (thus satisfying the practical aim).

The Structure of a Moral Theory

Finally, what Rawls calls the "structure" of a moral theory is a matter of how a theory connects the right and the good. As we shall see, some theories take the concept of the good to be more basic than the concept of the right and thus define or characterize the rightness of actions in terms of considerations of intrinsic goodness. Call such theories value-based moral theories. **Value-based moral theories** include versions of consequentialism, natural law theory, and virtue ethics. However, some moral theories do not define rightness in terms of goodness. Some theories are **duty-based moral theories**—theories that take the concept of duty to be basic and so define or characterize the rightness of actions independently of considerations of goodness. These theories are often called "deontological" moral theories (from *deon,* the Greek term for duty). The moral theory of Immanuel Kant (see later in this chapter) and theories inspired by Kant (Kantian moral theories) are arguably deontological.[5] And what is called the ethics of prima facie duty, if not a pure deontological theory, contains deontological elements, as we shall see when we discuss this theory later in section 2.

Brief Summary

Now that we have reviewed a few basic elements of moral theory, let us briefly sum up.

- *Main concepts of moral theory.* The two main concepts featured in moral theory are the concepts of the right (and wrong) and the good (and bad).
- *Two aims of moral theory.* A moral theory can be understood as having two central aims. The theoretical aim is to explain the underlying nature of the right and the good—specifying those features of actions or other items of evaluation that *make* an action or whatever right or wrong, good or bad. We call such features "criteria." The practical aim is to offer practical guidance for how we might arrive at correct or justified moral verdicts about matters of moral concern.
- *The role of moral principles.* A moral theory is typically composed of moral principles (sometimes a single, fundamental principle) that are intended to serve as criteria of the right and the good (thus satisfying the theoretical aim) and are also intended to be useful in guiding moral thinking toward correct, or at least justified conclusions about some moral issue.
- *The structure of a moral theory.* Considerations of structure concern how a moral theory connects the concepts of the right and the good. Value-based theories make the good (intrinsic value) more basic than the right and define or characterize the right in terms of the good. Duty-based theories characterize the right independently of considerations of value.

In the next section, we briefly examine six moral theories that play a large role in philosophical discussions of disputed moral issues. After presenting these theories, I devote the remaining section and an appendix to questions that are likely to occur to readers. First, there is the question of why studying moral theories is helpful in thinking about disputed moral issues when there is no *one* moral theory that is accepted by all those who study moral theory. Rather, we find a variety of apparently competing moral theories that sometimes yield conflicting moral verdicts about the same issue. So, how can appealing to moral theory really help in trying to think productively about moral issues? This is a fair question that I address in section 3. In the appendix,

I briefly present two moral theories whose guiding ideas will be familiar to most all readers—the divine command theory and ethical relativism. [. . .]

2. Six Essential Moral Theories

Six types of moral theory are prominently represented in our readings: consequentialism, natural law theory, Kantian moral theory, rights-based moral theory, virtue ethics, and the ethics of prima facie duty. Here, then, is an overview of these various theories that will provide useful background for understanding [many of the readings in this volume].

A. Consequentialism

In thinking about moral issues, one obvious thing to do is to consider the consequences or effects of various actions—the consequences or effects on matters that are of concern to us. **Consequentialism** is a type of moral theory according to which consequences of actions are all that matter in determining the rightness and wrongness of actions. Its guiding idea is this:

> C Right action is to be understood entirely in terms of the overall intrinsic value of the consequences of the action compared to the overall intrinsic value of the consequences associated with alternative actions an agent might perform instead. An action is right if and only if (and because) its consequences would be at least as good as the consequences of any alternative action that the agent might instead perform.

A number of important ideas are packed into C that we need to unpack—ideas that are present in the varieties of consequentialist moral theory presented next. Let us sort them out.

- First, consequentialist moral theory is a *value-based moral theory*: it characterizes or defines right action in terms of intrinsic value.
- Second, this sort of theory involves the fairly intuitive idea of *alternative actions* open to an agent: in circumstances calling for a moral choice, an agent is confronted by a range of alternative actions, any one of which she might choose to perform.

- Third (and relatedly), consequentialism is a *comparative* theory of right action: the rightness (or wrongness) of an action depends on how much intrinsic value it would likely produce (if performed) compared to how much intrinsic value alternative actions would likely produce (if performed).
- Fourth, the consequentialist account of right action is a *maximizing* conception: we are to perform that action, from among the alternatives, whose consequences will have *at least as much* overall value as any other.
- Fifth, and finally, consequentialism is a strongly *impartialist* moral theory in the sense that the rightness or wrongness of an action is made to depend on the values of the consequences for *everyone* who is affected by the action, where everyone affected counts *equally*. (This fifth point will become clearer when we consider particular versions of consequentialism.)

Consequentialism, we have noted, is a *general type* of moral theory that has a variety of species. For instance, consequentialists may differ over the issue of what has intrinsic value. Those versions that take happiness or welfare alone to have intrinsic value are versions of utilitarianism, whereas those that take human perfection to have intrinsic value are versions of perfectionism. Again, consequentialists may differ over the primary focus of consequentialist evaluation. Some versions focus on individual actions, other versions focus on rules. So, we can distinguish four main species of consequentialism. Let us explore further.

Utilitarianism has been perhaps the most prominent form of consequentialism, so let us begin with it.

Utilitarianism

Utilitarianism was originally developed and defended by Jeremy Bentham (1748–1832) and later refined by John Stuart Mill (1806–1873).[6] Their basic idea is that it is *human welfare* or *happiness* that alone is intrinsically valuable and that the rightness or wrongness of actions depends entirely on how they affect human welfare or happiness. As a consequentialist theory, utilitarianism requires that one *maximize* welfare where the welfare of *all* individuals

who will be affected by some action counts. We can sharpen our characterization of this theory by introducing the technical term "utility," which refers to the *net value* of the consequences of actions—how much overall welfare or happiness would likely result from an action, taking into account both the short-term and long-term effects of the action on the welfare of all who will be affected. The basic idea is that the moral status of an action—its rightness or wrongness—depends both on how much happiness (if any) it would likely produce for each individual affected were it to be performed, as well as how much unhappiness (if any) it would likely produce for each affected person were it to be performed. For each alternative action, then, we can consider the *net balance* of overall happiness versus unhappiness associated with that action. Call this overall net value the **utility** of an action. We can now formulate a generic statement of the basic utilitarian principle—the **principle of utility:**

> **U** An action is right if and only if (and because) it would (if performed) likely produce at least as high a utility (net overall balance of welfare) as would any other alternative action one might perform instead.[7]

Notice that the utility of an action might be negative. That is, all things considered, an action may produce a net balance of unhappiness over happiness were it to be performed. Moreover, since U (like all versions of C) is comparative, it may turn out that the right action in some unfortunate circumstance is the one that would likely bring about the least amount of overall negative utility.

As formulated, U leaves open questions about the nature of happiness and unhappiness about which there are different philosophical theories.[8] Bentham and (apparently) Mill held that happiness is entirely constituted by experiences of pleasure and unhappiness by experiences of displeasure or pain. And so their theory of intrinsic value is called **value hedonism:** *only* states of pleasure have positive intrinsic value and *only* states of pain have intrinsic negative value; anything else of value is of mere extrinsic value. So, for instance, for the value hedonist, any positive value that knowledge may have is extrinsic: it is only of positive value when it contributes to bringing about what has intrinsic value, namely pleasure (or the alleviation of pain). It should be noted that a value hedonist need not (and should not) take an excessively narrow view of pleasure and pain; the hedonist can follow Bentham and Mill in holding that in addition to such bodily pleasures of the sort one gets from eating delicious food or having a massage, there are aesthetic and intellectual pleasures such as appreciating a beautifully written poem. Moreover, the value hedonist will recognize not only passive pleasures of the sort just mentioned, but also active pleasures as when one plays a game or is involved in some creative activity. So value hedonism can recognize a broad range of pleasurable experiences that have positive intrinsic value and a broad range of painful experiences that have negative intrinsic value.

If we now combine the principle of utility (U) with value hedonism, we obtain **hedonistic utilitarianism:**

> **HU** An action is right if and only if (and because) it would likely produce (if performed) at least as high a net balance of pleasure (or less pain) as would any other alternative action one might do instead.

But as I hope my presentation has made clear, one need not accept hedonism as a theory of value in order to be a utilitarian. In fact, many contemporary utilitarians reject value hedonism and accept some other conception of happiness or welfare. But, again, what makes a theory a version of utilitarianism is that the theory accepts the basic consequentialist claim, C, together with the idea that it is human happiness or human well-being that has intrinsic value and is to be promoted in what we do.

Perfectionist Consequentialism

But a consequentialist need not be a utilitarian— she might hold that there are items having intrinsic value other than happiness that are important in determining the rightness or wrongness of action. To illustrate, I have chosen what is called **perfectionist consequentialism**—a species of the generic view that accepts a perfectionist theory of value.[9] According to a **value perfectionist,** it is states of

human perfection, including knowledge and achievement, that have intrinsic value.[10] One might come to have a great deal of knowledge and achievement in one's life, yet not be happy. So a perfectionist theory of the good is not the same as a happiness theory of the good. We might formulate the basic principle of perfectionist consequentialism as follows:

> **PC** An action is right if and only if (and because) it would (if performed) likely bring about a greater net balance of perfectionist goods than would any alternative action one might perform instead.

The distinction between utilitarianism and perfectionist consequentialism has to do with differences over what has intrinsic value for purposes of morally evaluating actions. And notice that the consequentialist principles presented thus far refer to particular concrete actions and their consequences, so the views (expressed in principles U, HU, and PC) are versions of **act consequentialism.** However, as mentioned at the outset, another important division within the ranks of consequentialists is between act and rule versions of the view. So let us turn from act versions to rule versions.

Rule Consequentialism

Moral rules—rules, for example, against lying, theft, and killing—are generally thought to be significant in thinking about particular moral issues. The importance of moral rules is emphasized by rule consequentialists. Whereas act consequentialism is the view that the rightness of a particular, concrete action—an actual or possible doing by a person at a time—depends on the value of its consequences, **rule consequentialism** is the view that the rightness or wrongness of an action depends on whether it is required, permitted, or prohibited by a rule whose consequences are best.[11] So rule consequentialism involves two levels of evaluation: first, rules that require, permit, or prohibit various courses of action are evaluated by reference to the values of their consequences, and second, a particular action is evaluated by determining whether it is required, permitted, or prohibited by a rule whose consequences are best. Let us explore this view a bit further.

The sense in which a rule can have consequences has to do with the fact that were people to accept the rule in question, this would influence what they do. So, we can evaluate a rule by asking what consequences would likely be brought about were it to be generally accepted in society. Call the value associated with rules their **acceptance value.** This idea is familiar. Think of debates in the sporting world about changing the rules of some sport. The focus in such debates is on the likely effects the proposed rule change would have on the game, were it to be accepted.

According to rule consequentialism, then, the morality of a particular action in some situation depends upon the acceptance values of various competing rules that are relevant to the situation in question. We can thus formulate this theory with the following principle of right conduct:

> RC An action is right if and only if (and because) it is permitted by a rule whose associated acceptance value is at least as high as the acceptance value of any other rule applying to the situation.

In order to better understand this principle, let us illustrate its application with a simple example.

Suppose that I have promised to help you move next Friday morning. Friday morning arrives, and many alternative courses of action are open to me. Among them are these:

A1. Keep my promise (and show up at your place),
A2. Break my promise (and do something else).

Corresponding to each of these alternative actions, we have these rules:

R1. Whenever one makes a promise, keep it,
R2. Whenever one makes a promise, break it if one feels like it.

Now consider the acceptance values associated with these rules. I think we can all agree that acceptance value of **R1** is far greater than that of **R2.** So (ignoring for the moment that there may be other competing rules to be considered in this situation) rule consequentialism implies that one ought to keep one's promise.

Finally notice that act and rule consequentialism may diverge in their moral implications. To stick with the previous example, suppose that by breaking my promise and instead hanging out with some friends at the local pool hall will likely produce a greater level of overall intrinsic value than would the backbreaking work of helping you move. Besides, you've lined up plenty of help; I won't be missed that much. Act consequentialism implies that it would be morally permissible to go ahead and break the promise; rule consequentialism by contrast implies that I am morally obliged to keep my promise.

Brief Summary

Let us pause for a moment to summarize (see Fig. 2) what we have covered. As we have seen, the basic consequentialist idea (C) can be developed in a variety of ways; we have considered four versions of this generic approach to ethics.

For now, the main idea to take away from this discussion is that for all varieties of consequentialism, the rightness or wrongness of an action depends entirely on the net intrinsic value of the consequences of either individual actions or rules. Consequentialist theories (and especially utilitarianism) are often discussed in articles and books about disputed moral issues. Some authors appeal to consequentialism to justify their particular views on some moral issue; other authors will contrast their approach with consequentialism.

Applying Consequentialism

To convey a sense of how one is to go about applying consequentialism to a particular moral issue, let us work with act utilitarianism as expressed earlier in U. And to make things fairly manageable, let us consider a rather simple case.

Suppose that I am in charge of inviting a guest philosopher to speak at my university and that I've narrowed the choices to two. On the one hand, I can invite Dr. Brilliant, a very well-known and innovative philosopher but whose manner of presentation is decidedly dull. The philosophy faculty will no doubt take pleasure in his presentation and will benefit intellectually from what he has to say, but others will be bored stiff and get little out of the talk. On the

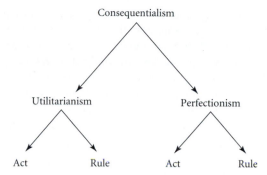

Figure 2. Some Forms of Consequentialism

other hand, I can invite Dr. Flash who is not nearly as accomplished as Dr. Brilliant but who I know is an extremely engaging speaker. Suppose that five professional philosophers and forty-five students are expected to attend the lecture no matter which of these two philosophers I invite.

Now if I apply U to my situation, it would have me invite the speaker whose talk will produce the greatest amount of overall happiness. A careful application of U would require that I consider each person who will be affected by the lecture of Dr. Brilliant and determine how much happiness (if any) that person would experience as a result of this lecture and then determine how much unhappiness (if any) that person would experience as a result of this lecture. Once I have done this calculation for each person, I then calculate how much total happiness the lecture would cause and how much total unhappiness it would cause in order to arrive at the overall net value associated with Dr. Brilliant's lecture. I do the same for Dr. Flash. The lecture I ought to sponsor and hence the philosopher I ought to invite depends on which talk will result in the greatest amount of intrinsic value.

Obviously, to apply U to one's own choices with any precision would require much factual information: information about one's circumstances, about the various alternative actions one might perform in one's particular circumstances, about the individuals who will be affected either negatively or positively were one to perform a particular action, and about the overall amount of happiness or unhappiness, both short term and long term, that would likely result from each of the various alternative actions. Some critics of consequentialism argue that

when it comes to satisfying the practical aim of moral theory—the aim of providing practical guidance for arriving at correct or justified verdicts for the further aim of acting on such verdicts—consequentialism makes implausible demands on what one needs to know in order to apply it to particular cases. Defenders reply that even if *precise* application of this sort of moral theory is not feasible, we can and do make rough estimates of the values of the consequences of various alternative actions, and that in doing so we must realize that the moral verdicts we reach as a result are likely to be highly fallible. But this, say the defenders, is something we just have to live with given our limited information about the effects of our actions.

B. Natural Law Theory

The idea that certain actions or practices are "natural" while others are "unnatural" is commonly offered as a reason why certain "unnatural" actions are wrong and that we ought to do what is natural. Think of popular arguments against homosexuality. This idea of morality being natural is associated with the **natural law theory.**[12]

This type of moral theory is often traced to the thirteenth-century philosopher and theologian St. Thomas Aquinas (1225–1274). It gets its name from the guiding idea that there are objectively true moral principles that are grounded in human nature.[13] Because there are objective facts about human nature that determine what our good consists in, and because moral requirements have to do with maintaining and promoting the human goods, these requirements, unlike the rules of some club or made-up game, are part of the natural order. Because the natural law theory bases right action on considerations of intrinsic value, it is a value-based theory of right conduct, as is consequentialism. However, as we shall see in setting out this theory, natural law theory is opposed to consequentialism—it denies that the *only* considerations that matter when it comes to right action are consequences. So, to understand this theory let us proceed by first presenting its theory of intrinsic value and then presenting its theory of right conduct in two parts: (a) first, the "core" of theory and then (b) the doctrine of double effect.

Theory of Intrinsic Value[14]

According to Aquinas's version of natural law theory, there are four basic intrinsic goods:

- Human life
- Human procreation (which includes raising children)
- Human knowledge
- Human sociability (this value has to do with associations and bonds with others, including friendship, social organizations, and political organizations)

Each of these items, then, has intrinsic value and their destruction is intrinsically bad or evil. These four values are the basis for the core of natural law theory.

The Core

We can state the basic principle of natural law theory roughly as follows:

> **NLT** An action is right if and only if (and because) in performing the action one does not directly violate any of the basic values.

Thus, killing a human being (with some exceptions explained later) is morally wrong. If we suppose, as many natural law theorists do, that the use of contraceptives thwarts human procreation, then their use is morally wrong. Interfering with the good of knowledge by distorting information or by lying is morally wrong. Destroying legitimate social bonds through the advocacy of anarchy is morally wrong.

But what about hard cases in which no matter what one does, one will violate at least one of the basic values and thus bring about evil through whichever action one chooses? Let us consider a much discussed case involving abortion. Suppose that a pregnant woman has cancer of the uterus and must have a hysterectomy (removal of her uterus) to save her life. Human life is one of the intrinsic goods, so having the operation will have at least one good effect. But suppose (just for the sake of the example) that from conception the fetus counts as a human life and so having the hysterectomy would bring about the death of the unborn human life. This effect, because it involves the destruction of

something having intrinsic value—human life—is an evil. And let us suppose that this moral dilemma is unavoidable in this case because there is no other way to save the woman's life while also preserving the life of her fetus. How does the natural law theory deal with this kind of case? After all, the core of the theory seems to say that any action that violates one or more of the basic goods is wrong, period. But if it really does say this, then we have to conclude that her having the operation is wrong, but also her not having the operation is wrong (because she will fail to preserve her own life). How can natural law theory deal with this moral dilemma?

If we go back and inspect the basic principle of natural law theory, NLT, we notice that what it prohibits are actions that *directly* violate one or more of the basic goods, thereby bringing about evil. But what counts as a direct violation? Can there be morally permissible "indirect" violations? These questions bring us to the next major component of natural law ethics—the doctrine of double effect.

The Doctrine of Double Effect

In addition to the core principle (NLT), the natural law theory also embraces the following set of provisions that compose the **doctrine of double effect**— so named because it concerns cases in which performing an action would have at least one good effect and one bad effect (where good and bad have to do with the theory's list of intrinsic goods). So this doctrine is meant to address the question of whether it is ever morally permissible to knowingly bring about bad or evil consequences where one's aim in action is to bring about or preserve one or more of the basic human goods. Here, then, is a statement of the various provisions making up the doctrine:

> **DDE** An action that would bring about at least one evil effect and at least one good effect is morally permissible if (and only if) the following conditions are satisfied:

> *Intrinsic permissibility:* The action in question, apart from its effects, is morally permissible;
> *Necessity:* It is not possible to bring about the good effect except by performing an action that will bring about the evil effect in question;

Nonintentionality: The evil effect is not intended—it is neither one's end nor a chosen means for bringing about some intended end;

Proportionality: The evil that will be brought about by the action is not out of proportion to the good being aimed at.

What this principle does is help define the idea of a direct violation of a human good which is the central idea in the core principle, NLT. We shall return to this point in a moment. For the time being, let us explain DDE by showing how it would apply to the case just described.

In applying DDE to our moral dilemma, we must ask whether all four of the doctrine's provisions are satisfied. Let us take them in order. (1) First, since having a hysterectomy is not an intrinsically wrong action, the first requirement is satisfied. (2) Furthermore, given my description of the case, the second requirement of DDE is met because having a hysterectomy is the *only* way to save her life. Were there some other operation or some medication that would both save the woman's life and preserve the life of the fetus, then the necessity condition would not be met and the hysterectomy would be wrong. But we are supposing that there are no such options in this case.

(3) The third requirement rests on the distinction between effects that one intends in action and effects that may be foreseen but are unintended. One intends some consequence or effect when either it is something one is aiming to bring about (an end) or it is one's chosen means for bringing about some desired end. Here is a simple, everyday example. I fire a rifle in order to hit the paper target, but in so doing I know that the noise from the rifle will frighten nearby wildlife. But even though I can foresee that my act of pulling the trigger will frighten those animals, this effect is not intended: it is not my purpose—my purpose is to hit the target, and their being frightened is not a means for achieving my end—the means is taking aim and firing. So the effect of my act of firing—frightening those animals—is not something I intend, rather it is a foreseen but unintended side effect of what I do.

Returning now to our example, we find that this third provision is satisfied because although the death of the unborn child is a foreseen effect of the hysterectomy, its death is not her chief aim or end (saving her own life), and it is not a means by which her life will be saved. After all, were she not pregnant, she would still have the operation to save her life, and so the death of the unborn is a mere unintended and unfortunate side effect of the operation. Removing the cancer is what will save her life.

(4) Finally, the evil that will result from the operation (loss of one innocent human life) is not grossly out of proportion to the good that will result (saving an innocent human life). (When DDE is applied to the morality of war activities, considerations of proportionality of evil to good become especially relevant. [. . .])

Having explained the DDE, we can now return to the core principle, NLT, and explain how these two elements are related in natural law ethics. The idea is that, according to NLT, we are not to *directly* violate any of the basic human goods. The DDE helps define what counts as a direct violation: direct violations are those that cannot be justified by the doctrine of double effect.

Before going on, it will be useful to pause for a moment to compare the natural law theory with consequentialism. In response to our moral dilemma involving the hysterectomy, an act consequentialist will say that we should consider the value of the consequences of the alternative actions (having a hysterectomy or refraining from this operation) and choose the action with the best consequences. In short, for the act consequentialist good results justify the means. But not for the natural law theorist, because on her theory one may not act in direct violation of the basic goods even if by doing so one would produce better consequences. Good ends do not always justify an action that is a means to those ends. For instance, I am not permitted to intentionally kill one innocent human being (do evil) even if by doing so I can save five others (bring about good). To see how consequentialism and natural law theory yield different verdicts about a difficult moral case, consider the case of a woman who is pregnant, but this time she is suffering from a "tubal" pregnancy, which means that her fetus is lodged in her fallopian tube and thus has not implanted itself into the uterine wall. If nothing is done, both fetus and woman will die. The only thing that can be done to save the woman is to remove the fetus, which will bring about its death. Exercise: apply act consequentialism and the natural law theory to this case to see whether they differ in their moral implications.

Applying Natural Law Theory

In applying the natural law theory to some case in order to determine whether a particular course of action is morally right, one begins with the core principle, NLT, and asks whether the action in question would violate any of the basic goods. If not, then the action is not wrong. But if it would violate one or more of the basic goods, then one has to determine whether the action would constitute a *direct* violation. And to do that, one makes use of the DDE. If the action satisfies all four provisions of DDE, then the violation is not direct and the action is morally permissible. If the action does not pass DDE, then the action involves a direct violation of one or more of the intrinsic goods and is, therefore, wrong.

Of course, as with all moral theories, applying the natural law theory is not a mechanical process. For one thing, one must address questions about the proper interpretation of the four basic human goods. Surely coming to have knowledge of the basic laws that govern the physical universe is intrinsically valuable, if any knowledge is. But what if, for example, I spend my time counting the number of needles on a cactus plant for no particular reason; is the knowledge I acquire about the number of needles really of any intrinsic value? One can raise similar questions about the other three basic human goods. Furthermore, applying the doctrine of double effect raises questions of interpretation. For instance, the proportionality provision requires that the evil caused by an action not be "out of proportion" to the good effects of that action. But, of course, determining when things are out of proportion requires sensitivity to particular cases and the use of good judgment.

These points about interpretation are not meant as a criticism of natural law theory; rather they call attention to the fact that applying it to particular moral issues requires that we interpret its various

elements. As we shall see, a similar point applies to Kantian moral theory.

C. Kantian Moral Theory

Most everyone has come across moral arguments that appeal to the **golden rule:** do unto others as you would have them do unto you. This rule encapsulates a kind of test for thinking about the morality of actions: it asks the individual making a moral choice that will affect others to consider how one would like it were one on the receiving end of the action in question. In the case of Thomas Youk with which we began the chapter, the golden rule would have Kevorkian consider what he would want done to (or for) him were he in Youk's situation. Various objections have been made to the golden rule—for instance, it suggests that the rightness or wrongness of an action depends simply on what one does or would desire. But people can have crazy desires. A masochist who inflicts pain on others might cheerfully say that he would have others do unto him as he is doing to them. Do we want to conclude that his causing others pain is morally right? Perhaps there is some interpretation of the golden rule that does not yield the wrong result in the case of the masochist or other examples that have been used against it. Nevertheless, there is something about the *spirit* of the golden rule that seems right. The idea suggested by this rule is that morality requires that we not treat people unfairly, that we respect other persons by taking them into account in our moral deliberations. This suggestion is quite vague but finds one articulation in Kantian moral theory to which we now turn.

Kantian moral theory derives from the moral writings of the German philosopher Immanuel Kant (1724–1804), which continue to have an enormous influence on contemporary ethics.[15] Central to Kant's moral theory is the idea that moral requirements can be expressed as commands or imperatives that categorically bid us to perform certain actions—requirements that apply to us regardless of what we might happen to want or desire or how such actions bear on the production of our own happiness. Kant thought that specific moral requirements could be derived from a fundamental moral principle that he called the **categorical imperative.**

Moreover, Kant offered various alternative formulations of his fundamental moral principle. The two I will consider are the ones that are most often applied to moral issues.

The Humanity Formulation

One of Kant's formulations of his categorical imperative is called the **Humanity formulation:**

> **H** An action is right if and only if (and because) the action treats persons (including oneself) as ends in themselves and not as mere means.

Obviously, to make use of this principle, we need to know what it means to treat someone as an end and what it means to treat someone as a mere means. Space does not permit a thorough discussion of these ideas, so a few illustrations will have to suffice.

Deception and coercion are two ways in which one can treat another person as a mere means—as an object to be manipulated. Deceiving someone in order to get him or her to do something he or she would otherwise not agree to do constitutes using the person as though that person were a mere instrument at one's disposal for promoting one's own ends. Again, many cases of coercing someone by threats involve attempting to manipulate that person for one's own purposes and hence constitutes an attempt to use him or her as a mere means to one's own ends.

But Kant's Humanity formulation requires not only that we not treat others as mere means to our own ends (a negative requirement), but also that we treat them as ends in themselves (a positive requirement). For Kant, to say that persons are ends in themselves is to say that they have a special worth or value that demands of us that we have a certain positive regard for them. Kant refers to this special worth as *dignity*.[16] So, for instance, if I fail to help those who need and deserve my help, I don't treat them as mere means, but I do fail to have a positive regard for their welfare and thus fail to properly recognize their worth as persons.

Applying Kant's Humanity Formulation

As just explained, applying the Humanity formulation requires consideration of the dual requirements that we not treat people as mere means and that we also not fail to treat them as ends in themselves—as

individuals who have dignity. Interpreting these requirements is where the hard work comes in: what are the boundaries when it comes to treating people as *mere* means? If, in walking by, I see that you are wearing a watch and ask you for the time, I am using you as a means for finding out what time it is, but I am not thereby using you as a *mere* means to my own ends. We have noted that deception and coercion represent main ways in which one might use someone as a mere means—as something to be manipulated. So we have a good start on interpreting the idea of treatment as mere means. Here is not the place to consider other ways in which our actions might involve treating someone as a mere means. Rather, the point I wish to make is that we have some idea of what it means to treat someone as a mere means and we must build on this understanding to apply the Humanity formulation to a range of moral issues.

Similar remarks apply to the requirement that we positively treat others as ends in themselves. Here it is interesting to note that Kant argued that in satisfying this requirement, we are obligated to adopt two very general goals—the goal of promoting the (morally permissible) ends of others, and the goal of self-perfection. Such wide-open goals allow a person much latitude in deciding in what ways and on what occasions to promote the ends of others and one's own self-perfection. For Kant, then, applying the positive requirement embedded in H is a matter of figuring out how best to integrate the promotion of the well-being of others and one's own self-perfection into a moral life.

The Universal Law Formulation

Kant's other main formulation of the categorical imperative, the **Universal Law formulation,** expresses a test whereby we can determine whether our actions are right or wrong.

> **UL** An action is right if and only if one can both (a) consistently conceive of everyone adopting and acting on the general policy (that, is the maxim) of one's action, and also (b) consistently will that everyone act on that maxim.[17]

This formulation will remind readers of the golden rule, though notice that UL does not refer to an agent's wants; rather it represents a kind of consistency test.[18]

Unfortunately, interpreting Kant's two-part test requires some explanation. So let me say a bit more about UL and then, using some of Kant's own examples, show how it can be applied.

According to Kant, when we act, we act on a general policy that is called a "maxim." To determine the morality of an action, one formulates the general policy of one's action and asks whether one could consistently both conceive of and will that everyone act on the same policy or, to put it in Kant's terms, one asks whether one could consistently conceive and will that the maxim of one's action become a "universal law" governing everyone's behavior. If so, then the action is right; if not, then the action is wrong. So UL expresses a two-part test one can use to determine the rightness or wrongness of actions. To make Kant's tests more concrete, let us consider a few of Kant's own sample applications of UL.

One of Kant's examples involves making a lying promise—that is, a promise that one has no intention of keeping. Consider a case in which I desperately need money right away and the only way I can get it is by getting a loan which I must promise to repay. I know, however, that I won't be able to repay the loan. The maxim corresponding to the action I am considering is:

M1 Whenever I need money and can get it only by making a lying promise, I will borrow the money by making a lying promise.

Kant's principle, UL, would have me test the morality of making a lying promise by asking whether I could *consistently conceive* and *will* that everyone act on M1—that everyone who needs money in such circumstances as mine make a lying promise. Let us first ask whether this is something I can consistently conceive. If it isn't, then I certainly can't consistently will that everyone adopt and act on it.

Kant claims that when I think through what would be involved in everyone acting on M1, I realize that I cannot even consistently conceive of a world in which everyone in need of money successfully makes lying promises. After all, a world in which everyone in need of money goes around trying to get the money by making a lying promise is one in which successful promising becomes impossible since, as Kant observes, "no one would believe

what was promised him but would laugh at all such expressions as vain pretenses."[19] Thus, trying to even conceive of a world in which everyone in need of money acts on M1 involves an inconsistency: it is a world in which (1) *everyone* in need gets money by making a lying promise, but because of the breakdown in the institution of promising that would result, it is a world in which (2) *not everyone* in need gets money by making a lying promise for the reason Kant gives. But if I can't consistently conceive of everyone acting on M1, then my maxim fails the first test mentioned in UL. And if I can't consistently conceive that everyone act on M1, this shows me that, in making a lying promise, I am acting on an immoral policy and that my action is wrong.

But why is the fact that one cannot consistently conceive that everyone act on one's maxim an indication that the action in question is wrong? Kant's idea here seems to be that in performing an action whose maxim I cannot consistently conceive everyone adopting, I am, in effect, proposing to make an exception of myself—an exception that I cannot justify. In making an exception of myself, I am failing to respect others because I'm taking advantage of the fact that many others do not make lying promises. And so these reflections lead us to conclude that making a lying promise is morally wrong.

Here is another example Kant uses to illustrate the application of UL that has to do with clause (b) of UL. Suppose I am in a position to help someone in need but would rather not be bothered. The maxim Kant has us consider is:

M2 Whenever I am able to help others in need, I will refrain from helping them.

Using UL, I am to consider whether I can consistently conceive of a world in which everyone adopts and acts on this maxim. Is such a world conceivable? It would seem so. Granted, a world in which people in need did not receive help from others would be a very unpleasant place. Perhaps the human race would not survive in such a world. But we can certainly conceive of a world in which the human race ceases to exist. So, M2 passes the first part of Kant's UL test.

But can one *will* that M2 be adopted and acted upon by everyone? Upon reflection I realize that if I will that everyone adopt and act on M2, I am thereby willing that others refuse to help me when I am in need. But willing that others refuse to help me is inconsistent with the fact that as a rational agent I do will that others help me when I am in need. That is, as a rational agent, I embrace the following maxim:

> RM I will that others who are able to do so help me when I am in need.

But an implication of my willing that everyone adopt and act on M2 would be:

> IM I will that others who are able to help me, refuse to do so when I am in need.

RM is inconsistent with IM—and IM an implication of willing that everyone adopt and act on M2. Thus, I cannot consistently will that everyone adopt and act on M2. Since I cannot consistently will that everyone adopt M2, then according to clause (b) of Kant's UL, my action of refusing to help others in need is morally wrong.

What is the point of Kant's UL formulation involving two tests? Kant thought that these two tests could distinguish between what he called "narrow" or "perfect" duty and "wide" or "imperfect" duty: maxims that one cannot consistently conceive as adopted and acted on by everyone involve actions that are contrary to narrow duty, whereas those that can be so conceived but which one cannot consistently will involve actions that are contrary to wide duty. The realm of narrow duty concerns those actions and omissions regarding which one has comparatively little room for when and how one complies with the duty. If I have promised to do something for you on a particular occasion—help you with your taxes—then to fulfill my obligation I must perform some rather specific action (helping you with your taxes) at a certain time. By contrast, a wide duty is one which can be fulfilled in a variety of ways and situations, giving one much leeway in how and when to fulfill the duty. Duties of charity—helping others—are like this.

It is important to notice that in his examples, Kant is not arguing that if everyone went around making lying promises the consequences would be bad and therefore making a lying promise is wrong. Again, he does not argue that the consequences of everyone refusing to help others in need would be bad and therefore refusing help to others is wrong. Such ways of arguing are characteristic of consequentialism, but Kant rejects consequentialism. He has us consider the implications of everyone acting on the general policy behind one's own action because he thinks doing so is a way of revealing any inconsistencies in what one wills, which in turn indicates whether an action fails to respect persons. So the test involved in the categorical imperative is meant to reveal whether one's action shows a proper respect for persons.

Applying the Universal Law Formulation

Since this formulation expresses tests for determining the rightness or wrongness of actions, I have been illustrating how it is to be applied in thinking through moral issues. If we step back from these illustrations, we can summarize the basic procedure to be followed. In applying UL to some actual or contemplated action of yours, here are the basic steps to follow:

- Formulate the maxim on which you are proposing to act, which will have the form "I will _____ whenever _____," where the blanks are filled with a description of your action and circumstances, respectively.
- Next, you consider the possibility of everyone in your circumstances adopting and acting on that same maxim. In particular, you ask yourself whether you can consistently *conceive* of a world in which everyone adopts and acts on the maxim in question. This is the test expressed in clause (a) of UL.
- If you cannot even conceive of such a world, then action on the maxim is morally wrong—a violation of narrow duty. The lying promise example illustrates this result.
- If you can consistently conceive of a world in which everyone adopts and acts on the maxim, then you are to ask yourself whether you could, even so, consistently will that everyone adopt and act on the maxim. This is the test expressed in clause (b) of UL.
- If you cannot consistently will that everyone adopt and act on that maxim, then action on

the maxim is wrong—a violation of wide duty. The case of refusing to help others illustrates this result.

- Finally, if your maxim is such that you can both consistently conceive of a world in which everyone adopts and acts on your maxim and consistently will this to be the case—if the maxim passes both tests—then action on the maxim is morally right.

The two main challenges for anyone applying the UL formulation to a particular issue is to correctly formulate one's maxim and then carefully think through Kant's two consistency tests.

How are the two formulations of the categorical imperative—H and UL—related? They are supposed to be alternative formulations of the same basic principle, rather than two entirely distinct principles. One way to see how this might be so is to notice that in cases in which I cannot consistently conceive or will that my maxim be adopted by everyone, I am making an exception of myself, and in doing so either I am treating someone as a mere means or I am failing to treat others as ends in themselves. And, of course, treating others as mere means and failing to treat them as ends in themselves is precisely what the Humanity formulation rules out.

D. Rights-Based Moral Theory

In our brief survey of moral theories up to this point, we have seen how those theories attempt to give accounts of the nature of right (and wrong) action, where "right" is being used in its adjectival sense. Nothing so far has been said about the notion of *a right* or *rights*. However, in moral theory we distinguish between the adjectival use of "right" as in *right action* and its use as a noun as in *a right to life*. One can hold that actions may or may not be right—actions that are either permissible or impermissible to do—without also holding that there are things called rights. Perhaps the most basic idea of a **right** is that of an *entitlement* to be free to engage in some activity, to exercise a certain power, or to be provided with some benefit. One's having such an entitlement typically imposes duties on others (including governments) either to refrain from interfering with one's freedom (or exercise of power) or to provide

one with some benefit, depending on the right in question. In explaining the idea of a right and how it figures both in moral theory and in moral controversies, it will be useful to briefly discuss the following topics: (1) some basic elements of a right, (2) categories of rights, (3) rights and moral theory, (4) the idea of a rights-based moral theory, (5) the application of rights-based theories in practice, and (6) so-called rights-focused approaches to moral issues.[20]

Rights: Some Basic Elements

A right has the following characteristics. First, there is the **rights holder,** the party who has or "holds" the right. If you own property, then as a property owner, then you hold a property right. A rights holder may be an individual or a group. Minority rights are one type of group rights. One of the most important philosophical questions about rights concerns the *scope* of rights holders—those beings that *have* rights. According to some views that would restrict the scope of rights holders, only those creatures that have a developed capacity to reason can be the holders of rights. Less restrictive views would allow that anything having interests, including certain nonhuman animals, can be rights holders. Among those who approach moral issues from the perspective of rights—including the issues of abortion, animals, and the environment—we find important differences in views about the requirements for holding rights and thus differences in views about the scope of rights holders.

A second element of a right is what we might call the **rights addressee,** that is, the individual or group with regard to whom the rights holder is entitled to certain treatment. If I have entered into a contract with you to provide you a service, then I am the addressee of your right; you are entitled to demand that I provide that service. The relationship between a rights holder and the corresponding rights addressee can most often be understood in terms of the idea of a *claim*. For instance, in light of a rights holder being entitled to certain treatment by others, we may say that the former has a valid *claim* on the behavior of the latter. And so, corresponding to a rights holder's claim, the addressee of a right has an obligation or duty to either perform or refrain from performing actions that would affect the rights holder and the treatment to which he or she is entitled. Thus, at least for most rights, there is a correlation between the rights of rights holders and certain duties on the part of addressees.

A third element is the **content** of a right, which refers to whatever action, states, or objects the right concerns. The right to freedom of expression differs in content from the right to life. And, of course, these rights differ in content from property rights, and so on.

Finally, another dimension of rights is that of **strength.** Think of a right as a claim on others that has a certain degree of strength in the sense that the stronger right, the stronger the justification needed to defeat the right in question. For instance, some hold the view that nonhuman animals as well as human beings have a right to life. Suppose this is correct. It may still be the case that the right to life of a human being is stronger than the right to life of, say, a dog or cat. The difference in strength here would be reflected, for example, by the fact that one would be arguably justified in euthanizing a dog or cat if the animal were no longer able to walk, while this same sort of reason would not be strong enough to euthanize a human being.

Related to the fact that rights come in degrees of strength is the fact that in some situations someone might be morally justified in performing an action that "goes against" another person's right. And when this occurs, let us say that the person's right has been infringed. So, for instance, suppose my property rights involve the claim that no one may enter my house and use my property without my consent. Now suppose that my next door neighbor's child has been seriously hurt and needs immediate medical attention, and so calling an ambulance is in order. Suppose also that the closest phone available to my neighbor is the one in my house, but I am not at home. Were the neighbor to break into my house to use my phone, he or she would be infringing upon my property rights. But assuming that the neighbor is morally justified in doing this, we may call this case of "going against" my right, a **rights infringement.** By contrast, **rights violations** involve cases where someone goes against another person's rights but is not morally justified in doing so. Thus, as we

are using these terms, rights infringements involve actions that are not morally wrong given the circumstances, while rights violations involve actions that are morally wrong.

Categories of Rights

It is common to recognize both negative and positive rights. A **negative right** is an entitlement of noninterference and thus involves a claim by the rights holder that others refrain from interfering with her or his engaging in some activity. Because such rights require that others *not* act in certain ways, they impose what are called negative duties. Rights that are correlated with negative duties are called negative rights. A right to certain liberties such as free speech is an example of a negative right—a right that imposes a duty on others not to interfere with one's expressing one's ideas. A **positive right,** by contrast, involves the rights holder being entitled to something and thus having a valid claim that some other party do or provide something (some service or some good) to that rights holder. Because the duty in question requires positive action on the part of the addressee, the corresponding right is called a positive right. For instance, Article 25 of the United Nations 1948 *Universal Declaration of Human Rights* states:

> Everyone has a right to a standard of living adequate for the health and well-being of himself and of his family, including food, clothing, housing, and medical care and necessary social services, and the right to security in the event of unemployment, sickness, disability, widowhood, old age, or other lack of livelihood in circumstances beyond his control.

This (alleged) right is supposed to be held by all human beings and presumably it is a right that one be provided certain necessities by one's nation or perhaps other nations in a position to provide such goods.

In addition to the distinction between negative and positive rights, it is also important to distinguish **moral rights** from legal rights. This distinction has to do with the source of a right. A so-called moral right is a right that a being has independently of any legal system or other set of conventions.[21] So, for instance, it is often claimed that all human beings, in virtue of facts about humanity, have certain rights, including the rights to life, liberty, and well-being. Such alleged universal rights of humanity[22] are typically referred to as **human rights.** A **legal right** is something that results or comes into existence as the result of a legal statute or some other form of governmental activity. One reason why it is important to distinguish moral from legal rights is that controversies over moral issues are often framed in terms of whether some individual (including nonhumans) or group has certain moral rights—rights that may or may not be recognized by some particular legal system and thus not (at the time in question) count as legal rights within the system in question. So, in debates over the morality of various activities and practices where talk of rights enter the discussion, one is mainly concerned with moral rights.

Another common distinction, often associated with human rights, is the distinction between "basic" and "nonbasic" rights. Roughly speaking, a **basic right** is a universal right that is especially important in the lives of individuals—rights such as the rights to life and to liberty, which arguably must be met in order to live a decent life. One's right to life and freedom from torture is clearly more important compared with one's right to be repaid a sum of money by a borrower. Just how to distinguish basic from nonbasic rights is controversial, and we need not examine various proposals here. It is enough for our purposes to leave the distinction at a more or less intuitive level and recognize that rights differ in their importance and thus in their comparative strengths.

Let us now turn from our general discussion of rights to their place in moral theory and in contemporary debates over particular moral issues.

Rights and Moral Theory

A great deal of contemporary discussion about moral issues is couched in terms of rights. Does a human fetus have a moral right to life? Does a terminally ill patient in severe pain have a moral right to die? Do people have a moral right to reproduce by cloning? Do animals have moral rights? In this subsection and the next, I want to explain how rights figure in moral theories. In doing so, I will make two main points: (1) All of the moral theories we have already surveyed

(as well as the two that follow) can recognize moral rights. (2) However, what is distinctive of a rights-based moral theory is that it takes rights to be in some sense more basic than such notions as value (including utility), dignity, and right action (including duty). Let us take these points one by one.

First, a utilitarian who recognizes moral rights will attempt to explain rights on the basis of utility by claiming that a moral right is a kind of entitlement that imposes various claims on addressees justified by the fact that its recognition will contribute to the maximization of overall welfare. This means that for the utilitarian—who, as a consequentialist, embraces a value-based moral theory—rights are derivative rather than basic in her moral theory. Similar remarks apply to the moral theories featured in this chapter. For instance, according to Kantian ethics, all human beings possess moral rights in virtue of having a certain status—being the sort of creature that possesses dignity. Having this sort of status, according to the Kantian, demands that persons be treated in certain ways and thus that they enjoy certain moral rights. Thus, utilitarians and Kantians can agree that persons have moral rights. They disagree in how they explain the basis of such rights. And notice that because utilitarians and Kantians purport to explain moral rights in terms of more basic elements—utility in the case of utilitarianism, the possession of dignity in the case of Kantians—it would be incorrect to think of these theories as rights-based.

Rights-Based Moral Theory

Might there be a **rights-based moral theory**—a moral theory according to which rights are more basic than utility, dignity, and even duty? Unlike the other theories featured in this chapter, rights-based theories are relatively underdeveloped despite the fact that appeals to rights are very common in discussions of moral issues. What we find in the writings of authors who appeal to rights in discussing particular moral issues is that they often fail to indicate the nature of rights—whether they have a consequentialist, natural law, Kantian, or some other basis on the one hand, or whether, on the other hand, they are conceived as basic in the theory. So let us consider the idea of a rights-based moral theory.

According to such a theory, rights are even more basic than right action and duty. But one might think that duties must be more basic than rights and so there cannot be a rights-based moral theory. After all, as explained above, a typical moral right is a claim one party has against others that they do or refrain from some activity, and it is natural to think of these burdens as duties or obligations that are owed to the rights-holder. If I have a right to free speech, then this seems to entail that others have a duty not to interfere with me in certain ways and thus that the concept of duty must be used to explain what a right is. If so, then duty is more basic than a right and so a rights-based theory is conceptually impossible.

Granted, it is common to explain the idea of a moral right of one party in terms of certain corresponding duties on the part of others. But as J. L. Mackie, a defender of rights-based moral theory explains, instead of thinking of rights in terms of duties, "we could look at it the other way round: what is primary is A's having this right in a sense indicated by the prescription 'Let A be able to do X if he chooses,' and the duty of others not to interfere follows from this."[23]

So let us follow Mackie and suppose that there is no conceptual barrier to there being a rights-based theory of right and wrong action. How might it be developed? The idea would be to begin with a list of moral rights, perhaps distinguishing such basic rights, including for instance the rights to life and to liberty, from nonbasic rights. Once one has identified the various moral rights, one could then proceed to define or characterize the concepts of right and wrong action in terms of moral rights. Here, then, is how we might express the basic idea of right conduct for a rights-based theory:

> R An action is right if and only if (and because) in performing it either (a) one does not violate the moral rights of others, or (b) in cases where it is not possible to respect all such rights because they are in conflict, one's action is among the best ways to protect the most important rights in the case at hand.

This principle—it is more of a *scheme*—all by itself is too abstract to be of any practical use. What needs to be added, of course, is a specification of the moral rights that figure in this scheme and their relative importance. Mackie proposes a single basic moral right: the right of persons to "choose how they shall live."[24] But this right to choose is wide open, and to work our way from it to specific moral obligations, we will need to specify what sorts of more specific rights people have in virtue of having this most basic right. Perhaps we can begin by recognizing the Jeffersonian moral rights to life, liberty, and the pursuit of happiness. And then, for each of these general rights, we might specify them further by recognizing a set of specific moral rights including, for example, a right to free speech.

So, specifying a single basic and perhaps very general moral right (or set of them) and working toward a specification of more specific moral rights is one task of a rights-based moral theory. However one works out the details of what the moral rights are, we must keep in mind the obvious fact that in some contexts moral rights will come into conflict. My right of free speech may conflict with the rights that others have to be safe from harm. Suppose, for instance, that on some occasion, my speaking out would seriously jeopardize the personal safety of others. If so, then in such circumstances, it is plausible to suppose that people's right of personal safety overrides a person's right to free speech. How is one to determine whether one right overrides another in cases of conflict? This question brings us to the issue of applying a rights-based theory to moral issues.

Applying a Rights-Based Moral Theory

Principle (or scheme) R purports to explain an action's being morally right (and by implication morally wrong) in terms of respecting fundamental moral rights. Clause (a) of R covers the easy case in which one's action simply does not come into contact with the moral rights of others. I get up in the morning and decide to eat Cheerios for breakfast. Unusual cases aside, this action has nothing to do with the moral rights of others—I'm morally free to eat the Cheerios or not. Clause (b), however, is where a rights-based approach to moral problems is most relevant: one can frame many of the disputed moral issues [. . .] as a conflict of rights: right to life versus right to choice; right to express oneself in speech and writing versus right to public safety, and so on.

So in applying R (supplemented with a theory of rights) to moral issues, the challenge is to find the best way of properly balancing competing rights claims in arriving at a moral verdict about what ought to be done. As I will explain more thoroughly below in connection with the ethics of prima facie duty, it is very doubtful that there is some fixed mechanical procedure that one can use in arriving at a correct or justified moral verdict in particular cases based on a consideration of competing rights. Rather, what one needs is what philosophers call **moral judgment**—roughly, an acquired skill at discerning what matters the most morally speaking and coming to an all-things-considered moral verdict where this skill cannot be entirely captured by a set of rules. The point to stress here is that, as with the other moral theories we are considering, applying a moral theory—its principles—to particular issues is not a mechanical process. But this does not take away from the value of such theories in guiding one's moral deliberations and subsequent choices.

Rights-Focused Approaches to Moral Issues

We have noted that talk of rights is very common in moral thought and discussion. However, we have also noted that in thinking about a moral issue in terms of competing rights claims, one need not accept a rights-based moral theory as just described. As noted earlier, consequentialists, Kantians, and natural law theorists can and do recognize rights—although on these theories rights are not what is most morally basic in the theory. So, because one may appeal to rights in discussing a moral issue without accepting a rights-based moral theory, we must recognize what we may call **rights-focused** approaches to moral issues. To say that an author's approach to a moral issue is rights-focused is simply to say that the author appeals to rights as a basis for taking a stand on the issue at hand—the author may or may not also embrace a rights-based moral theory. [. . .]

E. Virtue Ethics

Sometimes our moral thinking is dominated by thoughts about what sort of person one would be if one were to perform some action. The thought of living up to certain ideals or virtues of what a morally good person is like is crucial here. Being an unselfish person is an ideal that we may use in evaluating some course of action, and sometimes we may think, "Not helping her would be selfish on my part, so I'm going to help." When our moral thinking takes this turn, we are evaluating actions in terms of virtue and vice. The ideas of virtue and vice have played a negligible role in the moral theories we have surveyed (at least as I have presented them).[25] However, inspired primarily by the ethical views of the ancient Greek philosophers Plato and Aristotle, **virtue ethics** makes the concepts of virtue and vice central in moral theory. Such theories, as I will understand them, take the concepts of virtue and vice to be more basic than the concepts of right and wrong, and thus propose to define or characterize the latter in terms of the former.[26]

One might characterize right and wrong in terms of virtue and vice in different ways, but here (roughly) is how Rosalind Hursthouse [. . .] formulates a virtue ethical principle of right action:

> **VE** An action is right if and only if (and because) it is what a virtuous agent (acting in character) would not avoid doing in the circumstances under consideration.

How are we to understand the concept of a virtuous agent featured in this principle? One straightforward way is to say that the virtuous agent is one who has the virtues. But what is a virtue? And which ones does the virtuous agent have?

A **virtue** is a trait of character or mind that typically involves dispositions to act, feel, and think in certain ways and that is central in the *positive* evaluation of persons. Honesty and loyalty are two commonly recognized virtues. The trait of honesty, for instance, involves at a minimum being disposed to tell the truth and avoid lying, as well as the disposition to have certain feelings about truth telling (positive ones) and about lying (negative ones). Honesty, as a virtue, is a trait that has positive value and contributes to what makes someone a good person. In contrast to a virtue, a **vice** is a trait of character or mind which typically involves dispositions to act, feel, and think in certain ways, and that is central in the *negative* evaluation of persons. So, for instance, opposed to the virtue of honesty is the vice of dishonesty which may be understood as having inappropriate dispositions of action and feeling regarding truth telling and lying. Furthermore, as a vice, dishonesty has negative value and contributes to what makes someone a morally bad person. So, in general, virtues and vices are character traits that are manifested in having certain dispositions to act and feel in certain ways and that bear on what makes a person morally good or bad. Here, then, is a short (and by no means complete) list of fairly commonly recognized moral virtues and their corresponding vices:[27]

- Honesty/Dishonesty
- Courage/Cowardice
- Justice/Injustice
- Temperance/Intemperance
- Beneficence/Selfishness
- Humility/Arrogance
- Loyalty/Disloyalty
- Gratitude/Ingratitude

Applying Virtue Ethics

To apply VE to a particular case, then, we must first determine which character traits are the virtues that are possessed by the virtuous agent (we may begin with the previous list), and then determine how, on the basis of such traits, this agent would be disposed to act in the circumstances in question. An action that a virtuous agent, acting in character, would not fail to perform in some circumstance is morally required, an action she might or might not do at her discretion is morally optional, and one that she would avoid doing is morally wrong.

Of course, in applying virtue ethics to disputed moral issues, we encounter the fact that more than one virtue is relevant to the case at hand and that one of them—say, honesty—favors telling the truth, whereas one of the others—say, loyalty—favors telling a lie. In such cases of conflict among the virtues, we must examine the particular details of the case at hand and ask such questions as, "What is at stake here?" "How important is telling the truth in this case?" "How important is loyalty to an organization?" It is only by examining the details of such cases of conflict that we can come to

an all-things-considered moral evaluation of some particular action based on considerations of virtue. This point is reflected in VE's reference to a virtuous agent *acting in character*. Presumably, such an ideal agent has the sort of practical wisdom or judgment that is required in order for her to discern which virtue consideration, from among the competing virtue considerations in a particular case, has the most weight. As I have been noting all along in presenting the various moral theories— something that we explore a bit further in the next subsection—the application of moral theories to particular issues requires moral judgment.

F. Ethics of Prima Facie Duty

Whereas consequentialism, for instance, features a single moral principle of right conduct, what I am calling the **ethics of prima facie duty** features a plurality of basic moral principles of right conduct. The most famous version of this kind of view was developed by the twentieth-century British philosopher W. D. Ross (1877–1971). To understand the elements of Ross's view, we need to do the following: (1) explain what he means by talk of "prima facie duty"; (2) present his basic principles of prima facie duty; and then (3) explain the role of moral judgment in applying them in practice.

The Concept of a Prima Facie Duty

To say that one has a **prima facie duty** to perform some action is to say that one has *some* moral reason to perform the action, but the reason in question might be *overridden* by some other moral reason that favors not performing the action. The best way to understand the concept is with an example. Suppose I have promised to pick you up on Saturday by 10:00 A.M. so that you can get to a very important job interview (your car is in the shop). Ross would say that because of my having made a promise to you, I have a prima facie duty (of fidelity—see later discussion) to do what I said I would do: pick you up by 10:00 A.M. on Saturday. But now suppose that as I am about to leave to pick you up, my child falls off the roof of my house and needs immediate medical attention. Ross would say that here I have a prima facie duty to take my child to the emergency ward of the hospital. So, I have a prima facie duty to start out for your place and a conflicting prima facie duty to attend to my child: as things have turned out, I am not able to fulfill both prima facie duties. Now the point of calling a duty "prima facie" is that the moral reasons provided by such facts as that I've made a promise or that my child needs my help can be outweighed by other moral reasons that favor doing some other action. Ross puts this point by saying that a prima facie duty can be overridden—beat out—by a competing prima facie duty. In the case I've described, because it is my child and because she needs immediate medical attention, my prima facie duty to help her overrides my prima facie duty to come pick you up. When one prima facie duty prevails in some conflict of duties situation, it becomes one's *all-things-considered duty*—it is what you ought, all things considered, to do in that circumstance. So, for Ross, to say that one has a prima facie duty to perform action *A* on some occasion is to say that one has a moral reason to do *A,* and unless something comes up that is morally more important, one has an all-things-considered duty to do *A* on that occasion.

Ross's theory of right conduct, which is our main concern, is based partly on his theory of intrinsic value to which we now turn.

Ross's Theory of Intrinsic Value

Ross held that there are four basic intrinsic goods:

1. Virtue. The disposition to act from certain desires, including the desire to do what is morally right, is intrinsically good.
2. Pleasure. States of experiencing pleasure are intrinsically good.
3. Pleasure in proportion to virtue. The state of experiencing pleasure in proportion to one's level of virtue is intrinsically good.
4. Knowledge. Having knowledge (at least of a nontrivial sort) is intrinsically good.

The items on this list are the basis for some of Ross's basic prima facie duties—call them "value-based" prima facie duties. What Ross calls duties of "special obligation" are not based on his theory of intrinsic value.

Ross's Prima Facie Duties

Here, then, is Ross's list of basic prima facie duties, organized into the two categories just mentioned:

Basic Value-Based Prima Facie Duties
1. Justice: prima facie, one ought to ensure that pleasure is distributed according to merit.
2. Beneficence: prima facie, one ought to help those in need and, in general, increase the virtue, pleasure, and knowledge of others.
3. Self-improvement: prima facie, one ought to improve oneself with respect to one's own virtue and knowledge.
4. Nonmaleficence: prima facie, one ought to refrain from harming others.

Basic Prima Facie Duties of Special Obligation
5. Fidelity: prima facie, one ought to keep one's promises (including the implicit promise to be truthful).
6. Reparation: prima facie, one ought to make amends to others for any past wrongs one has done them.
7. Gratitude: prima facie, one ought to show gratitude toward one's benefactors.

The first four basic prima facie duties, then, make reference to what has intrinsic value according to Ross's theory of value. Ross himself points out that the prima facie duties of justice, beneficence, and self-improvement "come under the general principle that we should produce as much good as possible."[28] This part of Ross's theory fits the characterization of consequentialism.

The duties of special obligation do not make reference to what has intrinsic value; the duties of fidelity, reparation, and gratitude do not depend for their prima facie rightness on the values of the consequences of those actions. This part of Ross's theory is clearly duty-based or deontological. Overall, then, Ross's theory represents a hybrid: part consequentialist, part deontological.

Applying the Ethics of Prima Facie Duties

But how, on Ross's view, does one determine in some particular case that one prima facie duty overrides another, competing prima facie duty? Ross denies that there is any correct super-principle like the principle of utility or Kant's categorical imperative to which one might appeal to determine one's all-things-considered duty in cases of conflict. Nor is there any fixed ranking of the various prima facie duties such that the duty higher up on the list always beats out duties below it. Rather, according to Ross, in determining which prima facie duty is most "stringent" in some particular case and thus represents one's all-things-considered duty, one must examine the details of the case by using one's *judgment* about which of the competing duties is (in that situation) strongest. As mentioned earlier, moral judgment is a matter of discerning the morally important features of a situation and determining what ought or ought not to be done, where doing so cannot be fully captured in a set of rules. Judgment is largely a matter of skill that one may acquire through experience.

One final remark. One need not agree with Ross's own list of basic prima facie duties in order to accept the other tenets of Ross's view. For instance, Robert Audi has recently defended an ethic of prima facie duties that features ten basic prima facie duties.[29] Audi, unlike Ross, distinguishes duties not to lie from duties of fidelity, and he adds two additional duties to Ross's list. So were we to make the additions Audi proposes, we would have the following:

8. Veracity: prima facie, one ought not to lie.
9. Enhancement and preservation of freedom: prima facie, one ought to contribute to increasing or at least preserving the freedom of others with priority given to removing constraints over enhancing opportunities.
10. Respectfulness: prima facie, one ought, in the manner of our relations with other people, treat others respectfully.

The main point I wish to make here is that Ross's version of an ethic of prima facie duties is one version of this general sort of view. Audi's view attempts to build upon and improve Ross's view.

This completes our survey of some of the leading moral theories that figure importantly in many [contemporary debates]. As mentioned earlier, I recommend using these summaries of the six theories as an aid in understanding those writings in which an author appeals to one or other of them. The remaining section and the appendix address questions about moral theory that are likely to occur to the reader:

- What is the point of moral theory in thinking about disputed moral issues in light of the fact that there is a variety of competing moral theories?
- What about theories that appeal to the will of God or to the norms of society of culture in determining what is right or wrong?

3. Coping with Many Moral Theories

This chapter began with a brief overview of the central concepts and guiding aims of moral theory and then proceeded to survey six types of moral theory. In working through the various moral problems featured in this book, one will find that different moral theories often yield different and conflicting answers to questions about the morality of some action. The natural law theory, for instance, arguably condemns all homosexual behavior as morally wrong; a consequentialist approach does not. So the application of one theory to an issue may yield one moral verdict, while the application of another theory may yield a conflicting moral verdict. What, then, a student may ask, is the point of thinking about disputed moral issues from the perspective of moral theory? It all seems rather arbitrary.

This is a completely understandable question whose answer requires that one move from a focus on particular moral issues to questions about the nature and evaluation of moral theories. It is not possible to fully address such questions in a chapter whose aim is to provide students with a basic understanding of a range of moral theories. But because of its importance, the question does deserve to be addressed, even if briefly. In so doing, I will first offer some remarks about evaluating a moral theory, and then I will suggest a way of looking at the various moral theories for the illumination I think they provide in thinking about moral issues.

Evaluating a Moral Theory

Philosophers who develop a moral theory do not just state some moral principle or other and leave it at that; rather, they *argue* for whatever principles they are proposing. And we can critically evaluate their arguments. So the first point I wish to make is that there can be rational debate about a moral theory—not any old moral theory is as good as any other.

Furthermore, there are standards for evaluating a moral theory—standards that are not arbitrary but rather have to do with the guiding aims of a moral theory that we discussed in section 1 of this chapter. Corresponding to the theoretical aim of moral theory—the aim of explaining what makes something right or wrong, good or bad—is the principle of **explanatory power:**

> A moral theory should feature principles that explain our more specific considered moral beliefs, thus helping us understand *why* actions, persons, and other objects of moral evaluation are right or wrong, good or bad. The better a theory's principles in providing such explanations, the better the theory.

This principle appeals to our "considered" moral beliefs, which may be defined as those moral beliefs that are *deeply held* and *very widely shared.* I hope that everyone reading this text believes that murder is wrong, that rape is wrong, and that child molestation is wrong. The list could be extended. Moreover, such moral beliefs are (for those who have them) very likely deeply held convictions. The principle of explanatory power tells us to evaluate a moral theory by determining whether its principles properly explain why such actions are morally wrong. Similar remarks apply to widely shared and deeply held beliefs about our obligations. So we can help confirm a moral theory by showing that it can properly explain the rightness or wrongness of actions about whose moral status we are virtually certain. Correlatively, we can criticize a moral theory by showing that it does not properly explain the rightness or wrongness of actions about whose moral status we are virtually certain. Applying this principle requires that we can tell what counts as a good explanation of the rightness or wrongness of actions. This is a topic of lively and ongoing philosophical inquiry whose study would take us far beyond the scope of this book. But in thinking about moral issues from the perspective of moral theory, the reader is invited to consider not only what a theory implies about some action or practice, but also what explanation it provides for whatever verdict it reaches about the action or practice under consideration. (I return briefly to this matter toward the end of this section.)

According to the practical aim of moral theory, we want moral principles that will help guide our moral deliberations and subsequent choices. Corresponding to this aim is the principle of **practical guidance:**

> A moral theory should feature principles that are useful in guiding moral deliberation toward correct or justified moral verdicts about particular issues which we can then use to help guide choice. The better a theory's principles are in providing practical guidance, the better the theory.

Any moral theory that would yield inconsistent verdicts about some particular concrete action is obviously of no practical help on the issue at hand. Furthermore, a moral theory whose principles are so vague that it fails to have clear implications for a range of moral issues is again of no help in guiding thought about those issues. Finally, a moral theory whose principles are extremely difficult to apply because, for example, applying them requires a great deal of factual information that is humanly impossible to acquire, is at odds with the principle of practical guidance. These are three measures to consider in evaluating how well a moral theory does in satisfying the principle of practical guidance and thus how well it does in satisfying the practical aim of moral theory.

These brief remarks are only meant to indicate how one can begin to evaluate a moral theory. Hopefully, what I have said is enough to make a start on answering the challenge that began this section. Let us now move on to the second point I wish to make in response to the challenge.

Moral Theory and Moral Illumination[30]

I conclude with a plea for the importance of moral theory, even if there is no one theory that currently commands the allegiance of all philosophers who specialize in ethics. The plea is that moral theory can help focus and sharpen our moral thinking about particular issues, and it can thereby provide a kind of insight and illumination of moral issues that is otherwise easily missed. Let me explain.

No doubt readers of this chapter will have noticed that the various moral theories we have surveyed build on ideas that are very familiar. To see this, let us return to the case of euthanasia with which this chapter began. You may recall that in that case, Dr. Jack Kevorkian brought about the death of his patient Thomas Youk by a lethal injection. We described Kevorkian's action as an instance of voluntary active euthanasia. Now if one pays attention to on-line discussions and newspaper editorials that focus on this moral issue, and listens to the views of politicians and other social activists who discuss it, we find that some arguments appeal to the likely effects or consequences of allowing this practice. And of course, the idea that an action's rightness or wrongness is to be explained by reference to its likely consequences is the main idea of the various varieties of consequentialist moral theory. Similar remarks can be made about the other five types of moral theory presented in section 2. Some arguments over euthanasia focus on the intrinsic value of human life—one of the four basic human goods featured in natural law ethics. Related to questions about end-of-life moral decisions, some have argued that providing a terminal patient with painkilling drugs that will knowingly cause the patient to die of liver failure before succumbing to cancer is nevertheless permissible because death in this case is merely a foreseen side effect of the painkilling drug. Here we have a tacit appeal to the doctrine of double effect. Again, we find arguments that appeal to the special dignity and worth of human beings, as well as arguments that appeal to such alleged rights as the right to die or the right to die with dignity—arguments that tacitly appeal, respectively, to elements of Kantian moral theory and to rights-based moral theory (or at least rights-focused approaches to moral issues). Similar points can be made about virtue ethics and the ethics of prima facie duties.

So the first point I wish to make about studying moral issues from the perspective of moral theory is that one thereby gains greater insight and clarity into the kinds of arguments that one commonly reads and hears (and perhaps is disposed to give) over disputed moral issues. In fact, one may think of the various moral theories we have surveyed as attempts to develop such familiar ideas from moral thought and discourse in a rigorous philosophical manner. To really understand some moral issue for purposes of making up your own mind about it, you first have to understand the issue, which in turn requires that you consider the various reasons that reflective people bring to bear in thinking and debating the issue at hand. Such reasons, as I have just indicated, are often developed systematically in a moral theory. So coming to understand moral theory helps provide a kind of moral illumination or insight into moral issues.

The further point is this. Different moral theories differ partly because of how they propose to *organize* our moral thinking about practical issues. For instance, utilitarianism has us organize our moral thinking about some issue in terms of its likely effects on well-being or happiness. Virtue ethics, by contrast, has us organize our moral thinking around considerations of virtue and vice, asking us, for example, to view a proposed course of action in terms of what it would express about our characters. Rights-based moral theories have us think about an issue in terms of competing moral claims that can be made by various involved parties. Similar remarks apply to Kantian moral theory, natural law theory, and the ethics of prima facie duty. But let us put aside for the moment the fact that the various moral theories in question purport to provide competing answers to questions about the underlying nature of right and wrong, good and bad. If we do, we might then view these theories as providing different ways of diagnosing and thinking about a moral problem, where in some cases the best approach is utilitarian, whereas in others the best approach is from a virtue ethics perspective, and still in others, some other moral theory best gets at what is morally most important to consider. In other words, it strikes me that some practical moral questions are best approached from, say, the perspective of act utilitarianism, others not. [. . .] Alan M. Dershowitz [. . .] considers a "ticking bomb" scenario in which a captured terrorist very likely knows the whereabouts of a powerful explosive set to go off in a heavily populated city. Would it be morally permissible to torture this (uncooperative) individual in an attempt to extract information that might be used to locate and defuse the explosive? Given what is at stake in *this* particular case, I can well understand why one's moral thinking would be guided by essentially act utilitarian reasoning. But in other cases, thinking in these terms seems morally askew. Thomas E. Hill Jr. [. . .] argues that in thinking about how we ought to relate to the environment, utilitarianism fails to properly diagnose what is wrong with certain ways of treating the environment. He also argues that thinking in terms of rights fails to get at what is really morally important about our dealings with the environment. His proposal is to think in terms of virtue—ideals of excellence—rather than in terms of utility or rights. As explained in section 1 of this chapter, a moral theory is partly in the business of providing practical guidance for moral thinking and decision making. My suggestion is that in some contexts it makes sense to think as an act utilitarian, in other contexts it makes most sense to think in terms of rights, and in still other contexts, thinking in terms of virtue and excellence seems most illuminating. The same can be said about the other moral theories we have surveyed. Thinking exclusively about all moral issues in terms of some one particular moral theory assumes a *one-size-fits-all* approach to moral thinking. I am suggesting that this probably isn't the best way to use theory to illuminate practice.[31]

Returning now to the challenge that began this section, I have tried to address it in two ways. First, moral theory is not arbitrary in the sense that you can just pick and choose your favorite or make up your own: there are standards for evaluating moral theories that have to do with the theoretical and practical aims of moral theory. Second, the variety of moral theories on offer can positively aid in one's moral thinking about controversial moral issues in two ways. First, it can do so by providing rigorous articulations of common ideas about morality. And second, it can do so if one views these theories as diagnostic tools for getting to the heart of moral problems. Some tools are better for some jobs than other tools. My suggestion is that a particular moral theory may be a better tool than others when it comes to thinking through some particular issue, though a different theory may be better at helping one think through other issues.

APPENDIX: ETHICS BY AUTHORITY?
Divine Command Theory and Ethical Relativism

The idea that morality depends on some authority—whether the will of God or the norms of one's culture—is well known, even if not generally well understood. The readings in this collection by and large reflect the impact of the six moral theories presented in section 2 on philosophical thinking about disputed moral issues. This does not mean that other moral theories or approaches to moral issues are not worthy of philosophical attention. My presentation has been selective. However, because what I am calling ethics by authority in one form or another will likely occur to readers, I think it is important to explain why many who think about moral issues have grave reservations about both divine command theory and ethical relativism.

According to the **divine command theory,** what is right or wrong depends on God's commands in the sense that what *makes* an action right or wrong are mere facts about God's commands, nothing more. On this view, an action is wrong whenever (and because) God commands that we not do the action. An action is morally obligatory whenever (and because) God commands that we do it. Otherwise an action is morally optional. So the fundamental moral principle of this sort of theory can be expressed as follows:

> **DCT** An action is right if and only if (and because) God does not command that we not do that action.

For many people, being told that God does or does not command some action is crucial in their thinking about moral issues. But surely if God commands that we perform some action, there must be some reason why God issues this command—some reason that explains *why* the action is something we ought or ought not to do. But then, as philosophers, we can ask what it is about the action in question that makes it wrong and is a basis for God's command. And once we put the question to ourselves in this way, we are simply raising the general moral questions about the right and the good that we began with. So, appealing to God's commands (at least for believers) may help the believer decide what to do, but the fact that God commands this or that action does not answer the deep question about the underlying nature of right and wrong that a moral theory attempts to answer—it does not plausibly address the main *theoretical aim* of moral theory explained earlier.

Of course, someone sympathetic to DCT may claim that it is just God's commands that make an action right or wrong. But this won't be acceptable to a theist who thinks that God's actions are rational. After all, if one says that there is no reason behind God's commands, then one is saying that God has no good reason for commanding that we keep our promises and not commit murder, that God's commands are completely arbitrary. But this can't be right. So, a theist must say that there are facts about an action that make it wrong and that since God knows all facts, and since God is all-good, God commands that we do what is (independently of his commands) right and not do what is wrong.

As for **ethical relativism,** there is a good deal of confusion generated by the vague (and unfortunately popular) talk of morality being relative. Surely anyone can agree that whether a particular action— say, addressing a professor by her first name—is morally right may be importantly affected by what a society considers to be insulting. In the United States at present, the social norms that help specify what constitutes an insult do not seem to consider a student addressing a university professor by her first name as an insult. If that's right, then a student in a U.S. university would not be insulting a professor in addressing her by her first name (unless, perhaps, the professor had expressed a desire not to be so addressed). But in other countries (at present), the social norms governing student–professor relationships are such that the sort of address in question does constitute an insult. If we agree that insults are morally wrong [. . .], then we can easily see that the action of addressing a professor by her first name is morally wrong in some social circumstances (when in certain countries) and not in others (when in the United States). But this kind of context-sensitivity of morality according to which one's circumstances, including the social norms of one's culture, may have a bearing on what is right or wrong to do in

that culture is something that all of the moral theories we have considered do accept.

So if ethical relativism is to represent a moral theory that competes with the ones we have surveyed, what must it say? It must say something like this: (1) there are no correct moral norms or principles that are valid for all cultures at all times; rather (2) there are only the moral norms that some group or culture happens to accept, and these norms—*no matter what those norms say*—are what determine what is right or wrong for members of that group or culture. We can encapsulate these ideas in the following principle:

> **ER** An action (performed by members of a group G) is right if and only if the moral norms that are accepted by G permit the performance of the action.

Thus, if some culture accepts the moral norm that the enslavement of other human beings is morally right, then (according to the relativist) enslavement really *is* right—for those people.

Now relativism has its popular allure. Some people seem to take ethical relativism as an enlightened view about the true nature of morality. In order to disabuse the reader of the kind of simple ethical relativism just described, consider abortion. Suppose we find out that a majority of current U.S. citizens accept a set of moral norms that find nothing wrong with abortion. If we suppose that the moral norms of some culture are those norms that are held by a majority of its members, then according to ethical relativism, we would have to conclude that abortion (for members of U.S. culture) is morally right. Even if you think that abortion is morally right, do you (the reader) really think that the actual moral rightness and wrongness of an action depends on majority opinion? If so, then you might think we can settle moral issues by a vote. But this would mean that no matter what the majority of some group accepts as part of that group's moral norms—genocide, slavery, infanticide, lying, cheating, whatever—those actions would be right for members of that group. Granted, the members of some group may honestly *think* that genocide is morally right, but thinking something is right does not *make* it right. Right?

So, we can agree to the following thesis of **context-sensitivity:**

> **CS** The rightness or wrongness of an action may depend in part on facts about the agent and her circumstances, where her circumstances may include facts about the norms for what counts as constituting insults, a person's privacy, proper respect for others, and so forth.

The example of insulting behavior illustrates how CS can be true. But as we have already noted, CS is compatible with all of the nonrelativist moral theories that we have surveyed in section 2. According to each of those theories, there are basic moral principles or norms whose correctness is objective and not dependent on whether they happen to be accepted by some culture. Of course, in applying one of these principles to some particular case, we must consider various details of the case including facts about particular agents and their circumstances as well as facts about the society in which one happens to live.

Whether some version of ethical relativism can be defended is controversial and cannot be settled here. If so, it would have to improve upon ER. My main point was to note the important difference between CS and ER (they are often confused) and explain why CS is uncontroversial and why ER is problematic.

According to both divine command theory and ethical relativism, morality depends on the dictates of some authority—God or culture. I have tried to indicate very briefly why many moral philosophers are not satisfied with either of these theories.[32] [. . .]

NOTES

1. A few paragraphs of material in this essay are taken from my "Ethics" in *Reflections on Philosophy,* 2nd ed., ed. L. McHenry and T. Yagisowa (New York: Longman's Publishers, 2003), 103–25.
2. John Rawls, *A Theory of Justice* (Cambridge, MA: Harvard University Press, 1971), 24.
3. Given this understanding of the notions of intrinsic and extrinsic value, it is possible for something to have value of both sorts. Suppose, for example, that both happiness and knowledge have intrinsic positive value. Since knowledge can be of use in promoting happiness, knowledge can also have extrinsic value.
4. The "if and only if (and because) . . ." is meant to make clear that what follows the "and because" is meant to be a moral criterion that explains *why* the item being evaluated has whatever moral property (e.g., rightness) is mentioned in the first part of the principle.
5. To categorize Kant's ethical theory as deontological in the sense of being fundamentally duty-based may be inaccurate. Arguably, the notion of dignity—a kind of status that all persons have—is the explanatory basis of duties in Kant's ethical theory. Since dignity is a kind of value, this would make Kant's theory a certain kind of value-based theory, but nevertheless distinct from consequentialist views.
6. See Jeremy Bentham, *An Introduction to the Principles of Morals and Legislation* (New York: Hafner Press, 1948, originally published in 1789), and J. S. Mill, *Utilitarianism* (Indianapolis, IN: Hackett Publishing, 1979, originally published in 1861).
7. Another important distinction within consequentialism is between versions that appeal to the *actual* consequences (and associated value) that would occur were some action to be performed and versions that appeal to the *likely* consequences (and associated value) of actions—those consequences and their associated value that can be reasonably expected to follow from an action were it to be performed. I have chosen to formulate consequentialist principles in terms of likely consequences, since in applying a consequentialist theory to practice, we have to rely on our *estimates* of the consequences and associated value of actions.
8. I have explained utilitarianism in terms of *human* happiness or welfare, but a utilitarian may expand the scope of moral concern to all creatures for whom it makes sense to talk about their happiness or welfare.
9. For a recent defense of perfectionist consequentialism, see Tom Hurka, *Perfectionism* (Oxford: Oxford University Press, 1993).
10. What I am describing is a pure perfectionist account of value. It is, of course, possible to accept a hybrid view of intrinsic value according to which both happiness and perfectionist goods such as knowledge and achievement have intrinsic value.
11. For a recent defense of rule consequentialism, see Brad Hooker, *Ideal Code, Real World* (Oxford: Oxford University Press, 2000).

12. This is not to say that the best form of the natural law theory embraces the idea that "unnatural" actions are wrong and "natural" actions are right. The version I am about to present does not feature such ideas.

13. For a recent defense of natural law theory, see John Finnis, *Natural Law and Natural Rights* (Oxford: Oxford University Press, 1980).

14. Here is an appropriate place to clarify what I am calling theories of intrinsic value that figure importantly in those moral theories which feature value-based theories of right conduct. Ideally, a complete theory of intrinsic value would accomplish two related tasks: (1) provide a complete list of those types of things that have intrinsic value and also (2) specify those underlying features of intrinsically good and bad things *in virtue of which* they have whatever intrinsic value they do have. However, since our main concern in this chapter is with that part of a moral theory having to do with right and wrong action, we need only consider how a theory of intrinsic value responds to the first task—a specification of the types of things that have intrinsic value. So, for example, in what immediately follows, I will simply list the most basic types of items that have positive intrinsic value according to the natural law theory.

15. Kant's major writings in ethics include *Groundwork of the Metaphysics of Morals* (1785), *Critique of Practical Reason* (1790), and *The Metaphysics of Morals* (1797). All of these writings are included in Mary E. Gregor, trans., *Kant's Practical Philosophy* (Cambridge: Cambridge University Press, 1997). Page references to Kant's writings are to this volume. For a recent defense of Kantian ethics, see Onora O'Neill, *Towards Justice and Virtue* (Cambridge: Cambridge University Press, 1996).

16. See *Groundwork of the Metaphysics of Morals,* section II, 84–85.

17. I have left out the "and because" since arguably this formulation does not purport to express a moral criterion of right action—what *makes* an action right for Kant is expressed by the Humanity formulation; a *test* of an action's rightness is provided by the Universal Law formulation. For more on this, see my *Moral Theory: An Introduction,* chap. 5.

18. In the *Groundwork,* section II, in the footnote on p. 80, Kant raises objections to the golden rule.

19. *Practical Philosophy*, 74.

20. Readers should be aware that the topic of rights is extremely complex and contentious. In what follows, my aim is to introduce readers to some distinctions and to some observations about rights, moral theory, and moral controversies which, although elementary and perhaps contentious, are useful for understanding moral disputes that are framed in terms of rights.

21. Such rights are sometimes referred to as "natural rights."

22. *Universal* human rights are rights that are enjoyed by all human beings regardless of nationality, sex, race, religion, or other such distinctions. Universal rights, as universal, are contrasted with the particular rights of particular individuals, such as the rights that come with owning a house or having a certain occupation.

23. J. L. Mackie, "Can There Be a Rights-Based Moral Theory?" *Midwest Studies in Philosophy* 3 (1978): 351.

24. Mackie, "Rights-Based Moral Theory," 355.

25. This does not mean that such theories have little to say about such matters. For instance, Kant elaborates a theory of virtue in the "Doctrine of Virtue" which makes up part 2 of his 1797 *Metaphysics of Morals.*

26. For a recent defense of virtue ethics, see Rosalind Hursthouse, *On Virtue Ethics* (Oxford: Oxford University Press, 1999).

27. Defenders of virtue ethics often attempt to explain the basis of the virtues and vices (why some trait is a virtue or a vice) by appealing to the idea of human flourishing. The idea is that a trait of character or mind is a virtue because it contributes to or partly constitutes the flourishing of its possessor. [. . .]

28. W. D. Ross, *The Right and the Good* (Oxford: Oxford University Press, 1930), 27.

29. See Audi's *The Good in the Right* (Princeton, N.J.: Princeton University Press, 2004) for a recent defense of an ethic of prima facie duty that attempts to integrate this sort of view into a basically Kantian framework.

30. Special thanks to Jason Brennan and to Dave Schmidtz for very helpful conversations about moral theory and illumination.

31. These remarks suggest the possibility of combining certain elements from the various theories into one big super-theory featuring a plurality of principles, some having to do with duties, others with virtuous actions, others with rights, others with utility, and perhaps all of them unified by the Kantian idea of respect for persons, animals, and the environment. Doing so would still leave open the question of

whether some one element of the theory—duties, virtues, rights, etc.—is most basic in the theory. One possibility (and the one that strikes me as initially plausible) is a theory according to which these notions are "interpenetrating"—a full understanding of any one of them requires appeal to the others.

32. For a more detailed presentation and critique of divine command theory and ethical relativism, see chapters 2 and 3 of my *Moral Theory: An Introduction* (Lanham, MD: Rowman & Littlefield, 2002). This book also has chapters on utilitarianism, natural law theory, Kantian ethics, the ethics of prima facie duty (what I there call ethical pluralism), and virtue ethics.